INDEX TO *Resources for Further Investigation*

Eighth Edition

Psychology Applied to Teaching

Robert F. Biehler

Jack Snowman
Southern Illinois University

HOUGHTON MIFFLIN COMPANY BOSTON NEW YORK

Senior Sponsoring Editor: Loretta Wolozin
Senior Associate Editor: Janet Edmonds
Senior Project Editor: Janet Young
Editorial Assistant: Elizabeth M. Emmons
Senior Production/Design Coordinator: Sarah Ambrose
Senior Manufacturing Coordinator: Priscilla Bailey
Marketing Manager: David Lenehan

Cover design by Diana Coe.
Cover image: David Bohn, D. Bohn INK, "Man Sitting"
Part opener photos: pp. 29 and 237, Charles Gupton/Stock Boston; p. 273, M. Greenlar/The Image Works; pp. 437 and 477, Bob Daemmrich/The Image Works.
Additional credits appear following Index.

Printed in the U.S.A.

Library of Congress Catalog Card Number: 96-76870

ISBN:
Student Copy 0-395-77685-6
Exam Copy 0-395-84155-0

123456789-VH-00 99 98 97 96

Brief Contents

Contents

Preface

The hallmark of *Psychology Applied to Teaching* is its usefulness to teachers. It is written for students enrolled in an introductory educational psychology course, and it is at once a basic source of information for prospective teachers and a resource for their future use as classroom teachers.

Goals of the Text

This eighth edition of *Psychology Applied to Teaching* has been written to be used in three ways: 1) as a text that provides basic information, organized and presented so that it will be understood, remembered, and applied; 2) as a source of practical ideas about instructional techniques for student teachers and beginning teachers; and 3) as a means for teachers to improve their effectiveness as they gain experience in the classroom.

Major Features of the Revision

Because of its central role in American society, education is a dynamic enterprise. Tens of thousands of people—including classroom teachers, school administrators, state education officials, politicians, and educational and psychological researchers—are constantly searching for and trying out new ideas in an attempt to increase student learning and achievement. This searching about for ways to improve education is especially true of educational and psychological researchers. Since the last edition of this text, many new developments have occurred in social, emotional, and cognitive development (areas such as memory and problem solving); motivation; classroom assessment and management; multicultural education; inclusion of students with disabilities; and the use of computer-based technology to support student learning and achievement. The eighth edition of *Psychology Applied to Teaching* is extensively revised and updated, incorporating new developments in all its domains. Noteworthy themes of this revision include

- *Reflective teaching.* New coverage in Chapters 1 and 14 includes a graphic organizer in the opening chapter that helps readers implement their own Reflective Journal as they read, study, and gain teaching experience.
- *Technology.* New information is included throughout the text (identified by an "@" icon), and information in Applying Technology to Teaching

sections has been expanded. Technology coverage in this edition features ideas about how computers can support learning, as well as specific resources and addresses for such tools as sites on the World Wide Web.

- *Improved utility for novice readers.* Added structure within chapters guides readers easily through the material. A reduction in content helps students to focus on significant ideas.
- *Case in Print.* This new feature connects chapter content to today's issues and asks thought-provoking questions to make its topics meaningful to readers.

The major changes made to each chapter include the following:

CHAPTER 1: APPLYING PSYCHOLOGY TO TEACHING

This chapter was essentially rewritten 1) to introduce students to the discipline of educational psychology (and, by extension, to the topics in the text) and especially 2) to underscore this book's commitment to professional development. Special features in this book help students to become reflective teachers. To achieve the first purpose, we included a discussion of how knowledge of educational psychology is likely to make one a more effective teacher and a summary of research findings that prove the point. To help with the second purpose, we describe how to set up and use a Reflective Journal.

CHAPTER 2: STAGE THEORIES OF DEVELOPMENT

As part of the discussions of the theories of Erik Erikson, Jean Piaget, and Lawrence Kohlberg, this chapter features new research findings on aspects of sex-role development, identity formation, the relationship between cultural background and cognitive development, and moral development. Also new is a section that compares the views of Piaget and Lev Vygotsky on how social interaction and formal instruction affect cognitive development.

CHAPTER 3: AGE-LEVEL CHARACTERISTICS

As part of its discussion of the physical, social, emotional, and cognitive characteristics of students from preschool through high school, this chapter contains new material on the topics of gender differences in motor skills, obesity, peer group influences, friendships, self-concept, logical reasoning, and the cognitive styles of elementary grade students. A new section on characteristics of middle school students was created to help teachers understand the important transition from childhood to adolescence.

CHAPTER 4: UNDERSTANDING CULTURAL DIVERSITY

This chapter is now placed earlier in the book so that students can apply its concepts and ideas to later chapters on assessment, learning, and management. The section on the effects of social class on academic performance, particularly factors that relate to motivation and dropping out of school, has been expanded. Major additions to this chapter include a section on the role of teacher expectancy effects in culturally diverse classrooms and a section on the characteristics of effective multicultural teachers.

CHAPTER 5: ASSESSING STUDENT VARIABILITY

The discussion of the nature of standardized tests and the categories into which they fall is now clarified. A new section takes a critical look at the misuses of standardized test scores and covers, for instance, how pressures to raise standardized test scores lead to such abuses as test score pollution. A second major addition is a section covering new information on performance-based assessment and statewide performance testing.

CHAPTER 6: DEALING WITH STUDENT VARIABILITY

The discussion of the federal legislation that mandates the education of children with disabilities, the Individuals with Disabilities Education Act (Public Law 101-476), has been updated and reorganized. Specifically, we have added coverage of the pro and con arguments about and research on inclusion, and we have lengthened the discussion of the characteristics of children with mild retardation and children with learning disabilities.

CHAPTER 7: DEVISING AND USING OBJECTIVES

This chapter incorporates new content on outcome-based objectives, including discussion of the basic assumptions of OBE and the pros and cons of its application.

CHAPTER 8: BEHAVIORAL AND SOCIAL LEARNING THEORIES

New information has been added on the basic nature of and assumptions underlying operant conditioning. Research on the effects of computer-assisted instruction as an aid to learning is now examined in an expanded section. Also new is a section on the nature of self-efficacy and its relationship to modeling. Effects of modeling on persistence and self-confidence and on the learning of math skills are also discussed as part of revised coverage of social learning theory.

CHAPTER 9: INFORMATION-PROCESSING THEORY

A new section was added, covering how much of what students learn in school is remembered in later years, the conditions that affect retention, and new research on the effects of self-questioning and reciprocal teaching.

CHAPTER 10: COGNITIVE LEARNING THEORIES AND PROBLEM SOLVING

The discussion of constructivism now features a description of its various facets and the conditions that foster it. A new, extended example of constructivist teaching, from the Jasper Woodbury series created by the Center for Cognition and Technology at Vanderbilt University, provides a demonstration of a constructivist perspective, most specifically with problem-solving underpinnings.

CHAPTER 11: MOTIVATION

This extensively revised chapter has a new organization that more clearly reflects the major approaches to motivation: behavioral, cognitive, humanistic, and those based on self-perceptions and cooperative learning. The chapter also contains new material on need achievement and on beliefs about cognitive ability, self-esteem, self-efficacy, and cooperative learning. The chapter puts new emphasis on the role of self-perceptions in motivation and the impact of cooperative learning on motivation.

CHAPTER 12: ASSESSMENT OF CLASSROOM LEARNING

The discussion of the characteristics of authentic performance assessment and how classroom teachers can use it to assess student achievement has been greatly expanded. Among the topics of this discussion are active responding, a close link between teaching and assessment, and an emphasis on complex problems.

CHAPTER 13: CLASSROOM MANAGEMENT

New to this chapter are discussions of different approaches to management and classroom climate—authoritarian, laissez-faire, and authoritative. An expanded section on school violence looks at the multiple factors that underlie its causes; the section provides approaches to classroom management, current data on the nature and frequency of school violence, and descriptions of programs now being used in schools to reduce violence.

CHAPTER 14: BECOMING A BETTER TEACHER BY BECOMING A REFLECTIVE TEACHER

This chapter has been extensively revised to articulate today's theme of reflective teaching. It supplies students with self-assessment techniques and reflective teaching plans. In addition, it encourages students to use the section "Becoming a Reflective Teacher: Questions and Suggestions" in connection with the "Journal Entry" marginal note introduced in Chapter 1.

A final change that deserves mention is perhaps the most subtle and underappreciated, since it does not appear in any specific location. As anyone who has studied psychology or taught students at any level can attest, human behavior is the end result of many factors that interact with one another. We have tried to sensitize the reader to this fact both by pointing it out explicitly (see, for example, the discussion of the effects of computer-assisted instruction on achievement in Chapter 8) and by making cross-references to other chapters wherever possible. The topic of learning strategies, for example, is discussed primarily in Chapter 9 but is also mentioned in conjunction with the writing of instructional objectives (Chapter 7) and measuring classroom learning (Chapter 12).

Special Features of the Text

The following features, many of which were introduced in various earlier editions, have been selected, improved, and augmented to make this eighth edition more useful and effective than its predecessors.

Key Points At the beginning of each chapter, Key Points are listed under major headings. They also appear in the margins of pages opposite sections in which each point is discussed. The Key Points call attention to sections of the text that are considered to be of special significance to teachers and thus serve as instructional objectives.

Suggestions for Teaching in Your Classroom Most chapters include summaries of research findings and principles relating to a particular topic. These are followed by detailed descriptions of various ways in which the information and concepts might be applied in classrooms. Numerous examples of applications at different grade levels are supplied, and readers are urged to select and record applications that will fit their own particular personality, style, and teaching situation in a Reflective Journal. The Suggestions for Teaching are intended to be read while the book is used as a text and referred to by future teachers and in-service teachers after they have completed coursework. For ease in reference, these suggestions are surrounded by a colored border.

Case in Print New with this edition, this feature uses recent news articles to demonstrate how a basic idea or technique in a chapter was applied by educators from the primary grades through high school. Following each article are several open-ended questions designed to encourage the student to think more deeply about the issue in question. The purpose of the Case in Print feature is to illustrate to preservice teachers that the psychological theory and research that their instructors require them to learn does have real-world relevance. A Case in Print can be found in Chapters 2, 4, 5, 6, 7, 8, 9, 10, 11, and 13.

Journal Entries, Becoming a Reflective Teacher: Questions and Suggestions These two features facilitate the preparation and use of a Reflective Journal for teaching. Readers are urged to use the journal entries, which appear in the margins, to prepare a personal set of guidelines for reference before and during the student teaching experience and during the first years of teaching. The Questions and Suggestions in the Becoming a Reflective Teacher section are intended to help in-service teachers to analyze strengths and weaknesses and to plan how to improve their effectiveness as instructors. A guide for setting up and using these resources is included in Chapter 14, "Becoming a Better Teacher by Becoming a Reflective Teacher."

Applying Technology to Teaching Introduced in the last edition, this special feature is now expanded to suggest ways that teachers can use computer-based technology to enhance their students' learning. It appears near the end of each of the three learning theories chapters (Chapters 8–10) in Part 3.

Resources for Further Investigation At the end of each chapter an annotated bibliography is presented, offering sources of information on the major topics covered in the chapter. And starting with this edition, Internet addresses for World Wide Web and gopher sites that provide additional useful information are also listed in this section.

Summary A numbered set of summary statements appears after the Resources for Further Investigation. This feature is intended to help students review the main points of a chapter for upcoming examinations or class discussions.

Key Terms Appearing after the Summary is a list of topics that are key aspects of the chapter. Understanding these topics is an essential part of understanding the chapter as a whole. To facilitate use of this feature, the page where each term is initially defined and discussed appears in parentheses.

Discussion Questions This feature appears after the Key Terms. Because understanding and retention of new information is enhanced when learners actively relate it to known ideas and experiences, the Discussion Questions ask the reader to reflect on how previous experiences (or possible future experiences) relate to the chapter material. These questions can serve as the focus for in-class discussion and out-of-class discussion.

Glossary A glossary of key terms and concepts is provided at the back of the book as an aid in reviewing for examinations or classroom discussion.

Indexes In addition to the detailed name and subject indexes at the end of the book, indexes to Suggestions for Teaching in Your Classroom, Applying Technology to Teaching, Resources for Further Investigation, and Case in Print are included inside the front and back covers.

Instructional Components That Accompany the Text

Study Guide The Study Guide for the eighth edition of *Psychology Applied to Teaching* was designed to help students formulate and carry out a strategy for mastering the Key Points. Students are provided general guidelines for analyzing their resources and learning materials, planning a learning strategy, carrying out the strategy, monitoring their progress, and modifying their strategy if they are dissatisfied with the results. As an integral part of the suggested tactics for learning, original "concept maps" are supplied for each major section of each chapter. These concept maps are schematic representations of how major topics, subtopics, and Key Points of a chapter relate to each other. Also included in the Study Guide are exercises designed to help students enhance memory and understanding of Key Point material, and two sets of review questions (multiple-choice and short-answer) to support student efforts at self-monitoring. Feedback is provided following the multiple-choice questions, explaining to students why each choice is either correct or wrong and referring students to specific pages in the text for verification and additional information.

Instructor's Resource Manual This teaching aid provides for each chapter a detailed lecture outline with supplementary teaching suggestions, a specification of new material to aid users of the seventh edition of *Psychology Applied to Teaching* in making the transition to the current edition, coverage of Key

Points, supplementary discussion topics, student activities, extra references, listings of films and videotapes, and "Approaches to Teaching Educational Psychology," a compendium of teaching tactics from professors across the country.

Test Bank The thoroughly revised Test Bank includes test items consisting of multiple-choice items in alternate forms, short-answer questions, and essay questions. Consistent with this text's longstanding emphasis on mastery, each multiple-choice and short-answer question reflects a Key Point and either the Knowledge, Comprehension, Application, or Analysis level of Bloom's taxonomy. Feedback booklets allow instructors to point out misconceptions in students' reasoning.

Test Generator This component is an interactive computerized version of the Test Bank.

Transparencies An extensive set of colorful transparencies consisting of figures, charts, and instructional aids in the text, is available upon adoption of the text.

Videos Videos are available to course adopters.

Acknowledgments

While the content of a textbook is mostly the product of an author's knowledge, judgment, and communication skill, the suggestions of others play a significant role in shaping its final form. A number of reviewers made constructive suggestions and provided thoughtful reactions at various stages in the development of this manuscript. Thanks go out to the following individuals for their help:

William Hopkins, *State University of New York, Cortland*
Aileen Johnson, *University of Texas, Brownsville*
Adria Karle-Weiss, *Murrat State University*
David Larkin, *Bemidji State University*
Vickie Luttrell, *Southwest Missouri State University*
Sharon McNeeley, *Northeastern Illinois University*
James Rubovits, *Rhode Island College*
L.O. Soderberg, *University of Rhode Island*
Judy Speed, *University of California, Davis*
Julian Wilder, *Adelphi University*

I would also like to acknowledge the invaluable contributions and encouragement of the following members of the Houghton Mifflin editorial staff who helped make this text more accurate, readable, useful, and attractive than I could have made it myself: Janet Edmonds, Janet Young, Elizabeth Emmons, and Lisa Mafrici. I also extend thanks to Merryl Maleska Wilbur, Jess Lionheart, and Connie Gardner.

Finally, I would like to thank my wife, Ruth, for her encouragement, patience, and understanding, particularly for those times when I was convinced that this was the revision that would not end; and my children, Andrea and Jeffrey, who motivate me in their own ways. Four years ago at this time I noted in the Preface to the seventh edition that Andrea was starting college with an interest in psychology. As I write the Preface to this edition I am proud to say that she will graduate in a few days with a degree in psychology and will begin working on a master of social work degree in the fall. I am also proud to say that Jeffrey, who is now a sophomore in college, has decided to major in elementary education. It is for people like Andrea and Jeff that I write this book.

J.S.

Psychology Applied to Teaching

CHAPTER 1

Applying Psychology to Teaching

Key Points

These key points will help you learn the important information in this chapter. To help you study, they also appear in the margins of the pages, next to the text where they are discussed.

What Is Educational Psychology?

- Educational psychologists study how students learn in classrooms

How Will Learning About Educational Psychology Help You Be a Better Teacher?

- Teaching is complex work because it requires a wide range of knowledge and skills
- Research in educational psychology offers many useful ideas for improving classroom instruction
- Teachers who have had professional training are generally more effective

The Nature and Values of Science

- Unsystematic observation may lead to false conclusions
- Grade retention policies are influenced by unsystematic observation
- Scientific methods: sampling, control, objectivity, publication, replication

Complicating Factors in the Study of Behavior and Thought Processes

- Research focuses on a few aspects of a problem
- Constructivism: individuals differ in what they perceive and how they form ideas
- Differences of opinion due to selection and interpretation of data
- Accumulated knowledge leads researchers to revise original ideas

GOOD TEACHING IS PARTLY AN ART AND PARTLY A SCIENCE

- Teaching as an art: emotions, values, flexibility
- Research provides a scientific basis for "artistic" teaching
- Good teachers combine "artistic" and "scientific" characteristics

REFLECTIVE TEACHING: A PROCESS TO HELP YOU GROW FROM NOVICE TO EXPERT

- Reflective teachers think about what they do and why
- Reflective teachers have particular attitudes and abilities

---

As you begin to read this book, you may be asking yourself, "What will this book tell me about teaching that I don't already know?" The answer to that question depends on several factors, including your previous experiences with teaching and the number of psychology courses you have taken. Since you have been actively engaged in the process of formal education for a number of years, you already know a great deal about learning and teaching. You have had abundant opportunities to observe and react to more than one hundred teachers. You have probably read several hundred texts, finished all kinds of assignments, used a variety of software programs, and taken hundreds of examinations. Undoubtedly, you have also established strong likes and dislikes for certain subjects and approaches to teaching.

Yet despite your familiarity with education from the student's point of view, you have probably had limited experience with education from the teacher's point of view. Therefore, we will try to give you a better appreciation of what teachers have to know in order to help students achieve educational goals and objectives.

Throughout this book we will describe many different psychological theories, concepts, and principles and illustrate how you might apply them to teaching. The branch of psychology that specializes in understanding how different factors affect the classroom behavior of both teachers and students is **educational psychology**. In the next few sections we will briefly describe the nature of this field of study and highlight the different ways that you can use this book to become a more effective teacher.

What Is Educational Psychology?

Educational psychologists study how students learn in classrooms

Most educational psychologists, us included, would define their field as a scientific discipline that is concerned with understanding and improving how students acquire a variety of capabilities through formal instruction in classroom settings. According to David Berliner (1992), for example, educational psychology should "study what people think and do as they teach and learn in a particular environment where education and training are intended to take place." This description of educational psychology suggests that to become the most effective teacher possible, you will need to understand such aspects of the learner as physical, social, emotional, and cognitive development; cultural, social, emotional, and intellectual differences; learning and problem-solving processes; self-esteem; motivation; testing; and measurement.

We recognize that you may have some doubts right now both about your ability to master all of this material and the necessity to do so. To help you learn as much of this material as possible, we have incorporated into each chapter a number of helpful features that are described on pages 17–23. But first let's examine why the learning you will do in educational psychology is a worthwhile goal.

This book has been written so that you can use it as a student in a course in educational psychology, as a student teacher coping with all the new experiences of an "apprentice," and as a first-year teacher interested in perfecting instructional skills.

How Will Learning about Educational Psychology Help You Be a Better Teacher?

There's no question that knowledge about psychological concepts and their application to educational settings certainly has the potential to help you be a better teacher. Whether that potential is ever fulfilled depends on how willing you are to maintain an open mind and a positive attitude. We say this because many prospective and practicing teachers have anything but a positive attitude when it comes to using psychological knowledge in the classroom. One teacher, for example, notes that "educational psychology and research are relatively useless because they rarely examine learning in authentic classroom contexts" (Burch, 1993). As you read through the next few paragraphs, as well as the subsequent chapters, you will see that criticisms like this are easily rebutted. We will offer a three-pronged argument to explain how educational psychology can help you be a better teacher, whether you plan to teach in an elementary school, a middle school, or a high school.

TEACHING IS A COMPLEX ENTERPRISE

The first part of our argument is that teaching is not the simple, straightforward enterprise some people imagine it to be; in fact, it ranks in the top quartile on complexity for all occupations (Rowan, 1994). There are many reasons for this complexity. In increasing ways, teachers have daily responsibility for diverse populations of students with varied and sometimes contradictory needs. But perhaps most fundamentally, the complexity of teaching derives from its decision-making nature. Teachers are constantly making decisions—before and after instruction as well as on the spot. To be informed and effective, these decisions should be based on a deep reservoir of knowledge and a wide range of skills. According to a model of good teaching created by Andrew Porter and Jere Brophy (1988), a teacher's knowledge base should include (1) knowledge about the subject matter, (2) knowledge about instructional strategies, and (3) knowledge about the students, including both knowledge about the typical characteristics of children at a particular age and knowledge about the specific characteristics of the teacher's own students. While the complexity inherent in teaching makes it a difficult profession to master, making progress toward that goal is also one of teaching's greatest rewards.

Teaching is complex work because it requires a wide range of knowledge and skills

To help you prepare to take on these challenges and become an effective teacher, educational psychology offers not so much specific prescriptions about how to handle particular problems but general principles that you can use in a flexible manner. Fortunately, the research literature contains a wealth of these ideas.

RESEARCH THAT INFORMS TEACHERS

Contrary to the opinion ventured by the anonymous teacher quoted previously, the research literature contains numerous studies that were conducted under realistic classroom conditions and that offer useful ideas for improving one's instruction. There is consistent, classroom-based support for the following instructional practices (Porter & Brophy, 1988; Cruickshank, 1990. The number in parentheses after each entry refers to the chapter in which we discuss that particular practice):

Research in educational psychology offers many useful ideas for improving classroom instruction

1. Using more advanced students to tutor less advanced students (6)
2. Giving positive reinforcement to students whose performance meets or exceeds the teacher's objectives and giving corrective feedback to students whose performance falls short of the teacher's objectives (8)
3. Communicating to students what is expected of them and why (7)
4. Requiring students to respond to higher-order questions (7, 10)
5. Providing students with cues about the nature of upcoming tasks by giving them introductory information and telling them what constitutes satisfactory performance (8)
6. Teaching students how to monitor and improve their own learning efforts and offering them structured opportunities to practice independent learning activities (9)
7. Knowing the misconceptions that students bring to the classroom that will likely interfere with their learning of a particular subject matter (10)
8. Creating learning situations in which students are expected to organize information in new ways and formulate problems for themselves (10)
9. Accepting responsibility for student outcomes rather than seeing students as solely responsible for what they learn and how they behave (7, 11, 12)
10. Showing students how to work in small cooperative learning groups (4, 11)

COURSEWORK AND COMPETENCE

The third part of our argument concerns the courses you are currently taking, particularly this educational psychology course. Many researchers have asked the question, "How do the courses teachers take as students relate to how capable they perceive themselves to be as teachers?" One means that researchers have used to determine the answer has been to ask beginning teachers to rate how prepared they feel to handle a variety of classroom tasks.

Yona Leyser, Laura Frankiewicz, & Rebecca Vaughn (1992) found that about half of the first-year teachers they surveyed said that their teacher education classes had provided them with their first exposure to the instructional techniques they were now using in their own classrooms. In addition, most beginning teachers surveyed believed they were adequately or well prepared to deal with such tasks as understanding early adolescent development, assessing student achievement, understanding and responding to individual differences in ability, and promoting the social growth of students. Areas in which many felt uncomfortable included motivating students to learn, working with culturally diverse students, teaching exceptional students, managing the classroom, and teaching students how to use computers (e.g., Houston & Williamson, 1992–1993; Leyser, Frankiewicz, & Vaughn, 1992; Queen & Gretes, 1992; Scales, 1993). This textbook will address all of these issues, with special emphasis on most of those about which teachers reported discomfort. Our belief is that this course and this book will be one important means for helping you feel prepared to enter your first classroom.

Another way to gauge the value of teacher-education coursework is to look at the relationship between the courses teachers took as students and how effective they are as teachers. Patrick Ferguson and Sid Womack (1993) found that for students majoring in secondary education, the grades they received in their education courses were a better predictor of their subsequent effectiveness as teachers than either their grade-point average in their major (such as history, biology, math, English) or their specific knowledge (as measured by the specialty score on the National Teacher Examination).

Teachers who have had professional training are generally more effective

Finally, there are the cases of individuals who make dramatic improvements in teaching effectiveness as a result of specific courses in a teacher education program. Linda Valli (1993) describes one individual who stopped working on his bachelor's degree in mathematics to teach full-time at a parochial high school. After one year of teaching in which he described his classes as "basically out of control," he quit teaching, returned to college, and completed a teacher-education program in high school mathematics. Recalling the specific contributions of his educational psychology course, he judged his next teaching job as much more successful than the previous one.

Uses of This Book

This book has been written so that it can be used in three ways. First, it is a text for a course in educational psychology intended to help you master an organized sampling of scientific knowledge about development, learning, objectives, motivation, evaluation, and classroom management. Second, it is a source of practical ideas and suggestions for use during your time as a student teacher and during your first years of teaching. Third, it is a resource to help you reflect on and analyze your own teaching when used in conjunction with the compilation of a Reflective Journal.

USING THIS BOOK TO ACQUIRE SCIENTIFIC INFORMATION

A substantial amount of scientific knowledge is of potential value to teachers. This book offers a selection of information from this pool of knowledge, organized so that you can learn and remember what you read as easily and effectively as possible. Chances are that your instructor will present lectures, organize discussions, provide videotapes and software programs, and perhaps arrange field trips that will tie in with what is discussed in assigned chapters of this text. Depending on the purposes and organization of the educational psychology course you are taking, this book may also serve as the basis for examinations and/or other types of evaluation.

This book contains much scientific information and several features, such as suggestions for teaching, uses of technology, and suggestions for constructing a reflective journal, that will help you become an effective teacher during the early and later stages of your career.

The first way you can use this book, then, is to become well acquainted with an organized body of scientific information in the field of educational psychology. Since this book presently functions as the text for a course, you may be asked to learn some sections well enough to be able to answer test questions. Tests do, after all, act as incentives that motivate students to read with care, and they provide information about how well students understand what they have read. It is particularly desirable for you to read this book carefully during this quarter or semester so that you will become well acquainted with the second way of using the book.

USING THIS BOOK AS A SOURCE OF PRACTICAL IDEAS

The second way this book can be used is as a source of practical ideas on how to teach, especially in the diverse, demanding, and often technologically sophisticated classrooms of today. In addition to acquiring knowledge and learning principles that will serve as a general, all-purpose background for teaching, you should think of specific ways in which you might apply what you learn. Sooner or later you will engage in student teaching. You may be student teaching at the same time you are taking educational psychology. But it is more likely that you will student teach after you finish this book and that you will take one or more additional courses in methods of teaching. Your performance as a student teacher will probably be one of the most important factors considered when you apply for a teaching position. Furthermore, once you secure a job, your performance in the classroom will determine whether you will be offered a contract for a second year. Therefore, you will be eager to function as a prepared, confident, resourceful student teacher and first-year teacher. This book has been designed to help you get ready for your first teaching experiences and to enable you to find solutions to problems as they arise.

USING THIS BOOK TO BECOME A REFLECTIVE TEACHER

As you gain experience in the classroom, you should begin to observe your own teaching and reflect daily on what you feel is working and what is not. Because you cannot anticipate all the problems you will encounter in any classroom, you will need to continually make adjustments and engage in a process of trial and error. To make this process as constructive as possible, you should systematically analyze strengths and weaknesses in your teaching. The third way you can use this book (especially in conjunction with the compilation of your own Reflective Journal), then, is to analyze specific facets of your instructional techniques and plan how to correct errors and perfect successes.

The Nature and Values of Science

The various features of this book all summarize information supplied by psychologists. In addition, the observations of individuals not classified as psychologists will sometimes be mentioned. Indeed, people with many different kinds of backgrounds have taken an interest in education, and their ideas will occasionally be noted at appropriate places in the chapters that follow. The primary purpose of this book, however, is to offer suggestions on how psychology (the scientific study of behavior and mental processes) might be applied to teaching. This text is based on the premise that information reported by scientists can be especially useful for those who plan to teach. Some of the reasons for this conviction become apparent when the characteristics of science are examined.

The values of science become clear when one understands some of the limitations of casual observation—and of unsystematic applications of such observations to behavior—and sees how the scientist tries to correct these weaknesses.

LIMITATIONS OF UNSYSTEMATIC OBSERVATION

Unsystematic observation may lead to false conclusions

Those who make unsystematic observations of human behavior may be easily misled into drawing false conclusions. For instance, they may treat the first plausible explanation that comes to mind as the only possible explanation. Or they may mistakenly apply a generalization about a single episode to superficially similar situations. In the process, they may fail to realize that an individual's reactions in a given situation are due primarily to unrecognized idiosyncratic factors that may never occur again or that the behavior of one person under certain circumstances may not resemble that of other persons in the same circumstances. In short, unsystematic observers are especially prone to noting only evidence that fits their expectations and ignoring evidence that does not. Ignorance of what others have discovered may cause such individuals to start at the same point when confronted with a problem—and to make the same mistakes others have made as they struggled to find solutions.

A clear example of the limitation of unsystematic observation is the practice of retaining children for a second year in a given grade because of poor achievement. Grade retention has long been used as a way of dealing with individual differences in learning rate, emotional development, and socialization skills. According to one estimate, 15 to 19 percent of all schoolchildren in the United States are retained in any given year (Smith & Shepard, 1987). In some school districts the retention rate for a given grade level is reported to be as high as 50 percent (Schultz, 1989). The widespread use of retention in the United States and Europe continues even though most research clearly shows that low-achieving children who are promoted learn more the following year, have a stronger self-concept, and are better adjusted emotionally than similar children who are retained, even when the retention occurs as early as kindergarten (Haberman & Dill, 1993; Holmes, 1989; Mantzicopoulos & Morrison, 1992; Meisels & Liaw, 1993; Reynolds, 1992). Grade retention continues to be recommended by some parents, schools, administrators, and teachers for the very reasons just cited—common sense suggests that repeating a grade should be beneficial to a student, and people tend to overgeneralize from the exceptional case in which the outcome was positive (Haberman & Dill, 1993; Smith & Shepard, 1987; Tomchin & Impara, 1992).

Grade retention policies are influenced by unsystematic observation

STRENGTHS OF SCIENTIFIC OBSERVATION

Those who study behavior and mental processes scientifically are more likely to acquire trustworthy information than a casual observer is, and they are likely to apply what they learn more effectively because they follow the procedures of sampling, control, objectivity, publication, and replication. In most cases a representative sample of subjects is studied so that individual idiosyncrasies are canceled out. An effort is made to note all plausible hypotheses to explain a given type of behavior, and each hypothesis is tested under controlled conditions. If all factors but one can be held constant in an experiment, the researcher may be able to trace the impact of a given condition by comparing the behaviors of those who have been exposed to it and those who have not.

Scientific methods: sampling, control, objectivity, publication, replication

Observers make special efforts to be objective and to guard against being misled by predetermined ideas, wishful thinking, or selected evidence. Observations are made in a carefully prescribed, systematic manner, which makes it possible for observers to compare reactions.

Complete reports of experiments—including descriptions of subjects, methods, results, and conclusions—are published in professional journals. This dissemination allows other experimenters to replicate a study to discover if they obtain the same results. The existence of reports of thousands of experiments makes it possible to discover what others have done. This knowledge can then serve as a starting point for one's own speculations.

Complicating Factors in the Study of Behavior and Thought Processes

Although the use of scientific methods makes it possible to overcome many of the limitations of unscientific observation, the application of knowledge acquired in a scientific manner is subject to several complicating factors.

THE LIMITED FOCUS OF RESEARCH

Behavior is complex, changes with age, and has many causes. A student may perform poorly on a history exam, for example, for one or more of the following reasons: poorly developed study skills, inattentiveness in class, low interest in the subject, a poorly written text, low motivation to achieve high grades, vaguely worded exam questions, and/or difficulty with a particular type of exam question (compare-and-contrast essays, for example).

To understand how these factors affect performance on school-related tasks, research psychologists study at most only a few of them at a time under conditions that may not be entirely realistic. For example, a researcher who is interested in the effect of simulation software versus drill or tutorial software programs on conceptual understanding may recruit subjects who are equivalent in terms of social class, prior knowledge of the topic of the reading passage, and age; randomly assign them to one of two experimental groups; give them either a simulation program or a drill program to use; and then examine each group's responses to several types of comprehension items. As a consequence, most research studies provide specific information about a particular aspect of behavior. More comprehensive knowledge, however, is acquired by the combining and interrelating of separate studies that have looked at different aspects of a common problem.

Research focuses on a few aspects of a problem

INDIVIDUAL DIFFERENCES IN PERCEPTION AND THINKING

As we mentioned in the preceding section, researchers equate subjects in an experiment on one or more major characteristics (such as age, ability, gender, or prior knowledge) in order to draw unambiguous conclusions about the effect of a particular variable or procedure on a particular outcome. This

The constructivist view of learning holds that individual differences in such factors as age, gender, race, and ethnic background lead to differences in what people perceive and how they form ideas.

scientific tactic does not always produce clear-cut results, however, because of unforeseen differences between individuals. Such differences are largely a result of the fact that ideas are not given from one person to another like so many packages but rather are actively *constructed* by each person (Blais, 1988; Brooks, 1990; Wheatley, 1991). Many factors affect the form that an idea takes or whether it comes into existence at all. Some of these factors (which we will discuss at various points in the text) include age, gender, race, ethnic background, prior knowledge, problem-solving skills, and motivation. Because different factors come into play for different people and the same factors affect people differently, two people can read the same passage yet construct entirely different interpretations of its meaning. This concept (known as *constructivism)* is so fundamental to human behavior and to learning that we will return to it again and again in this text.

Constructivism: individuals differ in what they perceive and how they form ideas

SELECTION AND INTERPRETATION OF DATA

The amount of scientific information available on behavior and mental processes is so extensive that no individual could examine or interpret all of it. Accordingly, researchers learn to be highly selective in their reading. In addition, conclusions about the meaning of scientific results vary from one researcher to another. As you read this book, you will discover that there are differences of opinion among psychologists regarding certain aspects of development, motivation, and intelligence. Opposing views may be based on equally scientific evidence, but the way in which the evidence is selected and interpreted will vary. Just because a topic is studied scientifically does not necessarily mean that opinions about interpretations of the data will be unanimous.

Differences of opinion due to selection and interpretation of data

NEW FINDINGS MEAN REVISED IDEAS

Scientific information is not only voluminous and subject to different interpretations; it is also constantly being revised. A series of experiments may lead to the development of a new concept or pedagogical technique that is highly successful when it is first tried out. Subsequent studies, however, may reveal that the original research was incomplete, or repeated applications of a technique may show that it is less effective once the novelty has worn off. But frequent shifts of emphasis in education also reflect the basic nature of science. A quality of science that sets it apart from other intellectual processes is that the discoveries by one generation of scientists set the stage for more complete and far-reaching discoveries by the next. More researchers are studying aspects of psychology and education now than at any previous time in history. And thousands of reports of scientific research are published every month.

Accumulated knowledge leads researchers to revise original ideas

As our knowledge accumulates, it is inevitable that interpretations of how children learn and how we should teach will continue to change. We know more about development, learning, and teaching today than ever before, but because of the nature of some of the factors just discussed—and the complexity of human behavior—our answers are tentative and incomplete.

You should be aware, of course, that fads occur in education (just as they occur in other fields). Occasionally, national and/or international events cause changes in our political and social climate. These changes often result in pressures on education to "do something." And when large numbers of educators embrace a new practice without waiting for or paying attention to research findings, fads develop (see Slavin, 1989, for an example). One of our objectives in writing this text is to demonstrate the importance of basing your practices on principles that have some research support and, thereby, help you avoid contributing to fads.

In the last few pages we have asked you to consider some of the values of science, the strengths of scientific observation, and a few of the factors that complicate the scientific study of behavior and lead to frequent changes of emphasis in teaching techniques. These considerations help explain why this book stresses how psychology might be applied to teaching; they also support the position that information reported by scientists can be especially valuable for those who plan to teach. At the same time, our intention has been to acquaint you with a few of the limitations and sometimes unsettling by-products of science.

The science of psychology has much to offer educators, but a scientific approach to teaching does have its limits. Because teaching is a dynamic *decision-making process,* you will be greatly aided by a systematic, objective framework for making your decisions; research on teaching and learning can give you that framework. But for the reasons just cited, research cannot give you a prescription or a set of rules that specify how you should handle every situation. Often you will have to make on-the-spot, subjective decisions about how to present a lesson, explain a concept, handle mass boredom, or reprimand a student. This contrast between an objective, systematic approach to planning instruction and the need to make immediate (yet appropriate) applications and modifications of those plans calls attention to a question that has been debated for years: Is teaching primarily an art or a science—or a combination of both?

Good Teaching Is Partly an Art and Partly a Science

Some educators have argued that teaching is an art that cannot be practiced—or even studied—in an objective or scientific manner (Dawe, 1984; Flinders, 1989; Hansgen, 1991; Highet, 1957; Rubin, 1985). For example, Gilbert Highet, a distinguished critic and professor of literature, argues in *The Art of Teaching* that successful teaching must be considered an art because it involves two things that cannot be objectively and systematically manipulated: emotions and values. In Highet's view:

> Teaching is not like inducing a chemical reaction: it is much more like painting a picture or making a piece of music, . . . like planting a garden or writing a friendly letter. You must throw your heart into it, you must realize that it cannot all be done by formulas, or you will spoil your work, and your pupils, and yourself. (1957, p. viii)

Part of the art of teaching is knowing when to introduce an unusual assignment or activity that captures students' interest.

Examples of the emotions and values referred to by Highet include believing that teaching is one of society's most valuable and rewarding activities, that teaching must be done as well as possible every day, that it is important to get students excited about learning, and that there is no such thing as an unteachable student. When Highet states that teaching cannot all be done by formulas, he is urging teachers to be flexible. Flexibility, which can be thought of as a "feel" for doing the right thing at the right time, can take many forms. First, it means being able to choose from among all the techniques and information at your disposal to formulate effective lesson plans that take the diverse needs and interests of all your students into consideration. It means knowing, for example, when to present a formal lesson and when to let students discover things for themselves, when to be demanding and when to make few demands, when and to whom to give direct help and when and to whom to give indirect help.

Second, flexibility entails the communication of emotions and interest in a variety of ways. David Flinders (1989) describes a teacher who, when talking to students, would lean or step in their direction and maintain eye contact. At various times she would raise her eyebrows, nod her head, smile, and bring the index finger of her right hand to her lips, indicating serious consideration of the student's comments.

Third, flexibility includes the ability to improvise. When a lesson plan falls flat, the flexible teacher immediately thinks of an alternative presentation that recaptures the students' interest. Expert teachers actually plan improvisation into their lessons. Instead of writing out what they intend to do in great detail, expert teachers formulate general mental plans and wait to see how the students react before filling in such details as pacing, timing, and numbers of examples (Livingston & Borko, 1989; Westerman, 1991). Obviously, this type of high-wire act requires a great deal of experience and confidence.

Fourth, flexibility involves the willingness and resourcefulness to work around impediments. Teaching does not always occur under ideal circumstances, and teachers must sometimes cope with inadequate facilities, insufficient materials, interruptions, and other difficulties.Thus, **teaching as an art** involves emotions, values, and flexibility. Because these characteristics are intangible, they can be very difficult, if not impossible, to teach. Teachers must find these qualities within themselves.

Teaching as an art: emotions, values, flexibility

The argument for **teaching as a science** is equally persuasive. Scholars such as Paul Woodring (1957), Nathaniel Gage (1984), David Berliner (1986), and Lee Shulman (1986) agree that the science of teaching, as such, does not currently exist. But they contend that it is possible and good to have a scientific basis for the art of teaching. By drawing on established research findings, both prospective and practicing teachers can be taught many of the prerequisites that make "artistic" teaching possible. Also, as Robert Slavin (1989) persuasively argues, working from a scientific basis helps teachers avoid the pitfall of subscribing to the latest fad. This argument, of course, rests on the existence of a usable body of research findings, which educational psychologists believe does exist. As evidence, you might consult "The Quiet Revolution in Educational Research" (Walberg, Schiller, & Haertel, 1979) and "Productive Thinking and Instruction: Assessing the Knowledge Base" (Walberg, 1990). In both articles Herbert Walberg identifies dozens of research-validated instructional practices that have been shown to improve achievement. For example, twenty-four of twenty-five studies found that giving teachers more instructional time—that is, giving students more time to learn—leads to higher achievement. (This finding is often used to support proposals for a longer school year.)

Research provides a scientific basis for "artistic" teaching

Other studies have demonstrated the benefits of alerting students to important material through the use of objectives and pretests, getting students involved in a task through the use of questions and homework, and providing corrective feedback and reinforcement with written comments, verbal explanations, and praise. Another example of usable research can be found in the work of David Berliner (1986) and Lee Shulman (1986) on the characteristics of expert teachers. One reason some teachers are experts is that they can quickly and accurately recall relevant knowledge from two large areas: subject-matter knowledge and knowledge of classroom organization and management. From the research being done in this area, we are learning how expert teachers acquire this knowledge, recall it, and use it appropriately.

Look back at the heading of this section. Notice that it reads, "Good Teaching Is Partly an Art and Partly a Science," not "Teaching as an Art

Versus Teaching as a Science." Our choice of wording indicates our belief that good teaching is a skillful blend of artistic and scientific elements. The teacher who attempts to base every action on scientific evidence is likely to come across as rigid and mechanical—perhaps even indecisive (when the scientific evidence is lacking or unclear). The teacher who ignores scientific knowledge about teaching and learning and makes arbitrary decisions runs the risk of using methods and principles of teaching that are ineffective.

Good teachers combine "artistic" and "scientific" characteristics

Reflective Teaching: A Process to Help You Grow from Novice to Expert

This blending of artistic and scientific elements can be seen in recent discussions of what is called **reflective teaching** (see, for example, Eby, 1994; Hatton & Smith, 1995; Ross, Bondy, & Kyle, 1993; and Schon, 1987). Reflective teachers are constantly engaged in thoughtful observation and analysis of their actions in the classroom before, during, and after interactions with their students.

Reflective teachers think about what they do and why

Prior to instruction, reflective teachers may think about such things as the types of knowledge and skills students in a democratic society in the late 1990s need to learn, the kind of classroom atmosphere and teaching techniques that are most likely to produce this learning, and the kinds of assessments that will provide clear evidence that these goals are being accomplished (a topic that we discuss at some length in Chapter 12). Jere Brophy and Janet Alleman (1991) illustrate the importance of thinking about long-range goals by pointing out how the choice of goals affects content coverage and how content coverage affects teachers' choice of classroom activities. If, for example, one goal is for students to acquire problem-solving skills, students would likely be engaged in activities that call for inquiring, reasoning, and decision making. Debates, simulations, and laboratory experiments are just three examples of activities that might be used to meet such a goal. If, however, the goal is for students to memorize facts and information, students will likely be given activities that call for isolated memorization and recall. Worksheets and drill-and-practice exercises are typically used to meet this type of goal. The point here is that effective teachers are reflective—they think about these issues as a basis for drawing up lesson plans.

Reflective teachers set aside time to think about what they do in class, why they do it, and how their methods affect student performance.

As they interact with students, reflective teachers are highly aware of how students are responding to what they are doing and are prepared to make minor but significant changes to keep a lesson moving toward its predetermined goal. Consider an elementary school classroom in which some students are having difficulty understanding the relationship between the orbits of the planets around the sun and their position in the night sky. The teacher knows there is a problem because some students have a puzzled expression on their faces, while others cannot describe this phenomenon in their own words. Realizing that some students think in more concrete terms than others (a topic we will discuss in Chapter 2), the teacher decides to push the desks to the sides of the room and have the students simulate the planets by walking through their orbits. Notice how—all in the moment—this teacher engaged in thoughtful observation, spontaneous analysis, and flexible, resourceful problem solving.

For events that cannot be handled on the spot, some period of afterschool time should be set aside for reflection. This is the time to assess how well a particular lesson met its objective, to wonder why some students rarely participate in class discussions, to ponder the pros and cons of grouping students by ability, and to formulate plans for dealing with these concerns.

Reflective teachers have particular attitudes and abilities

To become a reflective teacher, you will need to acquire several attitudes and abilities. Three of the most important attitudes are an introspective orientation, an open-minded but questioning attitude about educational theories and practices, and the willingness to take responsibility for your decisions and actions. These attitudes need to be combined with the ability to view situations from others' perspectives (students, parents, principal, other teachers), the ability to find information that allows an alternative explanation of classroom events and that produces more effective instructional methods, and the ability to use compelling evidence in support of a decision (Eby, 1994; Ross, Bondy, & Kyle, 1993). We hasten to add that, while reflection is by nature largely a solitary activity, you should discuss your concerns with colleagues, students, and parents to get different perspectives on the nature of a problem and possible alternative courses of action.

As you can probably see from this brief discussion, the reflection process is likely to work well when teachers have command of a wide range of knowledge about the nature of students, the learning process, and the instructional process. By mastering much of the content of this text, you will be that much more prepared than your less knowledgeable peers to make productive use of the time you devote to reflection. Another factor that has been shown to contribute to teacher reflectivity is journal writing. Keeping a written journal forces you to express with some clarity your thoughts and beliefs about the causes of classroom events, how you feel about them, and what you might do about them (Bolin, 1990; Han, 1995). Thus, one potentially helpful way you might begin developing this reflective capacity is to follow our suggestion for compiling a Reflective Journal. Later in this chapter we will describe in more detail just how you might set this journal up.

The Contents of This Book

In speculating about ways that psychology might be applied to teaching, a number of theorists have proposed what are often referred to as *theories of instruction* or *models of instruction* (for example, see Mager, 1975; Carroll, 1963; Glaser, 1976; Bloom, 1976). The purpose of such theories or models is to provide a basic strategy for instruction.

Several theories of instruction will be discussed in subsequent chapters of this book. For now, however, note that these theories emphasize a basic four-step sequence that teachers might follow to make instruction as effective as possible:

1. Take into account what students are like and how much they know.
2. Specify what is to be learned.

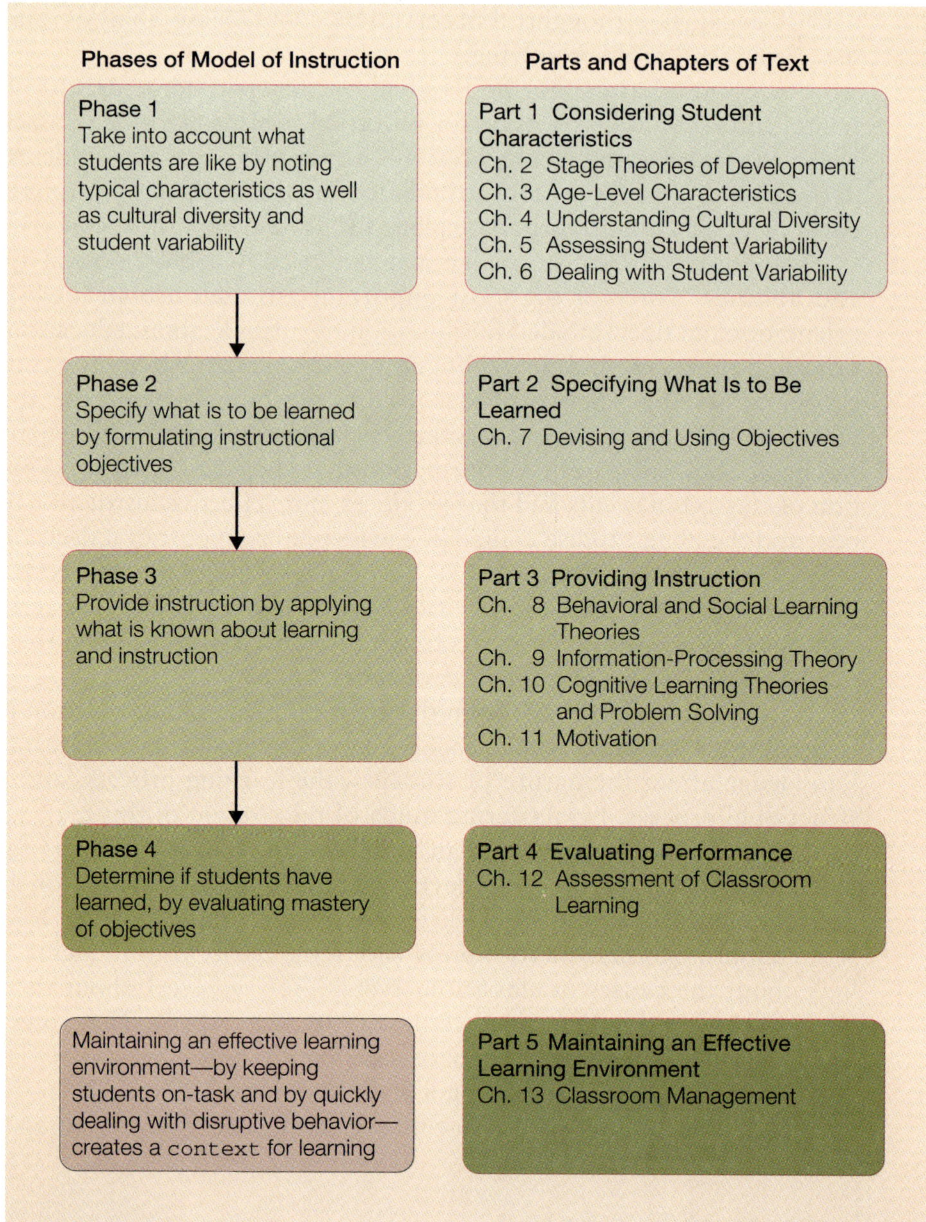

FIGURE 1.1 *The Model of Instruction Used in Organizing This Book*

3. Provide instruction by taking advantage of what has been discovered about learning, cognitive strategies, and motivation.
4. Determine if students have learned.

(Some models of instruction suggest that the first step is to specify what is to be learned. While this is often a logical place for teachers to begin when dealing with college students, it may not be the best first step when dealing with younger students of various ages. Indeed, younger students tend to benefit when teachers initially consider their personal traits—how much they already know, their cognitive characteristics, how they behave in classrooms, and so forth.)

The contents of this book are arranged with reference to the sequence just described. Chapters 2 through 12 are grouped (as diagrammed in Figure 1.1) to reflect and illustrate the four phases of the model of instruction featured in this text. Chapter 13 provides information about the context within which that learning will take place—that is, the management of a classroom conducive to learning. (Not shown in the figure are this first chapter and the final chapter, which offer you tools for your own learning, reflectivity, and growth as a practitioner.)

Special Features of This Book

Several distinctive features of this book are intended to be used in rather specialized ways. These features include Key Points, Suggestions for Teaching in Your Classroom, Applying Technology to Teaching, Resources for Further Investigation, and Journal Entries. In addition, your compilation of a separate component to accompany this book—the Reflective Journal—is recommended. This journal makes use of the text's Journal Entries, of the Suggestions for Teaching, and of the final chapter's special section, Questions and Suggestions for Becoming a Reflective Teacher.

KEY POINTS

At the beginning of each chapter, you will find a list of *Key Points.* The Key Points also appear within each chapter, printed in small type in the margins. These points have been selected to help you learn and remember sections of each chapter that are of special significance to teachers. (These sections may be stressed on exams, but they were originally selected not because they can serve as the basis for test items, but because they are important.) If you tried to learn everything in this book, you would be working against yourself because some of the information you might memorize would interfere with the acquisition of other information. To reduce forgetting due to such interference, you are asked to concentrate on only a few sections in each chapter. To grasp the nature of the Key Points, turn to pages 30–31, which list points stressed under the major headings of Chapter 2. Then flip through the chapter to see how the appearance of the Key Points in the margins calls attention to significant sections of the text.

SUGGESTIONS FOR TEACHING IN YOUR CLASSROOM

In most of the chapters of this book, you will find summaries of research that serve as the basis for related principles or conclusions. These sets of principles or conclusions, in turn, are the foundation for *Suggestions for Teaching in Your Classroom.* Each suggestion is usually followed by a list of examples illustrating how it might be applied. In most cases examples are provided for both elementary and secondary grades since there usually are differences in the way a principle might be applied in dealing with younger and with older pupils.

The principles, suggestions, and examples are intended to help you think about how you can apply psychology to teaching. The lists of Suggestions for Teaching in Your Classroom and the examples of some ways of applying principles are intended to help you compensate, at least partially, for lack of experience when you begin to teach. Since you will often want to find quick answers with a minimum of difficulty, applications of principles are first listed as sets of related ideas (which you can later refer to as reminders and as an "index" to detailed analyses of each point). Then each point is discussed and illustrated, in most cases by multiple examples. To permit you to find information relating to particular aspects of teaching, an index to the Suggestions for Teaching in Your Classroom is printed inside the front cover. To discover the nature of the Suggestions read the list on page 46, and then examine the detailed suggestions and examples of applications that follow.

CASE IN PRINT

This new feature presents a recent newspaper article that either 1) elaborates on an idea or technique described in the chapter or 2) shows how an idea was applied by public school educators.

@ APPLYING TECHNOLOGY TO TEACHING

As a teacher in the 1990s, you will want to be knowledgeable about the many ways educational technology can enhance your students' learning. We feel it is important for new teachers to recognize that the fundamentals of good teaching described in this book apply regardless of the tools that are used. For this reason, you will find a section called *Applying Technology to Teaching* in each of the learning theories chapters in Part 3. The suggestions in these sections give you an idea of how to use technology in your own classroom teaching, building on the same general concepts discussed in each of the chapters. You might wish to try some of the suggested software yourself to see how it functions—and to help you develop your ability to select good software. Note that all references to software and other forms of computer technology in this book will be marked with an "@" sign, as shown above.

RESOURCES FOR FURTHER INVESTIGATION

In the chapters that follow, you will find suggestions that cover many facets of teaching. You are likely to conclude, however, that some information on particular aspects of teaching is not complete enough. Despite the book's attempt to provide at least partial solutions to the most common difficulties faced by teachers, you are bound, sooner or later, to become aware of problems that are not discussed in these pages. You may want additional data on some aspects of teaching, either while you are taking this course or after you are experienced enough to have time for a detailed look at some facet of education, psychology, or instruction. To allow for instances where you will need additional information, an annotated bibliography is provided at the end of each chapter. *Resources for Further Investigation* lists articles, books, and, for the first time, on-line (Internet) sources you might consult. Instructions for do-it-yourself studies are also included at the end of many chapters.

Since the 1980s, computer-based technologies have played an increasingly larger role in classroom teaching and learning. In all likelihood, computers will one day be as common a part of classrooms as text-books are today.

Two important points should be mentioned regarding Internet sources of information. First, all the databases and resources listed or described throughout this book have been checked for accuracy as of its publication date. The world of on-line information, however, is in constant flux—databases are updated, moved, renamed, or deleted from the Internet network every day. If you're unable to find one of the resources mentioned, we recommend that you consult your school's computer support person or your colleagues (since the most current information is often passed by word of mouth).

This brings up the second important point about on-line information: it is not any more reliable (and in some cases is definitely less reliable) than what you may find in print. In particular, "newsgroups" and "discussion groups" are notorious for participants' distribution of incorrect, incomplete, or misleading advice or information. Our recommendation to you is to treat on-line information as you would print: try to stay with publishers or databases that are maintained by reputable sources, such as education or psychology departments of universities, major educational associations, the U.S. government, and so forth. Double-check the information you gather on-line—don't assume that because it appears on a computer that it is accurate! And remember that participating in a newsgroup discussion is most useful for generating new ideas or potential directions that you can pursue further on your own or with a group of classmates.

DEVELOPING A REFLECTIVE JOURNAL

We recommend that you develop a Reflective Journal for two basic purposes: (1) to serve as a repository of instructional ideas and techniques that you have either created from your own experiences or gleaned from other sources and (2) to give yourself a format for recording your observations and reflections on teaching. These two purposes can be separate from each other or, if you choose, related to each other in a cycle of reflectivity that we will describe. As you read this section, refer to Figure 1.2 for an illustration of how a journal page might look.

Journal Entry: *Ways to Teach Comprehension Tactics*
Source: *Chapter 9—Information-Processing Theory*

IDEAS FOR INSTRUCTION

Note: All the ideas you list here will pertain to the particular journal entry/instructional goal for this journal page.

- *Customized suggestions for teaching—those points, principles, activities, and examples taken from the text and the Suggestions for Teaching that are most relevant to your own situation.*
- *Ideas generated from past experiences as a student.*
- *Ideas provided by professional colleagues.*
- *Ideas collected from student-teaching experiences.*
- *Ideas gathered from methods textbooks.*

REFLECTIONS: QUESTIONS AND "RESTARTER" SUGGESTIONS FOR INSTRUCTION

Reflective Question (to focus observation of my teaching and my students' learning): *Do my students have difficulty understanding the meaning of what they read or of what I present in class?*

(Record your ongoing reflections, observations, and analytic notes about your instruction and your students' learning of this topic here. If necessary, you may need to "jump-start" or reorient your instruction. One possible idea follows.)

Suggested Action: *Schedule a series of sessions on how to study. Explain the purpose of various comprehension tactics, and provide opportunities for students to practice these skills on material they have been assigned to read. Give corrective feedback.*

FIGURE 1.2 *Sample Page for Your Reflective Journal*

Since you may need to concentrate on learning Key Points to demonstrate understanding on exams during the course you are now taking, you may not have time to prepare the journal this quarter or semester. But after you have read this book as a text, you might go through it a second time for the purpose of developing a custom-designed journal. To allow room for both expansion of your teaching ideas and the inclusion of your ongoing reflections, you might purchase a three-ring binder so that pages can be added or dropped. Alternatively, if you have regular access to a computer, you might want to create your Reflective Journal on electronic files, which would permit you unlimited capacity for interaction and expansion.

Journal Entries Within the margins of each chapter, you will find numerous instances of the phrase *Journal Entries.* These marginal headings are related to the material just opposite in the text. They are intended to serve as suggested wordings for the headings of pages in your Reflective Journal. You might print each heading at the top of a page; it can act as the title of the topic for both the reflections and the teaching ideas that you will include on that page. On page 349, for instance, you will find the Journal Entry "Ways to Teach Comprehension Tactics." That heading is intended to stimulate you to jot down your reflections about how well students seem to understand the meaning of what they are learning and to record specific ways to help your students improve their comprehension skills.

"Ideas": Suggestions for Teaching and Other Sources The Suggestions for Teaching in Your Classroom and the instructional examples in this text are intended as models and representative sample applications to help you prepare for your initial teaching experiences. Most of the time you will need to devise specific applications of principles that apply to your own teaching situations. For each Journal Entry, you can customize Suggestions for Teaching from the general list and include them under that topic. You can also list other specific techniques brainstormed with peers and colleagues, remembered from your own student days, or invented on your own. As it expands over time, this will become a repository of ideas that occur to you during methods courses, student teaching, and your first years as a full-time teacher. By writing out your own version of the suggestions, devising your own examples of applications, and perhaps even preparing an index, you will be equipping yourself with a custom-designed guidebook that should assist you in coping with many of the problems you will encounter when you first take over a classroom.

To grasp in more detail how you might proceed, let's use the Journal Entry from page 349 ("Ways to Teach Comprehension Tactics") mentioned previously. First, search your memory for techniques used by your former teachers. Did your fifth-grade teacher, for instance, have a clever way of relating new information to ideas that you had learned earlier in order to make the new information easier to understand? Describe the technique so you will remember to try it yourself. Did a high school teacher have an ingenious way of displaying the similarities and differences among a set of ideas? Exactly how did she or he do it? After you exhaust your own recollections, ask roommates or classmates if they can remember any successful ways that their teachers made learning easier.

Next, examine the examples opposite the Journal Entry. Which ones seem most appropriate for the grade level and subject you will be teaching? Jot them down. Do any of the examples suggest variations you can think of on your own? Write them down before you forget them.

Finally, add ideas that you pick up in methods classes or during your student-teaching experience. If you see a film in a methods class that shows how a teacher helps students understand a particular point, describe it in your journal. If your master teacher uses a successful technique to clarify difficult to understand material, record it. If you follow some or all of these suggestions for using the Journal Entries, you will have a rich source of ideas to turn to when you discover that your students seem confused and anxious because of poor comprehension and you find yourself wondering if there is anything you can do about it.

"Reflections": Questions and Suggestions for Becoming a Reflective Teacher

Good teachers never stop learning. They never stop questioning themselves, observing what works and what doesn't work with which students and in which situations, self-evaluating their own methods and styles. They maintain a mindful awareness of their own actions, and they monitor the reactions that their students have. They realize that often what appears to be a student's learning problem can turn out to be an instructional problem or just an instructional mismatch that they themselves must help resolve.

Even when teachers plan ahead for a given situation, they often discover that for one reason or another it is extremely difficult or impossible to put their ideas into practice. Sometimes they become so preoccupied with certain aspects of teaching that when they finally take stock, they realize they have slighted other facets of instruction.

For all these reasons, it will be to your advantage during the first months or years of your teaching career to make a systematic effort to evaluate selected aspects of your instructional technique. Otherwise, you may simply "do what comes naturally." Even with the guidance of this text, the Reflective Journal, and other books on teaching, you will not be able to think of everything at once. To enable you to analyze selected aspects of your teaching style over a period of time and to become a better reflective teacher, we recommend that you develop a regular habit of questioning yourself mindfully. To help you set up a cycle of questioning in your journal (see Figure 1.3), Chapter 14 provides an extensive set of questions cued to the Journal Entries. Each Journal Entry is accompanied by one or more questions; those questions are followed by a new Suggestion for Teaching. It or something like it of your own making can act to "restart" you in a different direction if that seems appropriate and help launch you in a new instructional and reflective cycle.

One final comment: remember that—like the suggestions themselves—these questions from Chapter 14 are intended only as models, samples, and examples. As you develop the ability to become reflective about your teaching, you will find yourself generating your own inquiries and creating original journal entries. You will have become an experienced self-observer.

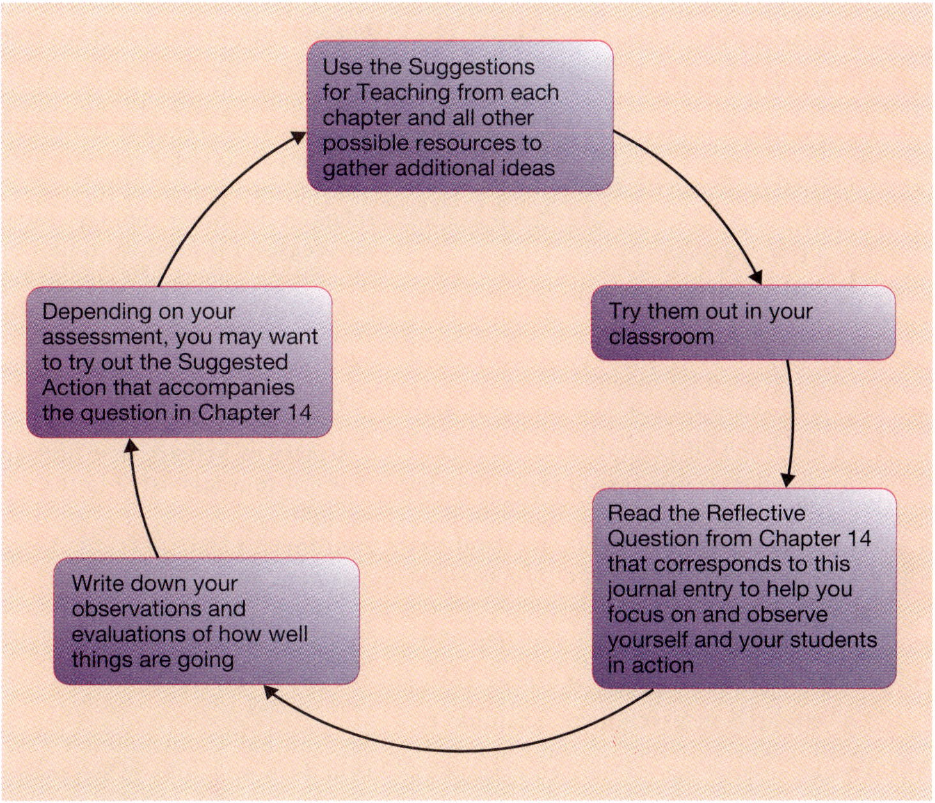

FIGURE 1.3 *How to Use Your Journal as Part of a Reflective Teaching Cycle*

Resources for Further Investigation

Professional Journals

To gain some direct experience with the raw material of psychology—the building blocks that are eventually combined to establish a principle or theory—you might examine one or more of the professional journals in psychology. These journals consist primarily of reports of experiments.

The following journals are likely to be found in a typical college library:

American Educational Research Journal

Behavioral Science

Child Development

Developmental Psychology

Educational and Psychological Measurement

Exceptional Child

Genetic Psychology Monographs

Harvard Educational Review

Journal of Abnormal and Social Psychology

Journal of Applied Behavior Analysis

Journal of Educational Psychology

Journal of Educational Research

Journal of Educational Sociology

Journal of Experimental Child Psychology

Journal of Experimental Education

Journal of Teacher Education

Merrill-Palmer Quarterly of Behavior and Development

Psychological Monographs

Psychological Review

Psychology in the Schools

Society for Research in Child Development Monographs

An excellent starting point for on-line research in education is the American Educational Research Association's database, which is located at http://info.asu.edu/aff/aera/home.html.[1] A Gopher version of the database can be found at gopher://info.asu.edu.:70/11/aff/aera.

To develop an awareness of the nature of research in psychology, examine recent issues of some of these journals. Then, select an article describing an experiment that intrigues you or appears to be relevant to your own interests, grade level, and subject. Finally, write an abstract (a brief summary of results) of the article, including the following:

Author of article

Title of article

Journal in which article appears (including date, volume number, and page numbers)

Purpose (or description of problem)

Subjects

Procedure (or methods)

Treatment of data

Results

Conclusions

Are there any criticisms that you can make of the procedure or conclusions?

1. Readers new to the Internet should note that end punctuation is not part of the address.

What inferences for your own teaching can you draw from this experiment?

Would you be willing to change your methods of teaching on the strength of this one article?

Journals of Abstracts and Reviews

Unless you are familiar with research in a particular aspect of educational psychology, you may find it difficult either to fit an individual study reported in a journal into a general framework or to relate it to other similar research. In most cases it is prudent to find out what other experiments of a similar type have revealed about a particular point before you generalize from the results of a single study. A variety of journals and reference works exist to assist you in doing this. The following journals consist of abstracts of articles that appear in the types of journals listed in the preceding section:

Child Development Abstracts and Bibliography

Exceptional Child Education Abstracts

Psychological Abstracts

Psyc SCAN

The journal *Contemporary Psychology* reviews new books in psychology, and the *Annual Review of Psychology* provides information reflected by the title—that is, a specialist in each of several areas of psychology reviews significant studies that have appeared during a given year. An on-line source for psychological abstracts is the American Psychological Association's (APA) database, whose address is http://www.apa.org. This site contains a large database of information published by the APA, as well as news and announcements of conferences and journals. The *Review of Educational Research* features articles that describe, relate, and analyze reports of studies on a particular theme.

To discover the nature of these journals and reference works, examine some of them and perhaps prepare a brief description of the most promising titles to save for future reference. Or select a topic of interest, search for reports of experiments, and summarize the conclusions you reach.

Journals That Describe Trends and Techniques

In addition to descriptions of actual experiments, "discussion" articles are published in some professional journals and in many teachers' magazines.

Journals Consisting of General Discussions of Trends, Developments, and Techniques

The following journals describe trends, developments, and techniques and also interpret research data. Some articles cite research studies; others offer interpretations of approaches to teaching without reference to specific data. Many of these journals also feature sections on tricks of the trade, and most provide book reviews. A comprehensive on-line source of pedagogical information is the "Best of the Internet K–12" gopher database, located at gopher://informns.k12.mns.us/11/best-k12.

Change in Higher Education

Clearing House (junior and senior high school teaching)

Contemporary Education

Elementary School Journal

Exceptional Children

Journal of General Education

Journal of Higher Education (college and university teaching)

Junior College Journal

Phi Delta Kappa

Teachers College Record

Theory into Practice

Journals Consisting of Brief Commentaries on Trends, Developments, and Techniques

The following journals consist of short articles (usually fewer than five pages each) on trends, developments, and techniques in education:

American Journal of Education

Childhood Education

Education

Educational Forum

Educational Leadership

Educational Record (college and university teaching)

Educational Technology (computer-assisted instruction, behavior modification)

Electronic Learning

High School Journal

Journal of Education

Education Digest is made up of condensations of articles selected from the types of journals listed in this section and the preceding one. Similarly, the on-line digest EduPage, located at http://www.educom.com, consists of brief summaries of news articles related to education and technology. It is published twice weekly.

Magazines for Teachers

The following publications provide articles, usually in magazine format, with emphasis on journalistic style, abundant illustrations, and colorful graphic design:

Instructor

Learning

NEA Today

Psychology Today

If you look through some recent issues of several of these journals, you will find typical trend-and-technique articles on psychology and education. For future reference, you might read an article that is relevant to your own interests, grade level, and subject and then write a synopsis of the author's arguments. If any of these arguments are pertinent to your own theorizing about teaching, briefly analyze your thoughts, perhaps by using the following outline:

Author of article

Name of article

Journal in which article appeared (including date, volume number, and page numbers)

Synopsis of arguments presented

Your reaction to the arguments

Specialized Publications for Teachers

Almost every field of study in education has one or more journals devoted to reports of research, reviews of related experimental studies, discussions of teaching techniques, descriptions of tricks of the trade, and analyses of subject matter.

A large number of such specialized publications are available on-line as well. Because of the ever-changing nature of the Internet, a sensible approach for finding good current information on a specialized topic is to do a key-word search through one of the major search services, such as Yahoo, which is located at http://www.yahoo.com/search.html. The following list of journals may help you discover what is available in your area or areas of interest (using their titles as key words in your on-line search is a good strategy, too):

African Studies Journal

Agricultural Education Magazine

American Biology Teacher

American Music Teacher

American Speech

American String Teacher

Arithmetic Teacher

Art Education

Business Education World

Communication Quarterly

Education and Training in Mental Retardation

Educational Theatre News

Elementary School Guidance and Counseling

English Language Teaching Journal

English Studies

Forecast (home economics)

French Review

Geography Teacher

Gifted Child Quarterly

History Teacher

Industrial Arts and Vocational Education

Instrumentalist

Journal of American Indian Education

Journal of Industrial Teacher Education

Journal of Negro Education

Journal of Nursing Education

Journal of Reading

Journal of Research in Science Teaching

Journal of School Health

Journal of Special Education

Journal of Vocational Education Research

Language Arts

Marriage and Family Living

Mathematics Teacher

Music Educators Journal

Physical Educator

Physics Teacher

Reading Teacher

Scholastic Coach

School Arts

School Counselor

School Musician Director and Teacher

School Science and Mathematics

School Shop–Technical Directions

Science Education

Swimming Technique

Teaching Exceptional Children

Tennis

Theatre World

Track Technique

To discover what is available, check titles that sound promising, spend some time in the periodicals section of your college library, and examine some recent issues. You might select an article you find interesting and write an abstract of it, together with your own interpretation. Or you might prepare a brief description of journals that impress you as worthy of attention. This list could serve as a source of information on what journals to consult after you begin your teaching career.

Educational Resources Information Center (ERIC)

As a number of journals listed on the preceding pages indicate, thousands of articles are published each year on every conceivable aspect of educational psychology and education. To assist psychologists and educators in discovering what has been published on a specific topic, the Educational Resources Information Center was established by the U.S. Office of Education (now called the U.S. Department of Education). ERIC publishes two sources of information.

Current Index to Journals in Education—Annual Cumulation contains an index of articles in more than three hundred education and education-oriented journals published in a given year. There are four sections in each volume: the Subject Index (which lists titles of articles organized under hundreds of subject headings), the Author Index, the Journal Contents Index (which lists the table of contents for each issue of journals published that year), and the Main Entry Section (which provides the title, author, journal reference, and a brief abstract of articles published in journals covered by the index).

Resources in Education lists curriculum guides, speeches, research reviews, convention papers, reports, and monographs not published in journals. The Document Resumé section presents descriptions of the documents arranged according to the ERIC classification scheme, together with information about where each can be obtained. There is also the Subject Index (in which titles of documents are listed according to the ERIC classification), the Author Index, the Institution Index (in which titles of articles are listed with reference to source), and the Publication Type Index. The documents cited in *Resources in Education* are available from the ERIC Document Reproduction Service in both microfiche and paper copy form.

You are urged to examine a recent issue of these publications to discover what is available in the ERIC network and how you might obtain information. An excellent on-line source for this information is the AskERIC Virtual Library, located at http://ericir.syr.edu/. It provides lesson plans, reviews, information about publications, and links to other databases and is a searchable database.

Summary

1. Educational psychology is a scientific discipline that attempts to understand and improve how students learn from instruction in classroom settings.
2. Learning about the research findings and principles of eductional psychology can help you be a better teacher because (a) teaching is complex work that requires a wide range of knowledge and skills, (b) the research literature contains numerous useful ideas for improving your instruction, and (c) teachers who have had professional training are often more effective than those who have not had such training.
3. Unsystematic observations of students may lead teachers to draw false conclusions because of limited cases, unrecognized or unusual factors, and a tendency to ignore contrary evidence.
4. Even though scientific evidence does not support the practice of grade retention, it remains popular among teachers and parents because of unsystematic observations about its effectiveness.
5. Scientifically gathered evidence is more trustworthy than casual observation because it involves sampling, control, objectivity, publication, and replication.
6. The scientific study of education is complicated by the limited focus of research, individual differences in perception and thinking, the inability of researchers to keep up with all published research, different interpretations of findings, and the ongoing accumulation of new knowledge.
7. Research on teaching and learning gives you a systematic, objective basis for making instructional decisions, but it cannot tell you how to handle every classroom situation. Many classroom decisions must be made on the spot. This contrast represents the science and the art of teaching.
8. Those who argue that teaching is an art point to communication of emotions, to values, and to flexibility as qualities that good teachers must possess but that are not easily taught.
9. Certain scholars contend that there is a scientific basis for teaching that can be taught and that draws on established research findings.
10. Good teachers strike a balance between the art and the science of teaching.

11. Reflective teachers constantly think about such issues as the worthwhileness of the goals they are trying to achieve, the types of teaching methods they use and how effective those methods are, and the extent to which their methods and goals are supported by scientific evidence.

Key Terms

educational psychology *(2)*
teaching as an art *(13)*
teaching as a science *(13)*
reflective teaching *(14)*

Discussion Questions

1. Imagine that you are a second-grade teacher at the end of the school year. You have just finished telling your principal about a student who performed so poorly during the year that you question whether the student is adequately prepared for third grade. The principal suggests that the child should repeat second grade next year. Given what you know about the research on retention, how would you respond to the principal's suggestion?
2. Think of or identify a popular instructional practice. Would you classify that practice as a fad or as the outgrowth of accumulated scientific knowledge? Why? How can you tell the difference between the two?
3. The effective teacher as artist displays enthusiasm and a sense of worthwhileness about content and teaching methods. At some point, however, you may be asked to teach a grade level or a subject for which you have little enthusiasm, or you may grow bored teaching the same grade level or subject in the same way year after year. How will you fulfill the role of teacher-artist if faced with these conditions?
4. The point was made in this chapter that good teachers strike a balance between the art and the science of teaching. How do they do so? Are they born with the right type of personality? Are they the products of good teacher-education programs? Or is some combination of these elements at work? If you believe that both factors play a role, which do you feel is more important?
5. The effective reflective teacher sets aside regular blocks of time to think about teaching activities and to make new plans. Most teachers complain about having insufficient time to reflect and plan. What would you do to make more time available?

Part 1

Considering Student Characteristics

CHAPTER 2

Stage Theories of Development

Key Points

These key points will help you learn the important information in this chapter. To help you study, they also appear in the margins of the pages, next to the text where they are discussed.

ERIKSON: PSYCHOSOCIAL DEVELOPMENT

- Erikson's theory encompasses the life span, highlights the role of the person and culture in development
- Personality development based on epigenetic principle
- Personality grows out of successful resolution of psychosocial crises
- 2 to 3 years: autonomy vs. shame and doubt
- 4 to 5 years: initiative vs. guilt
- 6 to 11 years: industry vs. inferiority
- 12 to 18 years: identity vs. role confusion
- Role confusion: uncertainty as to what behaviors others will react to favorably
- Identity: accepting body, having goals, getting recognition
- Gender roles establish patterns for many behaviors
- Traditionally, male identity linked to job, female identity linked to husband
- Female identity linked to job more now than in past
- American boys encouraged to be independent, active, exploratory; girls encouraged to be dependent, quiet
- Androgynous individuals more flexible and better adjusted than gender-typed individuals
- Occupational choice is a major commitment
- Psychosocial moratorium delays commitment
- Adolescents exhibit a particular process, called an identity status, for establishing an identity
- Individuals in identity diffusion avoid thinking about jobs, roles, values

- Individuals in moratorium suffer identity crises of various kinds
- Individuals who have reached identity achievement status have made their own commitments
- Individuals in foreclosure unquestioningly endorse parents' goals and values

PIAGET: COGNITIVE DEVELOPMENT

- Organization: tendency to systematize processes
- Scheme: organized pattern of behavior or thought
- Adaptation: tendency to adjust to environment
- Assimilation: new experience is fitted into existing scheme
- Accommodation: scheme is created or revised to fit new experience
- Equilibration: tendency to organize schemes to allow better understanding of experiences
- Sensorimotor stage: schemes reflect sensory and motor experiences
- Preoperational stage: child forms many new schemes but does not think logically
- Perceptual centration, irreversibility, egocentrism: barriers to logical thought
- Egocentrism: assumption that others see things the same way
- Concrete operational stage: child is capable of mentally reversing actions but generalizes only from concrete experiences
- Formal operational stage: child is able to deal with abstractions, form hypotheses, engage in mental manipulations
- Adolescent egocentrism: one's thoughts and actions are as central to others as to oneself
- Piaget's theory underestimates children's abilities
- Most adolescents are not formal operational thinkers
- Sequence of stages uniform across cultures but rate of development varies

PIAGET AND VYGOTSKY: THE ROLE OF SOCIAL INTERACTION AND INSTRUCTION IN COGNITIVE DEVELOPMENT

- Piaget: cognitive development more strongly influenced by peers than by adults
- Instruction can accelerate development of schemes that have begun to form
- Vygotsky: cognitive development more strongly influenced by those more intellectually advanced
- Vygotsky: cognitive development due to instruction in zone of proximal development

PIAGET, KOHLBERG, AND GILLIGAN: MORAL DEVELOPMENT

- Moral realism: sacred rules, no exceptions, no allowance for intentions, consequences determine guilt
- Moral relativism: rules are flexible, intent important in determining guilt
- Preconventional morality: avoid punishment, receive benefits in return
- Conventional morality: impress others, respect authority
- Postconventional morality: mutual agreements, consistent principles
- Moral education programs may produce modest acceleration in moral development
- Males and females may use different approaches to resolve real-life moral dilemmas
- Moral knowledge does not always result in moral behavior

Because the field of developmental psychology includes so many topics that have been studied intensively, separate courses are often given on infancy, early childhood, childhood, adolescence, and adulthood. If you have taken (or plan to take) one or more such courses, you will gain an understanding of the process of development and become familiar with the direction and significance of current research. The five chapters that make up Part 1 are intended to call your attention to aspects of human development that particularly concern teachers and to encourage you to make use of that knowledge.

For example, after you read these chapters, you should be able to answer the following questions:

> What psychosocial stages of development described by Erik Erikson are significant at the preschool, elementary, and secondary school levels?
>
> What are two key factors that contribute to an adolescent's sense of identity?
>
> What cognitive stages of development described by Jean Piaget are significant at the preschool, elementary, and secondary school levels?
>
> How does the moral reasoning of primary grade students differ from that of secondary grade students?
>
> How does the rate of physical development influence the behavior of boys and girls?
>
> What are some differences in the aptitudes of boys and girls and their attitudes toward school?
>
> How do students' cultural background and social class affect their classroom behavior?
>
> How can standardized test scores be used to design more effective forms of instruction for students?
>
> What sorts of emotional disorders are most common in male and female secondary school students?
>
> What is Public Law 101-476, and what significance does it have for teachers?

Human development is a difficult topic to discuss because, in addition to analyzing many different forms of behavior, one must trace the way each type of behavior changes as a child matures. Authors of books on development have adopted different strategies for coping with this problem. Some have described theories that outline stages in the emergence of particular forms of behavior. Others have summarized significant types of behavior at successive age levels. Still others have examined specific types of behavior, noting age changes for every topic. Each approach has advantages and disadvantages.

Theories call attention to the overall sequence, continuity, and interrelatedness of aspects of development, but they typically account for only limited facets of behavior. Texts organized in terms of age levels make the reader aware of varied aspects of children's behavior at a given age but sometimes tend to obscure how particular types of behavior emerge and change. And although texts organized according to types of behavior do not have the limitation of the age-level approach, they may make it difficult for the reader to grasp the overall pattern of behavior at a particular stage of development.

In an effort to profit from the advantages and to minimize the disadvantages of each approach, Chapters 2 and 3 present discussions of development that combine all three. Chapter 2 focuses principally on Erik Erikson's psychosocial stages and Jean Piaget's cognitive stages, including a comparison of Piaget's views of cognitive development with those of Lev Vygotsky. This chapter also describes Piaget's ideas about moral development, Lawrence Kohlberg's extension of Piaget's work, and Carol Gilligan's criticism and modification of Kohlberg's theory. Chapter 3 describes age-level characteristics of students at five levels—preschool, primary school, elementary school, middle school, and high school. Discussion at each age level focuses on four types of behavior—physical, social, emotional, and cognitive. The information in these chapters will help you adapt teaching techniques to the students who are in the age range that you expect to teach. The first two chapters in this part describe patterns of behavior exhibited by typical children and adolescents.

The following three chapters are devoted to student variability. Chapter 4 describes the characteristics of students from different ethnic and social-class backgrounds. Chapter 5 discusses the assessment of variability. And Chapter 6 describes types of students who vary from their classmates to such an extent that they may require special kinds of education.

Erikson: Psychosocial Development

Of all the developmental theories that we could have chosen to discuss, why did we choose to open this chapter with Erik Erikson's theory of psychosocial development? There are several reasons for this choice. First, Erikson described psychological growth from infancy through old age. Thus, one can draw out instructional implications for every level of education from preschool through adult education. Second, Erikson's theory portrays people as playing an active role in their own psychological development through their attempts to understand, organize, and integrate their everyday experiences. Third, this theory highlights the important role played by cultural goals, aspirations, expectations, requirements, and opportunities in personal growth (a theme we will discuss in Chapter 4) (Newman & Newman, 1991).

Erikson's theory encompasses the life span, highlights the role of the person and culture in development

FACTORS THAT INFLUENCED ERIKSON

Erik Erikson was born in Germany of Danish parents. An indifferent student, he left high school without graduating and spent several years wandering around Europe and attending various art schools. Eventually, while assisting a friend who was starting a school in Vienna, Erikson was introduced to Sigmund Freud. Freud was impressed by the young man and invited him to prepare for a career as a psychoanalyst. Erikson completed his training just at the time Adolf Hitler came to power, and to escape from the tension building up in Europe, Erikson decided to come to America. He taught at Harvard, Yale, and the University of California at Berkeley; did private counseling; and became interested in studying Native American tribes. He also did research on well-adjusted and emotionally disturbed children and served as a psychotherapist for soldiers during World War II.

These experiences led Erikson to conclude that Freud's tendency to stay in Vienna and interact with only a small and very select group of individuals had prevented the founder of psychoanalysis from fully appreciating how social and cultural factors (for example, values, attitudes, beliefs, and customs) influence behavior, perception, and thinking. Erikson decided to formulate a theory of development based on psychoanalytic principles but taking into account such influences.

BASIC PRINCIPLES OF ERIKSON'S THEORY

Personality development based on epigenetic principle

Epigenetic Principle Erikson based his description of personality development on the **epigenetic principle,** which states that in fetal development certain organs of the body appear at certain specified times and eventually "combine" to form a child. Erikson hypothesized that just as the parts of the body develop in interrelated ways in a human fetus, so the personality of an individual forms as the ego progresses through a series of interrelated stages. All these ego stages exist in some form from the very beginning, but each has a critical period of development.

Personality grows out of successful resolution of psychosocial crises

Psychosocial Crisis In Erikson's view, personality development occurs as one successfully resolves a series of turning points, or psychosocial crises. Although the word *crisis* typically refers to an extraordinary event that threatens our well-being, Erikson had a more benign meaning in mind. Crises occur when people feel compelled to adjust to the normal guidelines and expectations that society has for them but are not altogether certain that they are prepared to fully carry out these demands. For example, Western societies expect children of elementary and middle school age (roughly six to twelve years) to develop a basic sense of industry, mostly through success in school, rather than one of inferiority. Adolescents are expected to come to terms with such questions as "Who am I?" and "Where am I going?" Young adults are expected to establish a relationship with another person rather than live physically and emotionally apart from others (Newman & Newman, 1991).

Although Erikson described these crises in terms of desirable qualities and dangers, he did not mean to imply by this scheme that only positive qualities should emerge and that any manifestation of potentially dangerous traits is undesirable. He emphasized that people are best able to adapt to their world when they possess both the positive and negative qualities of a particular stage, provided the positive quality is significantly stronger than the negative quality. Try to imagine, for example, the personality of an individual who was never mistrustful (stage 1) or who never felt guilt (stage 3). Only when the negative quality outweighs the positive for any given stage or when the outcome for most stages is negative do difficulties in development and adjustment arise (Newman & Newman, 1991).

As you read through the following brief descriptions, keep in mind that a positive resolution of the issue for each stage depends on how well the issue of the previous stage was resolved. An adolescent who at the end of the industry versus inferiority stage strongly doubts her own capabilities and devalues the quality of her work, for example, may have trouble making the occupational commitments required for identity development (Marcia, 1991).

STAGES OF PSYCHOSOCIAL DEVELOPMENT

The following designations, age ranges, and essential characteristics of the stages of personality development are proposed by Erikson in *Childhood and Society* (1963).[1]

[1] All quotations in "Stages of Psychosocial Development" are drawn from Chapter 7 of *Childhood and Society*.

Trust Versus Mistrust (Birth to One Year) The basic psychosocial attitude to be learned by infants is that they can trust their world. Trust is fostered by "consistency, continuity, and sameness of experience" in the satisfaction by the parents of the infant's basic needs, which will permit children to think of their world as safe and dependable. Conversely, if care is inadequate, inconsistent, or negative, children will approach the world with fear and suspicion.

Autonomy Versus Shame and Doubt (Two to Three Years; Preschool) Just when children have learned to trust (or mistrust) their parents, they must exert a degree of independence. If toddlers are permitted and encouraged to do what they are capable of doing at their own pace and in their own way—but with judicious supervision by parents and teachers—they will develop a sense of autonomy. But if parents and teachers are impatient and do too many things for young children or shame young children for unacceptable behavior, feelings of self-doubt will develop.

2 to 3 years: autonomy vs. shame and doubt

Initiative Versus Guilt (Four to Five Years; Preschool to Kindergarten) The ability to participate in many physical activities and to use language sets the stage for initiative, which "adds to autonomy the quality of undertaking, planning, and 'attacking' a task for the sake of being active and on the move." If four- and five-year-olds are given freedom to explore and experiment, and if parents and teachers take time to answer questions, tendencies toward initiative will be encouraged. Conversely, if children of this age are restricted and made to feel that their activities and questions have no point or are a nuisance, they will feel guilty about acting on their own.

4 to 5 years: initiative vs. guilt

Industry Versus Inferiority (Six to Eleven Years; Elementary to Middle School) A child entering school is at a point in development when behavior is dominated by intellectual curiosity and performance. "He now learns to win recognition by producing things. . . . He develops a sense of industry." If the child is encouraged to make and do things well, helped to persevere, allowed to finish tasks, and praised for trying, industry results. If the child's efforts are unsuccessful or if they are derided or treated as bothersome, a feeling of inferiority results. Children who feel inferior may never learn to enjoy intellectual work and take pride in doing at least one kind of thing really well. At worst, they may believe they will never excel at anything.

6 to 11 years: industry vs. inferiority

Identity Versus Role Confusion (Twelve to Eighteen Years; Middle Through High School) The goal at this stage is development of those roles and skills that will prepare adolescents to eventually take a meaningful place in adult society. The danger at this stage is **role confusion:** having no clear conception of appropriate types of behavior that others will react to favorably. If adolescents succeed (as reflected by the reactions of others) in integrating roles in different situations to the point of experiencing continuity in their perception of self, identity develops. If they are unable to establish a sense of stability in various aspects of their lives, role confusion results.

12 to 18 years: identity vs. role confusion

Role confusion: uncertainty as to what behaviors others will react to favorably

Intimacy Versus Isolation (Young Adulthood) To experience satisfying development at this stage, the young adult needs to establish close and committed intimate relationships and partnerships with other people. The hallmark of intimacy is the "ethical strength to abide by such commitments, even though they may call for significant sacrifices and compromises." Failure to do so will lead to a sense of aloneness.

Generativity Versus Stagnation (Middle Age) "Generativity . . . is primarily the concern of establishing and guiding the next generation." Erikson's use of the term *generativity* is purposely broad. It refers, of course, to having children and raising them. In addition, it refers to the productive and creative efforts in which adults take part (for example, teaching) that have a positive effect on younger generations. Those unable or unwilling to "establish" and "guide" the next generation become victims of stagnation and self-absorption.

Integrity Versus Despair (Old Age) Integrity is "the acceptance of one's one and only life cycle as something that had to be and that, by necessity, permitted of no substitutions. . . . Despair expresses the feeling that the time is now short, too short for the attempt to start another life and to try out alternate roads to integrity."

FACTORS AFFECTING IDENTITY

The most complex of Erikson's stages is identity versus role confusion; he has written more extensively about this stage than any other. Because this stage is often misunderstood, let's use Erikson's own words to describe the concept of **identity:** "An optimal sense of identity . . . is experienced merely as a sense of psychosocial well-being. Its most obvious concomitants are a feeling of being at home in one's body, a sense of 'knowing where one is going' and an inner assuredness of anticipated recognition from those who count" (1968, p. 165). Even if you do not plan to teach middle school or high school stu-

Identity, as Erikson defines it, involves acceptance of one's body, knowing where one is going, and recognition from those who count. A high school graduate who is pleased with his or her appearance, who has already decided on a college major, and who is admired by parents, relatives, and friends is likely to experience a sense of psychosocial well-being.

dents, careful consideration of what Erikson and other psychologists have to say about identity may help you understand your own behavior better. We will use this section to examine two major influences on identity formation: gender and occupation.

Identity: accepting body, having goals, getting recognition

Gender Erikson believed that gender roles are particularly important in the development of identity because they establish a pattern for many types of behaviors. Until the early 1960s, there was little confusion about appropriate characteristics and activities for males and females in American society. Almost all adult males and females were expected to marry. Husband and wife would then take on well-defined and clearly established responsibilities: the man would function as the breadwinner; the woman would serve as the homemaker and child rearer. This certainty provided a clear code of behavior for those who had or were eager to develop those characteristics; but it created problems for those who did not, especially adolescent girls.

Gender roles establish patterns for many behaviors

The typical female adolescent in the America of the 1950s did not formulate as clear a sense of identity as the typical male adolescent because she assumed that what she would become as an adult would depend to a large extent on the man she married. The kind of job he secured after marriage and his success at that job would influence her conception of herself perhaps more than her own behavior (Douvan & Adelson, 1966).

Traditionally, male identity linked to job, female identity linked to husband

CHANGES IN GENDER ROLES. Over the last thirty years interpretations of appropriate behavior for men and women have changed dramatically. More than 60 percent of all mothers of school-age children now work outside the home. The high rate of divorce has led to a significant number of single-parent households. And in a growing number of families, both parents hold jobs. Several factors seem to be responsible for these trends: the need for increased family income to meet current lifestyles and future goals; a large increase in the number of jobs traditionally held by women (clerical workers, secretaries, telephone operators, teachers); increased opportunities for women in occupations that have been dominated by men; and a change in women's attitudes about the nature of the female gender role. A 1985 survey of women's attitudes found that 63 percent felt that combining marriage, career, and child rearing was the best alternative for a satisfying and interesting life (Borker, 1987).

Female identity linked to job more now than in past

Because of the changing attitude toward the role of women in our society, the young woman of the 1990s is more likely to feel that her destiny is in her own hands than her mother did when she was the same age. The opportunity for self-fulfillment obviously opens up many other opportunities. But change in social values is a gradual process. There are still many people who hold traditional views of male and female roles and believe in traditional approaches to child rearing. The end product can be confusion and problems, especially for the adolescent who is trying to develop a clear sense of what it means to be a male or a female.

FACTORS THAT PERPETUATE GENDER ROLES. Inge Broverman, Susan Vogel, Donald Broverman, Frank Clarkson, and Paul Rosenkrantz

(1972) analyzed perceptions of "typical" masculine and feminine traits. There was considerable unanimity of opinion from respondents of both sexes, all age levels, and all types of backgrounds: men were pictured as competent, rational, and assertive; women were thought of as warm and expressive. These gender role standards are remarkably robust and long-lived. David J. Bergen and John E. Williams (1991) replicated the Broverman et al. study in 1988 and found an almost identical pattern of responses despite the passage of sixteen years. John E. Williams and Deborah L. Best (1990) found similar perceptions in North and South America, Europe, Africa, Asia, and Australia.

What gives rise to these stereotypes is still an open question, although parenting behaviors are thought to be very influential. Parents, particularly fathers, emphasize achievement and exploration more for boys than for girls. Girls tend to be kept under closer supervision and are given more help in solving problems. As a consequence, they are much more likely than boys to ask for help—a tendency that is strengthened by the positive responses of adults. Boys, in contrast, are often told directly or indirectly to handle things themselves.

American boys encouraged to be independent, active, exploratory; girls encouraged to be dependent, quiet

In the area of play, boys generally are given toys or are encouraged to participate in activities that involve exploration of the physical world (for example, baseball, blocks, construction toys, cars, and science kits); girls are encouraged to participate in activities that involve quiet play and imitation of interpersonal behavior (for example, doll play, dressing up, drawing, and painting) (Block, 1973; Carter, 1987; Fagot, 1978; Fagot & Leinbach, 1987). There are indications that adolescents come under increasing pressure by family members, peers, and teachers to engage in gender-appropriate behavior. One indication is a noticeable increase in academically related and socially related gender-typed behaviors. Girls, for instance, become less interested than boys in math and science but more interested in intimate interpersonal relationships (Crockett, 1991). (See Case in Print: Gender and Education, pages 40–41.)

Social modeling (which we will discuss in detail in Chapter 8) is another process that has long been suspected of contributing to the formation of gender role stereotypes. Analyses of television programs, for example, have shown that the ratio of male to female characters is about 70 to 30 (despite the fact that females outnumber males 52 percent to 48 percent in the real world), that females occupy starring roles only about 30 percent of the time, that male characters are more often shown in high-status occupations, and that males are more likely to be shown as aggressive. Because of problems in defining and measuring gender role beliefs, there is no way to clearly determine the extent to which these factors contribute to gender role stereotypes (Durkin, 1985).

A major aspect of male-female gender role stereotypes is aggressive behavior. Contrary to earlier research findings, boys exhibit more physical *and* verbal aggression, although the difference is more pronounced for physical aggression. In addition, boys act more aggressively than girls following exposure to an aggressive model. Although gender differences in aggression decrease with age, researchers are not sure of the extent to which this narrowing is caused by social and/or hormonal factors (Hyde, 1986).

For those who believe gender role stereotyping is an obstacle to optimal identity formation, one solution is to change the way in which parents raise their children. This is more difficult to accomplish than you might realize. Beverly Fagot (1978) found that parents of preschoolers were often unaware that they were responding differently to boys and to girls. It is possible, then, that, although contemporary parents may *think* they have rejected traditional conceptions of gender roles, they are still encouraging girls to be dependent and passive and boys to be independent and active.

Given the ways in which society maintains gender role stereotypes and the difficulties they create for some adolescents in establishing an identity, many researchers have suggested that children and adolescents should acquire a gender role that *combines* traditional masculine and feminine traits. This idea is called **psychological androgyny.**

GENDER TYPING AND PSYCHOLOGICAL ANDROGYNY. The findings reported in the previous section reveal the extent to which traditional conceptions of gender roles are ingrained in the minds of many Americans. But not all individuals react the same way, as indicated in studies by Sandra Bem (1975, 1976). Bem found that adults varied in the extent to which they could be classified as *gender-typed* or as high in *psychological androgyny*. (*Androgyny* means possessing both male and female characteristics.) Gender-typed females (who endorse stereotyped conceptions of femininity) may refuse to nail two boards together because they feel it is a "masculine," rather than a "feminine," form of behavior. Gender-typed males may refuse to handle a baby or do household chores, presumably because these men feel that engaging in such behavior will make them appear less masculine. Only adults rated high in psychological androgyny appear able to move between masculine and feminine roles without difficulty or self-consciousness.

Because of this increased flexibility, proponents of androgyny argue that androgynous individuals are better adjusted than those who identify with traditional gender roles. Research findings seem to support this argument. In two studies conducted by James Dusek (1987), androgynous college students scored higher than gender-typed students on measures of trust versus mistrust, initiative versus guilt, identity versus role confusion, and intimacy versus isolation. In another study, male and female androgynous college students scored higher on a measure of intimacy than did their more gender-typed peers (Hodgson & Fischer, 1979). In terms of Erikson's theory, at least, these results suggest that androgynous individuals are better adjusted than gender-typed individuals.

Androgynous individuals more flexible and better adjusted than gender-typed individuals

How do you as a teacher help students develop more flexible conceptions of gender roles? In general, you can encourage girls to be more competitive and achievement oriented, particularly in math and science (two areas in which women are seriously underrepresented). And you can encourage boys to be more sensitive to the feelings of others and to take part in other than traditional masculine activities without being self-conscious. The study by Fagot (1978) and analyses of research by Felicisima Serafica and Suzanna Rose (1982) and Carol A. Dwyer (1982) call attention to the extent to which gender-typed behavior is shaped by the responses of parents and teachers.

Gender and Education

There are indications that adolescents come under increasing pressure by family members, peers, and teachers to engage in gender-appropriate behavior. One indication is a noticeable increase in academically related and socially related gender-typed behaviors. Girls, for instance, become less interested than boys in math and science but more interested in intimate interpersonal relationships. (p. 38)

"Why Can't Susie Do Calculus?"

MICKEY BACA

Merrimack Valley Sunday (Ipswich, MA) 8/7/94

Twelve-year-old Laura Young struggles to grip a small coated wire with a pair of wire snippers, as 13-year-old Juliana Cejka looks on.

The students are making telegraphs, using an electromagnet, a small battery and a washer suspended on an elastic: a typical science class exercise for middle school kids.

There is a difference in this classroom, however. There are no boys wielding the hammers and wire strippers.

This experimental two-week summer math and science program at the Nock Middle School in Newburyport is for girls only in hopes of making a dent in what most agree is a social failing in education. Somehow when girls reach middle school and early high school age, they begin falling behind in math and science.

By the time they reach high school and college, girls take a decided path away from the calculus, physics, biology and chemistry courses and instead select humanities and language courses.

In turn, researchers say, they are self-selecting themselves out of important and high-paying jobs in science and technology.

A growing body of research over the last decade suggests numerous reasons for the trend, from the different learning styles of girls and boys and social stereotyping of their abilities to teacher biases that channel more attention to boys.

Marcia O'Neil, an eighth grade language arts teacher at the Nock Middle School who has been following gender issues in education, proposed this ground-breaking summer program. . . . "If there were boys, I don't think the girls would be doing these projects. They'd be standing back and watching. A girl wouldn't have the hammer . . ."

In fact, a study of science classrooms cited by the American Association Of University Women found that 79 percent of student-assisted science demonstrations were carried out by boys.

Researchers have also found that, even when girls do well in math and science, they don't receive the encouragement they need in order to pursue scientific careers. . . .

Carol Sund of The Network, a nonprofit education research firm in Andover . . . says girls lower their sights in general when they hit adolescence: "If you talk to a girl who is 10, she can do anything. She has all these hopes and dreams. If you talk to her at 13, she has much lower expectations."

What's more, Sund notes, studies that date back to the 1970s show that teachers channel more attention to males, calling on them more often, expecting more from them in math and science.

"Again, it's the boys being taught and the girls watching the boys being taught. It's the cheerleader/football player syndrome," Sund says. "We've trained girls to think that they are invisible in the classroom."

Girls do have a different learning style than boys, Sund acknowledges, tending to do better in a cooperative setting rather than the competitive environment most classrooms foster.

Schools have been slow to change teaching styles to accommodate female learning styles, according to Sund, and even to attempt to give girls the same amount of attention as that received by boys. Teacher behavior is difficult to change, she says, and some teachers don't agree that it should be changed.

Sund still gets teachers in training sessions that say girls and boys were made differently, and girls should remain quiet and supportive, she says. . . .

O'Neil herself remembers having trouble with math growing up. "My view of myself as a math student was compromised by attitudes."

If the girls across the room studying probability are suffering from "math anxiety," they aren't showing it. They're too busy calculating the odds of rolling certain number combinations on dice and betting pieces of candy on the outcome.

. . . Besides getting hands-on experience with math, science and computers, the girls in the Stars program are getting to hear first hand from women who work in fields involving math and science.

Today's luncheon speaker is Ann Gothro, an engineer working on the Boston Harbor tunnel project. . . .

One of the most important things you can get, Gothro advises the students, is hands-on experience.

Gothro didn't shy away from math and science when she was in middle and high school. In fact, she had quite the opposite problem, she tells the girls.

"I always took math and science in high school mainly because my dad (an engineer) decided I should. I remember being a little upset because my brothers always got to take cooking classes," she says. . . .

Superintendent Paul Dulac says combating gender biases in the city's classrooms really boils down to teacher strategies.

For example, he says, boys are more aggressive in the classroom and tend to pose more discipline problems. That could be why teachers tend to call on boys more, to keep them more engaged and out of trouble.

If that's the case, the superintendent says, teachers need to be trained in other ways to engage boys without neglecting the girls. . . .

"The bottom line is that we need to pay more attention to both male and female development to make sure both are developing their potential in math and science," says [middle school principal Doug] Lay, adding that "I think it's an issue that's more relevant to young women right now."

Education can't continue to "deliver one menu to students and expect them to be successful," Lay says.

Questions and Activities

1. This article describes several environmental influences on learning and classroom behavior and at least one innate factor. Go through the article to list these various influences and factors. Describe how they might interact with one another to affect your students' learning differently depending on their gender. Does this jibe with your own experience as a student? Why or why not?

2. The overall message of this article and of the experimental program is that girls can do and can enjoy math and science if certain environmental factors are rearranged. What lessons can you draw from this in terms of the assumptions you make about your students and the goals you should set for them? How does the final quote in the article—from Principal Lay—speak to this issue, and how does it specifically address the teacher's role in helping diverse individuals reach their potential?

3. Write a dialogue that might occur between Carol Sund and one of the teachers who say that "girls and boys were made differently and that girls should remain quiet and supportive." Which position is more reflective of the theories in this chapter? Think of ways you might call on knowledge you glean from this chapter to support that position.

4. Why might the years between ten and thirteen bring "lower expectations" for a girl? Try writing out an answer to this question now and then again when you have finished studying both this chapter and Chapter 3. Combine new information you may have learned from these chapters with your own experiential knowledge. Reflect as you do so on ways in which you, as a future teacher, might be able to help reverse the direction of girls' lowered expectations.

Furthermore, observation of models has a significant impact on gender-typed behavior. A boy who watches his father unself-consciously care for an infant or wash the dishes is more likely to acquire a flexible view of gender roles than is a boy whose father is a gender-typed male. And a girl who sees her mother go off to work is less inclined to picture women solely as mothers and homemakers.

Occupational choice is a major commitment

Occupation The occupation we choose influences other aspects of our lives perhaps more than any other single factor. Our job determines how we will spend a sizable proportion of our time and how much money we earn; our income, in turn, affects where and how we live. Moreover, the last two factors determine, to a considerable extent, the people we interact with socially. All these elements together influence the reactions of others, and these reactions lead us to develop perceptions of ourselves. The choice of a career, therefore, may be the biggest commitment of a person's life.

But there are several factors that complicate the process of making an occupational choice in American society. First, adolescents do not have many opportunities to observe and interact with working adults because they are required to be in school seven hours a day until they are at least sixteen years old. Second, the types of jobs most readily available to adolescents are minimum-wage, service-oriented jobs. Third, because of the sheer number of possible occupations (the *Dictionary of Occupational Titles* lists more than forty-seven thousand) and the limited work experience of young people, most adolescents have little knowledge about which jobs they would enjoy and be able to do successfully, nor are they aware of the level of training required for a particular job. Fourth, because of gender role stereotyping, many adolescents exhibit relatively traditional gender-related occupational aspirations (for example, elementary school teacher for girls, manager and administrator for boys) (Brown, 1982; Conger, 1991).

FORMULATING AN IDENTITY

Psychosocial moratorium delays commitment

Taking a Psychosocial Moratorium For those individuals who are unprepared to make a career choice, Erikson suggested the possibility of a **psychosocial moratorium.** This is a period marked by a delay of commitment. Such a postponement occurred in Erikson's own life: after leaving high school, Erikson spent several years wandering around Europe without making any firm decision about the sort of job he would seek. Under ideal circumstances, a psychosocial moratorium should be a period of adventure and exploration, having a positive, or at least neutral, impact on the individual and society.

Establishing a Negative Identity In some cases, however, the young person may engage in defiant or destructive behavior. A young person who is unable to overcome role confusion—or to postpone choices leading to identity formation by engaging in a positive psychosocial moratorium—may attempt to resolve inner conflict by choosing what Erikson refers to as a **negative identity.**

> The loss of a sense of identity is often expressed in a scornful and snobbish hostility toward the roles offered as proper and desirable in one's family or

> immediate community. Any aspect of the required role, or all of it—be it masculinity or femininity, nationality or class membership—can become the main focus of the young person's acid disdain. (1968, pp. 172–173)

For example, an adolescent boy whose parents have constantly stressed how important it is to do well in school may deliberately flunk out or quit school. Erikson explains such choices by suggesting that the young person finds it easier to "derive a sense of identity out of total identification with that which he is least supposed to be than to struggle for a feeling of reality in acceptable roles which are unattainable with his inner means" (1968, p. 176). If the young person who chooses a negative identity plays the role only long enough to gain greater self-insight, the experience may be positive. In some cases, however, the negative identity may be "confirmed" by the treatment the adolescent receives from those in authority. If such an individual is contemptuously referred to as a "failure," "delinquent," "punk," "loser," or "slacker" and treated with excessive punishment by parents, teachers, or law enforcement agencies, for example, the "young person may well put his energy into becoming exactly what the careless and fearful community expects him to be—and make a total job of it" (1968, p. 196).

Adolescent Identity Statuses Erikson's observations on identity formation have been usefully extended by James Marcia's notion of *identity statuses* (1966, 1980, 1991). Identity statuses, of which there are four, are styles or processes "for handling the psychosocial task of establishing a sense of identity" (Waterman & Archer, 1990, p. 35). Marcia (1980) developed this idea as a way to scientifically test the validity of Erikson's notions about identity.

Adolescents exhibit a particular process, called an identity status, for establishing an identity

Marcia established the four identity statuses after he had conducted semistructured interviews with a selected sample of male youths. The interviewees were asked their thoughts about a career, their personal value system, their sexual attitudes, and their religious beliefs. Marcia proposed that the criteria for the attainment of a mature identity are based on two vari-

Adolescents who are dissatisfied with themselves and unable to focus on constructive goals may fashion a negative identity by engaging in forms of behavior that their parents oppose.

ables: crisis and commitment. "Crisis refers to times during adolescence when the individual seems to be actively involved in choosing among alternative occupations and beliefs. Commitment refers to the degree of personal investment the individual expresses in an occupation or belief" (1967, p. 119). After analyzing interview records with these two criteria in mind, Marcia established four identity statuses that vary in their degree of crisis and commitment: identity diffusion, moratorium, identity achievement, and foreclosure. The identity achievement and moratorium statuses are generally thought to be more developmentally mature than the foreclosure and identity diffusion statuses because those individuals exhibiting the former have either evaluated alternatives and made a commitment or are actively involved in obtaining and evaluating information in preparation for a commitment (Archer, 1982).

As you read the following brief descriptions of each identity type, keep a few points in mind. First, the more mature identity statuses are slow to evolve. Among sixth graders only about 11 percent are likely to show any evidence of either an identity achievement or a moratorium status. By twelfth grade, only about 20 percent will have attained either status (Archer, 1982). Second, an identity status is not a once-and-for-all accomplishment. If an ego-shattering event (loss of a job, divorce) later occurs, individuals who have reached identity achievement, for example, may find themselves uncertain about old values and behavior patterns and once again in crisis. But for most individuals, a new view of oneself is eventually created. This cycling between certainty and doubt as to who one is and where one fits in society may well occur in each of the last three of Erikson's stages (Stephen, Fraser, & Marcia, 1992). Third, because identity is an amalgam of commitments from a number of different domains, only a small percentage (about 20 percent) of adolescents will experience a triumphant sense of having "put it all together." To cite just one example, an adolescent is more likely to have made a firm occupational choice but to be indecisive about gender role or religious values (Waterman, 1988).

Individuals in identity diffusion avoid thinking about jobs, roles, values

Individuals in the **identity diffusion status** have yet to experience a crisis because they have not given much serious thought to an occupation, gender roles, or values. Their positions on these issues are only casually held and are readily subject to change in response to positive or negative feedback. These individuals have little self-direction, are disorganized and impulsive, are low in self-esteem, are likely to feel alienated from their parents, and avoid getting involved either in schoolwork or interpersonal relationships (Vondracek, Schulenberg, Skorikov, Gillespie, & Walheim, 1995).

Individuals in moratorium suffer identity crises of various kinds

Individuals in a **moratorium status** have given a certain amount of thought to identity questions, but they have not come up with any satisfactory answers. They are anxious, dissatisfied with school or college, change majors often, daydream a great deal, and engage in intense but short-lived relationships with others. They tend to have conflicting needs to conform and rebel and may temporarily reject parental values. After a period of experimentation and restless searching, these individuals typically come to grips with themselves and take on characteristics of people who have reached identity achievement. As improbable as it may seem, the daydreaming and fantasizing in which moratorium types engage may help them establish a more stable identity if these activities are used as a sort of simulation of reality (Bilsker & Marcia, 1991).

Individuals who have reached **identity achievement status** have made self-chosen commitments with respect to at least some aspects of their identity after considering and exploring distinctly different alternatives. They are reflective in their approach to decision making, have high self-esteem, work effectively under stress, are likely to form close interpersonal relationships, and are more likely than are adolescents in the other identity statuses to have formulated a career goal (Blustein & Palladino, 1991; Vondracek et al., 1995). This status is usually the last to emerge developmentally.

Individuals who have reached identity achievement status have made their own commitments

Individuals in the **foreclosure status** do not experience a crisis and may never suffer any doubts about occupational choice, gender roles, and values. The main reason for this lack of doubt about identity issues is that these individuals accept and endorse the values of their parents. Individuals in foreclosure are likely to be close-minded, authoritarian, and low in anxiety; to have difficulty solving problems under stress; to feel superior to their peers; and to be more dependent on their parents for direction and approval than are adolescents in the other identity statuses (Blustein & Palladino, 1991; Frank, Pirsch, & Wright, 1990).

Individuals in foreclosure unquestioningly endorse parents' goals and values

Although the foreclosure status is the historical norm for Western societies, things can and do change. For example, individuals in moratorium were more numerous during the 1960s and 1970s than during the 1980s (Scarr, Weinberg, & Levine, 1986; Waterman, 1988). Also, recent evidence indicates that African-American adolescents are now more likely to be either in a moratorium status, in an identity achievement status, or in transition between these two statuses than in the foreclosure status of earlier generations (Watson & Protinsky, 1991). Gender differences are most apparent in the areas of political ideology, family/career priorities, and sexuality. With respect to political beliefs, males are more likely to exhibit a foreclosure process and females a diffusion process. With respect to family/career priorities and sexuality, males are likely to be foreclosed or diffuse, whereas females are likely to express an identity achievement or a moratorium status (Archer, 1991).

A relevant question to ask about Marcia's identity statuses, particularly if you plan to teach in a foreign country or to instruct students with different cultural backgrounds, is whether these identity statuses occur only in the United States. The answer appears to be no. Researchers in such diverse countries as Korea, India, Nigeria, Japan, Denmark, and Holland report finding the same patterns (Scarr, Weinberg, & Levine, 1986).

CRITICISMS OF ERIKSON'S THEORY

Erikson's theory has been described as somewhat vague and difficult to test. As a result, researchers are not sure what the best way is to measure such complex qualities as initiative and integrity or which kinds of experiences should be studied to discover how people cope with and successfully resolve psychosocial conflicts (Ochse & Plug, 1986; Sigelman & Shaffer, 1991).

Although Erikson occasionally carried out research investigations, most of his conclusions are based on personal and subjective interpretations that have been only partly substantiated by controlled investigations of the type that are valued by American psychologists. As a result, there have been only limited checks on Erikson's tendency to generalize from limited experiences. Some of his observations on identity, for example, reflect his own indecision about occupational choice.

Some critics argue that Erikson's stages reflect the personality development of males more accurately than that of females. According to Carol Gilligan (1982, 1988), for example, Erikson's theory is a more accurate description of male psychosocial development than of female psychosocial development. In particular, she feels that the process and timing of identity formation are different for each gender. Marcia (1986) contends that beginning in about fourth grade (the industry versus inferiority stage), girls are as concerned with the nature of interpersonal relationships as they are with achievement, whereas boys focus mainly on achievement. And during adolescence, many young women seem to work through the crises of identity *and* intimacy simultaneously, whereas most young men follow the sequence described by Erikson—identity versus role confusion, then intimacy versus isolation (Gilligan, 1982; Ochse & Plug, 1986; Scarr, Weinberg, & Levine, 1986).

A final criticism is that Erikson's early stages, those covering ages two through eleven, seem to stress the same basic qualities. Autonomy, initiative, and industry all emphasize the desirability of permitting and encouraging children to do things on their own. Doubt, guilt, and inferiority all focus on the need for parents and teachers to provide sympathetic support.

If you keep these reservations in mind, however, you are likely to discover that Erikson's observations (as well as the identity statuses described by Marcia) will clarify important aspects of development. Suggestions for Teaching that take advantage of Erikson's observations are listed below. (These suggestions might also serve as the nucleus of a section in your Reflective Journal. Possible Journal Entries are indicated in the margins.)

Suggestions for Teaching in Your Classroom

Applying Erikson's Theory of Psychosocial Development

1. **Keep in mind that certain types of behaviors and relationships may be of special significance at different age levels.**

Journal Entry
Ways to Apply Erikson's Theory (Preschool and Kindergarten)

2. **With younger preschool children, allow plenty of opportunities for free play and experimentation to encourage the development of autonomy, but provide guidance to reduce the possibility that children will experience doubt. Also avoid shaming children for unacceptable behavior.**

3. **With older preschool children, encourage activities that permit the use of initiative and provide a sense of accomplishment. Avoid making children feel guilty about well-motivated but inconvenient (to you) questions or actions.**

4. During the elementary and middle school years, help children experience a sense of industry by presenting tasks that they can complete successfully.

Journal Entry
Ways to Apply Erikson's Theory (Elementary Grades)

Arrange such tasks so that students will *know* they have been successful. Play down comparisons and encourage cooperation and self-competition to limit feelings of inferiority. Also try to help jealous children gain satisfaction from their own behavior. (Specific ways to accomplish these goals will be described in several later chapters.)

5. At the secondary school level, keep in mind the significance of each student's search for a sense of identity.

The components of identity stressed by Erikson are acceptance of one's appearance, recognition from those who count, and knowledge about where one is going. Role confusion is most frequently caused by failure to formulate clear ideas about gender roles and by indecision about occupational choice.

Journal Entry
Ways to Apply Erikson's Theory (Secondary Grades)

The American school system, particularly at the high school level, has been described as a place where individual differences are either ignored or discouraged and where negative feedback greatly outweighs positive feedback (e.g., Boyer, 1983; Csikszentmihalyi & Larson, 1984; Friedenberg, 1963; Murphy, 1987). When John Murphy (1987), a professor of education at Brooklyn College, asked his students to recall positive learning experiences from high school, few were able to do so. But as "someone who counts" to your students, you can contribute to their sense of positive identity by recognizing them as individuals and praising them for their accomplishments. If you become aware that particular students lack recognition from peers because of abrasive qualities or ineptness, and if you have the time and opportunity, you might also attempt to encourage social skills.

An excellent book to consult for this purpose is *Skill-Streaming the Adolescent: A Structured Learning Approach to Teaching Prosocial Skills* (Goldstein, Sprafkin, Gershaw, & Nein, 1980). This volume describes fifty specific skills that fall into five general categories: social skills, skills for dealing with feelings, skill alternatives to aggression, skills for dealing with stress, and planning skills. Each skill is taught by a four-step method:

Modeling (imitating those who use social skills effectively)

Role playing (gaining practice in social skills in simulated situations)

Performance feedback (improving techniques by noting their effectiveness or ineffectiveness)

Transfer of training (applying a technique that was learned in role-playing situations to everyday interactions with others)

Since the techniques are planned and structured, you will probably obtain the best results by following the procedures outlined in the book. But don't be afraid to experiment or make spontaneous changes.

You might be able to reduce identity problems resulting from indecisiveness about gender roles by having class discussions (for example, in social science courses) centering on changes in attitudes regarding masculinity, femininity, and family responsibilities. Following the suggestions of Jeanne Block (1973), you can encourage boys to become more sensitive to the needs of others and girls to be more achievement oriented. In addition, you can acquaint members of both sexes with the concept of psychological androgyny and make them aware of the advantages of possessing both "masculine" and "feminine" characteristics.

Another forum for such discussion is an on-line bulletin board or group in a computer-based classroom. On-line writing can be conducive to explorations of sensitive issues because it provides a slightly slower, more thoughtful pace and also allows male and female students an equal voice, even those who feel shy about speaking out loud in class. An on-line discussion, when carefully moderated by an experienced teacher, can both model and explore the territory of psychological androgyny.

Working with your school counselor, you may in some cases be able to help students make decisions about occupational choice by providing them with information (gleaned from classroom performance and standardized test results) about intellectual capabilities, personality traits, interests, and values (Lambert & Mounce, 1987). Or you may be able to help students decide whether to apply for admission to a college instead of entering the job market just after graduation. There are many ways to enable students to work toward short term goals, particularly in your classroom. These will be described in detail in Chapters 7 and 11, which deal with instructional objectives and motivation.

6. **Remember, the aimlessness of some students may be evidence that they are engaging in a psychosocial moratorium. If possible, encourage such individuals to focus on short-term goals while they continue to search for long-term goals.**

7. **Try to be patient if you suspect that disruptive behavior on the part of a student may be due to the acting out of a negative identity.**

When you must control negative behavior to preserve a satisfactory learning environment for other students, try to do it in such a way that the troublemaker is not confirmed as a troublemaker. One way is to make clear that you do not hold a grudge and that you have confidence in the student's ability to make positive contributions in class. (If possible, arrange opportunities for troublemakers to carry out assignments that will be positive and constructive.)

8. **Remain aware that adolescents may exhibit characteristics of different identity status types.**

Some may drift aimlessly; others may be distressed because they realize they lack goals and values. A few high school students may have arrived at self-chosen commitments; others may have accepted the goals and values of their parents.

If you become aware that certain students seem depressed or bothered because they are unable to develop a satisfactory set of personal values, consult your school psychologist or counselor. In addition, you might use the techniques just summarized to help these students experience at least a degree of identity achievement. Perhaps the main value of the identity status concept is that it calls attention to individual differences in the formation of identity. Because students in the foreclosure status will pose few, if any, classroom problems, you must keep in mind that foreclosure is not necessarily desirable for the individual student. Those experiencing identity diffusion or moratorium may be so bothered by role confusion that they are unwilling to carry out even simple assignments—unless you supply support and incentives.

Piaget: Cognitive Development

FACTORS THAT INFLUENCED PIAGET

Piaget was born in the small university town of Neuchâtel, Switzerland, in 1896. His father was a professor of history who specialized in medieval literature, and young Jean was brought up in a scholarly atmosphere. His main boyhood interest was observation of animals in their natural habitat, an interest he pursued with considerable energy and sophistication.

Piaget earned undergraduate and graduate degrees from the University of Neuchâtel in natural science; he was awarded a Ph.D. at the age of twenty-one. At that point he became intrigued with psychology. This he studied in Zurich, where he was introduced to Freudian theory and wrote a paper relating psychoanalysis to child psychology. From Zurich he went to Paris to study abnormal psychology. Shortly after his arrival, he obtained a position preparing a French version of some reasoning tests developed in England. As he recorded the responses of his subjects, Piaget found that he was much more intrigued with wrong answers than with correct ones. He became convinced that the thought processes of younger children are basically different from those of older children and adults. His lifelong fascination with biology and his interest in studying the nature of knowledge led him to speculate about the development of thinking in children.

In 1921 an appointment as director of research at the Jean-Jacques Rousseau Institute in Geneva permitted Piaget to concentrate full-time on the study of cognitive development. He engaged in active study at the institute until 1975 and continued to analyze cognitive development in "retirement" until his death in 1980.

BASIC PRINCIPLES OF PIAGET'S THEORY

Piaget's conception of intellectual development reflects his basic interest in biology and knowledge. He postulated that human beings inherit two basic tendencies: **organization** (the tendency to systematize and combine processes into coherent general systems) and **adaptation** (the tendency to adjust to the environment). For Piaget, these tendencies govern both physiological functioning and mental functioning. Just as the biological process of digestion transforms food into a form that the body can use, so intellectual processes transform experiences into a form that the child can use in dealing with new

Activities that encourage children to create new ideas or schemes through experimentation, questioning, discussion, and discovery often produce meaningful learning because of the inherent drive toward equilibration.

situations. And just as biological processes must be kept in a state of balance (through homeostasis), intellectual processes seek a balance through the process of **equilibration** (a form of self-regulation that all individuals use to bring coherence and stability to their conception of the world).

Organization: tendency to systematize processes

Organization As we just stated, *organization* refers to the tendency of all individuals to systematize or combine processes into coherent (logically interrelated) systems. When we think of tulips and roses as subcategories of the more general category *flowers,* instead of as two unrelated categories, we are using organization to aid our thinking process. This organizational capacity makes thinking processes efficient and powerful and allows for a better "fit," or adaptation, of the individual to the environment.

Scheme: organized pattern of behavior or thought

Schemes These are organized patterns of behavior or thought that children formulate as they interact with their environment, parents, teachers, and agemates. **Schemes** can be behavioral (throwing a ball) or cognitive (realizing that there are many different kinds of balls). Whenever a child encounters a new experience that does not easily fit into an existing scheme, adaptation is necessary.

Adaptation: tendency to adjust to environment

Assimilation: new experience is fitted into existing scheme

Adaptation This is the process of creating a good fit or match between one's conception of reality (one's schemes) and the real-life experiences one encounters. Adaptation, as described by Piaget, is accomplished by two subprocesses: **assimilation** and **accommodation.** A child may adapt either by interpreting an experience so that it *does* fit an existing scheme (assimilation) or by changing an existing scheme to incorporate the experience (accommodation). Imagine a six-year-old who goes to an aquarium for the first time and calls the minnows "little fish" and the whales "big fish." In both cases the child is assimilating—attempting to fit a new experience into an existing scheme (in this case, the conception that all creatures that live in the water are fish). When her parents point out that, even though whales live in the water, they are mammals, not fish, the six-year-old begins to accommodate—to modify her existing scheme to fit the new experience she has encountered. Gradually (accommodations are made slowly, over repeated experiences), a new scheme forms that contains nonfish creatures that live in the water.

Accommodation: scheme is created or revised to fit new experience

Relationships Among Organization, Adaptation, and Schemes To give you a basic understanding of Piaget's ideas, we have talked about them as distinct elements. But the concepts of organization, adaptation, and schemes are all related. In their drive to be organized, individuals try to have a place for everything (accommodation) so they can put everything in its place (assimilation). The product of organization and adaptation is the creation of new schemes that allow individuals to organize at a higher level and to adapt more effectively.

Equilibration, Disequilibrium, and Learning Piaget believed that people are driven to organize their knowledge in order to achieve the best possible adaptation to their environment. He calls this process *equilibration*. But what motivates people's drive toward equilibration? It is a state of *disequilibrium*, or a perceived discrepancy between an existing scheme and something new. In other words, when people encounter something that is inconsistent with or contradicts what they already know or believe, this experience produces a disequilibrium that they are driven to eliminate (assuming they are sufficiently interested in the new experience to begin with). A student may wonder why, for example, tomatoes and cucumbers are referred to as fruits in a science text since she has always referred to them as vegetables and has distinguished fruits from vegetables on the basis of sweetness. This discrepancy may cause the student to read the text carefully or to ask the teacher for further explanation. Gradually, the student reorganizes her thinking about the classification of fruits and vegetables in terms of edible plant roots, stems, leaves, and ovaries so that it is more consistent with the expert view. These processes are two sides of the learning coin: For equilibration to occur, disequilibrium must already have occurred. Disequilibrium can occur spontaneously within an individual through maturation and experience, or it can be stimulated by someone else (such as a teacher).

Equilibration: tendency to organize schemes to allow better understanding of experiences

Constructing Knowledge Meaningful learning, then, occurs when people *create* new ideas, or knowledge (rules and hypotheses that explain things), from existing information (for example, facts, concepts, and procedures). To solve a problem, we have to search our memory for information that can be used to fashion a solution. Using information can mean experimenting, questioning, reflecting, discovering, inventing, and discussing. This process of creating knowledge to solve a problem and eliminate a disequilibrium is referred to by Piagetian psychologists and educators as **constructivism** (Blais, 1988; Brooks, 1990; Wheatley, 1991). It is a powerful notion that will reappear in a later chapter (Chapter 10) and in other forms. (The Discussion Questions at the end of each chapter are intended to stimulate constructivist thinking, as is the manner in which we encourage you to set up and use your journal for reflective thinking and teaching.)

STAGES OF COGNITIVE DEVELOPMENT

Organization and adaptation are what Piaget called *invariant functions*. This means that these thought processes function the same way for infants, children, adolescents, and adults. Schemes, however, are not invariant. They undergo systematic change at particular points in time. As a result, there are real differences between the ways younger children and older children think and between the ways children and adults think. The schemes of infants and toddlers, for example, are sensory and motor in nature. They are often referred to as *habits* or *reflexes*. In early childhood, schemes gradually become more mental in nature; during this period they are called *concepts* or *categories*. Finally, by late adolescence or early adulthood, schemes are very complex and result in what we call *strategic* or *planful* behavior.

On the basis of his studies, Piaget concluded that schemes evolve through four stages. Although these stages reflect a generally continuous pattern of cognitive development, children do not suddenly "jump" from one stage to the next. Their cognitive development follows a definite sequence, but they may occasionally use a more advanced kind of thinking or revert to a more primitive form. The *rate* at which a particular child proceeds through these stages varies, but Piaget believed the *sequence* is the same in all children.

Piaget's four stages are described in the following sections. To help you grasp the sequence of these stages, Table 2.1 briefly outlines the range of ages to which they generally apply and their distinguishing characteristics.

Sensorimotor stage: schemes reflect sensory and motor experiences

Sensorimotor Stage (Infants and Toddlers) Up to the age of two, children acquire understanding primarily through sensory impressions and motor activities. Therefore, Piaget called this the *sensorimotor stage*. Because infants are unable to move around much on their own during the first months of postnatal existence, they develop schemes primarily by exploring their own bodies and senses. After toddlers learn to walk and manipulate things, however, they get into everything and build up a sizable repertoire of schemes involving external objects and situations.

An important cognitive development milestone, *object permanence*, occurs between the fourth and eighth months of this stage. Prior to this point, the phrase "out of sight, out of mind" is literally true. Infants treat objects that leave their field of vision as if they no longer exist. When they drop an object from their hands or when an object at which they are looking is covered, for example, they do not search for it. During the same period, however, intentional search behaviors become increasingly apparent.

Most children under two are able to use schemes they have mastered to engage in mental as well as physical trial-and-error behavior. By age two, toddlers' schemes have become more mental in nature. You can see this in the way toddlers imitate the behavior of others. They imitate people they have

TABLE 2.1 ***Piaget's Stages of Cognitive Development***

Stage	Age Range	Characteristics
Sensorimotor	Birth to two years	Develops schemes primarily through sense and motor activities. Recognizes permanence of objects not seen.
Preoperational	Two to seven years	Gradually acquires ability to conserve and decenter but not capable of operations and unable to mentally reverse actions.
Concrete operational	Seven to eleven years	Capable of operations but solves problems by generalizing from concrete experiences. Not able to manipulate conditions mentally unless they have been experienced.
Formal	Eleven years	Able to deal with abstractions, form hypotheses, solve problems systematically, engage in mental manipulations.

not previously observed, they imitate the behavior of animals, and, most important, they imitate even when the model is no longer present (this is called *deferred imitation*). These types of imitative behaviors show toddlers' increasing ability to think in terms of symbols.

Preoperational Stage (Preschool and Primary Grades) The thinking of preschool and primary grade children (roughly two to seven years old) centers on mastery of symbols (such as words), which permits them to benefit much more from past experiences. Piaget believed that many symbols are derived from mental imitation and involve both visual images and bodily sensations (notice how the schemes of this stage incorporate and build on the schemes of the previous stage). Even though the thinking at this stage is much more sophisticated than that of one- and two-year-olds, preschool children are limited in their ability to use their new symbol-oriented schemes. From an adult perspective, their thinking and behavior are illogical.

Preoperational stage: child forms many new schemes but does not think logically

When Piaget used the term *operation,* he meant an action carried out through logical thinking. *Preoperational,* then, means prelogical. The main impediments to logical thinking that preschoolers have to overcome are *perceptual centration, irreversibility,* and *egocentrism*. You can see these impediments at work most clearly when children attempt to solve **conservation** problems, problems that test their ability to recognize that certain properties stay the same despite a change in appearance or position.

Perceptual centration, irreversibility, egocentrism: barriers to logical thought

One of the best known conservation problems is conservation of continuous quantity. A child is taken to a quiet place by an experimenter, who then pours water (or juice or beans or whatever) into identical short glasses until the child agrees that each contains an equal amount. Then the water is poured from one of these glasses into a tall, thin glass. At that point the child is asked, "Is there more water in this glass (the experimenter points to the tall glass) or this one?" Immediately after the child answers, the experimenter asks, "Why do you think so?" If the child's response is evasive or vague, the experimenter continues to probe until the underlying thought processes become clear.

In carrying out this experiment (and many others similar to it) with children of different ages, Piaget discovered that children below the age of six or so maintain that there is more water in the tall, thin glass than in the short, squat glass. Even though they agree at the beginning of the experiment that the water in the two identical glasses is equal, young children stoutly insist that after the water has been poured the taller glass contains more. When asked, "Why do you think so?" many preschool children immediately and confidently reply, "Because it's taller." Children over the age of six or so, by contrast, are more likely to reply, "Well, it *looks* as if there's more water in this one because it's taller, but they're really the same."

One reason preoperational stage children have difficulty solving conservation problems (as well as other problems that require logical thinking) is **perceptual centration.** This is the very strong tendency to focus attention on only one characteristic of an object or aspect of a problem or event at a time. The young child focuses only on the height of the water in the two containers and ignores the differences in width and volume. Another way to put this is to say that the child has not yet mastered **decentration**—the ability to think of more than one quality at a time—and is therefore not inclined to contemplate alternatives.

The second impediment to logical thinking is **irreversibility.** This means that young children cannot mentally pour the water from the tall, thin glass back into the short, squat one (thereby proving to themselves that the glasses contain the same amount of water). For the same reason, these youngsters do not understand the logic behind simple mathematical reversals ($4 + 5 = 9$; $9 - 5 = 4$).

Egocentrism: assumption that others see things the same way

The third major impediment is **egocentrism.** When applied to preschool children, *egocentric* does not mean selfish or conceited. It means that youngsters find it difficult, if not impossible, to take another person's point of view. In their conversations and in experimental situations in which they are asked to describe how something would look if viewed by someone else, preschool children reveal that they often have difficulty seeing things from another person's perspective (Piaget & Inhelder, 1956). They seem to assume that others see things the same way they see them. As a result, attempts to explain the logic behind conservation are usually met with quizzical looks and the insistence (some would mistakenly call it stubbornness) that the tall, thin glass contains more water.

Concrete operational stage: child is capable of mentally reversing actions but generalizes only from concrete experiences

Concrete Operational Stage (Elementary to Early Middle School) Through formal instruction, informal experiences, and maturation, children over the age of seven gradually become less influenced by perceptual centration, irreversibility, and egocentrism. Schemes are developing that allow a greater understanding of such logic-based tasks as conservation (matter is neither created nor destroyed but simply changes shape or form or position), class inclusion (the construction of hierarchical relationships among related classes of items), and seriation (the arrangement of items in a particular order).

But operational thinking is limited to objects that are actually present or that children have experienced concretely and directly. For this reason, Piaget described the stage from approximately seven to eleven years as that of *concrete operations*. The nature of the concrete operational stage can be illustrated by the child's mastery of different kinds of conservation.

Children who are within Piaget's preoperational stage of cognitive development have difficulty solving tasks that require logical reasoning because they focus on one aspect of a task at a time (perceptual centration), cannot reverse a sequence of steps in order to find the starting point of a problem (irreversibility), and cannot think of different ways of defining and solving problems (egocentrism).

By the age of seven most children are able to correctly explain that water poured from a short, squat glass into a tall, thin glass is still the same amount of water. Being able to solve the water-pouring problem, however, does not guarantee that a seven-year-old will be able to solve a similar problem involving two balls of clay. A child who has just explained why a tall glass of water contains the same amount as a short one may inconsistently maintain a few moments later that rolling one of two equally sized balls of clay into an elongated shape causes the rolled one to become bigger.

Children in the primary grades tend to react to each situation in terms of concrete experiences. The tendency to solve problems by generalizing from one situation to a similar situation does not occur with any degree of consistency until the end of the elementary school years. Furthermore, if asked to deal with a hypothetical problem, the concrete operational child is likely to be stymied. Seven-year-olds are not likely to be able to solve abstract problems by engaging in mental explorations. They usually need to manipulate concrete objects physically or to recollect specific past experiences in order to explain things to themselves and others. If, for example, you told a student at the concrete operational stage to assume that a feather could break a piece of glass and then asked him whether the deduction "If one hits the glass with a feather, then the glass will break" is true or false, he would likely respond that it is false because in his experience feathers do not break glass (Overton & Byrnes, 1991).

Formal Operational Stage (Middle School, High School, and Beyond) When children *do* reach the point of being able to generalize and to engage in mental trial and error by thinking up hypotheses and testing them in their heads, Piaget said they have reached the stage of *formal operations*. The term *formal* reflects the ability to respond to the *form* of a problem rather than its content and to *form* hypotheses. For example, the formal operational thinker can read the analogies "5 is to 15 as 1 is to 3" and "Penny is to dollar as year is to century" and realize that, despite the different content, the form of the two problems is identical (both analogies are based on ratios). In the same way, the formal thinker can understand and use complex language forms: proverbs ("Strike while the iron is hot"), metaphor ("Procrastination is the thief of time"), sarcasm, and satire.

Formal operational stage: child is able to deal with abstractions, form hypotheses, engage in mental manipulations

We can see the nature of formal operational thinking and how it differs from concrete operational thinking by looking at a simplified version of Piaget's rod-bending experiment. Adolescents are given a basin filled with water, a set of metal rods of varying length, and a set of weights. The rods are attached to the edge of the basin and the weights to the ends of the rods. The subject's task is to figure out how much weight is required to bend a rod just enough to touch the water. Let's say that our hypothetical subject picks out the longest rod in the set (which is 9 inches long), attaches it to the edge of the basin, and puts just enough weight on the end of it to get it to touch the water. This observation is then recorded. Successively shorter rods are selected, and the same procedure is carried out. At some point the subject comes to the 4-inch rod. This rod does not touch the water even when all of the weights have been attached to it. There are, however, three more rods, all of which are shorter than the last one tested.

This is where the formal and concrete operators part company. The formal operational thinker reasons that, if all of the available weights are not sufficient to bend the 4-inch rod enough to touch the water, the same will be true of the remaining rods. In essence, the rest of the experiment is done mentally and symbolically. The concrete operational thinker, however, continues trying out each rod and recording each observation independent of the others. Although both subjects reach the same conclusions, the formal operator does so through a more powerful and efficient process.

But remember that new schemes develop gradually. Even though adolescents can sometimes deal with mental abstractions representing concrete objects, most twelve-year-olds solve problems haphazardly, using trial and error. It is not until the end of the high school years that adolescents are likely to attack a problem by forming hypotheses, mentally sorting out solutions, and systematically testing the most promising leads.

Some interpreters of Piaget (for example, Ginsburg & Opper, 1988) note that a significant aspect of formal thought is that it causes the adolescent to concentrate more on possibilities than on realities. This is the ability that Erikson and others (for example, Kalbaugh & Haviland, 1991) suggest is instrumental in the emergence of the identity crisis. At the point when older adolescents can become aware of all the factors that have to be considered in choosing a career and can imagine what it might be like to be employed, some may feel so threatened and confused that they postpone the final choice. Yet the same capability can also help resolve the identity crisis because adolescents can reason about possibilities in a logical manner. An adolescent girl, for example, may consider working as a pediatrician, teacher, or child psychologist in an underprivileged environment because she has always enjoyed and sought out activities that allowed her to interact with children and has also been concerned with the effects of deprivation on development.

While mastery of formal thought equips the older adolescent with impressive intellectual skills, it may also lead to a tendency for the burgeoning formal thinker to become preoccupied with abstract and theoretical matters. Herbert Ginsburg and Sylvia Opper interpret some of Piaget's observations on this point in the following way:

> In the intellectual sphere, the adolescent has a tendency to become involved in abstract and theoretical matters, constructing elaborate political theories or inventing complex philosophical doctrines. The adolescent may develop plans for the complete reorganization of society or indulge in metaphysical speculation. After discovering capabilities for abstract thought, he then proceeds to exercise them without restraint. Indeed, in the process of exploring these new abilities the adolescent sometimes loses touch with real-

> ity and feels that he can accomplish everything by thought alone. In the emotional sphere the adolescent now becomes capable of directing emotions at abstract ideals and not just toward people. Whereas earlier the adolescent could love his mother or hate a peer, now he can love freedom or hate exploitation. The adolescent has developed a new mode of life: the possible and the ideal captivate both mind and feeling. (1988, pp. 202–203)

David Elkind (1968) suggests that unrestrained theorizing about ideals without complete understanding of realities tends to make the young adolescent a militant rebel with little patience for parents or other adults who fail to find quick solutions to personal, social, and other problems. Only when the older adolescent begins to grasp the complexities of interpersonal relationships and of social and economic problems does more tempered understanding appear.

Elkind also suggests that the egocentrism of early childhood reappears in a different form as **adolescent egocentrism.** This occurs when high school students turn their new powers of thought on themselves and become introspective. The strong tendency to analyze self is projected on others. This helps explain why adolescents are so self-conscious: they assume their thoughts and actions are as central to others as to themselves. The major difference between the egocentrism of childhood and that of adolescence is summed up in Elkind's observation: "The child is egocentric in the sense that he is unable to take another person's point of view. The adolescent, on the other hand, takes the other person's point of view to an extreme degree" (1968, p. 153).

Adolescent egocentrism: one's thoughts and actions are as central to others as to oneself

Elkind believes that adolescent egocentrism also explains why the peer group becomes such a potent force in high school. He observes:

> Adolescent egocentrism . . . accounts, in part, for the power of the peer group during this period. The adolescent is so concerned with the reactions of others toward him, particularly his peers, that he is willing to do many things which are opposed to all of his previous training and to his own best interests. At the same time, this egocentric impression that he is always on stage may help to account for the many and varied adolescent attention-getting maneuvers. (1968, p. 154)

Toward the end of adolescence, this form of exploitative egocentrism gradually declines. The young person comes to realize that other people are much more concerned with themselves and their problems than they are with him and his problems.

CRITICISMS OF PIAGET'S THEORY

Underestimating Children's Capabilities Among the thousands of articles that have been published in response to Piaget's findings are many that offer critiques of his work. Some psychologists argue that Piaget underestimated children's abilities not only because he imposed stringent criteria for inferring the presence of particular cognitive abilities, but also because the tasks he used were often complex and far removed from children's real-life experiences. The term *preoperational,* for instance, stresses what is absent rather than what is present. Within the last decade researchers have focused more on

Piaget's theory underestimates children's abilities

what preoperational children *can* do. The results (summarized by Bryant, 1984; Gelman & Baillargeon, 1983) suggest that preschoolers' cognitive abilities are more advanced in some areas than Piaget's work suggests.

Overestimating Adolescents' Capabilities Other evidence suggests that Piaget may have overestimated the formal thinking capabilities of adolescents. Research summarized by Constance Kamii (1984) revealed that only 20 to 25 percent of college freshmen were able to consistently use formal operational reasoning. Herman Epstein (1980) found that among a group of ninth graders, 32 percent were just beginning the concrete operational stage, 43 percent were well within the concrete operational stage, 15 percent were just entering the formal operational stage, and only 9 percent were mature formal operators. In addition, Norman Sprinthall and Richard Sprinthall (1987) reported that only 33 percent of a group of high school seniors could apply formal operational reasoning to scientific problem solving. Formal reasoning seems to be the exception, not the rule, throughout adolescence.

Most adolescents are not formal operational thinkers

Vague Explanations for Cognitive Growth Piaget's theory has also been criticized for its vagueness in specifying the factors that are responsible for cognitive growth. Why, for example, do children give up conserving responses in favor of nonconserving responses at a particular age? On the basis of recent research, Robert Siegler (1994) believes that variability in children's thinking plays an influential role. For example, it is not uncommon to hear children use on successive occasions different forms of a given verb, as in "I ate it," "I eated it," and "I ated it." Similar variability has been found in the use of memory strategies (five-year-old and eight-year-old children do not always rehearse information they want to remember), addition rules, time-telling rules, and block-building tasks. Siegler's explanation is that variability gives the child a range of plausible options about how to deal with a particular problem. The child then tries them out in an attempt to see which one produces the best adaptation. Note the use of the qualifying word *plausible.* Most children do not try out any and all possible solutions to a problem. Instead, they stick to possibilities that are consistent with a problem's underlying principles.

Cultural Differences Questions have also been raised as to whether children from different cultures develop intellectually in the manner described by Piaget. The answer at this point is both yes and no. The sequence of stages appears to be universal, but the rate of development may vary from one culture to another (Dasen & Heron, 1981; Hughes & Noppe, 1991; Leadbeater, 1991).

Sequence of stages uniform across cultures but rate of development varies

For example, Oglala Sioux children studied by Gilbert Voyat (1983) were quite similar to the Swiss schoolchildren Piaget studied in rate of cognitive development. In terms of performance on conservation, spatial relationship, class inclusion, and seriation tasks, all the four- and five-year-olds were preoperational, the six- and seven-year-olds were transitional, and the eight- and nine-year-olds were concrete operational. The average Eskimo child acquires the spatial concept of horizontalness faster than the average West African child. But many West African children (around the age of twelve or thirteen) understand conservation of quantity, weight, and volume sooner than Eskimo children do (Dasen & Heron, 1981). Although children in Western, industrialized societies (like ours) usually are not given baby-sitting responsibilities until they are at least ten years old because their high level of egocentrism prevents them from considering the needs of the other child, Mayan children in Mexican villages as young as five play this role because their culture stresses the development of cooperative behavior (Sameroff & McDonough, 1994).

Although there is some doubt that formal operational thinking occurs in every culture (Dasen & Heron, 1981; Leadbeater, 1991), you should be aware that what appears to be the absence of a more advanced level of thinking among people in a particular culture may actually be something quite different. Consider, for example, studies of the Kpelle people of Liberia (West Africa). When given a set of twenty familiar objects to sort into categories, they grouped them into small, functional categories (such as a knife and an orange, a potato and a hoe) rather than into the broader and more abstract taxonomic categories of food, tools, and so forth. When asked why they sorted the objects this way, many indicated that this is the way an intelligent person in their society would deal with the task. Then, when asked how an unintelligent person would sort the objects, the subjects sorted them taxonomically (Rogoff, 1990)!

Now that you are familiar with Piaget's theory of cognitive development, you can formulate specific classroom applications. You might use the Suggestions for Teaching for the grade level you expect to teach as the basis for a section in your journal.

Suggestions for Teaching in Your Classroom

Applying Piaget's Theory of Cognitive Development

General Guidelines

1. **Focus on what children at each stage can do and avoid what they cannot meaningfully understand.**

This implication must be interpreted carefully, as recent research has shown that children at the preoperational and concrete operational levels can do more than Piaget believes. In general, however, it is safe to say that since preoperational stage children (preschoolers, kindergartners, most first and some second graders) can use language and other symbols to stand for objects, they should be given many opportunities to describe and explain things through the use of artwork, body movement, role-play, musical performance, and speech. While the concepts of conservation, seriation, class inclusion, time, space, and number can be introduced, attempts at mastering them should probably be postponed until children are in the concrete operational stage.

Concrete operational stage children (grades 3–6) can be given opportunities to master such mental processes as ordering, seriating, classifying, reversing, multiplying, dividing, subtracting, and adding by manipulating concrete objects or symbols. Exercises that involve theorizing, hypothesizing, or generalizing about abstract ideas should be avoided.

Formal operational stage children (grades 7 through high school) can be given activities that require hypothetical-deductive reasoning, reflective thinking, analysis, synthesis, and evaluation.

Students at each of these stages can benefit from exploratory software programs, such as Millie's Math House (produced by Edmark) and Dinosaur Adventure or 3-D Dinosaur Adventure (Knowledge Adventure), that provide environments for children to try a variety of activities using colorful images, sounds, words, and games. When selecting software programs, teachers should look for ones that contain a variety of activities or lots of variation on the main activity, that give positive feedback at appropriate points, that allow the student to control the pace and goals of the activity, and that include engaging qualities such as humorous characters to help guide the student through the program or provide help and support. In other words, a quality software program is one whose characteristics and qualities reflect Piaget's principles of development and learning.

2. **Because individuals differ in their rates of intellectual growth, gear instructional materials and activities to each student's developmental level.**

3. **Because intellectual growth occurs when individuals attempt to eliminate a disequilibrium, instructional lessons and materials that introduce new concepts should provoke interest and curiosity and be moderately challenging in order to maximize assimilation and accommodation.**

4. **While information (facts, concepts, procedures) can be efficiently transmitted from teacher to student through direct instruction, knowledge (rules and hypotheses) is best created by each student through the mental and physical manipulation of information.**

   Accordingly, lesson plans should also indicate opportunities for activity, manipulation, exploration, discussion, and application of information. Small-group science projects are one example of how this implication can be implemented.

5. **Since students' schemes at any given time are an outgrowth of earlier schemes, point out to students how new ideas relate to old ideas and allow students a better understanding of something. Memorization of information for its own sake should be avoided.**

6. **Begin lessons with concrete objects or ideas and gradually shift explanations to a more abstract and general level.**

Preschool, Elementary, and Middle School Grades[2]

Journal Entry
Ways to Apply Piaget's Theory (Preschool, Elementary, and Middle School Grades)

1. **Become thoroughly familiar with Piaget's theory so that you will be aware of how your students organize and synthesize ideas. You may gain extra insight if you analyze your own thinking since you are likely to discover that in some situations you operate at a concrete, rather than an abstract, level.**

2. **If possible, assess the level and the type of thinking of each child in your class. Ask individual children to perform some of Piaget's experiments, and spend most of your time listening to each child explain her reactions.**

3. **Remember that learning through activity and direct experience is essential. Provide plenty of materials and opportunities for children to learn on their own.**

4. **Arrange situations to permit social interaction, so that children can learn from one another.**

   Hearing others explain their views is a natural way for students to learn that not everyone sees things the same way. The placement of a few advanced thinkers with less mature thinkers is more likely to facilitate this process than is homogeneous grouping.

5. **Plan learning experiences to take into account the level of thinking attained by an individual or group.**

   Encourage children to classify things on the basis of a single attribute before you expose them to problems that involve relationships among two or more attributes. Ask many questions, and give your students many opportunities to explain their interpretations of experiences so that you can remain aware of their level of thinking.

6. **Keep in mind the possibility that students may be influenced by egocentric speech and thought.**

   Allow for the possibility that each child may assume that everyone else has the same conception of a word that he has. If confusion becomes apparent or if a child becomes impatient about failure to communicate, request an explanation in different terms. Or ask several children to explain their conception of an object or a situation.

Middle School and Secondary Grades[3]

Journal Entry
Ways to Apply Piaget's Theory (Middle School and Secondary Grades)

1. **Become well acquainted with the nature of concrete operational thinking and formal thought so that you can recognize when your students are resorting to either type or to a combination of the two.**

[2] These guidelines are adapted from Bryant (1984); Bybee and Sund (1982); Elkind (1989); Ginsburg and Opper (1988); and Wadsworth (1989).
[3] Many of these suggestions are derived from points made in Chapter 7 of *Young Children's Thinking* (Almy, Chittenden, & Miller, 1966).

2. **To become aware of the type of thinking used by individual students, ask them to explain how they arrived at solutions to problems. Do this either as part of your classroom curriculum or in response to experimental situations similar to those devised by Piaget.**

3. **Teach students how to solve problems more systematically. (Suggestions for doing this will be provided in Chapters 9 and 10.)**

4. **Keep in mind that some high school students may be more interested in possibilities than in realities.**

   If class discussions become unrealistically theoretical and hypothetical, call attention to facts and practical difficulties. If students are contemptuous of unsuccessful attempts by adults to solve school, local, national, and international problems, point out the complexity of many situations involving conflicts of interest, perhaps by summarizing arguments from both sides.

5. **Allow for the possibility that younger adolescents may go through a period of egocentrism that will cause them to act as if they are always on stage and to be extremely concerned about the reactions of peers.**

Piaget and Vygotsky: The Role of Social Interaction and Instruction in Cognitive Development

From the time Piaget's work first became known to large numbers of American psychologists in the early 1960s until the 1980s, it was the dominant explanation of cognitive development. Not that Piaget didn't have his critics. As the last section made clear, many psychologists challenged one aspect or another of his work. But there were no competing explanations of cognitive development. Beginning in the early 1980s, however, the ideas of a Russian psychologist by the name of Lev Vygotsky began to appear in the psychological literature with increasing frequency. A contemporary of Piaget who died prematurely from tuberculosis in 1934, Vygotsky had very different views about the major forces that shape learning and thinking, particularly about the role of social interaction and formal instruction.

PIAGET'S VIEWS

Piaget believed that cognitive development is caused by two general factors: heredity and environmental experience. Heredity establishes the basic nature of physical structures (such as the brain), the development of physical structures, the existence of reflexes (sucking, grasping, crying), and the tendency to organize experiences and adapt to the environment (through assimilation, accommodation, and equilibration). Experience refers to the variety of interactions we have with the world. These interactions can be classified in three ways: physical experiences, mental experiences, and social experiences. Picking up a bunch of rocks and estimating their size and weight are physical experiences. Arranging the rocks in sequence from smallest to largest or lightest to heaviest is a mental experience. (Piaget used the term *logico-mathematical knowledge* because this type of knowledge is created from schemes based on logic and mathematics.) Watching other people behave, listening to other people's ideas, and discussing ideas with others are examples of social experience. Physical, mental, and social experiences occur spontaneously in the course of everyday living as well as formally as a part of classroom instruction.

Of these two general factors, Piaget believed that heredity is more influential than the various environmental experiences in determining the basic course and rate of cognitive development because heredity directly affects such fundamental processes as maturational growth, organization, and accommodation. Environmental experiences, particularly social interactions with adults and peers, have an indirect effect on cognitive development—they supply the stimulus for further development (Crain, 1992).

The Role of Social Interaction When it comes to social experiences, Piaget clearly believed that peer interactions do more to spur cognitive development than do interactions with adults. The reason is that children are more likely to discuss, analyze, and debate the merits of another child's view of some issue (such as who should have which toy or what the rules of a game should be) than they are to take serious issue with an adult. The balance of power between children and adults is simply too unequal. Not only are most children quickly taught that adults know more and use superior reasoning, but also the adult always gets to have the last word: argue too long and it's off to bed with no dessert. But when children interact with one another, the outcome is more dependent on how well each child uses her wits.

Piaget: cognitive development more strongly influenced by peers than by adults

It is the need to understand the ideas of a peer or playmate in order to formulate responses to those ideas that leads to less egocentrism and the development of new, more complex mental schemes. Put another way, a strongly felt sense of cognitive conflict automatically impels the child to strive for a higher level of equilibrium. Formal instruction by an adult expert simply does not have the same impact regardless of how well designed it might be. That is why parents and teachers are often surprised to find children agreeing on some issue after having rejected an adult's explanation of the very same thing. Thus, educational programs that are patterned after Piaget's ideas usually provide many opportunities for children to socially interact and to discover through these interactions basic ideas about how the world works (Crain, 1992; Rogoff, 1990; Tudge & Winterhoff, 1993).

As proof of the feasibility of this approach, William Damon and Erin Phelps (1991) describe a study they conducted in which fourth graders who worked collaboratively were more successful that similar students who did not work collaboratively at solving mathematical, spatial reasoning, and balance scale problems. As the authors put it, this "is a process that strongly facilitates intellectual growth, because it forces subjects to bring to consciousness the ideas that they are just beginning to grasp intuitively" (p. 182).

The Role of Instruction Even though Piaget believes that formal instruction by expert adults will not significantly stimulate cognitive development, not all American psychologists have been willing to accept this conclusion at face value. Over the past twenty years, dozens of experiments have been conducted to determine whether it is possible to teach preoperational stage children to understand and use concrete operational schemes or to teach students in the concrete operational stage to grasp formal operational reasoning.

The main conclusion of psychologists who have analyzed and evaluated this body of research is, unfortunately, one of uncertainty (see, for example, Case, 1975; Good & Brophy, 1995; Nagy & Griffiths, 1982; Sprinthall, Sprinthall & Oja, 1994). Because of shortcomings in the way some studies were carried out and disagreements about what constitutes evidence of true concrete operational thinking or formal operational thinking, a decisive answer to this question is just not available. Nevertheless, something of value can be gleaned from the research on cognitive acceleration. Two recent analyses of this literature (Sigelman & Shaffer, 1991; Sprinthall & Sprinthall, 1994) conclude that children who are in the process of developing the schemes that will govern the next stage of cognitive functioning can, with good-quality instruction, be helped to refine those schemes a bit faster than would normally be the case. For example, teachers can teach the principle of conservation by using simple explanations and concrete materials and by allowing children to manipulate the materials. This means that teachers should nurture the process of cognitive growth at any particular stage by presenting lessons in a form that is consistent with but slightly more advanced than the students' existing schemes. The objective here is to help students assimilate and accommodate new and different experiences as efficiently as possible.

Instruction can accelerate development of schemes that have begun to form

VYGOTSKY'S VIEWS

Whereas Piaget saw cognitive development arising from attempts to overcome cognitive conflict through the internal and genetically determined processes of assimilation, accommodation, and equilibration, Vygotsky believed that such development is largely due to social processes, particularly interactions with others who are more skilled and competent in what he called the technologies or psychological tools of a culture (Rogoff, 1990; Tudge & Winterhoff, 1993).

The Role of Social Interaction As cultures develop, people create such psychological tools as speech, writing, and numbering to help them master their environment. Early explorers, for example, created maps to help them represent where they had been, communicate that knowledge to others, and plan future trips. Children are first introduced to a culture's major psychological tools through social interactions with their parents and later through more formal interactions with classroom teachers.

Vygotsky: cognitive development more strongly influenced by those more intellectually advanced

Unlike Piaget, Vygotsky believed that children gain significantly from the knowledge and conceptual tools handed down to them by those who are more intellectually advanced, be they peers, older children, or adults. Consider, for example, a simple concept like grandmother. In the absence of formal instruction, a primary grade child's concept of grandmother is likely to be very narrow in scope because it is based on personal experience ("My grandmother is seventy years old, has gray hair, wears glasses, and makes the

Jean Piaget believes that children's schemes develop more quickly when children interact with one another than when they interact with adults. But Lev Vygotsky believes that children learn more from the instructional interactions they have with those who are more intellectually advanced, particularly if the instruction is designed to fall within the child's zone of proximal development.

best apple pie"). But when children are helped to understand the basic nature of the concept with such instructional tools as family tree diagrams, they understand the notion of grandmother (and other types of relatives) on a broader and more general basis. They can then use this concept to compare family structures with friends and, later on, do genealogical research. This example also reveals Vygotsky's basic view of instruction. Its basic purpose is not simply to add one piece of knowledge to another like pennies in a piggy bank, but to stimulate and guide cognitive development (Crain, 1992; Rogoff, 1990).

The Role of Instruction Vygotsky believes that well-designed instruction is like a magnet. If it is aimed slightly ahead of what children know and can do at the present time, it will pull them along, helping them master things they cannot learn on their own. We can illustrate this idea by paraphrasing an experiment described by Vygotsky (1986). He gave two eight-year-olds of average ability problems that were a bit too difficult for them to solve on their own. (Although Vygotsky did not specify what types of problems they were, imagine that they were math problems.) He then tried to help the children solve the problems by giving them leading questions and hints. With this aid he found that one child was able to solve problems designed for twelve-year-olds, whereas the other child could reach only a nine-year-old level.

Vygotsky: cognitive development due to instruction in zone of proximal development

Vygotsky referred to the difference between what a child can do on his own versus what can be accomplished with some assistance as the **zone of proximal development** (**ZPD**). The size of the first eight-year-old's zone is 4, whereas the second child has a zone of 1. According to Vygotsky, students with wider zones are likely to experience greater cognitive development when instruction is pitched just above the lower limit of their ZPD than will students with narrower zones because the former are in a better position to capitalize on the instruction.

Instructional methods that are likely to help students traverse their ZPD include modeling, the use of rewards and punishments, feedback, cognitive structuring (using such devices as theories, categories, labels, and rules for helping students organize and understand ideas), and questioning (Gallimore & Tharp, 1990; Ratner, 1991). The first three techniques will be discussed more fully in Chapter 8, questions will be discussed in Chapter 9, and cognitive structuring techniques will be discussed in Chapter 10. As students approach the upper limit of their ZPD, their behavior becomes smoother, more internalized, and more automatized. Any assistance offered at this level is likely to be perceived as disruptive and irritating.

Vygotsky's notion of producing cognitive development by embedding instruction within a student's zone of proximal development is an attractive one and has many implications for instruction. In Chapter 9, for example, we will describe how this notion was used to improve the reading comprehension skills of low-achieving seventh graders. Whether it can be used to greatly accelerate students' passage through Piaget's stages remains to be seen.

Piaget, Kohlberg, and Gilligan: Moral Development

PIAGET'S ANALYSIS OF THE MORAL JUDGMENT OF THE CHILD

Because he was intrigued by *all* aspects of children's thinking, Piaget became interested in moral development. He began his study of morality by observing how children played marbles. (He first took the trouble to learn the game himself, so that he would be able to understand the subtleties of the conception.) Piaget discovered that interpretations of rules followed by participants in marble games changed with age.

Age Changes in Interpretation of Rules Four- to seven-year-olds just learning the game seemed to view rules as interesting examples of the social behavior of older children. They did not understand the rules but tried to go along with them. Seven- to ten-year-olds regarded rules as sacred pronouncements handed down by older children or adults. At about the age of eleven or twelve, children began to see rules as agreements reached by mutual consent. Piaget concluded that younger children see rules as absolute and external.

Even though children ranging from the age of four to about ten do not question rules, they may frequently break them because they do not understand rules completely. After the age of eleven or so, children become increasingly capable of grasping why rules are necessary. At that point, Piaget concluded, they tend to lose interest in adult-imposed regulations and take delight in formulating their own variations of rules to fit a particular situation. Piaget illustrated this point by describing how a group of ten- and eleven-year-old boys prepared for a snowball fight (1965, p. 50). They divided themselves into teams, elected officers, decided on rules to govern the distances from which the snowballs could be thrown, and agreed on a system of punishments for those who violated the rules. Even though they spent a substantial amount of playtime engaging in such preliminary discussions, they seemed to thoroughly enjoy their newly discovered ability to make up rules to supplant those that had previously been imposed on them by their elders.

Moral Realism Versus Moral Relativism The way children of different ages responded to rules so intrigued Piaget that he decided to use the interview method to obtain more systematic information about moral development. He made up pairs of stories and asked children of different ages to discuss them. Here is a typical pair of stories:

> A: There was a little boy called Julian. His father had gone out and Julian thought it would be fun to play with father's ink-pot. First he played with the pen, and then he made a little blot on the table cloth.
>
> B: A little boy who was called Augustus once noticed that his father's ink-pot was empty. One day that his father was away he thought of filling the ink-pot so as to help his father, and so that he should find it full when he came home. But while he was opening the ink-bottle he made a big blot on the table cloth. (1965, p. 122)

After reading these stories, Piaget asked, "Are these children equally guilty? Which of the two is naughtiest, and why?" As was the case with interpretations of rules, Piaget found that younger children reacted to these stories differently from older children. The younger children maintained that Augustus was more guilty than Julian because he had made a bigger inkblot on the tablecloth. They took no account of the fact that Julian was misbehaving and that Augustus was trying to help his father. Older children, however, were more likely to base their judgment of guilt on the intent of each child.

Piaget referred to the moral thinking of children up to the age of ten or so as the **morality of constraint,** but he also calls it *moral realism.* (Remember our definition of *decentration* in the earlier discussion of Piaget's theory. How do you think the young child's lack of decentration might affect her moral reasoning?) The thinking of children of eleven or older Piaget called the **morality of cooperation.** He also occasionally used the term *moral relativism.* Piaget concluded that the two basic types of moral reasoning differ in several ways. We summarize these differences in Table 2.2, shown on the next page.

Moral realism: sacred rules, no exceptions, no allowance for intentions, consequences determine guilt

Moral relativism: rules are flexible, intent important in determining guilt

KOHLBERG'S DESCRIPTION OF MORAL DEVELOPMENT

Just as James Marcia has elaborated Erikson's concept of identity formation, Lawrence Kohlberg has elaborated Piaget's ideas on moral thinking.

Kohlberg's Use of Moral Dilemmas As a graduate student at the University of Chicago in the 1950s, Lawrence Kohlberg became fascinated by Piaget's

TABLE 2.2 *Morality of Constraint versus Morality of Cooperation*

Morality of Constraint (Typical of Six-year-olds)	Morality of Cooperation (Typical of Twelve-year-olds)
Holds single, absolute moral perspective (behavior is right or wrong)	Is aware of different viewpoints regarding rules
Believes rules are unchangeable	Believes rules are flexible
Determines extent of guilt by amount of damage	Considers the wrongdoers' intentions when evaluating guilt
Defines moral wrongness in terms of what is forbidden or punished	Defines moral wrongness in terms of violation of spirit and cooperation
(Notice that these first four differences call attention to the tendency for children below the age of ten or so to think of rules as sacred pronouncements handed down by external authority.)	
Believes punishment should stress atonement and does not need to "fit the crime"	Believes punishment should involve either restitution or suffering the same fate as one's victim
Believes peer aggression should be punished by an external authority	Believes peer aggression should be punished by retaliatory behavior on the part of the victim*
Believes children should obey rules because they are established by those in authority	Believes children should obey rules because of mutual concerns for rights of others
(Notice how these last three differences call attention to the tendency for children above the age of ten or so to see rules as mutual agreements among equals.)	

*Beyond the age of twelve, adolescents increasingly affirm that reciprocal reactions, or "getting back," should be a response to good behavior, not bad.

SOURCES: Freely adapted from interpretations of Piaget (1932) by Kohlberg (1969); and Lickona (1976).

studies of moral development. He decided to expand on Piaget's original research by making up stories involving moral dilemmas that would be more appropriate for older children. Here is the story that is most often mentioned in discussions of his work:

> In Europe a woman was near death from cancer. One drug might save her, a form of radium that a druggist in the same town had recently discovered. The druggist was charging $2,000, ten times what the drug cost him to make. The sick woman's husband, Heinz, went to everyone he knew to borrow the money, but he could only get together about half of what it cost. He told the druggist that his wife was dying and asked him to sell it cheaper or let him pay later, but the druggist said "No." The husband got desperate and broke into the man's store to steal the drug for his wife. Should the husband have done that? Why? (1969, p. 376)

Kohlberg's Six Stages of Moral Reasoning After analyzing the responses of ten- to sixteen-year-olds to this and similar moral dilemmas, Kohlberg (1963)

TABLE 2.3 *Kohlberg's Stages of Moral Reasoning*

LEVEL 1: PRECONVENTIONAL MORALITY. (Typical of children up to the age of nine. Called *preconventional* because young children do not really understand the conventions or rules of a society.)

Stage 1 Punishment-obedience orientation. The physical consequences of an action determine goodness or badness. Those in authority have superior power and should be obeyed. Punishment should be avoided by staying out of trouble.

Stage 2 Instrumental relativist orientation. An action is judged to be right if it is instrumental in satisfying one's own needs or involves an even exchange. Obeying rules should bring some sort of benefit in return.

LEVEL 2: CONVENTIONAL MORALITY. (Typical of nine- to twenty-year-olds. Called *conventional* since most of nine- to twenty-year-olds conform to the conventions of society because they *are* the rules of a society.)

Stage 3 Good boy–nice girl orientation. The right action is one that would be carried out by someone whose behavior is likely to please or impress others.

Stage 4 Law-and-order orientation. To maintain the social order, fixed rules must be established and obeyed. It is essential to respect authority.

LEVEL 3: POSTCONVENTIONAL MORALITY. (Usually reached only after the age of twenty and only by a small proportion of adults. Called *postconventional* because the moral principles that underlie the conventions of a society are understood.)

Stage 5 Social contract orientation. Rules needed to maintain the social order should be based not on blind obedience to authority but on mutual agreement. At the same time, the rights of the individual should be protected.

Stage 6 Universal ethical principle orientation. Moral decisions should be made in terms of self-chosen ethical principles. Once principles are chosen, they should be applied in consistent ways.*

*In an article published in 1978, several years after Kohlberg had originally descibed the six stages, he described the last stage as an essentially theoretical ideal that is rarely encountered in real life.

SOURCE: Based on descriptions in Kohlberg (1969, 1976, 1978).

eventually developed a description of six stages of moral reasoning. Be forewarned, however, that Kohlberg has revised some of his original stage designations and that descriptions of the stages have been modified since he first proposed them. In different discussions of his stages, therefore, you may encounter varying descriptions. The outline presented in Table 2.3 is a composite summary of the sequence of moral development as it has been described by Kohlberg, but you should expect to find differences if you read other accounts of his theory.

The scoring system Kohlberg developed to evaluate a given response to a moral dilemma is extremely complex. Furthermore, the responses of subjects are lengthy and may feature arguments about a particular decision. To help you understand a bit more about each Kohlberg stage, simplified examples of responses to a dilemma such as that faced by Heinz are noted. For maximum clarity, only brief typical responses to the question "Why shouldn't you steal from a store?" are mentioned.

Preconventional morality: avoid punishment, receive benefits in return

Stage 1: punishment-obedience orientation. "You might get caught." (The physical consequences of an action determine goodness or badness.)

Stage 2: instrumental relativist orientation. "You shouldn't steal something from a store, and the store owner shouldn't steal things that belong to you." (Obedience to laws should involve an even exchange.)

Conventional morality: impress others, respect authority

Stage 3: good boy–nice girl orientation. "Your parents will be proud of you if you are honest." (The right action is one that will impress others.)

Stage 4: law-and-order orientation. "It's against the law, and if we don't obey laws, our whole society might fall apart." (To maintain the social order, fixed rules must be obeyed.)

Postconventional morality: mutual agreements, consistent principles

Stage 5: social contract orientation. "Under certain circumstances laws may have to be disregarded—if a person's life depends on breaking a law, for instance." (Rules should involve mutual agreements; the rights of the individual should be protected.)

Stage 6: universal ethical principle orientation. "You need to weigh all the factors and then try to make the most appropriate decision in a given situation. Sometimes it would be morally wrong *not* to steal." (Moral decisions should be based on consistent applications of self-chosen ethical principles.)

Similarities and Differences Between Piaget and Kohlberg As you examined this list of stages and the examples of responses at each stage, you may have detected similarities between Piaget's and Kohlberg's descriptions of age changes in moral development. The first four of Kohlberg's stages are roughly equivalent to the moral realism described by Piaget. Kohlberg's preconventional and conventional moral thinkers and Piaget's moral realists all tend to think of rules as edicts handed down by external authority. The letter of the law is observed, and not much allowance is made for intentions or circumstances. Kohlberg's postconventional thinker shares some similarities with the older children observed by Piaget: rules are established by individuals who come to mutual agreement, and each moral decision takes special circumstances into account.

While there are similarities in the conclusions drawn by Piaget and Kohlberg, there are important differences as well. Piaget believes that moral thinking changes as children mature. He does not, however, believe that such changes are clearly related to specific ages, nor are they sequential. Piaget maintains that the different types of moral thinking he describes often overlap and that a child might sometimes function as a moral realist, sometimes as a more mature moral decision maker. Kohlberg (1969), by contrast, maintains that the order of the stages he has described is universal and fixed and that a person moves through the stages in sequence. Not everyone reaches the top stages, but all individuals begin at stage 1 and work their way upward.

Another difference concerns the acceleration of moral reasoning. Piaget believed that children in the preoperational and concrete operational stages cannot be helped to understand the logic behind moral relativism until the elements of formal operational schemes have begun to form. Kohlberg, however, believes that progress through his six stages can be accelerated with the proper type of instruction.

In some respects there are greater similarities between Piaget's description of *cognitive* development and Kohlberg's description of *moral* development than between the two outlines of moral development. Piaget described preoperational, concrete operational, and formal operational stages. Kohlberg describes preconventional, conventional, and postconventional levels. Even though Piaget did not stress an orderly sequence of *moral* development, he did believe that children go through the stages of *cognitive* development in a definite order. Both Piaget's formal operational stage and Kohlberg's postconventional level stress understanding and application of abstract principles and take into account unique circumstances in a given situation. A person cannot engage in postconventional moral reasoning, in fact, until she has mastered formal thinking.

Criticisms and Evaluations of Kohlberg's Theory Is Kohlberg's contention that moral reasoning proceeds through a fixed universal sequence of stages accurate? Based on analysis of research on moral development, Martin Hoffman (1980) feels that, although Kohlberg's sequence of stages may not be true of every individual in every culture, it may provide a useful general description of how moral reasoning develops in American society. Carol Gilligan (1979), whose position we will discuss in detail later on, has proposed two somewhat different sequences that reflect differences in male and female socialization.

What about Kohlberg's view that moral development can be accelerated through direct instruction? Is this another "mission impossible," as some critics contend? Research on this question has produced some limited but moderately positive results. Most of these studies have used a teaching method known as *direct discussion* or *dilemma discussion*. After reading a set of moral dilemmas (like the one about Heinz and the cancer drug) and identifying those issues that could help resolve the dilemma, students, under the teacher's guidance, discuss the different ways each of them chose to resolve the dilemma. This process can involve challenging one another's thinking, reexamining assumptions, building lines of argument, and responding to counterarguments.

Alan Lockwood (1978), after summarizing the findings of almost a dozen studies on acceleration of moral reasoning, concludes that the strongest effects (about half a stage increase in reasoning) occurred among individuals whose reasoning reflected stages 2 and 3. The effect of the treatment varied considerably from one subject to another. Some individuals showed substantial increases in reasoning; others showed no change. A more recent and comprehensive review of research on this topic by Andre Schlaefli, James Rest, and Stephen Thoma (1985) revealed similar conclusions. The authors found that moral education programs produced modest positive effects. They also found that the strongest effects were obtained with adult subjects.

Moral education programs may produce modest acceleration in moral development

Paul Vitz (1990) criticizes the use of moral dilemmas on the grounds that they are too far removed from the kinds of everyday social interactions in which children and adolescents engage. He prefers instead the use of narrative stories, be they fictional or real accounts of others, because they portray such basic moral values as honesty, compassion, fairness, and hard work in an understandable context.

Educational Implications of Kohlberg's Theory

THE JUST COMMUNITY. In the 1970s Kohlberg experimented with the use of discussion techniques to "teach" moral reasoning. An interesting outgrowth of that work (for example, see Blatt & Kohlberg, 1978) and his observations in 1969 of life on an Israeli kibbutz is the *just community*, an approach that brings students and teachers together to settle their own problems and make their own rules on a one-person, one-vote basis. (In one instance students and teachers discussed how to handle immoral and illegal actions, such as the theft of stereo equipment from a camp where students had gone for an outing.) While the just community approach seems to have met with some success (for example, see Kohlberg, 1978; Power, 1981, 1985), it is useful only when a school system agrees to give students the time and power to make many of their own decisions about school rules and interpersonal relationships. It does not seem likely at present that many school boards would be willing to agree to those terms. Perhaps this is why the concept has been tried in only a few, relatively small alternative schools.

Another problem with the just community has to do with the nature of participatory democracy. As soon as more than a few people become involved, participatory democracy becomes unwieldy. Piaget drew attention to this point when he described how a small group of ten-year-old boys spent as much time agreeing on rules to govern a snowball fight as they did actually playing. While rule making may be enjoyable when it is a novelty, those who have been involved in a participatory democracy for very long are likely to confess that they sometimes wish an external authority would simply tell them what the rules are so that they can go about their business.

USING MORAL DILEMMAS. Because of these potential weaknesses of the just community approach, teachers may find that other techniques of moral instruction based on Kohlberg's theory will be more workable. Carol Harding and Kenneth Snyder (1991) believe that teachers can make productive use of contemporary films mainly because film is an attractive medium to students and several types of moral dilemmas are often portrayed in the space of about two hours. To highlight the dilemma of the rights of the individual versus the rights of others in a community, Harding and Snyder recommend the films *Platoon* and *Wall Street*. The former is a story about the Vietnam War and contains scenes of American soldiers burning villages and abusing villagers who are suspected of having ties to or of being the enemy. In response to such scenes, students can be asked such questions as, "Should the enemy in war be granted certain rights, or is personal survival more important?" *Wall Street* is a story about a corporate raider who uses borrowed money to take control of public companies and then sells off the assets (thereby eliminating people's jobs) to enrich himself.

The Tom Snyder educational software company offers a series of computer-based programs titled "Decisions, Decisions" in which students identify and discuss moral dilemmas such as protecting the environment or using drugs. Students discuss each situation and choose a response within the program as a group. Each response is stored by the program and in turn affects the development and outcome of the following situations to illustrate that events do not occur in isolation and that all decisions have consequences.

If films or computer programs are not available but you occasionally wish to engage your students in a discussion of moral dilemmas, the daily newspaper is an excellent source of material. Biology teachers, for example, can point to stories of the conflicts produced by machines that keep comatose patients alive or by medical practices based on genetic engineering. Other science teachers might bring in articles that describe the moral dilemma produced by the debate over nuclear power versus fossil fuel. Civics or government teachers could use news items that reflect the dilemma that arises when freedom of speech conflicts with the need to curtail racism.

GILLIGAN'S VIEW OF IDENTITY AND MORAL DEVELOPMENT

Carol Gilligan (1982, 1988) argues that Erikson's view of identity development and Kohlberg's view of moral development more accurately describe what occurs with adolescent males than with adolescent females. In her view, Erikson's and Kohlberg's ideas emphasize separation from parental authority and societal conventions. Instead of remaining loyal to adult authority, individuals as they mature shift their loyalty to abstract principles (for example, self-reliance, independence, justice, and fairness). This process of detachment allows adolescents to assume a more equal status with adults. It's almost as if adolescents are saying, "You have your life, and I have mine; you don't intrude on mine, and I won't intrude on yours."

But, Gilligan argues, many adolescent females have a different primary concern. They care less about separation and independence and more about remaining loyal to others through expressions of caring, understanding, and sharing of experiences. Detachment for these female adolescents is a moral problem rather than a sought-after developmental milestone. The problem for them is how to become autonomous while also being caring and connected.

Given this view, Gilligan feels that adolescent females are more likely to resolve Erikson's identity versus role confusion and intimacy versus isolation crises concurrently rather than consecutively. The results of at least one study (Ochse & Plug, 1986) support this view. With respect to Kohlberg's theory, Gilligan argues that because females are socialized to value more highly the qualities of understanding, helping, and cooperation with others than that of preserving individual rights, and because this orientation is reflected most strongly in Kohlberg's two conventional stages, females are more likely to be judged to be at a lower level of moral development than males.

Carol Gilligan believes that Erikson's theory of identity development and Kohlberg's theory of moral development do not accurately describe the course of identity formation and moral reasoning in females. She believes that adolescent females place a higher value on caring, understanding, and sharing of experiences than they do on independence, self-reliance, and justice.

Stephen Thoma (1986) offers a partial answer to Gilligan's criticism. After reviewing more than fifty studies on gender differences in moral development, he draws three conclusions. First, the effect of gender on scores from the Defining Issues Test (the DIT is a device that uses responses to moral dilemmas to determine level of moral reasoning) was very small. Less than one-half of 1 percent of the differences in DIT scores was due to gender differences. Second, females almost always scored higher. This slight superiority for females appeared in every age group studied (middle school, high school, college, adults). Third, differences in DIT scores were strongly associated with differences in age and level of education. That is, individuals who were older and who had graduated from college were more likely to score at the postconventional level than those who were younger and who had less education. Thoma's findings suggest that females are just as likely as males to use justice and fairness concepts in their reasoning about *hypothetical* moral dilemmas.

Males and females may use different approaches to resolve real-life moral dilemmas

But there is one aspect of Gilligan's criticism that cannot be answered by Thoma's analysis of existing research. She argues that when females are faced with their own real-life moral dilemmas (abortion, civil rights, environmental pollution) rather than hypothetical ones, they are more likely to favor a caring/helping/cooperation orientation than a justice/fairness/individual rights orientation. Perhaps the best approach that educators can take when they involve students in discussions of moral issues is to emphasize the utility of *both* orientations.

DOES MORAL THINKING LEAD TO MORAL BEHAVIOR?

Hugh Hartshorne and Mark May (1929, 1930a, 1930b) observed thousands of children at different age levels reacting in situations that revealed their actual moral behavior. Hartshorne and May also asked the children to respond to questions about hypothetical situations to reveal how much they understood about right and wrong behavior. Elementary school children, for example, were allowed to correct their own papers or record their own scores on measures of athletic skill without being aware that accurate measures were being made independently by adult observers. The children were also asked what they *thought* was the right thing to do in similar situations.

A comparison of the two sets of data made it possible to determine, among other things, whether children practiced what they preached. What Hartshorne and May discovered, however, was that many children who were able to describe right kinds of behavior in hypothetical situations indulged in wrong behavior in real-life situations. Children reacted in specific, rather than consistent, ways to situations that called for moral judgment. Even a child who was rated as among the most honest in a group would behave in a dishonest way under certain circumstances. A boy who was an excellent student but an indifferent athlete, for example, would not cheat when asked to correct his own paper, but he *would* inflate scores on sports skills.

Moral knowledge does not always result in moral behavior

Another significant, and dismaying, discovery made by Hartshorne and May was that children who went to Sunday school or who belonged to such organizations as the Boy Scouts or Girl Scouts were just as dishonest as children who were not exposed to the kind of moral instruction provided by such organizations. Hartshorne and May concluded that one explanation for the ineffectiveness of moral instruction in the 1920s was that too much stress was placed on having children memorize values such as the Ten Commandments or the Boy Scout oath and law. The two researchers suggested that it would be more effective to invite children to discuss real-life moral situations as they occurred. Instead of children chanting, "Honesty is the best policy," for example, Hartshorne and May urged teachers to call attention to the positive consequences of honest acts. If a student in a school reported that she had found money belonging to someone else, the teacher might praise the child and ask everyone in the class to think about how relieved the person who had lost the money would be to get it back.

The necessity for teachers and parents to follow Hartshorne and May's suggestion of becoming directly involved in the moral education of children in both word and deed was made clear in two recent publications. In *The Moral Child,* William Damon argues that "children acquire moral values by actively participating in adult-child and child-child relationships that support, enhance, and guide their natural moral inclinations." (1988, p. 118). A critical aspect of these relationships is that parents, teachers, and other adults must explain the reasons for requiring children to exhibit certain moral behaviors. Fred Schab (1991) surveyed more than twelve hundred high school students in 1969 and 1989 on cheating in school and other aspects of dishonesty. Over that twenty-year period, he found that fear of failure was the most common reason for cheating and that it occurred most often in math and science classes. School was judged the worst place by these students to teach the value of honesty.

Piaget's description of cognitive development and Kohlberg's description of moral reasoning development help explain some of Hartshorne and May's conclusions. Elementary school children are in the concrete operational stage. They think in terms of actual experiences and treat situations that look different in different ways. Because many of these youngsters are also at Kohlberg's third stage (good boy–nice girl), their moral behavior is influenced by their eagerness to please or impress others. Thus, the inability of elementary school children to comprehend and apply general principles in varied situations and their desire to do what they think will please or impress authority figures may partly explain the ineffectiveness of moral instruction that stresses the memorization of abstract principles.

Suggestions for Teaching in Your Classroom

Encouraging Moral Development

Journal Entry
Ways to Encourage Moral Development

1. **Recognize that younger children will respond to moral conflicts differently from older children.**

2. **Try to take the perspective of students and stimulate their perspective-taking abilities.**

3. **Develop an awareness of moral issues by discussing a variety of real and hypothetical moral dilemmas and by using daily opportunities in the classroom to heighten moral awareness. (Moral education should be an integral part of the curriculum; it should not take place during a "moral education period.")**

4. **Create a classroom atmosphere that will enhance open discussion. (For example, arrange face-to-face groupings, be an accepting model, foster listening and communication skills, and encourage student-to-student interaction.)**

Specific suggestions for supervising classroom discussions offered by Richard Hersh, Diana Paolitto, and Joseph Reimer (1979) include the following:

Highlight the moral issue to be discussed. (Describe a specific real or hypothetical moral dilemma.)

Ask "why?" questions. (After asking students what they would do if they were faced with the moral dilemma under discussion, ask them to explain why they would act that way.)

Complicate the circumstances. (After students have responded to the original dilemma, mention a factor that might complicate matters—for example, the involvement of a best friend in the dilemma.)

Use personal and naturalistic examples. (Invite students to put themselves in the position of individuals who are confronted by moral dilemmas described in newspapers or depicted on television.)

Before you use any techniques of moral education in your classes, it would be wise to check with your principal. In some communities parents have insisted that they, not teachers, should take the responsibility for moral instruction.

Resources for Further Investigation

Erikson's Description of Development

Erik Erikson's books are of considerable significance for their speculations about development and education. In the first six chapters of *Childhood and Society* (2d ed., 1963), he describes how studying Native Americans and observing patients in treatment led him to develop the Eight Ages of Man (described in Chapter 7 of the book). In the final chapters of this book, Erikson uses his conception of development to analyze the lives of Hitler and Maxim Gorky. *Identity: Youth and Crisis* (1968) features a revised description of the eight stages of development, with emphasis on identity and role confusion. Erikson comments on many aspects of his work in an interview with Richard Evans, published under the title *Dialogue with Erik Erikson* (1967). And James Marcia reviews research on identity statuses in "Identity in Adolescence," in *Handbook of Adolescent Psychology* (1980), edited by Joseph Adelson.

Piaget's Theory of Cognitive Development

Jean Piaget has probably exerted more influence on theoretical discussions of development and on educational practices than any other contemporary psychologist. Of his own books, you might wish to consult *The Language and Thought of the Child* (1952a), *The Origins of Intelligence in Children* (1952b), and *The Psychology of the Child* (1969), the last of which was written in collaboration with Barbel Inhelder. Howard Gruber and Jacques Vonèche have edited *The Essential Piaget: An Interpretive Reference and Guide* (1977), which Piaget describes in the Foreword as "the best and most complete of all anthologies of my work." An inexpensive paperback that provides a biography of Piaget and an analysis of his work is *Piaget's Theory of Intellectual Development* (3d ed., 1988), by Herbert Ginsburg and Sylvia Opper. Other books about Piaget are *Piaget for Teachers* (1970), by Hans Furth; *Piaget's Theory of Cognitive and Affective Development* (4th ed., 1989), by Barry Wadsworth; *Theories of Developmental Psychology* (3d ed., 1993), by Patricia Miller; and *Piaget's Theory: Prospects and Possibilities* (1992), edited by Harry Beilin and Peter Pufall.

An on-line source of information and relevant publications for Piaget is the Jean Piaget Society database, located at http://www.wimsey.com/~chrisl/JPS/JPS.html. It contains electronic journals and conference information and is dedicated to "the presentation and discussion of scholarly work on issues related to human knowledge and its development."

Vygotsky's Theory of Cognitive Development

Comprehensive descriptions and analyses of Lev Vygotsky's ideas about cognitive development can be found in *Vygotsky and Education: Instructional Implications and Applications of Sociohistorical Psychology* (1990), edited by Luis Moll; *Vygotsky's Sociohistorical Psychology and Its Contemporary Application* (1991), by Carl Ratner; and *Lev Vygotsky: Revolutionary Scientist* (1993), by Fred Newman and Lois Holzman. The proceedings of an annual conference on Vygotsky and his work can be found on-line at http://www.glasnet.ru/~vega/vygodsky/index.html. The proceedings include a number of original papers, including one by Vygotsky's daughter.

Piaget's Description of Moral Development

Piaget describes his observations on moral development in *The Moral Judgment of the Child* (1948). Thomas Lickona summarizes research investigations stimulated by Piaget's conclusions in "Research on Piaget's Theory of Moral Development," in *Moral Development and Behavior: Theory, Research, and Social Issues* (1976), an excellent compilation of articles on all aspects of morality, which he edited.

Kohlberg's Stages of Moral Development

If you would like to read Kohlberg's own account of the stages of moral development, examine "Moral Stages and Moralization: The Cognitive-Developmental Approach," in *Moral Development and Behavior: Theory, Research, and Social Issues* (1976), edited by Thomas Lickona. Kohlberg discusses "Revisions in the Theory and Practice of Moral Development," in: *New Directions for Child Development*: Moral Development (1978), edited by William Damon. Techniques for encouraging moral development by taking account of Kohlberg's stages are described in *Promoting Moral Growth: From Piaget to Kohlberg* (1979), by Richard Hersh, Diana Paolitto, and Joseph Reimer. A discussion of current research on moral development can be found in *Approaches to Moral Development: New Research and Emerging Themes* (1993), edited by Andrew Garrod.

Kohlberg's Just Community

To learn more about the nature of a just community and how it works in practice, read "The Just Community Approach to Moral Education in Theory and Practice," by Kohlberg; and "Democratic Moral Education in the Large Public High School," by Clark Power. Both chapters appear in *Moral Education: Theory and Application* (1985), edited by Marvin Berkowitz and Fritz Oser.

Gilligan's Analysis of Adolescent Development

If you would like to know more about the basis of Carol Gilligan's critique of Erikson's and Kohlberg's theories and her arguments for a broader view of adolescent development, start with her widely cited book *In a Different Voice: Psychological Theory and Women's Development* (1982). Briefer and more recent analyses of this issue are "Adolescent Development Reconsidered," a chapter in *Adolescent Social Behavior and Health* (1987), edited by Charles Irwin Jr.; and "Exit Voice Dilemmas in Adolescent Development," a chapter in *Mapping the Moral Domain: A Contribution of Women's Thinking to Psychological Theory and Education* (1988), edited by Carol Gilligan, Janie Ward, Jill Taylor, and Betty Bardige.

Summary

1. Erikson's theory is notable because it covers the life span, it describes people as playing an active role in their own psychological development as opposed to passively responding to external forces, and it emphasizes the role played by cultural norms and goals.
2. Erikson's theory of personality development is based on the epigenetic principle of biology. Just as certain parts of the fetus are formed at certain times and combine to produce a biologically whole individual at birth, certain aspects of personality develop at certain times and combine to form a psychologically whole individual.
3. Erikson's theory describes eight stages, from birth through old age. The stages that deal with the personality development of school-age children are initiative versus guilt (four to five years), industry versus inferiority (six to eleven years), and identity versus role confusion (twelve to eighteen years).
4. Individuals with a strong sense of identity are comfortable with their physical selves, have a sense of purpose and direction, and know they will be recognized by others. Individuals with a poorly developed sense of identity are susceptible to role confusion.
5. Establishing a strong identity and avoiding role confusion are especially difficult for today's adolescents because of changing social values.
6. One solution to the conflict over appropriate gender role behavior is psychological androgyny.
7. When faced with making an occupational choice, some adolescents declare a psychosocial moratorium; others establish a negative identity.

8. Erikson's observations about identity were extended by Marcia, who described four identity statuses: identity diffusion, moratorium, identity achievement, and foreclosure.
9. Erikson's theory has been criticized for its heavy reliance on personal experience, for its inaccuracies in terms of female personality development, and for its failure to specify how individuals move from stage to stage.
10. Piaget believed that individuals inherit two basic intellectual tendencies: organization (the tendency to combine mental processes into more general systems) and adaptation (the tendency to adjust to the environment).
11. Adaptation occurs through the processes of assimilation (fitting an experience into an existing scheme) and accommodation (changing a scheme or creating a new one to incorporate a new experience).
12. A scheme is a mental framework that guides our thoughts and actions.
13. Equilibration is the process of trying to organize a system of schemes that allows us to adapt to current environmental conditions. Equilibration is produced by a state of disequilibrium.
14. Piaget concluded on the basis of his studies that schemes evolve through four stages: sensorimotor (birth to two years), preoperational (two to seven years), concrete operational (seven to eleven years), and formal operational (twelve to eighteen years).
15. During the sensorimotor stage, the infant and toddler use senses and motor skills to explore and understand the environment.
16. In the preoperational stage, the child masters symbol systems but cannot manipulate symbols logically.
17. In the concrete operational stage, the child is capable of logical thinking, but only with ideas with which he has had firsthand experience.
18. During the formal operational stage, the individual is capable of hypothetical reasoning, dealing with abstractions, and engaging in mental manipulations.
19. Systematic instruction may have modest positive effects on the rate of cognitive development as long as the schemes that will govern the next stage have already begun to develop.
20. Piaget's theory has been criticized for underestimating children's abilities, for overestimating the capability of adolescents to engage in formal operational thinking, for vague explanations of how individuals move from stage to stage, and for not addressing cultural differences.
21. Piaget identified two types of moral reasoning in children: morality of constraint (rules are inflexible and external) and morality of cooperation (rules are flexible and internal).
22. Kohlberg defined six stages in the development of moral reasoning: punishment-obedience, instrumental relativist, good boy–nice girl, law and order, social contract, and universal ethical principle.
23. Structured discussions based on moral dilemmas may have some positive effects on the rate of development of moral reasoning.
24. Carol Gilligan maintains that Erikson's theory of identity development and Kohlberg's theory of moral development more accurately describe male development than female development.
25. Studies show that children's moral behavior varies in different circumstances.

Key Terms

epigenetic principle *(34)*
role confusion *(35)*
identity *(36)*
psychological androgyny *(39)*
psychosocial moratorium *(42)*
negative identity *(42)*
identity diffusion status *(44)*
moratorium status *(44)*
identity achievement status *(45)*
foreclosure status *(45)*
organization *(49)*
adaptation *(49)*

equilibration *(50)*
schemes *(50)*
assimilation *(50)*
accommodation *(50)*
constructivism *(51)*
conservation *(53)*
perceptual centration *(54)*
decentration *(54)*
irreversibility *(54)*
egocentrism *(54)*
adolescent egocentrism *(57)*
zone of proximal development (ZPD) *(66)*
morality of constraint *(67)*
morality of cooperation *(67)*

Discussion Questions

1. According to Erikson, the way in which personality develops among six- to eleven-year-old children depends on their attaining a sense of industry and avoiding a sense of inferiority. Suppose you were an elementary school teacher. What kinds of things would you do to help your students feel more capable and productive? What kinds of things would you avoid doing?

2. Between the ages of twelve and eighteen, personality development revolves around establishing an identity and avoiding role confusion. American high schools are often criticized for not helping adolescents resolve this conflict. Do you agree? Why? What do you think could be done to improve matters?

3. From Piaget's point of view, why is it wrong to think of children as "small adults"?

4. In response to reports that American schoolchildren do not score as well as many European and Asian schoolchildren on standardized achievement tests, some critics of American education argue that we should begin formal schooling earlier than age five and that it should focus on mastery of basic reading and computation skills. How would Piaget respond to this proposal?

5. How would you respond to a parent (or colleague) who argued that students have better things to do in class than discuss ways of resolving moral dilemmas?

CHAPTER 3

Age-Level Characteristics

Key Points

These key points will help you learn the important information in this chapter. To help you study, they also appear in the margins of pages, next to the text where they are discussed.

PRESCHOOL AND KINDERGARTEN

- Large-muscle control better established than small-muscle control and eye-hand coordination
- Play patterns vary as a function of social class, gender, and age
- Gender differences in toy preferences and play activities noticeable by kindergarten
- Young children stick to own language rules

PRIMARY GRADES

- Primary grade children have difficulty focusing on small print
- Accident rate peaks in third grade because of confidence in physical skills
- Rigid interpretation of rules in primary grades
- To encourage industry, use praise, avoid criticism

ELEMENTARY GRADES

- Boys slightly better at sports-related motor skills; girls better at flexibility, balance, rhythmic motor skills
- Peer group norms for behavior begin to replace adult norms
- Self-concept becomes more generalized and stable; is based primarily on comparisons with peers
- Delinquents have few friends, are easily distracted, are not interested in schoolwork, lack basic skills
- Elementary grade students reason logically but concretely
- Cognitive styles are preferences for dealing with intellectual tasks in a particular way
- Field-independent students prefer their own structure; field-dependent students prefer to work within existing structure

Middle School

- Girls' growth spurt occurs earlier, and so they look older than boys of same age
- After growth spurt, boys have greater strength and endurance
- Early-maturing boys likely to draw favorable responses
- Late-maturing boys may seek attention
- Late-maturing girls likely to be popular and carefree
- Average age of puberty: girls, eleven; boys, fourteen
- Discussion of controversial issues may be difficult because of strong desire to conform to peer norms
- Teenagers experience different degrees of emotional turmoil
- Girls superior in language skills, math computation; boys superior in analogies, math reasoning, spatial orientation
- Self-efficacy beliefs for academic and social tasks become strong influences on behavior

High School

- Sexual activity among male, female teens due to different factors
- Adolescents likely to be confused about appropriateness of premarital sex
- Parents influence values, plans; peers influence immediate status
- Girls more likely than boys to experience anxiety about friendships
- Depression most common among females, teens from poor families
- Depression may be caused by negative set, learned helplessness, sense of loss
- Depression and unstable family situation place adolescents at risk for suicide
- Political thinking becomes more abstract, less authoritarian, more knowledgeable

The theories described in Chapter 2 call attention to stages of psychosocial, cognitive, and moral development. While these types of behavior are important, they represent only a small part of the behavior repertoire of a child or adolescent. To describe the many aspects of development that are of potential significance to teachers, we must analyze types of behavior that are not directly related to the theories already discussed or to those (learning and information processing) that will be discussed in Part 3. This chapter will present such an overview of types of behavior at different age and grade levels that are not directly related to any particular theory. In selecting points for emphasis, we used one basic criterion: Does this information about development have potential significance for teachers?

To organize the points to be discussed, we have divided the developmental span into five levels, corresponding to common grade groupings in schools: preschool and kindergarten (three to five years), primary grades (1, 2, and 3; six, seven, and eight years), elementary grades (4 and 5; nine and ten years), middle school grades (6, 7, and 8; eleven, twelve, and thirteen years), and high school grades (9, 10, 11, and 12; fourteen, fifteen, sixteen, and seventeen years). Because the way grades are grouped varies, you may find yourself teaching in a school system where the arrangement described in this chapter is not followed. In that case simply refer to the appropriate age-level designations and, if necessary, concentrate on two levels rather than one.

You should also read the rest of the chapter with care. Even though you presently anticipate that you will teach a particular grade level, you may at some point teach younger or older students. You may also gain awareness of continuities of development and come to realize how some aspects of the behavior of older children were influenced by earlier experiences. Indeed, even though a particular type of behavior is discussed at a level where it is considered to be of special significance, that behavior may be important at any age level.

Various types of behavior at each of the five levels are discussed under these headings: physical, social, emotional, and cognitive characteristics. Following each characteristic are implications for teachers. To help you establish a general conception of what children are like at each level, brief summaries of the types of behavior stressed by the theorists discussed in the preceding chapter are listed in a table near the beginning of each section (Tables 3.1, 3.2, 3.3, 3.4, and 3.7).

Preschool and Kindergarten (Three, Four, and Five Years)

PHYSICAL CHARACTERISTICS: PRESCHOOL AND KINDERGARTEN

1. *Preschool children are extremely active. They have good control of their bodies and enjoy activity for its own sake.* Provide plenty of opportunities for the children to run, climb, and jump. Arrange these activities, as much as possible, so that they are under your control. If you follow a policy of complete freedom, you may discover that thirty improvising three- to five-year-olds can be a frightening thing. In your Reflective Journal you might note some specific games and activities that you could use to achieve semicontrolled play.

Journal Entry
Active Games

2. *Because of an inclination toward bursts of activity, kindergartners need frequent rest periods. They themselves often don't recognize the*

Journal Entry
Riot-Stopping Signals and Activities

TABLE 3.1 *Applying Stage Theories of Development to the Preschool and Kindergarten Years*

Stage of psychosocial development: initiative vs. guilt. Children need opportunities for free play and experimentation as well as experiences that give them a sense of accomplishment.

Stage of cognitive development: preoperational thought. Children gradually acquire the ability to conserve and center but are not capable of operations and are unable to mentally reverse operations.

Stage of moral development: morality of constraint, preconventional. Rules are viewed as unchangeable edicts handed down by those in authority. Punishment-obedience orientation focuses on physical consequences rather than on intentions.

General factors to keep in mind: Children are having their first experiences with school routine and interactions with more than a few peers and are preparing for initial academic experiences in group settings. They need to learn to follow directions and get along with others.

Preschool and kindergarten children are very active and possess good gross motor skills. As a result, they enjoy activities that involve climbing, running, throwing, and kicking.

need to slow down. Schedule quiet activities after strenuous ones. Have rest time. Realize that excitement may build up to a riot level if the attention of "catalytic agents" and their followers is not diverted. In your journal you might list some signals for calling a halt to a melée (for example, playing the opening chords of Beethoven's Fifth Symphony on the piano) or for diverting wild action into more or less controlled activity (marching around the room to a brisk rendition of "Stars and Stripes Forever").

Journal Entry
Allowing for Large-Muscle Control

3. *Preschoolers' large muscles are more developed than those that control fingers and hands. Therefore, preschoolers may be quite clumsy at, or physically incapable of, such skills as tying shoes and buttoning coats.* Avoid too many small-motor activities, such as pasting paper chains. Provide big brushes, crayons, and tools. In your journal you might note other activities or items of king-sized equipment that would be appropriate for the children's level of muscular development.

4. *Young children find it difficult to focus their eyes on small objects. Therefore, their eye-hand coordination may be imperfect.* If possible, minimize the necessity for the children to look at small things. (Incomplete eye development is the reason for large print in children's books.) This is also important to keep in mind if you are planning to use computers or software programs—highly graphic programs requiring a simple "point and click" response are most appropriate for very young students.

Large-muscle control better established than small-muscle control and eye-hand coordination

5. *Although the children's bodies are flexible and resilient, the bones that protect the brain are still soft.* Be extremely wary of blows to the head in games or fights between children. If you notice an activity involving such a blow, intervene immediately; warn the class that this is dangerous and explain why.

6. *Although boys are bigger, girls are ahead of boys in practically all other areas of development, especially in fine motor skills, so don't be surprised if boys are clumsier at manipulating small objects.* It may be desirable to avoid boy-girl comparisons or competition involving such skills.

SOCIAL CHARACTERISTICS: PRESCHOOL AND KINDERGARTEN

1. *Most children have one or two best friends, but these friendships may change rapidly. Preschoolers tend to be quite flexible socially; they are usually willing and able to play with most of the other children in the class. Favorite friends tend to be of the same gender, but many friendships between boys and girls develop.* Young children are quite adept at figuring out which social and linguistic skills elicit responses from playmates. Typical gambits include inviting a peer to engage in rough-and-tumble play, offering an object to a playmate, offering to exchange objects with a playmate, sticking to the topic of a conversation, moving close to the person to whom one is speaking, and asking a question or

Young children engage in a variety of types of play. These play patterns may vary as a function of social class and gender.

giving a command (Guralnick, 1986). You might make it a habit to notice whether some children seem to lack the ability or confidence to join others. In some cases a child may prefer to be an observer. But if you sense that a child really wants to get to know others, you might provide some assistance.

Journal Entry
How Much Control Is Necessary?

2. *Play groups tend to be small and not too highly organized; hence they change rapidly.* You should not be concerned if children flit constantly from one activity to another. Such behavior is normal for this age group, although it may sometimes drive you wild. You might think about how much control you will want to exert over your students, particularly during free-play periods. At what point is insistence on silence and sedentary activities justifiable? Should you insist that students stick with self-selected activities for a given period of time?

3. *Younger children exhibit different types of play behavior.* Mildred Parten (1932) observed the free play of children in a preschool and noted the types of social behavior they engaged in. Eventually, she was able to write quite precise descriptions of six types of **play behavior:**

Unoccupied behavior. Children do not really play at all. They either stand around and look at others for a time or engage in aimless activities.

Solitary play. Children play alone with toys that are different from those used by other children within speaking distance of them. They make no attempt to interact with others.

Onlooker behavior. Children spend most of their time watching others. They may kibitz and make comments about the play of others, but they do not attempt to join in.

Parallel play. Children play *beside* but not really with other children. They use the same toys in close proximity to others but in an independent way.

Associative play. Children engage in rather disorganized play with other children. There is no assignment of activities or roles; individual children play in their own ways.

Cooperative play. Children engage in an organized form of play in which leadership and other roles are assigned. The members of the group may cooperate in creating some project, dramatize some situation, or engage in some sort of coordinated enterprise.

4. *Play patterns may vary as a function of social class and gender.* Kenneth Rubin, Terence Maioni, and Margaret Hornung (1976) observed and classified the free play of preschoolers according to their level of social and cognitive participation. The four levels of social participation they observed (solitary, parallel, associative, and cooperative) were taken from the work of Parten. The four levels of cognitive participation they observed were taken from the work of Sara Smilansky (1968) (who based them on Piaget's work) and were as follows:

Functional play. Making simple repetitive muscle movements with or without objects.

Constructive play. Manipulating objects to construct or create something.

Dramatic play. Using an imaginary situation.

Games with rules. Using prearranged rules to play a game.

The Parten and Rubin et al. studies found that children of lower socioeconomic status engaged in more parallel and functional play than their middle-class peers, whereas middle-class children displayed more associative, cooperative, and constructive play. Girls engaged in more solitary- and parallel-constructive play and in less dramatic play than did the boys. Boys engaged in more solitary-functional and associative-dramatic play than did girls.

Play patterns vary as a function of social class, gender, and age

These studies call attention to the variety of play activities common to preschool children. This knowledge may help you determine if a child *prefers* solitary play or plays alone because of shyness or lack of skills for joining in associative or cooperative play.

5. *Quarrels are frequent, but they tend to be of short duration and are quickly forgotten.* When thirty children are thrown together for the first time in a restricted environment with a limited number of objects to be shared, disputes over property rights and similar matters are inevitable. Do not be surprised if you find that the majority of quarrels and aggressive acts involve two or more boys. Research has shown that males are more likely than females to behave aggressively. The gender difference in aggression is greatest among preschoolers and least noticeable among college students (Hyde, 1986). Whenever possible, let the children settle these differences on their own; intervene only if a quarrel gets out of hand. If you do have to intervene, you might try one of two tactics: suggest that one or both children engage in another equally attractive activity, or impose a turn-taking rule. (Other methods of classroom control will be discussed in Chapter 13.)

6. *Awareness of gender roles and gender typing is evident.* By the time children enter kindergarten, most of them have developed awareness of gender differences and of masculine and feminine roles (Wynn & Fletcher, 1987). This awareness of **gender roles** shows up very clearly in the toys and activities that boys and girls prefer. Boys are more likely than girls to play outdoors, to engage in rough-and-tumble play, and to behave aggressively. Boys play with toy vehicles and construction toys, and they engage in action games (such as football). Girls prefer art activities, doll play, and dancing (Carter, 1987). As we pointed out in Chapter 2, gender role differences are often reinforced by the way parents behave. Boys are encouraged to be active and independent, whereas girls are encouraged to be more docile and dependent. Peers may further reinforce these tendencies. A boy or girl may notice that other children are more willing to play when he or she selects a gender-appropriate toy.

Gender differences in toy preferences and play activities noticeable by kindergarten

Therefore, if you teach preschool children, you may have to guard against a tendency to respond too soon when little girls ask for help. If they *need* assistance, of course you should supply it; but if preschool girls can carry out tasks on their own, you should urge them to do so. You might also remind yourself that girls need to be encouraged to become more achievement oriented and boys to become more sensitive to the needs of others.

Journal Entry
Encouraging Girls to Achieve, Boys to Be Sensitive

EMOTIONAL CHARACTERISTICS: PRESCHOOL AND KINDERGARTEN

1. *Kindergarten children tend to express their emotions freely and openly. Anger outbursts are frequent.* It is probably desirable to let children at this age level express their feelings openly, at least within broad limits, so that they can recognize and face their emotions. In *Between Parent and Child* (1965) and *Teacher and Child* (1972), Haim Ginott offers some specific suggestions on how a parent or teacher can help children develop awareness of their feelings. His books may help you work out your own philosophy and techniques for dealing with emotional outbursts.

Suppose, for example, that a boy who was wildly waving his hand to be called on during share-and-tell time later knocks down a block tower made by a girl who monopolized sharing time with a spellbinding story of a kitten rescued by firefighters. When you go over to break up the incipient fight, the boy angrily pushes you away. In such a situation Ginott suggests you take the boy to a quiet corner and engage in a dialogue such as this:

You: It looks as if you are unhappy about something, Pete.
Boy: Yes, I am.
You: Are you angry about something that happened this morning?
Boy: Yes.
You: Tell me about it.
Boy: I wanted to tell the class about something at sharing time, and Mary talked for three hours, and you wouldn't let me say anything.
You: And that made you mad at Mary and at me?
Boy: Yes.
You: Well, I can understand why you are disappointed and angry. But Mary had an exciting story to tell, and we didn't have time for anyone else to tell what they had to say. You can be the very first one to share something tomorrow morning. Now how about doing an easel painting? You always do such interesting paintings.

Journal Entry
Helping Students Understand Anger

Ginott suggests that when children are encouraged to analyze their own behavior, they are more likely to become aware of the causes of their feelings. This awareness, in turn, may help them learn to accept and control their feelings and find more acceptable means of expressing them. But because these children are likely to be in Piaget's preoperational stage of intellectual development, bear in mind that this approach may not be successful with all of them. The egocentric orientation of four- to five-year-olds makes it difficult for them to reflect on the thoughts of self or others. Anger outbursts are more likely to occur when children are tired, hungry, and/or exposed to too much adult interference. If you take such conditions into account and try to alleviate them (by providing a nap or a snack, for example), temper tantrums may be minimized.

Journal Entry
Ways to Avoid Playing Favorites

2. *Jealousy among classmates is likely to be fairly common at this age since kindergarten children have much affection for the teacher and actively seek approval. When there are thirty individuals competing for the affection and attention of just one, some jealousy is inevitable.* Try to spread your attention around as equitably as possible, and when you

praise particular children, do it in a private or casual way. If one child is given lavish public recognition, it is only natural for the other children to feel resentful. Think back to how you felt about teachers' pets during your own school years. If you have observed or can think of other techniques for minimizing jealousy, jot them down in your journal.

COGNITIVE CHARACTERISTICS: PRESCHOOL AND KINDERGARTEN

1. *Kindergartners are quite skillful with language. Most of them like to talk, especially in front of a group.* Providing a sharing time gives children a natural opportunity for talking, but many will need help in becoming good listeners. Some sort of rotation scheme is usually necessary to divide talking opportunities between the gabby and the silent extremes. You might provide activities or experiences for less confident children to talk about, such as a field trip, a book, or a film. In your journal you might note some comments to use if students start to share the wrong thing (such as a vivid account of a fight between their parents) or if they try to one-up classmates (for example, "Your cat may have had five kittens, but *our* cat had a *hundred* kittens"). For titillating topics, for instance, you might say, "There are some things that are private, and it's better not to talk about them to others."

Journal Entry
Handling Sharing

2. *Preschoolers may stick to their own rules in using language.* One of the most intriguing aspects of **early language development** is the extent to which children stick to their own rules. This tendency is so strong that Roger Brown (1973) concludes that efforts by parents and teachers to speed up acquisition of correct speech may not always be successful. Evidence to back up this conclusion is provided in an ingenious study by Jean Berko (1958). Berko found that when four-year-olds were shown pictures and told, for example, "Here is a goose, and here are two geese," and were then asked to complete the sentence "There are two _____," most said, "Gooses."

Young children stick to own language rules

Given this strong tendency of children to use their own rules of grammar, you should probably limit any attempts at grammar instruction to modeling the correct forms. The possibility of getting youngsters to use adult forms of grammar is outweighed by the risk of inhibiting their spontaneous use of language. Direct and systematic instruction in grammar should be delayed until second or third grade.

3. *Competence is encouraged by interaction, interest, opportunities, urging, limits, admiration, and signs of affection.* Studies of young children rated as highly competent (Ainsworth & Wittig, 1972; White & Watts, 1973) show that to encourage preschoolers to make the most of their abilities adults should

Interact with the child often and in a variety of ways

Show interest in what the child does and says

Journal Entry
Encouraging Competence

Provide opportunities for the child to investigate and experience many things

Permit and encourage the child to do many things

Urge the child to try to achieve mature and skilled types of behavior

Establish firm and consistent limits regarding unacceptable forms of behavior, explain the reasons for these as soon as the child is able to understand, listen to complaints if the child feels the restrictions are too confining and give additional reasons if the limits are still to be maintained as originally stated

Show that the child's achievements are admired and appreciated

Communicate love in a warm and sincere way

Diana Baumrind's analysis (1971) of authoritative, authoritarian, and permissive child-rearing approaches shows why such techniques seem to lead to competence in children. Baumrind found that parents of competent children were **authoritative parents**. They had confidence in their abilities as parents and therefore provided a model of competence for their children to imitate. When they established limits and explained reasons for restrictions, they encouraged their children to set standards for themselves and to think about *why* certain procedures should be followed. And because these parents were warm and affectionate, their positive responses were valued by their children as rewards for mature behavior.

Authoritarian parents, by contrast, made demands and wielded power, but their failure to take into account the children's point of view and their lack of warmth led to resentment and insecurity on the part of the children. Children of authoritarian parents might have done as they were told, but they were likely to do so out of compliance or fear, not out of a desire to earn love or approval.

Permissive parents, as defined by Baumrind, were disorganized, inconsistent, and lacked confidence. Their children were likely to imitate such behavior. Furthermore, such parents did not demand much of their children, nor did they discourage immature behavior.

You might refer to these observations not only when you plan how to encourage competence but also when you think about the kind of classroom atmosphere you hope to establish.

Primary Grades (1, 2, and 3; Six, Seven, and Eight Years)

PHYSICAL CHARACTERISTICS: PRIMARY GRADES

1. *Primary grade children are still extremely active. Because they are frequently required to participate in sedentary pursuits, energy is often released in the form of nervous habits—for example, pencil chewing, fingernail biting, and general fidgeting.* You will have to decide what noise and activity level should prevail during work periods. A few teachers insist on absolute quiet, but such a rule can make children work so hard at remaining quiet that they cannot devote much effort to their lessons. The majority of teachers allow a certain amount of moving about and talking. Whatever you decide, be on the alert for the point of diminishing returns—whether from too much or too little restriction.

Journal Entry
Building Activity into Classwork

To minimize fidgeting, avoid situations in which your students must stay glued to their desks for long periods. Have frequent breaks and try to work activity (such as bringing papers to your desk) into the lessons themselves.

TABLE 3.2 *Applying Stage Theories of Development to the Primary Grade Years*

Stage of psychosocial development: industry vs. inferiority. Students need to experience a sense of industry through successful completion of tasks. Try to minimize and correct failures to prevent development of feelings of inferiority.

Stage of cognitive development: transition from preoperational to concrete operational stage. Students gradually acquire the ability to solve problems by generalizing from concrete experiences.

Stage of moral development: morality of constraint, preconventional. Rules are viewed as edicts handed down by authority. Focus is on physical consequences, meaning that obeying rules should bring benefit in return.

General factors to keep in mind: Students are having first experiences with school learning, are eager to learn how to read and write, and are likely to be upset by lack of progress. Initial attitudes toward schooling are being established. Initial roles in a group are being formed, roles that may establish a lasting pattern (for example, leader, follower, loner, athlete, or underachiever).

2. *Children at these grade levels still need rest periods; they become fatigued easily as a result of physical and mental exertion.* Schedule quiet activities after strenuous ones (story time after recess, for example) and relaxing activities after periods of mental concentration (art after spelling or math).

3. *Large-muscle control is still superior to fine coordination. Many children, especially boys, have difficulty manipulating a pencil.* Try not to schedule too much writing at one time. If drill periods are too long, skill may deteriorate and children may develop a negative attitude toward writing or toward school in general.

4. *Many primary grade students may have difficulty focusing on small print or objects. Quite a few children may be far-sighted because of the shallow shape of the eye.* Try not to require too much reading at one stretch. Be on the alert for signs of eye fatigue (rubbing the eyes or blinking). When you are preparing class handouts, be sure to print in large letters or use a primary grade typewriter. Until the lens of the eye can be easily focused, young children have trouble looking back and forth from near to far objects.

Primary grade children have difficulty focusing on small print

Another vision problem encountered by preschool and primary grade children is amblyopia, or "lazy eye." In normal vision the muscles of the two eyes work together to fuse their two images into one. If the eye muscles are not coordinated, however, children may experience double vision. In their efforts to cope with this problem, children may try to eliminate one image by closing one eye, tilting their heads, or blinking or rubbing their eyes. You should watch for signs of amblyopia and let the parents know if you detect one or more signs of lazy eye in any of your students.

Although many children at this age have had extensive exposure to computer games and video games at home or outside of school, and therefore have begun to develop greater eye-hand coordination with images on-screen, it's still appropriate to select software programs that incorporate easy-to-see graphics and easy-to-click buttons to avoid frustration.

Journal Entry
Safe but Strenuous Game

5. *At this age children tend to be extreme in their physical activities. They have excellent control of their bodies and develop considerable confidence in their skills. As a result, they often underestimate the danger involved in their more daring exploits. The accident rate is at a peak in the third grade.* You might check on school procedures for handling injuries, but also try to prevent reckless play. During recess, for example, encourage class participation in "wild" but essentially safe games (such as relay races involving stunts) to help the children get devil-may-care tendencies out of their systems. In your journal you might list other games to use for this purpose.

Accident rate peaks in third grade because of confidence in physical skills

6. *Bone growth is not yet complete. Therefore, bones and ligaments can't stand heavy pressure.* If you notice students indulging in strenuous tests of strength (punching each other on the arm until one person can't retaliate, for example), you might suggest that they switch to competition involving coordinated *skills.* During team games, rotate players in especially tiring positions (for example, the pitcher in baseball).

SOCIAL CHARACTERISTICS: PRIMARY GRADES

The characteristics noted here are typical of both primary and elementary grade students and underlie the elementary-level characteristics described in the next section.

1. *Children become somewhat more selective in their choice of friends and are likely to have a more or less permanent best friend.* Friendships are typically same-sex relationships marked by mutual understanding, loyalty, cooperation, and sharing. Competition between friends should be discouraged as it can become intense and increase their dissatisfaction with each other. Although friends disagree with each other more often than with nonfriends, their conflicts are shorter, less heated, and less likely to lead to a dissolving of the friendship (Hartup, 1989).

Journal Entry
Using Sociometric Techniques

You might use a device called a sociogram to identify friendships, cliques, and children who are social isolates and then give tentative assistance to children who have difficulty in attracting friends. Also, be on the alert for feuds, which can develop beyond good-natured quarreling and teasing. For detailed information on how to construct and use sociograms, consult *Sociometry in the Classroom,* by Norman Gronlund (1959); or "Sociometrics: Peer-Referenced Measures and the Assessment of Social Competence," by Scott McConnell and Samuel Odom (1986).

Journal Entry
Enjoyable Team Games

2. *Children during this age span often like organized games in small groups, but they may be overly concerned with rules or get carried away by team spirit.* Keep in mind that, according to Piaget, children at this age practice the morality of constraint: they find it difficult to understand how and why rules should be adjusted to special situations. When you divide a class into teams, you may be amazed at the amount of rivalry that develops (and the noise level generated). One way to reduce both the rivalry and the noise is to promote the idea that games should be fun.

Rigid interpretation of rules in primary grades

Another technique is to rotate team membership frequently. If you know any especially good—but not excessively competitive—team games, note them in your journal. You might also consult *Cooperative Learning: Theory, Research, and Practice* (2d ed., 1995), by Robert Slavin, for descriptions of several team learning games that emphasize cooperation.

3. *Quarrels are still frequent. Words are used more often than physical aggression, but many boys (in particular) may indulge in punching, wrestling, and shoving.* Occasional fights are to be expected, but if certain children, especially the same pair, seem to be involved in one long battle, you should probably try to effect a truce. But give children a chance to work out their own solutions to disagreements as social conflict is effective in spurring cognitive growth (Smith, Johnson, & Johnson, 1981; Tudge & Rogoff, 1989).

Journal Entry
Handling Feuds and Fights

EMOTIONAL CHARACTERISTICS: PRIMARY GRADES

1. *Primary grade students are sensitive to criticism and ridicule and may have difficulty adjusting to failure.* Young children need frequent praise and recognition. Because they tend to admire or even worship their teachers, they may be crushed by criticism. Provide positive reinforcement as frequently as possible, and reserve your negative reactions for nonacademic misbehavior. Scrupulously avoid sarcasm and ridicule. Remember that this is the stage of industry versus inferiority; if you make a child feel inferior, you may prevent the development of industry.

Journal Entry
Avoiding Sarcasm and Extreme Criticism

To encourage industry, use praise, avoid criticism

2. *Most primary grade children are eager to please the teacher.* They like to help, enjoy responsibility, and want to do well in their schoolwork. The time-honored technique for satisfying the urge to help is to assign jobs (eraser cleaner, wastebasket emptier, paper distributor, and the like) on a rotating basis. In your journal you might note other techniques—for example, were there any particular responsibilities you enjoyed as a student?

Journal Entry
Spreading Around Responsibilities

Most elementary school students eagerly strive to obtain "helping" jobs around the classroom. Accordingly, you may wish to arrange a rotating schedule for such jobs.

3. *Children of this age are becoming sensitive to the feelings of others.* Unfortunately, this permits them to hurt others deeply by attacking a sensitive spot without realizing how devastating their attack really is. It sometimes happens that teasing a particular child who has reacted to a gibe becomes a group pastime. Be on the alert for such situations. If you are able to make a private and personal appeal to the ringleaders, you may be able to prevent an escalation of the teasing, which may make a tremendous difference in the way the victim feels about school.

COGNITIVE CHARACTERISTICS: PRIMARY GRADES

1. *Generally speaking, primary grade students are extremely eager to learn.* One of the best things about teaching in the primary grades is the built-in motivation of students. The teacher's problem is how to make the most of it. Suggestions for doing this will be offered in Part 3.

2. *Children of this age like to talk and have much more facility in speech than in writing.* Primary grade children are eager to recite, regardless of whether they know the right answer. The high school teacher may have difficulty stimulating voluntary class participation, but not the primary grade teacher. The problem here is more likely to be one of controlling participation so that children speak up only when called on. Frequent reminders to take turns and to be good listeners are often necessary. And even if you are successful in this area, you may feel a bit unsettled to find that a student, after wildly waving a hand or pumping an arm to be recognized, supplies a hopelessly wrong answer. You may want to develop some phrases that gently and/or humorously indicate that an answer is erroneous or irrelevant. If you come up with some good ones, jot them down in your Journal.

> *Journal Entry*
> Ways to Handle Wrong Answers

3. *Because of the literal interpretation of rules associated with this stage of development, primary grade children may tend to be tattletales.* Sometimes telling the teacher that someone has broken a school or class rule is due to a child's level of moral development, sometimes it is due to jealousy or malice, and sometimes it is simply a way to get attention or curry favor. If a child calls your attention to the misbehavior of others and you respond by saying, "Don't be a tattletale," the child may be hurt and confused. If you thank the child too enthusiastically and then proceed to punish the culprit, you may encourage most members of the class to begin to inform on each other. Perhaps the best policy is to tell an informant that you already are aware of the errant behavior and that you intend to do something about it. Then you might follow up by talking to the offending parties.

Elementary Grades (4 and 5; Nine and Ten Years)

PHYSICAL CHARACTERISTICS: ELEMENTARY GRADES

1. *Both boys and girls become leaner and stronger.* In general, there are a decrease in the growth of fatty tissue and an increase in bone and muscle development, although this process occurs more rapidly in boys. In a year's time the average child of this age will grow about 2 inches and gain about 5 pounds. As a result, they have a lean and gangly look. Beginning

TABLE 3.3 *Applying Stage Theories of Development to the Elementary Grade Years*

Stage of psychosocial development: industry vs. inferiority. Keep students constructively busy; try to play down comparisons between best and worse learners.

Stage of cognitive development: concrete operational. Except for the most intellectually advanced students, most will need to generalize from concrete experiences.

Stage of moral development: morality of constraint; transition from preconventional to conventional. A shift to viewing rules as mutual agreements is occurring, but "official" rules are obeyed out of respect for authority or out of a desire to impress others.

General factors to keep in mind: Initial enthusiasm for learning may fade as the novelty wears off and as the process of perfecting skills becomes more difficult. Differences in knowledge and skills of fastest and slowest learners become more noticeable. "Automatic" respect for teachers tends to diminish. Peer group influences become strong.

at about age nine and lasting until about age fourteen, girls are slightly heavier and taller than boys. Because secondary sex characteristics have not yet appeared, boys and girls can be mistaken for one another. This is particularly likely to happen when girls have close-cropped hair, boys have very long hair, and both genders wear gender-neutral clothing (Hetherington & Parke, 1993; Mitchell, 1990; LeFrançois, 1995).

2. *Obesity can become a problem for some children of this age group.* Because nine- and ten-year-olds have more control over their eating habits than younger children do, there is a greater tendency for them to overeat, particularly junk food (foods high in calories and fat but low in nutritional value). When this eating pattern is coupled with a relatively low level of physical activity (mainly because of television watching) and a genetic predisposition toward obesity, children become mildly to severely overweight. Not only do overweight children put themselves at risk for cardiovascular problems later in life, but they also become targets for ridicule and ostracism in the present from peers (Hetherington & Parke, 1993; Mitchell, 1990).

3. *Although small in magnitude, gender differences in motor skill performance are apparent.* Boys tend to outperform girls on tasks that involve kicking, throwing, catching, running, broad jumping, and batting. Girls surpass boys on tasks that require muscular flexibility, balance, and rhythmic movements. These differences may be due in part to the gender role stereotyping process that we discussed in Chapter 2. That is, because of socialization differences, girls are more likely to play hopscotch and jump rope, whereas boys are more likely to play baseball and basketball. One benefit of attaining mastery over large and small muscles is a relatively orderly classroom. Fourth and fifth graders can sit quietly for extended periods and concentrate on whatever intellectual task is at hand (Hetherington & Parke, 1993; Mitchell, 1990). Another benefit is that children enjoy arts and crafts and musical activities.

Journal Entry
Minimizing Gender Differences in Motor Skill Performance

Boys slightly better at sports-related motor skills; girls better at flexibility, balance, rhythmic motor skills

4. *This is a period of relative calm and predictability in physical development.* Growth in height and weight tends to be consistent, and

moderate, hormonal imbalances are absent; disease occurs less frequently than at any other period; and bodily coordination is relatively stable (Hetherington & Parke, 1993; Mitchell, 1990).

SOCIAL CHARACTERISTICS: ELEMENTARY GRADES

1. *The peer group becomes powerful and begins to replace adults as the major source of behavior standards and recognition of achievement.* During the early school years, parents and teachers set standards of conduct, and most children try to live up to them. But by the later elementary grades, children are more interested in getting along with one another without adult supervision. Consequently, children come to realize that the rules for behavior within the peer group are not quite the same as the rules for behavior within the family or the classroom.

Peer group norms for behavior begin to replace adult norms

This newfound freedom can have a down side. Because children of this age typically want to be accepted by their peers, have a relatively naive view of right and wrong, and do not have enough self-assurance to oppose group norms, they may engage in behaviors (shoplifting, fighting, prejudice against outsiders) that they would not exhibit at home or in the classroom (Mitchell, 1990).

Journal Entry
Moderating the Power of Peer Group Norms

2. *Friendships become more selective and gender based.* Elementary grade children become even more discriminating than primary grade children in the selection of friends and playmates as they associate mainly with peers of the same age and gender. Although children of this age will rarely refuse to interact with members of the opposite sex when directed to do so by parents and teachers, they will avoid each other's company when left to their own devices. Most children choose a best friend who is usually of the same gender. These relationships, based usually on common ideas, outlooks, and impressions of the world, may last through adolescence (Mitchell, 1990).

EMOTIONAL CHARACTERISTICS: ELEMENTARY GRADES

1. *During this period, children develop a global and moderately stable self-image.* Susan Harter (1988, 1990) and William Damon (1988) have made extensive studies of how children formulate their **self-image**. According to both researchers, the overall picture upper elementary grade children have of themselves, a mental self-portrait, so to speak, is made up of two components: a description of their physical, social, emotional, and cognitive attributes (normally referred to as **self-concept**) and the evaluative judgments they make about those attributes (normally referred to as **self-esteem**). They may, for example, describe themselves as being taller but clumsier than most others or as having a lot of friends because of superior social skills.

There are several important facts to keep in mind about the formulation of a child's self-portrait. First, it is more generalized than is the case for primary grade children because it is based on information gained over time, tasks, and settings. A child may think of herself as socially adept not just because she is popular at school but because she has always been well liked and gets along well with adults as well as peers in a variety of situations. It is this generalized quality that helps make self-portraits relatively stable. Second, as the previous paragraph implies, comparison

Self-concept becomes more generalized and stable; is based primarily on comparisons with peers with others is the fundamental basis of a self-portrait during the elementary grades. This orientation is due in part to the fact that children are not as egocentric as they were a few years earlier and are developing the capability to think in terms of multiple categories. It is also due to the fact that competition and individualism are highly prized values in many Western cultures. Consequently, children will naturally compare themselves to one another ("I'm taller than my friend") as well as to broad-based norms ("I'm tall for my age") in an effort to determine who they are. But, as William Damon and Hart (1988) point out, comparison is a less important basis for building a self-image in cultures where competition and individualism are downplayed.

Third, the self is described for the first time in terms of emotions (pride, shame, worry, anger, happiness) and how well they can be controlled. Fourth, a child's sense of self is influenced both by the information and attitudes that are communicated by such significant others as parents, teachers, and friends, and by how competent the child feels in areas where success is important. The implications of this fact will be discussed in many of the remaining chapters of the text.

Journal Entry
Ways to Improve Students' Self-Concept

Since major developmental changes usually do not occur during the elementary grades, and if there are no major changes in the child's home or social environment, a child's self-image will remain fairly stable for a few years. But, as you will see in the latter part of this chapter, the developmental changes that typically occur during the middle school and high school grades often produce dramatic changes in the sense of self.

2. *Disruptive family relationships, social rejection, and school failure may lead to delinquent behavior.* Gerald Patterson, Barbara DeBarsyshe, and Elizabeth Ramsey (1989) marshal a wide array of evidence to support their belief that delinquent behavior is the result of a causal chain of events that originates in childhood with dysfunctional parent-child relationships. In their view, poor parent-child relationships lead to behavior problems, which lead to peer rejection and academic failure, which lead to identification with a deviant peer group, which results in delinquent behavior. Parents of such children administer harsh and inconsistent punishment, provide little positive reinforcement, and do little monitoring and supervising of each child's activities.

Because these children have not learned to follow adult rules and regulations but have learned how to satisfy their needs through coercive behavior, they are rejected by their peers, are easily distracted when doing schoolwork, show little interest in the subjects they study, and do not master many of the basic academic skills necessary for subsequent achievement. Attempts at shortcircuiting this chain of events stand a greater chance of success if they begin early and are multifaceted. In addition to counseling and parent training, mastery of basic academic skills is important.

Delinquents have few friends, are easily distracted, are not interested in schoolwork, lack basic skills

COGNITIVE CHARACTERISTICS: ELEMENTARY GRADES

1. *The elementary grade child can think logically, although such thinking is constrained and inconsistent.* In terms of Piaget's stages, upper elementary grade children are concrete operational stage thinkers. Most will have attained enough mastery of logical schemes that they can understand and solve tasks that involve such processes as class inclusion

During the elementary years it becomes very apparent that students approach tasks in different ways. This preference for doing things in a particular way is often referred to as a cognitive style. Some students, for example, are impulsive thinkers who tend to react quickly when asked a question; other students are reflective thinkers who prefer to mull over things before answering.

(understanding the superordinate-subordinate relationships that make up hierarchies), seriation, conservation, and symbolic representation (reading maps, for example), provided that the content of the task refers to real, tangible ideas that the child has either experienced or can imagine. But general and abstract ideas often escape the elementary-age child. For example, sarcasm, metaphor, and allegory are usually lost on concrete stage thinkers. A similar fate usually befalls the idea that knowledge is often the product of inferential reasoning and may therefore be rejected as untrue if flaws in the reasoning can be shown. Concrete thinkers either accept or reject what authority figures tell them on the basis of rather arbitrary criteria.

Elementary grade students reason logically but concretely

The knowledge base of fourth- and fifth-grade children contains many misconceptions, and they may behave illogically. To prove a point or win a debate with a classmate or playmate, the upper elementary child may reel off a string of facts, some of which reflect authoritative sources, some of which are exaggerations, and some of which are invented on the spot. A ten-year-old may believe, for example, that people can live for several months without eating and that vacant houses are haunted. As John Mitchell (1990) humorously put it, "Many kids possess a gift for compressing the largest number of words into the smallest amount of thought." (p. 213)

Cognitive styles are preferences for dealing with intellectual tasks in a particular way

2. *Differences in cognitive style become apparent.* During this period, children also exhibit differences in **cognitive style**. Cognitive styles are tendencies or preferences to respond to a variety of intellectual tasks and

problems in a particular fashion. According to Jerome Kagan (1964a, 1964b), for instance, some children seem to be characteristically *impulsive,* whereas others are characteristically *reflective*. He notes that impulsive children have a fast conceptual tempo; they tend to come forth with the first answer they can think of and are concerned about giving quick responses. Reflective children take time before they speak; they tend to evaluate alternative answers and give correct, rather than quick, responses. Kagan discovered that when tests of reading and of inductive reasoning were administered in the first and second grades, impulsive students made more errors than reflective students. He also found that impulsiveness was a general trait; it appeared early in a person's life and was consistently revealed in a great variety of situations.

Another very popular cognitive style dimension, known as field dependence/field independence, was proposed by Herbert Witkin (Witkin, Moore, Goodenough, & Cox, 1977) and refers to the extent to which a person's perception and thinking about a particular piece of information are influenced by the surrounding context. For example, when some individuals are shown a set of simple geometric figures and asked to locate each one (by outlining it with a pencil) within a larger and more complex display of intersecting lines, those with a field-dependent style take significantly longer to respond and identify fewer of them than individuals with a field-independent style. The former are labeled field dependent because their perception is strongly influenced by the prevailing field. The latter are called field independent because they are more successful in isolating target information despite the fact that it is embedded within a larger and more complex context.

The significance of this difference in approach is clearly seen with materials and tasks that are poorly structured. Field-independent students usually perform better in these situations because of their willingness to create a more meaningful structure. In social situations field-dependent people, in comparison to field-independent people, spend more time looking directly at the faces of others, are more aware of prevailing attitudes, and are generally thought of as more considerate, socially outgoing, and affectionate.

Field-independent students prefer their own structure; field-dependent students prefer to work within existing structure

Awareness of varying cognitive styles may help you understand the need to use different teaching methods and approaches so that all students are comfortable some of the time. An impulsive boy, for example, may disrupt a class discussion by blurting out the first thing that pops into his head, thereby upstaging reflective individuals who are still in the process of formulating more searching answers. To minimize this possibility, you may want to have an informal rotation scheme for recitation. To give the impulsive style its place in the sun, you might schedule speed drills or question-and-answer sessions covering previously learned basic material.

Journal Entry
Allowing for Differences in Cognitive Style

If you (either on your own or with an instructional technology advisor) are involved in selecting software for your students, it will be useful to keep these styles in mind. Reviews of software programs for upper elementary and middle school students in publications such as *Electronic Learning* and *Technology and Education* can help you get a sense of which programs might be best suited to a particular learning style.

Middle School (Grades 6, 7, and 8; Eleven, Twelve, and Thirteen Years)

In this section we use the term *adolescent* for the first time. Although it may strike you as odd to think of eleven- and twelve-year-olds as adolescents, developmental psychologists typically apply this term to individuals as young as ten years of age. The reason they do is because the onset of puberty is taken as the primary characteristic that defines the passage from middle childhood to adolescence (Allen, Splittgerber, & Manning, 1993; Balk, 1995). While a variety of terms are used to denote the initial period of change that marks the adolescent years (ages ten to fourteen), we use two of the more popular: early adolescent and emerging adolescent.

TABLE 3.4 *Applying Stage Theories of Development to Middle School Years*

Stage of psychosocial development: transition from industry vs. inferiority to identity vs. role confusion. Growing independence leads to initial thoughts about identity. There is greater concern about appearance and gender roles than about occupational choice.

Stage of cognitive development: beginning of formal operational thought for some. There is increasing ability to engage in mental manipulations and test hypotheses.

Stage of moral development: transition to morality of cooperation, conventional level. There is increasing willingness to think of rules as flexible mutual agreements; "official" rules are still likely to be obeyed out of respect for authority or out of a desire to impress others.

General factors to keep in mind: Growth spurt and puberty influence many aspects of behavior. An abrupt switch occurs (for sixth graders) from being the oldest, biggest, most sophisticated students in elementary school to being the youngest, smallest, least knowledgeable students in middle school. Acceptance by peers is extremely important. Students who do poor schoolwork begin to feel bitter, resentful, and restless. Awareness grows of a need to make personal value decisions regarding dress, premarital sex, and code of ethics.

PHYSICAL CHARACTERISTICS: MIDDLE SCHOOL

Girls' growth spurt occurs earlier, and so they look older than boys of same age

1. *Physical growth tends to be both rapid and uneven.* During the middle school years, the average child will grow 2 to 4 inches per year and gain 8 to 10 pounds per year. But some parts of the body, particularly the hands and feet, grow faster than others. Consequently, middle school children tend to look gangly and clumsy (Ames & Miller, 1994). Because girls mature more rapidly than boys, their **growth spurt** begins at about age ten and a half, reaches a peak at about age twelve, and is generally complete by age fourteen (Dusek, 1991).

The result of this timing difference in the growth spurt is that many middle school girls look considerably older than boys of the same age. After the growth spurt, however, the muscles in the average boy's body are larger, as are the heart and lungs. Furthermore, the body of the mature male has a greater capacity than that of the female for carrying oxygen to the blood and for neutralizing the chemical products of muscular exercise, such as lactic acid. Thus, the average male has greater strength and endurance than the average female (Tanner, 1972).

After growth spurt, boys have greater strength and endurance

If you notice that students are upset about sudden growth (or lack of it), you might try to help them accept the situation by explaining that things will eventually even out. To reduce the unhappiness that arises from conflicts between physical attributes and gender roles, you might try to persuade students that being male or female should not in itself determine what a person does.

Journal Entry
Helping Students Adjust to the Growth Spurt

After reviewing research on early and later maturation, Norman Livson and Harvey Peskin (1980) conclude that differences in physical maturation are likely to produce specific differences in later behavior (see Table 3.5). The **early-maturing boy** is likely to draw favorable responses from adults (because of his adult appearance), which promotes confidence and poise (thus contributing to leadership and popularity with peers). The **late-maturing boy,** by contrast, may feel inferior and attempt to compensate for his physical and social frustration by engaging in bossy and attention-getting behavior. The very success of the early-maturing boy in

Early-maturing boys likely to draw favorable responses

Late-maturing boys may seek attention

TABLE 3.5 *The Impact of Early and Late Maturation*

Maturational Stage	Characteristics as Adolescents	Characteristics as Adults
Early-maturing boys	Self-confident, high in self-esteem, likely to be chosen as leaders (but leadership tendencies more likely in low-SES boys than in middle-class boys)	Self-confident, responsible, cooperative, sociable. But also rigid, moralistic, humorless, and conforming
Late-maturing boys	Energetic, bouncy, given to attention-getting behavior, not popular, lower aspirations for educational achievement	Impulsive and assertive. But also insightful, perceptive, creatively playful, able to cope with new situations
Early-maturing girls	Not popular or likely to be leaders, indifferent in social situations, lacking in poise (but middle-class girls more confident than those from low-SES groups), more likely to date, smoke, and drink earlier	Self-possessed, self-directed, able to cope, likely to score high in ratings of psychological health
Late-maturing girls	Confident, outgoing, assured, popular, likely to be chosen as leaders	Likely to experience difficulty adapting to stress, likely to score low in ratings of overall psychological health

SOURCES: Jones (1957, 1965); Mussen & Jones (1957); Peskin (1967, 1973); Clausen (1975); Livson & Peskin (1980); Peterson & Taylor (1980); Hetherington & Parke (1993).

high school, however, may cause him to develop an inflexible conception of himself, leading to problems when he must deal with new or negative situations later in life. The need for the late-maturing boy to cope with difficult adjustment situations in high school may equip him to adapt to adversity and change later in life.

Late-maturing girls likely to be popular and carefree

Livson and Peskin observe that the late-maturing boy is psychologically and socially out of step with peers, and the same applies to the **early-maturing girl**. The **late-maturing girl**, whose growth is less abrupt and whose size and appearance are likely to reflect the petiteness featured in stereotyped views of femininity, shares many of the characteristics (poise, popularity, leadership tendencies) of the early-maturing boy. The advantages enjoyed by the late-maturing girl are not permanent, however. Livson and Peskin report that "the stress-ridden early-maturing girl in adulthood has become clearly a more coping, self-possessed, and self-directed person than the late-maturing female in the cognitive and social as well as emotional sectors. . . . It is the late-maturing female, carefree and unchallenged in adolescence, who faces adversity maladroitly in adulthood" (1980, p. 72).

Journal Entry
Helping Early and Late Maturers Cope

If late-maturing boys in your classes appear driven to seek attention or inclined to brood about their immaturity, you might try to give them extra opportunities to gain status and self-confidence by succeeding in schoolwork or other nonathletic activities. If you notice that early-maturing girls seem insecure, you might try to bolster their self-esteem by giving them extra attention and by recognizing their achievements.

2. *Pubertal development is evident in practically all girls and in many boys.* From ages eleven through thirteen, most girls develop sparse pubic and underarm hair and exhibit breast enlargement. In boys the testes and scrotum begin to grow, and lightly pigmented pubic hair appears (Hetherington & Parke, 1993).

Average age of puberty: girls, eleven; boys, fourteen

3. *Concern and curiosity about sex are almost universal, especially among girls.* The average age of puberty for girls in the United States is eleven years (Dusek, 1991); the range is from eight to eighteen years. For boys the average age of puberty is fourteen years; the range is from ten to eighteen years. Since sexual maturation involves drastic biological and psychological adjustments, children are concerned and curious. It seems obvious that accurate, unemotional answers to questions about sex are desirable. However, for your own protection you should find out about the sex education policy at your school. Many school districts have formal programs approved by community representatives and led by designated educators. Informal spur-of-the-moment class discussions may create more problems than they solve.

SOCIAL CHARACTERISTICS: MIDDLE SCHOOL

1. *The development of interpersonal reasoning leads to greater understanding of the feelings of others.* Robert L. Selman (1980) has studied the development of **interpersonal reasoning** in children. Interpersonal reasoning is the ability to understand the relationship between motives and behavior among a group of people. The results of Selman's research are summarized in Table 3.6. The stages outlined there reveal that during

TABLE 3.6 *Stages of Interpersonal Reasoning Described by Selman*

Stage 0: egocentric level (about ages 4 to 6). Children do not recognize that other persons may interpret the same social event or course of action differently from the way they do. They do not reflect on the thoughts of self and others. They can label the overtly expressed feelings of others but do not comprehend cause-and-effect relations of social actions.

Stage 1: social information role taking (about ages 6 to 8). Children are able in limited ways to differentiate between their own interpretations of social interactions and the interpretation of others. But they cannot simultaneously think of their own view and those of others.

Stage 2: self-reflective role taking (about ages 8 to 10). Interpersonal relations are interpreted in specific situations whereby each person understands the expectations of the other in that particular context. Children are not yet able to view the two perspectives at once, however.

Stage 3: multiple role taking (about ages 10 to 12). Children become capable of taking a third-person view, which permits them to understand the expectations of themselves and of others in a variety of situations as if they were spectators.

Stage 4: social and conventional system taking (about ages 12 to 15+). Each individual involved in a relationship with another understands many of the subtleties of the interactions involved. In addition, a societal perspective begins to develop. That is, actions are judged by how they might influence *all* individuals, not just those who are immediately concerned.

SOURCE: Adapted from discussions in Selman (1980).

the elementary school years children gradually grasp the fact that a person's overt actions or words do not always reflect inner feelings. They also come to comprehend that a person's reaction to a distressing situation can have many facets. Toward the end of the elementary school years—and increasingly during adolescence—children become capable of taking a somewhat detached and analytical view of their own behavior as well as the behavior of others.

Not surprisingly, a child's interpersonal sensitivity and maturity seem to have an impact on relationships with others. Selman (1980) compared the responses of seven- to twelve-year-old boys who were attending schools for children with learning and interpersonal problems with the responses of a matched group of boys attending regular schools. The boys attending special schools were below average for their age in understanding the feelings of others.

Selman believes that teachers and therapists might be able to aid children who are not as advanced in role-taking skills as their age-mates by helping them become more sensitive to the feelings of others. If an eight-year-old boy is still functioning at the egocentric level, for example, he may fail to properly interpret the behavior of classmates and become a social isolate. Selman describes how one such boy was encouraged to think continually about the reasons behind his social actions and those of others and acquired sufficient social sensitivity to learn to get along with others.

During the middle school years, children acquire greater sensitivity to the beliefs and feelings of others.

Journal Entry
Ways to Promote Social Sensitivity

Discussion techniques Selman recommends can be introduced in a natural, rather than a formal, way. If you see a boy react with physical or verbal abuse when jostled by a playmate, for example, you might say, "You know, people don't always intentionally bump into others. Unless you are absolutely sure that someone has hurt you on purpose, it can be a lot pleasanter for all concerned if you don't make a big deal out of it."

Discussion of controversial issues may be difficult because of strong desire to conform to peer norms

2. *The desire to conform reaches a peak during the middle school years.* Early adolescents find it reassuring to dress and behave like others, and they are likely to alter their own opinions to coincide with those of a group. When you encourage student participation in class discussions, you may need to be alert to the tendency for students at these grade levels to be reluctant to voice minority opinions. If you want them to think about controversial issues, it may be preferable to invite them to write their opinions anonymously rather than voice them in front of the rest of the class.

EMOTIONAL CHARACTERISTICS: MIDDLE SCHOOL

1. *Some early adolescents go through a period of "storm and stress."* Starting with G. Stanley Hall, who wrote a pioneering two-volume text on adolescence in 1904, some theorists have described adolescence as a period of turmoil. Feelings of confusion, anxiety, and depression; extreme mood swings; and low levels of self-confidence are felt to be typical of this age group. Some of the reasons cited for this turbulence are rapid changes in height, weight, and body proportions; increases in hormone production; the task of identity formation; increased academic responsibilities; and the development of formal operational reasoning (Jackson & Bosma, 1990; Peterson, 1988; Susman, 1991).

Since the 1970s, however, a number of psychologists have questioned whether turmoil is universal during the emerging adolescent (and later) years (for example, see Hill, 1987; Jackson & Bosma, 1990; Peterson,

1988). In one study (Offer & Offer, 1975) 79 percent of a group of middle-class adolescent boys were classified as falling into one of three categories: *continuous growth, surgent growth,* and *tumultuous growth.* Boys in the continuous growth group (23 percent of the sample) were easily able to cope with the various physiological, social, emotional, and cognitive changes they experienced. Boys in the surgent growth group (35 percent) alternated between difficult and easy periods, although in general they were reasonably well adjusted. Only 21 percent, those in the tumultuous growth group, exhibited the type of chronic turmoil that marked early accounts of adolescent emotional development. (The remaining 21 percent could not be classified, although they were closest to the first two groups.)

Teenagers experience different degrees of emotional turmoil

Although the Offer and Offer study was limited to adolescent males, gender differences in psychological adjustment have been documented. Boys who exhibit problems during adolescence are more likely to have had similar problems in childhood, whereas girls are more likely to initially exhibit problems in adolescence. Achievement situations are more likely to produce anxiety responses in boys, whereas girls are more likely to become anxious in interpersonal situations. Finally, girls are more likely than boys to increasingly exhibit signs of depression (Peterson, 1988).

2. *As a result of the continued influence of egocentric thought, middle school students are typically self-conscious and self-centered.* Because emerging adolescents are acutely aware of the physical and emotional changes that are taking place within them, they assume that everyone else is just as interested in, and is constantly evaluating, their appearance, feelings, and behavior. Consequently, they are deeply concerned about such things as what type of clothing to wear for special occasions, with whom they should and should not be seen in public (they should never be seen with their parents at the mall, for example), and how they greet and talk with various people. Not surprisingly, what interests middle school students a great deal either does not interest or annoys adults.

Another manifestation of adolescent egocentrism is the assumption that adults do not, indeed cannot, understand the thoughts and feelings of early adolescence. It's as if the early adolescent believes she is experiencing things no one else has ever experienced before. Hence, a teen or preteen will likely say to a parent, "You just don't know what it feels like to be in love." (Wiles & Bondi, 1993).

COGNITIVE CHARACTERISTICS: MIDDLE SCHOOL

1. *There are gender differences in specific abilities, although they may be decreasing in number and magnitude.* Early research on gender differences in cognitive functioning found that during the elementary school years girls, on the average, were superior in verbal fluency, spelling, reading, and mathematical computation. Boys, on the average, were superior in mathematical reasoning, in tasks involving understanding of spatial relationships, and in the solving of insight problems (Bee, 1978; Block, 1976; Maccoby & Jacklin, 1974).

More recent research paints a similar picture. Alan Feingold (1988) analyzed the performance of eighth- through twelfth-grade students on

At the middle school level, girls typically outscore boys on tasks that involve language skills and mathematical computation, whereas boys achieve higher scores on tasks that involve mathematical reasoning and spatial abilities. Research evidence suggests that the magnitude of these differences has been decreasing in recent years and that the decline may be due to less gender stereotyping.

eight subtests of the *Differential Aptitude Test* for the years 1947, 1962, 1972, and 1980. At every grade level and year, he found that the girls outscored the boys on tests of spelling, language, and clerical speed and accuracy. The boys outscored the girls on the mechanical reasoning and spatial relations tests. The most interesting aspect of Feingold's analysis was the discovery that gender differences in cognitive abilities are decreasing. Between 1947 and 1980, the amount by which the girls outscored the boys, and vice versa, decreased at every grade level.

Girls superior in language skills, math computation; boys superior in analogies, math reasoning, spatial orientation

Diane Halpern (1992) concludes that, while the differences between males and females may be relatively small, females excel at tasks that involve the generation of synonyms, language production and word fluency, arithmetic computation, and the solving of anagrams. These tasks appear to be governed by the same cognitive process—rapid access to and retrieval of information from memory. Males outperform females on tasks that involve verbal analogies, mathematical problem solving, and mental rotation of objects in space. The cognitive process that seems to underlie these tasks is the maintenance and manipulation of a mental representation.

Journal Entry
Encouraging Girls to Excel in Math and Science

As to the question of whether gender differences are decreasing, Halpern is more cautious with an answer. She believes that it is premature to draw that conclusion because the nature of the test-taking population has changed over time (for example, colleges that used to have a predominance of male students now have more females), as has the nature of the tests (tests of mental rotation and word fluency, for example, are sufficiently new that they cannot be meaningfully compared with anything from earlier studies).

2. *Self-efficacy becomes an important influence on intellectual and social behavior.* As we mentioned in point 1 of social characteristics, middle school children become capable of analyzing both their own view of an interpersonal interaction and that of the other person. This newfound analytic ability is also turned inward, resulting in evaluations of one's intellectual and social capabilities. Albert Bandura (1986), a learning theo-

rist whom we will discuss in Chapter 8, coined the term **self-efficacy** to refer to how capable people believe they are at dealing with one type of task or another. Thus, a student may have a very strong sense of self-efficacy for math ("I know I can solve most any algebraic equation"), a moderate degree of self-efficacy for certain athletic activities ("I think I play baseball and basketball about as well as most kids my age"), and a low sense of self-efficacy for interpersonal relationships ("I'm just no good at making friends").

These self-evaluative beliefs influence what activities students chose and for how long they will persist at a given task, particularly when progress becomes difficult. Students with a moderate to strong sense of self-efficacy will persist at a task long enough to obtain the success or corrective feedback that leads to expectations of future success. Students with a low sense of self-efficacy, however, tend to abandon tasks at the first sign of difficulty, thereby establishing a pattern of failure, low expectations of future success, and task avoidance. Since self-efficacy beliefs grow out of personal performance, observation of other people doing the same thing, and verbal persuasion, you can help students develop strong feelings of self-efficacy by following the suggestions we will make in Chapters 8, 9, and 12 about modeling and imitation, learning strategies, and mastery learning, respectively.

Self-efficacy beliefs for academic and social tasks become strong influences on behavior

High School (Grades 9, 10, 11, and 12; Fourteen, Fifteen, Sixteen, and Seventeen Years)

PHYSICAL CHARACTERISTICS: HIGH SCHOOL

1. *Most students reach physical maturity, and virtually all attain puberty.* Although almost all girls reach their ultimate height, some boys may continue to grow even after graduation. Tremendous variation

TABLE 3.7 *Applying Stage Theories of Development to the High School Years*

Stage of psychosocial development: identity vs. role confusion. Concerns arise about gender roles and occupational choice. Different identity statuses become apparent.

Stage of cognitive development: formal thought for many students. There is increasing ability to engage in mental manipulations, understand abstractions, and test hypotheses.

Stage of moral development: morality of cooperation, conventional level. There is increasing willingness to think of rules as mutual agreements and to allow for intentions and extenuating circumstances.

General factors to keep in mind: achievement of sexual maturity has a profound effect on many aspects of behavior. Peer group and reactions of friends are extremely important. There is concern about what will happen after graduation, particularly for students who do not intend to continue their education. Awareness grows of the significance of academic ability and importance of grades for certain career patterns. There is a need to make personal value decisions regarding use of drugs, premarital sex, and code of ethics.

Many adolescents may experience confusion about sexual relationships. They are expected to be interested in sex, but at the same time attitudes towards sex are often imbued with strong moral overtones.

exists in height and weight and in rate of maturation. As noted earlier, late-maturing boys seem to have considerable difficulty adjusting to their slower rate of growth. There is still concern about appearance, although it may not be as strong as during the middle school years. Glandular changes leading to acne may be a source of worry and self-consciousness to some students. The most significant glandular change accompanying puberty is arousal of the sex drive.

2. *Many adolescents become sexually active but experience confusion regarding sexual relationships.* Recent surveys reveal that 78 percent of males and 63 percent of females have engaged in sexual intercourse at least once by age nineteen. The percentages for African-American, Hispanic-American, and white males are 92 percent, 78 percent, and 75 percent, respectively. For African-American, Hispanic-American, and white females, the percentages are 77 percent, 59 percent, and 61 percent, respectively (Irwin & Millstein, 1991). Comparable data for African-American and white males apparently do not exist at this point (Brooks-Gunn & Furstenberg, 1989).

Sexual activity among male, female teens due to different factors

For a group of eleven hundred adolescents, J. Richard Udrey (1990) found that initiation of sexual intercourse in white males was strongly related to hormone production and was only weakly related to the discouraging or encouraging efforts of parents, schools, friends, and the media. It was not unusual for adolescent males to experience a tenfold increase in testosterone levels over a period of six months. The initiation of sexual intercourse among white females, however, was more strongly associated with such social factors as grades in school and whether friends had engaged in sexual intercourse than with increases in hormone levels. For African-American females, the factors that best predicted onset of sexual intercourse were pubertal development and sexual intentions. The factors associated with initial sexual intercourse in African-American males could not be determined as most of them reported having had at least one sexual intercourse experience prior to the initial interview.

In a discussion of the development of sexuality in adolescence, Patricia Miller and William Simon (1980) point out that puberty, a biological event, causes adolescents to function as "self-motivated sexual actors," which is a social event. Miller and Simon comment that in technological societies "young people are defined as sexually mature while simultaneously being defined as socially and psychologically immature" (1980, p. 383). The result is that adolescents are pulled first one way and then another regarding sexual relationships.

Adolescents likely to be confused about appropriateness of premarital sex

These findings illustrate the pressing need for sex education during the high school years. In particular, adolescents need to understand the distinction between sex and mature love. A major characteristic of mature love is that "the well-being of the other person is just a little bit more important than the well-being of the self" (Gordon & Gilgun, 1987, p. 180).

3. *Increased sexual activity among adolescents has led to high rates of births outside of marriage and to sexually transmitted diseases.* Recent surveys indicate that about 65 percent of all adolescent mothers (about 307,000 as of 1991) are unmarried and that the rate at which babies are born to unmarried adolescent females has quadrupled since 1960. Younger white females and African-American females are most likely to be unmarried at the birth of their child (Coates & van Widenfeldt, 1991). Some factors that predict adolescent pregnancy include being a member of a particular race, having a mother who was pregnant as an adolescent, coming from a low-income family, coming from a one-parent family, and having low self-esteem (Coates & van Widenfeldt, 1991; Stiffman, Earls, Robins, Jung, & Kulbok, 1987). One factor contributing to the high rate of teenage pregnancies and births is the relatively low level of contraceptive use. Less than 50 percent of all adolescents regularly use some form of contraception (Conger, 1991).

The relatively high levels of sexual activity and low levels of regular contraception among adolescents are particularly worrisome as they put adolescents at risk for contracting **sexually transmitted diseases (STDs)**. According to some experts, STDs among adolescents in the United States have reached epidemic proportions. One estimate is that as many as 2.5 million teens are infected each year with an STD (Wiles & Bondi, 1993). The highest rates of STDs are found among younger adolescent females (fifteen years or younger) and inner-city minority youths. More than 60 percent of the STD cases reported annually occur among individuals under the age of twenty-five. And about 25 percent of the cases occur among individuals between the ages of fifteen and nineteen (Boyer & Hein, 1991).

The worst of the STDs is, of course, acquired immune deficiency syndrome (AIDS) because there is no known cure. Although the number of AIDS cases among adolescents is currently low, it will rise in the future, potentially becoming a major problem. The percentage of adolescents who test positive for human immunodeficiency virus (HIV, the viral cause of AIDS) ranges from about 2 percent to 6 percent (Rotheram-Borus & Koopman, 1991). Because HIV has a long incubation period,

AIDS symptoms may not show up for several years. Consequently, the proportion of today's teens who will be diagnosed with AIDS in their twenties will be more than the 2 percent to 6 percent figure just cited.

SOCIAL CHARACTERISTICS: HIGH SCHOOL

1. *Parents are likely to influence long-range plans; peers are likely to influence immediate status.* A number of studies have attempted to compare the beliefs, attitudes, and values of parents and those of their children and also to compare the extent to which parent-peer and peer-peer opinions agree and conflict. Studies of values (reviewed by Feather, 1980), of political thinking (reviewed by Gallatin, 1980), of moral development (reviewed by Hoffman, 1980), and of occupational choice (reviewed by Rogers, 1972) lead to the conclusion that high school students are probably influenced in these areas of their lives more by parents than by peers. But a visit to any high school will reveal that in terms of dress, hair styles, interests, social relationships, and the like, the influence of peers is extremely potent.

Not surprisingly, most conflicts between parents and their adolescent children are about such peer-influenced issues as personal appearance, friends, dating, hours, and eating habits (Hill, 1987). The hypothesis that parents and peers influence different aspects of adolescent behavior has been developed by Clay Brittain (1967), who suggests that parents have a greater impact on decisions that have implications for the future (such as choice of a career), whereas peers influence decisions that involve current status and identity needs (such as choice of friends). The influence of parents appears to be greatest when there are mutual affection and respect between parent and child (Baumrind, 1991; Hill, 1987).

Parents influence values, plans; peers influence immediate status

2. *Girls seem to experience greater anxiety about friendships than boys do.* Factors that cause girls to become concerned about the reactions of others were summarized in the preceding chapter. Adolescent girls tend to seek intimacy in friendships (Coleman, 1980). Boys, in contrast, often stress skills and interests when they form friendships, and their tendencies to be competitive and self-reliant may work against the formation of close relationships with male companions. Because adolescent girls often wish to form an intimate relationship with another girl, they are more likely than boys to experience anxiety, jealousy, and conflicts regarding friendships with same-sex peers. You should not be surprised, therefore, if secondary school girls are much more preoccupied with positive and negative aspects of friendships than boys are.

Girls more likely than boys to experience anxiety about friendships

3. *Many high school students are employed after school.* Part-time employment among adolescents who attend school has increased in recent years and is more prevalent in the United States than in other industrialized countries. Between 1953 and 1983 the percentage of sixteen- and seventeen-year-old boys who attended school and worked part-time grew from 29 to 36 percent. The increase for girls was even more dramatic—a doubling from 18 to 36 percent. By 1987 the combined part-time employment figure for both sexes was 41 percent. According to self-report data, about 60 percent of high school sophomores and 75 percent of seniors engage in part-time employment to some degree. Sophomore boys who work average about fifteen hours a week; senior boys average about

twenty-one hours a week. Sophomore and senior girls average about eleven and eighteen hours, respectively.

The pros and cons of after-school employment have been vigorously debated. On the positive side, it is thought to enhance self-discipline, a sense of responsibility, self-confidence, and attitudes toward work. On the negative side, part-time employment leaves less time for homework, participation in extracurricular activities, and development of friendships; it may also lead to increased stress, lower grades, and lower career aspirations (Mortimer, 1991).

EMOTIONAL CHARACTERISTICS: HIGH SCHOOL

1. *Many psychiatric disorders either appear or become prominent during adolescence. Included among these are eating disorders, substance abuse, schizophrenia, depression, and suicide.* Eating disorders are much more common in females than in males. *Anorexia nervosa* is an eating disorder characterized by a preoccupation with body weight and food, behavior directed toward losing weight, peculiar patterns of handling food, weight loss, intense fear of gaining weight, and a distorted perception of one's body. This disorder occurs predominantly in females (about 94 percent of the cases) and usually appears between the ages of fourteen and seventeen (Halmi, 1987).

Bulimia nervosa is a disorder in which binge eating (uncontrolled, rapid eating of large quantities of food over a short period of time), followed by self-induced vomiting, is the predominant behavior. Binges are typically followed by feelings of guilt, depression, self-disgust, and fasting. Bulimia is a disorder that also appears predominantly in adolescent females (Halmi, 1987).

Many high school students, girls in particular, experience periods of depression, loneliness, and anxiety. Because severe depression often precedes a suicide attempt, teachers should refer students they believe to be depressed to the school counselor.

Overall, *substance abuse* among adolescents has declined since 1980. Daily use of marijuana dropped from 11 percent of high school seniors to 5 percent between 1980 and 1984. Although sharp increases in cocaine use were reported between 1975 and 1985, usage rates declined throughout the rest of the 1980s. Approximately 5 percent of 1984 seniors reported drinking daily, and 39 percent admitted to having five or more drinks on one occasion within two weeks of being asked. Although cigarette smoking has declined slightly since 1975, the number of smokers increases with age. Among sixteen- and seventeen-year-olds, 31 percent of males and 26 percent of females smoked cigarettes at least weekly. Sixty-seven percent of the males and more than 50 percent of the females exceeded half a pack a day (Conger, 1991; Horan & Strauss, 1987).

Although *schizophrenia* (a thinking disorder characterized by illogical and unrealistic thinking, delusions, and hallucinations) is relatively rare among adolescents, it is the most frequently occurring psychotic disorder, and the number of cases diagnosed between the ages of twelve and eighteen is steadily increasing. In about half of the cases, behavioral abnormalities such as odd, unpredictable behavior; social isolation; and rejection by peers were first noticeable in childhood (Conger, 1991; Rutter, 1990).

2. *The most common type of emotional disorder during adolescence is depression.* Estimates of **depression** among high school youths range from 7 to 28 percent depending on the level of depression being examined and the criteria being used to measure depression. Individuals from low-income families are typically the most depressed. Depression in adolescents often precedes substance abuse (Petti & Larson, 1987). Prior to puberty, twice as many boys as girls exhibit depressive syndromes; after puberty the ratio is just the opposite (Rutter, 1990). Females may exhibit greater tendencies than males to feel depressed, but this does not mean that such reactions occur only in high school girls. Extreme feelings of depression are the most common reason that teenagers of both sexes are referred to psychiatric clinics.

Depression most common among females, teens from poor families

Common symptoms of depression include self-deprecation, crying spells, and suicidal thoughts, threats, and attempts. Additional symptoms are moodiness, social isolation, fatigue, hypochondriasis, and difficulty in concentrating (Petti & Larson, 1987). High school students who experience such symptoms typically try to ward off their depression through restless activity or flight to or from others. They may also engage in problem behavior or delinquent acts carried out in ways that make it clear they are appealing for help. (A depressed fifteen-year-old boy may carry out an act of vandalism, for instance, at a time when a school authority or police officer is sure to observe the incident.)

Aaron Beck (1972) suggests that depression consists of a *cognitive set* made up of negative views of oneself, the world, and the future. Martin Seligman (1975) proposes that depression is caused by *learned helplessness*, which leads to feelings of having no control over one's life. Irving Weiner (1975) emphasizes that depression typically involves a *sense of loss* that may have many causes. Depression may stem from the abrupt end of a personal relationship through death, separation, or broken

Depression may be caused by negative set, learned helplessness, sense of loss friendship. An individual may undergo a sharp drop in self-esteem as a result of failure or guilt. Or a person may experience a loss of bodily integrity following illness, incapacitation, or disfigurement.

Although many techniques exist for changing a negative self-concept to a positive view of self, one effective approach to minimizing depression is to help as many of your students as possible to experience success as they learn. Techniques to accomplish that goal will be discussed in the next six chapters of this book.

Journal Entry
Helping Students Overcome Depression

3. *If depression becomes severe, suicide may be contemplated.* Suicide is now a major cause of death among adolescents and young adults. Among high school students only motor vehicle accidents claim more victims. The number of reported suicides among fifteen- to twenty-four-year-olds has increased by 300 percent for males and by 230 percent for females in the last thirty-five years. Fortunately, the youth suicide rate has begun to level off and perhaps even to decline. Between 1980 and 1985 the rate dropped from 12.3 per 100,000 individuals in the fifteen to twenty-four year range to 12.0 per 100,000 (Blumenthal & Kupfer, 1988; Garfinkel et al., 1988).

Two or three times as many females as males *attempt suicide,* almost always by taking an overdose of drugs. But twice as many young males as females *complete suicide,* usually with a gun. Prior to age twelve, *completed suicides* are rare (0.06 cases per million). Between the ages of twelve and sixteen, however, there is a hundredfold increase and then an additional tenfold increase between the ages of sixteen and nineteen (76 cases per million) (Petti & Larson, 1987; Rutter, 1990).

The single most important signal of a youth at risk for suicide is depression. Along with the common symptoms noted earlier under point 2, signs of depression include poor appetite, weight loss, changes in sleeping patterns, difficulty in concentrating, academic problems, and poor self-concept. These symptoms take on added significance when accompanied by a family history of suicide or parents who commit abuse or use drugs and alcohol excessively (Strother, 1986).

Depression and unstable family situation place adolescents at risk for suicide

If you notice that a student in one of your classes seems extremely depressed, take the trouble to ask if there is anything you can do to provide support. Your interest and sympathy may prevent a suicide attempt. In addition, don't hesitate to refer a seemingly depressed student to the school guidance counselor or the school psychologist. Their training and skills equip them to diagnose and treat depression (Garfinkel et al., 1988; Strother, 1986). Finally, take seriously any threats or talk of suicide.

COGNITIVE CHARACTERISTICS: HIGH SCHOOL

1. *High school students become increasingly capable of engaging in formal thought, but they may not use this capability.* High school students are more likely than younger students to grasp relationships, mentally plan a course of action before proceeding, and test hypotheses systematically. Without supervision and guidance, however, they may not use such capabilities consistently. Accordingly, you might take advantage of opportunities to show students at these grade levels how they can function as formal thinkers. Call attention to relationships and to ways that previously acquired knowledge can be applied to new situations.

Provide specific instruction in techniques of problem solving. (Ways you might do this will be discussed in Chapter 10.) Although your advice may be ignored by some students, others will probably take it more seriously. Despite the constant attempts of adolescents to appear totally self-sufficient and independent, they still view parents and teachers as knowledgeable authority figures when it comes to school achievement (Amiram, Bar-Tal, Alona, & Peleg, 1990).

2. *Between the ages of twelve and sixteen, political thinking becomes more abstract, liberal, and knowledgeable.* Joseph Adelson (1972, 1986) used an interview approach to obtain information about the development of political thought during the adolescent years. At the start of the interviews, the subjects were requested to imagine that one thousand people had ventured to an island in the Pacific for the purpose of establishing a new society. The respondents were then asked to explain how these people might establish a political order; devise a legal system; establish a balance among rights, responsibilities, personal liberty, and the common good; and deal with other problems of public policy.

The analysis of the interview responses showed no significant gender differences in the understanding of political concepts and no significant differences attributable to intelligence and social class, although brighter students were better able to deal with abstract ideas and upper-class students were less likely to be authoritarian. The most striking and consistent finding was the degree to which the political thinking of the adolescent changed in the years between twelve and sixteen. Adelson concluded that the most significant changes were (1) an increase in the ability to deal with such abstractions as freedom of speech, equal justice under law, and the concept of community; (2) a decline in authoritarian views; (3) an increase in the ability to imagine the consequences of current actions; and (4) an increase in political knowledge.

Political thinking becomes more abstract, less authoritarian, more knowledgeable

Increased ability to deal with abstractions is a function of the shift from concrete to formal operational thought. When thirteen-year-olds were asked, "What is the purpose of laws?" a typical answer was "So people don't steal or kill" (Adelson, 1972, p. 108). A fifteen- or sixteen-year-old, by contrast, was more likely to say, "To ensure safety and enforce the government" (p. 108).

When considering punishment for crimes, younger children (Piaget's moral realists) hold the conviction that laws are immutable and that punishment should be stern. But by fourteen and fifteen, the adolescents interviewed by Adelson were more likely to consider circumstances and individual rights and to recommend rehabilitation rather than punishment.

If you will be teaching courses in social studies, you may find this information useful in lesson planning. It may also help you understand why students may respond to discussions of political or other abstract matters in different ways.

Resources for Further Investigation

Children's Play Behavior

In *Children, Play, and Development* (1991), Fergus Hughes discusses the history of play in the Western world; different theories of play; cultural differences in play behaviors; patterns of play among toddlers, preschoolers, school-age children, and adolescents; gender differences in play; and the play behaviors of children with disabilities. Sandra Heidemann and Deborah Hewitt (1992), in *Pathways to Play,* describe the play categories of Mildred Parten, the proper conditions for children's play (such as time, space, and props), a checklist for observing play behaviors, and how to use the results of the checklist for teaching children different play skills.

Cognitive Development

Henry Wellman and Susan Gelman (1992) describe what three- to five-year-olds understand about the workings of their own mind and those of others in "Cognitive Development: Foundational Theories of Core Domains," which is in volume 43 of the *Annual Review of Psychology.* Discussions of the biological, social, and school factors that influence cognitive development can be found in *Directors of Development: Influences on the Development of Children's Thinking* (1991), edited by Lynn Okagaki and Robert Sternberg.

Understanding and Dealing with Gender Stereotypes

Katherine Blick Hoyenga and Kermit Hoyenga (1993) discuss stereotypes and gender typing in Chapter 11 of *Gender-Related Differences: Origins and Outcomes.* In *We've All Got Scars* (1983), Raphaela Best, a reading specialist for an affluent school district, describes how the school's "second curriculum" (gender role socialization) and "third curriculum" (self-taught sex education) affect interpersonal relationships and classroom achievement in six-, seven-, and eight-year-old boys and girls.

In the *Sex Equity Handbook for Schools* (1982), Myra Pollock Sadker and David Miller Sadker provide an overview of those aspects of education where gender equity is most needed (for example, instructional materials and teacher-student interactions), describe strategies and lesson plans for eliminating gender bias in the classroom, and provide a directory of sources of nonsexist instructional materials and classroom strategies.

For any prospective or practicing teacher interested in learning how to reduce personal gender bias, as well as the gender bias of others, *Building Gender Fairness in Schools* (1988), by Beverly Stitt, is a useful resource. This book is made up of two parts. Part 1 contains a collection of six readings on various aspects of gender bias (for example, "Sexism in Education," "How Fair Is Your Language?" and "Confronting Sex Bias in Instructional Materials"). Part 2 contains a sequenced set of eleven instructional units, each of which presents a competency to be mastered by the preservice or in-service teacher. The competencies become increasingly complex and difficult. Unit 1, for example, attempts to develop an awareness of the effects of gender bias. The goal of Unit 5 is to identify gender-fair curriculum materials. And the goal of Unit 11 is to conduct applied research to develop policies and programs to achieve gender fairness.

Teaching the Middle School Grades

Transforming Middle Level Education (1992), edited by Judith L. Irvin, contains twenty chapters that discuss various aspects of middle school education. Chapters that might be of particular interest are "A Portrait of Diversity: The Middle Level Student" (Chapter 2), by Joel Milgram; "Young Adolescents' Perceptions of School" (Chapter 3), by Linda R. Kramer; "Appropriate Grouping Practices for Middle Level Students"

(Chapter 14), by Robert Spear; and "Developmentally Appropriate Instruction: The Heart of the Middle School" (Chapter 16), by Judith Irvin. In *Changing Middle Schools: How to Make Schools Work for Young Adolescents* (1994), Nancy Ames and Edward Miller describe the experiences of four urban Indiana middle schools that were part of a restructuring program called the Middle Grades Improvement Program.

Characteristics of Adolescence

For a good overall treatment of the major developmental changes that occur during adolescence—biological, cognitive, moral reasoning, self-concept and self-esteem, identity, gender role socialization, sexuality, vocational choice—consult the second edition of *Adolescent Development and Behavior* (1991), by Jerome Dusek.

Advanced treatments of biological development during adolescence can be found in *Handbook of Adolescent Psychology* (1987), edited by Vincent van Hasselt and Michel Hersen. In particular, consult Chapter 3, "Biological Theoretical Models of Adolescent Development," and Chapter 7, "Pubertal Processes: Their Relevance for Developmental Research."

Useful, though advanced, information about the emotional aspects of adolescence can be gleaned from several chapters of *Handbook of Adolescent Psychology* (1987), just mentioned. Chapter 9 covers adolescent sexuality, Chapter 16 discusses depression and suicide, and Chapter 17 discusses the causes and nature of substance abuse.

In *Adolescent Stress* (1991), edited by Mary Ellen Colton and Susan Gore, fourteen authors discuss such sources of adolescent stress as negative emotions, conflicts with parents, drug use, pregnancy, and abuse at home and how adolescents try to cope with them. Robert D. Ketterlinus and Michael E. Lamb (1994), in *Adolescent Problem Behaviors: Issues and Research,* describe how such factors as sexual behavior, delinquency, risk taking, and childhood victimization give rise to troublesome behaviors among adolescents.

Summary

1. Preschool and kindergarten children are quite active and enjoy physical activity. But incomplete muscle and motor development limits what they can accomplish on tasks that require fine motor skills, eye-hand coordination, and visual focusing.

2. The social behavior of preschool and kindergarten children is marked by rapidly changing friendships and play groups, a variety of types of play, short quarrels, and a growing awareness of gender roles.

3. Kindergartners openly display their emotions. Anger and jealousy are common.

4. Kindergartners like to talk and are reasonably skilled at using language. Preschoolers tend to apply their own rules of grammar. An authoritative approach by parents is more likely to produce competent preschoolers than either an authoritarian or a permissive approach.

5. Primary grade children exhibit many of the same physical characteristics as preschool and kindergarten children (high activity level, incomplete muscle and motor development, frequent periods of fatigue). Most accidents occur among third graders because they overestimate their physical skills and underestimate the dangers in their activities.

6. Friendships are typically same sex and are made on a more selective basis by primary grade children. Quarrels among peers typically involve verbal arguments, although boys may engage in punching, wrestling, and shoving.

7. Primary grade students are becoming more emotionally sensitive. As a result, they are more easily hurt by criticism, respond strongly to praise, and are more likely to hurt another child's feelings during a quarrel.

8. Primary grade students are eager to learn and like to speak up in class.

9. Elementary grade boys and girls become leaner and stronger and tend to have a gangly look. But some run the risk of becoming overweight because of poor eating habits and lack of exercise. Boys usually outperform girls on such sports-related motor skills as kicking, throwing, catching, running, and jumping, whereas girls often surpass boys on such play-related motor skills as flexibility, balance, and rhythm.
10. The peer group becomes a strong influence on the norms that govern the behavior of elementary grade children.
11. Friendships in the elementary grades become even more selective and gender based than they were in the primary grades.
12. A child's self-image (self-concept plus self-esteem) becomes more stable and generalized during the elementary grades. As a result of the decline of egocentric thought and the competitive nature of American society, self-image is based primarily on comparisons with peers.
13. Delinquency occurs more frequently among elementary grade children than at earlier ages and is associated with dysfunctional parent-child relationships and academic failure. About 10 percent of elementary grade children exhibit a behavior disorder.
14. The thinking of elementary grade children, although more logical, can be wildly inconsistent and is constrained by the limitations of Piaget's concrete operational stage. It is also influenced by cognitive styles—preferential ways of dealing with intellectual tasks.
15. Although most children grow rapidly during the middle school years, girls grow more quickly and begin puberty earlier than boys. Early versus late maturation in boys and girls may affect subsequent personality development.
16. The social behavior of middle school children is increasingly influenced by peer group norms and the development of interpersonal reasoning. Children are now capable of understanding why they behave as they do toward others and vice versa.
17. Because the peer group is the primary source for rules of acceptable behavior, conformity and concern about what peers think reach a peak during the middle school years.
18. Although anxiety, worry, and concern about self-esteem, physical appearance, academic success, and acceptance by peers are prominent emotions among many adolescents, some cope with these emotions better than others.
19. Although gender differences in cognitive abilities among elementary students have decreased over the past forty years, they are still noticeable, as are differences in cognitive style.
20. Self-efficacy beliefs, or how competent one feels at carrying out a particular task, begin to stabilize during the middle school years and influence the willingness of students to take on and persist at various academic and social tasks.
21. Physical development during the high school years is marked by physical maturity for most students and by puberty for virtually all. Sexual activity increases.
22. The long-range goals, beliefs, and values of adolescents are likely to be influenced by parents, whereas immediate status is likely to be influenced by peers. Many teens have part-time, after-school employment.
23. Eating disorders, substance abuse, schizophrenia, depression, and suicide are prominent emotional disorders among adolescents. Depression is the most common emotional disorder during adolescence. Depression coupled with an unstable family situation places adolescents at risk for suicide.
24. Cognitively, high school students become increasingly capable of formal operational thought, although they may function at the concrete operational level a good deal of the time. The influence of formal operational reasoning can be seen in political thinking, which becomes more abstract and knowledgeable.

Key Terms

play behavior *(86)*
gender roles *(87)*
early language development *(89)*
authoritative parents *(90)*
authoritarian parents *(90)*
permissive parents *(90)*
self-image *(96)*
self-concept *(96)*
self-esteem *(96)*
cognitive style *(98)*
growth spurt *(100)*
early-maturing boy *(101)*
late-maturing boy *(101)*
early-maturing girl *(102)*
late-maturing girl *(102)*
interpersonal reasoning *(102)*
self-efficacy *(107)*
sexually transmitted diseases (STDs) *(109)*
depression *(112)*

Discussion Questions

1. Given the physical, social, emotional, and cognitive characteristics of preschool and kindergarten children, what type of classroom atmosphere and instructional tactics would you use to foster learning and enjoyment of school?

2. The primary and elementary years correspond to Erikson's stage of industry versus inferiority. The implication of this stage is that educators should do whatever is necessary to encourage a sense of industry and competence in each student. On a scale of 1 to 10, where 1 is the low end of the scale, how well do you think schools accomplish this goal? If your rating was lower than 10, what is it that schools do (or not do) that prevented you from assigning a perfect rating?

3. During the middle school years, the peer group becomes the general source for rules of behavior. Why? What advantages and disadvantages are associated with a situation in which the peer group establishes the norms for behavior?

4. Given the high rates of illegitimate births and sexually transmitted diseases among high school students, you could persuasively argue that adolescents should receive more sex education than they do. What are the advantages and disadvantages of providing this education in the school instead of in the home?

CHAPTER 4

Understanding Cultural Diversity

Key Points

These key points will help you learn the important information in this chapter. To help you study, they also appear in the margins of the pages, next to the text where they are discussed.

The Rise of Multiculturalism

- Cultural pluralism assumes every culture has own logic, no culture inherently better, all people somewhat culture-bound
- U.S. becoming more culturally diverse because of changes in immigration, birthrates

Taking Account of Your Students' Cultural Differences

- Culture: how a group of people perceives, believes, thinks, behaves
- Ethnocentrism: belief that one's own culture is superior to other cultures
- Ethnic group members differ in verbal and nonverbal communication patterns
- Ethnic group members may hold different values
- Ethnic group members may favor different learning modes
- Many ethnic families of color earn less than white families
- Low-SES children more proficient with everyday language than with language of classroom
- Educationally disadvantaged children often lack motivation, academic skills
- Support from home, school helps educationally disadvantaged students stay in school
- Low-SES adolescents often have lower career aspirations
- Pygmalion effect: impact of teacher expectations leads to self-fulfilling prophecy
- Limited effect of teacher expectancy on IQ scores
- Strong effect of teacher expectancy on achievement, participation
- Teacher expectancies influenced by gender, attractiveness, achievement, social class, ethnic background

MULTICULTURAL EDUCATION PROGRAMS

- Multicultural programs aim to promote respect for diversity, reduction of ethnocentrism and stereotypes, improved learning
- Multicultural education can be approached in different ways
- Multicultural lessons organized around key concepts
- Peer tutoring improves achievement, interpersonal relationships, attitudes toward subjects
- Cooperative learning: students work together in small groups
- Cooperative learning fosters better understanding among ethnically diverse students
- Mastery learning: all students can master the curriculum
- Minority children score lower on tests, drop out of school sooner
- Minority dropout rate due to alienation, differences in values, poverty

BILINGUAL EDUCATION

- Two main approaches to bilingual education: transition, maintenance
- Transition programs focus on rapid shift to English proficiency
- Maintenance programs focus on maintaining native-language competence
- Bilingual education programs produce moderate learning gains

In the introduction to Chapter 2 we pointed out that if your instructional plans are to be effective, they have to take into account what your students are like. (The term *entering behavior* is typically used to refer to the characteristics students bring with them to class.) In Chapters 2 and 3 we described students in terms of their age-related differences in psychosocial, cognitive, and moral development, and we discussed how students typically are similar to and different from one another in terms of physical, social, and cognitive characteristics. In this chapter we will turn to two other important ways in which students differ—cultural background and language.

Culture is a term that describes how a group of people perceives the world; formulates beliefs; evaluates objects, ideas, and experiences; and behaves. It can be thought of as a blueprint that guides the ways in which individuals within a group do such important things as communicate with others (both verbally and nonverbally), handle time and space, express emotions, and approach work and play. The concept of culture typically includes ethnic group but can also encompass religious beliefs and socioeconomic status (Gollnick & Chinn, 1994).

Different groups of people will, of course, vary in their beliefs, attitudes, values, and behavior patterns because of differences in cultural norms. (By *norms* we mean the perceptions, beliefs, and behaviors that characterize most members of a group.) People who were raised with mainstream American values, for example, find acceptable the practice of adults gently patting children on the head but find unacceptable the practice of two boys holding hands. Most Vietnamese, in contrast, disapprove of the former but not the latter (Sadker & Sadker, 1991).

To provide the appropriate classroom and school conditions that will help your students from different cultural backgrounds master a common curriculum, you must come to understand and take into account your students' differing cultural backgrounds. For example, a culturally aware teacher will emphasize the way in which American society has been enriched by the contributions of many different ethnic groups (and place special emphasis on those ethnic groups to which the students belong) and will not schedule a major exam or field trip for a day when certain students are likely to be out of school in observance of a religious holiday.

The approach to teaching and learning that we will describe in this chapter, one that seeks to foster an understanding of and mutual respect for the values, beliefs, and practices of different cultural groups, is typically referred to as **multicultural education.** Because culturally diverse children often come to school with different language backgrounds, another related issue is bilingual education, described at the end of this chapter.

The Rise of Multiculturalism

FROM MELTING POT TO CULTURAL PLURALISM

More than most other countries, the United States is made up of numerous ethnic groups of widely diverse histories, cultural backgrounds, and values. In addition to the hundreds of thousands of African Americans who were brought to the United States as slaves, the United States was peopled by many waves of immigrants, mostly from Europe but also from Asia and Latin America. Throughout the eighteenth and nineteenth centuries, the United States needed large numbers of people to settle its western frontier, build its railroads, harvest its natural resources, and work in its growing factories. As Table 4.1 indicates, between 1820 and 1920 approximately 33 million people immigrated to the United States.

Throughout this period the basic view of American society toward immigrants was that they should divest themselves of their old customs, views, allegiances, and rivalries as soon as possible and adopt English as their primary language along with mainstream American ideals, values, and customs. This assimilation of diverse ethnic groups into one national mainstream was

TABLE 4.1 *Immigrants to the United States*

Immigration Totals by Decade

Years	*Number*	*Years*	*Number*
1820–1830	151,824	1911–1920	5,735,811
1831–1840	599,125	1921–1930	4,107,209
1841–1850	1,713,251	1931–1940	528,431
1851–1860	2,598,214	1941–1950	1,035,039
1861–1870	2,314,824	1951–1960	2,515,479
1871–1880	2,812,191	1961–1970	3,321,677
1881–1890	5,246,613	1971–1980	4,493,300
1891–1900	3,687,546	1981–1990	7,338,100
1901–1910	8,795,386	Total	56,994,020

SOURCE: U.S. Bureau of the Census (1975); U.S. Bureau of the Census (1993a).

Multicultural education programs have become more widespread because changing immigration patterns and birth rates have made the United States a more culturally diverse nation.

known as the **melting pot,** a term and viewpoint popularized in a 1909 play by Israel Zangwill called *The Melting Pot*. The main institution responsible for bringing about this assimilation was the public school (Levine & Havighurst, 1992).

The notion of America as a great melting pot was generally accepted until the social unrest of the late 1960s and early 1970s. As an outgrowth of urban riots and the civil rights movement, minority ethnic groups argued not only for bilingual education programs in public schools but also for ethnic studies. It might be said that many American citizens realized that they did not wish to fit the white Anglo-Saxon Protestant mold of a "traditional American" and began to express a desire to be Americans who have different characteristics. Michael Novak (1971) refers to this movement as the "rise of the unmeltable ethnics." Since the early 1970s factors such as discrimination, the desire to maintain culturally specific ideas and practices, and continued immigration from different parts of the world have served to maintain, if not accelerate, this trend toward cultural diversity (or **cultural pluralism,** to use the preferred term). Three basic principles on which cultural pluralism rests are (1) every culture has its own internal coherence, integrity, and logic; (2) no culture is inherently better or worse than another; and (3) all persons are to some extent culture-bound (Janzen, 1994).

Cultural pluralism assumes every culture has own logic, no culture inherently better, all people somewhat culture-bound

THE CHANGING FACE OF THE UNITED STATES

Given recent changes in birthrates and immigration patterns and population projections for the next thirty to fifty years, one could argue that the decline of the melting pot philosophy and the rise of cultural pluralism and multicultural education will only accelerate in the years ahead. Consider, for example, the following statistics.

Between 1981 and 1986, 89 percent of legal immigrants to the United States came from non-European countries. Most of these immigrants came from Asia (principally the Philippine Islands, Korea, and China) and the Americas (principally Mexico and Cuba) and settled in the major cities of California, New York, Texas, and Florida. Estimates are that in the ten-year period 1981–1990 almost 9 million legal immigrants arrived in the United States. If this estimate proves accurate, it will virtually match the all-time immigration record of 1901–1910. Immigrant mothers bore 10 percent of all babies born in the United States in 1986. Native-born women in 1986 averaged 67.5 births per 1,000, while foreign-born women averaged 98.9 per 1,000 (Banks, 1994b; Bennett, 1995; Kellogg, 1988).

Between 1988 and 2020 the number of white non-Hispanic-American children from birth through age seventeen is expected to decline by 27 percent from 44.5 million to 32.3 million (or from 70 percent of the school-age population to 49 percent). The number of Hispanic-American children is expected to almost triple, increasing from 6.8 million (11 percent of the school-aged population) to 18.6 million (28 percent of the school-age population). The population of African-American youths under age eighteen is expected to grow from 9.6 million to 10.5 million, an increase of 9 percent. By 2020 African-American youths should account for approximately 16 percent of the school-age population (see Figure 4.1). And by the year 2020 the number of Asian-American and other minority school-age children is expected to almost double, increasing by about 2.3 million children (Natriello, McDill, & Pallas, 1990). As these figures make clear, the United States is rapidly on its way to becoming an even more ethnically diverse nation than ever before.

U.S. becoming more culturally diverse because of changes in immigration, birthrates

FIGURE 4.1 *Projected Change in Percentage of Children under Eighteen from Three Ethnic Groups Between 1988 and 2020*

SOURCE: Adapted from Natriello, McDill & Pallas (1990).

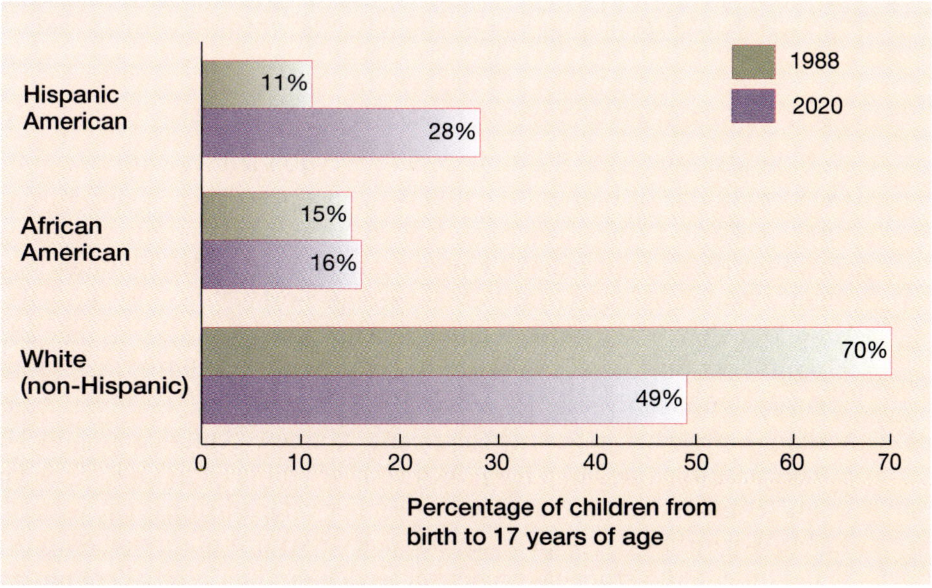

Taking Account of Your Students' Cultural Differences

As we pointed out in the opening paragraphs of this chapter, culture refers to the way in which a group of people perceives, thinks about, and interacts with the world. It is a way of giving meaning to experiences. As Donna Gollnick and Philip Chinn put it, "Culture gives us a certain lifestyle that is peculiarly our own. It becomes so peculiar to us that someone from a different culture can easily identify us as Americans" (1994, p. 5). Two significant factors that most readily distinguish one culture from another are ethnicity and social class.

Culture: how a group of people perceives, believes, thinks, behaves

Because of the demographic changes we discussed earlier, familiarity with the similarities and differences of students from different ethnic groups and social classes is a necessity. But for you and your students to benefit from your knowledge of cultural diversity, you must view it in the proper perspective. The perspective we encourage you to adopt is a twofold one. First, you should recognize that differences are not necessarily deficits. Students who subscribe to different value systems and who exhibit different communication patterns, time orientations, learning modes, motives, and aspirations should not be viewed as incapable students. Looking on ethnic and social-class differences as deficits usually stems from an attitude called *ethnocentrism.* This is the tendency of people to think of their own culture as superior to the culture of other groups. You may be able to moderate your ethnocentric tendencies and motivate your students to learn by consciously using instructional tactics that are congruent with the different cultural backgrounds of your students.

Ethnocentrism: belief that one's own culture is superior to other cultures

Second, note that, while our descriptions of various ethnic groups may accurately portray some general tendencies of a large group of people, they may apply only partly or not at all to given individuals. One must always be careful in applying general knowledge to particular cases. The Mexican-American high school student who vehemently opposes abortion, for example, may do so more because of his Roman Catholic faith than because of cultural values concerning family relationships (Chinn & Plata, 1987/1988).

THE EFFECT OF ETHNICITY ON LEARNING

An **ethnic group** is a collection of people who identify with one another on the basis of one or more of the following characteristics: country from which one's ancestors came, race, religion, language, values, political interests, economic interests, and behavior patterns (Banks, 1994b; Gollnick & Chinn, 1994). Viewed separately, the ethnic groups in the United States, particularly those of color, are numerical minorities; collectively, however, they constitute a significant portion of American society (Banks, 1994b). Most Americans identify with some ethnic group (Irish Americans, German Americans, Italian Americans, African Americans, Chinese Americans, and Hispanic Americans, to name but a few). As a teacher you need to know how your students' ethnicity can affect student-teacher relationships. Christine Bennett (1995) identifies five aspects of ethnicity that are potential sources of student-student and student-teacher misunderstanding: verbal communication,

Students from different ethnic groups sometimes exhibit learning modality preferences. Native-American, Mexican-American, and rural white students, for example, may favor a listening/speaking preference.

nonverbal communication, orientation modes, social value patterns, and intellectual modes.

Problems with verbal communication can occur in a number of ways. Children for whom English is a second language may not hear or accurately discriminate between certain speech sounds. Many African-American students are perceived as uneducated or less intelligent for no other reason than that they speak nonstandard English. Classroom discussions may not go as planned if teachers have students who do not understand or find confining the mainstream convention of "You take a turn and then somebody else takes a turn." Because of differences in cultural experiences, some students may be very reluctant to speak or perform in public, whereas others may prefer exchanges that resemble a free-for-all shouting match. Some Native American children, for example, prefer to work on ideas and skills in private. A public performance is given only after an acceptable degree of mastery is attained (Bennett, 1995; Vasquez, 1990). This last practice is not as unique to Native American culture as it might seem at first glance. Music lessons and practices are typically done in private, and public performances are not given until a piece or program is mastered.

Ethnic group members differ in verbal and nonverbal communication patterns

A form of nonverbal communication that is highly valued by mainstream American culture is direct eye contact. Most people are taught to look directly at the person to whom they are speaking, as this behavior signifies honesty on the part of the speaker and interest on the part of the listener. Among certain Native American, Hispanic, and Asian cultures, however, averting one's eyes is a sign of deference to and respect for the other person, whereas looking at someone directly while being corrected is a sign of defiance. Thus, an Asian-, a Hispanic-, or a Native American student who looks down or away when being questioned or corrected about something is not necessarily trying to hide guilt or ignorance or to communicate lack of interest (Bennett, 1995; Howe, 1994).

Mainstream American culture is very time oriented. People who know how to organize their time and work efficiently are praised and rewarded. We teach our children to value such statements as "Time is money" and "Never put off until tomorrow what you can do today." Nowhere is this time orientation more evident than in our schools. Classes begin and end at a specified time regardless of whether one is interested in starting a project, pursuing a discussion, or finishing an experiment. But for students whose ethnic cultures are not so time-bound (Hispanic Americans and Native Americans, for example), such a rigid approach to learning may be upsetting. Indeed, it may also be upsetting to some students who reflect the mainstream culture (Bennett, 1995).

Ethnic group members may hold different values

Two values that lie at the heart of mainstream American society are competition ("Competition brings out the best in people") and rugged individualism ("People's accomplishments should reflect their own efforts"). Since schools tend to reflect mainstream beliefs, many classroom activities are competitive and done on one's own for one's personal benefit. Mexican-American students, however, are more likely to have been taught to value cooperative relationships and family loyalty. These students may thus prefer group projects; they may also respond more positively to praise that emphasizes family pride rather than individual glory (Bennett, 1995; Vasquez, 1990).

Finally, ethnic groups may differ in terms of the value they place on different types of knowledge and the learning modes they prefer. Some groups may place a higher value on spiritual knowledge than on scientific knowledge; others may be more attracted to practical knowledge than to theoretical knowledge. Students who have adopted mainstream American values tend to favor a learning mode that is based largely on logical analysis of the written word.

According to research summarized by Christine Sleeter and Carl Grant (1994), most elementary teachers use a teacher-centered, large-group approach to instruction in which all students work from the same text, workbook, and worksheets. At the high school and middle school levels, the typical classroom arrangement is rows of chairs facing the front of the room and a teacher who governs exchanges with students by talking, asking questions, and listening to answers. These approaches to teaching are likely to be somewhat incompatible with the learning styles favored by students from other cultural backgrounds. African-American students, for example, seem to favor cooperative arrangements, content about people, discussion, and hands-on learning. One educational consequence of teaching students with this type of style might be, for example, the instruction of math concepts through descriptions of or active engagement in problems that involve buying, trading, or borrowing.

Ethnic group members may favor different learning modes

Some researchers have found that many Native Americans prefer visual imagery rather than verbal propositions as a way to mentally represent knowledge and deductively oriented rather than inductively oriented lessons.

That is, they perform better when lessons begin with an overview and proceed to an examination of the parts, as opposed to an approach that stresses the details first and then draws general conclusions. Because Navajo students are taught by their culture to treat serious learning as private, they may not fully participate in such traditionally Western activities as tests, debates, and contests (Bennett, 1995; Guild, 1994; Vasquez, 1990).

Students whose culture favors an aural/oral mode over a written mode (African American, Native American, and rural white, for example) are also likely to be at a disadvantage in the typical classroom. Christine Bennett (1995), for example, found that many African-American and Mexican-American eighth graders in Texas could better understand their U.S. history text if they listened to a tape of the text while they read it. Many white students, by contrast, preferred to read the text without listening to the tape.

THE EFFECT OF SOCIAL CLASS ON LEARNING

The social class from which a student comes also plays an influential role in a student's behavior. **Social class** is an indicator of an individual's or a family's relative standing in society. It is determined by such factors as annual income, occupation, amount of education, place of residence, types of organizations to which family members belong, manner of dress, and material possessions. The first three factors are used by the federal government to determine the closely related concept of **socioeconomic status (SES).** The influence of social class is such that the members of working-class Hispanic-American and Irish-American families may have more in common than the members of an upper-middle-class Hispanic-American family and those of a working-class Hispanic-American family (Gollnick & Chinn, 1994).

Because of the severe and long-lasting historic pattern of discrimination experienced by ethnic groups of color in the United States, many members of these groups have fewer years of education, a less prestigious occupation, and a lower income than the average white person. Significantly, more African-American, Hispanic-American, and Native American adolescents drop out of high school than do whites, thereby shortening their years of education. And because they have less education, people of color are more likely to be unemployed or working in such low-paying occupations as office clerk, private house cleaner, and manual laborer. According to the Census Bureau, the median income of Native American families who lived on reservations was $13,489. For those who lived in and around metropolitan areas, it was $21,750. For African-American and Hispanic-American families in 1989, median income was $22,429 and $25,064, respectively, as compared to a median income of $37,628 for white families. A similar discrepancy existed in ethnic poverty rates. In 1989, 30.9 percent of all nonreservation Native Americans (50.7 percent of those who lived on reservations), 29.5 percent of all African Americans, 25.3 percent of all Hispanic Americans, and 14.1 percent of all Asian Americans lived below the poverty line ($6,652 for an individual and $11,200 for a family of four) as compared to 9.2 percent of all white individuals. The poverty rates for families, which are

Many ethnic families of color earn less than white families

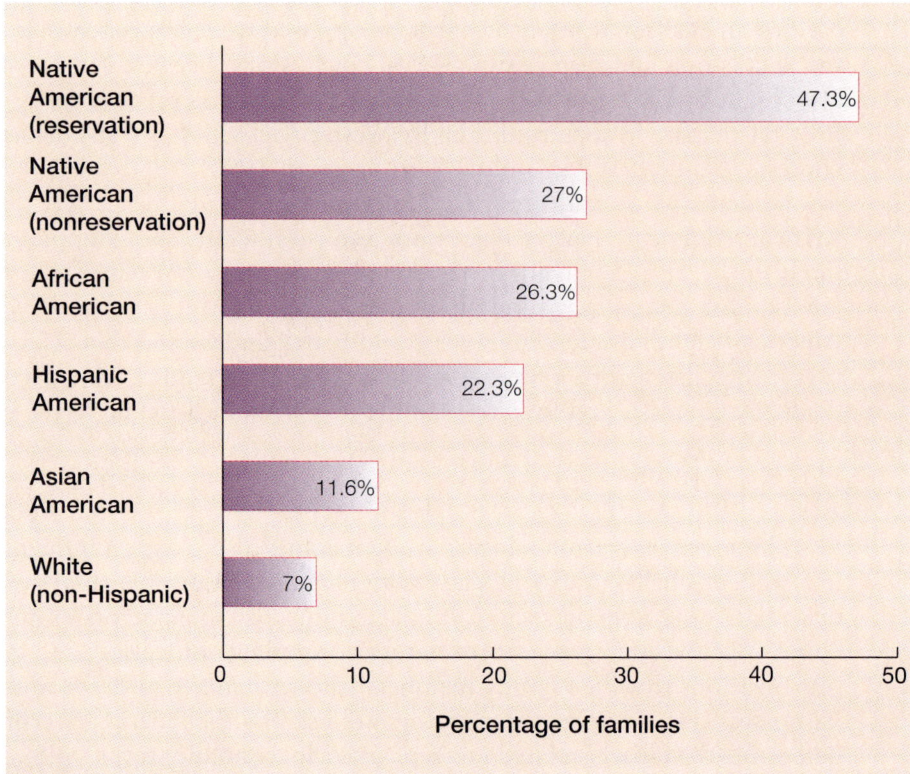

FIGURE 4.2 *Percentage of Families Within Ethnic Groups Living below Poverty Level in 1989*

SOURCE: U.S. Bureau of Census (1993).

portrayed in Figure 4.2, are similar. These factors place many ethnic individuals and families of color either in the working class (consisting of so-called blue-collar workers) or in what is called the underclass (Bureau of the Census, 1993).

Many low-SES students are what might be called educationally disadvantaged or educationally at-risk (Natriello, McDill, & Pallas, 1990) because they are continually exposed to various adverse factors that inhibit physical, social, emotional, and intellectual development. Before you read about some of these factors in the following paragraphs, we caution you to keep in mind that these differences appear to be largely due to environmental causes. On tests of cognitive development between low-SES children and those from more advantaged homes, significant score differences do not appear until after two years of age (Sanders-Phillips, 1989).

1. Many low-SES Americans do not receive satisfactory health care. For example, African-American women have a high level of such pregnancy complications as toxemia, hemorrhage, hypertension, heart disease, infection, and diabetes. In addition, inadequate diets during pregnancy are common (Sanders-Phillips, 1989). As a consequence, there is a greater incidence of premature births, birth defects, and infant mortality among low-SES children as compared to middle-class children (as

consistently revealed by National Institutes of Health statistics). Since poor children do not receive medical or dental care regularly, accurate statistics on general health are difficult to compile. It seems reasonable to assume, however, that the same inadequate nutrition and health care that leads to elevated infant mortality rates probably also leads to higher rates of illness in later years. In other words, low-SES children probably continue to suffer from untreated illnesses at a rate that may be at least twice that of middle-class children (Sanders-Phillips, 1989).

2. Educationally disadvantaged students are more likely than middle-class students to grow up in one-parent families (the father usually being the missing parent). While some studies have shown that the presence of only one parent may be a major factor contributing to low achievement, other studies have failed to confirm this finding (Levine & Havighurst, 1992).

3. Both low-SES and middle-SES children are adept at the language of ordinary conversation. Such interchanges are grammatically simple, utilize stereotyped expressions, do not communicate ideas or emotions precisely, and make heavy use of gesture and inflection to transmit meaning. This form of language is sometimes referred to as "public" or "restricted" language. However, low-SES children are much less proficient than middle-class children in the use of the "formal" or "elaborated" language of the classroom. Elaborated language is more precise in conveying meaning; it is also a more effective tool for organizing experiences because it includes the bases for associations among ideas (Levine & Havighurst, 1992).

Low-SES children more proficient with everyday language than with language of classroom

4. Educationally disadvantaged children typically have not been exposed to a wide variety of experiences. The parents of middle-class children in the United States frequently function as teachers, although *tutors* would be a more appropriate word, since instruction is often given to one child at a time. Every time they talk to their children, answer questions, take them on trips, and buy books or educational toys, parents provide knowledge and experiences that accumulate to make school learning familiar and easy. A child who does not receive such continual tutoring in the home is clearly at a disadvantage when placed in competitive academic situations (Levine & Havighurst, 1992). Furthermore, there has been an increasing concern about the development of a "technological underclass" of children whose families cannot afford to provide access to computers and on-line services at home.

5. Low-SES students may not be strongly motivated to do well in school, and they may not be knowledgeable about techniques for becoming successful in school. Middle-class parents who have benefited in a variety of ways from education serve as effective and enthusiastic advocates of schooling. Because doing well in school paid off for them, they are eager to persuade their children to do well academically in order to achieve similar or greater benefits. They also serve as positive role models. By contrast, low-SES parents who did not do well may describe school in negative terms and perhaps blame teachers for their failure in classrooms as well as for their difficulties later in life. If the parents were inept students, they are also unable to tell their children about how to study for exams, meet requirements, select courses, or acquire the general

Educationally disadvantaged children often lack motivation, academic skills all-around academic know-how that middle-class parents pass on to their offspring (Levine & Havighurst, 1992).

Support from home, school helps educationally disadvantaged students stay in school

Support for this argument comes from a recent study of factors that contributed to African-American seventh, eighth, and ninth graders staying in school (Connell, Halpern-Felsher, Clifford, Crichlow, & Usinger, 1995). These researchers found that support from parents at home and from teachers at school contributed to feelings of academic competence, autonomy (school work is related to important personal goals and/or is intrinsically interesting), and relatedness to others at school. Students with high levels of competence, autonomy, and relatedness were more likely to be successful in school and to stay in school than were students with low levels of these characteristics.

Low-SES adolescents often have lower career aspirations

6. Low-SES adolescents typically have low career aspirations. The impact of social class on career choice was revealed by a comprehensive study (Little, 1967) of all the graduating seniors in Wisconsin's public and private high schools. At the time of graduation, the students were asked to note the occupations they hoped to enter. Their choices were later compared with the jobs they actually attained. Students in the lower third of their graduating class in socioeconomic status had significantly lower aspirations than those in the middle and upper thirds. In addition, the later actual job attainments of the low-SES students were closer to their expectations.

7. Many educationally disadvantaged students feel role confusion and have poor self-esteem. As Erik Erikson has stressed, two key components of identity are being accepted by those who count and knowing where one is going. An educationally disadvantaged adolescent who has no definite career plans after leaving school (with or without a diploma) is more likely to experience role confusion than a sense of identity achievement. If such an adolescent is unable to find a job (a common occurrence, given that the unemployment rate for minority-group youths is typically several times greater than the average rate for that age group), low self-esteem may contribute to the formation of a negative identity.

A clear and chilling example of the last three characteristics is offered by Marc Elrich (1994), a sixth-grade teacher in a Maryland school district just outside of Washington, D.C. His class of twenty-nine students was composed almost entirely of African-American and Hispanic-American low-SES youths who saw no value in education and who exhibited low self-esteem and low expectations. To prompt a discussion of self-esteem, he showed them a film based on a Langston Hughes story about a black youth who attempts to steal the purse of an elderly black woman. Although he fails, the woman takes him into her home, where she tries to change his attitudes and behavior. The message of the film is that with love we all learn that we have it within ourselves to be better people. When Elrich asked for reactions to the film, this exchange occurred:

Student: As soon as you see a black boy, you know he's gonna do something bad.
Teacher: Just because he's black, he's bad?
Student: Everybody knows that black people are bad. That's the way we are. (p. 12)

When Elrich asked who else agreed with that assessment, twenty-four students raised their hands. Further discussion revealed that most of the students agreed with the following statements:

- Blacks are poor and stay poor because they're dumber than whites (and Asians).
- Black people don't like to work hard.
- Black men make women pregnant and leave.
- Black boys expect to die young and unnaturally.
- White people are smart and have money.
- Asians are smart and have money.
- Asians don't like blacks or Hispanics.
- Hispanics are more like blacks than whites. They can't be white so they try to be black.
- Hispanics are poor and don't try hard because, like blacks, they know it doesn't matter. They will be like blacks because when you're poor, you have to be bad to survive. (p. 13)

According to Elrich, his students' view of the world was that

> hard work does not equal success in their world; instead, it means that parents are gone and children take care of children, they told us. The people who have the material goods that reflect the good life get their money through guns and drugs. Wimps die young and live in fear. Tough guys die young but are proud. Bosses are white and workers are black, and black people don't do important things, except in school books. In their world, few aspire to be doctors, scientists, or lawyers. (1994, p. 14)

During the course of the year, Elrich prompted discussions of slavery, racism, and class. In an attempt to help his students understand that the effects of bigotry and racism are not necessarily permanent, he pointed out that two hundred years ago life for most whites was harsh and not terribly free, especially in Europe, and that ideas about race and class were taught and promoted in the interest of a few—primarily very wealthy and privileged—white men. But over time and with persistent effort, many of these barriers to personal advancement were either eliminated or drastically reduced. Therefore, his students could influence what they became if they worked at doing so.

THE EFFECT OF ETHNICITY AND SOCIAL CLASS ON TEACHERS' EXPECTATIONS

So far we have described how students' ethnic and social-class backgrounds influence their approach to and success with various learning tasks. Now we would like to tell you how those and other characteristics often affect (consciously and unconsciously) the expectations that teachers have for student performance and how those expectations affect the quantity and quality of work that students exhibit. This phenomenon has been extensively studied since 1968 and is known variously as the *Pygmalion effect,* the *self-fulfilling prophecy,* and the *teacher expectancy effect.* By becoming aware of the major factors that influence teachers' perceptions of and actions toward students, you may be able to reduce subjectivity to a minimum, particularly with students whose cultural backgrounds are very different from your own.

The Initial Study of Teachers' Expectancies In 1968 Robert Rosenthal and Lenore Jacobson published *Pygmalion in the Classroom,* in which they reported results of a study on the impact of teacher expectations. Rosenthal and Jacobson administered a little-known group test of intelligence (Flanagan's Test of General Ability) to children in grades one through six in a single San Francisco public school. The teachers of these children were not told the true name or nature of this test. Instead, they were told that the children had taken the "Harvard Test of Inflected Acquisition" and that on the basis of the test results certain students in each class were "likely to show unusual intellectual gains in the year ahead." In reality, however, there was no difference between the test performances of these "superior" students, who had been selected at random, and those of the other "average" children. At the end of the school year the same children took the Flanagan Test of General Ability a second time.

Pygmalion effect: impact of teacher expectations leads to self-fulfilling prophecy

Rosenthal and Jacobson reported that the students who were labeled potential achievers showed significant gains in intelligence quotient (IQ) and that the reason for these gains was that their teachers expected more of them. The authors referred to this phenomenon as the Pygmalion effect because they felt that teacher expectations had influenced the students to become intelligent in the same way that the expectations of the mythical Greek sculptor Pygmalion caused a statue he had carved to come to life. Another term frequently used for this phenomenon is **self-fulfilling prophecy** because a prophecy about behavior is often fulfilled. If teachers communicate the "prophecy" that certain students will behave intelligently, those students may behave in the expected manner.

Replications of the Teacher Expectancy Effect In the years following the publication of *Pygmalion in the Classroom,* hundreds of similar studies were carried out. Some attempted to replicate Rosenthal and Jacobson's findings, whereas others investigated the effects of teacher expectancy on other outcomes, such as classroom achievement and participation. Periodically, the results of these studies were reviewed and summarized (for example, by Braun, 1976; Brophy, 1983; Brophy & Good, 1974; Cooper, 1979; Raudenbush, 1984; Rosenthal, 1985). One review found that the effect of teacher expectancy on IQ scores was essentially limited to first- and second-grade students, was moderate in strength at those grade levels, and occurred only when it was induced within the first two weeks of the school year (Raudenbush, 1984). Apparently, once teachers have had an opportunity to observe and interact with their own students, they view these experiences as more credible and informative than the results of a mental ability test.

Limited effect of teacher expectancy on IQ scores

The tendency of teachers to form expectancies early in the school year is illustrated by Sonia Nieto (1992). She tells of a kindergarten teacher who established a set of expectations for each student in her class *by the eighth day of the term.* The teacher did this by comparing each child to a hypothetical "ideal student." An ideal student was one who conformed to middle-class characteristics. Those children who most closely matched this ideal were labeled "fast" learners, while the rest were labeled "slow" learners. Over the course of the year, the teacher interacted differently with students from each group. The "fast" learners received more attention, instructional time, and rewards. Since both the teacher and the students were African American, her expectations were based on differences in social class rather than race. After three years of similar behavior by other teachers, the children's actions more closely resembled the labels given them.

Extensions of the Teacher Expectancy Effect Reviews that have looked at the effect of teacher expectancy on classroom achievement and participation have generally found sizable positive *and* negative effects (for example, Braun, 1976; Brophy, 1983; Cooper, 1979; Rosenthal, 1985). In addition, it appears that teacher expectations are more likely to maintain already existing tendencies than to drastically alter well-established behaviors. For example, primary grade teachers react differently to students in the fast-track reading group than to students in the slow-track group. When working with the more proficient readers, teachers tend to smile, lean toward the students, and establish eye contact more often. Criticism tends to be given in friendlier, gentler tones. The oral reading errors of proficient readers are often overlooked. When corrections are given, they are made at the end of the sentence or other meaningful unit rather than in the middle of such units. And comprehension questions are asked more often than factual questions as a means of monitoring students' attention to the reading selection.

Strong effect of teacher expectancy on achievement, participation

In contrast, less proficient readers are corrected more often and in places that interrupt meaningful processing of the text, are given less time to decode difficult words or to correct themselves, and are asked low-level factual questions as a way of checking on their attention. Teachers' body posture is often characterized by frowning, pursing the lips, shaking the head, pointing a finger, and sitting erect. In sum, through a variety of subtle ways, teachers communicate to students that they expect them to perform well or poorly and then create a situation that is consistent with the expectation. As a result, initial differences between good and poor readers either remain or widen over the course of the school career (Wuthrick, 1990).

Factors That Help Create Expectancies In addition to documenting the existence of teacher expectancy effects and the conditions under which they occur, researchers have sought to identify the factors that might create high or low teacher expectations. Here is a list of some important factors taken from reviews by Carl Braun (1976), Jere Brophy and Tom Good (1974), Gloria Ladson-Billings (1994), and Sonia Nieto (1992):

Attractive children are often perceived by teachers to be brighter, more capable, and more social than unattractive children.

Teacher expectancies influenced by gender, attractiveness, achievement, social class, ethnic background

Teachers tend to approve of girls' behavior more frequently than they approve of boys' behavior.

Female teachers tend to perceive the behavior of girls as closer to the behavior of "ideal students" than do male teachers.

Middle-class students are expected to receive higher grades than low-SES students, even when their IQ scores and achievement test scores are similar.

Teachers expect more from white students than they do from African-American students.

Teachers are more influenced by negative information about students (for example, low test scores) than they are by neutral or positive information.

Teachers appear to spend more time and to interact more frequently with high achievers than with low achievers.

High-achieving students receive more praise than low-achieving ones.

It is important to bear in mind that these factors (plus others such as ethnic background, knowledge of siblings, and impressions of parents) usually operate *in concert* to produce an expectancy. A teacher may be influenced not just by a single test score but also by appearance, grades assigned by other teachers, and so forth.

Multicultural Education Programs

The concept of multicultural education has been around for some time. Many of the elements that constitute contemporary programs were devised sixty to seventy years ago as part of a then-current emphasis on international education (Gollnick & Chinn, 1994). In the next section we will give you some idea of what it might be like to teach today from a multicultural perspective by describing the basic goals, assumptions, and characteristics of modern programs.

ASSUMPTIONS AND GOALS

The various arguments in favor of multicultural education that are made by its proponents (for example, Banks, 1994a, 1994c; Bennett, 1995; Garcia, 1994; Gollnick & Chinn, 1994; Ogbu, 1992) stem from several assumptions. The most frequently mentioned are as follows:

1. The culture of the United States has been formed to a great extent by the contributions of many different cultural groups.
2. People must possess a degree of self- and group esteem to productively interact with members of other cultures.
3. Learning of the achievements of one's own cultural group will enhance self- and group esteem.
4. Interaction among members of culturally diverse groups is beneficial for the health and continued development of American society.
5. Cultural values and experiences predispose children to think and behave in particular ways. When these values and experiences are understood, accepted as worthwhile, incorporated into instructional lessons, and rewarded by the teacher, the students involved will perform better academically than they otherwise would.

In order for children to understand and appreciate different cultural values and experiences, those values and experiences have to be integrated into the curriculum and rewarded by the teacher.

These assumptions have given rise to several goals that proponents of multicultural education believe educators should strive to attain. Some of the most frequently mentioned are as follows:

1. Help students understand how the past and present experiences of various ethnic groups, including their own, have had or are having a significant impact on American society in order to promote self-acceptance and respect for the diverse ways in which other people live.
2. Help students understand how various historical events and artistic creations were influenced and perceived by various cultural groups in order to reduce ethnocentrism and foster productive relationships among members of those groups.
3. Help students combat such harmful stereotypes as African Americans are violent, southern whites are racially prejudiced, Jews are stingy, Asian Americans excel at math and science, and Hispanic Americans are hot-tempered.
4. Help teachers develop the attitudes, expectations, instructional practices, disciplinary policies and practices, and classroom climate that give *all* students a sense of being valued and accepted.
5. Help students master basic reading, writing, and computation skills by embedding them in a personally meaningful (that is, ethnically related) context.

Multicultural programs aim to promote respect for diversity, reduction of ethnocentrism and stereotypes, improved learning

BASIC APPROACHES AND CONCEPTS

Approaches James Banks (1994a, 1994c), a noted authority on multicultural education, describes four approaches to multicultural education. Most multicultural programs, particularly those in the primary grades, adopt what

Advocates of multicultural education believe that ethnic minority students learn more effectively when some of their learning materials and assignments contain ethnically related content.

he calls the *contributions approach*. Here, ethnic historical figures whose values and behaviors are consistent with American mainstream culture (for example, Booker T. Washington, Sacajawea) are studied, whereas individuals who have challenged the dominant view (such as W. E. B. DuBois, Geronimo) are ignored. A second approach, which incorporates the first, is called the *additive approach*. Here, an instructional unit composed of concepts, themes, points of view, and individual accomplishments is simply added to the curriculum. The perspective from which they are viewed, however, tends to be that of the mainstream.

Multicultural education can be approached in different ways

A third approach produces what Banks calls the *transformation approach*. Here, the assumption is that there is no one valid way of understanding people, events, concepts, and themes. Rather, there are multiple views, each of which has something of value to offer. For example, the view of the early pioneers who settled the American West could be summed up by such phrases as "How the West Was Won" and "The Westward Movement." But the Native American tribes who had lived there for thousands of years may well have referred to the same event as "How the West Was Taken" or "The Westward Plague." You may recognize that the transformation approach is based on the principle of constructivism (discussed in Chapters 1 and 2). Because this approach requires the concrete operational schemes described in Chapter 2, it is typically introduced at the middle school level. Finally, there is the *social action approach*. It incorporates all of the components of the previous approaches and adds the requirement that students make decisions and take actions concerning a concept, issue, or problem being studied.

Concepts Regardless of which approach you use, Banks (1994a) suggests that multicultural units and lessons be organized around a set of key concepts that incorporate a range of facts, generalizations, and subject-matter disciplines. These concepts can be used to analyze a particular ethnic group or to compare and contrast groups. The following set of key concepts and associated questions illustrates what Banks has in mind.

Multicultural lessons organized around key concepts

Identity: To what extent is the group aware of its ethnic identity, and how does the group express that identity?

Culture: What ethnic elements (for example, values, customs, perspectives) are present in the group's culture today? How is the group's culture reflected in its music, literature, and art?

Immigration: From what country or countries did this group originate? When and in what numbers did this group immigrate to the United States?

Ethnic community: To what extent are members of the group concentrated within particular geographic regions?

Racism and discrimination: In what ways has this group been subjected to racism and discrimination?

Communication: To what extent and why do members of the group encounter problems when communicating with other ethnic groups?

Self-concept: How have the group's societal experiences affected the self-concepts of its members?

Power: What is the group's social, political, and economic status? To what extent does the group exercise power within the community? Within the larger society?

Acculturation: To what extent has the group influenced and been influenced by the mainstream society?

For each key concept one would formulate a set of high-level,intermediate-level, and low-level generalizations; a set of cognitive and affective objectives (the nature of which will be described in Chapter 7); and a set of activities. Generalizations are summaries of facts that can be verified with empirical data. The difference among high-, intermediate-, and low-level generalizations is their range of applicability. Banks uses the concept of *social protest* by Mexican Americans to illustrate the different levels of generalization and an activity that might be used with each one.

Low-level generalization: Mexican-Americans have resisted Anglo discrimination since Anglo-Americans conquered and occupied the Southwest.

Activity: have students prepare an oral report that describes Chicano involvement in strikes and unions between 1900 and 1940.

Intermediate-level generalization: ethnic minorities have resisted discrimination in various ways throughout their time in the United States.

Activity: have students summarize and generalize how Mexican Americans have resisted Anglo discrimination in past and present American society.

High-level generalization: when individuals and groups are victims of discrimination, they tend to protest against their situation in various ways.

Activity: have students research the goals, tactics, and strategies used by various Mexican-American civil rights groups and write several generalizations about the activities of these groups.

CHARACTERISTICS OF EFFECTIVE TEACHERS

Although James Banks's ideas about how to structure multicultural education programs are well conceived, they require the efforts of effective teachers for their potential benefits to be realized. Eugene García (1994), on the basis of his own research and that of others, identifies several characteristics that contribute to the success some teachers have in teaching students from culturally diverse backgrounds. Briefly stated, the effective multicultural teacher:

1. Provides students with clear objectives.
2. Continuously communicates high expectations to the student.
3. Monitors student progress and provides immediate feedback.
4. Has several years experience in teaching culturally diverse students.
5. Can clearly explain why she uses specific instructional techniques (like the ones described in the next section).
6. Strives to embed instruction in a meaningful context. For example, a topic from one subject, such as controlling crop damaging insects with insecticide, would be extended to other subjects (examining the effects of insecticide on human health, graphing crop yields sprayed with various types and amounts of insecticides).
7. Provides opportunities for active learning through small-group work and hands-on activities. One teacher, for example, created writing workshops in which students wrote, revised, edited, and published their products for others to read.
8. Exhibits a high level of dedication. Effective multicultural teachers are among the first to arrive at school and among the last to leave, work weekends, buy supplies with their own money, and are constantly looking for opportunities to improve their instructional practices. If these characteristics sound familiar, it's because we discussed them in Chapter 1 as part of what makes teaching an art.
9. Enhances students' self-esteem by having classroom materials and practices reflect students' cultural and linguistic backgrounds.
10. Has a strong affinity for the students. Effective multicultural teachers describe their culturally diverse students in such terms as "I love these children like my own" and "We are a family here."

INSTRUCTIONAL TACTICS

The three instructional tactics that are recommended most often by proponents of multicultural education are peer tutoring, cooperative learning, and mastery learning. While each of these techniques can be used with any group of students and for most any purpose, they are particularly well suited to the goals of multicultural education.

Peer Tutoring As its name implies, **peer tutoring** involves the teaching of one student by another. The students may be similar in age or separated by one or more years. (The latter arrangement is usually referred to as cross-age tutoring.) The theoretical basis of peer tutoring comes from Jean Piaget's no-

Students from different cultural backgrounds who learn in small cooperative groups are more likely to make friends with one another than are culturally different students who do not interact with one another.

tions about cognitive development. Recall from our discussion of Piaget in Chapter 2 that cognitive growth depends on the presence of a disequilibrating stimulus that the learner is motivated to eliminate. When children with different cognitive schemes (because of differences in age, knowledge, or cultural background) are forced to interact with each other, cognitive conflict results. Growth occurs when children try to resolve this conflict (through assimilation and accommodation) by comparing and contrasting each other's views. The presumed benefits of peer tutoring include improved communication skills, an increased awareness of the perspectives of others, an increased ability to analyze ideas and provide feedback to others, higher levels of achievement, and a more positive attitude toward the subject being studied (Foot, Shute, & Morgan, 1990). This technique—as well as the one we will discuss next, cooperative learning—is effective for many different students, but especially Hispanic-American and Native American children, whose cultural backgrounds place a high value on cooperation and mentoring (Sadker & Sadker, 1991).

An early review of peer tutoring research (Cohen, Kulik, & Kulik, 1982) found that tutored students outscored nontutored students on classroom examinations by a fairly substantial margin in forty-five of fifty-two studies. The average student who was tutored scored at the 66th percentile, whereas the average nontutored student scored at the 50th percentile. Tutored students also demonstrated more positive attitudes toward the subject matter than nontutored students did. While the students who provided the tutoring did not benefit quite as much as the students who received it, they still scored higher on classroom tests than their nontutoring peers did.

Peer tutoring improves achievement, interpersonal relationships, attitudes toward subjects

Strong support for peer tutoring has been provided by subsequent studies involving a variety of students and yielding many different outcomes. In particular, peer tutoring has been shown to increase the arithmetic skills of low-achieving elementary school students from low-socioeconomic backgrounds (Fantuzzo, Polite, & Grayson, 1990); the self-esteem and achievement of students with learning disabilities (Beirne-Smith, 1991; Byrd, 1990); and the arithmetic accuracy, self-concept, attitude toward mathematics, and social interactions between tutor and tutee of students with behavioral disorders (Franca, Kerr, Reitz, & Lambert, 1990). Two conditions seem to account for the success of peer tutoring. One is the presence of an explicit set of guidelines that informs the tutor and tutee of their respective roles and responsibilities. The other is the holding of the tutor accountable for the performance of the tutee (Fantuzzo, Riggio, Connelly, & Dimeff, 1989).

Cooperative learning: students work together in small groups

Cooperative Learning Closely related to peer tutoring is cooperative learning. The general idea behind **cooperative learning** is that by working in small heterogeneous groups (of four or five students total) and by helping one another master the various aspects of a particular task, students will be more motivated to learn, will learn more than if they had to work independently, and will forge stronger interpersonal relationships than they would by working alone.

There are several forms of cooperative learning, one of which is Student Team Learning. Student Team Learning techniques are built on the concepts of team reward, individual accountability, and equal opportunities for success. *Team reward* means that teams are not in competition with one another for limited rewards. All of the teams, some of them, or none of them may earn whatever rewards are made available depending on how well the team's performance matches a predetermined standard. *Individual accountability* means that each member of the team must perform at a certain level (on a quiz, for example) for the team's effort to be judged successful. It is not permissible for one team member's above-average performance to compensate for another team member's below-average performance. Finally, *equal opportunities for success* allow students of all ability levels to contribute to their team's success by improving on their own past performances (Slavin, 1995).

Robert Slavin (1995), a leading exponent of cooperative learning, reports that cooperative learning produced significantly higher levels of achievement than did noncooperative arrangements in sixty-three of ninety-nine studies (64 percent). The results for the Student Team Learning programs have been the most consistently positive. Of particular relevance to this chapter are the findings that students who cooperate in learning are more apt to list as friends peers from different ethnic groups and are better able to take the perspective of a classmate than are students who do not work in cooperative groups.

Cooperative learning fosters better understanding among ethnically diverse students

Although cooperative learning is a generally effective instructional tactic, it is likely to be particularly useful with Hispanic-American and Native American students. Children from both cultures often come from extended families that emphasize cooperation and sharing. Thus, these students may be more prepared than other individuals to work productively as part of a group by carrying out their own responsibilities as well as helping others do the same (Sadker & Sadker, 1991; Soldier, 1989). We will have more to say about cooperative learning and its effects on motivation in Chapter 11.

Mastery Learning The third instructional tactic, **mastery learning,** is an approach to teaching and learning that assumes most students can master the curriculum if certain conditions are established. These conditions are that students (a) have sufficient aptitude to learn a particular task, (b) have sufficient ability to understand instruction, (c) are willing to persevere until they attain a certain level of mastery, (d) are allowed whatever time is necessary to attain mastery, and (e) are provided with good-quality instruction.

Mastery learning: all students can master the curriculum

Mastery learning proponents assume that all of these conditions can be created if they are not already present. Aptitude, for example, is seen as being partly determined by how well prerequisite knowledge and skills have been learned. And perseverance can be strengthened by the deft use of creative teaching methods and various forms of reward for successful performance. The basic mastery learning approach is to clearly specify what is to be learned, organize the content into a sequence of relatively short units, use a variety of instructional methods and materials, allow students to progress through the material at their own rate, monitor student progress in order to identify budding problems and provide corrective feedback, and allow students to relearn and retest on each unit until mastery is attained (Block, Efthim, & Burns, 1989). We will describe mastery learning in more detail in Chapter 12.

Like the research on peer tutoring and cooperative learning, the research on mastery learning has generally been positive. On the basis of a comprehensive review of this literature, Chen-Lin Kulik, James Kulik, and Robert Bangert-Drowns (1990) conclude that mastery learning programs produce moderately strong effects on achievement. The average student in a mastery learning class scored at the 70th percentile on a classroom examination, whereas the average student in a conventional class scored at the 50th percentile. The positive effect of mastery learning was slightly more pronounced for lower-ability students. As compared to students in conventional classes, those in mastery classes had more positive feelings about the subjects they studied and the way in which they were taught.

A RATIONALE FOR MULTICULTURAL EDUCATION

Some people seem to believe that multicultural education programs represent a rejection of basic American values and that this opposition to traditional values is the only rationale behind such programs. We feel this belief is mistaken on both counts. We see multicultural programs as being consistent with basic American values (such as tolerance of differences and equality of opportunity) and consider them to be justified in several ways.

One argument in favor of multicultural programs is that they foster teaching practices that are effective in general as well as for members of a particular group. For example, expressing an interest in a student through occasional touching and smiling and allowing the child to tutor a younger student are practices likely to benefit most students, not just those of Hispanic-American origin.

A second argument in favor of multicultural education is that all students may profit from understanding different cultural values. For example, the respect for elders that characterizes Native American and Asian-American

C A S E   I N   P R I N T

Confronting Multicultural Misunderstanding

A third argument in support of multicultural education programs is that the United States is becoming an increasingly multicultural society . . . and students thus need to understand and know how to work with people of cultures different from their own. (p. 144)

"Students Embrace Chance to Talk Out Frustrations"

PHILIP DINE

St. Louis Post-Dispatch 5/21/95

A lanky 15-year-old with a quick smile, Phuc Chau does not look like a youngster ready to fight. But after five years of school in St. Louis, fighting ranks high among skills he's learned—and now hopes to unlearn.

"Kids don't like us, don't like us Asians. White kids, black kids. I don't like kids calling me names, so I fight," he says, that smile never straying far from his lips.

Phuc, an eighth-grader at International Studies Middle school, says insults hurled at him or his 15 Vietnamese school buddies "make me very angry."

At least once a month, he says, two or three students approach him with hostile intentions.

They make fun of the way I talk or play with my friends," he says. "They call me 'Ching,' or they say 'Chung, chung, chung, bung, bung, bung.'" Things weren't too bad when he started in third grade at Hamilton Elementary, probably because the children were small, he says. But by sixth grade he found himself engaging in fisticuffs. In recent years, it seems, his temper has flashed as frequently as his smile. But that will stop, he abruptly lets on, fixing his black eyes on his listener. No more fighting, no more trouble.

"I know how to think," he confides. "I got to worry about my education."

And what brought this on?

A girlfriend, "kind of smart," who's given him a new perspective.

Phuc is one of a dozen youngsters gathered this particular day at an informal discussion group called "safehaven," held Friday afternoons in the basement of St. Pius V Church in south St. Louis. Ron Klutho, who teaches foreign students in area schools and started the sessions three years ago, worried that some kept their struggles bottled up when the school day ended.

Many left lands of devastating poverty or smoldering ethnic hatred. Yet what stands out are their descriptions of the chaos and wildness they find in American society and in the schools that have served as agents for assimilation for generations of immigrants.

Several praise their teachers but wonder about their schoolmates.

The Da Silva brothers, Claudio, 18, of Roosevelt High School, and Joao, 15, of Soldan High, grab chairs and want to talk.

Five years ago the brothers emigrated here from Angola with their parents, brother and three sisters after stops in Namibia and Botswana. Their father, a former educator fluent in six languages, works in a factory making cleaning products.

This country, the brothers assert, is full of opportunity. But they can't understand the way young people act, clowning around when the teacher is talking or taunting foreign students for supposedly getting government handouts.

Joao says that jabs about whether he lived in a hut or ever wrestled a lion stem from insecurity or ignorance. So he ignores them.

He has an engaging smile, is confident yet unassuming, and his rapid, nearly accentless English is spiced with "Hey oh" and "Check this out." It's easy to picture him in his drama class. Yet, he says, most of his friends are foreign classmates, who accept him more readily than do Americans.

"Vietnamese kids do good in school, in math for instance," Joao says. "Sometimes American kids become jealous. They say, 'Hey, you cheated.' They try to excuse themselves, instead of facing the fact that, hey, they don't study."

Another African student in the city's schools, a fourth-grader named John, joins the conversation.

The United States "is a good country," he says. "They have everything you need to live. Back home, school doesn't have so much. But they don't make fun of you. Everybody learns."

"Here, white people make fun of black people, black people make fun of white people. You get mad, say something out loud, you get in trouble."

The Da Silva brothers nod. Not a day goes by without the brothers thinking of the people dying back home from war and poverty—and hoping for the time their education will be finished so they can go back and make a difference.

That makes it all the harder, they say, to understand why people who have choices fight so much.

"This could be a great place," Claudio says.

Questions and Activities

1. In this article there are both indications of hope and indications of hopelessness in terms of young people's attitudes toward different races and cultures and how it might be possible to change these attitudes. Identify two positive and two negative aspects. Consider how your role as a teacher might come into play vis-à-vis these aspects. How might your role be different if you were an elementary school teacher, a middle school teacher, or a high school teacher?

2. Imagine that you had some of these students—both the foreign students and the American students they describe—in your class. Do you think the instructional tactics you have learned about in this chapter could be used to try to alter the non-minority students' negative behavior and attitudes as well as offer effective instruction to the minority students? Which ones might be most effective and why? Can you think of other tactics or methods that you would like to try?

3. As a future teacher, what important lesson do you draw from the fact that a "safehaven" environment for airing feelings that get "bottled up" has proved helpful for these students? Name some specific ways in which you might put this knowledge to use inside and outside your classroom.

4. In a related article, the reporter states that until a recent and ongoing influx of immigrants and refugees, St. Louis was a "decidedly monoglot area." In other words, the population was fairly homogeneous, and students were not exposed to different cultural groups. Although this certainly does not excuse negative and stereotyping behavior, it might help explain it. If you become a teacher in a homogeneous and non-culturally diverse district, how might you work toward building tolerance and dispelling cultural ignorance? Describe several ways in which you could put to use the tactics and approaches in this chapter to increase multicultural awareness in such a situation.

cultures is likely to become increasingly desirable as the percentage of elderly Americans increases over the years. Similarly, learning the Native American value of living in harmony with nature may come to be essential as we run out of natural resources and attempt to alleviate environmental pollution (Triandis, 1986).

A third argument in support of multicultural education programs is that the United States is becoming an increasingly multicultural society (because of the immigration and birthrate trends mentioned earlier) and students thus need to understand and know how to work with people of cultures different from their own. (See Case in Print, pages 142–143, for a discussion of how prevalent behavior based on stereotypes still is and how it can be confronted.)

A fourth argument for multicultural education programs is that they expose students to the idea that "truth" is very much in the eye of the beholder. From a European perspective, Christopher Columbus did indeed discover a new world. But from the perspective of the Arawak Indians who were native to the Caribbean, Columbus invaded territories that they had occupied for thousands of years. Similarly, one can describe the history of the United States as one in which continual progress toward democratic ideals has been made or as one in which progress has been interrupted by conflict, struggle, violence, and exclusion (Banks, 1993).

And last but not least, multicultural programs can encourage student motivation and learning. These programs demonstrate respect for a child's culture and teach about the contributions that the student's group has made to American society. Proponents argue that these features both personalize education and make it more meaningful. Conversely, when children perceive disrespect for their cultural background, the result can be disastrous. Consider the following comment by a New York City student:

> I came upon a world unknown to me, a language I did not understand, and a school administration which made ugly faces at me every time I spoke Spanish. Many teachers referred to us as animals. Believe me, maintaining a half-decent image of yourself wasn't an easy thing. . . . I had enough strength of character to withstand the many school personnel who tried to destroy my motivation. But many of my classmates didn't make it. (First, 1988, p. 210)

Statistical evidence of the need for multicultural programs can be seen in the disappointing academic performance of a significant number of minority-group students. Compared to white high school sophomores and seniors, African-American, Hispanic-American, and Native American students score lower on standardized tests of vocabulary, reading, writing, mathematics, and science (Levine & Havighurst, 1992). These differences appear early. Recent results from the National Assessment of Educational Progress reveal that the reading and writing skills of African-American and Hispanic-American children are substantially below those of white children as early as third grade (Pallas, Natriello, & McDill, 1989).

Given these achievement differences, it should come as no surprise that there are parallel differences in school dropout rates. Whereas 8.9 percent of whites drop out of school before graduation, 13.6 percent of African Americans, 35.3 percent of Hispanic Americans, and 44.5 percent of Native Americans do so (Bennett, 1995). Investigations into the reasons for which minority students leave school prematurely have found that individual factors, school environment factors, social-class factors, and economic factors may all play a role. Compared to white students who stay in school, minority dropouts have lower levels of motivation, lower self-esteem, and weaker academic skills; they are also more impulsive. In addition, dropouts nearly always report a sense of alienation from school because of low teacher expectations, expressions of racial or ethnic group prejudice from teachers and students, and unfair discrimination. Students required to repeat grades (recall our discussion of this topic in Chapter 1) are among the most likely to drop out of school.

Minority children score lower on tests, drop out of school sooner

Minority dropout rate due to alienation, differences in values, poverty

Differences in social-class values can also contribute to low levels of achievement and a subsequent early exit from school. Two middle-class values, order and discipline, fit nicely with the expectations and activities of schools. In contrast, values typically held by low-SES groups—such as avoiding trouble with authorities, developing physical prowess, and establishing independence from external control—are not likely to be as productive in achieving school success (Tidwell, 1989).

Finally, minority students who do poorly in school and leave early typically come from the poorest households. In 1988 the poverty rate for white children was 14.1 percent, whereas 37.6 percent of Hispanic-American children and 43.5 percent of African-American children were living in poverty (Sleeter & Grant, 1994). Multicultural theorists believe that the inclusion of ethnically related content and activities in the curriculum will make classroom assignments more meaningful and will help minority students master basic reading, writing, computational, and reasoning skills (Banks, 1994a; Vasquez, 1990).

Trends toward ethnic awareness mean that you may find yourself teaching in a system that has authorized some form of multicultural education. If the program is well established, you should be given instructions about how to work cultural and ethnic studies into the curriculum. Be aware, however, that people in some areas hold strong feelings against bilingual and multicultural education. If a formal program is absent and you want to incorporate some multicultural activities on your own, it would be wise to find out about prevailing attitudes in your school district first. If you discover that you have the green light in your school, you might institute a limited program intended to make students more familiar with the cultural backgrounds of their classmates. This limited approach is recommended by some experts. Nicholas Appleton (1983) and James Banks (Brandt, 1994), for example, feel that multicultural education should be seen as a long-term process that will produce gradual awareness rather than rapid, dramatic changes in students' perceptions and behaviors. Accordingly, they see nothing wrong with teachers starting off by supplementing their existing curriculum with small multicultural units. The following Suggestions for Teaching should help you get started.

Suggestions for Teaching in Your Classroom

Promoting Multicultural Understanding and Classroom Achievement

1. Use every possible means for motivating educationally disadvantaged students to do well in school.
2. Use a variety of instructional techniques to help educationally disadvantaged students master both basic and higher-order knowledge and skills.
3. Be alert to the potential dangers of labeling. Concentrate on individuals while guarding against the impact of stereotyping.
   a. Remember that in addition to being a skilled teacher, you are also a human being who may at times react subjectively to students.
   b. Take systematic steps to ensure that you treat all student equitably, regardless of their backgrounds.
   c. Use information about students' backgrounds to help them become more effective students.
4. Help make students aware of the contributions that specific ethnic groups have made to the development of the United States and the world.
5. Assign projects and activities that allow students to demonstrate culture-specific knowledge and skills and that encourage students to learn from and about each other's cultures.
6. Encourage students to identify with representatives of their ethnic group who have achieved success.
7. At the secondary level, involve students in activities that explore cultural differences in perceptions, beliefs, and values.

1. Use every possible means for motivating educationally disadvantaged students to do well in school.

Perhaps the major reason many educationally disadvantaged students do poorly in school is not lack of ability but lack of interest in learning. As the account of Marc Elrich (1994), the sixth-grade teacher whose experiences we summarized earlier, makes clear, a number of circumstances may conspire to prevent such students from acquiring a desire to do well in school: lack of encouragement from parents, the absence of role models in the form of parents and siblings who have benefited from schooling, a level of aspiration set low to avoid possible failure, and lack of success leading to a low need for achievement. One of the major tasks facing the teacher of educationally disadvantaged students is to arouse and sustain interest in learning. Techniques for doing so will be described in detail in Chapter 11.

2. Use a variety of instructional techniques to help educationally disadvantaged students master both basic and higher-order knowledge and skills.

Research from the 1970s (e.g., Brophy & Evertson, 1976) found that the classroom and standardized test performance of educationally disadvantaged students improves when teachers

- Eliminate distractions and maximize the amount of time students actually spend working on a task

- Determine what and how quickly subject matter is learned
- Establish high expectations and a classroom climate that supports achievement
- Break tasks down into small, easy-to-manage pieces and arrange the pieces in a logical sequence
- Have students work on specific exercises in small groups
- Ask direct questions that have direct answers
- Provide frequent opportunities for practice and review
- Provide timely corrective feedback

Designing classroom instruction along these guidelines has both benefits and costs. The benefits are that students spend more time on-task, success tends to be more consistent, and more students reach a higher level of mastery of content knowledge and skills. The main cost is the lack of transfer that usually occurs when knowledge and skills are learned as isolated segments in a nonmeaningful context. A second cost is that students have few opportunities to interact with each other (the benefits of which were mentioned in Chapter 2 and will be further described in Chapters 10 and 11).

Journal Entry
Using Productive Techniques of Teaching

If teachers combine the eight guidelines just mentioned with current learning theory and research (see, for example, Knapp & Shields, 1990; Knapp, Shields, & Turnbull, 1995; Means & Knapp, 1991; Natriello, McDill, & Pallas, 1990; as well as Chapters 9 and 10 of this book), they may be able to raise the basic skill level of educationally disadvantaged students *and* improve their ability to transfer what they have learned to meaningful and realistic contexts. To accomplish this goal, a teacher should also

- Provide opportunities for students to apply ideas and skills to real-life or realistic situations in order to make the lesson more meaningful. For example, students might, after collecting and analyzing information, write letters to the mayor and/or city council requesting more streetlights for increased safety at night or improvements to basketball courts and baseball fields.
- Allow students the opportunity to discuss among themselves the meaning of ideas and their potential applications. In making a request of a government official, students should be encouraged to discuss which arguments are likely to be most effective and how they would respond should the official turn their proposal down.
- Embed basic skills instruction within the context of complex and realistic tasks. Letter writing campaigns, for example, can be used to practice such basic English skills as vocabulary acquisition, spelling, punctuation, and grammar. Science projects can be used to practice a variety of mathematics skills.
- Point out how classroom tasks relate to students' out-of-school experiences. One example is to draw attention to the basic similarities between poetry and rap, a form of song common to many African-American students.
- Model for and explain to students the various thinking processes that are activated and used when one engages a complex task. As you will see when you read Chapter 9, effective learners approach tasks

strategically, which is to say they analyze the task, formulate a plan for dealing with it, use a variety of specific learning skills, and monitor their progress. These are fundamental learning processes that are almost never made explicit to students.

- Gradually ease students into the process of dealing with complex and realistic tasks. There is no question that the approach described in points (a)–(e) carries with it more risk for failure than was the case for the structured, small-scale approach of the 1970s. But much of this risk can be minimized by a technique called *scaffolding*. As its name suggests, the teacher initially provides a considerable amount of support through explanations, demonstrations, and prompts of various types. As students demonstrate their ability to carry out more of a task independently, the scaffolding is withdrawn.

3. Be alert to the potential dangers of labeling. Concentrate on individuals while guarding against the impact of stereotyping.

Although the practice of labeling students is often necessary in order to provide them with helpful specialized services (as you will see in Chapter 6), it can also serve as the basis for unfair treatment. The negative impact of labels can be minimized, however, if you use them to help students become more effective learners. Instead of thinking that an educationally disadvantaged student is beyond help, for example, you might ask yourself, "What kinds of disadvantages does this student need to overcome?" and "What kinds of strengths—or *advantages*—does this student have?" By asking these questions, you concentrate on *individuals,* which is the surest way to avoid succumbing to the perils of stereotyping.

a. Remember that in addition to being a skilled teacher, you are also a human being who may at times react subjectively to students.

Journal Entry
Ways to Minimize Subjectivity

Try to control the influence of such factors as name, ethnic background, sex, physical characteristics, knowledge of siblings or parents, grades, and test scores. If you think you can be honest with yourself, you might attempt to describe your prejudices so that you will be in a position to guard against them. (Do you tend to be annoyed when you read descriptions of the exploits of members of a particular religious or ethnic group, for example?) Try to think of a student independently of her siblings and parents.

b. Take systematic steps to ensure that you treat all students equitably, regardless of their backgrounds.

One way to be fair and consistent in the way you interact with students is to keep a Question and Recitation Record. By periodically referring to this record, you will know whether you are calling on all students about the same number of times. Strive to be consistently positive and enthusiastic when asking questions or responding to answers. Don't hesitate or introduce vocal inflections when calling on less capable students. Such public signs of hesitation or lack of confidence may be communicated to the student and contribute to a negative expectancy effect. Refer to Table 11.1, page 429, to make your praise effective.

Another technique you might use is a Positive Reinforcement Record in an effort to say favorable things about the work of all students. If after keeping such a record for two weeks, you discover that you have not said a single positive thing to one or more individuals, make it a point to praise them at least as regularly as you do others.

c. **Use information about students' backgrounds to help them become more effective students.**

If you become aware of students' previous low grades or are presented with low test scores, give individuals identified as poor learners the benefit of the doubt. Use the information to try to help low-scoring students improve their classroom performance, and keep in mind that many factors (such as anxiety, differences in cultural values about the importance of tests, and misunderstanding of instructions) may artificially lower test scores.

4. **Help make students aware of the contributions that specific ethnic groups have made to the development of the United States and the world.**

Journal Entry
Ways to Promote Awareness of Contributions of Ethnic Minorities

The first principle suggested by Nicholas Appleton (1983) for implementing a multicultural education program is that each student should examine his own ethnic background before examining the backgrounds of others. Appleton's rationale is that racism in the United States has had a negative impact on the self-concepts of ethnic minority children. Since self-concept is related to achievement, it is important to help students develop positive attitudes about their ethnic heritage. One suggestion for accomplishing this goal is to invite family members of students (and other local residents) of different ethnic backgrounds to the classroom. Ask them to describe the values subscribed to by members of their group and to explain how those values have contributed to life in the United States and to the world in general.

5. **Assign projects and activities that allow students to demonstrate culture-specific knowledge and skills and that encourage students to learn from and about each other's cultures.**

You might encourage students from similar ethnic and religious backgrounds to get together at designated periods and prepare presentations for the rest of the class. Ask them to illustrate and explain the art, music, beliefs, and ceremonies of their particular group. On special holidays honored by different groups, the entire class can take part in the celebration, perhaps including the preparation of appropriate decorations and food.

Another opportunity for cultural interaction is provided by the global Internet. For example, a database maintained by St. Olaf College in Minneapolis, Minnesota, is dedicated to matching students with intercultural pen pals. Such exchanges among students can promote shared cultural knowledge and understanding, especially in schools whose populations are relatively homogeneous. The Intercultural Pen Pal server is located at http://www.stolaf.edu/network/iecc/.

6. **Encourage students to identify with representatives of their ethnic group who have achieved success.**

Erikson has called attention to the role confusion experienced by many minority-group Americans. He has also concluded that one of the most important factors leading to a sense of identity is occupational choice. You might help minority-group students avoid role confusion and develop a sense of identity by acquainting them with the accomplishments of eminent and successful people who share their ethnic background. Models might practice in the professions, business, education, or the arts. Identifying with prominent people can help youngsters develop a sense of their group's identity as successful Americans. Once that identity is achieved, individuals can freely cherish the language and culture of their heritage without risking role confusion.

7. **At the secondary level, involve students in activities that explore cultural differences in perceptions, beliefs, and values.**

A well-conceived multicultural education program cannot, and should not, avoid or minimize the issue of cultural conflict. There are at least two reasons for helping students examine this issue. One is that conflict has been a constant and salient aspect of relationships among cultural groups. Another is that cultural conflicts often produce changes that benefit all members of a society (a prime example being the civil rights boycotts, marches, and demonstrations of the 1960s).

Cultural conflicts arise from differences in perceptions, beliefs, and values. American culture, for example, places great value on self-reliance. Americans generally respect and praise individuals who, through their own initiative, persistence, and ingenuity, achieve substantial personal goals; and they tend to look down on individuals who are dependent on others for their welfare. Consequently, American parents who are financially dependent on their children, even though the children may be prosperous enough to support them, would probably feel ashamed enough to hide the fact. The same situation in China would likely elicit a different reaction because of different values about self-reliance and family responsibilities. Chinese parents who are unable to provide for themselves in their old age but have children successful enough to support them might well brag about it to others (Appleton, 1983).

One technique for exploring cultural conflict is to have students search through newspapers and news magazines for articles that describe clashes. Ask them to identify the source of the conflict and how it might be positively resolved. Another technique is to involve students in games that simulate group conflict. Class members can, for example, play the role of city council members who represent the interests of diverse ethnic groups and who have been ordered by the federal government to integrate their school system (Appleton, 1983). Both the use of simulations and the discussion of newspaper articles will probably work best at the high school level because adolescents are better able than younger students to understand the abstract concepts involved in these activities.

Journal Entry
Ways to Help Students Explore Conflicts Between Cultures

Bilingual Education

As we mentioned earlier, almost one million legal immigrants a year for the ten-year period from 1981 through 1990 were estimated to have arrived in the United States. Not surprisingly, many of the school-age children of these families have either limited or no English proficiency. To address this need, the federal government provides financial support for the establishment of bilingual education programs. Because language is viewed as an important part of a group's culture, many school districts integrate bilingual education with multicultural education. In this section we will examine the nature and effectiveness of bilingual education programs.

Before we consider different approaches to bilingual education, there are three general points we would like you to keep in mind. First, bilingual programs have become an emotionally charged and politicized topic. Educators, parents, and legislators have strong opinions regarding what time and resources should be devoted to helping students master native-language skills and whether such programs should include cultural awareness goals. Some individuals favor moving students into all-English classes as quickly as possible; others believe that students should have a firm grasp of their native language *and* English before attempting to make the transition to regular classes. While research on this issue is helpful because it informs us about what *is,* such research cannot tell us what we *should do* about what we know. Second, some language-minority students may suffer from problems that bilingual education alone cannot solve. If (as noted earlier) parents do not model the types of behaviors valued by schools or encourage their children to exhibit such behaviors, learning difficulties often result. Finally, no one approach to bilingual education is likely to be equally effective for all language-minority students. What works well for some low-SES Puerto Rican children may not work well for middle-class Cuban children and vice versa.

HISTORICAL DEVELOPMENTS

In the introduction to this chapter we described a turn-of-the-century view of the United States as a great melting pot. Immigrants were expected to leave behind their old allegiances, languages, customs, and views and adopt English as their primary language as well as American values and ideals. To help immigrant schoolchildren make this linguistic and cultural transition as quickly as possible, many communities established bilingual schools. After World War I, however, public financing of bilingual schools was abruptly withdrawn, partly because of increasing nationalism and isolationism. Foreign languages were classified as electives to be studied in a superficial way only by students preparing for college. Most students were given intensive instruction only in English (Bennett, 1995).

This situation remained essentially unchanged until 1965. In that year Congress provided funds for the creation of bilingual education programs for low-SES students with limited English skills through Title VII of the Elementary and Secondary Education Act. Additional funds were authorized in

1968 with the passage of the Bilingual Education Act. The impetus for providing bilingual education programs to a wider audience came from the U.S. Supreme Court in 1974 in the case of *Lau* v. *Nicholls*. The Court ruled that *all* non- and limited-English-speaking children were entitled to some sort of appropriate language instruction in order to preserve their constitutional right to equal educational opportunities. In the same year Congress revised the Bilingual Education Act, creating a greater range of programs for a larger number of children. Since 1974 the federal government has provided hundreds of millions of dollars to states and local school districts in support of programs aimed at improving English language proficiency. The federal government currently sponsors bilingual programs for more than seventy Asian, Indo-European, and Native American languages, with Hispanic Americans being the single largest group served (Gollnick & Chinn, 1994; Levine & Havighurst, 1992; Scarcella, 1990).

GOALS AND APPROACHES

Most bilingual education programs have a common long-term goal but differ in their approach to that goal. The goal is to help minority-language students acquire as efficiently as possible the English skills they will need to succeed in school and society. The approaches to that goal fall into one of two categories: *transition* or *maintenance*.

Two main approaches to bilingual education: transition, maintenance

Programs that have a transition approach teach students wholly (in the case of non-English-proficient students) or partly (in the case of limited-English-proficient students) in their native language so as not to retard their academic progress, but only until they can function adequately in English. At that point they are placed in regular classes, where all of the instruction is in English. To make the transition time as brief as possible, some programs add an ESL (English as a second language) component. Supporters of this ap-

Transition programs focus on rapid shift to English proficiency

Some bilingual education programs emphasize using the student's native language competence to help the student learn English as quickly as possible. Other programs emphasize the maintenance or improvement of both the student's native language and English.

proach point out that much of what occurs in classrooms takes the form of verbal directions, descriptions, and explanations; question-and-answer sessions; and references to abstract ideas. The ability to speak a common language allows individuals to feel part of a larger group. Most current programs are transitional in nature, possibly because this was the goal espoused by such early legislation as the Bilingual Education Act of 1968 (Bowman, 1989; Hakuta & Garcia, 1989).

Maintenance programs focus on maintaining native-language competence

Programs that have a maintenance approach try to maintain or improve the students' native-language skills prior to instruction in English. Supporters of maintenance programs point to the results of psychological and linguistic studies that suggest that a strong native-language foundation supports the subsequent learning of both English and subject-matter knowledge. In addition, many proponents of multicultural education favor a maintenance approach because they see language as an important part of a group's cultural heritage (Hakuta & Garcia, 1989; Hakuta & Gould, 1987).

In addition to programs whose goal is exclusively or predominantly English acquisition, there are programs that combine cultural awareness goals with language acquisition goals and that are directed at a wider audience. Daniel Levine and Robert Havighurst (1992) describe a five-part classification scheme proposed by Josué Gonzalez, a former director of the U.S. Office of Bilingual Education, that encompasses all of these programs. The five types are as follows:

1. *Transitional bilingual:* students are taught wholly or partly in their native language only until they can function adequately in English.
2. *Bilingual maintenance:* teachers help students become fluent in English and maintain or improve their native-language skills.
3. *Bilingual/bicultural maintenance:* teachers help students become fluent both in English and their native language, and teach students about their cultural background.
4. *Bilingual/bicultural restorationist:* students are helped to become fluent in English and in a native language that has been lost through assimilation. Aspects of the students' lost culture are taught as well.
5. *Bilingual/bicultural culturally pluralistic:* all students in the program, regardless of their ethnic and linguistic backgrounds, learn to function in two languages and to appreciate one another's cultural background.

TEACHING METHODS

Robin Scarcella (1990) describes three methods of bilingual instruction that are currently in use. The preferred method is the three-part *Preview/Review* technique. The teacher summarizes the main points of the lesson in the students' primary language, presents the lesson in English, and then concludes with a review of the main points in the students' primary language. An alternative but less frequently used method is the *Alternate Language Method.* A lesson is presented in the students' native language one day and is repeated in English the next day. A third technique that is used but is considered less effective than either of the first two is the *Concurrent Method.* Small amounts of a lesson are given in the primary language, followed immediately by a translation. The problem with this method is that students tend to pay attention only to those portions of the lesson that are spoken in their native language.

RESEARCH FINDINGS

In comparison to immersion (English-only) programs, how successful have bilingual education programs been in helping non-English-speaking students learn English and other subjects? After analyzing twenty-three studies, Anne Willig (1985) concludes that participation in bilingual education programs produced small to moderate gains on tests of reading, language skills, mathematics, and total achievement when measured by tests in English. When measured by tests administered in the student's native language, however, participation in bilingual education led to significantly better performance on tests of listening comprehension, reading, writing, total language, mathematics, social studies, and attitudes toward school and self.

Bilingual education programs produce moderate learning gains

ESL programs appear to have a generally positive effect on a variety of reading comprehension skills. After reviewing sixty-seven studies, Jill Fitzgerald (1995) concludes that ESL students recognized cognate vocabulary (related words) fairly well (there was a wide range of proficiency for this outcome), demonstrated the ability to monitor their comprehension, and used prior knowledge to help them understand and remember what they read.

Resources for Further Investigation

Multicultural Education: Theory and Practice

James Banks offers a brief (seven chapters, 121 pages) introduction to multicultural education in *An Introduction to Multicultural Education* (1994a). A more detailed discussion can be found in his *Teaching Strategies for Ethnic Studies* (5th ed., 1991). Part 1 discusses goals for multicultural programs, key concepts, and planning a multicultural curriculum. Parts 2 through 5 provide background information about twelve ethnic groups and strategies for teaching about each group. Part 6 provides an example of a multicultural unit and an evaluation strategy. The book concludes with such useful appendices as a list of videotapes and films on U.S. ethnic groups, a bibliography of books about women of color, and a chronology of key events concerning ethnic groups in U.S. history.

Another practical book is *Comprehensive Multicultural Education: Theory and Practice* (3d ed., 1995), by Christine Bennett. Part 1 of this book (Chapters 1 to 3) presents the case for multicultural education. Part 2 (Chapters 4 to 6) describes culturally based individual differences that affect teaching and learning. Part 3 (Chapters 7 and 8) presents a model for multicultural education, guidelines for instruction, and a set of twenty-two illustrative lessons. The lessons include statements of goals and objectives, a description of the instructional sequence, a list of needed materials, and a means for evaluating how well the objectives were met.

Cultural Diversity in Schools: From Rhetoric to Practice (1994), edited by Robert DeVillars, Christian Faltis, and James Cummins, contains chapters on the use of cooperative learning in culturally diverse classrooms, the promotion of positive cross-cultural attitudes, the management of behavior in the culturally diverse classroom, and the use of computer technology in culturally diverse and bilingual classrooms.

A large number of multicultural resources are available on the Internet. Several good starting points include:

Multicultural Internet Sites:

http://www.qualcomm.com/users/gnash/mcult.html

Intercultural Pen Pals:

http://www.stolaf.edu/network/iecc

The TIME Project (Telecommunications in Multicultural Education):

http://www.cgrg.ohio-state.edu/~scott/timaeusl.html

Ethnic Minority Groups

American Indian Leaders: Studies in Diversity (1980), edited by R. David Edmunds, contains chapters on twelve Native American leaders from the mid-1700s to the present. For information about how to obtain books, films, and reports about African Americans, Asian Americans, Hispanic Americans, and Native Americans, consult *Guide to Multicultural Resources* (1989), edited by Charles Taylor. *Sourcebook of Hispanic Culture in the United States* (1982), edited by David Foster, contains several chapters on the history, anthropology, sociology, literature, and art of Hispanic-American groups living in the United States. Angela Carrasquillo provides a comprehensive discussion of Hispanic-American children and youths in the United States in *Hispanic Children and Youth in the United States: A Resource Guide* (1991). Chapter 12 contains the names and addresses as well as brief descriptions of fifteen Hispanic-American advocacy groups. For information about various aspects of development among African-American adolescents, see *Black Adolescence: Current Issues and Annotated Bibliography* (1990), by the Consortium for Research on Black Adolescence.

An Internet search using the names of particular cultural groups or names of individuals may be the best way to find specific resources on-line.

Bilingual Education

Deborah Sauvé provides a compilation of computer-assisted instruction programs in bilingual education, ESL, and second-language instructional settings in *Guide to Microcomputer Courseware for Bilingual Education* (revised and expanded, 1985). Each entry provides the name of the program; the producer's name, address, and telephone number; the type of computer needed; the type of instructional techniques used; the content area; the grade level or proficiency level of the program; and a brief abstract.

Judith Lessow-Hurley offers a brief (69 pages), readable overview and introduction to bilingual education in *A Commonsense Guide to Bilingual Education* (1991). Appendix A contains the addresses of two national Evaluation Assistance Centers that provide technical assistance to state and local education agencies concerning methods of assessing the needs of limited-English-proficiency students. Appendix B contains the addresses of sixteen Multifunctional Resource Centers that provide technical assistance to educational personnel in bilingual programs.

The political issues that often surround bilingual education as well as various programmatic and instructional issues are discussed in *Bilingual Education: Politics, Practice, and Research* (1993), edited by Beatriz Arias and Ursula Casanova. *Bilingual Education and English as a Second Language: A Research Handbook, 1988–1990* (1991), edited by Alba Ambert, contains ten chapters that discuss a variety of topics, among them early childhood education, bilingual gifted and talented students, and psychoeducational assessment of language-minority children. Appendix 1 contains the addresses of fifteen organizations that provide resource materials on specific topics (for example, counseling for limited-English proficiency students, educational technology in bilingual programs). Appendix 2 is a list of nine organizations that provide information on bilingual education. Appendix 3 is a list of sixteen journals and newsletters that specialize in bilingual education issues.

Teaching English as a Second Language: A Resource Guide (1994), by Angela Carrasquillo, contains eleven chapters that discuss such topics as language acquisition, individual differences in language learning, different types of ESL programs, and characteristics of ESL programs at different grade levels. Chapter 12 includes addresses for organizations that provide various publications and services to individuals involved in ESL programs.

An excellent on-line directory is maintained at the University of Texas, Austin. Its address is http://www.edb.utexas.edu/coe/depts/CI/bilingue/resources.html.

Summary

1. Culture refers to the perceptions, emotions, beliefs, ideas, experiences, and behavior patterns that a group of people has in common.

2. Beginning in the 1960s the notion of the United States as a cultural melting pot became less popular, and the concept of cultural diversity, or cultural pluralism, increased in popularity. As the latter became more widely accepted, calls were made for the establishment of multicultural education programs in American public schools.

3. The concept of cultural pluralism assumes that every culture is internally consistent and logical, that no culture is inherently inferior or superior to another, and that all people are somewhat culture-bound.

4. Because of immigration patterns and high birthrates in some ethnic groups, the United States is becoming an increasingly diverse country.

5. Two important factors that distinguish one culture from another are ethnicity and social class.

6. People of the same ethnic group typically share many of the following characteristics: ancestral country or origin, race, religion, values, political interests, economic interests, and behavior patterns.

7. Ethnic differences in communication patterns and preferences, time orientation, values, and thinking styles can lead to misunderstandings among students and between students and teachers.

8. Social class indicates an individual's or a family's relative position in society in terms of such factors as income, occupation, level of education, place of residence, and material possessions.

9. Educationally disadvantaged students often receive irregular health care, experience child-care practices that do not effectively prepare them for school, are not exposed to a wide variety of experiences, are not motivated to do well in school, and have low career aspirations.

10. The teacher expectancy effect, also known as the self-fulfilling prophecy or the Pygmalion effect, occurs when teachers communicate a particular expectation about how a student will perform and the student's behavior changes so as to be consistent with that expectation.

11. Although the effect of teacher expectancy on IQ scores originally reported by Rosenthal and Jacobson has never been fully replicated, research has demonstrated that teacher expectancy strongly affects classroom achievement and participation in both positive and negative ways.

12. Factors that seem to play a strong role in producing a teacher expectancy effect include a student's gender, compliance, achievement, attractiveness, social class, and ethnic background.

13. Multicultural education programs assume that minority students will learn more and have a stronger self-concept if teachers understand, accept, and reward the thinking and behavior patterns characteristic of the students' culture.

14. Effective multicultural teachers use such proven instructional techniques as providing clear objectives, communicating high expectations, monitoring progress, providing immediate feedback, and making lessons meaningful. In addition, they have experience in teaching culturally diverse classes, exhibit a high level of dedication, and have a strong affinity for their students.
15. Peer tutoring, cooperative learning, and mastery learning are three generally effective instructional tactics that are particularly well suited to multicultural education programs.
16. Calls for multicultural education were stimulated by changing immigration and birthrate patterns, low levels of school achievement by many ethnic minority children, and students' need to work productively with members of other cultures.
17. Most bilingual education programs reflect either a transition goal or a maintenance goal. Transition programs teach students in their native language only until they speak and understand English well enough to be placed in a regular classroom. Maintenance programs try to maintain or improve students' native-language skills prior to instruction in English.

Key Terms

culture *(120)*
multicultural education *(121)*
melting pot *(122)*
cultural pluralism *(122)*
ethnic group *(124)*
social class *(127)*
socioeconomic status (SES) *(127)*
self-fulfilling prophecy *(132)*
peer tutoring *(138)*
cooperative learning *(140)*
mastery learning *(141)*

Discussion Questions

1. Culture refers to the way in which a group of people views the world; formulates beliefs; evaluates objects, ideas, and experiences; and behaves. Ethnocentrism often causes people to view the cultural beliefs and practices of others as deficits. How can you use the concept of constructivism (mentioned in Chapters 1, 2, and 10) to help students overcome any ethnocentrism they may have and understand the beliefs and practices of other cultures?

2. The school dropout rate for African-American, Hispanic-American, and Native American students is two to three times the rate for white students. A likely contributing factor is the sense of alienation from school that grows out of low teacher expectations, expressions of racial or ethnic group prejudice, and discrimination. What steps might you take to reduce or eliminate this sense of alienation in students?

3. How have your experiences with members of ethnic or racial minority groups been similar or different from what you have heard and read about those groups?

4. On page 16 we briefly describe four approaches to multicultural education: contributions, additive, transformation, and social action. What advantages and disadvantages do you see for each approach? Which approach would you use? Why?

5. On pages 16–17 we describe a set of key concepts proposed by James Banks around which multicultural lessons and units can be organized. Why are these concepts so important that Banks labels them *key* concepts?

CHAPTER 5

Assessing Student Variability

Key Points

These key points will help you learn the important information in this chapter. To help you study, they also appear in the margins of pages, next to the text where they are discussed.

THE MEANING OF VARIABILITY

- Intraindividual variation: differences in a person's behavior over time and across situations
- Interindividual variation: differences between individuals at a given point in time

STANDARDIZED TESTS

- Standardized tests: items presented and scored in standard fashion, results reported with reference to standards
- Basic purpose of standardized test is to obtain accurate, representative sample of some aspect of a person
- Standardized test scores used to identify strengths and weaknesses, plan instruction, select students for programs
- Reliability: similarity between two rankings of test scores obtained from the same individual
- Validity: how accurately a test measures what users want it to measure
- Content validity: how well test items cover a body of knowledge and skill
- Predictive validity: how well a test score predicts later performance
- Construct validity: how accurately a test measures a particular attribute
- Meaningfulness of standardized test scores depends on representativeness of norm group
- Formal testing of young children is inappropriate because of rapid developmental changes
- Achievement tests measure how much of a subject or skill has been learned
- Diagnostic achievement tests designed to identify specific strengths and weaknesses

- Competency tests determine if potential graduates possess basic skills
- Aptitude tests measure predisposition to develop advanced capabilities in specific areas
- Norm-referenced tests compare one student with others
- Criterion-referenced tests indicate degree of mastery of objectives
- Percentile rank: percentage of scores at or below a given point
- Standard deviation: degree of deviation from the mean of a distribution
- z score: how far a raw score is from the mean in standard deviation units
- T score: how far a raw score is from the mean in numerical terms
- Stanine score: student performance indicated with reference to a 9-point scale based on normal curve

The Nature and Measurement of Intelligence

- Intelligence test scores most closely related to school success
- Intelligence tests not good predictors of job success, marital happiness, life happiness
- Intelligence involves more than what intelligence tests measure
- Triarchic theory: part of intelligence is ability to achieve personal goals
- Multiple intelligences theory: intelligence composed of 7 distinct forms of intelligence
- IQ scores can change with experience, training
- IQ test items based on knowledge and situations thought to be common to most children

A Critical Look at the Misuses of Standardized Tests

- Overreliance on test scores can bar gifted and talented minority children from special programs
- Understanding the assessment process leads to nondiscriminatory testing
- Test scores inappropriately used to evaluate quality of teachers, schools, school districts
- Test score pollution: test-related practices that cause test scores to vary independent of what test measures

Authentic and Performance-Based Assessments

- Performance tests measure how well students can use knowledge and skill to solve problems

Sit back for a few minutes, and think about some of your friends and classmates over the past twelve years. Make a list of their physical characteristics (height, weight, visual acuity, athletic skill, for example), social characteristics (outgoing, reserved, cooperative, sensitive to the needs of others, assertive), emotional characteristics (self-assured, optimistic, pessimistic, egotistical), and intellectual characteristics (methodical, creative, impulsive, good with numbers, terrible at organizing ideas). Now analyze your descriptions in terms of similarities and differences. In all likelihood these descriptions point to many ways in which your friends and classmates have been alike, but to even more ways in which they have differed from one another. Indeed, although human beings share many important characteristics, they also differ from one another in significant ways (and we tend to notice the differences more readily than the similarities).

Now imagine yourself a few years from now, when your job as a teacher is to help every student learn as much as possible despite all the ways in which your students differ from one another. The variability among any group of students is one reason that teaching is both interesting and challenging. Richard Snow, who has written extensively about individual differences in education and how to deal with them, summarizes the problem as follows:

> Individual differences among students present a pervasive and profound problem to educators. At the outset of instruction in any topic, students of any age and in any culture will differ from one another in various intellectual and psychomotor abilities and skills, in both general and specialized prior knowledge, in interests and motives, and in personal styles of thought and work during learning. These differences, in turn, appear directly related to differences in the students' learning progress. (1986, p. 1029)

The significance of these observations on variability is that, while you will have to plan lessons, assignments, and teaching techniques by taking into account *typical* characteristics, you will also have to expect and make allowances for differences among students. Students vary not only in terms of all the characteristics described in Chapters 2 and 3 but also in terms of general and specific learning abilities. That some students learn more easily and successfully than others is one of the major problems you will need to deal with as a teacher.

The Meaning of Variability

Intraindividual variation: differences in a person's behavior over time and across situations

When psychologists discuss variability, they often do so in terms of two broad categories. One category is called **intraindividual variation.** Since the prefix *intra* means within, the focus here is on how a given individual changes over time or acts differently in different situations. Can you recall, for example, any friends or classmates who gradually became more outgoing or who excelled in algebra but struggled to write a coherent paragraph in English composition? A student's attention span, interest level, or motivation may change over time and tasks because youngsters are sensitive to changes in such classroom variables as the subject matter, the pacing of instruction, the personality of the teacher, and the type of test being given. In Chapter 2 we pointed out how personality and thinking change with age and offered suggestions for teaching based on these differences. Likewise, in Chapter 3 we summarized physical, social, emotional, and intellectual changes (as well as similarities) as children progress from preschool through high school. In Chapters 8 through 11 we will mention intraindividual variability in learning and motivation.

Interindividual variation: differences between individuals at a given point in time

The second category is called **interindividual variation.** Since the prefix *inter* means between, the focus here is on differences between individuals at any given point in time. Keep in mind that some ways in which students differ from each other are more important than others. The ones you want to pay special attention to are those that relate strongly to classroom achievement. What follows is a *sample* (in alphabetical order) of points of individual difference that through extensive research have been related to achievement:

Throughout their school years, students are interested in how they perform academically compared to classmates.

- age
- attention span
- attitudes
- cognitive style
- ethnicity
- gender
- intelligence
- interest
- learning strategies
- learning style
- memory capacity
- motivation
- perceptual skill
- personality
- prior knowledge
- problem solving
- self-concept
- social class
- social competence
- stage of cognitive development
- values

Most of the research on interindividual variation revolves around scholastic aptitude (another term for intelligence) and achievement because large numbers of standardized tests have been constructed to measure these variables. These tests make it possible to identify both the range of variability among a group of students and the strengths and weaknesses of each student. Ideally, schools can use this information to select and place children in instructional programs that match their characteristics or to adjust programs to better meet individual needs.

Because standardized assessment of scholastic aptitude and achievement is such a popular practice in the United States (as well as in many other countries), this chapter will focus on the nature of standardized tests, how they are used to assess student variability, and how these test results can be employed in putting together effective instructional programs for "typical" students. The following chapter will describe techniques for dealing with the range of interindividual variability—intellectual, emotional, and cultural—that exists in the typical classroom and may in some cases require special kinds of instruction. As we will see, and as Richard Snow (1986) points out, the use of standardized tests to assess variability and guide the subsequent placement of students into different instructional programs is truly a double-edged sword: It has the potential to harm students as well as help them.

Standardized Tests

NATURE OF STANDARDIZED TESTS

Standardized tests: items presented and scored in standard fashion, results reported with reference to standards

The kinds of assessment instruments described in this chapter are typically referred to as **standardized tests,** although the term *published tests* is sometimes used (because they are prepared, distributed, and scored by publishing companies or independent test services). You have almost certainly taken several of these tests during your academic career, and so you are probably familiar with their appearance and general characteristics. They are called standardized tests for the following reasons:

1. They are designed by people with specialized knowledge and training in test construction.
2. Every person who takes the test responds to the same items under the same conditions.
3. The answers are evaluated according to the same scoring standards.
4. The scores are interpreted through comparison to the scores obtained from a group (called a norm group) that took the same test under the same conditions or (in the case of some achievement tests) to a predetermined standard.

Basic purpose of standardized test is to obtain accurate, representative sample of some aspect of a person

The basic purpose of giving a standardized test is to obtain an *accurate and representative sample* of how much of some characteristic a person possesses (such as knowledge of a particular set of mathematical concepts and operations). The benefit of getting an accurate measure from a test is obvious. When standardized tests are well designed, they are likely to be more accurate measures of a particular characteristic than nonstandardized tests. Standardized tests measure a *sample* of the characteristic since a comprehensive

When high school seniors take exams such as the Scholastic Aptitude Test (or the equivalent) the results are reported in terms of norm-referenced scores. Each student's performance is compared to that of the sample of students who made up the standardization group when the test was devised.

measure would be too expensive, time-consuming, and cumbersome to administer (Walsh & Betz, 1995).

PREVALENCE OF STANDARDIZED TESTING

No one knows for certain how many students are tested in a given year or how many tests the typical student takes because comprehensive and unambiguous data are not available. (If a student takes an achievement battery that covers four subjects, does that count as one test or four?) Nevertheless, Walter Haney, George Madaus, and Robert Lyons (1993) provide low and high estimates of such usage on the basis of late-1980s data for four kinds of testing: state-mandated testing programs, school district testing programs, testing of special populations, and college admissions testing. On the low end, they estimate that slightly more than 143 million students a year were tested and that the average child took 2.7 tests per year. On the high end, they estimate that just over 395 million students a year were tested and that the average child took 5.4 tests per year. In either case it is clear that American schools engage in a substantial amount of standardized testing.

USES OF STANDARDIZED TESTS

Historically, standardized test scores, particularly achievement tests, have been used by educators for a variety of instructionally related purposes. Teachers, guidance counselors, and principals have used test data to identify general strengths and weaknesses in student achievement, inform parents of their child's general level of achievement, plan instructional lessons, group students for instruction, and recommend students for placement in special programs (a use we will describe in more detail in the next chapter). To cite just one example, when a child moves to a different neighborhood within a city or a different city within a state or a different part of the country, it is highly desirable to have some idea as to what the child knows about basic subjects. Standardized achievement tests do an effective job of providing information about the mastery of general subject matter and skills and thus can be used for planning, grouping, placement, and instructional purposes.

Standardized test scores used to identify strengths and weaknesses, plan instruction, select students for programs

When you read the test profiles that report how students in your classes have performed on standardized tests, you will get a general idea of some of your students' strengths and weaknesses. If certain students are weak in particular skill areas and you want to help them overcome those weaknesses, test results *may* give you *some* insights into possible ways to provide remedial instruction. If most of your students score below average in certain segments of the curriculum, you will know that you should devote more time and effort to presenting those topics and skills to the entire class. You can and should, of course, supplement what you learn from standardized test results with your own tests and observations in order to design potentially effective forms of remedial or advanced instruction.

CRITERIA FOR EVALUATING STANDARDIZED TESTS

Like most things, standardized tests vary in quality. To use test scores wisely, you need to be an informed consumer—to know what characteristics distinguish well-constructed from poorly constructed tests. Four criteria are widely used to evaluate standardized tests: reliability, validity, normed excellence, and examinee appropriateness. Each of these criteria will be explained individually.

Reliability A basic assumption that psychologists make about human characteristics (such as intelligence and achievement) is that they are relatively stable, at least over short periods of time. For most people this assumption seems to be true. Thus, you should be able to count on a test's results being consistent, just as you might count on a reliable worker doing a consistent job time after time. This stability in test performance is known as **reliability.** It is one of the most important characteristics of standardized tests and can be assessed in a number of ways.

To illustrate the importance of reliability, imagine that you wish to form cooperative learning groups for mathematics. Since these types of groups should be composed of five to six students who differ on a number of characteristics, including achievement, you use the students' most recent scores from a standardized mathematics test to assign two high, medium, and low achievers to each group. One month later the children are retested, and you now find that many of those who scored at the top initially (and whom you thought were very knowledgeable about mathematics) now score in the middle or at the bottom. Conversely, many students who initially scored low now have average or above-average scores. What does that do to your confidence in being able to form heterogeneous groups based on scores from this test? If you want to be able to consistently differentiate among individuals, you need to use an instrument that performs consistently.

Psychologists who specialize in constructing standardized tests assess reliability in a variety of ways. One method is to administer the same test to the same people on two occasions and measure the extent to which the rankings change over time. This approach results in *test-retest reliability.* Another method is to administer two equivalent forms of a test to the same group of students at the same time. This approach results in *alternate-form reliability.* A third approach is to administer a single test to a group of students, create two scores by dividing the test in half, and measure the extent to which the rankings change from one half to the other. This method results in *split-half reliability* and measures the internal consistency of a test.

Reliability: similarity between two rankings of test scores obtained from the same individual

Regardless of which method is used to assess reliability, the goal is to create two rankings of scores and to see how similar the rankings are. This degree of consistency is expressed as a correlation coefficient (abbreviated with a lower-case r) that ranges from 0 to 1. Well-constructed standardized tests should have correlation coefficients of about 0.95 for split-half reliability, 0.90 for test-retest reliability, and 0.85 for alternate-form reliability (Kubiszyn & Borich, 1993). Bear in mind, however, that a particular test may not report all three forms of reliability and that reliabilities for subtests and for younger age groups (kindergarten through second grade) are likely to be lower than these overall figures.

Validity: how accurately a test measures what users want it to measure

Validity A second important characteristic of a test is that it accurately measure what it claims to measure. A reading comprehension test should measure just that—nothing more, nothing less. Whenever we speak of a test's accuracy, we are referring to its **validity.** Since most of the characteristics we are interested in knowing something about (such as arithmetic skills, spatial aptitude, intelligence, and knowledge of the American Civil War) are internal and hence not directly observable, tests are indirect measures of those attributes. Therefore, any test-based conclusions we may draw about how much of a characteristic a person possesses, or any predictions we may make about how well a person will perform in the future (on other types of tests, in a job, or in a specialized academic program, for example), are properly referred to as *inferences.* So when we inquire about the validity of a test by asking, "Does this test measure what it claims to measure?" we are really asking, "How accurate are the inferences that I wish to draw about the test taker?" (See, for example, Messick, 1989.) The degree to which these inferences can be judged accurate, or valid, depends on the type and quality of the supporting evidence that we can muster. Three kinds of evidence that underlie test-based inferences are content validity evidence, predictive validity evidence, and construct validity evidence.

CONTENT VALIDITY EVIDENCE. This kind of evidence rests on a set of judgments about how well a test's items reflect the particular body of knowledge and skill (called a *domain* by measurement specialists) about which we want to draw inferences. If a test on the American Civil War, for example, contained no items on the war's causes, its great battles, or the years it encompassed, some users might be hesitant to call someone who had achieved a high score knowledgeable about this topic. Then again, other users might not be nearly so disturbed by these omissions (and the inference that would be drawn from the test score) if they considered such information to be relatively unimportant.

Content validity: how well test items cover a body of knowledge and skill

PREDICTIVE VALIDITY EVIDENCE. This evidence allows us to make probabilistic statements ("Based on his test scores, there is a strong likelihood that Yusef will do well in the creative writing program next year") about how well students will behave in the future. Many colleges, for example, require students to take the *American College Testing Program* (ACT) or the *Scholastic Aptitude Test* (SAT) and then use the results (along with other information) to predict each prospective student's grade-point average at the end of the freshman year. All other things being equal, students with higher test scores are expected to have higher grade-point averages than students with lower test scores and thus stand a better chance of being admitted.

Predictive validity: how well a test score predicts later performance

CONSTRUCT VALIDITY EVIDENCE. This evidence indicates how accurately a test measures a theoretical description of some internal attribute of a person. Such attributes—for example, intelligence, creativity, motivation, and anxiety—are called constructs by psychologists. To illustrate the nature of construct validity, we will use a hypothetical theory of intelligence called the Perfectly Valid theory. This theory holds that highly intelligent individuals should have higher-than-average school grades now and in the future, demonstrate superior performance on tasks that involve abstract reasoning, and be able to distinguish worthwhile from nonworthwhile goals. They may or may not, however, be popular among their peers. If the Perfectly Valid

Construct validity: how accurately a test measures a particular attribute

theory is accurate and if someone has done a good job of constructing an intelligence test based on this theory (the Smart Intelligence Test), people's scores on the Smart Test should vary in accordance with predictions derived from the Perfectly Valid theory. We should see, for example, a strong positive relationship between intelligence quotient (IQ) scores and grade-point average but no relationship between IQ scores and measures of popularity. As more and more of this type of evidence is supplied, we can feel increasingly confident in drawing the inference that the Smart Intelligence Test is an accurate measure of the Perfectly Valid theory of intelligence.

Normed Excellence For a test score to have any meaning, it has to be compared to some yardstick or measure of performance. Standardized tests use the performance of a norm group as the measure against which all other scores are compared. A **norm group** is a sample of individuals carefully chosen so as to reflect the larger population of students for whom the test is intended. In many cases the larger population consists of all elementary school children or all high school children in the United States. The norm group must closely match the larger population it represents on such major demographic variables as age, sex, race, region of country, family income, and occupation of head of household. These variables are considered major because they are strongly associated with differences in school performance. If, for example, the U.S. Census Bureau reports that 38 percent of all Hispanic-American males between the ages of six and thirteen live in the southwestern region of the country, a good test constructor testing in the Southwest will try to put together a norm group that contains the same percentage of six- to thirteen-year-old Hispanic-American males.

Meaningfulness of standardized test scores depends on representativeness of norm group

As you might suspect, problems of score interpretation arise when the major demographic characteristics of individuals who take the test are not reflected in the norm group. Suppose you were trying to interpret the score of a fourteen-year-old African-American male on the EZ Test of Academic Achievement. If the oldest students in the norm group were twelve years of age and if African-American children were not part of the norm group, you would have no way of knowing if your student's score is below average, average, or above average, compared to the norm.

Examinee Appropriateness Because developing a standardized test is a substantial undertaking that requires a considerable investment of money, time, and expertise, most tests of this type are designed for nationwide use. But the curriculum in school districts in different types of communities and in different sections of the country varies to a considerable extent. Therefore, it is important to estimate how appropriate a given test is for a particular group of students. When you are estimating the content validity of a test, you should pay attention not only to how well the questions measure what they are supposed to measure, but also to whether they are appropriate in terms of level of difficulty and the vocabulary and characteristics of your students. For example, the administration of readiness tests to preschool and kindergarten children to determine whether they are ready to begin school or should be promoted to first grade has been heavily criticized on the basis of examinee

Formal testing of young children is inappropriate because of rapid developmental changes appropriateness. A major problem with the use of tests for the making of admission and retention decisions in the early grades is their low reliability. Young children change physically, socially, emotionally, and intellectually so rapidly that many of them score very differently when retested six months later (Schultz, 1989).

TYPES OF STANDARDIZED TESTS

In this section we will examine two major categories of standardized tests—achievement tests and aptitude tests—each of which has several varieties. We will also examine two approaches to the interpretation of test scores—norm referenced and criterion referenced.

Achievement Tests One type of standardized test that you probably took during your elementary school years was the **single-subject achievement test,** designed to assess how much you had learned—or achieved—in a particular basic school subject. The very first standardized test you took was probably designed to evaluate aspects of reading performance. Then at intervals of two years or so, you probably worked your way tensely and laboriously through **achievement batteries** designed to assess your performance in reading as well as math, language, and perhaps other subjects. During your high school years, you may have taken one or more achievement batteries that evaluated more sophisticated understanding of basic reading-writing-arithmetic skills as well as course content in specific subjects.

Achievement tests measure how much of a subject or skill has been learned

At some point during your elementary school years, you may also have been asked to take a **diagnostic test,** a special type of single-subject achievement test intended to identify the source of a problem in basic subjects and perhaps in study skills as well.

Diagnostic achievement tests designed to identify specific strengths and weaknesses

Depending on when and where you graduated from high school, you may have been asked to take a **competency test** a few months before the end of your senior year. Competency tests came into use in the mid-1970s when it was discovered that many graduates of American high schools were unable to handle basic skills. In many school districts, therefore, students were asked to prove that they were competent in reading, writing, and arithmetic before they were awarded diplomas.

Competency tests determine if potential graduates possess basic skills

You may have earned some of your college credits by taking the *College-Level Examination Program*, a **special-purpose achievement test.** Depending on the state in which you choose to teach, you may be required to take and pass another special-purpose achievement test, the *National Teacher Examination*, before being granted a teaching certificate.

Aptitude Tests An aptitude is an underlying predisposition to respond to some task or situation in a particular way; it makes possible the development of more advanced capabilities (Snow, 1992). The word *aptitude* is derived from the Middle English apte, which meant to grasp or to reach, and is related to the French *apropos*, which means appropriate, fitting, or suited to a purpose. For the last several decades, aptitudes have come to be identified entirely with cognitive predispositions. But Richard Snow (1992) argues for a broader conception that also includes affective and motivational

Aptitude tests measure predisposition to develop advanced capabilities in specific areas predispositions. In his scheme, which we find attractive, such characteristics of people as extroversion, conformity, independence, production of mental images, attention span, beliefs, and fear of failure would also be considered aptitudes because they are fairly broad and stable predispositions to respond to tasks in certain ways.

Educators use **aptitude tests** to give themselves some idea of the level of knowledge and skill an individual could acquire with effective instruction. Thus, your teachers may have discovered that your aptitude for music was higher than normal and urged you to join the school band. Conversely, low scores on tests of mechanical reasoning and space relations may have dissuaded you from majoring in architecture in college.

It is almost certain that some time during your senior year of high school you took a test required by the admissions committee of the college you hoped to attend. You probably took either the *Scholastic Aptitude Test* (or the *American College Testing Assessment Program*). If you decide to continue on to graduate school, you can expect to take the *Graduate Record Exam* (GRE).

As part of your school district's annual or semiannual testing program, you may have taken a **group test of scholastic aptitude,** such as the *Otis-Lennon Mental Ability Tests,* in addition to an achievement battery. If there was a substantial discrepancy between your scores on these two tests, or if you were ever considered for a special program of some sort, you may have been asked to take an **individual intelligence test,** such as the *Stanford-Binet* or the *Wechsler Intelligence Scale for Children—III* (1991). Although both of these instruments are called intelligence tests, they are essentially tests of scholastic aptitude for the reasons given previously; they are used primarily to predict how successfully students will cope with academic demands in classroom settings. Because individual tests typically provide extensive explanations and illustrations of how to respond to items, allow the examiner to provide some degree of corrective feedback, and suggest ways of establishing a testing atmosphere in which the student will feel comfortable, they contain less measurement error than do group tests.

Norm-referenced tests compare one student with others

Norm-Referenced Tests Most of the achievement and aptitude tests just described are referred to as **norm referenced tests** since one's performance is evaluated with reference to norms—the performance of others—established when the final form of the test was administered to the sample of students who made up the standardization group. After taking an achievement battery in the elementary grades, for example, you were probably told that you had performed as well on reading comprehension questions as 80 percent (or whatever) of all of the students who took the test. If you take the GRE, you will be told how far from the average score of 500 you are (in terms of a score to be described shortly). Thus, you will learn just where you stand in a distribution of scores arranged from lowest to highest. Tests that are constructed according to norm-referenced criteria tend to cover a broad range of knowledge and skill but have relatively few items for each topic or skill tested. But in the last twenty years or so, an alternative approach to reporting achievement scores has been developed.

Criterion-Referenced Tests A different approach to reporting achievement test scores is used by **criterion-referenced tests.** When a test is scored in this manner, an individual's performance is not compared with the performance of others. Instead, students are evaluated according to how well they have mastered specific objectives in various well-defined skill areas. Because of this feature, you may find criterion-referenced tests more useful than norm-referenced tests in determining who needs how much additional instruction in what areas (provided, of course, that the test's objectives closely match your own). The criterion-referenced approach is intended to reduce overtones of competition and emphasize mastery of objectives at a rate commensurate with students' abilities. Tests that have criterion-referenced scoring systems tend to cover less ground than norm-referenced tests but contain more items for the objectives they do assess. Because norm-referenced and criterion-referenced scoring systems provide different types of information about student achievement, many testing companies provide both types of scores.

Criterion-referenced tests indicate degree of mastery of objectives

A new development in criterion-referenced testing has occurred within several states. In states such as Kentucky, statewide assessment systems that are known as **performance-based or authentic assessment** are being put into place in an attempt to counter some of the disadvantages of traditional norm-referenced standardized testing. We will look at these new tests in greater detail at the end of this chapter.

INTERPRETING STANDARDIZED TEST SCORES

Scores on the most widely used standardized tests are typically reported on student profile forms that summarize and explain the results. While most profiles contain sufficient information to make it possible to interpret scores without additional background, you should know in advance about the kinds of scores you may encounter, particularly since you may be asked to explain scores to students as well as to their parents.

Grade Equivalent Scores The **grade equivalent score** interprets test performance in terms of grade levels. A student who makes a grade equivalent score of 4.7 on an achievement test, for example, got the same number of items right on this test as the average fourth grader in the standardization group achieved by the seventh month of the school year. The grade equivalent score was once widely used at the elementary level, but because it may lead to misinterpretations, this score is not as popular as it once was. One problem with grade equivalent scores is the tendency to misinterpret a score above a student's actual grade level as an indication that the student is capable of consistently working at that level. This kind of assumption might lead parents or perhaps teachers themselves to consider accelerated promotion. Remember that, while such scores may show that a student did somewhat better on the test than the average student a grade or two above her, they do not mean that the student tested has acquired knowledge of all the skills covered in the grade that would be skipped.

Percentile rank: percentage of scores at or below a given point

Percentile Ranks Probably the most widely used score for standardized tests is the **percentile rank.** This score indicates the percentage of students who are at and below a given student's score. It provides specific information about relative position. Students earning a percentile rank of 87 did as well as or better than 87 percent of the students in the particular normative group being used. They did not get 87 percent of the questions right—unless by coincidence—and this is the point parents are most likely to misunderstand. Parents may have been brought up on the percentages grading system, in which 90 or above was A, 80 to 90 was B, and so on down the line. If you report that a son or daughter has a percentile rank of 50, some parents are horrorstruck or outraged, not understanding that the child's score on this test is average, not a failure. In such cases the best approach is to emphasize that the percentile rank tells the percentage of cases at or below the child's score. You might also talk in terms of a hypothetical group of 100; for example, a child with a percentile rank of 78 did as well as or better than 78 out of every 100 students who took the test.

Although the percentile rank gives simple and direct information on relative position, it has a major disadvantage: the difference in achievement among students clustered around the middle of the distribution is often considerably less than the difference among those at the extremes. The reason is that *most* scores are clustered around the middle of most distributions of large groups of students. The difference in raw score (number of items answered correctly) between students at percentile ranks 50 and 51 may be 1 point. But the difference in raw score between the student ranked 98 and one ranked 97 may be 10 or 15 points because the best (and worst) students scatter toward the extremes. This quality of percentile ranks means that ranks on different tests cannot be averaged. To get around that difficulty, standard scores are often used.

Standard deviation: degree of deviation from the mean of a distribution

Standard Scores Standard scores are expressed in terms of a common unit—the **standard deviation.** This statistic indicates the degree to which scores in a group of tests (a distribution) differ from the average or mean. (The *mean* is the arithmetical average of a distribution and is calculated by adding all scores and dividing the total by the number of scores.) The standard deviation is most valuable when it can be related to the normal probability curve. Figure 5.1 shows a normal probability curve indicating the percentage of cases to be found within 3 standard deviations above and below the mean. The **normal curve** is a mathematical concept that depicts a hypothetical bell-shaped distribution of scores. Such a perfectly symmetrical distribution rarely, if ever, occurs in real life. However, since many distributions of human characteristics and performance closely *resemble* the normal distribution, it is often assumed that such distributions are typical enough to be treated as "normal." Thus, information derived by mathematicians for the hypothetical normal distribution can be applied to the approximately normal distributions that are found when human attributes are measured. When very large numbers of students are asked to take tests designed by specialists who go to great lengths to cancel out the impact of selective factors, it may be appropriate to interpret the students' scores on such tests with reference to the normal curve.

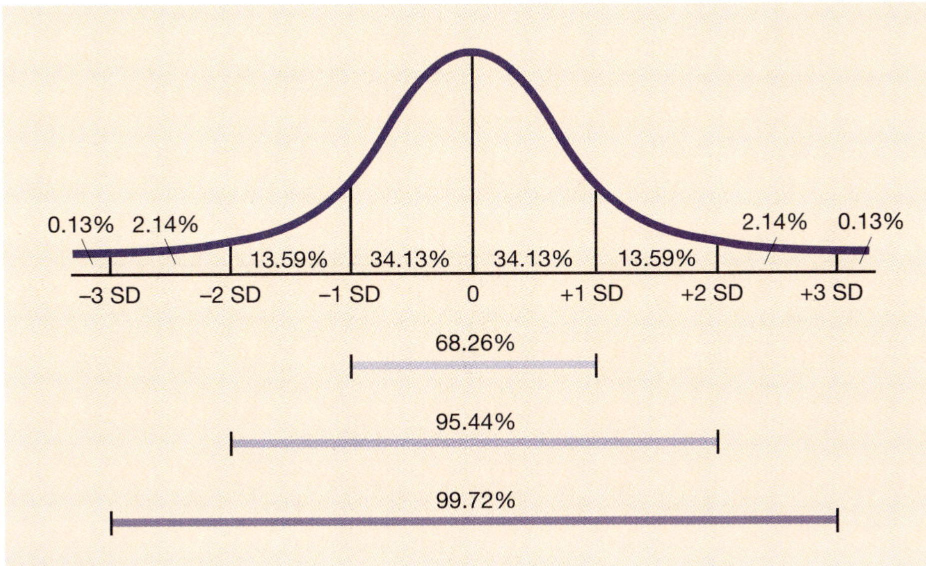

FIGURE 5.1 *The Normal Probability Curve*

For purposes of discussion, and for purposes of acquiring familiarity with test scores, it will be sufficient for you to know about two of the standard scores that are derived from standard deviations. One, called a **z score,** tells how far a given raw score is from the mean in standard deviation units. A z score of -1.5, for example, would mean that the student was 1.5 standard deviation units below the mean. Because some z scores (such as the one in the example just given) are negative and involve decimals, **T scores** are often used instead. T scores range from 0 to 100 and use a preselected mean of 50 to get away from negative values. Most standardized tests that use T scores offer detailed explanations, either in the test booklet or on the student profile of scores, of how they should be interpreted. In fact, many test profiles adopt the form of a narrative report when explaining the meaning of all scores used.

z score: how far a raw score is from the mean in standard deviation units

T score: how far a raw score is from the mean in numerical terms

To grasp the relationship among z scores, T scores, and percentile ranks, examine Figure 5.2. The diagram shows each scale marked off below a normal curve. It supplies information about the interrelationships of these various scores, provided that the distribution you are working with is essentially normal. In a normal distribution, for example, a z score of +1 is the same as a T score of 60 or a percentile rank of 84; a z score of -2 is the same as a T score of 30 or a percentile rank of about 2. (In addition, notice that the distance between the percentile ranks clustered around the middle is only a small fraction of the distance between the percentile ranks that are found at the ends of the distribution.)

Stanine Scores During World War II, Air Force psychologists developed a statistic called the **stanine score** (an abbreviation of standard nine-point scale), reflecting the fact that it is a type of standard score and divides a population into nine groups. Each stanine is one-half of a standard deviation unit, as indicated in Figure 5.3.

Stanine score: student performance indicated with reference to a 9-point scale based on normal curve

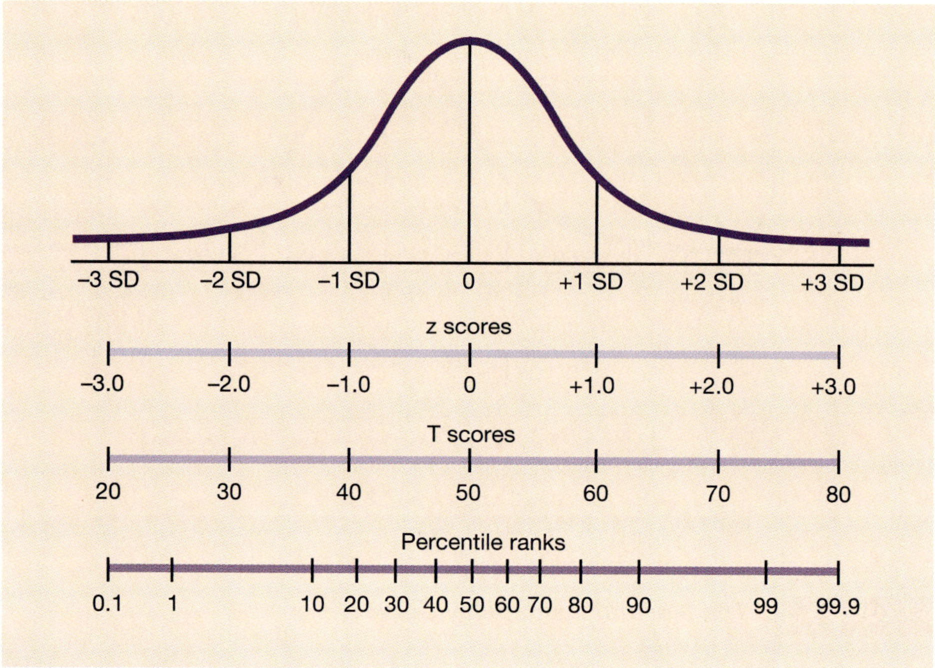

FIGURE 5.2 *Relationship Among z Scores, T scores, and Percentile Ranks*

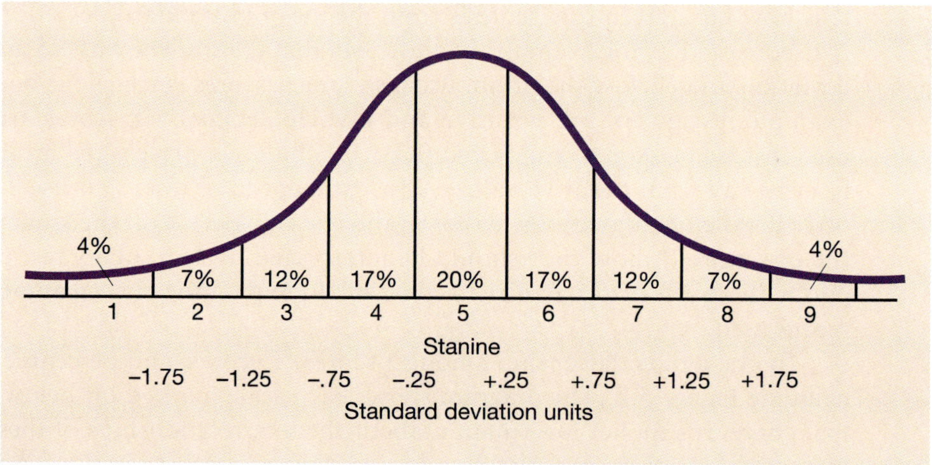

FIGURE 5.3 *Percentage of Cases in Each Stanine (with Standard Deviation Units Indicated)*

When stanines were first introduced on test profiles reporting the performance of public school children on standardized tests, they were often used to group students. (Students in stanines 1, 2, and 3 would be placed in one class; those in 4, 5, and 6 in another class; and so on.) For reasons to be described later in this chapter as well as in the next, grouping has become a highly controversial issue in American schools. Consequently, stanine scores are now used to indicate relative standing. They are easier to understand than z scores or T scores since any child or parent can understand that stanines represent a 9-point scale with 1 as the lowest, 5 as the average, and 9 as the highest. Furthermore, unlike percentile ranks, stanine scores can be averaged. In those cases when it is desirable to have more precise information about relative standing, however, percentile ranks may be more useful, even though they cannot be averaged.

Local and National Norms Percentile ranks and stanines are often used when local norms are prepared. As noted in our earlier description of how standardized tests are developed, the norms used to determine a student's level of performance are established by asking a representative sample of students to take the final form of the test. Inevitably, there will be differences between school systems (in texts used and the time during a school year or years when certain topics are covered, for instance). Accordingly, some test publishers report scores in terms of local as well as national norms. Each student's performance is thus compared not only with the performance of the members of the standardization group but also with the performance of all students in the same school system.

At the beginning of this section, we pointed out that standardized tests can be used in several ways to support the instructional goals of a school and a teacher. In instances where teachers fully understand the characteristic being measured; where reliable, valid, and well-normed tests are readily available; and where teachers know how to appropriately interpret test results, this strategy for dealing with individual differences can work quite well, particularly when it is supplemented with teacher observations and informal assessments. Effective remedial reading and math programs, for example, are based to a large extent on scores from diagnostic reading and math tests. But when the characteristic being measured and the nature of the test are poorly understood, inappropriate decisions and controversy often result. Nowhere are these negative outcomes more likely than in the assessment of intelligence. Since many instructional and placement decisions are based on intelligence test scores, you must clearly understand this characteristic and how it is measured. Hence, this is the topic of the next section.

The Nature and Measurement of Intelligence

THE ORIGIN OF INTELLIGENCE TESTING

The form and content of contemporary intelligence tests owe much to the pioneering work of French psychologist Alfred Binet. In 1904 Binet was appointed to a commission of experts charged by the minister of public instruction for the Paris school system with figuring out an accurate and objective way of distinguishing between children who could profit from normal classroom instruction and those who required special education. Since the point of this project was to predict degree of future academic success, Binet created a set of questions and tasks that reflected the same cognitive processes as those demanded by everyday classroom activities. Thus, Binet's first scale measured such processes as memory, attention, comprehension, discrimination, and reasoning.

In 1916 Lewis Terman of Stanford University published an extensive revision of Binet's test. This revision, which came to be known as the Stanford-Binet, proved to be extremely popular. One reason for its popularity was that Terman, following the 1912 suggestion of a German psychologist named William Stern, expressed a child's level of performance as a global figure called an intelligence quotient (Seagoe, 1974).

Intelligence test scores most closely related to school success

Intelligence tests not good predictors of job success, marital happiness, life happiness

We have provided this abbreviated history lesson to illustrate two important points. First, the form and function of contemporary intelligence tests have been directly influenced by the task Binet was given more than ninety years ago. Intelligence test items are still selected on the basis of their relationship to school success. Thus, predictions about job success, marital bliss, happiness in life, or anything else made on the basis of an IQ score are attempts to make the test do something for which it was not designed. As some psychologists have pointed out, this type of test might better have been called a test of scholastic aptitude or school ability rather than a test of intelligence. The second point concerns Stern and Terman's use of the IQ as a quantitative summary of a child's performance. Binet, worried that educators would use a summary score as an excuse to ignore or get rid of uninterested or troublesome students, never endorsed this application. His intent "was to identify in order to help and improve, not to label in order to limit" (Gould, 1981, p. 152). Later in this section we will see that Binet's concern was well placed. First, however, we will turn to a more detailed consideration of what intelligence tests do and do not measure.

Individually administered intelligence tests (such as the one shown here) are usually given to determine eligibility for a special class because they were designed to predict, and are moderately good predictors of, academic performance.

WHAT INTELLIGENCE TESTS MEASURE

In 1904 British psychologist Charles Spearman noticed that children given a battery of intellectual tests (such as the memory, reasoning, and comprehension tests used by Binet and Terman) showed a strong tendency to rank consistently from test to test: children who scored high (or average or below average) on memory tests tended to score high (or average or below average) on reasoning and comprehension tests. Our use of the words *tendency* and *tended* indicates, of course, that the rankings were not identical. Some children scored well on some tests but performed more poorly on others. Spearman explained this pattern by saying that intelligence is made up of two types of factors: a general factor (abbreviated as *g*) that affected performance on all intellectual tests and a set of specific factors (abbreviated as *s*) that affected performance only on specific intellectual tests. Spearman ascribed to the *g* factor the tendency for score rankings to remain constant over tests. That the rankings varied somewhat from test to test, he said, resulted from individual differences in specific factors. Not surprisingly, Spearman's explanation is called the two-factor theory of intelligence.

When you examine such contemporary intelligence tests as the Stanford-Binet, the Wechsler Intelligence Scale for Children—III, or the Wechsler Adult Intelligence Scale—Revised (1981), you will notice that the items in the various subtests differ greatly from one another. They may involve performing mental arithmetic, explaining the meanings of words, describing how two things are alike, indicating what part is missing from a pictured object, reproducing a pictured geometric design with blocks, or tracing a path through a maze. These varied items are included because, despite their apparent differences, they relate strongly to one another and to performance in the classroom. In other words, intelligence tests still reflect Binet's original goal and Spearman's two-factor theory. In practice, the examiner can combine the scores from each subtest into a global index (the IQ score), offer a prediction about the tested individual's degree of academic success for the next year or so, and make some judgments about specific strengths and weaknesses.

CONTEMPORARY VIEWS OF INTELLIGENCE

David Wechsler's Global Capacity View However, as David Wechsler (1975) persuasively points out, *intelligence is not simply the sum of one's tested abilities*. Wechsler defines intelligence as the global capacity of the individual to act purposefully, to think rationally, and to deal effectively with the environment. Given this definition, which is endorsed by many psychologists, an IQ score reflects just one facet of a person's global capacity—the ability to act purposefully, rationally, and effectively on academic tasks in a *classroom* environment. However, people display intelligent behavior in other settings (at work, home, and play, for example), and other characteristics contribute to intelligent behavior (such as persistence, realistic goal setting, the productive use of corrective feedback, creativity, and moral and aesthetic values). A true assessment of intelligence would take into account behavior related to these other settings and characteristics.

Intelligence involves more than what intelligence tests measure

That such an assessment would be highly subjective and take a great deal of time is one reason current intelligence tests assess only a small sample of cognitive abilities. But if recent formulations of intelligence by psychologists Robert Sternberg (1988) and Howard Gardner (1983) become widely accepted, future intelligence tests may be broader in scope than those in use today. Even before such tests are devised, these theories serve a useful purpose by reminding us that intelligence is multifaceted and can be expressed in many ways.

Robert Sternberg's Triarchic Theory Robert Sternberg's (1988) *triarchic theory of intelligence* has, as its name suggests, three main parts. Two of the three parts deal with thinking processes that we will describe in Chapters 9 and 10 and so will not be described here. The third part, the contextual subtheory, focuses on an aspect of intelligence that has been and still is largely overlooked.

In describing the contextual subtheory, Sternberg argues that part of what makes an individual intelligent is the ability to achieve personal goals (for example, graduating from high school or college with honors, working for a particular company in a particular capacity, or having a successful marriage). One way to accomplish personal goals is to understand and adapt to the values that govern behavior in a particular setting. For example, if most teachers in a particular school (or executives in a particular company) place a high value on conformity and cooperation, the person who persistently challenges authority, suggests new ideas without being asked, or operates without consulting others will, in all likelihood, receive fewer rewards than

Triarchic theory: part of intelligence is ability to achieve personal goals

Contemporary theories typically view intelligence as being composed of several types of capabilities. Howard Gardner's theory of multiple intelligences, for example, describes seven different ways of expressing intelligent behavior.

those who are more willing to conform and cooperate. According to Sternberg's theory, this person would be less intelligent.

Where a mismatch exists and the individual cannot adapt to the values of the majority, the intelligent person explores ways to make the values of others more consistent with his own values and skills. An enterprising student may try to convince her teacher, for example, that short-answer questions are better measures of achievement than essay questions or that effort and classroom participation should count just as much toward a grade as test scores. Finally, where all attempts at adapting or attempting to change the views of others fail, the intelligent person seeks out a setting where his behaviors are more consistent with those of others. For instance, many gifted and talented students will seek out private alternative schools where their particular abilities are more highly prized.

Sternberg's basic point is that intelligence should be viewed as a broad characteristic of people that is evidenced not only by how well they answer a particular set of test questions but also by how well they function in different settings. The individual with average test scores who knows how to get people to do what she wants is, in this view, at least as intelligent as the person who scores at the 99th percentile of a science test.

Multiple intelligences theory: intelligence composed of 7 distinct forms of intelligence

Howard Gardner's Multiple Intelligences Theory Howard Gardner's (1983) conception of intelligence, like Sternberg's, is broader than traditional conceptions. It is different from Sternberg's, however, in that it describes at least seven separate types of intelligence. Accordingly, Gardner's work is referred to as the *theory of multiple intelligences*. The intelligences described by Gardner are linguistic, logical-mathematical, spatial, musical, bodily-kinesthetic, interpersonal (understanding of others), and intrapersonal (understanding of self). Since these intelligences are presumed to be independent of one another, an individual would likely exhibit different levels of skill in each of these domains. One student, for example, may show evidence of becoming an outstanding trial lawyer, novelist, or journalist because his linguistic intelligence produces a facility for vividly describing, explaining, or persuading. Another student may be able to manipulate aspects of sound (such as pitch, rhythm,

and timbre) to produce musical experiences that people find highly pleasing. And the student who is adept at understanding her own and others' feelings and how those feelings relate to behavior would be exhibiting high intrapersonal and interpersonal intelligence. Like Sternberg's work, Gardner's theory cautions us against focusing on the results of IQ tests to the exclusion of other worthwhile behaviors. (See Case in Print for a real-life implementation of Gardner's work.)

Gardner and his colleagues are now in the process of trying to validate the theory of multiple intelligences. In one program, called Arts PROPEL, junior and senior high school students in the Pittsburgh public schools were assessed for growth in the areas of music, creative writing, and the visual arts. In a second project, all students in an Indianapolis elementary school were exposed to special classes and enrichment activities designed to enhance the various intelligences. A third effort, called Project Spectrum, is aimed at preschool and kindergarten children. Spectrum classrooms are equipped with a variety of materials that invite children to use one or another intelligence. For example, household objects that can be taken apart and reassembled afford children the opportunity to exercise spatial intelligence. Unlike traditional intelligence testing, where students respond to fairly brief written or spoken questions that are taken out of their naturally occurring context (where else would someone ask you to put together a puzzle in a limited amount of time?), Gardner and his associates measure intelligence by observing and evaluating what students do as they work through a variety of everyday tasks and projects. A preliminary assessment of Project Spectrum children provided partial support for Gardner's theory (Blythe & Gardner, 1990; Gardner & Hatch, 1989).

LIMITATIONS OF INTELLIGENCE TESTS

So where does all this leave us in terms of trying to decide what intelligence tests do and do not measure? Five points seem to be in order.

1. The appraisal of intelligence is limited by the fact that it cannot be measured directly. Our efforts are confined to measuring the overt

C A S E   I N   P R I N T

Multiple Answers to the Question of Who Is Smartest

Howard Gardner's (1983) conception of intelligence . . . is broader than traditional conceptions. . . . It describes at least seven separate types of intelligence. . . . Gardner's theory cautions us against focusing on the results of IQ tests to the exclusion of other worthwhile behaviors. (pp. 176–177)

"Intelligence Goes Way Beyond Test Scores"

CHARLES M. MADIGAN

Chicago Tribune 4/24/940

Two 3rd-grade classes from Carpenter School dropped in at the Chicago Children's Museum one bright morning a few days ago to visit an exhibit aimed at checking up on their "smarts" and how they might use them.

Four boys moved into a section full of big foam blocks, first creating a horse, then a castle, then a building just for knocking down, then a whole spectrum of devices secret to everyone but them.

At another station, girls in headphones listened to a beat, then recorded their own rap songs, playing them back, and editing them to create the variations on themes.

What was this all about?

On one level, it was play, most simply defined as "work for children." But the other answer is more complicated. Think of it as another way of measuring intelligence.

A few weeks ago Howard Gardner spoke to a standing room-only crowd at the museum about his theory of intelligence. . . .

Gardner, a Harvard psychologist, researcher, neurologist and successful author, believes there are at least seven paths of intelligence in everyone. Sometimes some of the paths are stronger than others. They are linguistic, logical mathematical, musical, spatial, bodily kinesthetic, interpersonal and intrapersonal.

At the Children's Museum, these are translated into the "smarts"—words, numbers, music, space, body, people and feelings. . . .

Gardner has found a telling way to make his point.

He presents the cover of a *Parade* magazine that asks "Are These the Smartest People in America?" The group includes retired Gen. Norman Schwartzkopf, mastermind of Operation Desert Storm; comedian George Burns; retired Supreme Court Justice William Brennan; author Toni Morrison; some Nobel prize winners; artists; and other performers.

"So," Gardner asks, "which of these people is smarter?"

Schwartzkopf has the highest IQ in the group at about 167. But Gardner says the question is stupid, because the people on the list are so different.

Stormin' Norman might be just the man to invite for an evening of beef and tactics, but no one would expect him to match George Burns on wit and timing or William Brennan on perception of the law and its significance. . . .

Each of these people is noted for a different kind of intelligence, Gardner points out. Society is willing, and sometimes eager, to embrace these different performances in adults.

But it won't do that for children.

They are measured by a different set of standards, generally on tests that, Gardner and his advocates argue, are terrific at showing how well a person takes tests, but not much of an indicator about how their lives will turn out. . . .

"If you just want to find out people of a certain type, schools do a pretty good job. But the hidden cost is that people that don't think that way, who can't learn to be scholastic, get lost on the sidelines. . . ."

He has a different message in two parts, both tied to his theories of intelligence.

The first is the importance of something he calls "personalization." Every person truly is an individual. But factory models of education don't work very well because they are predicated not on the differences, but on the assumption of the sameness in people.

The second part is that the goal of education is "understanding.". . .

"Intelligence is the ability to solve a problem or make something valued in at least one culture of a community," he says.

"There is no way to test that in a few minutes. . . . All we have are certain latent potentials which are or are not brought out. If Bobby Fischer lived in a culture without chess, you know, he would probably have been just another nerd."

. . .Teachers Nancy McAuliff and Nathalie Morgan see these theories playing out every day, but in some ways, they are powerless to respond to them.

Because there is no music program for 3rd-graders at Carpenter, for example, the teachers do the best they can to channel their students with musical interests to help, or to lessons outside of school.

But not having a music program may not be the biggest problem.

Most public schools and private schools work on assumptions about what it is that society values, one of the teachers pointed out. If society values high test scores, word smarts and math, it presents problems for the student whose strongest path of intelligence is artistic. . . .

Teachers are bound to teach the curriculum.

Gardner's theory argues that the need to follow the plan at any expense is the greatest barricade to the kind of teaching he advocates. His model would use those natural avenues of intelligence to teach to a student's strength.

There would be lots of things for children to do, lots of avenues for them to pursue.

Questions and Activities

1. In addition to the kinds of museum exhibits and explorations described in the article, what are some possible applications of Gardner's theory about multiple intelligences? Try to think of uses and experiences that apply inside the classroom and outside it.

2. You've learned that what has traditionally been called "intelligence" might better be called "scholastic aptitude." Gardner's exploration of multiple intelligences was in part a reaction against the traditional definition. How can it best coexist with current "scholastic" classrooms? With classrooms of the future? With your own view of the ideal classroom?

3. Imagine a conversation between two teachers, one a strong advocate of the traditional view of intelligence and the other a supporter of the multiple intelligences view. List about four or five differences in instructional assumptions, pedagogical values, and teaching strategies that might characterize these teachers.

4. During your student teaching, observe several students over a prescribed period of time with Gardner's seven categories in mind. Try to evaluate these students' particular strengths and identify their intelligences. Compare your evaluations with your master teacher's (who may have already used the students' numerical IQ scores to form opinions).

   Later in your own teaching (when you may have access to students' traditional IQ scores), do the same kind of observation *before* checking the numerical scores. Use this as a way to "unquantify" your opinion or to balance out the effect an IQ number may have on your view of an individual student.

manifestations (responses to test items) of what is ultimately based on brain function and experience.

2. The intelligence we test is a sample of intellectual capabilities that relate to classroom achievement better than they relate to anything else. That is why, as stated earlier, many psychologists prefer the terms *test of scholastic aptitude* or *test of school ability*.

3. No intelligence test score is an absolute measure. Many people—parents, especially—fail to grasp this fact. An IQ score is not a once-and-for-all judgment of how bright a child is. It is merely an estimate of how successful a child is in handling certain kinds of problems at a particular time on a particular test *as compared with other children of the same age*.

IQ scores can change with experience, training

4. Since IQ tests are designed to predict academic success, anything that enhances classroom performance (such as a wider range of factual information or more effective learning skills) will likely have a positive effect on intelligence test performance. In other words, IQ scores are not necessarily permanent. Research on the stability of IQ scores shows that, while they do not change significantly for most people, they can change dramatically for given individuals, and changes are most likely to occur among individuals who were first tested as preschoolers (Brody, 1992). This last point is often used to support early intervention programs like Head Start and Follow-Through.

IQ test items based on knowledge and situations thought to be common to most children

5. Since those who construct intelligence tests are primarily interested in a general capacity, they want to avoid, as much as possible, measuring abilities that are largely the result of a particular set of home or school experiences. If test makers ask questions too directly related to a specific kind of home or curriculum, they will measure only how well children have responded to these experiences. Children who have not had these experiences may then be unfairly judged as lacking in scholastic aptitude. To avoid this sort of error, test makers try to base the questions on knowledge and situations common to practically all children.

Given all these constraints and qualifications, you may be wondering whether the information that intelligence tests provide is worth knowing. While every person must decide that for himself, we believe that if you are fully aware of the nature and limitations of intelligence tests, they can be an effective tool for analyzing how individuals differ. Despite the shortcomings of these tests, we believe they provide an objective, economical, and timely assessment of an individual's current level of intellectual functioning. Because their appropriate use as well as that of other kinds of standardized tests is a topic of continued heated debate, however, we will spend the next section taking a critical look at certain important issues.

A Critical Look at the Misuses of Standardized Tests

Two types of misuses of standardized testing stand out as particularly important. First, we will look at the discriminatory judgments that have been made about certain groups of children when standardized test scores are the sole or primary basis for making educational decisions. Second, we will look at how standardized test scores have been used to make inappropriate judgments about the quality of teachers or school systems.

POTENTIAL DISCRIMINATORY MISUSE OF STANDARDIZED TESTS

On the average, American children who come from upper- and middle-SES homes perform better in school and on standardized tests than do children who come from lower-SES homes. Some critics of tests argue that improperly used test scores perpetuate or increase such differences. Some cite the overrepresentation of minority-group students in programs for the mentally retarded and their underrepresentation in programs for the gifted and talented as examples of how overreliance on a narrow range of test scores can harm students. Selection for gifted and talented programs is often based largely on classroom performance, standardized achievement test scores, and intelligence test scores. But talented members of minorities often hold values about school and academic achievement that differ from the norm. Their classroom performance and test scores may suffer as a result, thereby making them ineligible for these programs (Whitmore, 1987).

Overreliance on test scores can bar gifted and talented minority children from special programs

Consider Sioux children, for example. If they succeed in school, their Sioux peers think of them as lacking in independent thought, spontaneity, and creativity. Many Cherokee youngsters do not believe that success in school will have a positive impact on the quality of their lives on the reservation (Brantlinger & Guskin, 1985). Gifted and talented lower-SES African-American children may not embrace such traditional middle-class values as deferring immediate gratification (as in "Study first; then go out and play"), accepting the importance of symbolic indicators of success (such as grades or test scores), and focusing on the future (as in "Learning geometry and trigonometry now will help you become an engineer later") (Frasier, 1987; Stronge, Lynch, & Smith, 1987).

However, defenders of standardized tests maintain that tests, if interpreted properly, can be used to help *reduce* differences in academic performance. If a test accurately reveals that a student is below average in ability, for example, it is often wise to acknowledge that fact and arrange instructional experiences accordingly. If teachers assume that no differences in ability exist, they might be inclined to expose all students to the same sequences of educational experiences presented in the same way. In such a situation more capable and better prepared students are likely to thrive and less capable students with inadequate backgrounds are likely to fall further and further behind. Busing, Head Start and Follow-Through programs, continuation schools, and equal opportunity and affirmative action regulations are all based on the premise that some American children are raised in learning environments that are less desirable than others and that such students need assistance if they are to compete against more favored age-mates.

The basic issue here is whether reliance on standardized test scores, particularly IQ scores, helps or harms students. You should recognize that this issue cannot be resolved to everyone's satisfaction. Every psychologist, teacher, parent, lawyer, or legislator must take her own position on the basis of available evidence. Our view is that standardized tests can benefit students if those who use the scores understand fully both the nature of the characteristic being measured and the nature of the test.

Much of the criticism and controversy that has arisen over the use of standardized tests could perhaps have been avoided if the assessment principles proposed by Ronald Samuda, Shiu Kong, Jim Cummins, John Lewis, and Juan Pascual-Leone (1991, p. 182) had been followed. They believe that nondiscriminatory assessment results from the application of the following five principles:

Understanding the assessment process leads to nondiscriminatory testing

1. Use test scores to plan effective forms of instruction rather than as a basis for assigning students to existing programs.
2. Understand the nature of both the test being used and the student being tested.
3. Give students a comprehensive assessment that includes both standardized tests and informal measures.
4. Use the best data available to make decisions about students, regardless of whether the data reflect formal or informal assessment methods.
5. Assess a student's capacity to learn and develop in addition to his current knowledge and level of functioning.

AVOIDING TEST SCORE MISINTERPRETATION AND TEST SCORE POLLUTION

Over the last several years various individuals and groups have expressed strong dissatisfaction with the levels of achievement demonstrated by many students. To rectify matters, many of these individuals and groups feel that at least two things should be done. First, schools should provide tangible evidence (meaning scores from standardized tests) that students are mastering much of the curriculum to which they are exposed. Second, teachers whose students score at or above the norm on standardized achievement tests should be rewarded, while teachers whose students score below the norm should not be rewarded or should even be punished.

These pressures have led to an increase in the frequency of testing and to additional (and inappropriate) uses of standardized test scores. Many principals, for example, evaluate the quality of teachers' instruction on the basis of how the students in those classes score (above the norm, around the norm, below the norm). Schools, school districts, and states are likewise evaluated by superintendents, boards of education, state departments of education, legislatures, and the press.

Test scores inappropriately used to evaluate quality of teachers, schools, school districts

The use of standardized achievement test scores to draw inferences about how well teachers, schools, school districts, and states educate their children is inappropriate because the tests were not designed to support such use. There are many factors that are not assessed by these instruments, such as the physical facilities of a school and a student's home environment, that help determine the quality of teaching and learning (Feuer, Fulton, & Morison, 1993). The pressure to test more often (at least once every year in many districts) and to produce ever-increasing scores affect the students as well. By the time students get to high school, many have become suspicious and cynical about the purpose of standardized testing. Low achievers, in particular, become so anxious about their performance that they either cheat or approach the test with a blasé attitude. The result, of course, is that the test loses much of its validity (Paris, Lawton, Turner, & Roth, 1991). Nevertheless, principals and especially teachers feel compelled to raise students' scores as high as possible. The steps that some educators take to deal with this pressure result in a phenomenon called *test score pollution* (Haladyna, Nolen, & Haas, 1991).

Test score pollution refers to test-related practices that cause scores to go up or down but that are unrelated to what the test measures. Coaching students with items similar to those on the test, developing a curriculum based on the content of the test, dismissing low-achieving students on the day the test is given, and helping students choose the correct response to one or more questions are examples of practices that contribute to test pollution. These practices result in a meaningless score in the same way that students not taking a test seriously does. If you knew that Mr. Wallace engaged in some of the test polluting practices just mentioned but that Ms. Chang did not, and if the students in Mr. Wallace's class scored at the 74th percentile on a test of English grammar, whereas the students in Ms. Chang's class scored at the 57th percentile, would you be willing to conclude that Mr. Wallace's students learned more English grammar than did Ms. Chang's students? Of course not. But suppose you had no knowledge of Mr. Wallace's teaching and testing practices? Perhaps now you see the problems that are created with these practices, particularly when test scores are used to compare teachers, schools, and school districts.

Test score pollution: test-related practices that cause test scores to vary independent of what test measures

Although the likelihood of your engaging in any of the test polluting practices just mentioned is small, you should recognize that teachers are acutely aware of the pressure to raise scores. Consider, for example, the following exchange reported by Mary Lee Smith between a primary grade teacher and an interviewer concerning the use of scores from the Iowa Test of Basic Skills (ITBS):

Interviewer: Do the ITBS scores ever get used against you?

Teacher: Well, the first year I used Math Their Way (a program designed for conceptual understanding of math concepts through the manipulation of concrete materials), I was teaching a second grade class and they scored at grade level. But other second grades in that school scored higher than grade level, and I had to do an awful lot of talking before they allowed me to use that program again.

Interviewer: So they were willing to throw out the program on the basis of the scores. How did you feel?

Teacher: I was angry. I was really angry because so many of the things I had taught those children about math were not on the test—were not tested by the test. And, indeed, the following year they did extremely well in the third grade. I had no children who were in any of the low math classes and a great many of my children were in the advanced classes doing better than some of the children who had scored higher than they had on the ITBS. (1991, p. 8)

Because traditional standardized tests provide little or no information on how well students can use the knowledge they have acquired in school, educators are increasingly using performance tests. Popular types of performance tests include compiling portfolios of writing and math assignments, making a product, and conducting scientific experiments.

According to figures cited by Thomas Haladyna, Susan Nolen, and Nancy Haas (1991), 8.5 percent of secondary level teachers and 10 percent of elementary grade teachers engaged in the highly unethical practice of teaching students the actual items from the current year's test. In addition, 8 percent of the elementary teachers reported deviating from a test's standard directions or increasing the amount of time allotted to students.

Authentic and Performance-Based Assessments

As we noted at the beginning of this chapter, standardized testing is a prominent part of the American school experience; the typical student may take two or more such tests per year. But many educators have been dissatisfied for some time with the information that traditional standardized achievement tests provide and are experimenting with alternatives. These are commonly referred to as either performance-based assessment or authentic assessment. In this section, we will briefly discuss the nature of performance tests, how they are being used in state-mandated assessment programs, and why they are being increasingly looked to as a replacement for the traditional standardized achievement test. Because Chapter 12 will deal with classroom assessment (tests made up and administered by the teacher to assess mastery of material recently taught in class), we will revisit this topic in more detail.

WHAT IS PERFORMANCE ASSESSMENT?

Performance tests measure how well students can use knowledge and skill to solve problems

Performance tests attempt to assess how well students can use the knowledge and skills they have learned in the classroom to solve a problem or complete a task. They may, for example, be asked to interpret data from a graph, conduct an experiment in order to answer one or more questions about some

PAPER TOWELS INVESTIGATION—HANDS-ON SCORE FORM

Student ____________ Observer____________ Score ____________ Script ________

1. Method — A. Container — B. Drops — C. Tray (surface)

A. Container: Pour water in/put towel in; Put towel in/pour water in; 1 pitcher or 3 beakers/glasses

C. Tray (surface): towel on tray/pour water on; pour water on tray/wipe up

2. Saturation — A. Yes — B. No — C. Controlled

3. Determine Result

A. Weight
B. Squeeze towel/measure water (weight or volume)
C. Measure water in/out
D. Time to soak up water
E. No measurement
F. Count # drops until saturated
G. See how far drops spread out
H. Other ____________

4. Care in Measuring — Yes — No

5. Correct Result — Yes — No

Grade	Method	Saturate	Determine Result	Care in Measuring	Correct Answer
A	Yes	Yes	Yes	Yes	Yes
B	Yes	Yes	Yes	No	Yes/No
C	Yes	Yes/Controlled	Error		Yes/No
D	Yes	No	Missing		Yes/No
F	----------	----------	No Attempt	----------	----------

FIGURE 5.4 *Example of a Performance-Based Assessment*

SOURCE: Shavelson & Baxter (1992).

phenomenon, explain what they do to figure out the meaning of an unfamiliar word or reference in a story, construct a portfolio of a writing project that illustrates its different phases (outline, first draft, second draft, final draft), or solve mathematics problems and explain why they chose the solution procedure they did (O'Neil, 1992). When these performances are given under realistic conditions (such as access to reference materials and other people, generous time limits, opportunity to use corrective feedback to refine a product), they are also called authentic assessments. Perhaps the clearest way to distinguish between traditional norm-referenced achievement tests and performance tests is to say that the former measure how much students *know* compared to one another, whereas the latter measure what students *can do* with what they know compared to preexisting standards. See Figure 5.4 for an example of one variation of performance-based assessment.

In recent years several states have moved to statewide assessments that are either primarily or totally performance based. Vermont's assessment program, for example, is based entirely on the evaluation of math and writing portfolios. Kentucky requires writing portfolios and performances in science, social studies, and mathematics. Maryland's program incorporates performance assessments of writing and reading comprehension (O'Neil, 1992). The reasons that performance assessment is becoming a popular testing format for statewide assessments will be noted in the following discussion.

REASONS FOR THE GROWTH OF PERFORMANCE TESTING

Emphasis on Accountability As far back as the 1960s, groups of parents, teachers, and educational critics were calling for better ways to define and measure student achievement than traditional norm-referenced written tests could provide. Two responses that were popular in the 1960s and 1970s were the specification of student outcomes in terms of behavioral objectives and the use of criterion-referenced tests. In the 1980s many states mandated that students pass minimal competency tests before being awarded a high school diploma. In this decade much is being written about outcome-based education (described in Chapter 7) and, of course, performance assessment as ways to determine the extent to which educational goals are being achieved (Stiggins, 1994).

Limitations of Standardized Tests Traditional norm-referenced multiple-choice tests are designed to measure generally accepted goals rather than the specific objectives to which a school or district might subscribe. Consequently, these tests assess a broad array of basic factual knowledge and skills in order to appeal to the greatest number of school districts. Subject areas are not assessed in depth, and no evidence is collected as to what students can do with the knowledge they acquire. In addition, these tests do not allow teachers the opportunity to probe the reasoning behind a response. Although such tests partly satisfy demands for accountability since direct comparisons between schools and districts can be made, they do not address the concern that too many students are graduating from high school without having demonstrated that they know how to use the knowledge they have acquired (Worthen, 1993).

Dissatisfaction with Levels of Achievement A basic assumption on which conventional classroom testing rests is that individuals who achieve high scores have learned a variety of facts, concepts, principles, and procedures that they will be able to apply in other settings. But this assumption is not always true. For example, in Chapter 10 we will recount an anecdote by Richard Feynman (1985), a Nobel Prize–winning physicist, about the inability of his classmates at the Massachusetts Institute of Technology to recognize a specific application of a general mathematical formula they all had learned in a previous class. He refers to his classmates' knowledge as "fragile." John Bransford, an educational psychologist, has observed the same inability among many students and characterizes them as having "inert knowledge" (Bransford, Sherwood, Vye, & Rieser, 1986).

The gap between expectation and result started becoming apparent in the 1970s. Colleges and businesses complained that many high school and college graduates were not prepared to handle the tasks given to them by instructors or supervisors because of an inability to productively use whatever knowledge and skill they had acquired in school. Colleges felt compelled to establish learning skills programs, and the business community spent hundreds of millions of dollars a year to teach new employees the thinking skills it felt the schools had neglected. Performance testing is expected to help teachers produce more students who can use what they know to solve a variety of problems in various settings because it emphasizes a closer relationship between teaching and testing.

In the next section we offer several Suggestions for Teaching that will help you and your students appropriately use standarized test scores.

Suggestions for Teaching in Your Classroom

Using Standardized Tests

1. Before you give a standardized test, emphasize that students should do their best, and give them suggestions for taking such tests.

2. Examine the test booklet and answer sheet in advance so that you are familiar with the test.

3. Be cautious when interpreting scores, and always give the student the benefit of the doubt.

4. Do your best to control the impact of negative expectations.

5. If student folders contain individual intelligence test scores, ask for an interpretation by the psychometrist who administered the test (or ask an equally knowledgeable person).

6. Be prepared to offer parents clear and accurate information about their children's test scores.

7. Create lessons that emphasize different intelligences.

Journal Entry
Using Standardized Tests

1. Before you give a standardized test, emphasize that students should do their best, and give suggestions for taking such tests.

For maximum usefulness, scores on standardized tests should be as accurate a representation of actual ability as possible.

Accordingly, the day before a standardized test is scheduled, tell your students that they should do their best. Emphasize that the scores will be used to help them improve their school performance and that they should concentrate on answering questions as well as they can without feeling that they are competing against others. You may be able to partly reduce the anxiety and tension that are almost inevitable under formal testing conditions by giving some test-taking hints in advance. Robert Linn and Norman Gronlund note the following skills that might be stressed (depending on the type of test and the grade level of the student):

Journal Entry
Explaining Test-Taking Skills

1. Listening to or reading directions carefully
2. Listening to or reading test items carefully
3. Setting a pace that will allow time to complete the test
4. Bypassing difficult items and returning to them later
5. Making informed guesses rather than omitting items

6. Eliminating as many alternatives as possible on multiple-choice items before guessing
7. Following directions carefully in marking the answer sheet (tell students to darken the entire space, for example)
8. Checking to be sure the item number and answer number match when marking an answer
9. Checking to be sure the appropriate response was marked on the answer sheet
10. Going back and checking the answers if time permits (1995, p. 430)

2. **Examine the test booklet and answer sheet in advance so that you are familiar with the test.**

Ideally you might take the test yourself so that you become thoroughly familiar with what your students will be doing. If there are any aspects of recording scores that are especially tricky, you might mention these when you give your test-taking skills presentation or when you hand out examination booklets and answer sheets.

3. **Be cautious when interpreting scores, and always give the student the benefit of the doubt.**

Journal Entry
Interpreting Test Scores

The profiles or reports you will receive a few weeks after a test has been administered will contain information that is potentially beneficial to you and to your students. If misused or misinterpreted, however, the information is potentially harmful. Misinterpretations of scores can lead to complaints by parents. Therefore, as you examine the scores concentrate on ways you can make positive use of the results. Look for areas of weakness in student performance that need special attention. At the same time, do your best to avoid forming negative expectations. Chances are that the overall test scores will often reinforce your own impressions of the general abilities of students. You can't help forming such impressions, and they can work to the advantage of students. If a student has had trouble with almost every assignment and classroom test you have given, it is often the case that test scores will reflect that level of performance. If such a student scores higher than expected, however, you might ask yourself if your expectations for that student have been too low and make a resolution to give extra help and encouragement, using the test scores to provide direction.

If a student's test scores are lower than you expected them to be, examine them to discover areas of weakness, but guard against thinking, "Well, I guess he had me fooled. He's not as sharp as I thought he was. Maybe I had better lower grades a notch on the next report card." There are many reasons a student may not do well on a test (for example, anxiety, fatigue, illness, worry about some home or school interpersonal situation), and scores may not be an accurate reflection of current capability. Thus, whenever there is a discrepancy between test scores and observed classroom performance, always assume that the more favorable impression is the one to use as an indication of general capability. Try to use indications of below-average performance in constructive ways to help students overcome inadequacies.

4. **Do your best to control the impact of negative expectations.**

As you peruse student test scores, do your best to resist the temptation to label or categorize students, particularly those who have a consistent pattern of low scores. Instead of succumbing to thoughts that such students are incapable of learning, you might make an effort to concentrate on the idea that they need extra encouragement and individualized attention. Use the information on test profiles to help them overcome their learning difficulties, not to justify fatalistically ignoring their problems.

5. **If student folders contain individual intelligence test scores, ask for an interpretation by the psychometrist who administered the test (or ask an equally knowledgeable person).**

Because the concept of intelligence is complex and emotionally charged, you should be extremely careful about how you interpret scores on tests such as the Stanford-Binet or WISC—III. Such scores are not likely to be found in the folders of more than a few of your students; but when they *are* included, ask for an interpretation by a qualified person, particularly if the parents ask for an explanation.

6. **Be prepared to offer parents clear and accurate information about their children's test scores.**

For a variety of reasons, misconceptions about the nature of standardized tests are common. As a result, many parents do not fully understand what their children's scores mean. Parent-teacher conferences are probably the best time to correct misconceptions and provide some basic information about the meaning of standardized test scores. In an unobtrusive place on your desk, you might keep a brief list of points to cover as you converse with each parent. In one way or another you should mention that test scores should be treated as *estimates* of whatever was measured (achievement, for example). There are two reasons for representing test scores in this fashion. First, tests do not (indeed, they cannot) assess everything that students know or that makes up a particular capability. Standardized achievement tests, for example, tend to cover a relatively broad range of knowledge but do not assess any one topic in great depth. Therefore, students may know more than their scores suggest. Second, all tests contain some degree of error because of such factors as vaguely worded items, confusing directions, and low motivation on the day the test is administered.

Remember that a student's test score reflects the extent to which the content of that test has been mastered at about the time the test was taken. A student may have strengths and weaknesses not measured by a particular test, and because of changes in such characteristics as interests, motives, and cognitive skills, test scores can change, sometimes dramatically. The younger the student is and the longer the interval is between testings (on the same test), the greater the likelihood that a test score will change significantly.

What a test score means depends on the nature of the test. If an intelligence or a scholastic aptitude test was taken by your students, point out that such tests measure the current status of those cognitive skills that most closely relate to academic success. Also mention that IQ scores are judged to be below average, average, or above average on the basis of how they compare to the scores of a norm group. You might use personal wealth as an analogy to illustrate this last point. Whether someone is considered poor, financially comfortable, or wealthy depends on how much money everyone else in that person's reference group possesses. A net worth of $100,000 is considered wealthy in some circles but barely adequate in others.

If you are discussing achievement test scores, make sure you understand the differences among diagnostic tests, norm-referenced tests, and criterion-referenced tests. Scores from a diagnostic achievement test can be used to discuss a student's strengths and weaknesses in such skills as reading, math, and spelling. Scores from a norm-referenced achievement test can be used to discuss general strengths and weaknesses in one or more content areas. For achievement tests that provide multiple sets of norms, start your interpretation at the most local level (school norms, ideally) since they are likely to be the most meaningful to parents, and then move to a more broad-based interpretation (district, state, or national norms). Scores from a criterion-referenced achievement test can be used to discuss how well a student has mastered the objectives on which the test is based. If there is a close correspondence between the test's objectives and those of the teacher, the test score can be used as an indicator of how much the student has learned in class.

The instructional decisions you make in the classroom will be *guided* but not dictated by the test scores. Many parents fear that if their child obtains a low score on a test, she will be labeled a slow learner by the teacher and will receive less attention than higher-scoring students. This is a good opportunity to lay such a fear to rest in two ways. First, note that test scores are but *one* source of information about students. You will also take into account how well they perform on classroom tests, homework assignments, and special projects as well as in classroom discussions. Second, emphasize that you are committed to using test scores not to classify students but to help them learn (and think of Alfred Binet as you say this).

7. Create lessons that emphasize different intelligences.

As Howard Gardner and others point out, most of the tasks that we ask students to master reflect the linguistic and/or logical-mathematical forms of intelligence. But there are five other ways that students can come to know things and demonstrate what they have learned. Potentially, lesson plans for any subject can be designed that incorporate each of Gardner's seven intelligences. Here are a few examples suggested either by Thomas Armstrong (1994) or David Lazear (1992).

Elementary Grades: Punctuation Marks

Bodily-kinesthetic: students use their bodies to mimic the shape of various punctuation marks.

Musical: students make up different sounds and/or songs for each punctuation mark.

Interpersonal: in small groups of four to six students teach and test each other on proper punctuation usage.

Middle School Grades: American History

Linguistic: students debate the pros and cons of key historical decisions (such as Abraham Lincoln's decision to use military force to prevent the Confederate states from seceding from the Union, the Supreme Court decision in *Plessy* v. *Ferguson* that allowed separate facilities for African Americans and whites, President Harry Truman's decision to drop the atomic bomb on Japan).

Musical: students learn about and sing some of the songs that were popular at a particular point in a country's history.

Spatial: students draw murals that tell the story of a historical period.

High School Grades: Boyle's Law (Physics)

Logical-mathematical: students solve problems that require the use of Boyle's Law (for a fixed mass and temperature of gas, the pressure is inversely proportional to the volume, or P x V = K).

Bodily-kinesthetic: students breathe air into their mouths, move it to one side of their mouths (so that one cheek is puffed out), indicate whether the pressure goes up or down, distribute it to both sides of their mouths, and indicate again whether the pressure goes up or down.

Intrapersonal: students describe times in their lives when they felt they were either under a lot of psychological pressure or little pressure and whether they felt as if they had either a lot of or a little psychological space.

Resources for Further Investigation

Technical and Specialized Aspects of Testing

For more information about standardized tests and how to appropriately use the information they provide, consult one or more of these books: *Psychological Testing* (6th ed., 1988), by Anne Anastasi; *Essentials of Psychological Testing* (5th ed., 1990), by Lee Cronbach; *Essentials of Educational Measurement* (5th ed., 1991), by Robert Ebel and David Frisbie; *Measurement and Assessment in Teaching* (7th ed., 1995), by Robert Linn and Norman Gronlund; and *Tests and Assessment* (3d ed., 1995), by W. Bruce Walsh and Nancy Betz.

For information about issues surrounding the testing of minority students, examine *Psychological Testing of Hispanics* (1992), edited by Kurt Geisenger; *Assessment and Placement of Hispanics* (1992), edited by Kurt Geisenger; and *Assessment and Placement of Minority Students* (1991), by Ronald Samuda and associates.

Critiques of Standardized Testing

A critical view of the nature of standardized tests and how they might be changed can be found in *Standardized Tests and Our Children: A Guide to Testing Reform* (1990), by the organization FairTest.

References for Evaluating Standardized Tests

To obtain the information necessary for evaluating standardized tests, examine *Ninth Mental Measurements Yearbook* (1985), edited by James Mitchell, Jr.; *Tenth Mental Measurements Yearbook* (1989), edited by Jane Close Conoley and Jack Kramer; and *Test Critiques* (Vols. 1–8) (1984–1991), edited by Daniel Keyser and Richard Sweetland.

You may have to check earlier editions of *Mental Measurements Yearbook* and *Test Critiques* for information on a specific test since there are far too many tests available for either publication to review in a single edition.

Some additional on-line resources for you to explore include the ERIC/AE Test Locater, whose address is gopher://vms-gopher.cua.edu/11gopher_root_eric_ae:[_tc].

The American Educational Research Association has an excellent index to test information, including a Code of Fair Testing Practices, found at gopher://vms-gopher.cua.edu/00gopher_root_eric_ae%3a%5b_tc%5d_code.txt.

More information about standardized tests, such as the SAT, developed by the Educational Testing Service (ETS) can be found at http://hub.terc.edu/ra/ets.html.

Taking an Intelligence Test

If you wonder what it is like to take an individual test of intelligence, you might check on the possibility that a course in individual testing needs subjects for practice purposes. (In most courses of this type, each student is required to give several tests under practice conditions.) Look in a class schedule for a course in psychology or education designated as Individual Testing, Practicum in Testing, or something similar. Contact the instructor and ask whether she wants subjects. If you do find yourself acting as a guinea pig, jot down your reactions to the test immediately after you take it. Would you feel comfortable having the score used to determine whether you are admitted to some program or qualify for a promotion? Did the test seem to provide an adequate sample of your intelligence? Were the kinds of questions appropriate for your conception of intelligence? Write down comments on the implications of your reactions.

Summary

1. Two types of student variability can be observed: intraindividual and interindividual. Intraindividual variability refers to differences in an individual's behavior over time and across situations. Interindividual variability refers to the differences between individuals at a given point in time.

2. Most of the research on interindividual variation revolves around scholastic aptitude, achievement, and their assessment with standardized tests.

3. Standardized tests are designed by people with specialized training in test construction, are given to everyone under the same conditions, are scored the same for everyone, and are interpreted with reference either to a norm group or a set of predetermined standards.

4. The purpose of giving a standardized test is to obtain an accurate and representative sample of some characteristic of a person, since it is impractical to measure that characteristic comprehensively.

5. Standardized tests are typically used to identify students' strengths and weaknesses, inform parents of their child's general level of achievement, plan instructional lessons, and place students in special groups or programs.

6. One of the most important characteristics of a standardized test is its reliability—the similarity between two rankings of test scores obtained from the same individuals.

7. Another important characteristic of standardized tests is validity. A valid test accurately measures what its users intend it to measure and allows us to draw appropriate inferences about how much of some characteristic the test taker possesses. Three types of evidence that contribute to accurate inferences are content validity evidence, predictive validity evidence, and construct validity evidence.

8. A third important characteristic of a standardized test is its norm group—a sample of students specially chosen and tested so as to reflect the population of students for whom the test is intended. The norm group's performance becomes the standard against which scores are compared.

9. Standardized achievement tests measure how much has been learned about

a particular subject. The major types of achievement tests are single subject, batteries, diagnostic, competency, and special purpose.

10. Diagnostic tests identify specific strengths and weaknesses in basic learning skills.
11. Competency tests measure how well high school students have acquired such basic skills as reading, writing, and computation.
12. Aptitude tests estimate an individual's predisposition to acquire additional knowledge and skill in specific areas with the aid of effective instruction.
13. Tests that use a norm-referenced scoring system compare an individual's score to the performance of a norm group.
14. Tests that use a criterion-referenced scoring system judge scores in terms of mastery of a set of objectives.
15. Percentile rank indicates the percentage of scores that are at or below a person's score.
16. A z score is a standard score that indicates how far in standard deviation units a raw score is from the mean.
17. A T score is a standard score that indicates in whole positive numbers how far a raw score is from the mean.
18. A stanine score indicates in which of nine normal-curve segments a person's performance falls.
19. One of the most widely used but poorly understood standardized tests is the intelligence, or IQ, test.
20. The first practical test of intelligence was devised by Alfred Binet to identify students who would be best served in a special education program.
21. Because of a focus on academic success, intelligence tests are not good predictors of anything else, such as job success, marital happiness, and life satisfaction.
22. Intelligence, broadly defined, is the global capacity of the individual to act purposefully, think rationally, and deal effectively with the environment.
23. The intelligence that we test is but a sample of intellectual skills—those that closely relate to classroom achievement.
24. Robert Sternberg's triarchic theory of intelligence holds that an important part of intelligence is the ability to adapt to one's environment in order to achieve personal goals.
25. Howard Gardner's multiple intelligences theory holds that each person has seven distinct intelligences, some of which are more well developed than others.
26. As a person's intellectual skills improve with experience and/or training, the individual's IQ score may improve.
27. When test scores are the sole or primary basis for making educational decisions, unfair practices can result. For example, in some areas lower-SES and ethnic minority students are overrepresented in classes for the mentally retarded and underrepresented in classes for the gifted and talented.
28. In recent years test scores have been inappropriately used to assess the quality of instruction provided by teachers, schools, school districts, and entire states.
29. This constant pressure on educators to raise test scores to please critics has led to test score pollution—test preparation and test-taking practices that artificially inflate or deflate scores.
30. In recent years several statewide assessment programs have replaced their traditional norm-referenced, multiple-choice achievement tests with one or more types of performance tests. A performance test assesses how well students can use the knowledge and skill they have learned in the classroom to solve different types of problems and complete various tasks.

Key Terms

intraindividual variation *(160)*
interindividual variation *(160)*
standardized tests *(162)*
reliability *(164)*
validity *(165)*
norm group *(166)*
single-subject achievement test *(167)*
achievement battery *(167)*
diagnostic test *(167)*
competency test *(167)*
special-purpose achievement test *(167)*
aptitude tests *(168)*
group test of scholastic aptitude *(168)*
individual intelligence test *(168)*
norm-referenced test *(168)*
criterion-referenced test *(169)*
performance-based or authentic assessment *(169)*
grade equivalent score *(169)*
percentile rank *(170)*
standard deviation *(170)*
normal curve *(170)*
z score *(171)*
T score *(171)*
stanine score *(171)*
test score pollution *(183)*

Discussion Questions

1. If you are like most people, you took a variety of standardized tests throughout your elementary and high school years. The results of those tests were probably used to help determine what you would be taught and how. Do you think that those tests adequately reflected what you had learned and were capable of learning and, therefore, were always used in your best interest? What can you do to increase the chances you will use that test scores to help *your* students fulfill their potential?

2. Think about norm-referenced tests and criterion-referenced tests. Which do you think you prefer? Why? Can you describe a set of circumstances in which a norm-referenced test would be clearly preferable to a criterion-referenced test and vice versa?

3. If you had to tell parents about the results of a standardized test, which type of score could you explain most clearly: raw score, percentile rank, z score, T score, or stanine score? Which do you think would be most informative for parents? For you as a teacher? If you do not understand completely the one that you think most informative, what can you do about this situation?

4. Imagine that you are sitting in the faculty lounge listening to a colleague describe one of her students. Your colleague points out that this student has a C+ average and received an IQ score of 92 (low average) on a recently administered test. She concludes that since the student is working up to his ability level, he should not be encouraged to set higher goals because that would only lead to frustration. Your colleague then asks for your opinion. How do you respond?

CHAPTER 6

Dealing with Student Variability

Key Points

These key points will help you learn the important information in this chapter. To help you study, they also appear in the margins of pages, next to the text where they are discussed.

Ability Grouping

- Ability grouping assumes intelligence is inherited, reflected by IQ, unchangeable, and instruction will be superior
- No research support for between-class ability grouping
- Joplin Plan and within-class ability grouping for math produce moderate increases in learning
- Between-class ability grouping negatively influences teaching goals and methods
- Joplin Plan and within-class ability grouping may allow for better-quality instruction

The Individuals with Disabilities Education Act (PL 101-476)

- Before placement, student must be given complete, valid, and appropriate evaluation
- IEP must include objectives, services to be provided, criteria for determining achievement
- Students with disabilities must be educated in least restrictive environment
- Mainstreaming: policy of placing students with disabilities in regular classes
- Inclusion policy aims to keep students with disabilities in regular classroom for entire day
- Procedural safeguards intended to protect rights of student
- Students who are learning disabled, speech impaired, mentally retarded, or emotionally disturbed most likely to be served under PL 101-476

- Students who are speech impaired, learning disabled, otherwise health impaired, or visually impaired are most likely to attend regular classes
- Multidisciplinary assessment team determines if student needs special services
- Classroom teacher, parents, several specialists prepare IEP

STUDENTS WITH MENTAL RETARDATION

- Students with mild retardation may frustrate easily, lack confidence and self-esteem
- Students with mild retardation tend to oversimplify, have difficulty generalizing
- Give students with mild retardation specific assignments that can be completed quickly

STUDENTS WITH LEARNING DISABILITIES

- Learning disabilities: disorders in basic processes that lead to learning problems not due to other causes
- Students with learning disabilities have problems with perception, attention, memory, metacognition
- Help students with learning disabilities to reduce distractions, attend to important information

STUDENTS WITH EMOTIONAL DISTURBANCE

- Emotional disturbance: poor relationships, inappropriate behavior, depression, fears
- Term *behavior disorder* focuses on behavior that needs to be changed, objective assessment
- Students with behavior disorders tend to be either aggressive or withdrawn
- Foster interpersonal contact among withdrawn students
- Use techniques to forestall aggressive or antisocial behavior

GIFTED AND TALENTED STUDENTS

- Gifted and talented students show high performance in one or more areas
- Minorities underrepresented in gifted classes because of overreliance on test scores
- Gifted and talented students have stronger academic self-concept but average physical, social self-concepts
- Separate classes for gifted and talented students aid achievement but may lower academic self-concept

If you have had the opportunity to observe or work in an elementary, middle, or secondary classroom recently, you know that today's teacher can expect to have a wide variety of students who differ in abilities, talents, and backgrounds. The reasons for such diversity include compulsory attendance laws, patterns of immigration, and laws that govern which students can and cannot be placed in special classes, not to mention normal variations in physical, social, emotional, and cognitive development. The task of guiding each member of a diverse group of students toward high levels of learning is one of teaching's major challenges. We hope to help you meet this challenge by making you aware in this chapter of different ways of dealing with student variability.

Historical Developments

Prior to the turn of the century, dealing with student variability was an issue few educators had to face. Most communities were fairly small, and students in a given school tended to come from similar ethnic and economic backgrounds. In addition, poorer families often viewed a child's labor as more important than a complete, formal education, and many states had not yet enacted compulsory attendance laws. As a result, many low–socioeconomic status (SES) children did not attend school regularly or at all. In 1900, for example, only 8.5 percent of eligible students attended high school (Boyer, 1983), and these students were almost entirely from the upper and middle classes (Gutek, 1992). In comparison with today's schools, then, earlier student populations were considerably less diverse.

THE GROWTH OF PUBLIC EDUCATION AND AGE-GRADED CLASSROOMS

By 1920 this picture had changed, largely because of three developments. First, by 1918 all states had passed compulsory attendance laws. Second, child labor laws had been enacted by many states, as well as by Congress in 1916, to eliminate the hiring of children and adolescents in mines and factories. Third, large numbers of immigrant children arrived in the United States from 1901 through 1920. During those years, 14.5 million individuals, mostly from eastern and southern Europe, arrived on U.S. shores (Morris, 1961). The result was a vast increase in the number and diversity of children attending elementary and high school.

Educators initially dealt with this growth in student variability by forming age-graded classrooms. Introduced in the Quincy, Massachusetts, schools in the mid-1800s, these classrooms grouped all students of a particular age together each year to master a certain portion of the school's curriculum (Gutek, 1992). The main assumptions behind this approach were that teachers could be more effective in helping students learn and that students would have more positive attitudes toward themselves and school when classrooms were more *homogeneous* than *heterogeneous* (Oakes, 1985; Peltier, 1991). Regardless of whether these assumptions were well founded (an issue we will address shortly), they were (and still are) so widely held by educators that two additional approaches to creating even more homogeneous groups were eventually implemented—ability grouping and special class placement.

ABILITY-GROUPED CLASSROOMS

Ability grouping involved the use of standardized mental ability or achievement tests to create groups of students who were considered very similar to each other in learning ability. In elementary and middle schools, students typically were (and frequently still are) placed in a low-, average-, or high-ability groups. At the high school level, students were placed into different tracks that were geared toward such different post–high school goals as college, secretarial work, or vocational school.

Ability grouping was another means for school authorities to deal with the large influx of immigrant students. Since many of these children were not fluent in English and had had limited amounts of education in their native countries, they scored much lower on standardized tests when compared to American test norms. In addition, many of these children came from poor homes and were in poor health. At the time their assignment to a low-ability group seemed both the logical and appropriate thing to do (Wheelock, 1994).

In the first major part of this chapter, we will look at current applications of ability grouping, which nowadays takes several forms and is still used to reduce the normal range of variability in cognitive ability and achievement found in the typical classroom.

SPECIAL EDUCATION

For more or less normal children, age grading and ability testing were seen as workable approaches to creating more homogeneous classes. But compulsory attendance laws also brought to school many children with mild to severe mental and physical disabilities. These students were deemed incapable of profiting from any type of normal classroom instruction and so were assigned to special schools. Unfortunately, and as Alfred Binet feared, the labeling of a student as mentally retarded or physically disabled often resulted in a vastly inferior education. Early in this century, special schools served as convenient dumping grounds for all kinds of children who could not adapt to the regular classroom (Ysseldyke & Algozzine, 1995).

In the latter two-thirds of this chapter, we will detail the varied types and degrees of special class placement for children whose intellectual, social, emotional, or physical development falls outside (above as well as below) the range of normal variation. In discussing this approach, we pay particular attention to Public Law (PL) 101-476, which was enacted to counter past excesses of special class placement and to encourage the placement of children with disabilities in regular classes to the greatest extent possible.

Ability Grouping

Ability grouping is a widespread practice (e.g., Oakes, Quartz, Gong, Guiton, & Lipton, 1993; Wheelock, 1994). For example, 60 percent of all elementary schools use some form of between-class ability grouping, in the middle grades some form of ability grouping exists in 82 percent of schools, and approximately 80 percent of all high schools place students into tracks on the basis of standardized test scores. In this section we will describe the most common ways in which teachers group students by ability, examine the assumptions that provide the rationale for this practice, summarize research findings on the effectiveness of ability grouping, and look at alternative courses of action.

TYPES OF ABILITY GROUPS

Four approaches to ability grouping are popular among educators today: *between-class ability grouping, regrouping,* the *Joplin Plan,* and *within-class grouping.* Given their widespread use, you may be able to recall a few classes in which one or another of these techniques was used. If not, you will no doubt encounter at least one of them during your first year of teaching.

In ability grouping, students are selected and placed in homogeneous groups with other students who are considered to have very similar learning abilities.

Between-Class Ability Grouping The goal of **between-class ability grouping** is that each class be made up of students who are homogeneous in standardized intelligence or achievement test scores. Three levels of classes are usually formed—high, average, and low. Students in one ability group typically have little or no contact with students in others during the school day. Although each group covers the same subjects, a higher group does so in greater depth and breadth than lower groups. At the high school level, this approach is often called *tracking*. Groups are usually referred to as college preparatory, business/secretarial, vocational/technical, and general.

Regrouping The groups formed under a **regrouping** plan are more flexible in assignments and are narrower in scope than between-class groups. Students of the same age, ability, and grade but from different classrooms come together for instruction in a specific subject, usually reading or mathematics. If a student begins to significantly outperform the other members of the group, a change of group assignment is easier since it involves just that particular subject. Regrouping has two major disadvantages, however. First, it requires a certain degree of planning and cooperation among the teachers involved. They must agree, for example, to schedule reading and arithmetic during the same periods. Second, many teachers are uncomfortable working with children whom they see only once a day for an hour or so.

Joplin Plan The **Joplin Plan** is a variation of regrouping. The main difference is that regroupings take place *across* grade levels. For example, all third, fourth, and fifth graders whose grade equivalent scores in reading are 4.6 (fourth grade, sixth month) would come together for reading instruction. The same would be done for mathematics. The Joplin Plan has the same advantages and disadvantages as simple regrouping.

Within-Class Ability Grouping The most popular form of ability grouping, occurring in almost all elementary school classes, **within-class ability grouping** involves the division of a single class of students into two or three groups for reading and math instruction. Like regrouping and the Joplin Plan, within-class ability grouping has the advantages of being flexible in terms of group assignments and being restricted to one or two subjects. In addition, it eliminates the need for cooperative scheduling. One disadvantage of this approach is that the teacher needs to be skilled at keeping the other students in the class productively occupied while working with a particular group.

ASSUMPTIONS UNDERLYING ABILITY GROUPING

Ability grouping assumes intelligence is inherited, reflected by IQ, unchangeable, and instruction will be superior

When ability grouping was initiated earlier in this century, much less was known about the various factors that affect classroom learning. Consequently, educators simply assumed certain things to be true. One of those assumptions was that intelligence, which affects the capacity to learn, was a fixed trait and that little could be done to change the learning capacity of individuals. A second assumption was that intelligence was adequately reflected by an intelligence quotient (IQ) score. A third assumption was that all students would learn best when grouped with those of similar ability (Marsh & Raywid, 1994; Oakes & Lipton, 1992). Although these assumptions are still believed to be true by many educators, the research evidence summarized here and elsewhere in this book casts doubt on their validity.

EVALUATIONS OF ABILITY GROUPING

Because ability grouping has been practiced in one form or another for several decades and occurs in virtually all school districts, its effects have been intensively studied (e.g., Dawson, 1987; Hoffer, 1992; Kulik & Kulik, 1991; Marsh & Raywid, 1994; Raudenbush, Rowan, & Cheong, 1993; Slavin, 1990). The main findings of these analyses are as follows:

No research support for between-class ability grouping

1. There is little to no support for between-class ability grouping. Students assigned to low-ability classes generally performed worse than comparable students in heterogeneous classes. Students assigned to average-ability classes performed at about the same level as their nongrouped peers. High-ability students sometimes performed slightly better in homogeneous classes than in heterogeneous classes.
2. Regrouping for reading or mathematics can be effective if the instructional pace and level of the text match the student's actual achievement level rather than the student's nominal grade level. In other words, a fifth grader who scores at the fourth-grade level on a reading test should be reading out of a fourth-grade reading book.

Joplin Plan and within-class ability grouping for math produce moderate increases in learning

3. The Joplin Plan yields moderately positive effects compared with instruction in heterogeneous classes.
4. Within-class ability grouping in mathematics in grades 3 through 6 produced moderately positive results compared with instruction in heterogeneous classes. Low achievers appeared to benefit the most from this arrangement. Because within-class ability grouping for

reading is an almost universal practice at every grade level, researchers have not had the opportunity to compare its effectiveness with whole-class reading instruction. Nevertheless, it would be reasonable to expect pretty much the same results for reading as were found for mathematics.

5. Students in homogeneously grouped classes scored the same as students in heterogeneously grouped classes on measures of self-esteem.
6. Students in high-ability classes had more positive attitudes about school and higher educational aspirations than did students in low-ability classrooms.
7. Ability grouping affected the quality of instruction received by students.
   a. The best teachers were often assigned to teach the highest tracks, whereas the least experienced or weakest teachers were assigned to teach the lowest tracks.
   b. Teachers of high-ability classes stressed critical thinking, self-direction, creativity, and active participation, whereas teachers of low-ability classes stressed working quietly, following rules, and getting along with classmates. This effect was particularly noticeable in math and science.
   c. Teachers of low-ability groups covered less material and simpler material than did teachers of high-ability groups.
   d. Teachers of low-ability students expected and demanded less of them than did teachers of high-ability students.

Between-class ability grouping negatively influences teaching goals and methods

TO GROUP OR NOT TO GROUP?

The findings just summarized suggest three courses of action. The first course is to discontinue the use of full-day, between-class ability groups. Despite the fact that almost 60 percent of the nation's elementary schools, 82 percent of its middle schools, and 80 percent of its high schools continue to use this form of ability grouping, students do not learn more or feel more positively about themselves and school. This is a case in which even widely held beliefs must be modified or eliminated when the weight of evidence goes against them.

The second course of action is to use only those forms of ability grouping that produce positive results: within-class grouping and the Joplin Plan, especially for reading and mathematics. We don't know at present why these forms of ability grouping work. It is *assumed* that the increase in class homogeneity allows for more appropriate and potent forms of instruction (for example, greater flexibility in moving students into and out of a particular group, greater availability of high-achieving role models, and greater effort by the teacher to bring lower-achieving groups up to the level of higher-achieving groups). If this assumption is correct, within-class ability grouping and the Joplin Plan must be carried out in such a way that homogeneous groups are guaranteed to result. The best way to achieve similarity in cognitive ability among students is to group them on the basis of past classroom performance, standardized achievement test scores, or both. The least

Joplin Plan and within-class ability grouping may allow for better-quality instruction desirable (but most frequently used) approach is to base the assignments solely on IQ scores.

The third course of action is to dispense with all forms of ability grouping and use a variety of organizational and instructional techniques that will allow the teacher to cope with a heterogeneous class or to use these same techniques in conjunction with the Joplin Plan or within-class grouping. For instance, you might use with all students instructional techniques that are associated with high achievement. These would include making clear presentations, displaying a high level of enthusiasm, reinforcing students for correct responses, providing sufficient time for students to formulate answers to questions, prompting correct responses, providing detailed feedback about the accuracy of responses, requiring a high level of work and effort, and organizing students into small, heterogeneous learning groups (a technique known as cooperative learning, which we discuss in detail in Chapter 11).

The Individuals with Disabilities Education Act (PL 101-476)

Many of the criticisms and arguments marshaled against ability grouping have come to be applied as well to special classes for students with disabilities. In addition, the elimination of racially segregated schools by the U.S. Supreme Court in the case of *Brown* v. *Board of Education* (1954) established a precedent for providing students with disabilities an equal opportunity for a free and appropriate education (Ornstein & Levine, 1993). As a result, influential members of Congress were persuaded in the early 1970s that it was time for the federal government to take steps to correct the perceived inequities and deficiencies in our educational system. The result was a landmark piece of legislation called Public Law 94-142, the Education for All Handicapped Children Act. PL 94-142 has been revised and expanded twice since it was signed into law in November 1975—initially in 1986 as the Handicapped Children's Protection Act (PL 99-457) and most recently in October 1990 as the Individuals with Disabilities Education Act (IDEA, PL 101-476). Since all of the features that were written into PL 94-142 and PL 99-457 were carried over into PL 101-476, we will use that name and public law number in the description and discussion that follow.

MAJOR PROVISIONS OF PUBLIC LAW 101-476

A Free and Appropriate Public Education The basic purpose of PL 101-476 is to ensure that all individuals from birth through age twenty-one who have an identifiable disability, regardless of how severe, receive at public expense supervised special education and related services that meet their unique educational needs. These services can be delivered in a classroom, at home, in a hospital, or in a specialized institution and may include physical education and vocational education as well as instruction in the typical academic subjects (Office of the Federal Register, 1994).

Preplacement Evaluation Before an individual with a disability can be placed in a program that provides special education services, "a full and individual evaluation of the child's educational needs" must be conducted. Such an evaluation must conform to the following rules:

Before placement, student must be given complete, valid, and appropriate evaluation

1. Tests must be administered in the child's native language.
2. A test must be valid for the specific purpose for which it is used.
3. Tests must be administered by trained individuals according to the instructions provided by the test publisher.
4. Tests administered to students who have impaired sensory, manual, or speaking skills must reflect aptitude or achievement rather than the impairment.
5. No single procedure (such as an IQ test) can be the sole basis for determining an appropriate educational program. Data should be collected from such nontest sources as observations by other professionals (such as the classroom teacher), medical records, and parental interviews.
6. Evaluations must be made by a multidisciplinary team that contains at least one teacher or other specialist with knowledge in the area of the suspected disability.
7. The child must be assessed in all areas related to the suspected disability (Office of the Federal Register, 1994).

When you deal with students whose first language is not English, it is important to realize that standardized tests are designed to reflect cultural experiences common to the United States and that English words and phrases may not mean quite the same thing when translated. Therefore, these tests may not be measuring what they were developed to measure. In other words, they may not be valid. The results of such assessments should therefore be interpreted very cautiously (Nuttall, 1987; Wilen & Sweeting, 1986).

Individualized Education Program Every child who is identified as having a disability and who receives special education services must have an **individualized education program (IEP)** prepared. The IEP is a written statement that describes the educational program that has been designed to meet the child's unique needs. The IEP must include the following elements:

1. A statement of the child's present levels of educational performance
2. A statement of annual goals, including short-term instructional objectives
3. A statement of the specific special education and related services to be provided to the child and the extent to which the child will be able to participate in regular educational programs
4. The projected dates for initiation of services and the anticipated duration of the services
5. Appropriate objective criteria and evaluation procedures and schedules for determining, on at least an annual basis, whether short-term objectives are being achieved (Code of Federal Regulations, 1994)

IEP must include objectives, services to be provided, criteria for determining achievement

The IEP is to be planned by the student's classroom teacher in collaboration with a person qualified in special education, one or both of the student's parents, the student (when appropriate), and other individuals at the discretion of the parents or school. (An example of an IEP is depicted on page 212.)

The least restrictive environment provision of the Individuals with Disabilities Education Act (PL 101-476) has led to mainstreaming—the policy that children with disabilities should attend regular classes to the maximum extent possible.

Least Restrictive Environment According to the 1994 *Code of Federal Regulations* that governs the implementation of PL 101-476, educational services must be provided to children with disabilities in the **least restrictive environment** that their disability will allow. A school district must identify a continuum of increasingly restrictive placements (instruction in regular classes, special classes, home instruction, instruction in hospitals and institutions) and, on the basis of the multidisciplinary team's evaluation, select the least restrictive setting that will best meet the student's special educational needs. This provision is often referred to as **mainstreaming** since the goal of the law is to have as many children with disabilities as possible, regardless of the severity of the disability, enter the mainstream of education by attending regular classes with nondisabled students.

Students with disabilities must be educated in least restrictive environment

Mainstreaming: policy of placing students with disabilities in regular classes

Although PL 101-476 clearly allows for *more restrictive* placements than those of the regular classroom "when the nature or severity of the disability is such that education in regular classes with the use of supplementary aids and services cannot be achieved satisfactorily" (Office of the Federal Register, 1994, p. 54), there has been a movement in recent years to eliminate this option. Known variously as **full mainstreaming, inclusion**, or **full inclusion**, this extension of the mainstreaming provision has become one of the most controversial outgrowths of PL 101-476. As most proponents use the terms, *full mainstreaming* and *inclusion* tend to be synonymous and mean keeping special education students in regular classrooms and bringing support services to the children rather than the other way around. Full inclusion is sometimes used as a synonym for inclusion (which makes things more than a bit confusing). It usually refers to the practice of eliminating all pull-out programs (that is, programs that occur outside the classroom) *and* special education teachers and of providing regular classroom teachers with training in teaching special needs students so that they can teach these students in the

Inclusion policy aims to keep students with disabilities in regular classroom for entire day regular classroom (Rogers, 1993; Smelter, Rasch, & Yudewitz, 1994; Staub & Peck, 1994/1995).

The proponents of inclusion often raise three arguments to support their position. First, research suggests that special needs students who are segregated from regular students perform more poorly academically and socially than comparable students who are mainstreamed. Second, given the substantial body of evidence demonstrating the propensity of children to observe and imitate more competent children (see, for example, Schunk, 1987), it can be assumed that students with disabilities will learn more by interacting with nondisabled students than by attending homogeneous classes. Third, the Supreme Court in *Brown* v. *Board of Education* declared the doctrine of "separate but equal" to be unconstitutional. Therefore, pull-out programs are a violation of the civil rights of children with special needs because these programs segregate them from their nondisabled peers in programs that are assumed to be separate but equal (Smelter et al., 1994; Staub & Peck, 1994/1995). The opponents of inclusion often cite cases of students who fail to learn basic skills, of students whose disabilities interrupt the normal flow of instruction, or of teachers who are ill-prepared to adequately assist the various special needs students who are placed in their classes (e.g., Baines, Baines, & Masterson, 1994; Idstein, 1993; Ohanian, 1990).

The evidence that bears on the inclusion issue is somewhat limited and inconsistent, but it seems to indicate, at least for now, that inclusion is a mostly workable and somewhat beneficial practice. The anecdotal evidence is perhaps the most inconsistent, as the article in Case in Print demonstrates. On the basis of the anecdotal and experimental evidence (e.g., Baker, Wang, & Walberg, 1994/1995; Ohanian, 1990; Raison, Hanson, Hall, & Reynolds, 1995; Staub & Peck, 1994/1995; Stevens & Slavin, 1995), two conclusions seem warranted. One is that mainstreaming may not be an appropriate course of action for every child with a disability, although it can probably be made to work for many such students. The other is that for students who are mainstreamed, IEPs should be written so as to better reflect what a given student probably can and cannot accomplish.

Procedural safeguards intended to protect rights of student

Procedural Safeguards The basic purpose of the various procedural safeguards that were written into PL 101-476 is to make sure that parents are fully informed about the actions a school district intends to take to classify their child as having a disability, to protect the legal rights of parents and their child, and to provide a way to resolve disputes about any aspect of the process. Among other rights, parents have the right to inspect their child's education records; obtain an independent assessment of their child; obtain written prior notice of identification, assessment, and placement procedures; request a due process hearing; appeal the results of a due process hearing; or file a lawsuit in state or federal court. A due process hearing is a fact-finding procedure that is intended to resolve disagreements between the school district and the parents of a child with a disability. Such hearings are usually composed of a hearing officer, the parents of the disabled child, school district personnel (such as the classroom teacher, the principal, and the school psychologist), and attorneys for the parents and the school district.

CASE IN PRINT

Inclusion—"Dumping" Students or Helping Them Reach Their Potential?

The evidence that bears on the inclusion issue is somewhat limited and inconsistent, but it seems to indicate, at least for now, that inclusion is a mostly workable and somewhat beneficial practice. (p. 205)

"Teaching the Disabled: How Far Must Schools Go?"

KILEY ARMSTRONG, AP

St. Louis Post-Dispatch 4/26/94

It was a touching moment—Anastasia Somoza, looking up from her wheelchair at the White House to plead that her more severely disabled twin, Alba, be allowed to attend regular school.

President Bill Clinton's eyes filled up with tears. And her wish, expressed at a town meeting last year, was soon granted.

But this fairy tale and its 10-year-old heroines have not yet found a happy ending. Alba's parents claim she was "dumped" into the regular classroom without the help she needs to succeed.

Her mother, Mary Somoza, promotes a concept called "inclusion": allowing children, whatever the nature of their handicap, to spend their entire day in a regular classroom, with special services brought to them.

The family contends that the city's Board of Education has violated Alba's rights. Somoza attorney Salem Katsh says the law requires "every effort" to include disabled children in regular classrooms, with whatever help they might need.

Katsh said the Somozas are "asking for compensatory services: special tutoring, special training for communications, an outside consultant to monitor the board's compliance with relief. We are asking for a motorized wheelchair . . . to prevent fatigue."

"For too long, these children were shunted aside," agreed Larry Becker, attorney for the city Board of Education. But he argues that inclusion is "a theory, not a legal mandate. Federal law says handicapped children should be educated in "the least restrictive environment"—and "least restrictive," Becker says, should not mean "regular classroom."

The Board of Education is holding on the case; no ruling is expected until May, at the earliest.

In the meantime, the Somozas claim that the schools continue to fail their daughter, as they have failed her since she was 5 years old.

The girls are great-granddaughters of Nicaraguan dictator Anastasio Somoza, who was assassinated in 1956. One of his sons, Anastasio, the girls' great-uncle, was overthrown by the Sandinistas in 1979.

Anastasia and Alba have cerebral palsy. Anastasia, who has a milder form of the disease, speaks clearly—at times eloquently—and has attended regular classes from the start.

Alba, a quadriplegic, cannot speak but communicates with nods, moans, and glances toward symbols on her "communication board." Experts say both sisters have above-average IQs.

Luanna Meyer, a special education teacher from Syracuse University who testified for the family, said that Alba "understands virtually everything said to her in English and Spanish."

"She laughs at a joke, frowns or nods her head appropriately," said Meyer. Despite her physical limitations, Alba "is a very bright little girl. . . . With today's technology, she could become a rocket scientist."

Mary Somoza said Alba functioned at a normal grade level after preschool. But "when she started public school, year after year she regressed."

She was placed in a special education class with one teacher and 15 students who ranged from the learning disabled to the emotionally disturbed to those with speech or physical impairments.

Her individualized education plan, said Mary Somoza, was poorly coordinated and "inadequately written." During the years she was "in segregated classrooms, she didn't receive any education," Katsh contends.

Last June, four months after Anastasia's chat with the president, the school system decided to allow Alba into a regular fourth-grade class at Public School 234 in Manhattan.

The family says the school system merely responded to the publicity with "window dressing"—"dumping" Alba into the classroom.

Does she like her new class? Alba answered yes "with a smiling face," said Anastasia, who often acts as her sister's interpreter.

"Socially, of course, she's better off," said Mary Somoza. But "academically, it's the same."

Mary Somoza estimates that, despite her intelligence, Alba is doing schoolwork at only the first-or second- grade level. Said Meyer: "There seems to have been a judgment that she wasn't able to learn certain things, such as literacy."

Not surprisingly, the Board of Education's lawyer disagrees with any suggestion that the schools are at fault.

"We don't think it's dumping when you plan for the child's enrollment, plan for a special teacher, for integrated therapy in the classroom, for communication devices and a communication specialist," Becker said.

He said a special education teacher works with both Alba and her classroom teacher. The curriculum has been adapted for Alba. An aide helps her with health needs. And an occupational therapists, physical therapist and communication specialist are at her service.

Becker said the board is fulfilling its legal requirements toward Alba.

But not enough, says Alba's mother.

Questions and Activities

1. Consider the points made in this chapter by the proponents and the opponents of inclusion, and apply them to this particular situation. List the specific pros and cons for Alba and for her classmates of her being educated in the regular classroom. You might extend your analysis into a debate between both sides in this article. You could use as a take-off point for one position the attorney's statement that the "least restrictive environment should not always mean 'regular classroom'"; and for the other position, the special education teacher's observation that in the right environment Alba "could become a rocket scientist."
2. Alba's mother makes the comment in this article that "socially, of course [Alba's] better off" than she was in the segregated special education classroom. What does this comment imply to you about how inclusion works on a personal and a social basis? Can you think of some personal benefits that might emerge from inclusion for the other students as well as for the students with special needs?
3. Imagine that you are Alba's regular fourth-grade classroom teacher. You have twenty-five other students in your class. What is the greatest challenge you might face in terms of Alba's education? How might you best balance Alba's needs and those of your other students? Try to devise some solutions to these challenges, and reconsider and augment these when you have finished studying this chapter.
4. According to research results reported earlier in this chapter, ability grouping affects the quality of instruction students receive, including the fact that "teachers of low-ability students expected and demanded less of them than did teachers of high-ability students." How might this finding relate to the fact that Alba regressed when she was in the segregated special education classroom? Does it form a strong argument in your own mind for inclusion? If not, why not? What important lessons can you draw from this finding about your own expectations of your students, whether they be special education or regular education students?

WHAT PL 101-476 MEANS TO REGULAR CLASSROOM TEACHERS

By the time you begin your teaching career, the original legislation governing the delivery of educational services to the disabled, PL 94-142, will have been in effect for more than twenty years. Each state was required to have established laws and policies for implementing the various provisions by 1978. Thus, the trial-and-error process that inevitably follows a radical departure from previous routine will have taken place by the time you enter a classroom. The first guiding principle to follow, therefore, is *"Find out what the local ground rules are."* You will probably be told during orientation meetings about the ways PL 101-476 is being put into effect in your state and local school district. But if such a presentation is not given or is incomplete, it would be wise to ask about guidelines you should follow. Your second guiding principle, then, should be *"When in doubt, ask."* With these two caveats in mind, consider some questions you may be asking yourself about the impact of PL 101-476 as you approach your first teaching job.

What Kinds of Disabling Conditions Are Included Under PL 101-476? According to the Department of Education (1995), during the 1993–1994 academic year 5.37 million children and youths from birth through age twenty-one (about 12.2 percent of the total number of individuals in this age group) received special education services under PL 101-476. Most of these children (4.54 million) were between the ages of six and seventeen.

PL 101-476 recognizes thirteen categories of students with disabilities. Many states use the same categories. Others use fewer, more inclusive classification schemes. The thirteen categories described in the legislation are listed as follows in alphabetical order, with brief definitions of each type:

Autism. Significant difficulty in verbal and nonverbal communication and social interaction that adversely affects educational performance.

The decision as to whether a child qualifies for special education services under PL 101-476 is made largely on the basis of information supplied by the interdisciplinary assessment team. Classroom teachers typically contribute information about the child's academic and social behavior.

Deaf-blindness. Impairments of both hearing and vision, the combination of which causes severe communication, developmental, and educational problems. The combination of these impairments is such that a child's educational and physical needs cannot be adequately met by programs designed only for deaf children or blind children.

Deafness. Hearing impairment so severe that, even with hearing aids, a child has problems processing speech.

Hearing impairment. Permanent or fluctuating difficulty in understanding speech that adversely affects educational performance and is not included under the definition of deafness.

Mental retardation. Significant subaverage general intellectual functioning accompanied by deficits in adaptive behavior (how well a person functions in social environments).

Multiple disabilities. Two or more impairments (such as mental retardation—blindness and mental retardation—orthopedic, but not deaf-blindness) that cause such severe educational problems that a child's needs cannot be adequately met by programs designed solely for one of the impairments.

Orthopedic impairments. Impairment in a child's ability to use arms, legs, hands, or feet that significantly affects that child's educational performance.

Other health impairments. Conditions such as asthma, hemophilia, sickle cell anemia, epilepsy, heart disease, and diabetes that so limit the strength, vitality, or alertness of a child that educational performance is significantly affected.

Serious emotional disturbance. Personal and social problems exhibited in an extreme degree over a period of time that adversely affect a child's ability to learn and get along with others.

Specific learning disability. A disorder in one or more of the basic psychological processes involved in understanding or using language that leads to learning problems not traceable to physical disabilities, mental retardation, emotional disturbance, or cultural/economic disadvantage.

Speech or language impairment. A communication disorder such as stuttering, impaired articulation, or a language or voice impairment that adversely affects educational performance.

Traumatic brain injury. A brain injury due to an accident that causes cognitive or psychosocial impairments that adversely affect a child's educational performance.

Visual impairment including blindness. A visual impairment so severe that, even with corrective lenses, a child's educational performance is adversely affected.

The percentages of each type of student who received special educational services during the 1993–1994 school year are indicated in Table 6.1. As you can see, the most common types of children with disabilities receiving services (92.4 percent of the total) were those classified as having a specific learning disability, a speech or language impairment, mental retardation, or a serious emotional disturbance.

Students who are learning disabled, speech impaired, mentally retarded, or emotionally disturbed most likely to be served under PL 101-476

TABLE 6.1 ***Students Receiving Special Education Services, 1993–1994***

Disabling Condition	Percentage of Total School Enrollment	Percentage of Students with Disabilities Served
Specific learning disabilities	5.55	51.1
Speech or language impairments	2.29	21.1
Mental retardation	1.25	11.6
Serious emotional disturbance	0.95	8.6
Multiple disabilities	0.25	2.3
Other health impairments	0.19	1.7
Hearing impairments	0.14	1.3
Orthopedic impairments	0.12	1.2
Visual impairments	0.05	0.5
Autism	0.04	0.4
Traumatic brain injury	0.01	0.1
Deaf-blindness	0.00	0.0
Total	10.84	100.0

*Percentages are based on disabled children aged 6–21 as a percentage of total school enrollment for kindergarten through twelfth grade.

SOURCE: Department of Education (1995).

Students who are speech impaired, learning disabled, other health impaired, or visually impaired most likely to attend regular classes

Which Types of Students Are Most Likely to Attend Regular Classes? As you can see from Figure 6.1, those students most likely to spend most or part of each day in a regular classroom are classified as speech or language impaired, learning disabled, other health impaired, or visually impaired. Those students least likely to attend regular classes are classified as mentally retarded, multiply disabled, deaf-blind, or autistic. These figures also indicate that, at least for now, inclusion (meaning full-time placement in a regular classroom despite the nature and severity of the disability) is more the exception than the rule.

What Are the Regular Classroom Teacher's Responsibilities Under PL 101-476? Regular classroom teachers may be involved in activities required directly or indirectly by PL 101-476 in four possible ways: referral, assessment, preparation of the IEP, and implementation and evaluation of the IEP.

REFERRAL. The first step leading to the provision of services under PL 101-476 is referral—someone (for example, parent, teacher, specialist) comes to the conclusion that a child differs from the norm to the point that special instruction may be required. At this point information that is relevant to the referral is assembled by all parties. As the classroom teacher, you will be expected to gather information about the student's current educational status (this would include attendance records, scores from tests and quizzes, and evaluation of homework assignments) and about how the student has responded to various instructional strategies. Also important is any information provided to you by the parents (Kubiszyn & Borich, 1993; Langone, 1990). If a referral is seen as appropriate by the person or persons delegated to process referrals, the next step is assessment.

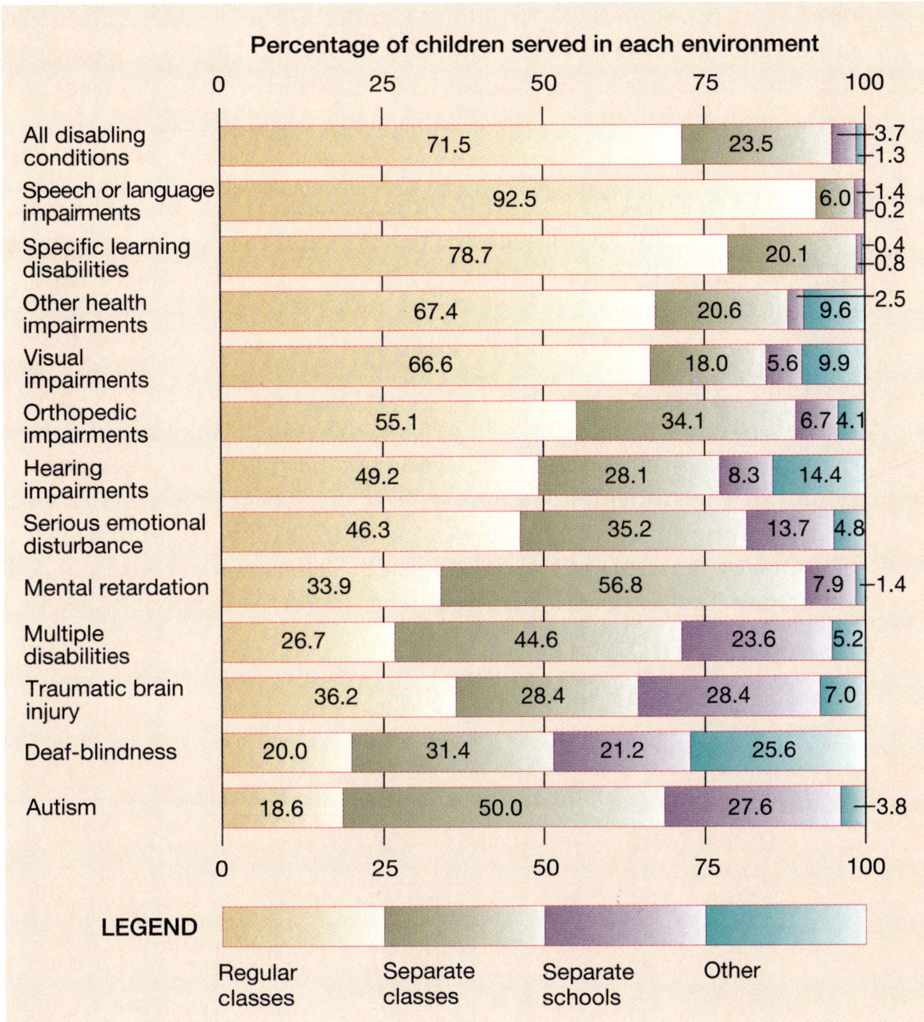

FIGURE 6.1 ***Environments in Which 6- to 21-Year-Old Children with Disabilities Were Served During the School Year 1992–1993***

SOURCE: Department of Education (1995).

ASSESSMENT. The initial assessment procedures, which must be approved by the child's parents, are usually carried out by school psychologists who are certified to administer tests. As many as a dozen tests may typically be given. If the initial conclusions of the school psychologist support the teacher's perception that the student needs special services, the **multidisciplinary assessment team** required under PL 101-476 will be formed. Depending on the type of personnel available and the nature of the child's disabling condition, a multidisciplinary team may consist of several of the following specialists: school psychologist, guidance counselor, classroom teacher, school social worker, school nurse, learning disability specialist, speech therapist, physician, psychiatrist. As the classroom teacher, you should be prepared to provide such information as the quality of the child's homework and his test scores, ability to understand and use language, ability to perform various

Multidisciplinary assessment team determines if student needs special services motor functions, alertness at different times of the day, and interpersonal relationships with classmates (Kubiszyn & Borich, 1993; Langone, 1990). If the team decides that the student *does* qualify for special services, the next step is preparation of the individualized education program.

Classroom teacher, parents, several specialists prepare IEP

PREPARATION OF THE IEP. At least some, if not all, of the members of the assessment team work with the teacher (and the parents) in preparing the IEP. The necessary components of an IEP were described earlier, and they are illustrated in Figure 6.2.

IMPLEMENTATION AND EVALUATION OF THE IEP. Depending on the nature and severity of the handicap, the student may spend part or all of the school day in a regular classroom or be placed in a separate class or school. If the student stays in a regular classroom, the teacher will be expected to put into practice the various instructional techniques listed in the IEP. One or more of the specialists listed earlier may give assistance by providing part-time instruction or treatment and/or by supplying specific advice.

FIGURE 6.2 *Example of an Individualized Education Program (IEP)*

INDIVIDUAL EDUCATIONAL PLAN 11/11/96
DATE

STUDENT: Last Name First Middle
School of Attendance: Home School — Grade Level: 5 — Birthdate/Age: 8-4-81
School Address — School Telephone Number

Child Study Team Members

Name	Title	Name	Title
	Homeroom	Case Manager	L D Teacher
	Facilitator		Parents
	Speech		

Summary of Assessment results

IDENTIFIED STUDENT NEEDS: Reading from last half of DISTAR II - present performance level

LONG TERM GOALS: To improve reading achievement level by at least one year's gain. To improve math achievement to grade level. To improve language skills by one year's gain.

SHORT TERM GOALS: Master Level 4 vocabulary and reading skills. Master math skills in basic curriculum. Master spelling words from Level 3 list. Complete units 1-9 from Level 3 curriculum.

MAINSTREAM MODIFICATIONS:

White Copy—Cumulative Folder
Pink Copy—Special Teacher
Goldenrod Copy—Case Manager
Yellow Copy—Parent

Description of Services to Be Provided

Type of Service	Teacher	Starting Date	Amt. of time per day	OBJECTIVES AND CRITERIA FOR ATTAINMENT
SLD level III	LD Teacher	11-11-96	2 1/2 hrs	Reading: will know all vocabulary through the "Honeycomb" level. Will master skills as presented through Distar II. Will know 1 2 3 second - symbols presented in "Sound Way to Reading." Math: will pass all tests at Basic 4 level. Spelling: 5 words each week from level 3 lists Language: will complete Units 1 - 9 of the 4th grade language program. Will also complete supplemental units from "Language Step by Step."

Mainstream Classes	Teacher	Amt. of time per day	OBJECTIVES AND CRITERIA FOR ATTAINMENT
		3 1/2 hrs	Out of seat behavior: Sit attentively and listen during mainstream class discussions. A simple management plan will be implemented if he does not meet this expectation. Mainstream modifications of Social Studies: will keep a folder in which he expresses through drawing the topics his class will cover. Modified district Social Studies curriculum. No formal testing will be made.

The following equipment and other changes in personnel, transportation, curriculum methods, and educational services will be provided: Distar II Reading Program, Spelling Level 3, "Sound Way to Reading" Program, Vocabulary tapes

Substantiation of least restrictive alternatives: The planning team has determined academic needs are best met with direct SLD support in reading, math, language, and spelling

ANTICIPATED LENGTH OF PLAN 1 yr. The next periodic review will be held: May 1997
DATE/TIME/PLACE

☐ I approve this program placement and the above IEP
☐ I do not approve this placement and/or the IEP
☐ I request a conciliation conference

PARENT/GUARDIAN

Principal or Designee

Form 2011

The classroom teacher may also be expected to determine if the listed objectives are being met and to furnish evidence of attainment. Various techniques of instruction as well as approaches to evaluation that stress student mastery of individualized assignments will be discussed in several of the chapters that follow. Specific techniques that you might use when instructing exceptional students most likely to be placed in regular classrooms, including some who qualify under the provisions of PL 101-476, will be summarized later in this chapter.

Because the IEP is planned by a multidisciplinary team, you will be given direction and support in providing regular class instruction for students who have a disabling condition as defined under PL 101-476. Thus, you will not be expected to start from scratch or to handle planning and instructional responsibilities entirely by yourself.

The types of atypical students you will sometimes be expected to teach in your classroom will vary. Some will be special education students who are being mainstreamed for a certain part of the school day. Others, while different from typical students in some noticeable respect, will not qualify for special education services under PL 101-476. The remainder of this chapter will describe atypical students from both categories and techniques for teaching them. Students with mental retardation, learning disabilities, and/or emotionally disturbance often require special forms of instruction, and we will focus on these categories in the remainder of this chapter. In addition, though not mentioned in PL 101-476, students who are gifted and talented require special forms of instruction, as we will also discuss.

Students with Mental Retardation

CLASSIFICATION OF CHILDREN WITH MENTAL RETARDATION

Despite the trend away from the rigid use of classification schemes in American education, the need to classify children with mental retardation has been recognized by the American Association on Mental Deficiency (AAMD) in order to plan and finance special education for them. The AAMD applies the term **mental retardation** to individuals who have IQ scores of 67 and below and who have concurrent problems functioning in social environments. The AAMD uses the following classifications:

Mild retardation: IQ score between 67 and 52

Moderate retardation: IQ score between 51 and 36

Severe retardation: IQ score between 35 and 20

Profound retardation: IQ score of 19 and below

As a result of legal challenges to IQ testing and special class placement as well as to the trend toward mainstreaming, students classified as mildly retarded who were once separated are more likely now to be placed in regular classes. You probably will not encounter a great many mainstreamed children classified as moderately or severely retarded because of the specialized forms of care and instruction they need. You may, however, be asked to teach for at least part of the day one or more of the higher-scoring children with mild retardation.

CHARACTERISTICS OF CHILDREN WITH MILD RETARDATION[1]

Students who have below-average IQ scores follow the same general developmental pattern as their peers with higher IQ scores, but they differ in the rate and degree of development. Accordingly, students with low IQ scores may possess characteristics typical of students with average IQ scores who are younger than they are. One general characteristic of such students, therefore, is that they often appear immature compared with their age-mates. Immature students are likely to experience frustration frequently when they find they are unable to do things their classmates can do, and many students with mild retardation tend to have a low tolerance for frustration and a tendency toward low self-esteem, low confidence, and low motivation. These feelings in conjunction with the cognitive deficits outlined in the next paragraph sometimes make it difficult for the child with mild retardation to make friends and get along with peers of average ability.

Students with mild retardation may frustrate easily, lack confidence and self-esteem

The cognitive characteristics of children with mild retardation include a limited amount of knowledge about how one learns and the factors that affect learning (this concept is known as *metacognition* and will be discussed more fully in Chapter 9), a tendency to oversimplify concepts, limited ability to generalize, smaller memory capacity, shorter attention span, the inclination to concentrate on only one aspect of a learning situation and to ignore other relevant features, the inability to formulate learning strategies that fit particular situations, and delayed language development. Several of these deficits often operate in concert to produce or contribute to the learning problems of students with mild retardation. Take, for example, the problem of generalization (also known as transfer). This refers to the ability of a learner to take something that has been learned in one context, such as paper-and-pencil arithmetic skills, and use it to deal with a similar but different task, such as knowing whether one has received the correct change after making a purchase at a store. Students with mild mental retardation may not spontaneously exhibit transfer because (1) their metacognitive deficits limit their tendency to look for signs of similarity between two tasks, (2) their relatively short attention span prevents them from noticing similarities, and (3) their limited memory capacity and skills lessens their ability to recall relevant knowledge (Hunt & Marshall, 1994).

Students with mild retardation tend to oversimplify, have difficulty generalizing

These characteristics can be understood more completely if they are related to Jean Piaget's description of cognitive development. Middle and high school students with mild retardation may never move beyond the level of concrete operations. They may be able to deal with concrete situations but

1. Many of the points in this section are based on a discussion of characteristics of mentally retarded children in *Special Education: A Practical Approach for Teachers* (3d edition, 1995), by James Ysseldyke and Bob Algozzine; *Exceptional Children and Youth* (1994), by Nancy Hunt and Kathleen Marshall; and *Educating Exceptional Children* (7th edition, 1993), by Samuel Kirk, James Gallagher, and Nicholas Anastasiow.

find it difficult to grasp abstractions, generalize from one situation to another, or state and test hypotheses. Younger children with retardation tend to classify things in terms of a single feature.

The following Suggestions for Teaching take into account the characteristics just described, as well as points made by Samuel Kirk, James Gallagher, and Nicholas Anastasiow (1993, pp. 205–210); Nancy Hunt and Kathleen Marshall (1994, pp. 165–167; and James Ysseldyke and Bob Algozzine (1995, pp. 306–338).

Suggestions for Teaching in Your Classroom

Instructing Students with Mild Retardation

1. As much as possible, try to avoid placing students with mild retardation in situations that are likely to lead to frustration. When, despite your efforts, such students indicate that they are close to their limit of frustration tolerance, encourage them to engage in relaxing change-of-pace pursuits or in physical activities.

2. Do everything possible to encourage a sense of self-esteem.

3. Present learning tasks that contain a small number of elements, at least some of which are familiar to students.

4. Give a series of brief lessons that can be completed in short periods of time instead of comprehensive assignments that require sustained concentration and effort.

5. Try to arrange what is to be learned into a series of small steps, each of which leads to immediate feedback.

6. Teach simple techniques for improving memory, and consistently point out how use of these techniques leads to more accurate recall.

7. Devise and use record-keeping techniques that make it clear that assignments have been completed successfully and that progress is taking place.

Children with mild retardation are more likely to respond to instruction if they are presented with simple learning tasks and provided with immediate feedback.

1. **As much as possible, try to avoid placing students with mild retardation in situations that are likely to lead to frustration. When, despite your efforts, such students indicate that they are close to their limit of frustration tolerance, encourage them to engage in relaxing change-of-pace pursuits or in physical activities.**

Journal Entry
Helping Students with Mild Retardation Deal with Frustration

Since children with retardation are more likely to experience frustration than their more capable peers, try to minimize the frequency of such experiences in the classroom. Probably the most effective way to do this is to give students with mild retardation individual assignments so that they are not placed in situations where their work is compared with that of others. No matter how hard you try, however, you will not be able to eliminate frustrating experiences, partly because you will have to schedule some all-class activities and partly because even individual assignments may be difficult for a child with mild retardation to handle. If you happen to notice that such a student appears to be getting more and more bothered by an inability to complete a task, you might try to divert attention to a less demanding form of activity or have the student engage in physical exercise of some kind.

2. **Do everything possible to encourage a sense of self-esteem.**

Children with mild retardation are prone to devalue themselves because they are aware that they are less capable than their classmates at doing many things. One way to combat this tendency toward self-devaluation is to make a point of showing that you have positive feelings about less capable students. If you indicate that you have positive feelings about an individual, that person is likely to acquire similar feelings about herself.

Journal Entry
Combating the Tendency to Communicate Low Expectations

As you saw in Chapter 4, many teachers, usually without realizing it, tend to communicate low expectations to students of low ability. To avoid committing the same error, you might do one or more of the following: make it clear that you will allow plenty of time for all students to come up with an answer to a question, repeat the question and give a clue before asking a different question, remind yourself to give frequent personal attention to students with mild retardation, and/or try to convey to these students the expectation that they *can* learn. Perhaps the best overall strategy to use in building self-esteem is to help children with retardation successfully complete learning tasks. Suggestions 3 through 7 offer ideas you might use.

3. **Present learning tasks that contain a small number of elements, at least some of which are familiar to students.**

Journal Entry
Giving Students with Mild Retardation Simple Assignments

Since students with retardation tend to oversimplify concepts, try to provide learning tasks that contain only a few elements, at least some of which have been previously learned. For example, you might ask middle or secondary school social studies students with mild retardation to prepare a report on the work of a single police officer, as opposed to preparing an analysis of law enforcement agencies (which might be an appropriate topic for the best student in the class).

4. **Give a series of brief lessons that can be completed in short periods of time instead of comprehensive assignments that require sustained concentration and effort.**

Students with retardation tend to have a short attention span. If they are asked to concentrate on demanding tasks that lead to a delayed payoff, they are likely to become distracted or discouraged. Therefore, it is better to give a series of short assignments that produce immediate feedback than to use any sort of contract approach or the equivalent in which the student is expected to engage in self-directed effort leading to a remote goal. For instance, with elementary school students who have mild retardation, you might make frequent use of curriculum materials that consist of a series of short, quickly graded tasks that call attention to progress.

Give students with mild retardation specific assignments that can be completed quickly

5. **Try to arrange what is to be learned into a series of small steps, each of which leads to immediate feedback.**

Students who lack confidence, tend to think of one thing at a time, are unable to generalize, and have a short memory and attention span usually respond quite positively to programmed instruction and linear forms of computer-assisted instruction (to be described more completely in Chapter 8). Linear computer programs offer a systematic step-by-step procedure that emphasizes only one specific idea per step or frame. They also offer immediate feedback. These characteristics closely fit the needs of children who are mildly retarded. You might look for computer programs in the subject or subjects you teach or develop your own materials, perhaps in the form of a workbook of some kind.

Other types of programs that can be used with students with mild retardation are those that emphasize the beginning steps of a larger process, such as counting, learning the alphabet, or grouping. Ready for Letters (The Learning Company) and Math Rabbit (Broderbund) are examples of computer-based programs that might be used with elementary and middle school students. Laureate and the Hanover Corporation offer programs for adult learners that concentrate on language and life skills development. Be careful, however, to avoid any student's perception that these are "baby" or "little kid" programs. Instead, emphasize the student's ability to work with the class in the computer lab and to use the computer.

6. **Teach simple techniques for improving memory, and consistently point out how use of these techniques leads to more accurate recall.**

In Chapter 9 we will describe a set of memory aids called mnemonic devices. Used for thousands of years by scholars and teachers in different countries, most are fairly simple devices that help a learner organize information, encode it meaningfully, and generate cues that allow it to be retrieved from memory when needed. The simplest mnemonic devices are rhymes, first letter mnemonics (also known as acronyms), and sentence mnemonics. For example, a first letter mnemonic or acronym for the Great Lakes is *HOMES*: *H*uron, *O*ntario, *M*ichigan, *E*rie, *S*uperior.

7. **Devise and use record-keeping techniques that make it clear that assignments have been completed successfully and that progress is taking place.**

Journal Entry
Giving Students with Mild Retardation Proof of Progress

Students who are experiencing difficulties in learning are especially in need of tangible proof of progress. When, for instance, they correctly fill in blanks in a programmed workbook and discover that their answers are correct, they are encouraged to go on to the next question. You might use the same basic approach in more general ways by having students with retardation keep records of progress. (This technique might be used with *all* students in a class.) For example, you could make individual charts for primary grade students. As they successfully complete assignments, have them color in marked-off sections, paste on gold stars or the equivalent, or trace the movement of animal figures, rockets, or whatever toward a destination.

Students with Learning Disabilities

By far the greatest number of students who qualify for special education under PL 101-476 are those classified as learning disabled. According to Department of Education (1995) figures, the number of students identified as learning disabled increased from approximately 800,000 in 1976–1977 to 2,444,020 in 1993–1994. In the 1976–1977 school year students with learning disabilities accounted for about 24 percent of the handicapped population. By the 1993–1994 school year that estimate had grown to a little more than 51 percent. Especially because so many students are now classified as learning disabled, it is important to define and explore the characteristics of students with **learning disabilities.**

CHARACTERISTICS OF STUDENTS WITH LEARNING DISABILITIES

In the early 1960s groups of concerned parents called attention to a problem in American education: a significant number of students in public schools were experiencing difficulties in learning but were not eligible for special classes or remedial instruction programs. These children were not mentally retarded, deaf, blind, or otherwise disabled, but they were unable to respond to aspects of the curriculum presented in regular classrooms. In 1963 parents of such children formed the Association for Children with Learning Disabilities to call attention to the scope of these problems not traceable to any specific cause. Their efforts were rewarded in 1968 when the National Advisory Committee on the Handicapped of the U.S. Office of Education developed a definition of specific learning disabilities, which was utilized by Congress the following year in the Learning Disability Act of 1969. That definition was revised and inserted in PL 94-142 (the predecessor of PL 101-476). It stresses the following basic points:

Learning disabilities: disorders in basic processes that lead to learning problems not due to other causes

1. The individual has a *disorder in one or more of the basic psychological processes.* (These processes refer to intrinsic prerequisite abilities such as memory, auditory perception, visual perception, and oral language.)

2. The individual has *difficulty in learning,* specifically in the areas of speaking, listening, writing, reading (word recognition skills and comprehension), and mathematics (calculation and reasoning).
3. A *severe discrepancy exists between the student's apparent potential for learning and low level of achievement.*
4. The problem is *not due primarily to other causes,* such as visual or hearing impairments, motor handicapped, mental retardation, emotional disturbance, or economic, environmental, or cultural disadvantage.

Some people dismiss the notion of a learning disability as a fiction since everyone at one time or another has misread numbers, letters, and words; confused pronunciations of words and letters; and suffered embarrassing lapses of attention and memory. But students with learning disabilities really are different from others—in degree mostly rather than in kind. While the nondisabled individual may occasionally exhibit lapses in basic information processing, the learning disabled individual does so consistently and with little hope of self-correction.

PROBLEMS WITH BASIC PSYCHOLOGICAL PROCESSES

The fundamental problem that underlies a learning disability is, as the law states, "a disorder in one or more basic psychological processes." Although this phrase is somewhat vague, it generally refers to problems with how students receive information, process it, and express what they have learned. Specifically, many students with learning disabilities have deficits in perception, attention, memory encoding and storage, and metacognition.

Some students with learning disabilities have great difficulty perceiving the difference between certain sounds (*f* and *v*, *m* and *n*, for example) or letters (*m* and *n*, *b*, *p*, and *d*, for example). As a result, words that begin with one letter (such as *v*ase) are sometimes perceived and pronounced as if they begin with another letter (as in *f*ase). As you can no doubt appreciate from this simple example, this type of deficit makes learning to read and reading with comprehension a long and frustrating affair for some students (Hunt & Marshall, 1994).

Many students with learning disabilities also have difficulty with attention—focusing on a task, noticing important cues and ideas, and staying with the task until it is completed. The source of the distraction may be objects and activities in the classroom, or it may be unrelated thoughts. In either case the student misses much of what the teacher says or what is on a page of text or misinterprets directions. Children with extreme deficits in attention may be diagnosed as having attention deficit disorder or attention deficit with hyperactivity disorder (Hunt & Marshall, 1994). Services for children with attention deficit disorders can be funded under the "seriously emotionally disturbed" category, the "specific learning disabilities" category, or the "other health impaired" category (Lerner, Lowenthal, & Lerner, 1995).

Because so many students with learning disabilities have problems with perception and attention, they also have problems with accurate recall of information. Because accurate recall is heavily dependent on what gets stored in memory in the first place and where in memory information is stored

(Hunt & Marshall, 1994), students who encode partial, incorrect, or unimportant information have memory problems.

Students with learning disabilities have problems with perception, attention, memory, metacognition

Like students with mild retardation, many students with learning disabilities have a deficit in metacognitive skills (Hunt & Marshall, 1994). As a result, their learning activities are like those of young children—chaotic. For example, they may begin a task before they have thought through all of the steps involved.

Students with learning disabilities tend to be characterized as passive and disorganized: passive in the sense that they take few active steps to attend to relevant information, store it effectively in memory, and retrieve it when needed; and disorganized in the sense that their learning activities are often unplanned and subject to whatever happens to capture their attention at the moment.

The following Suggestions for Teaching will give you some ideas about how to help students with learning disabilities improve their learning skills and feel better about themselves.

Suggestions for Teaching in Your Classroom

Instructing Students with Learning Disabilities

1. Structure learning tasks to help students with learning disabilities compensate for weaknesses in psychological processes.
2. Look for opportunities to bolster the self-esteem of students with learning disabilities.

1. Structure learning tasks to help students with learning disabilities compensate for weaknesses in psychological processes.

Journal Entry
Helping Students with Learning Disabilities Improve Basic Learning Processes

Because of their weaknesses in basic psychological processes, students with learning disabilities are often distractible, impulsive, forgetful, disorganized, poor at comprehension, and unaware of the factors that affect learning. But these deficits can be moderated to some extent by implementing one or more of the procedures that follow.

EXAMPLES

For students who have difficulty distinguishing between similar looking or sounding stimuli (such as letters, words, or phrases), point out and highlight their distinguishing characteristics. For example, highlight the circular part of the letters *b, p,* and *d,* and place a directional arrow at the end of the straight segment to emphasize that they have the same shape but differ in their spatial orientation. Or highlight the letters *t* and *r* in the words *though, thought,* and *through* to emphasize that they differ from each other by the absence or presence of one letter.

For students who are easily distracted, instruct them to place only the materials being used on top of the desk or within sight.

For students who seem unable to attend to important stimuli such as significant sections of a text page, show them how to underline or outline in an effort to distinguish between important and unimportant material. Or suggest that they use a marker under each line as they read so that they can evaluate one sentence at a time. To help them attend to important parts of directions, highlight or write key words and phrases in all capitals. For especially important tasks, you might want to ask students to paraphrase or repeat directions verbatim.

Help students with learning disabilities to reduce distractions, attend to important information

For students who have a short attention span, give brief assignments and divide complex material into smaller segments. After each short lesson segment, provide both immediate positive feedback and tangible evidence of progress. (Many sets of published materials prepared for use with students with learning disabilities are designed in just this way.)

To improve memory and comprehension of information, teach students memorization skills and how to relate new information to existing knowledge schemes to improve long-term storage and retrieval. Also, make frequent use of simple, concrete analogies and examples to explain and illustrate complex, abstract ideas. (We will describe several techniques for enhancing memory and comprehension in Chapter 9.)

To improve organization, suggest that students keep a notebook in which to record homework assignments, a checklist of materials needed for class, and books and materials that need to be brought home for studying and homework.

To improve general awareness of the learning process, emphasize the importance of thinking about the factors that could affect one's performance on a particular task, of forming a plan before actually starting to work, and of monitoring the effectiveness of learning activities.

Consider the variety of learning environments increasingly available through multimedia software programs. Some students with learning disabilities may respond better to a combination of visual and auditory information, while others may learn best in a hands-on setting. Multimedia programs provide options to address these different styles and also allow the student to control the direction and pace of learning. Some excellent examples for young children are the Living Books series (Broderbund).

2. **Look for opportunities to bolster the self-esteem of students with learning disabilities.**

Students with learning disabilities may show signs of low self-esteem because they realize that they make mistakes on or are unable to complete assignments with which most classmates have little difficulty. While the techniques just mentioned will help in this regard, there is at least one other specific technique that you may want to try. If the opportunity arises, have a student with a learning disability tutor either a low-achieving classmate in a subject that is not affected by the tutor's disability or a younger student in a lower grade. As we pointed out in Chapter 4, students with learning disabilities can fill the role of tutor as effectively as non–learning disabled students and typically experience increases in self-esteem and achievement as a result of doing so.

Students with Emotional Disturbance

ESTIMATES OF EMOTIONAL DISTURBANCE

In a 1995 report to Congress on the implementation of PL 101-476, the Department of Education noted that 414,279 students were classified as seriously emotionally disturbed for the 1993–1994 school year. This figure accounted for 8.6 percent of all schoolchildren classified as handicapped and slightly less than 1 percent of the general school-age population. Not everyone agrees, however, that these figures accurately reflect the scope of the problem. Other estimates range from 1 percent to 20 percent (Kirk et al., 1993). Frank Wood and Robert Zabel (1978) offer an explanation for these differences between estimates and classifications by suggesting that most identification procedures ask teachers to rate children in their classes at a particular point in time. Some identification procedures, however, stress recurrent problems. It seems possible, therefore, that, while perhaps one out of five students attending public schools may sometimes exhibit emotional problems, only two or three out of one hundred will display severe, persistent problems.

DEFINITIONS OF EMOTIONAL DISTURBANCE

Two other reasons that estimates of **emotional disturbance** vary are the lack of any clear descriptions of such forms of behavior and different interpretations of the descriptions that do exist. Children with *serious emotional disturbance* are defined in PL 101-476 in this way:

Emotional disturbance: poor relationships, inappropriate behavior, depression, fears

(i) The term means a condition exhibiting one or more of the following characteristics over a long period of time and to a marked degree that adversely affects a child's educational performance:

(A) An inability to learn that cannot be explained by intellectual, sensory, or health factors;

(B) An inability to build or maintain satisfactory interpersonal relationships with peers and teachers;

(C) Inappropriate types of behavior or feelings under normal circumstances;

(D) A general pervasive mood of unhappiness or depression; or

(E) A tendency to develop physical symptoms or fears associated with personal or school problems.

(ii) The term includes schizophrenia. The term does not apply to children who are socially maladjusted, unless it is determined that they have a serious emotional disturbance. (Office of the Federal Register, 1994, pp. 13–14)

Several special education scholars (e.g., Hunt & Marshall, 1994, pp. 247–248; Kirk et al., 1993, pp. 410–412; Ysseldyke & Algozzine, 1995, pp. 345–346) point out the difficulties caused by vague terminology in distinguishing between students who have emotional disturbance and students who are normal. The phrase *a long period of time,* for example, is not de-

Students who have an emotional disturbance tend to be either aggressive or withdrawn. Because withdrawn students tend to be anxious and fearful about interpersonal relationships, they may need to be encouraged to interact with their classmates.

fined in the law (although many special education experts use six months as a rough rule of thumb). Behaviors such as *satisfactory interpersonal relationships, a general pervasive mood,* and *inappropriate types of behavior or feelings under normal circumstances* are difficult to measure objectively and can often be observed in normal individuals. Since long-term observation of behavior is often critical in making a correct diagnosis of emotional disturbance, you can aid the multidisciplinary assessment team in this task by keeping a behavioral log of a child you suspect may have this disorder.

That many educators and psychologists use such terms as *emotionally disturbed, socially maladjusted,* and *behavior disordered* synonymously makes matters even more confusing. The term **behavior disorder** has many adherents and has been adopted by several states for two basic reasons. One reason is that it calls attention to the actual behavior that is disordered and needs to be changed. The second reason is that behaviors can be directly and objectively assessed. While there are subtle differences between the terms *emotionally disturbed* and *behavior disorder,* they are essentially interchangeable, and you can probably assume that those who use them are referring to children who share similar characteristics. Because of the nature of bureaucracies, however, it may be necessary for anyone hoping to obtain special assistance for a child with what many contemporary psychologists would call a behavior disorder to refer to that child as *seriously emotionally disturbed* since that is the label used in PL 101-476.

Term *behavior disorder* focuses on behavior that needs to be changed, objective assessment

CHARACTERISTICS OF STUDENTS WITH A SERIOUS EMOTIONAL DISTURBANCE

Several classifications of emotional disturbance (or behavior disorders) have been made (see, for example, Achenbach & Edelbrock, 1983; Quay, 1986; Wicks-Nelson & Israel, 1991). Most psychologists who have attempted to classify such forms of behavior describe two basic patterns: externalizing and internalizing. Externalizing students are often aggressive, uncooperative, restless, and negativistic. They tend to lie and steal, to defy teachers, and to be

Students with behavior disorders tend to be either aggressive or withdrawn hostile to authority figures. Sometimes they are cruel and malicious. Internalizing students, by contrast, are typically shy, timid, anxious, and fearful. They are often depressed and lack self-confidence. Teachers tend to be more aware of students who display aggressive disorders because their behavior often stimulates or forces reactions. The withdrawn student, however, may be more likely to develop serious emotional problems such as depression and may even be at risk of suicide during the adolescent years.

In the next section are Suggestions for Teaching to help you teach both the withdrawn student and the aggressive student.

Suggestions for Teaching in Your Classroom

Instructing Students with Emotional Disturbance[2]

Instructing Students Who Are Withdrawn

1. Design the classroom environment and formulate lesson plans to encourage social interaction and cooperation.
2. Prompt and reinforce appropriate social interactions.
3. Train other students to initiate social interaction.

Instructing Students Who Are Aggressive

4. Design the classroom environment to reduce the probability of disruptive behavior.
5. Reinforce appropriate behavior, and, if necessary, punish inappropriate behavior.
6. Use group contingency-management techniques.

1. Design the classroom environment and formulate lesson plans to encourage social interaction and cooperation.

Foster interpersonal contact among withdrawn students

Students whose emotional disturbance manifests itself as social withdrawal may stay away from others on purpose (perhaps because they find social contacts threatening), or they may find that others stay away from them (perhaps because they have poorly developed social skills). Regardless of the cause, the classroom environment and your instructional activities can be designed to foster appropriate interpersonal contact.

Journal Entry
Activities and Materials That Encourage Cooperation

EXAMPLES

Preschool and elementary school teachers can use toys and materials as well as organized games and sports that encourage cooperative play and that have a reduced focus on individual performance. Toys might include dress-up games or puppet plays; games might include soccer, variations of "it" (such as tag), and kickball or softball modified such that everyone on the team gets a turn to kick or bat before the team plays in the field.

2. Most of these suggestions were derived from points made in Chapters 7 and 10 of *Strategies for Managing Behavior Problems in the Classroom* (2d ed., 1989), by Mary Margaret Kerr and C. Michael Nelson.

Elementary and middle school teachers can use one or more of several team-oriented learning activities. See *Cooperative Learning* (2d ed., 1995), by Robert Slavin, for details on using such activities as Student Teams-Achievement Divisions, Jigsaw, and Team Accelerated Instruction.

2. Prompt and reinforce appropriate social interactions.

Prompting and positive reinforcement are basic learning principles that will be discussed at length in Chapter 8. Essentially, a prompt is a stimulus that draws out a desired response, and positive reinforcement involves giving the student a positive reinforcer (which is something the student wants) immediately after a desired behavior. The aim is to get the student to behave that way again. Typical reinforcers include verbal praise, stickers (with pictures of gold stars and smiley faces, for instance), and small prizes (such as a pencil with the child's name engraved on it).

EXAMPLE

You can also set up a cooperative task or activity: "Marc, I would like you to help Carol and Jane paint the scenery for next week's play. You can paint the trees and flowers, Carol will paint the grass, and Jane will do the people." After several minutes say something like, "That's good work. I am really pleased at how well the three of you are working together." Similar comments can be made at intervals as the interaction continues.

3. Train other students to initiate social interaction.

In all likelihood you will have too many classroom responsibilities to spend a great deal of time working directly with a withdrawn child. It may be possible, however, using the steps that follow, to train other students to initiate contact with withdrawn students.

EXAMPLES

First, choose a student who interacts freely and well, who can follow your instructions, and who can concentrate on the training task for at least ten minutes. Second, explain that the goal is to get the withdrawn child to work or play with the helping student but that the helper should expect rejection, particularly at first. Role-play the actions of a withdrawn child so that the helper understands what you mean by rejection. Emphasize the importance of making periodic attempts at interaction. Third, instruct the helper to suggest games or activities that appeal to the withdrawn student. Fourth, reinforce the helper's attempts to interact with the withdrawn child.

Journal Entry
Getting Students to Initiate Interaction with a Withdrawn Child

4. Design the classroom environment to reduce the probability of disruptive behavior.

Use techniques to forestall aggressive or antisocial behavior

The best way to deal with aggressive or antisocial behavior is to nip it in the bud. This strategy has at least three related benefits. One benefit of fewer disruptions is that you can better accomplish what you had planned for the day. A second benefit is that you are likely to be in a more positive frame of mind than if you spend half the day acting as a referee. A third benefit is that, because of fewer disruptions and a more positive attitude, you may be less inclined to resort to physical punishment (which, as we will point out in Chapter 8, often produces undesirable side effects).

EXAMPLES

With student input, formulate rules for classroom behavior and penalties for infractions of rules. Remind all students of the penalties, particularly when a disruptive incident seems about to occur, and consistently apply the penalties when the rules are broken.

Place valued objects and materials out of reach when they are not needed or in use.

Minimize the aggressive student's frustration with learning by using some of the same techniques you would use for a child with mild retardation: break tasks down into small, easy-to-manage pieces; provide clear directions; and reinforce correct responses.

5. Reinforce appropriate behavior, and, if necessary, punish inappropriate behavior.

In suggestion 2 we described the use of positive reinforcement to encourage desired behavior. Reinforcement has the dual effect of teaching the aggressive student which behavior is appropriate and reducing the frequency of inappropriate behavior as it is replaced by desired behavior. Disruptive behavior will still occur, however. Three effective techniques for suppressing it while reinforcing desired behaviors are contingency contracts, token economies and fines, and time-out. Each of these techniques will be described in Chapter 8 of this book.

6. Use group contingency-management techniques.

Up to now we have suggested methods that focus on the aggressive student. In addition, you may want to reward the entire class when the aggressive student behaves appropriately for a certain period of time. Such rewards —which may be free time, special classroom events, or certain privileges—should make the aggressive student the hero and foster better peer relationships.

Gifted and Talented Students

Students who learn at a significantly faster rate than their peers or who possess superior talent in one or more areas also need to be taught in special ways if they are to make the most of their abilities. Unlike students with mental retardation, learning disabilities, and emotional disturbance, however, students with superior capabilities are not covered by PL 101-476. Instead, the federal government provides technical assistance to states and local school districts in establishing programs for superior students. Although most states have such programs, some experts in special education (for example, Horowitz & O'Brien, 1986) feel that they are not given the resources they need to adequately meet the needs of all gifted and talented students. The Suggestions for Teaching that follows a bit later reflects this situation. All of the suggestions are inexpensive to implement and require few additional personnel.

A definition of the term **gifted and talented** was part of a bill passed by Congress in 1988:

> The term *gifted and talented children and youth* means children and youth who give evidence of high performance capability in areas such as intellectual, creative, artistic, or leadership capacity, or in specific academic fields, and who require services or activities not ordinarily provided by the school in order to fully develop such capabilities. (Title IV-H.R.5, 1988, pp. 227–228)

Gifted and talented students show high performance in one or more areas

IDENTIFICATION OF GIFTED AND TALENTED STUDENTS

The AAMD classification of mental retardation refers to specific IQ scores for use in establishing the upper and lower limits of various categories. But it is not possible to be that specific about the test scores of atypically bright students. From the 1920s through the 1950s an IQ score of 140 was commonly accepted for classifying children as gifted. Beginning in the early 1960s, however, this dividing line was increasingly criticized. A number of psychologists (such as Getzels & Jackson, 1962) called attention to the fact that many children who deserved to be classified as gifted did not earn IQ scores of 140 or above, primarily because the tests used to measure IQ seemed to discriminate against divergent thinkers.

Because of these criticisms, only four states use some sort of numerical cutoff score for identification (Cassidy & Johnson, 1986). While this is seen as a step in the right direction, critical weaknesses in the identification of gifted and talented children remain, particularly gifted children from minority cultures. One remaining problem is the historical emphasis on IQ. Achievement and mental ability are still often looked to as indicators of giftedness at the expense of such other relevant characteristics as motivation, creativity, leadership, and critical thinking ability (Frasier, 1991). A second problem is educators' unfamiliarity with ways of measuring human characteristics other than by standardized tests. Checklists, rating scales, and nominations by peers and adults can also be used (Baldwin, 1991). A third problem is a general ignorance of characteristics that are more highly valued

Minorities underrepresented in gifted classes because of overreliance on test scores by a minority culture than by the majority culture. Members of many Native American tribes, for example, place as much value on a child's knowledge of tribal traditions, storytelling ability, and artistic ability as they do on problem-solving ability and scientific reasoning (Tonemah, 1987). A child's giftedness may, therefore, be evident in such "unmeasurable" skills.

CHARACTERISTICS OF GIFTED AND TALENTED STUDENTS

On average, gifted and talented students are physically, socially, and emotionally indistinguishable from the general student population. Some are healthy and well coordinated, whereas others are not. Some are extremely popular and well liked, but others are not. Some are well adjusted; others are not (Piechowski, 1991; Ysseldyke & Algozzine, 1995).

Cognitively and academically, however, gifted and talented students are often noticeably different. Gifted students are quick to understand abstract concepts and to organize them into complex, efficient schemes. Hence, they can understand and manipulate such abstract concepts as symbiosis, probability, and conservation. In addition, gifted students are quick to generalize their knowledge to new but related tasks and settings.

Gifted and talented students have stronger academic self-concept but average physical, social self-concepts

For the most part gifted and talented students see themselves as they were described in the preceding two paragraphs. In comparison to intellectually average students, they have a moderately stronger academic self-concept but score at about the same level on measures of physical and social self-concepts (Hoge & Renzulli, 1993).

Some gifted students think in orthodox ways. Given some information and a problem, they excel at coming up with the one correct answer. In terms of J. P. Guilford's (1967) description of intellectual operations, such students might be classified as extremely competent *convergent* thinkers. When teachers are asked to nominate the most capable students in their classes, they tend to choose children of this type. Other gifted learners do *not* respond to instruction in expected ways. Instead, they often respond to questions and problems in unorthodox or unsettling ways and perhaps give the impression that they are uncooperative or disruptive. Many students of this type might be classified as brilliant *divergent* thinkers.

INSTRUCTIONAL OPTIONS

Gifted and talented students, whether convergent thinkers or divergent thinkers, constantly challenge a teacher's skill, ingenuity, and classroom resources. While trying to instruct the class as a whole, the teacher is faced with the need to provide more and more interesting and challenging materials and ideas to the gifted student. In this section we will examine three possible solutions to this problem.

Accelerated Instruction Accelerated instruction is often suggested as a solution to this problem. For many people, the phrase *accelerated instruction* means allowing the student to skip one or more grades, which often happens. But there are at least three other ways of accomplishing the same goal. The curriculum can be compressed, allowing gifted and talented students to com-

Because gifted and talented students understand and integrate abstract ideas more quickly than do their nongifted classmates, they are capable of successfully completing tasks that older students routinely carry out.

plete the work for more than one grade during the regular school year; the school year can be extended by the use of summer sessions; and students can take college courses while still in high school.

Whatever the form of accelerated instruction, this is always a hotly debated topic, with pros and cons on each side. Two often quoted advantages for giving gifted students the opportunity to work on complex tasks are that (1) it keeps them from becoming bored with school and (2) it produces more positive attitudes toward learning. On the negative side, two frequent arguments are that (1) a gifted student may have trouble with the social and emotional demands of acceleration and (2) acceleration produces an undesirable sense of elitism among gifted students. (Kulik & Kulik, 1984; Benbow; 1991) As with all informed educational decisions, the unique needs of the individual and the situation must be considered before the best course of action can be determined.

Gifted and Talented Classes and Schools Some public school districts offer separate classes for gifted and talented students either as an alternative to accelerated instruction or as something that follows accelerated instruction. In addition, so-called magnet schools are composed of students whose average level of ability is higher than that found in a typical elementary, middle, or high school. Finally, many states sponsor high-ability high schools, particularly in mathematics and science.

Separate classes for gifted and talented students aid achievement but may lower academic self-concept of some students

Recent findings suggest that such placements do not produce uniformly positive results and should be made only after the characteristics of the student and the program have been carefully considered. In terms of achievement, the typical gifted student can expect to score moderately higher (about one-third of a standard deviation) on tests than comparable students who remain in heterogeneous classes (Kulik & Kulik, 1991). But the effects of separate class or school placement on measures of academic self-concept have been inconsistent; some researchers find them to be higher than those of students who remain in heterogeneous classes, whereas other researchers have found either no differences or declines (Hoge & Renzulli, 1993; Marsh, Chessor, Craven, & Roche, 1995; Kulik & Kulik, 1991).

Enrichment Techniques and Programs In two books (Renzulli & Reis, 1985; Reis & Renzulli, 1985), Joseph Renzulli and Sally Reis describe three levels of curriculum enrichment for gifted and talented learners. The first level (type I enrichment) involves exploratory activities that are designed to expose students to topics, events, books, people, places, and such not ordinarily covered in the regular curriculum. The basic purpose of these activities is to stimulate new interests. Among the many suggestions Renzulli and Reis offer are having students view and write reports on films and videocassettes (such as *The Eagle Has Landed: The Flight of Apollo 11*) and having a local resident make a presentation on his occupation or hobby.

The second level (type II enrichment) involves instructional methods and materials that are aimed at the development of such thinking and feeling processes as thinking creatively, classifying and analyzing data, solving problems, appreciating, and valuing. Renzulli and Reis list the names and addresses of 125 publishers and distributors from which instructional materials can be obtained. For example, a program called Techniques of Problem Solving I, which is designed to enhance the problem-solving and decision-making skills of fourth through eighth graders, can be obtained from Resources for the Gifted.

The third level (type III enrichment) consists of activities in which students investigate and collect data about a real topic or problem. For example, a student may decide to document the history of her school, focusing on such issues as changes in size, instructional materials and methods, and curriculum.

Several databases on the Internet are now devoted to long distance education, enrichment, and tutoring. You might explore the Global Network Academy (http://www.gnacademy.org/), which offers on-line courses in a wide range of areas. The International Tutoring Foundation (http://edie.cprost.sfu.ca/it/programs.html), a nonprofit organization based at the University of Toronto, provides tutoring for all age and grade levels, including special programs for gifted students (as well as for students with disabilities).

The following Suggestions for Teaching provide ideas for working with gifted and talented students.

Suggestions for Teaching in Your Classroom

Instructing Gifted and Talented Students

1. Consult with gifted and talented students regarding individual study projects, perhaps involving a learning contract.
2. Encourage supplementary reading and writing.
3. Have gifted students act as tutors.

1. Consult with gifted and talented students regarding individual study projects, perhaps involving a learning contract.

Journal Entry
Individual Study for Students Who Are Gifted and Talented

One of the most effective ways to deal with gifted students is to assign individual study projects. These assignments should probably be related to some part of the curriculum. If you are studying Mexico, for example, a gifted student could devote free time to a special report on some aspect of Mexican life that intrigues him. In making these assignments, you should remember that even very bright students may not be able to absorb, organize, and apply abstract concepts until they become formal thinkers. Thus, up until early middle school years, it may be preferable to keep these assignments brief rather than comprehensive.

To provide another variation of the individual study project, you could ask the gifted student to act as a research specialist and report on questions that puzzle the class. Still another individual study project is the creation of an open-ended, personal yearbook. Any time a gifted student finishes the assigned work, she might be allowed to write stories or do drawings for such a journal. When possible, however, unobtrusive projects are preferable. Perhaps you can recall a teacher who rewarded the fast workers by letting them work on a mural (or the equivalent) covering the side board. If you were an average student, you can probably attest that the sight of the class "brains" having the time of their lives was not conducive to diligent effort on the part of the have-nots sweating away at their workbooks. Reward assignments should probably be restricted to individual work on unostentatious projects.

Finally, you might set up independent study projects by using the contract approach (described more completely in Chapters 8 and 13). Consult with students on an individual basis, and agree on a personal assignment that is to be completed by a certain date.

2. Encourage supplementary reading and writing.

Encourage students to spend extra time reading and writing. A logical method of combining both skills is the preparation of book reports. It is perhaps less threatening to call them book *reviews* and emphasize that you are interested in personal reaction, not in a précis or an abstract. Some specialists in the education of the gifted have suggested that such students be urged to read biographies and autobiographies. The line of reasoning here is that potential leaders might be inspired to emulate the exploits of a famous person. Even if such inspiration does not result, you could recommend life stories simply because they are usually interesting.

If your school has a computer network, or is connected to the Internet, other possibilities for writing are e-mail exchanges with other students, siblings at college, or friends in different areas. Or a student may write a review of a World Wide Web site that she has discovered. If the appropriate software and support are available, students could be encouraged to create "home pages" or World Wide Web sites for themselves, either on a topic mutually selected with the teacher or on their personal interests (the latter would be much like a yearbook entry).

3. **Have gifted students act as tutors.**

Depending on the grade, subject, and personalities of those involved, gifted students might be asked to act occasionally as tutors, lab assistants, or the equivalent. Some bright students will welcome such opportunities and are capable of providing instruction in such a way that their peers do not feel self-conscious or humiliated. Others, however, may resent being asked to spend school time helping classmates and/or may lack skills in interpersonal relationships. If you do decide to ask a gifted student to function as a tutor, therefore, it would be wise to proceed tentatively and cautiously.

Resources for Further Investigation

Ability Grouping

Additional discussions of ability grouping and alternatives to it can be found in a number of books and journal articles. For a comprehensive treatment of this topic, look at *Crossing the Tracks: How "Untracking" Can Save America's Schools* (1992), by Anne Wheelock. In Part 1 Wheelock describes the nature of tracking; its origins, prevalence, and negative effects; and alternative methods of organizing classrooms for the purpose of instruction. Part 2 describes how to organize and teach heterogeneous classrooms. Wheelock covers many of the same topics in *Alternatives to Tracking and Ability Grouping* (1994), but in far fewer pages (285 versus 77). Jeannie Oakes, a leading authority on tracking and ability grouping, discusses its effects and how schools can eliminate the practice in *Educational Researcher* (1992a) and *Phi Delta Kappan* (1992b).

Texts on the Education of Exceptional Children

The following books provide general coverage of the education of exceptional children: *Exceptional Children and Youth* (1994), by Nancy Hunt and Kathleen Marshall; *Educating Exceptional Children* (7th ed., 1993), by Samuel Kirk, James Gallagher, and Nicholas Anastasiow; *Special Education: A Practical Approach for Teachers* (3d ed., 1995), by James Ysseldyke and Bob Algozzine.

A book that emphasizes general teaching techniques for students with special needs is Deborah Deutsch Smith, *Teaching Students with Learning and Behavior Problems* (2d ed., 1989). Part 1 describes general teaching and classroom skills that all teachers of students with special needs should possess. Part 2 presents techniques for managing disruptive behavior and teaching appropriate social skills. Part 3 describes techniques for improving reading, writing, mathematics, and study skills.

Mainstreaming and Inclusion

For ideas about how to teach students with disabilities in a regular classroom setting, consult *Curriculum Considerations in Inclusive Classrooms* (1992), by Susan Stainback and William Stainback; and *Cooperative Learning and Strategies for Inclusion* (1993), edited by JoAnne Putnam. The entire December 1994/January 1995 issue of *Educational Leadership* is devoted to the inclusive school. Eighteen articles present various pro and con arguments that summarize the relatively limited amount of research on this topic. A useful book for anyone interested in teaching at the high school level is *Students with Mild Disabilities in the Secondary School* (1991), by Paul Retish, William Hitchings, Michael Horvath, and Bonnie Schmalle.

On-line information on the Americans with Disabilities Act can be found at http://www.public.iastate.edu/~sbilling/ada.html. Edlaw, a national legal organization and publisher, has created a site dedicated to following developments in IDEA and legal requirements for educators and administrators of special education programs. It can be found at http://access.digex.net/~edlawinc/. Information on all types of adaptive and assistive technology to promote inclusion can be located on-line at http://www.gsa.gov/coca/cocamain.htm, the Clearinghouse on Computer Accommodation.

Teaching Students with Mental Retardation

Specialized techniques for teaching students with mental retardation can be found in *Strategies for Teaching Students with Mild to Severe Mental Retardation* (1993), edited by Robert Gable and Steven Warren; and *Mental Retardation* (4th ed., 1994), by Mary Beirne-Smith, James Patton, and Richard Ittenbach.

Two excellent on-line sources of information, materials, publications, and so on are (1) ARC Online, a national organization on mental retardation (http://fohnix.metronet.com/~thearc/welcome.html); and also (2) University of Kansas Special Education Department (http://www.sped.ukans.edu/spedadmin/welcome.html). These sites also contain information relevant to students with learning disabilities.

Teaching Students with Learning Disabilities

The following books provide information about the nature of learning disabilities and how to teach students with learning disabilities: *Learning Disabilities; Theories, Diagnosis, and Teaching Strategies* (6th ed., 1993), by Janet Lerner; *Students with Learning Disabilities* (4th ed., 1991), by Cecil Mercer; and *Learning Disabilities: Characteristics, Identification, and Teaching Strategies* (2d ed., 1995), by William Bender. Information on the nature and teaching of students with attention deficits is offered by Janet Lerner, Barbara Lowenthal, and Sue Lerner (1995) in *Attention Deficit Disorders: Assessment and Teaching.*

Teaching Students with Behavior Disorders

Information on the nature of behavior disorders and on how the regular classroom teacher can deal with such students can be found in *Antisocial Behavior in School: Strategies and Best Practices* (1995), by Hill Walker, Geoff Colvin, and Elizabeth Ramsey; *Teaching Students with Behavior Disorders: Techniques and Activities for Classroom Instruction* (2d ed., 1995), by Patricia Gallagher; and *Characteristics of Emotional and Behavioral Disorders of Children and Youth* (5th ed., 1993), by James Kauffman.

Teaching Gifted and Talented Learners

These books describe various techniques to use in instructing gifted and talented learners: *Handbook of Gifted Education* (1991), edited by Nicholas Colangelo and Gary Davis; *Curriculum Development for the Gifted* (1982), by C. June Maker; *Programs and Practices in Gifted Education* (1992), edited by Sandra Berger; and *Teaching the Gifted Child* (3d ed., 1985), by James Gallagher.

Summary

1. Three early attempts at dealing with student variability were age-graded classrooms, ability grouping, and special class placement. Age-graded classrooms grouped together student who were roughly the same age. Ability grouping sorted normal students into separate classes according to mental ability test scores. Special class placement was used to separate normal students from those with mental and physical disabilities.

2. Ability grouping at the high school level is referred to as tracking and sorts students into groups such as college, secretarial, and vocational.

3. The four currently popular approaches to ability grouping are between-class ability grouping, regrouping, the Joplin Plan, and within-class ability grouping. In one form or another, ability grouping is widely practiced in the United States.

4. Ability grouping is based on the assumptions that intelligence is genetically determined, is reflected by an IQ score, and is unchangeable and that instruction is more effective with homogeneous groups of students.

5. There is no research support for between-class ability grouping and limited support for regrouping. Moderately positive results have been found for the Joplin Plan as well as within-class ability grouping.

6. Students in low ability groups often receive lower-quality instruction.

7. In light of research findings on ability grouping, educators may choose to discontinue the use of between-class ability grouping, use only within-class grouping and the Joplin Plan, or discontinue all forms of ability grouping.

8. The Education for All Handicapped Children Act (Public Law 94-142) was enacted in 1975 to ensure that students with disabling conditions receive the same free and appropriate education as nondisabled students. It was last revised in 1990 as PL 101-476, the Individuals with Disabilities Education Act (IDEA).

9. Major provisions of PL 101-476 include the right to a free and appropriate public education, an appropriate and valid preplacement evaluation, the development of an individualized education program, the education of students with disabilities in the least restrictive environment (also known as mainstreaming), and procedural safeguards.

10. In some school districts mainstreaming has been extended to the point where students with disabilities are taught only in regular classrooms by regular and special education teachers. This practice is known variously as full mainstreaming, inclusion, or full inclusion.

11. The evidence on mainstreaming and inclusion, while somewhat limited and inconsistent, indicates that they produce at least moderate benefits for students with disabilities.

12. Students who have speech or language impairments, a learning disability, other health impairments, or visual impairments are most likely to attend regular classes.

13. The regular classroom teacher's responsibilities under PL 101-476 may include participation in referral, assessment, preparation of the IEP, and implementation of the IEP.

14. Children with mild mental retardation are likely to be mainstreamed for some part of the school day and week. They are likely to have a low tolerance for frustration, to lack confidence and self-esteem, to oversimplify matters, and to have difficulty generalizing from one situation to another.

15. Students with learning disabilities account for more than half of all students with disabilities. They have a disorder in one or more of such basic psychological processes as perception, attention, memory, and metacognition, which leads to learning problems not attributable to other causes.

16. The true number of schoolchildren with serious emotional disturbance is

unknown because of variation in identification procedures, vague definitions of emotional disturbance, and differences in interpretation of definitions.

17. Most classifications of disturbed behavior focus on aggressive behavior or withdrawn behavior.

18. Students who are gifted and talented excel in performing tasks that require intellectual, creative, artistic, or leadership ability.

19. Minorities are underrepresented in gifted and talented classes because standardized test scores are emphasized at the expense of other indices such as creativity, leadership, communication skill, critical-thinking ability, and persistence.

20. The academic needs of students who are gifted and talented are usually met through accelerated instruction, placement in classes or schools for the gifted and talented, or classroom enrichment activities. Special classes and schools typically produce moderate achievement benefits but can also produce declines in academic self-concept.

Key Terms

between-class ability grouping *(199)*
regrouping *(199)*
Joplin Plan *(199)*
within-class ability grouping *(200)*
individualized education program (IEP) *(203)*
least restrictive environment *(204)*
mainstreaming *(204)*
full mainstreaming *(204)*
inclusion *(204)*
full inclusion *(204)*
multidisciplinary assessment team *(211)*
mental retardation *(213)*
learning disabilities *(218)*
emotional disturbance *(222)*
behavior disorder *(223)*
gifted and talented *(227)*

Discussion Questions

1. You probably experienced ability grouping, in one form or another, at the elementary and secondary levels. Try to recall the ability grouping used in your schools. Think about whether it might have been between-class grouping, regrouping, the Joplin Plan, or within-class grouping. Could you tell which group you were in? Did you have feelings about being in that group? How did you feel about classmates who were in other groups? Do you think this practice aided or hindered your educational progress? Why? Given your own experiences as a student and what you have learned from this chapter, would you advocate or employ some form of ability grouping for your own students someday?

2. Many regular classroom teachers say that, while they agree with the philosophy behind PL 101-476, they feel that their training has not adequately prepared them for meeting the needs of students with disabling conditions. Would you say the same about your teacher education program? Why? If you feel that your training is not adequately equipping you to teach students who are mentally retarded, learning disabled, or emotionally disturbed, what might you do to prepare yourself better?

3. Relatively little money is spent on programs for the gifted and talented compared to the amounts made available for the disabled. Defenders of this arrangement sometimes argue that since money for educational programs is always short, and since gifted students have a built-in advantage rather than a disability, we *should* invest most of our resources in programs and services for the disabled. Do you agree or disagree? Explain why.

Part 2

Specifying What Is to Be Learned

CHAPTER 7
Devising and Using Objectives

CHAPTER 7

Devising and Using Objectives

Key Points

These key points will help you learn the important information in this chapter. To help you study, they also appear in the margins of pages, next to the text where they are discussed.

Taxonomies of Objectives

- Taxonomy: categories arranged in hierarchical order
- Cognitive taxonomy: knowledge, comprehension, application, analysis, synthesis, evaluation
- Taxonomy of affective objectives stresses attitudes and values
- Psychomotor taxonomy outlines steps that lead to skilled performance

Ways to State and Use Objectives

- Mager: state specific objectives that identify act, define conditions, state criteria
- Gronlund: state general objectives, list sample of specific learning outcomes
- Mager-style objectives useful in arranging classroom exercises
- Gronlund-type objectives lead to comprehensive coverage of a skill or topic

Multiple Values of Objectives

- Using objectives can lead to improved planning, instruction, evaluation, learning

Evaluations of the Effectiveness of Objectives

- Objectives work best when students are aware of them
- Arranging objectives in strict hierarchical order does not seem to be essential
- Most test questions stress knowledge, ignore higher levels of cognitive taxonomy

OUTCOME-BASED EDUCATION: OBJECTIVES THAT ARE NOT CURRICULUM DRIVEN

- Outcome-based education assumes most students can master curriculum, mastery and self-concept affect each other, instruction more effective when aligned with tests
- Outcome-based education specifies student competencies first, then curriculum issues

SUGGESTIONS FOR TEACHING IN YOUR CLASSROOM

- Before devising objectives, examine curriculum materials, find out about tests
- Check on availability of appropriate lists of objectives
- Use taxonomies to make survey of what students should be able to do
- Use specific learning-outcome descriptions to arrange learning experiences

In Chapter 1 we mentioned models of instruction. The purpose of such models is to provide a basic strategy of instruction that consists of four phases:

1. Take into account what students are like and how much they know.
2. Specify what is to be learned.
3. Provide instruction to help students achieve specified objectives by taking advantage of what has been discovered about learning, cognitive strategies, and motivation.
4. Determine if students have achieved specified objectives.

Part 1 (Chapters 2–6) was devoted to the first phase of our instructional model—descriptions of what students are like and how they differ. It is now time to turn to the second phase and consider ways to specify what is to be learned.

Reasons for Thinking About Objectives

To grasp why this chapter on objectives appears before chapters on learning, motivation, and evaluation, imagine that it is your first day in your own classroom. If you plan to teach in the primary and elementary grades, you will observe (probably with mixed feelings of excitement, curiosity, and a bit of anxiety) the arrival of the twenty-five or so children who will be spending up to five hours a day in your room for the next nine months. If you expect to teach at the middle school level, you will have two or three groups of students to whom you will teach two or three subjects a day. At the high school level, you can expect to experience the same feelings as you observe the arrival of the first of (typically) five batches of students whose destiny has been linked to yours by a computer and/or an administrator. They will size you up probably even more keenly than you will sort out your first impressions of them.

If you remember some of what you read in Chapters 2 and 3 of this book, you will be familiar with at least some of the characteristics of the students who will seat themselves in front of you. If you recall the emphasis on variability stressed in Chapters 4, 5, and 6, you may detect, even on the basis of extremely brief first impressions, noticeable differences between students. You might find yourself thinking, "Juan will probably enjoy the cooperative learning projects I have planned since he is such an outgoing and friendly boy," or "I'll bet Keesha's going to be a sharp student," or "That boy looks so scared and unhappy about being back in school; I wonder if he has learning problems."

After the bell rings and you conclude that all your students are present, you will close the door, walk to the front of the room, and introduce yourself. You will either call roll or otherwise check that all students are present or accounted for. You will probably need to make some announcements; then you will explain classroom routine and pass out books and materials. Eventually, however, the moment of truth will arrive: you will have to start teaching. When that climactic moment comes, you had better convey the impression that you know what you are doing and make clear to your students exactly what you want them to do. This chapter on objectives is intended to help you achieve both of those goals not only the first day but also *every* day in the classroom.

Your reactions at this point may be "Well, sure, of course I'm going to have planned what I'm going to do the first day and at least for the next few days after that." But the plans you make for presenting lessons are likely to be much more effective if you take into account the value of stating instructional objectives in specific terms. Furthermore, the objectives you devise are more likely to be effective if you first think about what you want your students to be able to do at the *end* of an instructional sequence rather than just taking a stab at formulating a beginning. To grasp that point, suppose that you follow the common practice of many teachers and prepare lesson plans by examining texts and other curriculum materials in order to devise an instructional sequence. Probably your first inclination is to concentrate on what is going to happen tomorrow and to put off thinking about what is going to happen two weeks or a month ahead when the time comes to evaluate what students have learned. You might reason that there is no point in thinking about tests until it is time to prepare tests.

Quite a few teachers operate in such a one-thing-at-a-time way, and you are probably familiar with the results-disorganized lessons, lectures, and assignments, followed by exams that may not have much to do with what you think you were supposed to have learned. You can avoid falling into that common trap by concentrating at the very beginning on what you want your students to be able to do at the end of a unit of study. If you decide in advance what you desire your students to achieve, you can prepare lessons that logically lead to a particular result and also use assessment techniques efficiently designed to determine if achievement has occurred.

To help you grasp why and how objectives can be used to make teaching and testing effective, a history of various approaches to and arguments for goals and objectives will be presented as background for the specific suggestions that follow. As you read the following section and the rest of the chapter, we also encourage you to examine the Key Points in light of what you're learning about instructional objectives. Because these Key Points call your attention to sections of the text that are considered to be particularly important and are likely to be stressed on examinations, they function as a type of instructional objective. Try to reflect consciously on how they help you focus your reading and your studying.

Goals Listed by Educational Leaders

Most discussions of what children should learn in school take the form of lists of general goals of education. And from time to time such lists have been proposed by educational leaders or government officials who have been invited to Washington to participate in what are referred to as White House Conferences on Education.

A recent discussion of education goals by government officials occurred at the University of Virginia in September 1989. At the invitation of President George Bush, members of his cabinet and the nation's governors attended what was called an education summit to propose a set of national education goals. After several months of discussion, the summit concluded that the following six goals should be achieved by the year 2000:

1. All children will be ready to learn when they start school.
2. At least 90 percent of all students will graduate from high school.
3. At the end of the fourth, eighth, and twelfth grades, students will demonstrate their competency in such basic subjects as English, mathematics, science, history, and geography. In addition, students will acquire the thinking skills that will allow them to become responsible citizens, independent learners, and productive workers.
4. U.S. students will be ranked first in the world in science and mathematics achievement.
5. All adults will be sufficiently literate, knowledgeable, and skilled to compete in a global economy and behave as responsible citizens.
6. All schools will be free of drugs and violence and will offer an environment conducive to learning.

Note: The current status of the Goals 2000 project is distributed via an online database managed by the Department of Education. It can be found at http://www.ed.gov/legislation/GOALS2000/index.html.

This list clearly mentions skills, attitudes, and interests that are desirable, if not essential, for someone who hopes to live successfully and happily in America. Unfortunately, these statements do not provide very useful guidelines for teachers charged with the responsibility for achieving them. Precisely how, for example, are you supposed to make students independent learners and responsible citizens?

Taxonomies of Objectives

In the early 1950s, awareness of the vagueness of such goals stimulated a group of psychologists who specialized in testing to seek a better way to describe educational objectives. They reasoned that group tests used to measure school achievement could be made more effective and accurate if they were based on a school curriculum derived from a systematic list of objectives. The fact that psychologists interested in testing took the lead in describing specific objectives illustrates the point made a bit earlier that you should start at the end rather than just jumping in at the beginning. It makes more sense to decide in advance what is important enough to be tested rather than simply teaching an assortment of information and skills and then discovering in hit-or-miss fashion how much has been achieved.

After experimenting with various ways to prepare lists of objectives that would be more useful to teachers than vaguely worded sets of goals, the test specialists decided to develop taxonomies of educational objectives. A **taxonomy** is a classification scheme with categories arranged in hierarchical order. Because the goals of education are extremely diverse (take another look at those listed by the Education Summit participants), the decision was made to prepare taxonomies in three *domains:* cognitive, affective, and psychomotor. The taxonomy for the **cognitive domain** stresses knowledge and intellectual skills, the taxonomy for the **affective domain** concentrates on attitudes and values, and the taxonomy for the **psychomotor domain** focuses on physical abilities and skills.

Taxonomy: categories arranged in hierarchical order

TAXONOMY FOR THE COGNITIVE DOMAIN

The taxonomy for the cognitive domain was prepared by Benjamin Bloom, Max Englehart, Edward Furst, Walker Hill, and David Krathwohl (1956). It consists of six hierarchically ordered levels of instructional outcomes: knowledge, comprehension, application, analysis, synthesis, and evaluation. The taxonomy is described as a hierarchy because it was reasoned that comprehension relies on prior mastery of knowledge or facts, application depends on comprehension of relevant ideas, and so on through the remaining levels. An abridged outline of the taxonomy for the cognitive domain follows.

Cognitive taxonomy: knowledge, comprehension, application, analysis, synthesis, evaluation

Taxonomy of Educational Objectives: Cognitive Domain

1.00 *Knowledge.* Remembering of previously learned information.

1.10 *Knowledge of specifics.*

1.11 *Knowledge of terminology.* What terms and symbols will your students need to know (for example, verbs, nouns, +, –, H_2SO_4)?

1.12 *Knowledge of specific facts.* What specific facts will your students need to know (for example, names of the states, chief exports of Brazil, and properties of H_2SO_4)?

1.20 *Knowledge of ways and means of dealing with specifics.*

1.21 *Knowledge of conventions.* What sets of rules will your students need to know (for example, rules of etiquette, rules of punctuation)?

1.22 *Knowledge of trends and sequences.* What awareness of trends and sequences will your students need to have (for example, nature of evolution and changes in attitudes about the role of women in American society)?

1.23 *Knowledge of classifications and categories.* What classifications and category schemes will your students need to know (for example, types of literature, types of business ownership, and types of government)?

1.24 *Knowledge of criteria.* What sets of criteria will your students need to be able to apply (for example, factors to consider in judging the nutritional value of a meal or the qualities of a work of art)?

The taxonomy of objectives for the cognitive domain calls attention to the fact that instructional outcomes can range from such basic capabilities as verbatim recall and comprehension to such higher-level capabilities as application of knowledge and skill, analysis of complex ideas into their component parts, synthesis of different ideas into an integrated whole, and evaluation of the quality of ideas.

1.25 *Knowledge of methodology.* What sorts of methodology will your students need to master (for example, ways to solve problems in math and how to set up an experiment in chemistry)?

1.30 *Knowledge of the universals and abstractions in a field.*

1.31 *Knowledge of principles and generalizations.* What general principles will your students need to know (for example, laws of heredity and laws of motion)?

1.32 *Knowledge of theories and structure.* What general theories will your students need to know (for example, nature of free enterprise system, theory of evolution)?

2.00 *Comprehension.* Ability to grasp the meaning of information.

2.10 *Translation.* Ability to put communication into another form (for example, stating problems in own words, reading a musical score, translating words and phrases from a foreign language, interpreting a diagram, and grasping the meaning of a political cartoon).

2.20 *Interpretation.* Ability to reorder ideas and comprehend interrelationships (for example, giving own interpretation of a novel or a poem, gathering data from a variety of sources, and preparing an organized report).

2.30 *Extrapolation.* Ability to go beyond given data (for example, theorizing about what might happen if ... , drawing conclusions from given sets of data, and predicting trends).

3.00 *Application.* Applying knowledge to actual situations (for example, taking principles learned in math and applying them to laying out a baseball diamond and applying principles of civil liberties to current events).

4.00 *Analysis.* Breaking down objects or ideas into simpler parts and seeing how the parts relate and are organized (for example, discussing how the public and the private sectors differ and detecting logical fallacies in an argument).

5.00 *Synthesis.* Rearranging component ideas into a new whole (for example, planning a program or panel discussion and writing a comprehensive term paper).

6.00 *Evaluation.* Making judgments based on internal evidence or external criteria (for example, evaluating a work of art, editing a term paper, and detecting inconsistencies in the speech of a politician).

TAXONOMY FOR THE AFFECTIVE DOMAIN

Taxonomy of affective objectives stresses attitudes and values

In addition to arranging instructional experiences to help students achieve cognitive objectives, virtually all teachers are interested in encouraging the development of attitudes and values. To clarify the nature of such objectives, a taxonomy for the affective domain was prepared (Krathwohl, Bloom, & Masia, 1964). Affective objectives are more difficult to define, evaluate, or encourage than cognitive objectives because they are often demonstrated in subtle or indirect ways. Furthermore, certain aspects of value development are sometimes considered to be more the responsibility of parents than of teachers. Finally, because values and attitudes involve a significant element of personal choice, they are often expressed more clearly out of school than in the classroom. The complete taxonomy for the affective domain stresses out-of-school values as much as, if not more than, in-school values. The following abridgment concentrates on the kinds of affective objectives you are most likely to be concerned with as a teacher. You will probably recognize, however, that there is not much you can do to substantially influence the kinds of objectives described in the higher levels of the taxonomy since they

The taxonomy of objectives for the affective domain emphasizes that *receiving* (attending) and *responding* typically precede *valuing* (by which a person expresses support for a particular point of view).

represent a crystallization of values formed by experiences over an extended period of time.

Taxonomy of Educational Objectives: Affective Domain

1.0 *Receiving (attending).* Possessing a willingness to receive or attend.

1.1 *Awareness.* Being aware of distinctive features (for example, listening attentively and concentrating on distinctive features of a complex stimulus).

1.2 *Willingness to receive.* Showing a willingness to consider various interpretations and the opinions of others (for example, listening to discussions of controversial issues with an open mind and respecting the rights of others).

1.3 *Controlled or selected attention.* Actively attending to experiences or presentations of the ideas of others (for example, willingly participating in class discussions and reading articles that present both sides of a controversial issue).

2.0 *Responding.* Indicating positive response or acceptance of an idea or a policy.

2.1 *Acquiescence in responding.* Exhibiting acceptance of expectations and responsibilities (for example, completing homework assignments and obeying school rules).

2.2 *Willingness to respond.* Voluntarily or willingly choosing to respond (for example, willingly participating in class discussion and voluntarily completing optional assignments).

2.3 *Satisfaction in response.* Experiencing a sense of satisfaction or enjoyment by responding in a particular way (for example, showing enjoyment when working on a self-selected project and enthusiastically participating in group activities).

3.0 *Valuing.* Expressing a belief or attitude about the value or worth of something.

3.1 *Acceptance of value.* Endorsing a basic proposition or assumption (for example, endorsing the concept of democratic forms of government and accepting the idea that good health habits are important).

3.2 *Preference for a value.* Expressing willingness to be identified with a value (for example, expressing support for a particular point of view and defending an opinion questioned by another student).

3.3 *Commitment.* Expressing a strongly held value or conviction (for example, participating in a campaign to clean up the playground and volunteering to serve on a school committee formed to raise funds for homeless people in your community).

4.0 *Organization.* Organizing various values into an internalized system.

4.1 *Conceptualization of a value.* Understanding how a value relates to values already held (for example, recognizing the need to seek a balance between economic growth and conservation of natural resources).

4.2 *Organization of a value system.* Bringing several, possibly disparate, values together into a consistent system (for example, recognizing own abilities, limitations, and values and developing realistic aspirations).

5.0 *Characterization by a value or value complex.* Governing daily behavior according to a system of values.

5.1 *Generalized set.* Exhibiting a predisposition to act in certain ways (for example, a person's lifestyle influences reactions to many different kinds of situations).

TAXONOMY FOR THE PSYCHOMOTOR DOMAIN

Psychomotor taxonomy outlines steps that lead to skilled performance

Cognitive and affective objectives are important at all grade levels, but so are psychomotor objectives. Regardless of the grade level or subject you teach, at some point you will want to help your students acquire physical skills of various kinds. In the primary grades, for example, you will want your students to learn how to print legibly. And in many subjects in middle school and in high school, psychomotor skills (for example, driving a car, playing a violin, adjusting a microscope, manipulating a computer keyboard, operating a power saw, throwing a pot) may be essential. Recognition of the importance of physical skills prompted Elizabeth Simpson (1972) to prepare a taxonomy for the psychomotor domain. An abridged version of the taxonomy follows.

Taxonomy of Educational Objectives: Psychomotor Domain

1.0 *Perception.* Using sense organs to obtain cues needed to guide motor activity.

1.1 *Sensory stimulation.* Interpreting a sensory stimulus (for example, listening to the sounds made by violin strings before tuning them).

1.2 *Cue selection.* Identifying relevant cues and associating them with appropriate behavior (for example, recognizing sounds that indicate malfunctioning of equipment).

1.3 *Translation.* Relating sensory cues to performing a motor act (for example, relating musical tempo and rhythm to dance forms).

A basic instructional technique for helping students master psychomotor objectives is to demonstrate a skill and then give guidance as students try out the skill.

2.0 *Set.* Being ready to perform a particular action.

2.1 *Mental set.* Being mentally ready to perform (for example, knowing the steps to follow in order to replace a muffler).

2.2 *Physical set.* Being physically ready to perform in terms of body position, posture, focusing of visual and auditory attention (for example, having instrument ready to play and watching conductor at start of a musical performance).

2.3 *Emotional set.* Being willing and eager to perform (for example, exhibiting eagerness to use a sewing machine to make a garment).

3.0 *Guided response.* Performing under guidance of a model.

3.1 *Imitation.* Copying the performance of someone else (for example, swinging a tennis racket just after observing an expert's stroke).

3.2 *Trial and error.* Trying various responses until the correct one is selected (for example, experimenting with various ways to use a saw with a particular type of material).

4.0 *Mechanism.* Being able to perform a task habitually with some degree of confidence and proficiency (for example, demonstrating the ability to get the first tennis serve in the service area 70 percent of the time).

5.0 *Complex or overt response.* Performing a task with a high degree of proficiency and skill (for example, typing all kinds of business letters and forms quickly with no errors).

6.0 *Adaptation.* Using previously learned skills to perform new but related tasks (for example, using skills developed while using a word processor to do desktop publishing).

7.0 *Origination.* Creating new performances after having developed skills (for example, creating a new form of modern dance).

The hierarchically arranged lists of objectives you have just examined clearly provide more tangible descriptions of objectives than the goals listed by the participants in the Education Summit. The next section will describe how you can write and profitably use such objectives.

Ways to State and Use Objectives

Many psychologists have offered suggestions for use of objectives, but the following discussion is limited to recommendations made by two of the most influential writers on the subject: Robert Mager and Norman Gronlund.

MAGER'S RECOMMENDATIONS FOR USE OF SPECIFIC OBJECTIVES

With the publication of a provocative and unorthodox little treatise titled *Preparing Instructional Objectives* (1962), Mager sparked considerable interest in the use of objectives. The revised second edition of this book opens with the following statement:

> Once you decide to teach someone something, several kinds of activity are indicated if your instruction is to be successful. For one thing, you must assure yourself that there is a need for the instruction, making certain that (1)

Mager recommends that teachers use objectives that identify the behavioral act that indicates achievement, define conditions under which the behavior is to occur, and state the criterion of acceptable performance.

> your students don't already know what you intend to teach and (2) instruction is the best means for bringing about a desired change. For another, you must clearly specify the outcomes or objectives you intend your instruction to accomplish. You must select and arrange learning experiences for your students in accordance with principles of learning and must evaluate student performance according to the objectives originally selected. In other words, first you decide where you want to go, then you create and administer the means of getting there, and then you arrange to find out whether you arrived. (1984, p. 1)

As you undoubtedly recognized, this is a description of the model of instruction that is being used as the organizational frame of reference for this book, and Mager was one of several psychologists who were given credit in Chapter 1 for suggesting the model.

Having described his model of instruction, Mager then emphasizes the importance of objectives, pointing out that "you cannot concern yourself with the problem of selecting the most efficient route to your destination [of having students exhibit knowledge or perform a skill] until you know what your destination is" (1984, p. 1). Next, having described how important it is to state objectives at the beginning of a unit of study, Mager then offers these suggestions for writing **specific objectives** of instruction:

Mager: state specific objectives that identify act, define conditions, state criteria

1. Describe what you want learners to be doing when demonstrating achievement, and indicate how you will know they are doing it.
2. In your description, identify and name the behavioral act that indicates achievement, define the conditions under which the behavior is to occur, and state the criterion of acceptable performance. (The criterion of acceptable performance can be stated as a time limit, a minimum number of correct responses, or a proportion of correct responses.)

3. Write a separate objective for each learning performance.

Here are some examples of the types of objectives Mager recommends:

> Correctly solves at least seven addition problems consisting of three two-digit numbers within a period of three minutes
>
> Correctly answers at least four of the five questions on the last page of story booklet 16 in the Reading Comprehension series of booklets
>
> Given pictures of ten trees, correctly identifies at least eight as either deciduous or evergreen
>
> Correctly spells at least 90 percent of the words on the list handed out last week
>
> Given an electric typewriter or a computer and word processing program, sets it up to type a business letter (according to specifications provided in a text) within two minutes :

Mager's proposals were widely endorsed immediately after the publication of *Preparing Instructional Objectives,* but in time it became apparent that the very specific kinds of objectives he recommended were most useful in situations where students were asked to acquire knowledge of factual information or learn simple skills. Norman Gronlund concluded that a different type of objective was more appropriate for more complex and advanced kinds of learning.

GRONLUND'S RECOMMENDATIONS FOR USE OF GENERAL OBJECTIVES

Gronlund (1995) has developed a two-step procedure for writing a more general type of objective. He suggests that teachers follow this procedure:

1. Examine what is to be learned with reference to lists of objectives such as those included in the three taxonomies. Use such lists to formulate **general objectives** of instruction that describe types of behavior students should exhibit to demonstrate that they have learned.

Gronlund: state general objectives, list sample of specific learning outcomes

2. Under each general instructional objective, list up to five *specific learning outcomes* that begin with an *action verb* and indicate specific, observable responses. These sets of learning outcomes should provide a representative sample of what students should be able to do when they have achieved the general objective.

If you were teaching an educational psychology course and you wanted to write a Gronlund-type objective that reflected an understanding of the four stages of Jean Piaget's theory of cognitive development, it might look like this:

1.0 The student will understand the characteristics of Piaget's four stages of cognitive development.

- 1.1 Describes in her own words the type of thinking in which students at each stage can and cannot engage.
- 1.2 Predicts behaviors of students of different ages.
- 1.3 Explains why certain teaching techniques would or would not be successful with students of different ages.

However, if you wanted to cover the same outcome with a list of Mager-type objectives, it might look like this:

1. Given a list of the names of each of Piaget's four stages of cognitive development, the student, within twenty minutes, will describe in his own words two problems that students at each stage should and should not be able to solve.
2. Given a videotape of kindergarten students presented with a conservation-of-volume problem, the student will predict the response of 90 percent of the students.
3. Given a videotape of fifth-grade students presented with a class inclusion problem, the student will predict the response of 90 percent of the students.
4. Given eight descriptions of instructional lessons, two at each of Piaget's four stages, the student will be able to explain in each case why the lesson would or would not succeed.

Gronlund gives several reasons for beginning with general objectives. First, most learning activities are too complex to be described in terms of a specific objective for every learning outcome, as proposed by Mager. Second, the kind of specific objective advocated by Mager may tend to cause instructors and students to concentrate on memorizing facts and mastering simple skills. As indicated earlier, these types of behaviors are at the lowest levels of the taxonomies of objectives. Third, specific objectives can restrict the flexibility of the teacher. Gronlund's objectives, for example, allow performance criteria to be kept separate from the objective so that a teacher can revise performance standards as needed without having to rewrite the objective. This feature is useful if the same behavior is to be evaluated several times over the course of a unit of instruction, with successively higher levels of performance required. Fourth, general objectives help keep the teacher aware that the main target of her instructional efforts is the general outcome (such as comprehension, application, or analysis).

To illustrate the differences between general objectives and specific outcomes, Gronlund has prepared lists of phrases and verbs that can be used in writing each type of objective for each of the levels of all three taxonomies of educational objectives. These lists can be found in Chapter 4 of Gronlund's *How to Write and Use Instructional Objectives* (5th ed., 1995); and in Appendix E of Robert Linn and Gronlund's *Measurement and Assessment in Teaching* (7th ed., 1995). The lists in Tables 7.1, 7.2, and 7.3 are abridged and paraphrased versions of those devised by Gronlund.

USING GENERAL OBJECTIVES AND SPECIFIC OUTCOMES

To illustrate how you might take advantage of the information just summarized, we now provide a few examples of the use of objectives and specific outcomes at different grade levels and with different subjects.

Third-Grade Mathematics To begin, you might refer to the taxonomy for the cognitive domain and peruse the various descriptions under the headings of knowledge, comprehension, and application. (Since third graders are con-

TABLE 7.1 *Taxonomy for the Cognitive Domain: Objectives and Outcomes*

Level of Taxonomy	General Objectives	Specific-Outcome Action Verbs
Knowledge	Knows terms Knows specific facts Knows rules Knows trends and sequences Knows classifications and categories Knows methods and procedures	Defines, names, states, identifies, describes, outlines, reproduces
Comprehension	Translates communications Interprets relationships Understands facts	Paraphrases, converts, explains, predicts, generalizes, infers
Application	Applies principles	Uses, solves, constructs, prepares, demonstrates
Analysis	Analyzes organization and relationships Recognizes unstated assumptions	Discriminates, outlines, diagrams, differentiates, infers, subdivides
Synthesis	Produces new arrangements	Designs, organizes, rearranges, compiles, modifies, creates
Evaluation	Judges on basis of external criteria	Appraises, compares, contrasts, discriminates, criticizes, justifies
Example: comprehension	Judges on basis of evidence Understands the meaning of a constitutional democracy	Paraphrases, the contents of a country's constitution Explains the functions of various branches of government Gives an example of a constitutional democracy Explains how to convert a dictatorship into a constitutional democracy

crete operational thinkers, you reason that the analysis, synthesis, and evaluation objectives are too advanced to be appropriate.) Using the knowledge heading of the taxonomy as a guide, you might ask yourself what terms, symbols, and rules your students need to know and what methods they need to know how to use. Next, you refer to Mager's suggestions for preparing objectives to see if his approach would be appropriate. You conclude that his recommendations might be very useful in arranging short classroom exercises. You devise a page of addition and subtraction problems and plan to hand them out the next day with the announcement that anyone who gets

Mager-style objectives useful in arranging classroom exercises

TABLE 7.2 *Taxonomy for the Affective Domain: Objectives and Outcomes*

Level of Taxonomy	General Objectives	Specific-Outcome Action Verbs
Receiving (attending)	Shows awareness of distinctive features Shows willingness to receive Indicates attention	Describes, identifies, selects, points to
Responding	Accepts need for regulations and responsibilities Chooses to respond in acceptable ways Shows interest in responding	Complies, tells, performs
Valuing	Endorses propositions Shows preference for values Expresses commitment to values	Explains, justifies, shares, initiates
Organization	Understands relationships between values Develops a value system	Explains, defends, organizes
Value complex	Acts in ways consistent with values	Displays, practices, performs
Example: valuing	Shows concern for the welfare of people who are less fortunate	Reads reports on causes of homelessness Attends local government hearings on proposed policies toward people who are poor and homeless Joins organizations that serve those who are less fortunate Donates money to organizations that serve people who are less fortunate Lobbies politicians to support building of low-cost housing

more than eight out of ten correct will earn a passing grade. You also announce that similar exercises will be handed out every day and that those who get a passing grade on four in a row will not have to complete the exercise scheduled for Friday.

Gronlund-type objectives lead to comprehensive coverage of a skill or topic

Next, you refer to the lists of objectives and outcomes derived from Gronlund's description, paying particular attention to the knowledge category of the taxonomy for the cognitive domain. You decide that "Knows methods and procedures" is especially important, so you write it down, fol-

TABLE 7.3 *Taxonomy for the Psychomotor Domain: Objectives and Outcomes*

Level of Taxonomy	General Objectives	Specific-Outcome Action Verbs
Perception	Recognizes significant cues Relates cues to actions	Chooses, detects, identifies, differentiates, demonstrates
Set	Displays mental readiness to perform Displays physical readiness to perform Displays emotional readiness to perform	Begins, proceeds, starts, volunteers, shows, demonstrates
Guided response	Imitates a response Experiments with responses	Assembles, fixes, manipulates
Mechanism	Performs task habitually	Assembles, fixes, manipulates
Complex or overt response	Performs with confidence and proficiency	Assembles, fixes, manipulates, mends
Adaptation	Adapts skills to fit situation	Alters, varies, revises
Origination	Creates new performance	Originates, composes, constructs, devises
Example: adaptation	Adjusts tennis game to counteract opponent's style	Changes racquet grip to impart different spin Alters stance to better return opponent's serve Rushes net more often than usual

lowed by these specific outcomes (which you devise after referring to the complete list of specific-outcome action verbs):

1. Identifies plus and minus signs in problems
2. Describes how to add and subtract numbers
3. Demonstrates ability to add and subtract numbers
4. Shows ability to take sets of numbers supplied and arrange them to be added or subtracted by self or others
5. Explains how to use knowledge of addition and subtraction to handle situations outside of school (for example, deciding if enough money has been saved to buy three different objects of known value)

Middle School Music Even though you don't know a great deal about musical performance and had only a brief unit on music in an education course, you suddenly discover that you are supposed to present a unit on musical knowledge to your sixth- or seventh-grade class. You decide that a logical first objective is "Is knowledgeable about some musical instruments," and you refer to the list of objectives and specific outcomes relating to knowledge in the taxonomy for the cognitive domain to devise these specific outcomes:

1. Names the instruments of an orchestra when pictures of each are displayed
2. Identifies the instruments of an orchestra when each is played on a recording
3. States differences between the instruments of an orchestra and those of a band
4. Differentiates between recordings played by an orchestra and those played by a band

Middle School Literature You begin by examining the taxonomy for the cognitive domain as well as that for the affective domain. You conclude that the comprehension, application, analysis, synthesis, and evaluation levels from the cognitive domain may all be appropriate, at least to some extent. The receiving, responding, and valuing levels of the affective domain also seem worth examining. A brief look at Mager's recommendations leads you to conclude that his approach is not appropriate for your classes, so you concentrate on the lists of general objectives and specific outcomes for the levels of the taxonomies you have selected. Since *values* is, in your estimation, an important outcome for a literature class, you peruse the outline for the affective domain and record the general objective "Values well-written short stories." Under that statement you list these specific outcomes:

1. Selects a well-written short story from a book containing stories of varying quality
2. Identifies well-written and poorly written short stories
3. Explains why a short story identified as good is superior to one identified as poorly written
4. Tells classmates why a particular short story is good
5. Justifies preference for a favorite short story

High School Social Studies You begin by examining the outline of the taxonomy for the cognitive domain and concentrate on the analysis, synthesis, and evaluation levels. Using the lists of objectives and outcomes as a guide, you select the general objective "Judges on basis of evidence," and you list these specific outcomes:

1. Identifies limitations of evidence given in an article to justify statement
2. Distinguishes between evidence and opinions
3. Relates evidence to conclusions
4. Detects conclusions based on insufficient or irrelevant evidence
5. Explains why it is not always possible to determine the direction of cause-and-effect relationships
6. Criticizes statements made by public figures that cannot be backed up by evidence

High School Physical Education Since you are about to introduce archery as an activity for the first time, you turn directly to the taxonomy for the psychomotor domain. You realize that most of your students have never had a bow in their hands, so you decide to concentrate on the first two levels (perception and set) the first day. You jot down the general objective "Relates cues to actions," and you list these specific outcomes:

1. Detects balance point of bow
2. Differentiates between feel of moderate and extreme string pressure
3. Identifies correct placement of arrow in bow and above hand
4. Chooses proper stance to achieve good balance

Multiple Values of Objectives

These brief examples, because they illustrate only selected aspects of a few limited teaching units, give only a sketchy idea of the usefulness of objectives. Even so, these examples are sufficient to reveal the potential of objectives. If you follow the procedures just illustrated in systematic and comprehensive ways as you prepare lessons, you will develop firsthand appreciation of the values of objectives, and you and your students will also be likely to benefit in a variety of ways. To get maximum value from objectives, it would be to your advantage to follow this procedure.

First, examine the texts and curriculum materials you will be asked to use. Then, look over the curriculum outlines and lesson plan instructions that may have been supplied by your supervisors. Next, note your own general ideas about what should be included in lessons and assignments. In addition,

Well-written objectives help students formulate effective learning plans. They provide detailed information about the content on which students will be tested and the way in which students will be expected to demonstrate what they have learned.

look through teachers' journals for your grade level or subject area. Quite often individuals or groups present lists of objectives they have devised through a process of trial and error. If you are unable to find lists in journals but still desire at least some direction, write to one or more of the organizations that specialize in providing objectives for teachers. (Names and addresses are supplied in Resources for Further Investigation.)

After you have found helpful lists of objectives and/or developed your own, systematically go through all three taxonomies of objectives, and begin to develop a master set of instructional goals. Make it a point to include objectives from all three taxonomies (if appropriate) as well as at least some objectives from higher levels (depending on the stage of cognitive development of your students). Then, refer to the suggestions offered by Mager and Gronlund, and begin to experiment with various ways to actually write objectives.

Regardless of how much assistance you get from other sources, you and your students will benefit if you make an effort to devise lists of objectives that are custom designed for use in your classroom. That statement is based on several assumptions.

1. You are more likely to arrange learning experiences in a logical and comprehensive order if you devise sets of objectives than if you operate on a one-thing-at-a-time basis.

2. You will provide yourself with leads for developing specific classroom activities and perhaps get clues you can use with students experiencing learning difficulties. The description of objectives for third-grade math, for instance, illustrates how taking the trouble to list specific outcomes not only provides ideas for class exercises but also might give you information about sources of learning problems. Asking students to explain *how* they add and subtract, for example, might reveal why some students are unable to solve problems consistently. The description of objectives for teaching literature in middle school illustrates how an apparently elusive goal such as encouraging appreciation of good literature might be made quite tangible and attainable.

3. You will give yourself guidelines for doing an effective job of evaluation. For instance, if you ask students to *supply* answers (for example, to name or define), you know in advance that you should use short-answer questions or the equivalent. If you ask them to *identify* or *differentiate,* you know you can logically use multiple-choice questions. If you ask them to *perform* in some way (for example, to demonstrate), you know that you should develop ways to evaluate performance. Quite often you will discover that *what* you should evaluate also has been specified by your objectives. Take the middle school music unit. To evaluate achievement in that unit, all you would need to do is follow the objectives in order. That is, first ask students to write down the various instruments of an orchestra as you hold up pictures. Then, ask students to identify the instruments when you play a recording. Next, ask students to explain the differences between instruments used in an orchestra and those used in a band. Finally, play band and orchestra recordings, and ask students to differentiate between the two.

Using objectives can lead to improved planning, instruction, evaluation, learning

4. You will help your students become more effective strategic learners. As we will point out in Chapter 9, a strategic learner is one who analyzes

> the factors that bear on a particular task, formulates a plan for mastering the task, and skillfully implements the plan. One important factor that affects performance, and that, therefore, needs to be accounted for in the development of a learning plan, is the nature of the expected outcome. By telling students that they will have to supply or identify answers for this or that content, or that they will have to exhibit a particular type of performance, you are providing them with information that is critical to the formulation of an effective learning plan. The alternative is to leave the situation so vague that students are forced to guess about what and how to study. Inevitably, some of them will guess wrong.

In addition to reasoning about potential values of objectives, however, you should take into account the available research on their effectiveness. A brief analysis of such research will now be provided.

Evaluations of the Effectiveness of Objectives

EARLY AMBIGUOUS RESULTS

The publication of the various taxonomies and of books by Mager, Gronlund, and others led to widespread use of objectives in American schools and colleges. To determine if objectives were as useful as enthusiasts claimed or implied, many psychologists compared the achievement of students who had and students who had not been provided with specific instructional goals. The results of such research proved to be inconclusive. In one review of over fifty studies, for example, the authors (Duchastel & Merrill) note: "A number of studies have shown facilitative effects. However, an equal number of studies have failed to demonstrate any significant difference" (1973, p. 54). The authors conclude that since "objectives sometimes help and are almost never harmful. . . . One might as well make them available to students" (1973, p. 63). It is probably safe to assume that the supporters of objectives were less than pleased with this conclusion.

REFINING THE STUDIES: POSITIVE CONCLUSIONS EMERGE

The main reason that early studies on the effectiveness of objectives produced such inconsistent results was that the researchers were not asking quite the right question. For example, four variables that work in combination with objectives are individual differences (in ability or motivation, for instance), variations in the subject matter under study, variations in the type of objective provided, and variations in the outcome that is measured (which might be recall, recognition, comprehension, or problem solving). When researchers simply ask whether students who receive objectives will learn more than students who do not, they are assuming such variables to be of little or no importance. It would be nice if the world were that simple. But it is not—particularly when classroom learning is the phenomenon under study. More consistent and useful results were produced when researchers began asking more pointed questions, such as: For what type of learner will objectives work best? What types of things are learned with different types of objectives? For what types of subjects will objectives produce the best results? Later reviews (for example, Faw & Waller, 1976; Klauer, 1984; Melton, 1978) were able to draw the following conclusions:

Objectives work best when students are aware of them

1. Objectives seem to work best when students are aware of them, treat them as directions to learn specific sections of material, and feel they will aid learning.
2. Objectives seem to work best when they are clearly written and the learning task is neither too difficult nor too easy.
3. Students of average ability seem to profit more from being given objectives than do students of higher or lower ability.
4. Objectives lead to an improvement in intentional learning (what is stressed as important) but to a decline in incidental learning (what is not emphasized by the teacher). General objectives of the type recommended by Gronlund seem to lead to more incidental learning than do specific objectives of the type recommended by Mager.

Research results can be supplemented when we examine the kinds of outcomes that were typically measured. That is, most of the research investigations on which the conclusions summarized earlier were based concentrated on student *achievement* as the measure of the impact of objectives. Researchers often fail to take into account less easily measured factors such as positive student response to explicit directions, the teacher's feelings of confidence and satisfaction when presenting well-organized lessons, or the ease and efficiency with which evaluations can be made. When these not-so-easy-to-prove factors are added to evidence from the better-designed studies, it seems quite reasonable to say that there are definite advantages to using objectives.

USING OBJECTIVES APPROPRIATELY

Arranging objectives in strict hierarchical order does not seem to be essential

The three taxonomies described earlier were designed as cumulative hierarchies. That is, they were based on the assumption that learning experiences ideally should be systematically arranged so that lower-level skills are acquired as background for advanced skills. Evaluations of efforts to use the taxonomies to develop highly systematic hierarchies of learning experiences lead to the conclusion that it is rarely possible to use them exactly as published to plan a completely consistent overall curriculum (Furst, 1981). It appears, therefore, that, while there are some benefits to be gained by analyzing sequences of things to be learned, you should not attempt to devise a perfectly ordered set of objectives, with each item in a series preparing the way for the next. You are likely to find that this approach doesn't work, and you may get discouraged about using objectives.

At the same time, you should habitually make it a point to analyze the kinds of abilities represented by each of the levels in the various taxonomies, particularly the taxonomy for the cognitive domain. This will help you avoid a common instructional failing: instruction and classroom testing that overemphasize the lowest level of the cognitive domain. According to Benjamin Bloom, organizer and driving force of the team that prepared the first taxonomy:

> After the sale of over one million copies of the *Taxonomy of Educational Objectives-Cognitive Domain* [Bloom et al., 1956] and over a quarter of a century of use of this domain in preservice and in-service teacher training, it is estimated that over 90% of test questions that U.S. public school students are *now* expected to answer deal with little more than information. Our instructional material, our classroom teaching methods, and our testing methods rarely rise above the lowest category of the Taxonomy-knowledge. (1984, p. 13)

Most test questions stress knowledge, ignore higher levels of cognitive taxonomy

Outcome-Based Education: Objectives That Are Not Curriculum Driven

At the beginning of this chapter, we stated that you would likely be more effective as a teacher and that your students would probably learn more if you did *last things first.* That is, you should begin your instructional planning by focusing on what students should know and be able to do, in fairly specific and observable terms, after a unit of instruction. But in everyday practice the objectives you eventually set will draw from a preestablished curriculum. That is, there are certain basic curricular expectations (subject matter, content areas, and so on), usually established on a schoolwide or school-district-wide basis, that form the context within which and from which you as a classroom teacher will create your own objectives.

In recent years, however, a new approach to generating instructional objectives that is not based on a set curriculum has grown. It is usually referred to as **outcome-based education (OBE).** In the following section we will briefly examine four assumptions that form the foundation for this approach, and then we will define it in greater detail.

BASIC ASSUMPTIONS

There are four assumptions that underlie outcome-based education:

1. Most students can master most, if not all, of a typical school's curriculum. (We will describe the basis for this belief, called mastery learning, in Chapter 12.)
2. Academic mastery and self-concept are intertwined. That is, success in learning enhances self-concept and self-esteem, which maintains persistence at learning, which maintains a strong self-concept, and so on.
3. Instruction becomes more effective when it is aligned with objectives and tests. What is taught in classes, the content of tests, and the types of tests that are used (also discussed in Chapter 12) should relate directly to the objectives that students are given.
4. Schools can significantly improve the learning conditions for all students by taking such steps as clearly specifying what students will be expected to do, providing students with however much time they need to master tasks, providing students with corrective feedback, and expecting all students to learn at high levels (Ellis & Fouts, 1993; Spady, 1988; Spady & Marshall, 1991).

Outcome-based education assumes most students can master curriculum, mastery and self-concept affect each other, instruction more effective when aligned with tests

THE OBE IDEAL

Outcome-based education specifies student competencies first, then curriculum issues

There are three hallmark characteristics of outcome-based education. First, instead of conducting business as usual, which is to write objectives for a curriculum that is already in place, OBE proponents argue that the educational establishment (meaning teachers, administrators, school board members, and parents) start with a blank slate. Throw away, or at least hold in abeyance, all assumptions of what subjects should or should not be taught and the conditions under which they should be taught, OBE proponents say. Instead, focus first on what students should know and be able to do after so many hours, units, or credits of instruction. Then, decide on such things as what courses should be taught, in what sequence they should be taught, for how long, and how student competence will be evaluated, and use a variety of teaching methods—lecture, discussion, cooperative learning, problem-solving activities—to actually implement instruction. The important point for OBE enthusiasts is that the desired outcomes drive the curriculum rather than the other way around.

Second, some form of performance-based assessment to evaluate how well students have learned what you intend them to learn should be used. Performance-based assessment—such as asking students to build prototype models or solve real-life problems—involves actual demonstrations of the intended *outcomes* of learning. Third, the concept of mastery learning is almost always included because of OBE's focus on mastering objectives and the expectation that all students will learn at high levels (Spady & Marshall, 1991).

To illustrate this process, Arthur Ellis and Jeffrey Fouts (1993) use the objective of teaching students to think spatially. The traditional approach would be to suggest that all students take geometry because it seems to require spatial reasoning and, most important, because it is already in the curriculum. An OBE approach would be to examine as many different options as possible and to select the one or ones that would likely result in the greatest number of students mastering the objective. It might be geometry or architecture and design or sculpture or some combination of the above. Students would have multiple opportunities to master spatial reasoning and could demonstrate that mastery by designing an object of their choice (if architecture and design is the course to teach this skill).

Ordinarily we would follow this description of OBE with a summary of research findings. But according to Ellis and Fouts, "There is little to nothing to report at the basic or pure research level" (1993, p.99). Given the stir that OBE has created in the educational community, there may be something to report in a few years. For now we will have to rely on a few anecdotal reports at the classroom level. See, for example, volume 46, number 2 of *Educational Leadership* and Case in Print, pages 268–269, for a detailed description of how OBE is playing out in one county. We can also draw inferences from the research we reviewed earlier on the effectiveness of objectives at the classroom level and from the research on mastery learning (which will be discussed in Chapter 12).

Now that you are familiar with the types of objectives, various recommendations for using them, and evaluations of their effectiveness, it is time to turn to specific applications. Suggestions for Teaching in Your Classroom summarizes and reinforces points already discussed.

Suggestions for Teaching in Your Classroom

Using Instructional Objectives

1. To get a general picture of what you want your students to achieve, look over texts, curriculum guides, and report cards (for the primary and elementary grades); ask about achievement and competency tests; and think about your own goals.

2. Check to see if appropriate and useful lists of objectives for your subject and grade level have been developed by others.

3. Examine the taxonomies of objectives for the three domains, and make a preliminary outline of objectives and activities.

4. Refer to the listings of objectives and specific outcomes in Tables 7.1, 7.2, and 7.3, and begin to write sets of objectives.
   a. Describe a general objective in brief terms.
   b. Under that general objective, list from three to five specific outcomes that begin with an action verb. Try to write specific outcomes that reflect a representative sample of what a student should do when demonstrating achievement of the objective.

5. Examine your lists of objectives to determine how they might be converted into specific classroom learning exercises and/or examination questions.

6. Examine your lesson plans to determine if you should occasionally use specific objectives that include a statement of the criterion of acceptable performance.

7. Develop your own variations of the types of instructional objectives described in this and other books.

8. Keep in mind that measurement and evaluation of classroom learning must accurately reflect your learning objectives.

1. To get a general picture of what you want your students to achieve, look over texts, curriculum guides, and report cards (for the primary and elementary grades); ask about achievement and competency tests; and think about your own goals.

Before devising objectives, examine curriculum materials, find out about tests

At the beginning of this chapter we made the point that you will not be able to determine at the end of a report period or year whether your students have achieved specific objectives unless you describe those objectives before you start. Perhaps the most logical way to begin formulating objectives is to insti-

The first step in using instructional objectives is to get a general picture of what you want your students to achieve. You can do this by looking over texts and curriculum guides and by inquiring about standardized tests your students will be asked to take.

tute a survey of general goals and progressively refine them until you have devised specific objectives and learning outcomes. It would be wise to first find out what others have already decided you should do. Most of the texts you will be asked to use probably will have been selected by state and/or local committees. It is quite likely that you will be asked to follow curriculum guides developed for use in your school system. At the elementary level, the kinds of report cards you will be expected to fill out and/or the kinds of points you will be expected to stress in parent conferences often will indicate what your students will be expected to achieve.

It would also be prudent to find out whether your students will be asked to take achievement or competency tests. At present in American education there is quite a bit of stress on measuring student competency in basic skills. Even though it is usually unwise and ineffective to try to "teach to a test" (for reasons we mentioned in Chapter 5), it does make sense to stress the kinds of abilities that are measured by tests used to evaluate student (and perhaps teacher) achievement. If you will be teaching high school English, for example, and you discover that students in your school will not graduate unless they pass a competency test that includes questions designed to measure their ability to write clearly and accurately, it would be sensible to treat that skill as an important objective. Finally, you might note some of your own general goals that are not directly related to texts, curriculum guides, or examinations. For example, two possible such goals might be "Applies at least some of the things learned in class to out-of-class situations" and "Works diligently and cooperatively in the classroom." Although a bit vague, such goals can help you formulate and express a general conception of what you want your students to achieve by the last day of class.

2. Check to see if appropriate and useful lists of objectives for your subject and grade level have been developed by others.

After you have outlined the general objectives you want your students to achieve in your particular school and classroom, it makes sense to check on the availability of objectives prepared by experienced educators. You should ask experienced teachers or supervisors in your school if they know of lists of objectives that have proved useful. In addition, review recent issues of teachers' journals for articles on objectives. If you are unable to find any sets of goals that provide helpful leads, you might also check on-line databases of teaching materials or join a Usenet discussion group related either to the topic you wish to teach or to educational practice generally, such as "k12.chat.teacher" or "k12.ed.science."

Check on availability of appropriate lists of objectives

3. Examine the taxonomies of objectives for the three domains, and make a preliminary outline of objectives and activities.

The taxonomies of objectives for the cognitive, affective, and psychomotor domains can be used as all-purpose guides for translating general goals into specific objectives and classroom practices. After you have made your general survey of what you want your students to achieve, for example, you might systematically work your way through the taxonomy for the cognitive domain and jot down brief answers to the following questions:

What sorts of terms and symbols will my students need to know?
What specific facts will they need to know?
What sets of rules will they need to know?
What awareness of trends and sequences will they need to have?
What classifications and categories will they benefit from knowing?
What sets of criteria will they need to be able to apply?
What methods will they need to master?
What general principles will they benefit from knowing?
What theories will they benefit from knowing?
What sorts of translations will they need to perform?
What sorts of interpretations will they need to make?
What sorts of extrapolations will they need to make?
What sorts of applications should they be able to make?
What kinds of analyses will they need to make?
What kinds of syntheses should they be able to make?
What kinds of evaluations should they be able to make?

Use taxonomies to make survey of what students should be able to do

Journal Entry
Using the Taxonomy of Cognitive Objectives

You might follow a similar procedure for the various categories in the affective and psychomotor domains. In preparing such lists, you must remember to take into account the cognitive abilities of your students so that you do not waste time speculating about higher levels of a taxonomy if these are not appropriate. If you will be teaching students in the middle school or junior high school grades or beyond, however, pay *special* attention to the higher-level categories. Devising lists of objectives under analysis, synthesis, and evaluation categories may be more difficult than devising lists under the knowledge category, but higher-level skills are too often omitted (as noted by Bloom) when examinations are prepared.

4. Refer back to the listings of objectives and specific outcomes in Tables 7.1, 7.2, and 7.3 (pages 251–253), and begin to write sets of objectives.

a. Describe a general objective in brief terms.

b. Under that general objective, list from three to five specific outcomes that begin with an action verb. Try to write specific outcomes that reflect a representative sample of what a student should do when demonstrating achievement of the objective.

Since selected examples of objectives for different grade levels and subject areas were given earlier, and since it is impossible to provide further examples for all subjects at all grades, the following examples are based on material in this chapter. The general objectives and specific outcomes are written so that they can be applied to almost any subject matter. The examples in parentheses refer to points covered in this chapter. Thus, the examples serve to review what has been covered, permit you to test your knowledge, and help you prepare for exams.

Knows essential terms: (1) defines essential terms (for example, taxonomy, cognitive, affective, psychomotor, domain, and transfer); (2) distinguishes between similar terms (for example, explain difference between specific objectives and general objectives).

Knows methods and procedures: (1) describes how to use knowledge of procedures (for example, tell where to look for information about hierarchies and lists of objectives); (2) states procedure to follow when provided with problems (for example, describe how to proceed when instructed to teach math in third grade, music in sixth grade, and so forth).

Interprets ideas and concepts to display comprehension: (1) converts suggestions described for one situation to another (for example, take example for teaching a sixth-grade unit on music, and apply it to teaching a ninth-grade unit on art appreciation); (2) explains how to adapt given procedures to special circumstances (for example, describe how to use Mager-style objectives when teaching typing).

Applies principles to hypothetical or actual situations: (1) uses principles to develop procedures (for example, explain how to prepare objectives for a unit on general science); (2) demonstrates ability to apply principles (for example, develop a set of Gronlund-style objectives for a unit you expect to teach).

Analyzes organization and relationships: (1) outlines nature of relationships in a given set of data (for example, explain hierarchical arrangement of taxonomies); (2) differentiates between organizational schemes (for example, explain differences among the taxonomies for the cognitive, affective, and psychomotor domains).

Produces new arrangements: (1) combines separate sets of ideas into a new pattern (for example, tell how you might use techniques recommended by both Mager and Gronlund in the same teaching unit); (2) creates custom-designed approach by modifying original description (for example, take examples given in this chapter, and modify them so that they fit your own teaching situation).

Judges on basis of criteria or evidence: (1) criticizes misuse of a given technique (for example, specify when Mager-style objectives are not appropriate); (2) discriminates between proper and improper applications (for example, make judgments about whether the cognitive level of students is likely to permit them to engage in analysis, synthesis, and evaluation); (3) evaluates criticisms (for example, evaluate the conclusions of research on the effectiveness of use of objectives).

Journal Entry
Using the Taxonomy of Affective Objectives

After you have prepared sets of objectives for the cognitive domain, examine the affective and psychomotor taxonomies to determine if there are attitudes and skills you will want your students to acquire along with subject matter. The first level in the taxonomy of affective objectives, for instance, is *receiving* or *attending,* which includes showing willingness to receive and indicating attention. Suppose you conclude that many of your students need to pay closer attention to class demonstrations. You might devise an objective, "Observes attentively," as follows:

- Puts away distracting material when a demonstration is announced
- Observes demonstration with alertness
- Describes procedure accurately after having seen a demonstration
- Answers questions about how to proceed after having seen a demonstration
- Correctly carries out a procedure shown in a demonstration

Or suppose you want to encourage your students to develop an appreciation for the values of science. You might devise an objective, "Appreciates the values of scientific methods and discoveries," as follows:

- Describes the characteristics of scientific methods
- Distinguishes between scientific and nonscientific conclusions
- Explains why conclusions based on scientific evidence are more trustworthy than conclusions based on hunches or opinions

Suppose you notice that your students seem to be having trouble with the sequence of steps in carrying out some activity. You might devise a psychomotor objective, "Knows sequence of steps in a procedure," in this way:

- Describes correct sequence of steps
- Explains how to carry out each step
- Shows how to carry out each step
- Combines all steps in correct order with confidence

Journal Entry
Using the Taxonomy of Psychomotor Objectives

You might write other objectives derived from the taxonomies for the affective and psychomotor domains by referring to Tables 7.2 and 7.3.

5. **Examine your lists of objectives to determine how they might be converted into specific classroom learning exercises and/or examination questions.**

As you looked over the various examples of objectives provided earlier, you may have noticed that many of them give specific leads for arranging classroom learning experiences and for devising exams. The objective "Knows terms," for example, could be converted into this announcement:

Use specific learning-outcome descriptions to arrange learning experiences

> Here is a list of the most important terms in the next chapter of the text. As you read the chapter, write down the definition of each term. I will give you my definitions after you finish, and we can discuss differences between yours and mine. You will be asked to define five terms selected from this list on the exam scheduled for Friday.

When you take the trouble to describe specific learning outcomes, you not only give yourself instructions on ways to present lessons, but you also pretty much determine in advance how you will evaluate achievement.

You undoubtedly recognized as you read the suggestions just offered that the basic procedure outlined so far is based on Gronlund's recommendations for using objectives. His approach is quite versatile and has many advantages, but you should also consider other alternatives.

6. **Examine your lesson plans to determine if you should occasionally use specific objectives that include a statement of the criterion of acceptable performance.**

As noted in the discussion of Mager's recommendations and in the section on evaluations of objectives, too much stress on specific objectives tends to discourage incidental learning and to cause teachers to concentrate on knowledge and simple skills. Even so, there are times when you may find it desirable to describe precisely what you want your students to do and specify the criterion for acceptable performance. Here are three examples:

EXAMPLES

"To pass this unit, you will have to spell correctly at least eighteen of these twenty words on the quiz to be given on Friday."

"By the end of this month you should be able to type a 240-word selection in less than six minutes with no errors."

"After you watch this film, you should be able to list five basic kinds of crops and give an example of each within three minutes."

7. **Develop your own variations of the types of instructional objectives described in this and other books.**

The top levels of the various taxonomies stress the creation of something new or at least the modification of something already existing to fit particular situations. As a result of reading this chapter, therefore, you might devise your own variations of the techniques described. Here are a few variations you might consider as examples of ways you might modify the basic suggestions that have been supplied. They all stress objectives, but in different ways than those already described.

EXAMPLE

Variation 1. To help students study texts and respond selectively to lectures and assignments, go through a new text before you distribute it, and underline all terms that some students may not understand. List and define these terms; then give an informal quiz to determine if students have learned them.

Invite students to list all terms that they are not sure about as they read or listen. Suggest that they look up such terms in a dictionary or encyclopedia. Perhaps invite discussion of different interpretations of the same terms and decide on an "official" definition that will be used in class discussions or on exams.

Go through each chapter in a text, and list Key Points under major headings. If you plan to use these as the basis for exam questions, inform students of that fact. Look over lecture notes, and select the most important points. List these on the board before you begin to lecture.

Say to your students, "There may seem to be an overwhelming amount of factual information in this book. Here are the facts that I want you to concentrate on when you prepare for exams." Then hand out an organized list of these facts.

EXAMPLE

Variation 2. The basic goal of a unit on poetry is to help students learn to appreciate and enjoy it. Let them know that when they have finished the unit, they should be able to distinguish between superior and inferior poetry, give reasons for classifying a poem as superior or inferior, explain why they like some poems better than others, and find books and magazines that contain poems they are likely to enjoy.

EXAMPLE

Variation 3. You can focus on just one of the key verbs in the taxonomy for the cognitive domain and use it to develop a teaching exercise in any one of the following ways:

"Here is an excerpt from a recent speech by the president. *Translate* it into your own words."

Ask students to write their own brief summary of a chapter, their *interpretation* of a poem, or the meaning of a short story. Then arrange students in small groups to compare how they interpreted others' information.

Show a political cartoon from a newspaper, and ask students to give their *interpretation* of what the cartoonist intended to convey.

"As you read the next two chapters, I want you to draw up your own *analysis* of what is covered. Try to pick out points that are important, and organize them into an outline."

"Here are copies of three different newspaper reports of the same event. I'd like you to prepare a *synthesis* of the points made and write your own composite interpretation of what occurred."

"Your political science assignment this week is to watch the presidential candidates debate on television this Wednesday and *evaluate* the arguments of each candidate. On Thursday morning we will divide into small groups to compare our evaluations, and then we will have a class election to find out which candidate 'won.'"

8. **Keep in mind that measurement and evaluation of classroom learning must accurately reflect your learning objectives.**

In the opening to this chapter we pointed out that there are three related benefits to writing objectives: (a) it helps you identify in advance a body of knowledge and skill that students must learn, (b) it helps you prepare lessons that directly relate to the objectives, and (c) it helps you identify the content of your exams. By teaching for one thing but testing for something else (a common flaw, unfortunately), you do yourself and your students a great disservice. As we will point out in Chapter 9, forcing students to guess at the content of an exam makes it more difficult for them to be strategic learners.

As you write objectives, note how you intend to evaluate students' mastery of them, and use these notes when you prepare your assessment procedure. We will describe this process in more detail in Chapter 12. Finally, as you develop objectives, keep in mind the variability and diversity of your students. For example, write objectives that are consistent with your students' stage of cognitive development, that reinforce an understanding of and respect for cultural diversity, and that allow students to capitalize on cultural characteristics.

CASE IN PRINT

Outcome-Based Education: Doing Last Things First

Instead of conducting business as usual, which is to write objectives for a curriculum that is already in place, OBE proponents argue that the educational establishment . . . start with a blank slate. . . . Focus first on what students should know and be able to do. . . . Then, decide on such things as what courses should be taught, in what sequence they should be taught, for how long. (p. 260)

"Blackboard Jungle: Teaching Approach Divides Schools"

JO MANNIES AND JOAN LITTLE

St. Louis Post-Dispatch 1/2/94

In Franklin County, 350 parents crowd into the cafeteria at St. Clair High School. In west St. Louis County, hundreds pack the Ballwin Baptist Church. . . .

The topic: outcome-based education.

Most people in Missouri and Illinois probably have never heard of it. But "outcome-based education" is a loaded term in many states—splitting communities, pitting parents against schools and putting politicians on the hot seat. . . .

Outcome-based education, dubbed OBE, is a teaching philosophy that changes how students are taught, what they are taught and how their progress is assessed.

Some schools here have adopted parts of the philosophy. But educators in both states know of only a few—including Parkway South here and Arlington Heights High School near Chicago—that have embraced the philosophy in a big way.

Robert Bartman, Missouri's top educator, defines outcome-based education this way: A district or state sets up "outcomes" for students to master by graduation, then creates teaching methods or courses to get there.

Many see OBE as adapting for education the business principle of management by objective, or MBO: Decide on a goal or result, then develop a plan to achieve it.

. . . Some schools using the outcome-based approach drop all grades lower than a "B" or "C." Students retake tests or the course until they make the grade. . . .

Here are other earmarks of OBE:

- Special programs for "gifted students" are out.
- Group learning is in. That can mean students trade an individual grade for a team grade on a project.
- Memorization is out and hands-on, real-life applications are in.
- Keeping portfolios of individual students' work is in.
- Learning at an individual pace is in. But all students must meet specified outcomes before graduating.

At Parkway South High School, all students must display certain masteries before passing a course or graduating. For example, all freshmen must write a two-paragraph composition on an assigned topic. The teacher judges their ability to write clearly based on six skills. . . .

In Missouri, critics point to some outcomes state educators included in a draft sent to school districts in 1992. Among other things, they called for students to:

- "Use ethical, aesthetic and practical values to guide their behavior."
- Demonstrate "effective job-seeking skills. . . . "
- Manage "stress and time."
- Develop "skills needed for effective parenting."

"That's laudable, but how do you test for that?" asked Donna Hearne of St. Louis, who has served on several advisory boards with the U.S. Department of Education. "How do you test for a positive attitude?"

Bartman says the draft has been thrown out.

Supporters of outcome-based education contend that parents and educators need to get away from the traditional approach to learning, where somebody wins and somebody loses.

"So much of what has been passed off as learning is really an accelerated 'Trivial Pursuit,'" said Bert Schulte, associate superintendent of instruction for the Columbia, Mo., School District, which supports outcome-based education. . . .

Critics here see it differently. They complain that outcomes often are vague and that teaching methods "dumb-down" academic standards and discourage individual achievement.

OBE's backers and opponents don't line up behind typical conservative-liberal labels.

Supporters include many business leaders, former President Bush and many education-reform activists. Critics include Phyllis Schlafly's conservative Eagle Forum, the head of the American Federation of Teachers union and the admissions departments at many universities.

The universities complain that they find it difficult to pick out the best students at some high schools using outcome-based education.

Educators are divided. . . .

Illinois adopted its "State Goals for Learning" in 1986. Among the 34 academic items is a language-arts goal that graduates should "write standard English in a grammatical, well-organized, and coherent manner. . . . "

Ray Schaljo, an aide with the state Board of Education, said the state avoids prescribing specific learning methods. Illinois officials are well aware of the OBE debate, he added.

In Missouri, Bartman notes that the education tax package the Legislature passed last spring makes no reference to OBE. It does require the state to adopt up to 75 "performance standards" that local schools will have to meet.

"We're trying to avoid calling them 'outcomes' because there's so much baggage with that term," Bartman said.

. . . Bartman said U.S. Secretary of Education Richard Riley recommended during a recent visit that Missouri's performance standards "not try to challenge people's feelings and belief systems."

"Squishy stuff," committee member Frances Shands calls them. . . .

One proposed standard, Shands said, is "the ability to acquire and apply life skills for personal and economic independence."

Others include "the ability to apply for and hold jobs. The ability to balance a checkbook."

Those are worthy skills, but not as state standards, she said.

"And this is social studies," Shands said. "Where's something about the Constitution or the Bill of Rights? If they don't have this knowledge, how can they think critically?"

Bartman urges critics to withhold judgment.

The state will adopt only standards that are widely accepted. Once standards are written, individual districts will choose how to meet them.

Some districts may choose teaching methods associated with outcome-based education, he said. Some may not.

"It doesn't mean we're going to have to stop handing out grades," Bartman said, adding, "Kids have got to be able to write when they get out of high school—I think everybody agrees with that."

Questions and Activities

1. Because outcome-based education is frequently used in conjunction with such teaching techniques as cooperative learning, critics argue that it lowers academic standards and discourages individual achievement. Using the information we will present in Chapter 11 on the nature and effectiveness of cooperative learning as well as any other sources of which you may be aware, construct a rebuttal.

2. Some colleges and universities have opposed outcome-based education because its emphasis on mastery learning results in a narrower range of grades than is usually the case, thereby making it more difficult for them to select the top students. To what extent should public schools identify levels of student achievement for the benefit of other aspects of society? Why?

3. The outcomes of OBE that have attracted the most criticism are the affective ones (moral, ethical, and aesthetic). They have been criticized as being irrelevant (they have nothing to do with the primary goal of schools—helping students acquire cognitive knowledge and skills); inappropriate (these sorts of outcomes are best handled by parents); and difficult to accurately measure (how does one accurately measure a positive attitude?). Construct pro and con arguments for each of these criticisms.

4. Identify a set of criteria (such as "provides necessary job skills," "improves a person's ability to get along with others") that could be used to determine whether a proposed educational outcome should be adopted by a school system.

Resources for Further Investigation

Taxonomy of Educational Objectives: Cognitive Domain

This chapter presented an abridged outline of the taxonomy developed by Benjamin Bloom and several associates in *Taxonomy of Educational Objectives: The Classification of Educational Goals. Handbook I: Cognitive Domain* (1956). To better understand the taxonomy and to gain insight into coordinating objectives and evaluation, examine Bloom's book, particularly Chapter 1, "The Nature and Development of the Taxonomy," and Chapter 2, "Educational Objectives and Curriculum Development." The remainder of the book consists of definitions of the general and specific classifications, followed by illustrations and exam questions.

Taxonomy of Educational Objectives: Affective Domain

To become more familiar with the possible values of the *Taxonomy of Educational Objectives. Handbook II: Affective Domain* (1964), refer to the complete list and explanation of objectives in this book by David Krathwohl, Benjamin Bloom, and Bertram Masia.

Taxonomy of Educational Objectives: Psychomotor Domain

The Psychomotor Domain (1972), by Elizabeth Simpson, gives a complete description of the taxonomy for the psychomotor domain noted in this chapter. A different *Taxonomy of the Psychomotor Domain: A Guide for Developing Behavioral Objectives* (1972) has been developed by Anita Harrow.

Mager and Gronlund on Objectives

If you would like to read Robert Mager's complete description of his recommendations for writing specific objectives, peruse his brief paperback *Preparing Instructional Objectives* (rev. 2d ed., 1984). Norman Gronlund explains his approach to using objectives in *How to Write and Use Instructional Objectives* (5th ed., 1995); and in *Measurement and Assessment in Teaching* (7th ed., 1995), which he coauthored with Linn.

Outcome-Based Education

Information about outcome-based education for students with disabilities can be found at the National Center for Educational Outcomes for Students with Disabilities at the University of Minnesota. The center can be contacted through James Ysseldyke, Department of Education, 345 Elliott Hall, 75 East River Road, Minneapolis, MN 55455, (612) 626-1530 or on-line at http://www.coled.umn.edu/CARE|www/k12ns/NATIONALCENTER.html.

Summary

1. Early attempts at specifying the outcomes of education focused on general goals that meant different things to different people.
2. The vagueness of such goals stimulated psychologists to formulate taxonomies of specific, clearly stated objectives in each of three domains: cognitive, affective, and psychomotor.
3. The taxonomy for the cognitive domain that was prepared by Benjamin Bloom and several associates is composed of six levels: knowledge, comprehension, application, analysis, synthesis, and evaluation.
4. The taxonomy for the affective domain that was prepared by David Krathwohl and several associates is composed of five levels: receiving, responding, valuing, organization, and characterization by a value or value complex.
5. The taxonomy for the psychomotor domain that was prepared by Elizabeth Simpson is composed of seven levels:

perception, set, guided response, mechanism, complex or overt response, adaptation, and origination.

6. Robert Mager states that well-written objectives should specify what behaviors the learner will exhibit to indicate mastery, the conditions under which the behavior will be exhibited, and the criterion of acceptable performance.

7. Norman Gronlund believes that complex and advanced kinds of learning do not lend themselves to Mager-type objectives. Complex outcomes are so broad in scope that it is impractical to ask students to demonstrate everything they have learned. Instead, Gronlund suggests that teachers first state a general objective and then specify a sample of related specific outcomes.

8. Formulating objectives helps you plan a logical sequence of instruction, provides you with ideas for classroom activities and remedial instruction, and helps you specify tests that will determine if learning has occurred.

9. Objectives work best when students are aware of them and understand their intent, when they are clearly written, when they are provided to average students for tasks of average difficulty, and when intentional learning is measured.

10. Most teachers use test questions that measure knowledge-level objectives, largely ignoring higher-level outcomes.

11. Outcome-based education is a school-based and district-based approach to providing instruction that takes as its starting point the specifying of important educational outcomes, or objectives. These objectives then guide such curriculum matters as the choice of subject matter, course length, sequencing of courses, and the like. Although a variety of instructional methods are compatible with the practice of outcome-based education. Mastery learning is almost always made a part of it.

Key Terms

taxonomy *(242)*
cognitive domain *(242)*
affective domain *(242)*
psychomotor domain *(242)*
specific objectives *(248)*
general objectives *(249)*
outcome-based education (OBE) *(259)*

Discussion Questions

1. Based on the content of this chapter and your own experiences as a student, do you agree that writing objectives and providing them to students are worthwhile expenditures of a teacher's time and effort? If so, then what steps will you take to ensure that, unlike many teachers today, you will make writing objectives a standard part of your professional behavior?
2. One criticism of writing objectives is that it limits the artistic side of teaching. That is, objectives lock teachers into a predetermined plan of instruction and eliminate the ability to pursue unplanned topics or interests. Can you respond to this criticism by recalling a teacher who provided you and your classmates with objectives but was still enthusiastic, flexible, spontaneous, and inventive?
3. Although, for the sake of clarity and simplicity, textbooks discuss objectives in terms of separate domains, many educational outcomes are in reality a combination of cognitive, affective, and psychomotor elements. Can you describe a few instructional outcomes that incorporate objectives from two or three domains (such as playing a piece of music "with feeling")?
4. As Benjamin Bloom has pointed out, over 90 percent of the test questions teachers write reflect the lowest level of the cognitive taxonomy. How can you avoid doing the same thing?

Part 3

Providing Instruction

CHAPTER 8

Behavioral and Social Learning Theories

Key Points

These key points will help you learn the important information in this chapter. To help you study, they also appear in the margins of the pages, next to the text where they are discussed.

Operant Conditioning

- Operant conditioning: voluntary response strengthened or weakened by consequences that follow
- Positive reinforcement: strengthen a target behavior by presenting a positive reinforcer after the behavior occurs
- Negative reinforcement: strengthen a target behavior by removing an aversive stimulus after the behavior occurs
- Punishment: weaken a target behavior by presenting an aversive stimulus after the behavior occurs
- Time-out: weaken a target behavior by temporarily removing a positive reinforcer after the behavior occurs
- Extinction: weaken a target behavior by ignoring it
- Spontaneous recovery: extinguished behaviors may reappear spontaneously
- Generalization: responding in similar ways to similar stimuli
- Discrimination: responding in different ways to similar stimuli
- Complex behaviors are shaped by reinforcing closer approximations to terminal behavior
- Fixed interval schedules: reinforce after regular time intervals
- Variable interval schedules: reinforce after random time intervals
- Fixed ratio schedules: reinforce after a set number of responses
- Variable ratio schedules: reinforce after a different number of responses each time

EDUCATIONAL APPLICATIONS OF OPERANT CONDITIONING PRINCIPLES

- Programmed instruction: arrange material in small steps; reinforce correct responses
- Linear programs provide one path; branching programs have multiple paths
- CAI-taught students learn more with simulation programs than with drill-and-practice programs
- CAI works best for elementary grade students, especially low achievers
- CAI not meant to replace teachers
- Behavior modification: shape behavior by ignoring undesirable responses, reinforcing desirable responses
- Premack principle: required work first, then chosen reward
- Token economy is a flexible reinforcement system
- Contingency contracting: reinforcement supplied after student completes mutually agreed on assignment
- Time-out works best with disruptive, aggressive children
- Punishment is likely to be ineffective because of temporary impact, side effects

SOCIAL LEARNING THEORY

- People learn to inhibit or make responses by observing others
- Processes of observational learning: attention, retention, production, motivation
- Imitation is strengthened through direct reinforcement, vicarious reinforcement, self-reinforcement
- Self-efficacy: how capable one feels one is for handling particular kinds of tasks
- Self-efficacy influenced by past performance, persuasion, emotional reactions, observation of models
- Self-efficacy affects one's goals, thought processes, persistence, emotions
- Persistence, self-confidence, cognitive skills can be learned by observation of models

Now that you are familiar with how students develop from preschool through high school, with some of the major ways in which students differ from one another, and with a variety of ways to specify what is to be learned, it is time to turn to the third phase in our learning and instruction model. This third step, helping students achieve specified objectives, will demand most of your attention when you begin to teach. To understand why, think for a moment about what you will be doing then. If you obtain a position in an elementary or a middle school, you will be responsible for teaching some, or perhaps all, of the following subjects: reading, writing, math, science, social studies, foreign languages, citizenship, arts and crafts, music, and physical education. If you accept a position in a high school, you will specialize in advanced instruction of one or more of the subjects just listed or in courses in vocational education.

Now think for a moment about the kinds of tasks you and your students will spend much of each day dealing with. At the elementary and middle school levels, you will ask your students to read texts (once they have learned to read), complete exercises in workbooks, watch demonstrations, practice skills, participate in group work, engage in class discussions, work on individual and group projects, and prepare for and take exams. At the secondary school level, you will carry out more advanced and sophisticated variations of these activities. In addition, you may sometimes present lectures similar to those in college courses. You may also ask students to spend a good proportion of class time completing experiments or creating products. That is why this part begins with three chapters on learning. You will also work to keep your students actively engaged in mastering your objectives for up to five hours a day. That is why this part ends with a chapter on motivation.

In 1879 in Leipzig, Germany, Wilhelm Wundt opened the first laboratory devoted to the scientific study of human behavior. Since then, learning has been studied more extensively by more psychologists than any other aspect of human behavior. It probably will not surprise you to discover that over the decades different psychologists have had different ideas about how learning occurs in animals and human beings and how it should be studied. As a result, there are varied, seemingly conflicting, opinions about how teachers should arrange learning activities in classrooms. Such differences of opinion are not necessarily a problem since different theories and the approaches to teaching that flow from them complement, rather than compete with, one another. Think of these different theories as something like a jigsaw puzzle. To see the entire picture, you need to have all the pieces, and you need to know how to put them together. We hope that you will have some sense of how to do that by the end of this part.

This chapter is devoted to two theories of learning—a type of behavioral learning theory known as operant conditioning and social learning theory. Although different, they share certain assumptions about and principles of learning.

Operant Conditioning

In 1913 with the publication of an article titled "Psychology as the Behaviorist Views It," the influential American psychologist John Watson argued that psychology would quickly lose credibility as a science if it focused on internal mental and emotional states that could not be directly observed or accurately measured. The solution was to study what could be directly observed and objectively and accurately measured—the external stimuli that people experienced and what people did in response. In a word, behavior. From this point until the late 1960s, behavioral theories of one sort or another dominated the psychology of learning and culminated in the work of B. F. Skinner.

BASIC NATURE AND ASSUMPTIONS

Operant conditioning: voluntary response strengthened or weakened by consequences that follow

B.F. Skinner put together a theory that not only successfully combines many different ideas but also serves as the basis for a variety of applications to human behavior. Skinner's theory, **operant conditioning,** takes as its starting point that many of the voluntary responses of animals and humans are strengthened when they are reinforced (followed by a desirable consequence) and weakened when they are either ignored or punished. In this way organisms learn new behaviors and when to exhibit them and "unlearn" existing behaviors. The term *operant conditioning* refers to the fact that organisms learn to "operate" on their environment (make a particular response) in order to obtain or avoid a particular consequence. Some psychologists use the term *instrumental* since the behavior is instrumental in bringing about the consequence.

FIGURE 8.1 *A Rat in a Skinner Box*

The rat's behavior is reinforced with a food pellet when it presses the bar under conditions preselected by the experimenter. In the process of exploring the Skinner box, the rat is almost certain to touch the bar. When that occurs, the experimenter supplies a food pellet and bar-pressing behavior is reinforced. Eventually, the rat may be reinforced only when a particular sequence of actions (for example, pressing the bar five times in succession) is performed.

Most of the experiments on which the principles of operant conditioning are based involved an ingenious apparatus invented by Skinner and appropriately referred to as a Skinner box (see Figure 8.1). This is a small enclosure that contains only a bar (or lever) and a small tray. Outside the box is a hopper holding a supply of food pellets that are dropped into the tray when the bar is pressed under certain conditions.

A hungry rat is placed in the box, and when in the course of exploring its new environment, the rat approaches and then presses the bar, it is rewarded with a food pellet. The rat then presses the bar more frequently than it did before being rewarded. If food pellets are supplied under some conditions when the bar is pushed down—for example, when a tone is sounded—but not under others, the rat learns to discriminate one situation from the other, and the rate of bar pressing drops noticeably when the tone is not sounded. If a tone is sounded that is very close in frequency to the original tone, the rat generalizes (treats the two tones as equivalent) and presses the bar at the same rate for both. But if the food pellets are not given after the rat presses the bar, that behavior stops, or is extinguished.

The Skinner box's prominent role in operant conditioning experiments reflects Skinner's view of psychology as a natural science. One important assumption that underlies all natural sciences is that natural phenomena (such as weather patterns, earthquakes, and human behavior) may appear on the surface to be random but really operate according to set laws. What psychology needed, in Skinner's view, was the means by which a researcher could control the environment to observe the lawful and hence predictable influence of environmental factors on behavior.

A second assumption underlying Skinner's work is that a science develops most effectively when scientists study some phenomenon at its most simple, fundamental level. What is learned at this level can then be used to understand more complex processes.

A third assumption is that principles of learning that arise from experiments with animals *should* apply to humans. Note, however, the conditional phrasing of the last sentence. While Skinner accepted the usefulness of animal research, he was always careful to point out that such principles needed to be tested again at the human level.

A fourth assumption is that a change in an organism's behavior pattern is the only basis for concluding that learning has occurred. While admitting the existence of such internal processes as thoughts, motives, and emotions, Skinner has two objections to including them in his theoretical system. First, such processes have no place in the scientific study of learning since they cannot be directly observed or measured. Second, he believes that his experiments with rats in the Skinner box show that learning is caused not by internal processes but by the environmental consequences that follow behavior.

BASIC PRINCIPLES OF OPERANT CONDITIONING

To repeat the basic idea behind operant conditioning: all behaviors are accompanied by certain consequences, and these consequences strongly influence (some might say determine) whether these behaviors are repeated and at what level of intensity. In general, the consequences that follow behavior are either pleasant and desirable or unpleasant and aversive. Depending on conditions that we will discuss shortly, these consequences either increase (strengthen) or decrease (weaken) the likelihood that the preceding behavior will recur under the same or similar circumstances. When consequences strengthen a preceding behavior, *reinforcement* has taken place. When consequences weaken a preceding behavior, *punishment* and *extinction* have occurred. There are two forms of reinforcement and two forms of punishment. This section will describe both forms of reinforcement, both forms of punishment, extinction, and several related principles that can be applied to aspects of human learning.

Positive Reinforcement Although the term *positive reinforcement* may be unfamiliar to you, the idea behind it probably is not. If you can recall spending more time studying for a certain subject because of a compliment from the teacher or a high grade on an examination, you have experienced positive reinforcement. Specifically, **positive reinforcement** involves strengthening a target behavior—that is, increasing and maintaining the probability that a particular behavior will be repeated—by presenting a stimulus (called a *positive reinforcer*) immediately after the behavior has occurred. Praise, recognition, and the opportunity for free play are positive reinforcers for many (but not all) students. The term *positive* as used by Skinner refers to the act of presenting a stimulus (think of positive as *adding* here); it does not refer to the pleasant nature of the stimulus itself. You will understand better why this distinction is very important as we consider the other form of reinforcement.

Positive reinforcement: strengthen a target behavior by presenting a positive reinforcer after the behavior occurs

Negative Reinforcement People frequently have difficulty understanding the concept of negative reinforcement, most often confusing it with punishment,

Students are likely to be motivated to learn if they are positively reinforced for completing a project or task. Awards and praise from the teacher and one's peers are strong positive reinforcers for many students.

so we will examine it carefully here. The goal of **negative reinforcement** is the same as positive reinforcement—to *increase* the strength of a particular behavior. The method, however, is different. Instead of supplying a desirable stimulus, *one removes an unpleasant and aversive stimulus* whenever a target behavior is exhibited. As you study this definition, pay special attention to the removing action. Just as positive refers to adding, negative refers to the act of *removing* a stimulus. By removing something unwanted, you encourage the student to learn new behaviors.

Negative reinforcement: strengthen a target behavior by removing an aversive stimulus after the behavior occurs

In everyday life negative reinforcement occurs quite frequently. A child picks up his clothes or toys to stop his parents' nagging. A driver uses a seat belt to stop the annoying buzzer sound. Later in the chapter we will describe how educators use negative reinforcement. We will also discuss its desirability relative to positive reinforcement.

Punishment There are three procedures that reduce the likelihood of a particular behavior being repeated. The first is **punishment**, also known as Type I punishment or presentation punishment. Punishment is defined by operant psychologists as the presentation of an aversive stimulus (such as scolding, paddling, ridiculing, or making a student write five hundred times "I will not chew gum in class") that reduces the frequency of a target behavior. From an operant perspective, you can claim to have punished someone else only if the target behavior is actually reduced in frequency. (Note that whether these methods of punishment do achieve their goal and are effective and whether they are ethical are other issues—ones that we will discuss later in this chapter.)

Punishment: weaken a target behavior by presenting an aversive stimulus after the behavior occurs

Many people confuse negative reinforcement with punishment. Both involve the use of an aversive stimulus, but the effects of each are opposite. Remember that negative reinforcement strengthens a target behavior, whereas punishment weakens or eliminates a behavior.

Time-out: weaken a target behavior by temporarily removing a positive reinforcer after the behavior occurs

Time-Out The second procedure that decreases the frequency of or eliminates a target behavior is another form of punishment, called **time-out.** But, instead of presenting an aversive stimulus, time-out *temporarily removes the opportunity to receive positive reinforcement.* (Time-out is sometimes called Type II punishment or removal punishment.) For instance, a student who frequently disrupts classroom routine to get attention may be sent to sit in an empty room for five minutes. Removal from a reinforcing environment (as well as the angry tone of voice and facial expression that normally accompany the order to leave the classroom) is usually looked on as an aversive consequence by the individual being removed. An athlete who is suspended from competition is another example of this form of punishment.

Extinction: weaken a target behavior by ignoring it

Extinction A third consequence that weakens undesired behavior is **extinction.** Extinction occurs when a previously reinforced behavior decreases in frequency, and eventually ceases altogether, because reinforcement is withheld. Examples of extinction include a mother ignoring a whining child or a teacher ignoring a student who spontaneously answers a question without waiting to be called on. Both extinction and time-out are most effective when combined with other consequences, such as positive reinforcement. To help yourself define and remember the distinguishing characteristics of positive reinforcement, negative reinforcement, punishment, and extinction, study Table 8.1.

TABLE 8.1 ***Conditions That Define Reinforcement, Punishment, and Extinction***

Type of Stimulus +	Action +	Effect on Behavior =	Result
Desirable	Present	Strengthen	Positive reinforcement
Aversive	Remove	Strengthen	Negative reinforcement
Aversion	Present	Weaken	Type I (presentation) punishment
Desirable	Remove	Weaken	Type II (removal) punishment (also called time-out)
Desirable	Withhold	Weaken	Extinction

Spontaneous recovery: extinguished behaviors may reappear spontaneously

Spontaneous Recovery When used alone, extinction is sometimes a slow and difficult means of decreasing the frequency of undesired behavior because extinguished behaviors occasionally reappear without having been reinforced (an occurrence known as **spontaneous recovery**). Under normal circumstances, however, the time between spontaneous recoveries lengthens, and the intensity of the recurring behavior becomes progressively weaker. If the behavior undergoing extinction is not terribly disruptive, and if the teacher (or parent, counselor, or supervisor) is willing to persevere, these episodes can sometimes be tolerated on the way to more complete extinction.

Generalization When an individual learns to make a particular response to a particular stimulus and then makes the same or a similar response in a slightly different situation, **generalization** has occurred. For example, students who were positively reinforced for using effective study skills in history go on to use those same skills in chemistry, social studies, algebra, and so on. Or, to use a less encouraging illustration, students ignore or question a teacher's every request and direction because they have been reinforced for responding that way to their parents at home. The less similar the new stimulus is to the original, however, the less similar the response is likely to be.

Generalization: responding in similar ways to similar stimuli

Discrimination When inappropriate generalizations occur, as in the preceding example, they can be essentially extinguished through discrimination training. Quite simply, in **discrimination** individuals learn to notice the unique aspects of seemingly similar situations (for example, that teachers are not parents, although both are adults) and to respond differently to each situation. Teachers can encourage this process by reinforcing only the desired behaviors (for instance, attention, obedience, and cooperation) and withholding reinforcement following undesired behaviors (such as inattention or disobedience).

Discrimination: responding in different ways to similar stimuli

Shaping Up to now, we have not distinguished relatively simple behaviors learned from more complex ones. A bit of reflection, however, should enable you to realize that many of the behaviors human beings learn (such as playing a sport or writing a term paper) are complex and are acquired gradually. The principle of **shaping** best explains how complex responses are learned.

In shaping, actions that move progressively closer to the desired *terminal behavior* (to use Skinner's term) are reinforced. Actions that do not represent closer approximations of the terminal behavior are ignored. The key to success is to take one step at a time. The movements must be gradual enough so that the person or animal becomes aware that each step in the sequence is essential. This process is typically called *reinforcing successive approximations to the terminal behavior.*

Complex behaviors are shaped by reinforcing closer approximations to terminal behavior

At least three factors can undermine the effectiveness of shaping. First, too much positive reinforcement for early, crude responses may reduce the learner's willingness to attempt a more complex response. Second, an expectation of too much progress too soon may decrease the likelihood of an appropriate response. If this results in a long period of nonreinforcement, what has been learned up to that point may be extinguished. For example, expecting a student to work industriously on a homework assignment for ninety minutes just after you have shaped forty-five minutes of appropriate homework behavior is probably too big a jump. If it is, the student may revert to her original level of performance owing to the lack of reinforcement. Third, delay in the reinforcement of the terminal behavior allows time for additional, unrelated behaviors to occur. When the reinforcement eventually occurs, it may strengthen one or more of the more recent behaviors rather than the terminal behavior.

Schedules of Reinforcement If you have been reading this section on basic principles carefully, you may have begun to wonder if the use of operant conditioning principles, particularly positive reinforcement, requires you to be present every time a desired response happens. If so, you might have some justifiable reservations about the practicality of this theory. The answer is yes, up to a point, but after that, no. As we have pointed out, when you are trying to get a new behavior established, especially if it is a complex behavior that requires shaping, learning proceeds best when every desired response is positively reinforced and every undesired response is ignored. This is known as a *continuous reinforcement* schedule.

Once the behavior has been learned, however, positive reinforcement can be employed on a noncontinuous or intermittent basis to perpetuate that behavior. There are four basic *intermittent reinforcement* schedules: fixed interval (FI), variable interval (VI), fixed ratio (FR), and variable ratio (VR). Each schedule produces a different pattern of behavior.

Fixed interval schedules: reinforce after regular time intervals

FIXED INTERVAL SCHEDULE. In this schedule, a learner is reinforced for the first desired response that occurs after a predetermined amount of time has elapsed (for example, five minutes, one hour, or seven days). Once the response has occurred and been reinforced, the next interval begins. Any desired behaviors that are made during an interval are ignored. The reinforced behavior occurs at a lower level during the early part of the interval and gradually rises as the time for reinforcement draws closer. Once the reinforcer is delivered, the relevant behavior declines in frequency and gradually rises toward the end of that next interval.

FI schedules of reinforcement occur in education when teachers schedule exams or projects at regular intervals. The grade or score is considered to be a reinforcer. As you are certainly aware, it is not unusual to see little studying or progress occur during the early part of the interval. However, several days before an exam or due date, the pace quickens considerably.

Variable interval schedules: reinforce after random time intervals

VARIABLE INTERVAL SCHEDULE. If you would like to see a more consistent pattern of behavior, you might consider using a variable interval schedule. With a VI schedule, the length of time between reinforcements is essentially random but averages out to a predetermined interval. Thus, four successive reinforcements may occur at the following intervals: one week, four weeks, two weeks, five weeks. The average interval is three weeks. Teachers who give surprise quizzes or who call on students to answer oral questions on the average of once every third day are invoking a variable interval schedule.

Fixed ratio schedules: reinforce after a set number of responses

FIXED RATIO SCHEDULE. Within this schedule, reinforcement is provided whenever a predetermined number of responses are made. A rat in a Skinner box may be reinforced with a food pellet whenever it presses a lever fifty times. A factory worker may earn $20 each time he assembles five electronic circuit boards. A teacher may reinforce a student with praise for every ten arithmetic problems correctly completed. FR schedules tend to produce high response rates since the faster the learner responds, the sooner the reinforcement is delivered. However, a relatively brief period of no or few responses occurs immediately after the reinforcer is delivered.

VARIABLE RATIO SCHEDULE. Like a variable interval schedule, this schedule tends to eliminate irregularities in response rate, thereby producing a more consistent rate. This is accomplished through reinforcement after a different number of responses from one time to the next according to a predetermined average. If you decided to use a VR fifteen schedule, you might reinforce a desired behavior after twelve, seven, twenty-three, and eighteen occurrences, respectively (that is, after the twelfth, nineteenth, forty-second, and sixtieth desired behaviors). Because the occurrence of reinforcement is so unpredictable, learners tend to respond fairly rapidly for long periods of time. If you need proof, just watch people play the slot machines in Las Vegas.

Variable ratio schedules: reinforce after a different number of responses each time

Educational Applications of Operant Conditioning Principles

In the late 1940s when Skinner's daughter was in elementary school, he observed a number of instructional weaknesses that concerned him. These included the excessive use of aversive consequences to shape behavior (students studying to avoid a low grade or embarrassment in the classroom), an overly long interval between students taking tests or handing in homework and getting corrective feedback, and poorly organized lessons and workbooks that did not lead to specific goals. Skinner became convinced that if the principles of operant conditioning were systematically applied to education, all such weaknesses could be either reduced or eliminated.

That belief, which he then reiterated consistently until his death in 1990 (see, for example, Skinner, 1984), is based on four prescriptions that come straight from his laboratory research on operant conditioning: (1) be clear about what is to be taught, (2) teach first things first, (3) allow students to learn at their own rate, and (4) program the subject matter. The primary means for accomplishing this group of goals are programmed instruction and teaching machines (that is, computer-assisted instruction). The next few sections will describe the nature of these applications and assess the extent to which they improve classroom learning. In addition, we will discuss behavior modification, a general application of operant conditioning principles.

@ COMPUTER-ASSISTED INSTRUCTION

The Precursor: Skinner's Programmed Instruction The key idea behind Skinner's approach to teaching is that learning should be *shaped*. Programs of stimuli (material to be learned) and consequences should be designed to lead students step by step to a predetermined end result. In the mid-1950s Skinner turned this shaping approach into an innovation called **programmed instruction**. This method of instruction presents small amounts of specially designed written material to the student in a predetermined sequence, provides prompts to draw out the desired written response, calls for the response to be repeated in several ways in order to produce mastery, immediately reinforces correct responses, and allows the student to work through the program at her own pace.

Programmed instruction: arrange material in small steps; reinforce correct responses

According to Skinner (1968, 1986), when programmed materials are well designed and appropriately used, they produce the following effects:

1. Reinforcement for the right answer is immediate.
2. The teacher can monitor each student's progress more closely.
3. Each student learns at his own rate, completing as many problems as possible within the allotted time.
4. Motivation stays high because of the high success level designed into the program.
5. Students can easily stop and begin at almost any point.
6. Learning a complex repertoire of knowledge proceeds efficiently.

When programmed materials were first made commercially available during the mid-1950s, they were designed to be presented to students in one of two ways: in book form or as part of mechanical teaching machines. The earliest teaching machines were simple mechanical devices. A program was inserted in the machine, and the first statement or question was "framed" in a viewing window. (That is why the individual steps of a program are referred to as **frames.**) Today programmed instruction in book format is very uncommon, and the early mechanical teaching machines have been almost totally supplanted by the computer, particularly the microcomputer, because computers can do everything the books or the machine could do—and far more. Therefore, we will spend the remainder of this section exploring the relationship between computers and programmed instruction. Before we do so, we will take a brief look at what is involved in the development of a program.

Developing a Program Programmers begin developing a program by defining precisely what is to be learned (the terminal behavior). They then arrange facts, concepts, and principles in a sequence designed to lead students to the desired end result. This requires programmers to make the steps (the knowledge needed to go from frame to frame) small enough so that reinforcement occurs with optimal frequency and then arrange the steps so that students will be adequately prepared for each frame, or numbered problem, when they reach it.

Linear programs provide one path; branching programs have multiple paths

In arranging the sequence of steps, programmers may use a **linear program,** which tries to ensure that every response will be correct since there is only one path to the terminal behavior. Or they may use a **branching program,** in which there is less concern that all responses be right. If students give a wrong answer, the program provides a branching set of questions to enable them to master the troublesome point. Another type of branching program provides students with a more complete explanation of the misunderstood material and then urges them to go back and study the original explanations more carefully.

Do Computers Aid Learning? A teaching machine, either mechanical or electronic, is only as good as the instructional software program that runs it.[1]

1. In case you have never understood the terms *hardware* and *software* when used with reference to computers, *hardware* refers to the machine itself and other electronic devices, and *software* refers to the program language or instructions used to make the machine operate.

Computer-assisted instruction can effectively supplement conventional classroom teaching, particularly for elementary students of all ability levels and for low-achieving students.

And as we point out on pages 308–311, high-quality instructional programs are the exception rather than the rule. With this caveat in mind, we now ask, How effective is **computer-assisted instruction (CAI),** which is also known as computer-based instruction (CBI)? The answer to this question, like the answers to most of the questions posed in this book, is that it depends—in this case, largely on the type of program with which students interact, the grade level of the students, and the ability level of the students.

A review of twenty-five CAI studies conducted in elementary through college classrooms (Khalili & Shashaani, 1994) found that the average student who learned through a simulation program scored at the 78th percentile on a classroom examination, whereas the average student in a typical teacher-led lecture/discussion class scored at the 50th percentile. But the same large difference was not found for drill-and-practice programs. (We will describe both simulation and drill-and-practice programs later on in this chapter.) The average student who worked through a computerized version of drill and practice scored at the 54th percentile, whereas the average student who used the traditional worksheets scored at the 50th percentile.

CAI-taught students learn more with simulation programs than with drill-and-practice programs

In a review of CAI research done in actual classrooms in grades one through six, James Kulik, Chen-Lin Kulik, and Robert Bangert-Drowns (1985) found a fairly substantial advantage for CAI. The typical CAI-taught student scored at the 68th percentile on a classroom examination, whereas the average student in a conventionally taught class scored at the 50th percentile. CAI-taught students also scored higher than conventionally taught students when retested some weeks later. And low-aptitude students benefited more from CAI than did high-aptitude students. These results were obtained with a rather modest amount of input. In the typical study, students received a total of about twenty-six hours of CAI: fifteen minutes a day, four days a week, for twenty-six weeks.

CAI works best for elementary grade students, especially low achievers

In a companion review of CAI research done with students in grades seven through twelve, Bangert-Drowns, Kulik, and Kulik (1985) again found an advantage for CAI, although not as large as was the case for elementary school students. At this level the difference between CAI-taught and conventionally taught students on examination scores was about 10 percentile ranks. Once again, low-aptitude students gained more from CAI than did high-aptitude students.

Finally, there is evidence that learning various subjects through a CAI format also boosts performance on tests of such cognitive skills as planning, problem solving, and reasoning. The typical CAI-taught student scored at the 68th percentile on tests of these skills in comparison to the 50th percentile performance of the average control group student (Liao, 1992).

These findings suggest that CAI, when properly designed, can effectively supplement a teacher's attempts to present, explain, apply, and reinforce knowledge and skills. The relatively high degree of structure inherent in CAI seems to be particularly helpful to low-achieving and younger students. These findings also reaffirm what was suggested in Chapter 1 about good teaching being partly an art and partly a science. Whenever you as a teacher apply any psychological principle in your classroom, you will need to ask yourself, For whom is this instructional technique likely to be beneficial? With what materials? For what outcome? As the options for using CAI expand, with more varied and complex programs available, the ability of teachers to answer these questions will become increasingly important.

However, because computers and software are tools, CAI's potential is in large part determined by the teacher's ability to integrate them into an effective instructional environment. This responsibility involves all phases of the instructional process, including selecting appropriate and good quality software, introducing it clearly to students, providing initial guidance as students struggle, setting time for extended practice, and assessing students' learning. In other words, CAI is not a magic bullet that in itself guarantees quick or successful learning (regardless of the enthusiastic claims of its proponents). The following is a brief summary of the issues involved in effective use of CAI.

First, while we have learned quite a bit about the circumstances under which CAI is most effective, it is clear that these depend on numerous variables, such as students' skills and motivation, the type of program being used, the teacher's philosophical approach and comfort level with the technology, and even the physical setup of the classroom and school day schedule. For example, most newer programs use color, animation, and sound effects intended to motivate students and produce learning gains. However, not all students will react with interest to these features, despite teachers' frequently expressed belief in the existence of an "MTV generation" or a "video game generation" of students highly dependent on them. Many software programs (unintentionally) base their content, characters, and structure on cultural assumptions of mainstream middle-class America, which may be unfamiliar to culturally diverse students. And we do not know if highly entertaining programs will depress students' interest in tasks that do not possess such features (Lepper & Chabay, 1985; Lepper & Gurtner, 1989).

Second, there is a set of skills the teacher needs to master in order to integrate computers successfully in a classroom. As we noted in Chapter 1, and as Larry Cuban (1986) points out in a provocative book about the relationship between teachers and machines, successful teaching often depends on the ability of a live teacher to establish a positive emotional climate (by communicating interest, excitement, expectations, and caring), to monitor student actions and reactions (by "reading" students' verbal and nonverbal communications), and to orchestrate the sequence and pace of instructional events (by making additions, deletions, and modifications in lesson plans). If one thinks of the computer as simply another tool or material to work with, then each type of computer program—simulations, tutorials, drills—requires teachers to plan learning activities, interact with students, provide encouragement and feedback, and design assessment. While acquiring these skills may be a challenge, many teachers feel that being able to give their students meaningful access to such powerful learning tools is a significant reward. (Grabe & Grabe, 1995).

CAI not meant to replace teachers

BEHAVIOR MODIFICATION

Though applied in many ways, the term **behavior modification** basically refers to the use of operant conditioning techniques to (as the phrase indicates) modify behavior. Since those who use such techniques attempt to manage behavior by making rewards contingent on certain actions, the term *contingency management* is also sometimes used.

After Skinner and his followers had perfected techniques of operant conditioning in modifying the behavior of animals, they concluded that similar techniques could be used with humans. We will briefly discuss several techniques in this section that teachers may use to strengthen or weaken specific behaviors. Techniques applied in education to strengthen behaviors include shaping, token economies, and contingency contracts. Techniques that aim to weaken behaviors include extinction and punishment.

Behavior modification: shape behavior by ignoring undesirable responses, reinforcing desirable responses

Shaping You may want to take a few minutes now to review our earlier explanation of shaping. Most attempts at shaping important classroom behaviors should include at least the following steps (Walker & Shea, 1991):

1. Select the target behavior.
2. Obtain reliable baseline data (that is, determine how often the target behavior occurs in the normal course of events).
3. Select potential reinforcers.
4. Reinforce successive approximations of the target behavior each time they occur.
5. Reinforce the newly established target behavior each time it occurs.
6. Reinforce the target behavior on a variable reinforcement schedule.

To illustrate how shaping might be used, imagine that you are a third-grade teacher (or a middle or high school teacher) with a chronic problem: one of your students rarely completes more than a small percentage of the arithmetic (or algebra) problems on the worksheets you distribute in class, even though you know the student possesses the necessary skills. To begin, you decide that a reasonable goal would be for the student to complete at least 85 percent of the problems on a given worksheet. Next, you review the student's work for the past several weeks and determine that, on average, he completed only 25 percent of the problems per worksheet. Your next step is to select positive reinforcers that you know or suspect will work.

Reinforcers come in a variety of forms. Most elementary school teachers typically use such things as stickers, verbal praise, smiles, and classroom privileges (for example, feed the gerbil, clean the erasers). Middle school and high school teachers can use letter or numerical grades, material incentives (such as board games and computer games, so long as school policy and your financial resources allow it), and privately given verbal praise. With certain reservations, public forms of recognition can also be used. The reservations include the following: any public display of student work or presentation of awards should be made to several students at the same time (to avoid possible embarrassment among adolescents) (Emmer, Evertson, Clements, & Worsham, 1994), awards should be made without letter grades; and awards should be given with an awareness that public displays of recognition are not appropriate or comfortable for all cultures.

One popular shaping technique that has stood the test of time involves having students first list favorite activities on a card. Then they are told that they will be able to indulge in one of those activities for a stated period of time after they have completed a set of instructional objectives. This technique is sometimes called the **Premack principle** after psychologist David Premack (1959), who first proposed it. It is also called *Grandma's rule* since it is a variation of a technique that grandmothers have used for hundreds of years ("Finish your peas, and you can have dessert").

Premack principle: required work first, then chosen reward

Once you have decided on a sequence of objectives and a method of reinforcement, you are ready to shape the target behavior. For example, you can start by reinforcing the student for completing five problems (25 percent) each day for several consecutive days. Then you reinforce the student for completing five problems and starting a sixth (a fixed ratio schedule). Then you reinforce the student for six completed problems and so on. Once the student consistently completes at least 85 percent of the problems, you provide reinforcement after every fifth worksheet on the average (a variable ratio schedule).

Although you control the classroom environment while students are in school, this accounts for only about half of their waking hours. Accordingly, parents might supplement your efforts at shaping behavior. The first step in a home-based reinforcement program is obtaining the parents' and student's formal agreement to participate. Then you typically send home a brief note or form on a regular basis (daily, weekly) indicating whether the student exhibited the desired behaviors. For example, in response to the items "Was prepared for class" and "Handed in homework," you would circle "yes" or "no." In response to a homework grade or test grade, you would circle the appropriate letter or percent correct designation. The parents are then responsible for providing the appropriate reinforcement or punishment (temporary loss of a privilege, for example). This procedure has been successful in both reducing disruptive classroom behavior and increasing academic performance (longer time on tasks and higher test scores, for example). Some studies suggest that it may not be necessary to target both areas, as improved academic performance often results in decreased disruptiveness (Kelley & Carper, 1988).

Token Economies A second technique used to strengthen behavior in the classroom, the **token economy,** was introduced first with people who had been hospitalized for emotional disturbances and then with students in special education classes. A token is something that has little or no inherent value but can be used to "purchase" things that do have inherent value. In society, money is our most ubiquitous token. Its value lies not in what it is made of but in what it can purchase—a car, a house, or a college education. By the same token (if you will excuse the pun), students can accumulate check marks, gold stars, or happy faces and "cash them in" at some later date for any of the reinforcers already mentioned.

One reason for the advent of the token economy approach was the limited flexibility of more commonly used reinforcers. Candies and cookies, for instance, tend to lose their reinforcing value fairly quickly when supplied continually. It is not always convenient to award free time or the opportunity to engage in a highly preferred activity immediately after a desired response. And social rewards may or may not be sufficiently reinforcing for some individuals. Tokens, however, can always be given immediately after a desirable behavior, can be awarded according to one of the four schedules mentioned earlier, and can be redeemed for reinforcers that have high reinforcing value.

Token economy is a flexible reinforcement system

Token economies are effective in reducing such disruptive classroom behaviors as talking out of turn, being out of one's seat, fighting, and being off task. They are also effective in improving academic performance in a variety of subject areas. Token economies have been used successfully with individual students, groups of students, entire classrooms, and even entire schools. Some studies have shown that awarding tokens for group efforts is at least as effective and possibly more effective than awarding them to individuals. See Case in Print for an illustration of one token economy in action in a school system. Accordingly, token economies can be easily used in conjunction with the cooperative learning technique that was briefly mentioned in Chapter 4 and that will be described in detail in Chapter 11 (McLaughlin & Williams, 1988; Shook, LaBrie, Vallies, McLaughlin, & Williams, 1990).

Contingency Contracting A third technique teachers use to strengthen behavior is **contingency contracting.** A contingency contract is simply a more formal method of specifying desirable behaviors and consequent reinforcement. The contract, which can be written or verbal, is an agreement worked out by two people (teacher and student, parent and child, counselor and client) in which one person (student, child, client) agrees to behave in a mutually acceptable way and the other person (teacher, parent, counselor) agrees to provide a mutually acceptable form of reinforcement. For example, a student may contract to sit quietly and work on a social studies assignment for thirty minutes. When the student is done, the teacher may reinforce the child with ten minutes of free time, a token, or a small toy.

Contingency contracting: reinforcement supplied after student completes mutually agreed on assignment

Contracts can be drawn up with all members of a class individually, with selected individual class members, or with the class as a whole. As with most

CASE IN PRINT

Learning Is a Rewarding Experience for Some Students

Token economies are effective in reducing such disruptive behaviors as talking out of turn, being out of one's seat, fighting, and being off task. They are also effective in improving academic performance in a variety of subject areas. Token economies have been used successfully with individual students, groups of students, entire classrooms, and even entire schools. (p. 289)

"Studying's Rewards"

SACHA PFEIFFER

Boston Globe 1/3/96

NEWTON — Life, David Morris will tell you, is all about incentive.

Give him a scenario, be it the classroom or in the workplace, and the 18-year-old Newton North High School senior will give you an example of a society motivated by the prospect of gain—a better school, a better job, a better income.

Now, in a program designed by Morris, honor roll students at Newton North have an additional enticement: a coupon book containing more than $300 worth of gifts tailored to the teen-age appetite.

The book offers more than mere discounts and buy-one, get-one-free offers. Bearers are entitled to such things as free pizzas, ice cream, bagels, car washes, movie rentals, beeper services, health club visits and limousine rentals.

"All around us, there are different types of incentives, whether they are varsity letters or merit scholarships," said Morris, who, perhaps not surprisingly, is bound for the University of Pennsylvania's Wharton School of Business next fall. "So why not reward those students who think academics are important?"

The ultimate reward of the program, dubbed the Newton North High School Honor Roll Card Coupon Book, is a scholarship fund for college-bound seniors created by a $200 mandatory contribution from participating businesses.

The dual membership requirement for merchants presented a tough challenge to Morris and his small but growing sales staff.

"Most stores would immediately say, 'Wait, you want me to give money and a discount?'" recalled junior Noam Schimmel, who will run the program next year. "Their usual response was, 'Hi, thanks for calling, but that's a lot of money.'"

But hard work pays off, as the program's motto proclaims, and 50 merchants from Newton and beyond eventually agreed to participate. Collectively, those businesses made a $10,000 infusion to the fund last year—more than half of which was given to academically eligible, financially needy students.

The program, now entering its fourth grading period, weathered its share of criticism before getting off the ground.

"We had to ask ourselves if we were selling grades," said high school principal V. James Marini, echoing the concerns of educators who believe academic achievement should not be a material pursuit.

But recalling a discussion he had with Morris, Marini said the entrepreneurial student countered that young people are always told hard work will yield rewards. "How can you argue with that?" the principal said.

By the accounts of students, teachers and administrators, the program has been a roaring success, and may be a factor motivating some of Newton North's 1,800 high schoolers to study that extra hour. The school experienced a 37 percent jump in the number of seniors named to the honor roll last grading period, and a 21 percent increase among juniors.

The coupon book "definitely entices kids to want to succeed," said junior Daniel Steinberg. "If you give kids the book and say, 'Here, take this as a sign of your accomplishment,' you give them a better reason to feel better about themselves."

Even senior Josh Newman, who says he was skeptical that the book would catch on among students, now calls himself a coupon convert.

"I never thought it would work and I didn't think kids would even come pick the books up," admitted Newman, who said he has friends who raised their grades to become part of the program. "But the free stuff is great . . . and a larger amount of kids are trying harder in school because of it."

And, Morris boasts, not a penny of school or scholarship money was spent to run the program. All goods and services, from display easels to adhesive tapes, were donated. . . .

Student Schimmel says he is confident the program will continue with the same success when he takes it over next year.

"This program is a community-wide acknowledgment of academic achievement and educational excellence," said Schimmel. "It's an innovative way of saying, 'Thank you, good job.' And kids realize that beyond the little slice of pizza they got, there's something to perseverance and working hard."

Questions and Activities

1. Although the coupon book program had been in operation for only three grading periods at the time the article was written, it appeared to be quite successful. Do you think reinforcement programs like this one are likely to be successful over an extended period of time? Why or why not?

2. Students are typically given reinforcers by teachers in school-based token economies. Is there any reason that the behavior of teachers and administrators should not be reinforced by students when the occasion warrants? What might be the advantages (and disadvantages) of a token economy that runs in both directions?

3. The principal in this article is portrayed as being initially hesitant to implement the coupon book incentive program as it might have been perceived by some as the equivalent of bribing students to learn. But the student who created the program argued that it should be tried since adults constantly tell young people that if they work hard and succeed, they will be rewarded by society. These two views suggest that the token economy has potential advantages and disadvantages as a way to motivate students to learn. Based on the material in the chapter and your own experiences, write down as many advantages and disadvantages as you can think of.

The time-out procedure recommended by behavior modification enthusiasts involves weakening an undesirable form of behavior (such as shoving on the playground) by temporarily removing positive reinforcement (by having the misbehaving student remain in a corner of the classroom for five minutes while the rest of the class continues to enjoy another activity).

contracts, provisions can be made for renegotiating the terms. Moreover, the technique is flexible enough to incorporate the previously discussed techniques of token economies and shaping. It is possible, for example, to draw up a contract that provides tokens for successive approximations to some target behavior.

Extinction, Time-Out, and Response Cost The primary goal of behavior modification is to strengthen desired behaviors. Toward that end, techniques such as shaping, token economies, and contingency contracts are likely to be very useful. There will be times, however, when you have to weaken or eliminate undesired behaviors because they interfere with instruction and learning. For these occasions, you might consider some form of extinction. The most straightforward approach is to simply ignore the undesired response. If a student bids for your attention by clowning around, for instance, you may discourage repetition of that sort of behavior by ignoring it. It is possible, however, that classmates will not ignore the behavior but laugh at it. Such response-strengthening reactions from classmates will likely counteract your lack of reinforcement. Accordingly, you need to observe what happens when you try to extinguish behavior by not responding.

If other students are reinforcing a youngster's undesired behavior, you may want to apply the time-out procedure briefly discussed earlier. Suppose a physically active third-grade boy seems unable to keep himself from shoving classmates during recess. If verbal requests, reminders, or warnings fail to limit shoving, the boy can be required to take a five-minute time-out period immediately after he shoves a classmate. He must sit alone in the classroom for that period of time while the rest of the class remains out on the playground. Time-out appears to be most effective when it is used with aggressive, group-oriented children who want the attention of the teacher and their peers (Walker & Shea, 1991). The rules for the procedure should be clearly explained, and after being sentenced to time-out (which should last no more than five minutes), a child should be given reinforcement for agreeable, helpful behavior—for example, "Thank you for collecting all the playground balls so nicely, Tommy."

Time-out works best with disruptive, aggressive children

Another technique, **response cost**, is similar to time-out in that it involves the removal of a stimulus. It is often used with a token economy. With this procedure, a certain amount of positive reinforcement (for example, 5 percent of previously earned tokens) is withdrawn every time a child makes an undesired response. Anyone who has been caught exceeding the speed limit and been fined at least $50 can probably attest to the power of response cost as a modifier of behavior.

Punishment Punishment is one of the most common behavior modification techniques, particularly when it takes the form of corporal punishment. It is also one of the most controversial. At the present time corporal punishment has been banned in twenty-seven states either by state law or by state department of education regulation (Evans & Richardson, 1995). The remaining twenty-three states either explicitly permit schools to physically punish students or are silent on the matter. In states that allow corporal punishment, local school districts may regulate, but not prohibit, its use. Where states have not addressed the issue, local districts may regulate the use of corporal punishment or ban it altogether.

Although corporal punishment is actually fairly widely used in classrooms where it is permitted, considerable laboratory evidence, collected from human and animal subjects, suggests that it is likely to be ineffective in modifying behavior. The following reasons are typically cited:

1. Mild punishment (which is the kind usually applied) does not permanently eliminate undesirable behaviors. At best, it suppresses them temporarily.
2. Punished behaviors may continue to occur when the punisher is not present.
3. Punishment may actually increase the strength of undesirable behavior. Many teachers assume that a public reprimand is aversive. But for some students, teacher and peer attention, regardless of the form it takes, acts as a positive reinforcer and thus tends to increase behaviors the teacher seeks to eliminate.
4. Punishment may produce undesirable emotional side effects. Just as a shocked rat comes to fear a Skinner box, punished children may perceive the teacher and the school as objects to fear and avoid. The result is truancy, tardiness, and high levels of anxiety, all of which impair the ability to learn.
5. Punishers model a type of behavior (physical aggression) that they do not want students to exhibit.
6. To be effective, punishment must often be severe and must occur immediately after an undesirable response. Legal, ethical, and moral restrictions do not allow severe punishment.

Punishment is likely to be ineffective because of temporary impact, side effects

Should You Use Behavior Modification? This may seem a strange question to ask given the number of pages we have just spent covering behavior modification methods. Obviously, we feel that the results of decades of research on these techniques justify their use by teachers. Nevertheless, there are criticisms of behavior modification that are not adequately addressed by research findings and that you should carefully consider.

One criticism is that many students, including those in the primary grades, will eventually catch onto the fact that they get reinforced only when they do what the teacher wants them to do. Some may resent this and misbehave out of spite. Others may weigh the amount of effort required to earn a favorable comment or a privilege and decide the reinforcer isn't worth the trouble. Still others may develop a "What's in it for me?" attitude. That is, some students may come to think of learning as something they do only to earn an immediate reinforcer. The potential danger of using behavior modification over an extended period of time is that learning may come to an abrupt halt when no one is around to supply reinforcement (Kohn, 1993). (This point will be addressed by the next theory to be examined, social learning theory.)

A second major criticism is that behavior modification methods, because of their potential power, may lend themselves to inappropriate or even unethical uses. For example, teachers may shape students to be quiet and obedient because it makes their job easier, even though such behaviors do not always produce optimum conditions for learning.

In response to these criticisms, Skinner and other behavioral scientists (see Chance, 1993, for example) argue that if we do not systematically use what we know about the effects of stimuli and consequences on behavior, we will leave things to chance. In an uncontrolled situation some fortunate individuals will have a favorable chain of experiences that will equip them with desirable attitudes and skills; but others will suffer an unfortunate series of experiences that will lead to difficulties and disappointment. In a controlled situation it may be possible to arrange experiences so that almost everyone acquires desirable traits and abilities. What behavioral psychologists seem to be saying is that educators could be accused of being unethical for not making use of an effective learning tool. The challenge, of course, is to use it wisely.

Despite the popularity of operant conditioning among many American psychologists, a number of researchers, beginning in the 1940s, were eager to study types of human behavior that could not be readily explained in terms of principles of operant conditioning. They shared the desire of Skinner and his followers to study behavior as objectively as possible, but they wanted to analyze human behavior in social settings—to see how children acquire acceptable forms of social behavior (or become socialized). Together, these researchers contributed to the development of a set of ideas about human learning that borrowed from operant conditioning but was different from it as well. These ideas came to be called social learning theory.

Social Learning Theory

Albert Bandura, the acknowledged spokesperson for the social learning theory point of view, presents what is generally considered to be the definitive exposition of this theory in *Social Foundations of Thought and Action: A Social Cognitive Theory* (1986). In essence, **social learning theory** deemphasizes the role of reinforcement in learning by attributing initial changes in behavior to the observation and imitation of a model (which explains why social learning is also called **observational learning**).

In the sections that follow we will discuss some of the main features of Bandura's social learning theory and examine some of the research it has spawned. First, we will describe the various ways in which observational learning occurs: inhibition, disinhibition, facilitation, and true observational learning. Following this, we will describe the four processes that underlie observational learning: attention, retention, production, and motivation.

TYPES OF OBSERVATIONAL LEARNING EFFECTS

Inhibition In many instances we learn *not* to do something that we already know how to do because a model we are observing refrains from behaving, is punished for behaving, or does something different from what we intended to do. Consider the following example: a ten-year-old is taken to her first symphony concert by her parents. After the first movement of Beethoven's

Fifth Symphony, she is about to applaud but notices that her parents are sitting quietly with their hands in their laps. She does the same.

Disinhibition On occasion we learn to exhibit a behavior that is usually disapproved of by most people because a model does the same without being punished. For example, a student attends his school's final football game of the season. As time expires, thousands of students run onto the field and begin tearing up pieces of turf to take home as a souvenir. Noticing that the police do nothing, the student joins in.

Facilitation This effect occurs whenever we are prompted to do something that we do not ordinarily do because of insufficient motivation rather than social disapproval. For example, a college student attends a lecture on reforming the American education system. Impressed by the lecturer's enthusiasm and ideas, the student vigorously applauds at the end of the presentation. As several members of the audience stand and applaud, so does the student.

People learn to inhibit or make responses by observing others

True Observational Learning This effect occurs when we learn a *new* behavior pattern by watching and imitating the performance of someone else. A teenage girl learning how to hit a top-spin forehand in tennis by watching her instructor do the same is an example of observational learning. The four processes that make this form of learning possible will be discussed next.

PROCESSES IN OBSERVATIONAL LEARNING

Attention Clearly, if learning is *observational,* paying attention to a model's behavior is a critical first step. What factors, then, affect the willingness of a child to observe and mimic the behavior of a model? The most important factor seems to be the degree of similarity between the model and the observer. On the basis of an extensive review and analysis of previous research, Dale Schunk (1987) drew the following conclusions about the effect of observer-model similarity on observational learning:

1. When children are concerned about the appropriateness of a behavior, or when they have self-doubts about their capabilities, they are more likely to model a peer than an older child or adult.
2. Age similarity seems less important for the learning of skills, rules, and novel responses than does the competence of the model. When children question the competence of peers, they tend to model the behavior of adults.
3. Children learn academic skills from models of either sex, but they are more apt to perform behaviors displayed by models whom they believe are good examples of their gender role.
4. Children who have a negative self-concept, or who have had learning problems in the past, are more likely to imitate a peer who exhibits some initial learning difficulties and overcomes them (a coping model) than a peer who performs flawlessly (a mastery model). Improvements in self-concept and achievement are more likely to occur in response to coping models than to master models.

When teaching students a potentially dangerous skill, it is particularly important to remember the principles of observational learning noted by Bandura: make sure everyone is paying attention, have each student give a "dry run" demonstration, have students reproduce the correct procedures, and provide reinforcement for correct performance.

Processes of observational learning: attention, retention, production, motivation

Retention Once we have noticed a model's behavior with the intention of imitating it, we must encode that behavior in memory. Encoding may encompass just the observed behaviors, or it may also include an explanation of why, how, and when something is done. In the case of behavior, the encoding may be visual (that is, mental pictures) and/or verbal. In the case of behavioral rules, the encoding will likely be in terms of verbal propositions. The benefit of encoding behavioral rules is the ability to generalize the response. Modeled behaviors may be unitary, terminal behaviors (for example, working on a problem until it is solved), or they may be components of a complex behavior (such as striking a golf ball with a golf club). Once the behavior has been modeled, the observer should have several opportunities to engage in overt and/or covert rehearsal.

Production Bandura divides production into (1) selecting and organizing the response elements and (2) refining the response on the basis of informative feedback. The smooth operation of the production process is based on the assumption that the necessary response elements have been previously acquired (for example, gripping a golf club, addressing the ball, executing the swing, following through).

Motivation Like Skinner, Bandura acknowledges the motivational value of reinforcement and incorporates it into his theory. Unlike Skinner, however, Bandura thinks of reinforcement in broader terms. As a result, he talks about direct reinforcement, vicarious reinforcement, and self-reinforcement.

As part of observational learning, **direct reinforcement** occurs when an individual watches a model perform, imitates that behavior, and is reinforced (or punished) by the model or some other individual. A primary grade student, for example, may be told by the teacher to observe how a fellow student cleans up his desk at the end of the day. If that behavior is imitated, the teacher will praise the child. **Vicarious reinforcement** refers to a situation in which the observer anticipates receiving a reward for behaving in a given way because someone else has been so rewarded. A middle school student, for example, who observes that a classmate is praised by the teacher for completing an assignment promptly may strive to work quickly and diligently on the next assignment in anticipation of receiving similar praise. **Self-reinforcement** refers to a situation in which the individual strives to meet personal standards and does not depend on or care about the reactions of others. A high school student may strive to become as skillful as a classmate at word processing primarily because of an internal desire to prove that she can master that skill.

Imitation is strengthened through direct reinforcement, vicarious reinforcement, self-reinforcement

THE EFFECT OF SELF-EFFICACY ON OBSERVATIONAL LEARNING AND BEHAVIOR

Unlike self-concept, which we described in Chapter 3 as the *overall* or *global* picture that people have of themselves, *self-efficacy* refers to how capable or prepared we believe we are for handling *particular* kinds of tasks (Bandura 1982, 1986, 1989). For example, a student may have a high level of self-efficacy for mathematical reasoning—a feeling that she can master any math task that she might encounter in a particular course—but have a low level of self-efficacy for critical analysis of English literature. There are at least two reasons for Bandura's interest (and for general interest as well) in this phenomenon: (1) self-efficacy appears to strongly affect a variety of behaviors, and (2) an individual's level of self-efficacy can be influenced by several factors, one of which is observing the behavior of a model.

Self-efficacy: how capable one feels one is for handling particular kinds of tasks

Factors That Affect Self-Efficacy One obvious way in which we develop a sense of what we can and cannot do in various areas is by thinking about how well we have performed in the past on a given task or a set of closely related tasks. If, for example, my friends are always reluctant to have me on their team for neighborhood baseball games, and if I strike out or ground out far more often than I hit safely, I will probably conclude that I just don't have whatever skills it takes to be a competitive baseball player. Conversely, if my personal history of performance in school is one of mostly grades of A and of consistently being among the top ten students, my sense of academic self-efficacy is likely to be quite high.

A second source of influence mentioned by Bandura—verbal persuasion—is also fairly obvious. We frequently try to convince a child, student, relative, spouse, friend, or coworker that he has the ability to perform some task at a creditable level, and he in turn frequently tries to convince us of the same thing. Perhaps you can recall feeling somewhat more confident about your ability to handle some task (like college classes) after having several family members and friends express their confidence in your ability.

A third source of influence is more subtle. It is the emotions we feel as we prepare to engage a task. Individuals with low self-efficacy for science may become anxious, fearful, or restless prior to attending chemistry class or to taking an exam in physics. Those with high self-efficacy may feel assured,

Self-efficacy influenced by past performance, persuasion, emotional reactions, observation of models

comfortable, and eager to display what they have learned. Some individuals are acutely aware of these emotional states and infer from them high or low capabilities for performing specific tasks.

Finally, our sense of self-efficacy may be influenced by observing the successes and failures of individuals with whom we identify—what Bandura refers to as vicarious experience. If I take note of the fact that a sibling or neighborhood friend who is like me in many respects but is a year older has successfully adjusted to high school, I may feel more optimistic about my own adjustment the following year.

Types of Behaviors That Are Affected by Self-Efficacy Bandura has identified four types of behaviors that are at least partly influenced by an individual's level of self-efficacy: the goals and activities in which the person chooses to engage, the kind of thought processes she uses, how hard and how long she strives to achieve a goal, and the kinds of emotional reactions she experiences when she takes on certain tasks.

Individuals with a strong sense of self-efficacy, particularly if it extends over several areas, are more likely than others to consider a variety of goals and participate in a variety of activities. They may, for example, think about a wide range of career options, explore several majors while in college, take a variety of courses, participate in different sporting activities, engage in different types of social activities, and have a wide circle of friends.

Self-efficacy affects one's goals, thought processes, persistence, emotions

One way in which the thinking of high self-efficacy individuals differs from that of their low self-efficacy peers is in their tendency to use higher-level thought processes (such as the analysis, synthesis, and evaluation levels of Bloom's Taxonomy) to solve complex problems. Thus, in preparing a classroom report or a paper, low self-efficacy students may do little more than repeat a set of facts found in various sources (because of their belief that they are not capable of more), whereas high self-efficacy individuals discuss similarities and differences, inconsistencies, and contradictions and make evaluations about the validity and usefulness of the information they have found. Another difference is that high self-efficacy people are more likely to visualize themselves being successful at some challenging task, whereas low self-efficacy individuals are more likely to imagine disaster. This leads to differences in the next category of behaviors—motivation.

Those who rate their capabilities as higher than average can be expected to work harder and longer to achieve a goal than those who feel less capable. This difference should be particularly noticeable when individuals experience frustrations (poor-quality instruction, for example), problems (coursework being more difficult than anticipated), and setbacks (a serious illness). When faced with a challenging task, the high self-efficacy individual is more likely to experience excitement, curiosity, and an eagerness to get started rather than the sense of anxiety, depression, and impending disaster that many low self-efficacy individuals feel.

RESEARCH ON SOCIAL LEARNING THEORY

The research that has been stimulated by social learning theory supports Bandura's basic view that we can and do learn many types of behaviors by watching what other people do and the consequences they experience. In this section we will summarize several studies that, taken together, illustrate the wide range of this form of learning.

Effects of Modeling on Aggression The essential principles of social learning theory as described by Bandura can be illustrated by a series of three classic experiments he carried out in the 1960s. In the first experiment (Bandura, Ross, & Ross, 1961), a child was seated at a table and encouraged to play with a toy. The model sat at a nearby table and either played quietly with Tinker Toys for ten minutes or played with the Tinker Toys for a minute and then played aggressively with an inflatable clown "Bobo" doll for several minutes, punching, kicking, and sitting on it and hitting it with a hammer. In a subsequent, structured play situation, children who did not observe a model as well as those who observed a nonaggressive model displayed little aggression. By contrast, children exposed to the aggressive model behaved with considerably more aggression toward the Bobo doll and other toys.

The second study (Bandura, Ross, & Ross, 1963a) obtained similar results in response to children viewing a film of either an adult or an adult dressed as a cartoon character engaging in aggressive behavior. The third study (Bandura, Ross, & Ross, 1963b) attempted to determine how rewarding the model for aggressive behavior would affect children's imitative behavior. In general, children were more aggressive after they saw an aggressive model positively rewarded than when the model was punished. These studies, as you may have realized, illustrate the disinhibition effect described earlier.

These three studies stimulated hundreds of other investigations of the same type, particularly because of the implication that viewing aggressive behavior in a film or television program would lead to violence. Reviews of this research, such as those by T. H. A. van der Voort (1986), have found that exposure to repeated scenes of violence *can* engender violent behavior if the right set of conditions is in place. These conditions include the nature of the television program being watched (if the violent behavior is realistic and appears to be justified by the circumstances), the characteristics of the individual child (some children are more aggressive than others), the child's family, the child's neighborhood, and the reactions of others who are watching the program with the child.

Effects of Modeling on Persistence and Self-Confidence Social learning theorists have investigated a variety of academically related behaviors, including the effects of modeling on persistence and self-confidence. Barry Zimmerman and Roberta Blotner (1979), for example, had first- and second-grade children watch a model work for fifteen minutes at separating two interlocked rings and then succeed. Children in this group worked considerably longer at solving a similar puzzle than did children who watched a model work for only thirty seconds at separating the rings, regardless of whether the thirty-second model was successful. In a follow-up study, Barry Zimmerman and Jeffrey Ringle (1981) found that a model's persistence and statements of confidence in being able to solve a wire-puzzle problem increased first- and second-grade children's degree of persistence on both a wire puzzle and a word puzzle. The main implication of these two studies is that to the degree that academic success depends on persistent effort and self-confidence, students who have seen these behaviors modeled are likely to be more successful than students who have not.

Persistence, self-confidence, cognitive skills can be learned by observation of models

Effects of Modeling on the Learning of Math Skills At some point characteristics such as persistence and self-confidence have to be supplemented by effective cognitive skills. This raises at least two basic questions: Can cognitive skills be learned through modeling? And will such modeling improve achievement? A study by Dale Schunk (1981) provides an answer. Schunk arranged for nine-, ten-, and eleven-year-old children who had done poorly in math to receive one of two types of instruction. Children in the modeling condition received written materials that explained how to solve long-division problems, and they observed an adult model. While solving a series of problems, the model verbalized the underlying cognitive operations (such as estimating the quotient and multiplying the quotient by the divisor). The children then practiced what they had observed, with the researchers providing corrective modeling for any operations the youngsters failed to grasp. Children in the nonmodeling condition received the same written materials, which they studied on their own. When comprehension problems arose, these children were told to review the relevant section of the written instructions. In comparison to pretest scores, both treatments enhanced persistence, self-confidence, and accuracy of performance. The modeling condition, however, produced greater gains in accuracy than the nonmodeling condition did. (For additional examples of how modeling aids achievement, see Schunk, 1991, pp. 108–112.)

Another illustration of how students learn what their teachers model (and do not learn what they do not model) was offered by Diane Miller (1993). She described a middle school math teacher who was upset because his students did not use such terms as *numerator* and *denominator* in their writings about fractions. Instead, they substituted the phrases *the number on the top* and *the number on the bottom.* But when the teacher was observed reviewing a unit on fractions, he never used the terms *numerator* and *denominator.* When asked after class why he had avoided using these two terms, he said that he thought he had used them and was quite surprised to learn otherwise.

Effects of Modeling on Self-Efficacy Dale Schunk and Antoinette Hanson (1989) confirmed Bandura's contention that an individual's self-efficacy can be enhanced by watching a competent model. Nine- to twelve-year-old children whose math achievement was below the 35th percentile on a standardized test watched a videotape of a similar child receiving instruction in how to do subtraction with regrouping problems and then solving similar problems. In comparison to a group of similar children who saw a videotape of a teacher solving subtraction with regrouping problems and a group that did not see a model, those who saw a peer model had significantly higher self-efficacy ratings.

Now that you are familiar with operant conditioning and social learning theory, it is time to examine several Suggestions for Teaching derived from the principles and research findings that have just been discussed.

Suggestions for Teaching in Your Classroom

Applying Behavioral Learning Theory and Social Learning Theory in the Classroom

1. Remain aware that behavior is the result of particular conditions.

2. Use reinforcement, and use it appropriately to strengthen behaviors you want to encourage.

3. Take advantage of knowledge about the impact of different reinforcement schedules to encourage persistent and permanent learning.
   a. When students first attempt a new kind of learning, supply frequent reinforcement. Then supply rewards less often.
   b. If you want to encourage periodic spurts of activity, use a fixed interval schedule of reinforcement.

4. Give students opportunities to make overt responses, and provide prompt feedback.
   a. Require students to make frequent, overt, and relevant responses.
   b. Provide feedback so that correct responses will be reinforced and students will become aware of and correct errors.

5. When students must struggle to concentrate on material that is not intrinsically interesting, use special forms of reinforcement to motivate them to persevere.
   a. Select, with student assistance, a variety of reinforcers.
   b. Establish, in consultation with individual students, an initial contract of work to be performed to earn a particular reward.
   c. Once the initial reward is earned, establish a series of short contracts leading to frequent, immediate rewards.

6. To reduce the tendency for students to engage in undesirable forms of behavior, first try withholding reinforcement and calling attention to rewards that will follow completion of a task. If that does not work, consider the possibility of taking away a privilege or resorting to punishment.

7. Remember the basic processes of observational learning, and make effective use of observation and imitation.

1. Remain aware that behavior is the result of particular conditions.

Unlike the controlled environment of a Skinner box, many causes of behavior in a real-life classroom may not be observable or traceable. You might as well accept the fact, therefore, that quite often you are going to be a haphazard shaper of behavior. Nevertheless, there will be times when you and your students may benefit if you say to yourself, "Now, there *have* to be some causes for that behavior. Can I figure out what they are and do something about changing things for the better? Am I doing something that is leading to types of behavior that are making life difficult for some or all of us in the room?" When you are engaging in such speculations, keep in mind that reinforcement strengthens behavior. And check to see if you are inadvertently rewarding students for misbehavior (by calling attention to them, for example, or failing to reinforce those who engage in desirable forms of behavior).

Journal Entry
Checking on Causes of Behavior

EXAMPLES

If you become aware that it takes a long time for your students to settle down at the beginning of a period and that you are reacting by addressing critical remarks specifically to those who dawdle the longest, ignore the dawdlers, and respond positively to those who are ready to get to work.

Let's say that you have given students thirty minutes to finish an assignment. To your dismay, few of them get to work until almost the end of the period, and you find that you have to do a lot of nagging to hold down gossip and horseplay. When you later analyze why this happened, you conclude that you actually encouraged the time-killing behavior because of the way you set up the lesson. The next time you give a similar assignment, tell the students that as soon as they complete it, they can have class time to work on homework, a term project, or the equivalent and that you will be available to give help or advice to those who want it.

2. **Use reinforcement, and use it appropriately to strengthen behaviors you want to encourage.**

Why would we remind you to do something as obvious as reinforce behaviors you want students to acquire and exhibit in the future? Wouldn't you do that almost automatically? Well, we certainly hope so, but statistics suggest otherwise. A large team of researchers headed by John Goodlad (1984) observed the classroom behavior of 1,350 teachers and 17,163 students in thirty-eight schools from seven sections of the country. What they found may surprise you. Teachers' praise of student work occurred about 2 percent of the observed time in the primary grades and about 1 percent of the time in high school.

One of the basic principles of instruction derived from operant conditioning experiments is that teachers should provide elementary grade students with immediate reinforcement for correct responses.

Once you have resolved to reinforce desired behavior systematically, you need to be sure that you do it appropriately. Although reinforcement is a simple principle that can be readily understood at an intuitive level, it has to be used in the right way to produce desired results. Paul Chance (1992) offers seven guidelines for the effective use of positive reinforcement:

Journal Entry
Ways to Supply Reinforcement

- Use the weakest reward available to strengthen a behavior. In other words, don't use material rewards when you know that praise will be just as effective a reinforcer. Save the material rewards for that special behavior for which praise or other reinforcers may not be effective.
- When possible, avoid using rewards as incentives. What Chance means is don't get into the habit of automatically telling the student that if she does what you want, you will provide a specific reward. Instead, sometimes ask the student to do something (like work quietly or help another student), and then provide the reinforcer.
- Reward at a high rate in the early stages of learning, and reduce the frequency of rewards as learning progresses. We will discuss the reasons for this in suggestion seven.
- Reward only the behavior you want repeated. Although you may not realize it, students are often very sensitive to what is and is not being reinforced. If you decide that one way to encourage students to be more creative in their writing is to tell them not to worry about spelling and grammar errors, then don't be surprised to see many misspelled words and poorly constructed sentences. Or if you decide to reward only the three highest scorers on a test, reasoning that competition brings out the best in people, be prepared to deal with the fact that competition also brings out some of the worst in people (like cheating and refusing to help others).
- Remember that what is an effective reinforcer for one student may not be for another. For some students, comments such as "Very interesting point," "That's right," or "That was a big help" will strengthen the target behavior. But for others, something less overt, such as smiling encouragingly, may be just right.
- Set standards so that success is a realistic possibility for each student. Because classrooms are becoming increasingly diverse, you may have students whose English proficiency is limited or who have disabilities related to learning and intellectual functioning. One way to deal with such diversity is to reward students for making steady progress from whatever their baseline level of performance was at the beginning of the term.
- An often-mentioned goal of teachers is to have students become intrinsically motivated or to take personal pride and satisfaction in simply doing something well. You can use natural instructional opportunities to point this out—for example, explore with students how satisfying it is to write a clear and interesting story *as* they are writing.

3. Take advantage of knowledge about the impact of different reinforcement schedules to encourage persistent and permanent learning.

a. When students first attempt a new kind of learning, supply frequent reinforcement. Then supply rewards less often.

Keep in mind the impact of different schedules of reinforcement so that you can use the same techniques of reinforcement effectively in your classroom. For example, when students first try a new skill or type of learning, praise almost any genuine attempt, even though it may be inept. Then as they become more skillful, reserve your praise only for especially good performances. Avoid a set pattern of commenting on student work. Make favorable remarks at unpredictable intervals.

b. **If you want to encourage periodic spurts of activity, use a fixed interval schedule of reinforcement.**

Occasionally, you will want to encourage students to engage in spurts of activity since steady output might be too demanding or fatiguing. In such cases supply reinforcement at specified periods of time. For example, when students are engaging in strenuous or concentrated activity, circulate and provide praise and encouragement by following a set pattern that will bring you in contact with each student at predictable intervals.

4. Give students opportunities to make overt responses, and provide prompt feedback

a. **Require students to make frequent, overt, and relevant responses.**

The tendency of teachers is to talk and to do so for large chunks of time. Those who advocate a programmed approach to teaching recommend that teachers limit the amount of information and explanation they give to students and substitute opportunities for students to overtly respond. In addition, the responses should be directly related to the objectives. If your objectives emphasize the application of concepts and principles, then most of the responses students are asked to make should be about applications. The reason for this suggestion is that the delivery of corrective feedback and other forms of positive reinforcement can be increased when students make frequent responses, thereby accelerating the process of shaping.

EXAMPLES

Instead of lecturing for twenty to thirty minutes at a time about the development of science and technology in the twentieth century, present information in smaller chunks, perhaps eight to ten minutes at a time, and then ask students to describe how an everyday product or service grew out of a particular scientific principle.

Periodically ask students to summarize the main points of the material you presented over the last several minutes.

Journal Entry
Ways to Supply Immediate Feedback

b. **Provide feedback so that correct responses will be reinforced and students will become aware of and correct errors.**

Since the key principle of operant conditioning is reinforcement, it is essential to provide feedback to strengthen correct responses and inform students when their responses are incorrect. Therefore, you should try to supply frequent, specific, and prompt feedback. In addition, use techniques such as in the following examples.

EXAMPLES

Immediately after students read a chapter in a text, give them an informal quiz on the key points you listed. Then have them pair off, exchange quizzes, and correct and discuss them.

As soon as you complete a lecture or demonstration, ask individual students to volunteer to read to the rest of the class what they wrote about the points they were told to look for. Indicate whether the answer is correct; and if it is incorrect or incomplete, ask (in a relaxed and nonthreatening way) for additional comments. Direct students to amend and revise their notes as they listen to the responses.

5. When students must struggle to concentrate on material that is not intrinsically interesting, use special forms of reinforcement to motivate them to persevere.

For a variety of reasons, some students may have an extraordinarily difficult time concentrating on almost anything. And, as we all know, to master almost any skill or subject, we have to engage in a certain amount of tedious effort. Accordingly, you may sometimes find it essential to use techniques of behavior modification to help students stick to a task. If and when that time comes, you might follow these procedures.

Journal Entry
Ways to Encourage Perseverance

a. **Select, with student assistance, a variety of reinforcers.**

A behavior modification approach to motivation appears to work most successfully when students are aware of and eager to earn a payoff. Because students react differently to rewards and because any reward is likely to lose effectiveness if used to excess, it is desirable to list several kinds of rewards and permit students to choose. Some behavior modification enthusiasts (for example, Walker & Shea, 1991) even recommend that you make up a *reinforcement preference list* for each student. If you allow your students to prepare individual reinforcement menus themselves, they should be instructed to list school activities they really enjoy doing. It would be wise, however, to stress that entrées on anyone's menu must be approved by you so that they will not conflict with school regulations or interfere with the rights of others. A student's reward menu might include activities such as these: read a book of one's choice, work on an art of craft project, or view a videotape in another room. A reinforcement menu can be used in conjunction with Grandma's rule (the Premack principle). Set up learning situations, particularly those that are not intrinsically appealing, by telling students that as soon as they finish their broccoli (for example, doing a series of multiplication problems), they can have a chocolate sundae (an item from their reinforcement menu).

b. **Establish, in consultation with individual students, an initial contract of work to be performed to earn a particular reward.**

Once you have established a list of payoffs, you might consult with students (on an individual basis, if possible) to establish a certain amount of work that must be completed for students to obtain a reward selected from the menu.

(Refer in Chapters 3–6 to Mager's suggestions for preparing specific objectives for guidelines.) To ensure that students will earn the reward, the first contract should not be too demanding. For example, it might be something as simple as "successfully spell at least seven out of ten words on a list of previously misspelled words", or "correctly answer at least six out of ten questions about the content of a textbook chapter."

c. **Once the initial reward is earned, establish a series of short contracts leading to frequent, immediate rewards.**

The results of many operant conditioning experiments suggest that the frequency of reinforcement is of greater significance than the amount of reinforcement. Therefore, having students work on brief contracts that lead to frequent payoffs immediately after the task is completed is preferable to having them work toward a delayed, king-sized award.

6. To reduce the tendency of students to engage in undesirable forms of behavior, first try withholding reinforcement and calling attention to rewards that will follow completion of a task. If that does not work, consider the possibility of taking away a privilege or resorting to punishment.

Students often engage in types of behavior that are disruptive in one way or another. Theoretically, such behavior will tend to extinguish if it is not reinforced. Therefore, your first reaction might be to ignore it. Unfortunately, however, you will not be the only reinforcing agent in the classroom. As noted earlier, you may ignore a wisecrack, but classmates sitting around the culprit may respond enthusiastically and strengthen the tendency to wisecrack. Furthermore, in some cases you simply cannot ignore behavior. If a student is on the verge of destroying school property or injuring a classmate, you must respond immediately.

Journal Entry
Ways to Use Behavior Modification to Maintain Control

You may need to follow a sequence something like the following when confronted by undesirable but relatively minor misbehavior, such as two boys fooling around when assigned to work together on a chemistry experiment. First, ignore the behavior. Second, remind the class that those who finish the experiment early earn five bonus points and will be allowed to see a film. Third, approach the boys and tell them (privately and nicely) that they are disturbing others and making life difficult for themselves because if they do not complete the experiment in the allotted time, they will have to make it up at some other time. Fourth, resort to punishment by informing the boys (in a firm but not nasty way) that they must leave the classroom immediately and report to the vice principal to be assigned to a study hall for the rest of the class period. Tell them they will have to complete the experiment when the rest of the class has free experiment time. Finish by pointing out that once the work is made up, they will be all caught up and in a good position to do above-average work the rest of the period.

This sequence is based on studies (for example, Hall et al., 1971) that suggest that punishment is most effective when it occurs immediately after a response, cannot be avoided, is as intense as seems necessary, and provides the individual with an alternative and desirable response. An alternative to this sequence is negative reinforcement, which is not punishment but is designed to strengthen an escape response. Suppose you had said, "If you don't stop that fooling around and finish that experiment, I'll give you both an F for this unit." That would be an application of negative reinforcement because if the boys responded as planned, they would do the experiment not to gain a reward but to avoid negative consequences. Negative reinforcement is sometimes effective, but it may be risky because you can not always predict the kind of escape behavior that it will precipitate. In this case the boys might literally escape from the whole situation by not coming to class for several days. Thus, because both punishment and negative reinforcement have drawbacks, whenever possible use positive reinforcement and stress the rewards that will follow desired activities.

7. **Remember the basic processes of observational learning, and make effective use of observation and imitation.**

You can enhance learning of skills and promote desirable kinds of behavior if you take into account the four basic processes of observational learning: attention, retention, production, and motivation. If you plan to demonstrate the correct way to perform some skill or process, first make sure you have the attention of everyone in the class. (Techniques for securing attention will be discussed in the analysis of information processing in Chapter 9.) Then, after explaining what you are going to do (perhaps noting particular points students should look for), demonstrate. Immediately after you demonstrate, have all the students in the class try out the new skill to foster retention. Or, for complex skills, have them write down the steps to follow before they try the activity on their own. Finally, arrange for all the students to get feedback and experience satisfaction and/or reinforcement immediately after they imitate your behavior by proving to themselves that they can carry out the activity on their own.

EXAMPLES

Show primary grade students how to solve multiplication problems by first placing a large, colorful poster on a bulletin board with a diagram of the process. Explain the diagram, and then demonstrate how to solve some simple problems. As soon as you finish, hand out a worksheet containing several simple problems similar to those you just demonstrated.

Have students work on the problems for a specified period of time, and then secure their attention once again and demonstrate on the board the correct procedure for solving each problem. Have students correct their own papers as you demonstrate, point out that they now know how to do multiplication problems, and praise them for learning the skill so rapidly.

In a high school business class, follow a similar procedure when showing students how to set up a word processor to type a form letter. Make sure everyone is paying attention. Demonstrate the correct procedure. Have students write down the steps they should follow to imitate your actions. Have them study the steps before setting up their own word processor. Have them reproduce the letter. Provide reinforcement to supplement their own satisfaction in having completed the task successfully.

Select low-achieving students who have mastered a skill to demonstrate the skill to other low-achieving students.

A final point to remember about observational learning is that, in the lower grades particularly, you will be an admired model your students will be inclined to imitate. If you are well organized and businesslike, but also thoughtful and considerate, your students may act that way themselves.

@ APPLYING TECHNOLOGY TO TEACHING

Using Computers in Your Classroom

We mentioned earlier that under the right conditions computers can effectively supplement classroom instruction. If you are now thinking that you might like to use computers in your own classroom, there are a few additional things you need to know before you get started. You should know something about the types of programs that exist, their general quality, and how you can identify the best available programs.

USES OF COMPUTERS

Perhaps the most general distinction that can be made about the use of computers in schools is *learning about computers* versus *learning with computers*. The first approach, used primarily at the high school levels, emphasizes two things: understanding how computers work and learning how to use computers for such everyday purposes as word processing, data analysis, production of graphic material, and information organization. The second approach, computer-assisted instruction, has students use the computer and instructional programs to master typical school subject matter. CAI is typically found at the elementary and middle school levels (Hassett, 1984) and relies on one or more of the following types of programs: drill and practice, tutorials, and simulations and games.

Drill-and-Practice Programs These programs provide students with opportunities to practice knowledge and skills that were presented earlier by the teacher or by a textbook. The computer presents, for example, an arithmetic problem or a question about English vocabulary or a spelling exercise; the student types an answer; and the computer checks the accuracy of the response, provides feedback, and then presents the next item. Some programs keep track of how many errors a student makes, provide help when a student gets stuck, and adjust the difficulty level of the problems or questions to the proficiency level of the student. Some drill-and-practice programs are designed to look like arcade games, presumably to increase students' interest in using them, although the game usually has little or no connection to the educational content. For example, a math program requires a student to type in the correct answer to a multiplication problem in order to save a space station from being destroyed by a meteor (Doll, 1987; Willis, Hovey, & Hovey, 1987). Slightly over 50 percent of CAI programs in use are classified as drill and practice (Price, 1991).

Tutorial Programs These programs go one step beyond drill and practice in that they attempt to teach new material (for example, facts, definitions, concepts). Tutorial programs may be written in either a linear or a branching format. When a branching format is chosen, students who respond incorrectly are routed through supplementary frames of material that attempt to reteach a concept rather than continue with material that has already proved too difficult to understand. Branching decisions can also be made based on pretest information. (Grabe & Grabe 1995). Since branching tutorial programs are more complex, they take longer to develop (one hour of tutorial instruction often requires several thousand hours of development time on the part of a computer programmer, teaching methods specialist, and content area specialist) and generally tend to be more expensive than simple linear programs.

Some tutorial programs are referred to as *dialogue programs* because they mimic the instructional interchange that often occurs between student and teacher. For example, a program in reading instruction would begin with the computer examining a student's file to determine current reading level and then displaying appropriate reading exercises. The student reads the material, is presented with a set of questions, and types responses on the keyboard. The computer evaluates the responses and displays the results of the evaluation. If the student's responses are correct, the computer provides more difficult passages and questions. If the responses are incorrect, hints or less difficult exercises are presented (Doll, 1987; Willis et al., 1987).

Problem-Solving Programs: Simulations and Games Simulations and games are types of programs that have been growing in popularity as CAI formats. They are popular because they tend to be highly individualizable to each student's needs or interests, they allow for more flexibility in presenting content, and they give students the chance to solve problems in an actual (but simulated) setting. Simulations and games usually teach new material and then provide opportunities for the learner to apply what has been learned. They may also require the student to use existing knowledge, perhaps in a new way, to discover the solution to a problem. And they allow the learner to create and test hypotheses on the outcome of a particular situation with a particular set of variables. Simulations are particularly useful when students are denied firsthand experience because of factors such as cost (for example, diagnose and repair a malfunctioning car), danger (for example, operate a nuclear reactor), and time constraints (for example, recreate a Civil War battle) (Doll, 1987; Neill & Neill, 1990; Willis et al., 1987).

APPLYING TECHNOLOGY TO TEACHING, *continued*

PROGRAM QUALITY

After the teacher, the most important elements in CAI are clearly the programs themselves. The quality of software your students use is more important than how much information the classroom computer can store, how many disk drives it has, how many columns of characters it can display on its screen, and so on.

The unfortunate reality of educational software is that the not-so-good programs significantly outnumber the excellent ones. Why are good programs in such short supply? One reason is because their development requires a set of capabilities that are difficult to find in one person or among a small group of people. However, in recent years several large developers of educational software have successfully produced high-quality programs by including programmers, instructional designers, teachers, and students as members of their development teams.

Another reason that good CAI programs are in short supply is that a crucial step in the development process—the field test—is often eliminated. Even though a new program may have been revised several times by its author and reviewed by a panel of experts, its effectiveness as instructional material is still essentially unknown. The best way to identify and eliminate problems of step size, clarity, sequencing, feedback, attention getting, motivation, and so on, is to try the program out on a representative group of students. While a field test strikes people as so obviously necessary that they just assume it is a standard part of instructional software development, it may not be. The use of field testing is one criterion to look for when you select an instructional program, and most developers will provide you with information on their testing process.

The importance of integrating learning principles into the design of instructional programs has been discussed by Julie Vargas (1986). She finds that poor-quality programs often overlook such basic operant conditioning principles as offering maximum opportunities for active responding, providing immediate feedback, and shaping behavior. Some drill-and-practice programs, for example, incorporate into their lessons a variety of attention-getting features (such as familiar tunes, trains that puff across the screen, and animal characters that gesture or make facial expressions) in an attempt to keep the student interested and motivated. But the more often these features are used, the more time students spend watching them rather than practicing skills. As a result, it takes longer for students to make basic cognitive skills automatic (such as adding or multiplying numbers or recognizing and spelling words). Even worse, students may become distracted altogether from the goal of the drill if the motivational features are too numerous and compelling. It is also crucial to integrate learning principles in the *use* of programs. For example, tutorials and simulations often put students in an environment that requires

TABLE 8.2 **Eight Points to Consider When Choosing a CAI Program**

1. Does the software require a high frequency of responding (as opposed to screens of material to read)? For tutorials and drills, how many problems does a student actually do in a 10-minute session?
2. Is the responding relevant to your goals? (Do students do what they are to learn?)
3. Do students have to respond to the critical parts of the problems?
4. Is most of the screen content necessary for the response, or does the program assume that students will learn content without having to respond overtly to it?
5. Does the screen ask students to discriminate between at least two responses?
6. Can students see their progress as they work with the program from day to day or session to session?
7. Are students mostly successful going through the program (as opposed to becoming frustrated)? Do they enjoy using the program?
8. For series, or lessons to be used repeatedly, does the program adjust according to the performance level or progress of the student?

SOURCE: Vargas (1986).

them to experiment or explore, and the teacher must be prepared to act as a guide to this learning, to provide prompts, and to model approaches to solving the problems found in the simulation. To help you evaluate the quality of instructional software you may one day want to use in your classroom, a checklist devised by Julie Vargas appears in Table 8.2.

IDENTIFYING HIGH-QUALITY PROGRAMS

If and when you find yourself in a position to employ computer-assisted instruction, take the time and effort to identify well-designed programs. Four publications can help you in this effort. *Only the Best: Preschool–Grade 12,* by Shirley Boes Neill and George Neill, is an annual guide to educational software that has been judged to be of high quality by two or more educational organizations. *The Latest and Best of TESS: The Educational Software Selector* (1993) is a comprehensive guide to educational software published by the Educational Products Information Exchange Institute (EPIE), a nonprofit organization. This volume contains more than seventy-seven hundred descriptions of programs in more than one hundred subject areas. While the descriptions are brief, each contains upwards of fourteen pieces of relevant information. Hundreds of these summaries include a rating based on the evaluations of trained analysts. Detailed reports of these evaluated programs can be found in EPIE's periodical *MICROgram.* In addition, volume 17, number 3 (1990) of another EPIE publication, *EPIEgram,* describes the twelve criteria used by EPIE analysts to evaluate the quality of educational software. *Software Reports,* which is published by Trade Service Corporation, 10096 Torreyana Road, San Diego, CA 92121, provides program evaluations in twenty subject areas that cover every grade level. Each review includes a summary of the program's features, a description of the program, a graded evaluation, and comments made by the evaluator.

Resources for Further Investigation

B. F. Skinner

In three highly readable volumes, *Particulars of My Life* (1976), *The Shaping of a Behaviorist* (1979), and *A Matter of Consequences* (1983), B. F. Skinner describes his interests, aspirations, triumphs, and failures; the people and events that led him into psychology; and the forces that led him to devise operant conditioning.

A highly readable summary and critical analysis of Skinner's brand of operant conditioning can be found in Robert Nye, *What Is B. F. Skinner Really Saying?* (1979). According to Nye, "Two major thoughts accompanied the writing of this book: a growing sense of the importance of Skinner's work and the awareness that his ideas are often misjudged" (p.4).

The Technology of Teaching (1968) is B. F. Skinner's most concise and application-oriented discussion of operant conditioning techniques related to pedagogy.

In *Walden Two* (1948), B. F. Skinner describes his conception of a utopia based on the application of science to human behavior. To get the full impact of the novel and of Skinner's ideas, you should read the entire book. However, if you cannot read the whole thing at this time, Chapters 12 through 17, which describe the approach to child rearing and education at Walden Two, may be of special interest to you as a future teacher.

Behavior Modification

If the possibilities of behavior modification seem attractive, you may wish to examine issues of the journals *Behavior Modification, Behavior Research and Therapy, Child Behavior Therapy, Journal of Applied Behavior Analysis,* and *Journal of Behavioral Education.* If you browse through the education and psychology sections of your college bookstore, you are likely to find a number of books on behavior modification. Or you might look for these titles in the library: *Classroom Management for Elementary Teachers* (3d ed., 1994), by Carolyn Evertson, Edmund Emmer, Barbara Clements, and Murray Worsham; *Classroom Management for Secondary Teachers* (3d ed., 1994), by Edmund Emmer, Carolyn Evertson, Barbara Clements, and Murray Worsham; *Achieving Educational Excellence: Using Behavioral Strategies* (1986), by Beth Sulzer-Azaroff and G. Roy Mayer; and *Making It Till Friday: A Guide to Successful Classroom Management* (4th ed., 1989), by James Long, Virginia Frye, and Elizabeth Long. And, as the title suggests, *Beyond Behavior Modification: A Cognitive-Behavioral Approach to Behavior Management in the School* (2d ed., 1991), by Joseph Kaplan, goes beyond the typical behavior modification book. It includes chapters on assessing the classroom and school environment and teaching students how to use self-management, social, and stress-management skills.

Software Programs to Explore

@

The following are a few software programs whose excellence is generally recognized. They cover the range of drills, tutorials, simulations, and games.

Operation: Frog (Scholastic): allows students to simulate the dissection of a frog, complete with full graphics and video. Students can also "rebuild" the frog to practice locating its organs.

MathMagic (MindPlay Methods): offers an addition/subtraction drill program with an arcade game format, appropriate for elementary school students.

Oregon Trail (MECC): enables students to experience the journey from Independence, Missouri, to Oregon as the pioneers did in 1865. Students are responsible for stocking a wagon, avoiding obstacles on the trail, making decisions about how to cross rivers and catch food, and so forth.

SimCity, SimLife, SimAnt, and so forth (Maxis): allow students to control a large number of variables in complex simulations. The simulations are challenging, but the extensive tutorials and touch of humor in the programs reduce the risk of frustration. Excellent for group work.

Where in the World Is Carmen Sandiego? (Broderbund): requires students to interpret clues, put new or known facts (such as the location of cities) to use, and problem solve creatively.

Reviews of new software programs are found in journals such as *Electronic Learning* and *Computing Teacher.*

Internet Site for Social Learning

If you would like to pursue further information and materials relating to social learning, the Oregon Social Learning Center can be found at http//tiEEer. ogslc.org/publications, links.

Summary

1. Operant conditioning is a theory of learning devised by B. F. Skinner. It focuses on how voluntary behaviors are strengthened (made more likely to occur in the future) or weakened by the consequences that follow them.
2. Operant conditioning assumes that human behavior is a natural phenomenon that can be explained by a set of general laws, that the best way to understand complex behaviors is to analyze and study the components that make them up, that the results of animal learning studies are potentially useful in understanding human learning, and that learning is the ability to exhibit a new behavior pattern.
3. Basic learning principles that derive from Skinner's work are positive reinforcement, negative reinforcement, punishment (Type I or presentation), time-out (Type II or removal punishment), extinction, spontaneous recovery, generalization, and discrimination.
4. Positive reinforcement and negative reinforcement strengthen behaviors. Punishment, time-out, and extinction weaken target behaviors.
5. Complex behaviors can be learned by the reinforcement of successive approximations to the terminal (final) behavior and by the ignoring of nonapproximate behaviors, a process called shaping.
6. Once a new behavior is well established, it can be maintained at that level by the supplying of reinforcement on an intermittent schedule. The four basic schedules are fixed interval, variable interval, fixed ratio, and variable ratio.
7. Skinner's interest in educational applications of operant conditioning grew out of his disappointment with the quality of instruction his daughter was receiving in public school.
8. One of the first educational applications of operant conditioning principles was programmed instruction. It involves presenting written material in small steps according to a predetermined sequence, prompting the correct response, and presenting positive reinforcement in the form of knowledge of results.
9. Linear programs contain only one sequence of frames leading to the terminal behavior. They use extremely small steps and heavy prompting since they make no provision for incorrect responses.
10. Branching programs use larger steps and less prompting. If an incorrect response to a frame occurs, the learner is routed through a "branch"—a supplementary set of frames that attempts to reteach the misunderstood material—before proceeding further.
11. In recent years programmed materials have been designed for presentation by computer, an innovation generally referred to as computer-assisted instruction.
12. CAI-taught students seem to learn more from simulation programs than from drill-and-practice programs.

13. Computer-assisted instruction can be an effective supplement to regular classroom instruction, particularly for low-achieving students.
14. Another application of operant conditioning principles is behavior modification. The goal of behavior modification is for the teacher to help students learn desirable behaviors by ignoring or punishing undesired behaviors and reinforcing desired ones. Techniques for achieving this goal include shaping, token economies, contingency contracts, extinction, and punishment.
15. Social learning theory, which was devised largely by Albert Bandura, explains how individuals learn by observing a model (who may or may not be reinforced for the behavior involved) and imitating the model's behavior.
16. The processes involved in social learning (also called observational learning) are attention, retention, production, and motivation (reinforcement). The reinforcement can come from observing someone else (direct), from anticipating that one will be treated as the model was (vicarious), or from meeting personal standards (self-reinforcement).
17. Self-efficacy refers to how capable people believe they are for handling a particular task.
18. An individual's sense of self-efficacy is likely to be affected by a combination of past performance, persuasive comments from others, emotional reactions about an imminent task, and observation of the behavior of models judged to be similar to the individual.
19. Self-efficacy can affect an individual's choice of goals and activities, thought processes, willingness to persist at difficult tasks, and emotional reactions.
20. Research suggests that many social behaviors, such as aggression, may be learned by imitation of a model. Many academic-related behaviors, such as persistence, self-confidence, cognitive skills, and self-efficacy, can also be learned by observing and imitating a model.

Key Terms

operant conditioning *(276)*
positive reinforcement *(278)*
negative reinforcement *(279)*
punishment *(279)*
time-out *(280)*
extinction *(280)*
spontaneous recovery *(280)*
generalization *(281)*
discrimination *(281)*
shaping *(281)*
programmed instruction *(283)*
frames *(284)*
linear program *(284)*
branching program *(284)*
computer-assisted instruction (CAI) *(285)*
behavior modification *(287)*
Premack principle *(288)*
token economy *(289)*
contingency contracting *(289)*
response cost *(292)*
social learning theory *(294)*
observational learning *(294)*
direct reinforcement *(296)*
vicarious reinforcement *(297)*
self-reinforcement *(297)*

Discussion Questions

1. The theory of operant conditioning holds that we learn to respond or not respond to certain stimuli because our responses are followed by desirable or aversive consequences. How many of your own behaviors can you explain in this fashion? Why, for example, are you reading this book and answering these questions?
2. Many educators have a negative attitude toward operant conditioning because they feel it presents a cold, dehumanizing picture of human learning and ignores the role of such factors as free will, motives, and creativity. Did you feel this way as you read through the chapter? Do you think positive attributes of operant conditioning balance out possible negative aspects of the theory?

3. Skinner has argued that society too frequently uses aversive means to shape desired behavior (particularly punishment) rather than the more effective positive reinforcement. As you think about how your behavior has been shaped by your parents, teachers, friends, supervisors at work, law enforcement officials, and so on, would you agree or disagree with Skinner's observation? Can you think of some possible reasons we tend to use punishment more frequently than positive reinforcement?

4. Can you recall a teacher whom you admired so much that you imitated some aspects of her behavior (if not immediately, then sometime later)? What was it about this teacher that caused you to behave in the same way? How might you have the same effect on your students?

CHAPTER 9

Information-Processing Theory

Key Points

These key points will help you learn the important information in this chapter. To help you study, they also appear in the margins of pages, next to the text where they are discussed.

THE INFORMATION-PROCESSING VIEW OF LEARNING

- Information processing: how humans attend to, recognize, transform, store, retrieve information

A MODEL OF INFORMATION PROCESSING

- Sensory register: stimuli held briefly for possible processing
- Recognition: noting key features and relating them to stored information
- Attention: focusing on a portion of currently available information
- Information in long-term memory influences what we attend to
- Short-term memory: about seven bits of information held for about twenty seconds
- Maintenance rehearsal: hold information for immediate use
- Elaborative rehearsal: use stored information to aid learning
- Organizing material reduces number of chunks, provides recall cues
- Meaningful learning occurs when organized material is associated with stored knowledge
- Long-term memory: permanent storehouse of unlimited capacity
- Information in long-term memory organized as schemata
- Students remember much of what they learn in school, especially if mastery and active learning are emphasized

Metacognition

- Metacognition: knowledge of how we think
- Insight into one's learning processes improves with age

Helping Students Become Strategic Learners

- Strategy: plan to achieve a long-term goal
- Tactic: specific technique that helps achieve long-term goal
- Rote rehearsal not a very effective memory tactic
- Acronym: word made from first letters of items to be learned
- Acrostic: sentence made up of words derived from first letters of items to be learned
- Loci method: visualize items to be learned stored in specific locations
- Keyword method: visually link pronunciation of foreign word to English translation
- Mnemonic devices meaningfully organize information, provide retrieval cues
- Self-questioning aids comprehension under right circumstances
- Taking notes and reviewing notes aid retention and comprehension
- Learning strategy components: metacognition, analysis, planning, implementation, monitoring, modification
- Reciprocal teaching: students learn to summarize, question, clarify, predict as they read

Suggestions for Teaching in Your Classroom

- Unpredictable changes in environment usually command attention
- Attention span can be increased with practice
- Distributed practice: short study periods at frequent intervals
- Serial position effect: tendency to remember items at beginning and end of a long list
- Concrete analogies can make abstract information meaningful

In the previous chapter we noted that operant conditioning emphasizes the role of external factors in learning. Behavioral psychologists focus on the nature of a stimulus to which a student is exposed, the response that the student makes, and the consequences that follow the response. They see no reason to speculate about what takes place in the student's mind before and after the response. The extensive Suggestions for Teaching in Your Classroom presented at the end of the chapter on behavioral learning theories serve as evidence that conclusions and principles based on analyses of external stimuli, observable responses, and observable consequences can be of considerable value to teachers.

But cognitive psychologists, meaning those who study how the mind works and influences behavior, are convinced that it is possible to study nonobservable behavior, such as thought processes, in a scientific manner. Some cognitive psychologists focus on how people use what they know to solve different kinds of problems in different settings; their work will be discussed in the next chapter. Many cognitive psychologists are especially interested in an area of study known as **information-processing theory,** which seeks to understand how people acquire new information, how they store information and recall it from memory, and how what they already know guides and determines what and how they will learn.

Information-processing theory became a popular approach to the study of learning because it provided psychologists with a framework for investigating the role of a variable that behaviorism had ignored—the nature of the learner. Instead of being viewed as relatively passive organisms that respond in fairly predictable ways to environmental stimuli, learners were now seen as highly active interpreters and manipulators of environmental stimuli. The stage was set for psychology to study learning from a broader and more complicated perspective—namely, as an *interaction* between the learner and the environment.

The Information-Processing View of Learning

Information processing: how humans attend to, recognize, transform, store, retrieve information

Information-processing theory rests on a set of assumptions of which three are worth noting. First, information is processed in steps or stages. The major steps typically include attending to a stimulus, recognizing it, transforming it into some type of mental representation, comparing it with information already stored in memory, assigning meaning to it, and acting on it in some fashion (Searleman & Herrmann, 1994). At an early processing stage, human beings encode information (represent it in thought) in somewhat superficial ways (as when they represent visual and auditory stimuli as true-to-life pictures and sounds) and at later stages in more meaningful ways (as when they grasp the gist of an idea or its relationship to other ideas). Second, there are limits on how much information can be processed at each stage. Although the absolute amount of information human beings can learn appears to be limitless, it must be acquired gradually. Third, the human information-processing system is interactive. Information already stored in memory influences and is influenced by perception and attention. We see what our prior experiences direct us to see, and, in turn, what we see affects what we know.

Thus, according to the information-processing view, learning results from an interaction between an environmental stimulus (the *information* that is to be learned) and a learner (the one who *processes*, or transforms, the information). What an information-processing psychologist wants to know, for instance, is what goes on in a student's mind as a teacher demonstrates how to calculate the area of a triangle or as the student reads twenty pages of a social studies text or responds to test questions.

A great many studies have looked at the various information-processing decisions that different types of learners make when confronted with a learning task. As you read this book, for example, numerous other stimuli may compete for your attention. Will you close the book because someone just turned on the television or because you feel drowsy or because you were just invited out for pizza? If you decide to read, do you underline key points, take notes, organize your notes into a topical outline, think of analogies for abstract ideas, or imagine yourself applying educational psychology principles in your own classroom?

We believe that this is one chapter you ought to read very carefully because the information-processing decisions you make affect when you learn, how much you learn, how well you learn—indeed, whether you learn at all. To give you an appreciation of the information-processing approach to learning and how it can help teachers and students do their jobs, the next section will describe several basic cognitive processes and their role in how people store and retrieve information. The section following that will describe research on selected learning tactics and discuss the nature of strategic learning.

A Model of Information Processing

As mentioned earlier, information processing psychologists assume that people process new information in stages, that there are limits on how much information can be processed at each stage, and that previously learned information affects how and what people currently learn. Consequently, many psychologists think of information as being held in and transferred among three memory stores—a sensory register, a short-term store, and a long-term store. Each store varies as to the processes required to move information into and out of it, how much information it can hold, and for how long it can hold information. A symbolic representation of these memory stores and their associated processes appears in Figure 9.1. Called a *multi-store* model, it is based on the work of several theorists (for example, Atkinson & Shiffrin, 1968; Norman & Rumelhart, 1970). Note that our use of the term *memory stores* is not meant to suggest specific locations in the brain where information is held; it is simply a metaphorical device for classifying different memory phenomena.

Shortly after the introduction of multi-store models, information-processing theorists divided themselves into two groups. In one camp are those

FIGURE 9.1 *An Information-Processing Model of Learning*

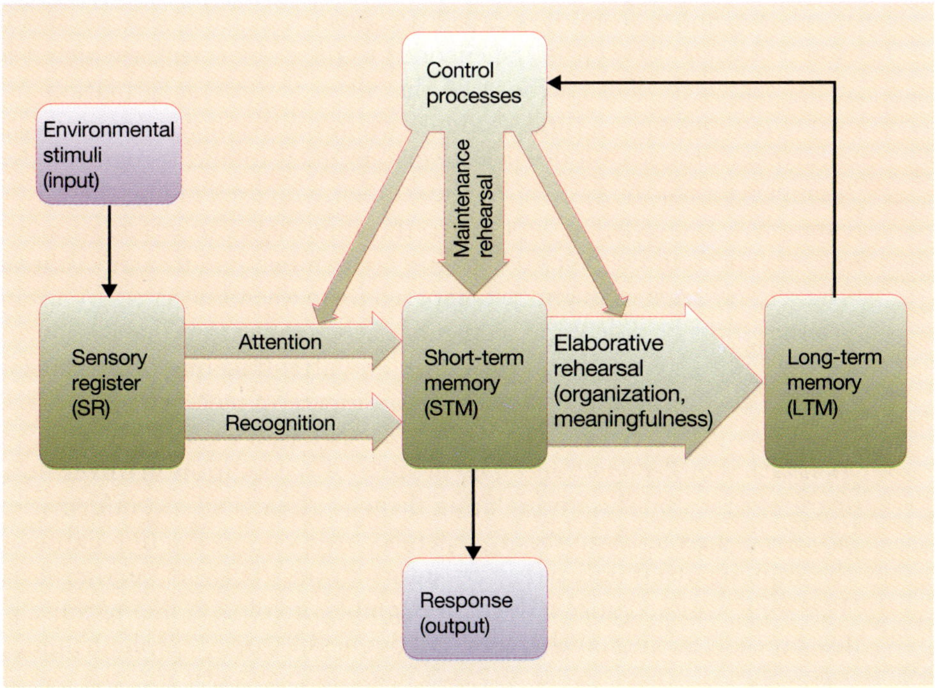

who believe that a multi-store model is the best way to explain a variety of memory phenomena. In the other camp are those who favor a theoretically leaner, single memory system. Although this debate has yet to be firmly resolved, the multi-store model is seen as having enough validity that it can be productively used to organize and present much of what is known about how humans store, process, and retrieve information from memory (Searleman & Herrmann, 1994; Spear & Riccio, 1994).

Control processes govern both the manner in which information is encoded and its flow between memory stores. These processes include *recognition, attention, maintenance rehearsal, elaborative rehearsal* (also called *elaborative encoding*), and retrieval. Elaborative rehearsal is a general label that includes a variety of organizational and meaning-enhancing encoding techniques. Each control process is associated primarily with a particular memory store. The control processes are an important aspect of the information-processing system for two reasons. First, they determine the quantity and quality of information that the learner stores in and retrieves from memory. Second, it is the learner who decides whether, when, and how to employ them. That the control processes are under our direct, conscious control will take on added importance when we discuss educational applications a bit later. Before we get to applications, however, we need to make you more familiar with the three memory stores and the control processes specifically associated with each of them.

THE SENSORY REGISTER AND ITS CONTROL PROCESSES

The Sensory Register A description of how human learners process information typically begins with environmental stimuli. Our sense receptors are constantly stimulated by visual, auditory, tactile, olfactory, and gustatory stimuli. These experiences are initially recorded in the **sensory register (SR)**, the first memory store. It is called the sensory register because the information it stores is thought to be encoded in the same form in which it is originally perceived. The purpose of the SR is to hold information just long enough (about one to three seconds) for us to decide if we want to attend to it further. Information not selectively attended to and recognized decays or disappears from the system. At the moment you are reading these words, for example, you are being exposed to the appearance of letters printed on paper, to sounds in the place where you are reading, and to many other stimuli. The sensory register might be compared to an unending series of instant-camera snapshots or videotape segments, each lasting from one to three seconds before fading away. If you recognize and attend to one of the snapshots, it will be "processed" and transferred to short-term memory.

Sensory register: stimuli held briefly for possible processing

The Nature of Recognition The process of **recognition** involves noting key features of a stimulus and relating them to already stored information. This process is interactive in that it depends partly on information extracted from the stimulus itself and partly on information stored in long-term memory. The ability to recognize a dog, for example, involves noticing those physical features of the animal that give it "dogness" (for example, height, length,

Recognition: noting key features and relating them to stored information number of feet, type of coat) and combining the results of that analysis with relevant information from long-term memory (such as that dogs are household pets, are walked on a leash by their owners, are used to guard property). To the degree that an object's defining features are ambiguous (as when one observes an unfamiliar breed of dog from a great distance) or a learner lacks relevant prior knowledge (as many young children do), recognition and more meaningful processing will suffer. Recognition of words and sentences during reading, for example, can be aided by such factors as clear printing, knowledge of spelling patterns, knowledge of letter sounds, and the frequency with which words appear in natural language. The important point to remember is that recognition and meaningful processing of information are most effective when we make use of all available sources of information (Driscoll, 1994).

One implication of this work to be discussed in more detail in this and other chapters is that, according to the information-processing view, elementary school students need more structured learning tasks than middle school or high school students. Because of their limited store of knowledge in long-term memory and narrow ability to logically relate what they do know to the task at hand, younger students should be provided with clear, complete, explicit directions and learning materials (see, for example, Doyle, 1983).

The Impact of Attention The environment usually provides us with more information than we can deal with at one time. From the multitude of sights, sounds, smells, and other stimuli impinging on us at a given moment, only a fraction are noticed and recorded in the sensory register. At this point yet another reduction typically occurs. We may process only one-third of the already-selected information recorded in the SR. We continually focus on one

Under normal circumstances, our environment contains a wealth of stimuli. Attending to and processing one of those stimuli usually means that the rest are ignored and not stored in memory.

thing at the expense of something else. This selective focusing on a portion of the information currently stored in the sensory register is what we call **attention.**

Attention: focusing on a portion of currently available information

As with any human characteristic, there are individual differences in attention. Some people can concentrate on a task while they are surrounded by a variety of sights and sounds. Others need to isolate themselves in a private study area. Still others have difficulty attending under any conditions. What explains these differences? Again, information from long-term memory plays an influential role. According to Ulric Neisser, "Perceivers pick up only what they have schemata for, and willy-nilly ignore the rest" (1976, p. 79). In other words, we choose what we will see (or hear) by *anticipating* the information it will provide. Students daydream, doodle, and write letters rather than listen to a lecture because they anticipate hearing little of value. Moreover, these anticipatory schemata are likely to have long-lasting effects. If someone asked you now to read a book about English grammar, you might recall having been bored by diagramming sentences and memorizing grammatical rules in elementary school. If that was the case, you might not read the grammar text very carefully. A basic challenge for teachers is to convince students that a learning task will be useful, enjoyable, informative, and meaningful. Later in this chapter we will present some ideas as to how this might be accomplished.

Information in long-term memory influences what we attend to

SHORT-TERM MEMORY AND ITS CONTROL PROCESSES

Short-Term Memory Once information has been attended to, it is transferred to **short-term memory (STM)**, the second memory store. Short-term memory can hold about seven unrelated bits of information for approximately twenty seconds. While this brief time span may seem surprising, it can be easily demonstrated. Imagine that you look up and dial an unfamiliar phone number and receive a busy signal. If you are then distracted by something or someone else for fifteen to twenty seconds, chances are you will forget the number. Short-term memory is often referred to as *working memory* since it holds information we are currently aware of at any given moment.

Short-term memory: about seven bits of information held for about twenty seconds

The following analogy also may help you grasp the nature of short-term memory. Visualize your STM as a filing cabinet with a capacity of seven pictures that will hold their image for about twenty seconds. As new items are placed in the file, either they are incorporated into one of the existing pictures, or they push out one that was previously encoded.

Rehearsal A severe limitation of short-term memory, as you can see, is how quickly information disappears or is forgotten in the absence of further processing. This problem can be dealt with through *rehearsal.* Most people think of rehearsal as repeating something over and over either in silence or out loud. The usual purpose for such behavior is to memorize information for later use, although occasionally we simply want to hold material in short-term memory for immediate use (for example, to redial a phone number after getting a busy signal). Rehearsal can serve both purposes, but not in the same way. Accordingly, cognitive psychologists have found it necessary and useful to distinguish two types of rehearsal: maintenance and elaborative.

Maintenance rehearsal (also called *rote rehearsal* or *repetition*) has a mechanical quality. Its only purpose is to use mental and verbal repetition to hold information in short-term memory for some immediate purpose. While this is a useful and often-used capability (as in the telephone example), it has no effect on long-term memory storage.

Maintenance rehearsal: hold information for immediate use

Elaborative rehearsal (also called *elaborative encoding*) consciously relates new information to knowledge already stored in long-term memory. Elaboration occurs when we use information stored in long-term memory to add details to new information, clarify the meaning of a new idea, make inferences, construct visual images, and create analogies (King, 1992b). In these ways we facilitate both the transfer of information to LTM and its maintenance in STM. For example, if you wanted to learn the lines for a part in a play, you might try to relate the dialogue and behavior of your character to similar personal experiences you remember. As you strive to memorize the lines and actions, your mental "elaborations" will help you store your part in long-term memory so that you can retrieve it later. Elaborative rehearsal, whereby information from long-term memory is used in learning new information, is the rule rather than the exception. Mature learners don't often employ maintenance rehearsal by itself. The decision to use one or the other, however, depends on the demands you expect the environment to make on you. If you need to remember things for future use, use elaborative rehearsal; if you want to keep something in consciousness just for the moment, use rote rehearsal.

Elaborative rehearsal: use stored information to aid learning

It is important for you to keep in mind that younger children may not use rehearsal processes in the same way as more mature learners. Kindergarten students rarely engage in spontaneous rehearsal. By the age of seven, however, children do typically use simple rehearsal strategies. When presented with a list of items, the average seven-year-old rehearses each word by itself several times. From the age of ten, rehearsal becomes more like that of an adult. Several items may be grouped together and rehearsed as a set.

So far, we have explained the effect of elaborative rehearsal in terms of relating new information to information already stored in long-term memory. That's fine as a very general explanation. But to be more precise, we need to point out that elaborative rehearsal is based on *organization* (as in the preceding example where several items were grouped together on some basis and rehearsed as a set) and *meaningfulness* (as in the earlier example where lines in a play were related to similar personal experiences).

Organization Quite often the information we want to learn is complex and interrelated. We can simplify the task by organizing several separate chunks of information into a few "clumps" of information, particularly when each part of a clump helps us remember other parts. The value of organizing material was illustrated by an experiment (Bower, Clark, Lesgold, & Winzenz, 1969) in which two groups of subjects were asked to learn 112 words in four successive lists but under different conditions. One group was given each of the four lists for four trials in the hierarchical arrangement displayed in Figure 9.2. The other group was given the same lists and the same hierarchical tree arrangement, but the words from each list were randomly arranged over the four levels of the hierarchy. As you can see, through the first three trials

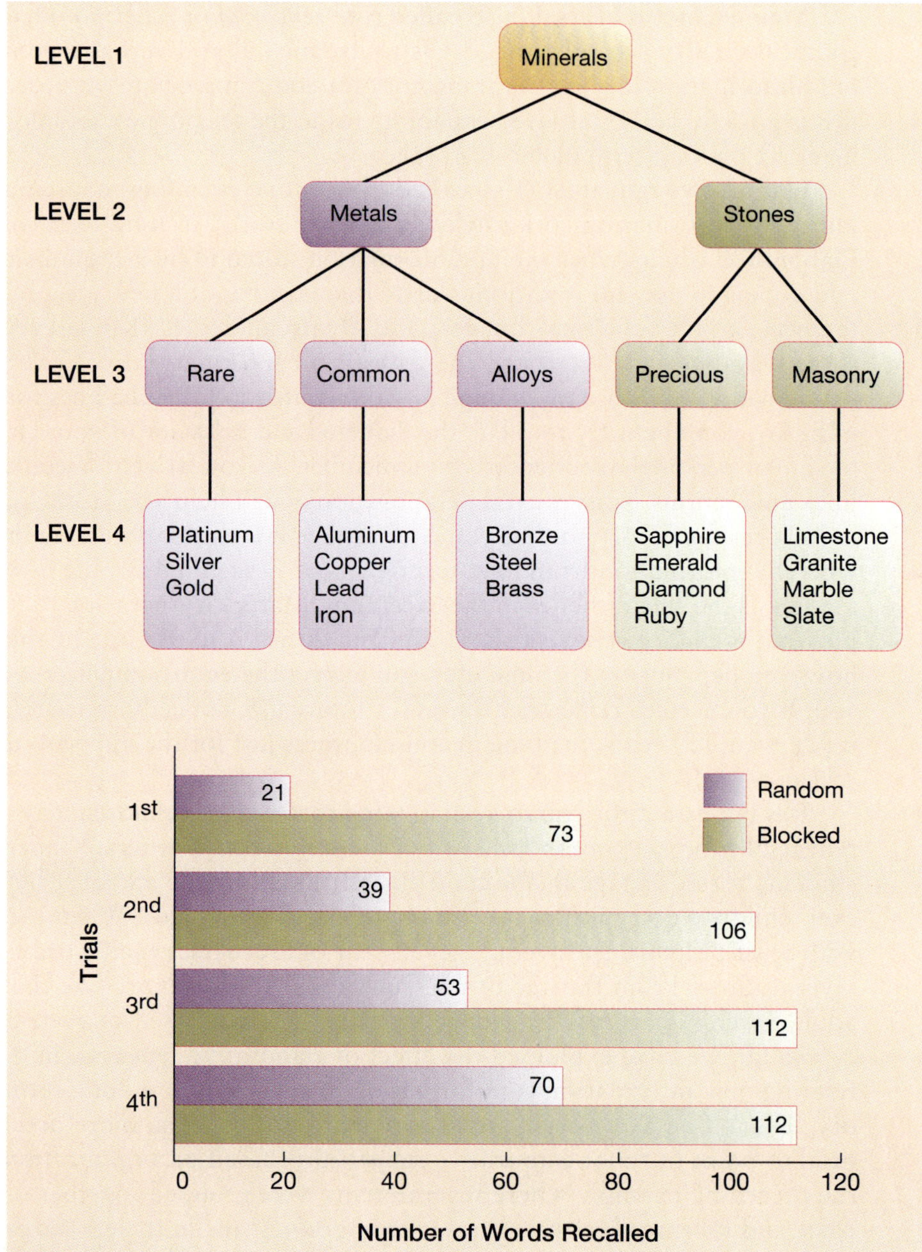

FIGURE 9.2 *Hierarchical Arrangement of Words Produces Superior Recall*

SOURCE: Bower et al. (1969).

Organizing material reduces number of chunks, provides recall cues

the first group recalled more than twice as many words as the second and achieved perfect recall scores for the last two trials. The organized material was much easier to learn not only because there were fewer chunks to memorize but also because each item in a group served as a cue for the other items. When you decide to store pertinent material from this chapter in your long-term memory in preparation for an exam, you will find the job much easier if you organize what you are studying. To learn the various parts of the

To help students encode information, teach them how to group objects and ideas according to some shared feature.

information-processing model under discussion, for instance, you might group the ideas being described under the various headings used in this chapter (as we do in the *Study Guide*).

Meaningfulness The meaningfulness of new information that one is about to learn has been characterized as "potentially the most powerful variable for explaining the learning of complex verbal discourse" (Johnson, 1975, pp. 425-426). According to David Ausubel (Ausubel, Novak, & Hanesian, 1978), meaningful learning occurs when a learner encounters clear, logically organized material and consciously tries to relate the new material to ideas and experiences stored in long-term memory. You might, for example, imagine yourself using learning theory principles to teach a lesson to a group of students. Or you might modify a previously constructed flow chart on the basis of new information. The basic idea behind meaningful learning is that the learner actively attempts to associate new ideas to existing ones. The questions that we pose to you at the end of each chapter, for example, are designed to foster meaningful encoding by getting you to relate text information with relevant prior experience.

Meaningful learning occurs when organized material is associated with stored knowledge

This brief description of meaningfulness and its role in learning contains a strong implication for teaching in culturally diverse classrooms. You can foster meaningful learning for students from other cultures by pointing out similarities between ideas presented in class and students' culture-specific knowledge. For example, you might point out that September 16 has the same significance to people of Mexican origin as July 4 has to U.S. citizens since the former date commemorates Mexico's revolution against and independence from Spain.

LONG-TERM MEMORY

We have already referred, in a general way, to the third memory store, **long-term memory (LTM)**, which is perhaps the most interesting of all. On the basis of neurological, experimental, and clinical evidence, most cognitive psychologists believe that the storage capacity of long-term memory is unlimited and contains a permanent record of everything an individual has learned, although some doubt exists about the latter point (see, for example, Loftus & Loftus, 1980).

Long-term memory: permanent storehouse of unlimited capacity

The neurological evidence comes from the work of Wilder Penfield (1969), a Canadian neurosurgeon who operated on more than one thousand patients who experienced epileptic seizures. To determine the source of the seizures, Penfield electrically stimulated various parts of the brain's surface. During this procedure, many patients reported vivid images of long-dormant events from their past. It was as if a neurological videotape had been turned on.

The experimental evidence, while less dramatic, is just as interesting. In a typical memory study (such as Tulving & Pearlstone, 1966), subjects receive a list of nouns to learn. After giving subjects ample opportunity to recall as many of the words as possible, researchers provide retrieval cues—for instance, category labels such as "clothing," "food," or "animals." In many cases cued subjects quickly recall additional items. Experiments on how well people recognize previously seen pictures have produced some startling findings. Thirty-six hours after viewing over 2,500 pictures, a group of college students correctly identified an average of about 2,250, or 90 percent (Standing, Conezio, & Haber, 1970). In fact, it has been estimated that if one million pictures could be shown, recognition memory would still be 90 percent or better (Standing, 1973). Finally, psychiatrists and psychotherapists have reported many case histories of individuals who have been helped to recall seemingly forgotten events through hypnosis and other techniques (Erdelyi & Goldberg, 1979).

How Information Is Organized in Long-Term Memory As you have seen, long-term memory plays an influential role throughout the information-processing system. The interests, attitudes, skills, and knowledge of the world that reside there influence what we perceive, how we interpret our perceptions, and whether we process information for short-term or long-term storage. In most instances retrieval of information from long-term memory is extremely rapid and accurate, like finding a book in a well-run library. Accordingly, we can conclude that information in long-term memory must be organized. The nature of this organization is a key area in the study of memory. The insights it provides help illuminate the encoding and retrieval processes associated with long-term memory.

Information in long-term memory organized as schemata

Many cognitive psychologists believe that our store of knowledge in long-term memory is organized in terms of **schemata** (which is plural for *schema* and is related in meaning to Jean Piaget's *scheme*). Richard Anderson (1984) defines a schema as an abstract structure of information. It is abstract because it summarizes information about many different cases or examples of something, and it is structured because it represents how its own informational components are interrelated. Schemata give us expectations about objects and events (dogs bark, birds fly, students listen to their teachers and study industriously). When our schemata are well formed and a specific event is consistent with our expectation, comprehension occurs. When schemata

Because people interpret new information and experience on the basis of existing long-term memory schemes, and because no two people's schemes are identical, each person is likely to represent the same idea or experience in a unique fashion.

are poorly structured or absent, learning is slow and uncertain. The following example should make this notion of schemata more understandable.

For most everyone raised in the United States, the word *classroom* typically calls to mind a scene that includes certain people (teacher, students), objects (desks, chalkboard, books, pencils), rules (attend to the teacher's instructions, stay in the classroom unless given permission to leave), and events (reading, listening, writing, talking, drawing). This is a generalized representation, and some classrooms may contain fewer or more of these characteristics. However, as long as students and teachers share the same basic classroom schema, each will generally know what to expect and how to behave in any given classroom. It is when people do not possess an appropriate schema that comprehension, memory, and behavior problems arise.

This notion was first investigated during the early 1930s by Sir Frederick Bartlett (1932), an English psychologist. In one experiment Bartlett had subjects read and recall a brief story, entitled "The War of the Ghosts," that was based on North American Indian folklore. Since Bartlett's subjects had little knowledge of Native American culture, they had difficulty accurately recalling the story; they omitted certain details and distorted others. The distortions were particularly interesting because they reflected an attempt to interpret the story in terms of the logic and beliefs of Western culture. Similar studies, conducted more recently with other kinds of reading materials, have reported similar results (di Sibio, 1982). The conclusion that Bartlett and other researchers have drawn is that remembering is not simply a matter of retrieving a true-to-life record of information. People often remember their *interpretations* or *constructions* of something read, seen, or heard. In addition, when they experience crucial gaps in memory, people tend to fill in these blanks with logical reconstructions of what they think must have been. People then report these reconstructions as memories of actual events (di Sibio, 1982).

A study cited by Mary di Sibio (1982) illustrates how prior knowledge may come into play during recall and lead subjects to guess at what they learned based on their schemata. When this happens, the typical result is distorted recall. In this study two groups of college subjects read the same biographical passage. One group was told that the passage was about a fictitious dictator named Gerald Martin. The other group was told that the passage was about Adolf Hitler. Subjects were tested either five minutes or one week after reading. They were asked to distinguish sentences taken from the passage ("old" sentences) from sentences that had not appeared but were consistent with the topic ("new" sentences). Subjects in both groups could accurately distinguish old from new sentences after the five-minute delay. After one week, however, subjects who read the Adolf Hitler passage were far more likely to mistakenly recognize a new sentence such as "He hated the Jews particularly and so persecuted them."

These experiments and the Case in Print feature on pp. 330–331 vividly demonstrate the interactive nature of memory. What we know influences what we perceive and how we interpret and store those perceptions. And because our memories of specific events or experiences are assembled, constructed, and sometimes reassembled by the brain over time, accurate and complete recall of information we once stored is not always possible. As a teacher, then, you should pay deliberate attention to how your students use their background knowledge, helping them to use it as accurately and completely as possible to process new information.

How Well Do We Remember What We Learn in School? Conventional wisdom (which is often wrong, by the way) holds that much of the information that we learn in school is forgotten soon after a unit of instruction or course has ended. You may have felt the same way yourself on more than one occasion. But is this belief true? To answer this question, George Semb and John Ellis (1994) reviewed the results of fifty-six research articles published between 1930 and 1993. Their main findings are very consistent with the information-processing principles that you have read about and should at least partially reassure you that you haven't been wasting your time all these years.

1. More than seven out of ten studies reported less than a 20 percent loss of what was learned when measured with a recognition task. One-half of the studies reported less than a 20 percent loss of what was learned when measured with free recall.
2. Subject matter that had a higher than average level of unfamiliar facts and associations (such as zoology, anatomy, and medical terminology) and for which students would have little relevant prior knowledge (such as electricity, mechanics, and linguistics) was associated with increased levels of forgetting.
3. Most of the forgetting of information occurred within four weeks after the end of a unit of instruction. Additional declines in recall occurred more slowly.

Students remember much of what they learn in school, especially if mastery and active learning are emphasized

4. Less forgetting occurred among students who learned the material to a high level either by being required to achieve a high score on an exam before moving on to the next unit of instruction, by having to teach it to less knowledgeable students, or by taking advanced courses.

5. Less forgetting occurred in classes where students were more actively involved in learning (as in a geography field trip where students had to observe, sketch, record, and answer questions).

The instructional implications that flow from these findings include an emphasis on mastery learning, peer tutoring, frequent testing with corrective feedback, and forms of instruction that actively involve students in learning.

The discussion up to this point has focused on a general explanation of how people attend to, encode, store, and retrieve information. In a word, we have described some of the major aspects of *thinking*. During the last twenty years, researchers have inquired into how much knowledge individuals have about their own thought processes and what significance this knowledge has for learning. The term that was coined to refer to how much we know of our own thought processes is *metacognition*. As we will see, it plays a very important role in learning.

Metacognition

THE NATURE AND IMPORTANCE OF METACOGNITION

The notion of metacognition was proposed by developmental psychologist John Flavell (1976) to explain why children of different ages deal with learning tasks in different ways. For example, when seven-year-olds are taught how to remember pairs of nouns using both a less effective technique (simply repeating the words) and a more effective technique (imagining the members of each pair doing something together), most of these children will use the less effective technique when given a new set of pairs to learn. Most ten-year-olds, however, will opt to use the more effective method (Kail, 1990). The explanation for this finding is that the seven-year-old has not had enough learning experiences to recognize that some problem-solving methods are

Metacognition refers to the knowledge we have about how we learn. It is a key component of our ability to regulate our learning processes.

"Remembering" Things That Never Were

People often remember their interpretations or constructions of something read, seen, or heard. In addition, when they experience crucial gaps in memory, people tend to fill in these blanks with logical reconstructions of what they think must have been. People then report these reconstructions as memories of actual events. (p. 327)

"You Must Remember This"

SHARON BEGLEY WITH MARTHA BRANT

Newsweek 9/26/94

At first, Chris had only the foggiest recollection of getting lost in the Spokane shopping mall at the age of 5. His older brother, a psychology student at the University of Washington, was doing an experiment on memory; would Chris, 14, read this brief account of an incident from his childhood, and write down everything he could remember about it? After reading about getting lost in the mall, Chris wrote variations on "I sort of remember the stores." But a few weeks later, pressed by his brother, he offered a richly detailed narrative: "I think I went over to look at the toy store, the Kay-Bee store and, uh, we got lost. . . . and then this old man, I think he was wearing blue flannel, came up to me. . . . He was kind of old. He was kind of bald on top. . . . He had like a ring of gray hair. . ."

Chris had never been lost at a mall. But now he was sure that he had. . . .

Glimmers of how memories might be created out of mere wisps of suggestion began to emerge this summer, after a May conference at Harvard Medical School on the neurological bases of false memories. Start with how normal memory is thought to work: bits and pieces of an experience are parceled out to different regions of the brain. Memories of its sound settle in the auditory cortex, and memories of its appearance into the visual cortex . . . "Each neuron represents a little bit of the memory," explains psychologist James McClelland of the Center for the Neural Basis of Cognition in Pittsburgh. But all the scattered fragments remain physically linked. The job of assembling them falls to a part of the brain called the limbic system. Like a neural file clerk, it pulls disparate aspects of each memory from the separate file drawers scattered throughout the cortex, gathering them into a cohesive whole.

Whatever reason evolution had for creating this scheme, it practically guarantees people will "remember" things that never happened. For one thing, people routinely take perfectly accurate snippets and assemble them incorrectly. Suppose you saw an accident in which a car ran a red light; a year later someone asks, "Remember when that guy ran the stop sign?" Neurons connected to the memory of the accident click in—but so do memories of stop signs. Time goes by. The next time you recall the accident, neurons holding memories of stop signs get activated, too—and suddenly you remember a car running a stop sign. Most chilling, says psychologist Michael Nash of the University of Tennessee, is that "there may be no structural difference between" a memory of a true event and a false one.

False memories commonly arise in a condition called "source amnesia." Thanks to the brain's frontal lobes, most people can distinguish the memory of a dream from the memory of a real event: these gelatinous folds of gray matter tag each incoming image with how, when and where it was acquired. But if the frontal lobes are damaged, their owners cannot remember where a memory came from, explains psychologist Daniel Schacter of Harvard. The patients retrieve bits and pieces of a memory—the face of an old teacher, a cinematic rape—and cannot distinguish which fragment came from where. "You could be remembering a dream, a fear or something someone talked about," says Schacter. "What gives the memory a feeling of authenticity is that authentic parts are included." Even in people with perfectly fine frontal lobes, a memory's origin deteriorates more quickly than its other aspects, says psychologist Stephen Ceci of Cornell University. (Do you remember your first day of kindergarten? Or is it your mother's endless recounting that you recall?) Source memory is also highly prone to suggestion—that the vision of a man by your bed is a real memory, for instance, and not an image drawn from hearing tales of abuse. "If you've imagined it enough and you lose the source of the information [your imagination]," says Ceci, "then you have a false memory."

Although not everyone is so suggestible—75 percent of the people in Loftus's lost-in-the-mall study refused to "remember" what had never been—certain conditions can make them do so. "Severe emotional stress overcomes internal checks on plausibility, and you are left with a false memory," says neurologist Marsel Mesulam of Northwestern University. From transcripts and session notes, Loftus, a psychologist at the University of Washington, found therapists who routinely told patients that if they cannot remember abuse, they should *imagine* it as an aid to memory. "Picture [your father] approaching the bed," one told her patient, Loftus reports. "Think about what happened in the bathtub," said another; "If you can't remember any details, just try to imagine what it must have been like." Many therapists also use hypnosis, which makes patients willing to internalize suggestions and to call any image they see a memory. "Under hypnosis," says psychiatrist David Spiegel of Stanford University, "you can create [memories] rather than retrieve them."

. . . Such skepticism about retrieved memories rankles people who counsel survivors of abuse. Harvard psychiatrist Judith Herman, for instance, says "scientists have no business using the term false memory. We have no way of judging independently [reports of] childhood experiences." That's OK if memories are used solely in therapy, and treated as mere expressions of the mind. But "memories" are sending people to jail: 700 civil and criminal cases have been filed based on retrieved memories of childhood abuse, according to the False Memory Syndrome Foundation. Some of the accused have been convicted and sentenced to 40 years, as in a case decided last week, based on nothing more substantial than retrieved memories. At least, the accusers thought they were memories.

Questions and Activities

1. Since people interpret experiences on the basis of their long-term memory schemes and, on occasion, add extraneous information to create a more meaningful and logical recollection, it is not surprising that disagreements occur about the details of an event. Teachers sometimes find themselves in such situations as, for example, when parents confront a teacher and demand to know why the teacher embarrassed their child in front of the rest of the class. The teacher is dumbfounded by the accusation and replies that she did no such thing. What might you do to avoid such confrontations by assuring that you and your students have a common understanding of important or sensitive events?

2. What kinds of classroom situations are most likely to be interpreted differently and hence remembered differently by teachers and students?

3. If you plan to have students view a film or videotape as part of a lesson, you may be able to demonstrate the phenomenon of false memory. Two weeks after students have viewed the film or tape, and without prior warning, announce that a prize will be awarded to the student who recalls the most information from the film. Have students write down as much as they can recall of what they saw and heard. Then give them a list of all the ideas that actually occurred in the film. Have them compare both lists and make a tally of both how many actual ideas they recalled *and* how many ideas they recalled that had never appeared.

better than others. To the younger child, one means is as good as another. This lack of metacognitive knowledge makes true strategic learning impossible for young children.

One way to grasp the essence of metacognition is to contrast it with cognition. The term *cognition* is used to describe the ways in which information is processed—that is, the ways it is attended to, recognized, encoded, stored in memory for various lengths of time, retrieved from storage, and used for one purpose or another. **Metacognition** refers to our knowledge about those operations and how they might best be used to achieve a learning goal. As Flavell has put it:

> I am engaging in metacognition . . . if I notice that I am having more trouble learning A than B; if it strikes me that I should double-check C before accepting it as a fact; if it occurs to me that I had better scrutinize each and every alternative in any multiple-choice type task situation before deciding which is the best one; if I become aware that I am not sure what the experimenter really wants me to do; if I sense that I had better make a note of D because I may forget it; if I think to ask someone about E to see if I have it right. Such examples could be multiplied endlessly. (1976, p. 232)

Metacognition: knowledge of how we think

Metacognition is obviously a very broad concept. It covers everything an individual can know that relates to how information is processed. To get a better grasp of this concept, you may want to use the three-part classification scheme proposed by Flavell (1987): knowledge of person variables, task variables, and strategy variables. An example of knowledge of person variables is that one is good at learning verbal material but poor at learning mathematical material. Another example is knowing that information not rehearsed or encoded is quickly forgotten. An example of knowledge of task variables is that passages with long sentences and unfamiliar words are usually harder to understand than passages that are more simply written. An example of knowledge of strategy variables is knowing that one should skim through a text passage before reading it to determine its length and difficulty level. Recent research indicates significant differences in what younger and older children know about metacognition. What follows is a discussion of some of these differences.

AGE TRENDS IN METACOGNITION

Two reviews of research on metacognition (Duell, 1986; Kail, 1990) examined how students of different ages use memorization techniques and how well they understand what they are doing. Following are some of the reviews' key conclusions.

1. In terms of diagnosing task difficulty, most six-year-olds know that more familiar items are easier to remember than less familiar items and that a small set of items is easier to recall than a large set of items. What six-year-olds do not yet realize is that the amount of information they can recall immediately after they study it is limited.

2. Similar findings have been obtained for reading tasks. Most second graders know that interest, familiarity, and story length influence comprehension and recall. However, they are relatively unaware of the effect

of how ideas are sequenced, of the introductory and summary qualities of first and last paragraphs, and of the relationship between reading goals and tactics. Sixth graders, by contrast, are much more aware of the effects of these variables on comprehension and recall. Partly because of these differences in metacognitive knowledge, young children tend to treat reading as a task of decoding symbols rather than of constructing and comprehending meaning. Recent research has clearly shown that children's metacognitive awareness about reading is positively related to performance on a variety of reading tasks.

3. Most children know very little about the role their own capabilities play in learning. For example, not until about nine years of age do most children realize that their recall right after they study something is limited. Consequently, children through the third grade usually overestimate how much they can store in and retrieve from short-term memory. One likely reason for this developmental difference is that younger children base their prediction on irrelevant personal characteristics (such as "I'm pretty smart"), whereas older children focus more on relevant task characteristics.

4. There are clear developmental differences in how well students understand the need to tailor learning tactics to task demands. For example, four- and six-year-old children in one study cited by Robert Kail (1990) did not alter how much time they spent studying a set of pictures when they were told that a recognition test would follow either three minutes later, one day later, or one week later. Eight-year-olds did use that information to allocate less or more study time to the task. In another study children of various ages were trained to use interactive visual imagery to learn a list of concrete noun pairs. When given a similar task and left on their own, most of those below ten years of age reverted to the less effective technique of rote rehearsal.

5. In terms of monitoring the progress of learning, most children younger than seven or eight are not very proficient at determining when they know something well enough to pass a memory test. Also, most first graders typically don't know what they don't know. When given multiple opportunities to study and recall a lengthy set of pictures, six-year-olds chose to study pictures they had previously seen and recalled as well as ones they hadn't. Thus, they wasted time studying things they already knew. Third graders, by contrast, focused on previously unseen pictures.

The general conclusion that emerges from these findings is that the youngest school-age children have only limited knowledge of how their cognitive processes work and when to use them. Consequently, primary grade children do not systematically analyze learning tasks, formulate plans for learning, use appropriate techniques of enhancing memory and comprehension, or monitor their progress because they do not (some would say cannot) understand the benefits of doing these things. But as children develop and gain more experience with increasingly complex academic tasks, they acquire a greater awareness of metacognitive knowledge and its relationship to classroom learning. In this process teachers can assist their students and guide them toward maximum use of their metacognitive knowledge. To help you understand how, the next section will discuss learning tactics and strategies.

Insight into one's learning processes improves with age

Helping Students Become Strategic Learners

With some effort and planning, a teacher can make logically organized and relevant lessons. However, this is only half the battle since students must then attend to the information, encode it into long-term memory, and retrieve it when needed. Getting students to use the attention, encoding, and retrieval processes discussed in the previous section is not always easy. The sad fact is that most children and adults are inefficient learners (as evidenced, for example, by Bond, Miller, & Kennon, 1987; Davies, 1984; Brown, Campione, & Day, 1981; Covington, 1985; Selmes, 1987; Simpson, 1984). Their attempts at encoding rarely go beyond rote rehearsal (for example, rereading a textbook chapter), simple organizational schemes (outlining), and various cueing devices (underlining or highlighting). When the nature of the learning task changes, few students think about changing their encoding techniques accordingly.

One reason for this state of affairs is that students are rarely taught how to make the most of their cognitive capabilities. In one study sixty-nine kindergarten through sixth-grade teachers were observed giving strategy instruction in only 9.5 percent of the times they were observed. Rationales for strategy use were given less than 1 percent of the time, and 10 percent of the teachers gave no strategy instructions at all. Moreover, the older the students were, the less likely they were to receive strategy instruction (Moely et al., 1992). Findings such as these are surprising, not to mention disappointing, since it is widely recognized that the amount of independent learning expected of students increases consistently from elementary school through high school and into college. The rest of this chapter will try to convince you that it need not be this way, at least for your students. The rise of information-processing theory has led researchers to study how cognitive processes can be taught to and used by students as learning tactics and strategies.

THE NATURE OF LEARNING TACTICS AND STRATEGIES

Strategy: plan to achieve a long-term goal

Tactic: specific technique that helps achieve long-term goal

A **learning strategy** is a general *plan* that a learner formulates for achieving a somewhat distant academic goal (like getting an A on your next exam). Like all strategies, it specifies what will be done to achieve the goal, where it will be done, and when it will be done. A **learning tactic** is a specific *technique* (like a memory aid or a form of notetaking) that a learner uses to accomplish an immediate objective (such as to understand the concepts in a textbook chapter and how they relate to one another). As you can see, tactics have an integral connection to strategies. They are the learning tools that move you closer to your goal. Thus, they have to be chosen so as to be consistent with the goals of a strategy. If you had to recall verbatim the preamble to the U.S. Constitution, for example, would you use a learning tactic that would help you understand the gist of each stanza or one that would allow for accurate and complete recall? It is surprising how often students fail to consider this point. Because understanding the different types and roles of tactics will help you better understand the process of strategy formulation, we will discuss tactics first.

TYPES OF TACTICS

Most learning tactics can be placed in one of two categories based on each tactic's intended primary purpose. One category, called *memory-directed tactics,* contains techniques that help produce accurate storage and retrieval of information. The second category, called *comprehension-directed tactics,* contains techniques that aid in understanding the meaning of ideas and their interrelationships (Levin, 1982). Within each category there are specific tactics from which one can choose. Because of space limitations, we cannot discuss them all. Instead, we have chosen to briefly discuss a few that are either very popular with students or have been shown to be reasonably effective. The first two, rehearsal and mnemonic devices, are memory-directed tactics. Both can take several forms and are used by students of almost every age. The last two, notetaking and self-questioning, are comprehension-directed tactics and are used frequently by students from the upper elementary grades through college.

Rehearsal The simplest form of rehearsal—rote rehearsal—is one of the earliest tactics to appear during childhood and is used by most everyone on occasion. It is not a particularly effective tactic for long-term storage and recall because it does not produce distinct encoding or good retrieval cues (although, as discussed earlier, it is a useful tactic for purposes of short-term memory). According to research reviewed by Kail (1990), most five- and six-year-olds do not rehearse at all. Seven-year-olds sometimes use the simplest form of rehearsal. By eight years of age, instead of rehearsing single pieces of information one at a time, youngsters start to rehearse several items together as a set. A slightly more advanced version, called *cumulative rehearsal,* involves rehearsing a small set of items for several repetitions, dropping the item at the top of the list and adding a new one, giving the set several repetitions, dropping the item at the head of the set and adding a new one, rehearsing the set, and so on. By early adolescence rehearsal reflects the learner's growing awareness of the organizational properties of information. When given a list of randomly arranged words from familiar categories, thirteen-year-olds will group items by category to form rehearsal sets. This version of rehearsal is likely to be the most effective because of the implicit association between the category members and the more general category label. If at the time of recall the learner is given the category label or can generate it spontaneously, the probability of accurate recall of the category members increases significantly.

Rote rehearsal not a very effective memory tactic

Mnemonic Devices A **mnemonic device** is a memory-directed tactic that helps a learner transform or organize information to enhance its retrievability. Such devices can be used to learn and remember individual items of information (a name, a fact, a date), sets of information (a list of names, a list of vocabulary definitions, a sequence of events), and ideas expressed in text. These devices range from simple, easy-to-learn techniques to somewhat complex systems that require a fair amount of practice. Since they incorporate visual and verbal forms of elaborative encoding, their effectiveness is due to the same factors that make imagery and category clustering successful—organization and meaningfulness.

Although mnemonic devices have been described and practiced for over two thousand years, they were rarely made the object of scientific study until the 1960s (see Yates, 1966, for a detailed discussion of the history of mnemonics). Since that time, however, mnemonics have been frequently and intensively studied by researchers. In recent years there have been several reviews of mnemonics research (for example, Bellezza, 1981; Higbee, 1979; Pressley, Levin, & Delaney, 1982; Snowman, 1986). In the next few pages, we will briefly discuss five mnemonic devices: rhymes, acronyms, acrostics, the loci method, and the key-word method.

RHYMES, ACRONYMS, AND ACROSTICS. Most students learn a few time-honored *rhyme* mnemonics during their elementary school years. The spelling rule "*i* before *e* except after *c*" and the calendar rule "Thirty days hath September, April, June, and November" are but two examples.

Acronym: word made from first letters of items to be learned

Another class of mnemonics is the *acronym,* or first-letter mnemonic. With this technique, you take the first letter from each of a set of items to be learned and make up a word (it doesn't have to be a real word). For example, take the first letter from each of the Great Lakes—Huron, Ontario, Michigan, Erie, Superior. Combined, they form the word *HOMES.* In this case you can add imagery by visualizing five homes on the shore of a lake. Surveys of mnemonic use among college students have found the acronym technique to be very well known and widely used. It appears to be most effective for recalling a short set of items, particularly abstract items, in serial order.

Acrostic: sentence made up of words derived from first letters of items to be learned

If an acronym is not feasible, you can construct an *acrostic,* or sentence mnemonic. Simply make up a sentence such that each word begins with the first letter of each item to be learned. To learn and remember the nine planets, the sentence "Men Very Easily Make Jugs Serve Useful New Purposes" (*M*ercury, *V*enus, *E*arth, *M*ars, *J*upiter, *S*aturn, *U*ranus, *N*eptune, *P*luto) works quite well. A variation of the acrostic is to embed information to be learned in a meaningful sentence. For instance, when trying to decide whether the port or starboard side of a ship is left or right, just remember one of the following sentences: "The ship *left port,*" or "The *star boarder* is always *right.*" The acrostic is most useful for recalling abstract items of information.

THE LOCI METHOD. The oldest known mnemonic, the loci (pronounced *low-sigh* and meaning places) method, is also one of the most popular. The loci method is a peg-type mnemonic in that the loci, or places, serve as memory pegs. Commonly used loci are rooms in a house, buildings on a campus, or stores on a street. First, form a set of memory locations that constitute a natural series, are numbered, are highly familiar, and can be easily imagined. Second, images of the things you want to remember (for example, objects, events, or ideas) should be generated and placed in each location as you mentally walk from one location to another. Within each location there should be particular pieces of furniture (chair, table, piano) or architectural

Loci method: visualize items to be learned stored in specific locations features (fireplace, mantel, archway, lobby) on, in, or under which one or more images can be placed. Third, when you want to recall, simply retrace your steps through each location, retrieve each image from where it was originally placed, and decode each image into a written or spoken message. The loci method is an effective memory-directed tactic for children, college students, and the elderly. When combined with an outlining tactic, it can be used to recall ideas from prose. It works for both free recall and serial recall.

THE KEYWORD METHOD. The last mnemonic to be discussed is also the newest to be devised. Called the *keyword method,* it first appeared in 1975 as a means for learning foreign language vocabulary (Atkinson, 1975; Atkinson & Raugh, 1975; Raugh & Atkinson, 1975). The technique is fairly simple and involves two steps. First, isolate some part of the foreign word that, when spoken, sounds like a real English word. This is the keyword. Second, form an interacting visual image between the key word and the English translation of the foreign word. Thus, the foreign word becomes associated to the key word by an acoustic link, and the keyword becomes associated to the English translation by an imagery link.

Keyword method: visually link pronunciation of foreign word to English translation

As an example, take the Spanish word *pato* (pronounced *pot-o*), which means "duck" in English. The key word in this case is *pot.* The next step, generating a visual image combining pot and duck, can be satisfied by imagining a duck with a pot over its head (other combinations, such as a duck simmering in a pot, are also possible). As a more meaningful example, assume that you have to recall the basic facts of the intelligence theorists mentioned in Chapter 5. To recall that Charles Spearman proposed a two-factor theory that was composed of a *g* factor and an *s* factor, you generate "spear" as a key word and a visual image of a spear being thrown at a *gas* can (Carney, Levin, & Levin, 1994).

The keyword mnemonic has proved effective in one form or another with preschoolers, elementary school children, adolescents, and college students. For children who cannot spontaneously generate visual images (preschool through fourth grade), two variations have been devised. In one, children are given the keyword and a picture that incorporates the keyword and the English translation. The other variation uses sentences instead of pictures. The sentence variation can also be used to remember abstract material. The keyword is a very flexible mnemonic. Besides foreign language vocabulary, it facilitates the recall of cities and their products, states and their capitals, medical definitions, and famous people's accomplishments.

WHY MNEMONIC DEVICES ARE EFFECTIVE. Mnemonic devices work so well because they enhance the encodability and retrievability of information. First, they provide a context (such as acronyms, sentences, mental walks) in which apparently unrelated items can be organized. Second, the meaningfulness of material to be learned is enhanced through associations with more familiar, meaningful information (for example, memory pegs or loci). Third, they provide distinctive retrieval cues that must be encoded with the material to be learned. Fourth, they force the learner to be an active participant in the learning process (Morris, 1977).

Mnemonic devices meaningfully organize information, provide retrieval cues

Despite the demonstrated effectiveness of mnemonic devices, many people argue against teaching them to students. They feel that students should learn the skills of critical thinking and problem solving rather than ways to reliably recall isolated bits of verbatim information. We feel this view is shortsighted for two reasons. First, it ignores the fact that effective problem solving depends on ready access to a well-organized and meaningful knowledge base. Second, it focuses only on the "little idea" that mnemonic usage aids verbatim recall of bits of information. The "big idea" is that students come to realize that the ability to learn and remember large amounts of information is an acquired capability. Too often students (and adults) assume that an effective memory is innate and requires high intelligence. Once they realize that learning is a skill, students may be more inclined to learn how to use other tactics and how to formulate broad-based strategies.

Self-Questioning Since students are expected to demonstrate much of what they know by answering written test questions, self-questioning can be a valuable learning tactic. The key to using questions profitably is to recognize that different types of questions make different cognitive demands. Some questions require little more than verbatim recall or recognition of simple facts and details. If an exam is to stress factual recall, then it may be helpful for a student to generate such questions while studying. Other questions, however, assess comprehension, application, or synthesis of main ideas or other high-level information. Since many teachers favor higher-level test questions, we will focus on self-questioning as an aid to comprehension.

Much of the research on self-questioning addresses two basic questions: Can students as young as those in fourth grade be trained to write comprehension questions about the content of a reading passage? And does writing such questions lead to better comprehension of the passage in comparison to students who do not write questions? The answer to both questions is yes if certain conditions are present. Research on teaching students how to generate questions as they read (see, for example, Wong, 1985; Mevarech and Susak, 1993) suggests that the following conditions play a major role in self-questioning's effectiveness as a comprehension-directed learning tactic:

Self-questioning aids comprehension under right circumstances

1. *The amount of prior knowledge the questioner has about the topic of the passage.* The more a student knows about a topic, the easier it is to formulate questions that reflect factual knowledge, comprehension of main ideas, similarities and differences among different ideas, and so on.
2. *The amount of metacognitive knowledge the questioner has compiled.* Before effective self-questioning is possible, a student has to be aware of, for example, the types of questions that could be asked (such as questions dealing with knowledge level, comprehension level, or application level) and the reasons for asking them.
3. *The clarity of instructions.* Students should be given clear and detailed instructions in how to write good questions of a particular type.
4. *The instructional format.* Students should be allowed to work in small cooperative groups in which they practice and evaluate each

TABLE 9.1 ***Self-Questioning Stems***

What is a new example of . . . ?
How would you use . . . to . . . ?
What would happen if . . . ?
What are the strengths and weaknesses of . . . ?
What do we already know about . . . ?
How does . . . tie in with what we learned before?
Explain why . . . .
Explain how . . . .
How does . . . affect . . . ?
What is the meaning of . . . ?
Why is . . . important?
What is the difference between . . . and . . . ?
How are . . . and . . . similar?
What is the best . . . , and why?
What are some possible solutions to the problem of . . . ?
Compare . . . and . . . with regard to . . . ?
How does . . . cause . . . ?
What do you think causes . . . ?

SOURCE: King (1992b).

other's questions. (We describe this instructional arrangement in more detail in Chapter 11.)

5. *The amount of practice allowed the student.* Students should be given enough practice in writing questions to develop high proficiency.
6. *The length of each practice session.* Each practice session should be long enough for all students to comfortably read the passage and think of good questions. Giving students twenty minutes to read a fourteen-hundred-word passage and write six comprehension questions is likely to produce poorly framed questions.

To ensure that students fully understood how to write comprehension-aiding questions (suggestion 3 in the preceding list), Alison King (1992b) created a set of question stems (see Table 9.1) that were intended to help students identify main ideas and think about how those ideas related to each other and to what the student already knew. When high school and college students used these question stems, they scored significantly better on tests of recall and comprehension of lecture material than did students who simply reviewed the same material.

Notetaking As a learning tactic, notetaking comes with good news and bad. The good news is that notetaking can benefit a student in two ways. First, the process of taking notes while listening to a lecture or reading a text leads to better retention and comprehension of the noted information than just listening or reading does. Second, the process of reviewing notes produces additional chances to recall and comprehend the noted material. The bad news is that we know very little at the present time about the specific conditions that make notetaking an effective tactic.

Taking notes and reviewing notes aid retention and comprehension

This uncertainty as to what constitutes a good set of notes probably explains the results obtained by King (1992a) in a comparison of self-questioning, summarizing, and notetaking. One group of students was given a set of question stems, shown how to generate good questions with them, and allowed to practice. A second group was given a set of rules for creating a good summary (identify a main idea or subtopic and related ideas, and link them together in one sentence), shown how to use them to create good summaries, and allowed to practice. A third group, however, was told to simply take notes as group members normally would in class. Both the self-questioning and summarizing groups scored significantly higher on an immediate and one-week-delayed retention test.

On the basis of this brief review, we would like to draw two conclusions. One is that students need to be systematically taught how to use learning tactics to make connections among ideas contained in text and lecture as well as between new and previously learned information. No one expects students to teach themselves to read, write, and compute. So why should they be expected to teach themselves how to use a variety of learning tactics? The second conclusion is that learning tactics should not be taught as isolated techniques, particularly to high school students. If tactics are taught that way, most students probably will not keep using them for very long or recognize that as the situation changes, so should the tactic. Therefore, as we implied at the start of this section, students should be taught how to use tactics as part of a broader learning strategy.

USING LEARNING STRATEGIES EFFECTIVELY

The Components of a Learning Strategy As noted, a learning strategy is a plan for accomplishing a learning goal. It consists of six components: metacognition, analysis, planning, implementation of the plan, monitoring of progress, and modification. To give you a better idea of how to formulate a learning strategy of your own, here is a detailed description of each of these components (Snowman, 1986, 1987).

Learning strategy components: metacognition, analysis, planning, implementation, monitoring, modification

1. *Metacognition.* In the absence of some minimal awareness of how we think and how our thought processes affect our academic performance, a strategic approach to learning is simply not possible. We need to know, at the very least, that effective learning requires an analysis of the learning situation, formulation of a learning plan, skillful implementation of appropriate tactics, periodic monitoring of our progress, and modification of things that go wrong. In addition, we need to know why each of these steps is necessary, when each step should be carried out, and how well prepared we are to perform each step. Without this knowledge, students who are taught one or more of the learning tactics mentioned earlier do not keep up their use for very long, nor do they apply the tactics to relevant tasks.

2. *Analysis.* Any workable plan must be based on relevant information. By thinking about the type of task that one must confront, the type of material that one has to learn, the personal characteristics that one possesses, and the way in which one's competence will be tested, the strategic learner can generate this information by playing the role of an

Students can formulate strategic learning plans that identify and analyze the important aspects of a task. Then, they can tailor these plans to their own strengths and weaknesses as learners.

investigative journalist and asking questions that pertain to what, when, where, why, who, and how. In this way the learner can identify important aspects of the material to be learned (what, when, where), understand the nature of the test that will be given (why), recognize relevant personal learner characteristics (who), and identify potentially useful learning activities or tactics (how).

3. *Planning.* Once satisfactory answers have been gained from the analysis phase, the strategic learner then formulates a learning plan by hypothesizing something like the following: "I know something about the material to be learned (I have to read and comprehend five chapters of my music appreciation text within the next three weeks), the nature of the criterion (I will have to compare and contrast the musical structure of symphonies that were written by Beethoven, Schubert, and Brahms), my strengths and weaknesses as a learner (I am good at tasks that involve the identification of similarities and differences, but I have difficulty concentrating for long periods of time), and the nature of various learning activities (skimming is a good way to get a general sense of the structure of a chapter; mnemonic devices make memorizing important details easier and more reliable; notetaking and self-questioning are more effective ways to enhance comprehension than simple rereading). Based on this knowledge, I should divide each chapter into several smaller units that will take no longer than thirty minutes to read, take notes as I read, answer self-generated compare-and-contrast questions, use the loci mnemonic to memorize details, and repeat this sequence several times over the course of each week."

4. *Implementation of the plan.* Once the learner has formulated a plan, each of its elements must be implemented *skillfully.* A careful analysis and a well-conceived plan will not work if tactics are carried out badly.

Of course, a poorly executed plan may not be entirely attributable to a learner's tactical skill deficiencies. Part of the problem may be a general lack of knowledge about what conditions make for effective use of tactics (as is the case with notetaking).

5. *Monitoring of progress.* Once the learning process is under way, the strategic learner assesses how well the chosen tactics are working. Possible monitoring techniques include writing out a summary, giving an oral presentation, working practice problems, and answering questions.

6. *Modification.* If the monitoring assessment is positive, the learner may decide that no changes are needed. If, however, attempts to memorize or understand the learning material seem to be producing unsatisfactory results, the learner will need to reevaluate and modify the analysis. This, in turn, will cause changes in both the plan and the implementation.

There are two points we would like to emphasize about the nature of a learning strategy. The first is that learning conditions constantly change. Subject matters have different types of information and structures, teachers use different instructional methods and have different styles, exams differ in the kinds of demands they make, and the interests, motives, and capabilities of students change over time. Accordingly, strategies must be *formulated* or constructed anew as one moves from task to task rather than *selected* from a bank of previously formulated strategies. The true strategist, in other words, is very mentally active.

The second point is that the concept of a learning strategy is obviously complex and requires a certain level of intellectual maturity. Thus, you may be tempted to conclude that, although *you* could do it, learning to be strategic is beyond the reach of most elementary and high school students. Research evidence suggests otherwise, however. A study of high school students in Scotland, for example, found that some students are sensitive to contextual differences among school tasks and vary their approach to studying accordingly (Selmes, 1987). Furthermore, as we are about to show, research in the United States suggests that elementary grade youngsters can be trained to use many of the strategy components just mentioned.

Research on Learning Strategy Training An ambitious project to teach third- and fifth-grade children how, when, and why to use various elements of a reading comprehension strategy was evaluated on two occasions by Scott Paris and his associates (Paris, Cross, & Lipson, 1984; Paris & Oka, 1986). Over the course of an academic year, several hundred third- and fifth-grade children participated either in a supplemental reading comprehension training program called Informed Strategies for Learning (ISL) or in a control condition.

The basic purposes of the ISL program were to increase the students' metacognitive awareness of reading strategies, convince them that reading strategies are useful skills, and teach them how to use strategic skills to improve reading comprehension. The major findings from this program are mostly positive:

1. As measured by a twenty-item test, ISL children showed a much greater awareness than control group children of why one should

use strategic reading skills, when such skills should be used, how to use them, and what benefits to expect from them.

2. Fifth-grade ISL children showed more metacognitive awareness than third-grade ISL children.
3. Third-grade and fifth-grade ISL children scored higher on two different measures of reading comprehension than did third-grade and fifth-grade control group children.
4. Children's comprehension strategies, metacognitive knowledge, and motivation were all significantly related to achievement.
5. ISL did not improve self-perception about reading or perceived self-competence.

Another study of strategy training aimed at improving reading comprehension is the *reciprocal teaching* (RT) program of Annemarie Palincsar and Ann Brown (1984). As the title of this program indicates, students learn certain comprehension skills by demonstrating them to each other. Palincsar and Brown trained a small group of seventh graders whose reading comprehension scores were at least two years below grade level to use the techniques of summarizing, self-questioning, clarifying, and predicting to improve their reading comprehension. These four methods were chosen because they can be used by students to improve *and* monitor comprehension.

Reciprocal teaching: students learn to summarize, question, clarify, predict as they read

During the early training sessions, the teacher explained and demonstrated the four methods while reading various passages. The students were then given gradually increasing responsibility for demonstrating these techniques to their peers, with the teacher supplying prompts and corrective feedback as needed. Eventually, each student was expected to offer a good summary of a passage, pose questions about important ideas, clarify ambiguous words or phrases, and predict upcoming events, all to be done with little or no intervention by the teacher. (This approach to strategy instruction, by the way, is based on the zone of proximal development concept that we first mentioned in Chapter 2.)

Palincsar and Brown found that the RT program produced two general beneficial effects. First, the quality of students' summaries, questions, clarifications, and predictions improved. Early in the program students produced overly detailed summaries and many unclear questions. But in later sessions concise summaries and questions dealing explicitly with main ideas were the rule. For example, questions on main ideas increased from 54 percent to 70 percent. In addition, the questions were increasingly stated in paraphrase form rather than as verbatim statements from the passage. Second, RT-trained students scored as well as a group of average readers on tests of comprehension (about 75 percent correct for both groups) and much better than a group taught how to locate information that might show up in a test question (75 percent correct versus 45 percent correct). Most impressively, these levels of performance held up for at least eight weeks after the study ended (no measures were taken after that point) and generalized to tests of social studies and science (20 percent correct prior to training versus 60 percent correct after training).

Subsequent research on the effectiveness of RT has continued to produce positive findings across a broad age spectrum (fourth grade through college).

On the average, RT students have scored at the 62nd percentile on standardized reading comprehension tests (compared to the 50th percentile for the average control student) and at the 81st percentile rank on reading comprehension tests that were created by the experimenters (Rosenshine & Meister, 1994).

The message of strategy training programs like Informed Strategies for Learning and reciprocal teaching is that knowledge of the learning process and the conditions that affect it should be as much a part of the curriculum as learning to read, write, and compute. Proponents have argued persuasively that mastery of traditional basic skills is influenced by the nontraditional but more basic skills of strategic reasoning (see, for example, Bracey, 1983). Accordingly, children should gradually be made aware of the general relationship between cognitive means and academic ends, the potential range of application of various learning tactics, how to determine if learning is proceeding as planned, and what to do if it is not.

In the following section we offer several Suggestions for Teaching that will help your students become more strategic and efficient learners.

Suggestions for Teaching in Your Classroom

Helping Your Students Become Efficient Information Processors

1. Develop and use a variety of techniques to attract and hold attention, and give your students opportunities to practice and refine their skills in maintaining attention.
   a. Be aware of what will capture your students' attention.
   b. To maintain attention, emphasize the possible utility of learning new ideas.
   c. Teach students how to increase their span of attention.
2. Point out and encourage students to recognize that certain bits of information are important and can be related to what is already known.
3. Use appropriate rehearsal techniques, including an emphasis on meaning and chunking.
4. Organize what you ask your students to learn, and urge older students to organize material on their own.
5. As much as possible, stress meaningfulness.
6. Demonstrate a variety of learning tactics, and allow students to practice them.
   a. Teach students how to use various forms of rehearsal and mnemonic devices.
   b. Teach students how to formulate comprehension questions.
   c. Teach students how to take notes.
7. Encourage students to think about the various conditions that affect *how* they learn and remember.
8. Each time you prepare an assignment, think about learning strategies that you and your students might use.

1. Develop and use a variety of techniques to attract and hold attention, and give your students opportunities to practice and refine their skills in maintaining attention.

a. **Be aware of what will capture your students' attention.**

Journal Entry
Techniques for Capturing Attention

The ability to capture your students' attention is affected by characteristics of the information itself and by the learners' related past experiences. Learners are more likely to attend to things they expect to find interesting or meaningful. It is also true that human beings are sensitive to abrupt, sudden changes in their environment. Thus, anything that stands out, breaks a rhythm, or is unpredictable is almost certain to command students' attention.

Unpredictable changes in environment usually command attention

EXAMPLES

Print key words or ideas in extra-large letters on the board.

Use colored chalk to emphasize important points written on the board.

When you come to a particularly important part of a lesson, say, "Now really concentrate on this. It's especially important." Then present the idea with intensity and emphasis.

Start off a lesson with unexpected remarks, such as "Imagine that you have just inherited a million dollars and . . . "

b. **To maintain attention, emphasize the possible utility of learning new ideas.**

Journal Entry
Techniques for Maintaining Attention

While it is possible to overdo attempts at making the curriculum relevant, it never hurts to think of possible ways of relating school learning to the present and future lives of students. When students realize that the basic purpose of school is to help them adapt to their environment, they are more apt to pay close attention to what you are trying to do.

EXAMPLE

Teach basic skills—such as arithmetic computation, arithmetic reasoning, spelling, writing, and reading—as part of class projects that relate to students' natural interests (for example, keeping records of money for newspaper deliveries; measuring rainfall, temperature, and wind speed; writing letters to local television stations to express opinions on or request information about television shows).

c. **Teach students how to increase their span of attention.**

Journal Entry
Techniques for Increasing Attention Span

Remember that paying attention is a skill that many students have not had an opportunity to refine. Give your students plenty of opportunities to practice and improve their ability to maintain attention.

EXAMPLES

Institute games that depend on maintaining attention, such as playing Simon Says, keeping track of an object hidden under one of several boxes (the old shell game), or determining whether two pictures are identical or different. At first, positively reinforce students for all correct responses. Then reinforce only for improvements in performance. Remind students that their success is a direct result of how well they pay attention.

Attention span can be increased with practice

Read a short magazine or newspaper story, and ask students to report who, what, where, when, and why.

2. **Point out and encourage students to recognize that certain bits of information are important and can be related to what is already known.**

Attention is one control process for the sensory register; the other is recognition. Sometimes the two processes can be used together to induce students to focus on important parts of material to be learned. Sometimes you can urge your students to recognize key features or familiar relationships on their own.

EXAMPLES

Have students practice grouping numbers, letters, or classroom items according to some shared feature, such as odd numbers, multiples of five, letters with circles, or things made of wood.

Say, "This math problem is very similar to one you solved last week. Does anyone recognize something familiar about this problem?"

Say, "In this chapter the same basic point is made in several different ways. As you read, try to recognize and write down as many variations on that basic theme as you can."

3. **Use appropriate rehearsal techniques, including an emphasis on meaning and chunking.**

Journal Entry
Ways to Use Chunking to Facilitate Learning

The power of chunking information into meaningful units was demonstrated in a study conducted with a single college student of average memory ability and intelligence (Ericsson, Chase, & Faloon, 1980). Over twenty months he was able to improve his memory for digits from seven to almost eighty. Being a track and field buff, he categorized three- and four-digit groups as running times for imaginary races. Thus, 3,492 became "3 minutes and 49.2 seconds, near world record time." Number groups that could not be encoded as running times were encoded as ages. These two chunking techniques accounted for almost 90 percent of his associations.

Distributed practice: short study periods at frequent intervals

Serial position effect: tendency to remember items at beginning and end of a long list

The main purpose of chunking is to enhance learning by breaking tasks into small, easy-to-manage pieces. To a large degree, students who are ten and older can learn to do this for themselves if you show them how chunking works. In addition, you can help by not requiring students to learn more than they can reasonably handle at one time. If you have a list of fifty spelling words to be learned, it is far better to present ten words a day, five days in a row, during short study periods than to give all fifty at once. This method of presentation is called **distributed practice.** In distributed practice, it is usually necessary to divide the material into small parts, which—because of the serial position effect—seems to be the best way for students to learn and retain unrelated material (for example, spelling words). The **serial position effect** refers to people's tendency to learn and remember the words at the beginning and end of a list more easily than those in the middle. By using short lists, then, you in effect eliminate the hard-to-memorize middle ground. A description of the positive effect of distributed practice on classroom learning and an explanation of why educators do not make greater use of it have been offered by Frank Dempster (1988).

Distributed practice may not be desirable for all learning tasks, however. If you ask students to learn roles in a play, short rehearsals might not be effective because students may have a difficult time grasping the entire plot. If you allow enough rehearsal time to run through a whole act, your students will be able to relate one speech to another and comprehend the overall structure of the play. When students learn by way of a few rather long study periods, spaced infrequently, psychologists call it **massed practice.**

You might also tell your students about the relative merits of distributed versus massed practice. Robert Bjork (1979) has pointed out that most students not only are unaware of the benefits of distributed study periods but also go to considerable lengths to block or mass the study time devoted to a particular subject.

4. **Organize what you ask your students to learn, and urge older students to organize material on their own.**

At least some items in most sets of information that you ask your students to learn will be related to other items, and you will find it desirable to call attention to interrelationships. The Bower et al. (1969) experiment described earlier in which one group of students was given a randomly arranged set of items to learn and another group was presented the same items in logically ordered groups illustrates the value of organization. By placing related items in groups, you reduce the number of chunks to be learned and also make it possible for students to benefit from cues supplied by the interrelationships between items in any given set. And by placing items in logical order, you help students grasp how information at the beginning of a chapter or lesson makes it easier to learn information that is presented later.

Journal Entry
Organizing Information into Related Categories

EXAMPLES

If students are to learn how to identify trees, birds, rocks, or the equivalent, group items that are related (for example, deciduous and evergreen trees). Call attention to distinctive features and to organizational schemes that have been developed.

Print an outline of a chapter on the board, or give students a duplicated outline, and have them record notes under the various headings. Whenever you give a lecture or demonstration, print an outline on the board. Call attention to the sequence of topics, and demonstrate how various points emerge from or are related to other points.

5. **As much as possible, stress meaningfulness.**

When you present material to be learned, emphasize the logic behind it, and urge students to look for meaning on their own. Concrete analogies offer one effective way to add meaning to material. Consider someone who has no knowledge of basic physics but is trying to understand a passage about the flow of electricity through metal. For this person, statements about crystalline lattice arrays, free-floating electrons, and the effects of impurities will

Concrete analogies can make abstract information meaningful

mean very little. However, such abstract ideas can be explained in more familiar terms. You might compare the molecular structure of a metal bar to a Tinker Toy arrangement, for example, or liken the effect of impurities to placing a book in the middle of a row of falling dominoes. Such analogies increase recall and comprehension (Royer & Cable, 1975, 1976).

EXAMPLES

Give students opportunities to express ideas in their own words and to relate new knowledge to previous learning.

When you explain or demonstrate, express complex and abstract ideas several different ways. Be sure to provide plenty of examples.

Construct essay tests and homework assignments that emphasize comprehension and application. Give credit for thoughtful answers even though they do not exactly match the answer you would have given.

For topics that are somewhat controversial (for example, nuclear energy, genetic engineering, pesticide use), require students to present both pro and con arguments.

Journal Entry
Ways to Stress Meaningfulness

6. Demonstrate a variety of learning tactics, and allow students to practice them.

a. Teach students how to use various forms of rehearsal and mnemonic devices.

Journal Entry
Ways to Teach Memory Tactics

At least two reasons recommend the teaching of rehearsal. One is that maintenance rehearsal is a useful tactic for keeping a relatively small amount of information active in short-term memory. The other is that maintenance rehearsal is one of a few tactics that young children can learn to use. If you do decide to teach rehearsal, we have two suggestions. First, remind young children that rehearsal is something that learners consciously decide to do when they want to remember things. Second, remind students to rehearse no more than seven items (or chunks) at a time.

Upper elementary grade students (fourth, fifth, and sixth graders) can be taught advanced forms of maintenance rehearsal, such as cumulative rehearsal, and forms of elaborative rehearsal, such as rehearsing sets of items that form homogeneous categories. As with younger students, provide several opportunities each week to practice these skills.

As you prepare class presentations or encounter bits of information that students seem to have difficulty learning, ask yourself if a mnemonic device would be useful. You might write up a list of the devices discussed earlier and refer to it often. Part of the value of mnemonic devices is that they make learning easier. They are also fun to make up and use. Moreover, rhymes, acronyms, and acrostics can be constructed rather quickly. You might consider setting aside about thirty minutes two or three times a week to teach mnemonics. First, explain how rhyme, acronym, and acrostic mnemonics work, and then provide examples of each. For younger children use short, simple rhymes like "Columbus crossed the ocean blue in fourteen hundred ninety-two." For older students, the rhymes can be longer and more complex.

Acrostics can be used to remember particularly difficult spelling words. The word *arithmetic* can be spelled by taking the first letter from each word of the following sentence: *a* rat *i*n *t*he *h*ouse *m*ay *e*at *t*he *i*ce *c*ream. Once students understand how the mnemonic is supposed to work, have them construct mnemonics to learn various facts and concepts. You might offer a prize for the most ingenious mnemonic.

b. **Teach students how to formulate comprehension questions.**

We concluded earlier that self-questioning could be an effective comprehension tactic if students were trained to write good comprehension questions and given opportunities to practice the technique. We suggest you try the following instructional sequence:

Journal Entry
Ways to Teach Comprehension Tactics

1. Discuss the purpose of student-generated questions.
2. Point out the differences between knowledge-level questions and comprehension-level questions. An excellent discussion of this distinction can be found in the *Taxonomy of Educational Objectives, Handbook I: Cognitive Domain* (Bloom et al., 1956).
3. Provide students with a sample paragraph and several comprehension questions. Again, good examples of comprehension questions and guidelines for writing your own can be found in the *Taxonomy.*
4. Hand out paragraphs from which students can practice constructing questions.
5. Provide corrective feedback.
6. Give students short passages from which to practice.
7. Provide corrective feedback (André & Anderson, 1978/1979).

c. **Teach students how to take notes.**

Despite the limitations of research on notetaking, mentioned earlier, three suggestions should lead to more effective notetaking. First, provide students

Research findings demonstrate that notetaking in one form or another is an effective tactic for improving comprehension of text and lecture material. Consequently, students should be taught the basic principles that support effective notetaking.

with clear, detailed objectives for every reading assignment. The objectives should indicate what parts of the assignment to focus on and how that material should be processed (whether memorized verbatim, reorganized and paraphrased, or integrated with earlier reading assignments). Second, inform students that notetaking is an effective comprehension tactic when used appropriately. Think, for example, about a reading passage that is long and for which test items will demand analysis and synthesis of broad concepts (as in "Compare and contrast the economic, social, and political causes of World War I with those of World War II"). Tell students to concentrate on identifying main ideas and supporting details, paraphrase this information, and record similarities and differences. Third, provide students with practice and corrective feedback in answering questions that are similar to those on the criterion test.

7. Encourage students to think about the various conditions that affect *how* they learn and remember.

The very youngest students (through third grade) should be told periodically that such cognitive behaviors as describing, recalling, guessing, and understanding mean different things, produce different results, and vary in how well they fit a task's demands. For older elementary school and middle school students, explain the learning process more simply, focusing on the circumstances in which different learning tactics are likely to be useful. Then, have students keep a diary or log in which they note when they use learning tactics, which ones, and with what success. Look for cases where good performance corresponds to frequent reported use of tactics, and positively reinforce those individuals. Encourage greater use of tactics among students whose performance and reported use of them are below average.

While this same technique can be used with high school and college students, they should also be made aware of the other elements that make up strategic learning. Discuss the meaning of and necessity for analyzing a learning task, developing a learning plan, using appropriate tactics, monitoring the effectiveness of the plan, and implementing whatever corrective measures might be called for.

8. Each time you prepare an assignment, think about learning strategies that you and your students might use.

Journal Entry
Ways to Teach Learning Strategies

As noted in our earlier discussion of age trends in metacognition, virtually all elementary school students and many high school students will not be able to devise and use their own coordinated set of learning strategies. Accordingly, you should devise such strategies for them, explain how the strategies work, and urge them to use these techniques on their own. With high school students, you might consider giving a how to study lecture at the beginning of a report period to provide your students with general information about learning strategies. Even if you do give such an orientation, however, it would still be wise to give specific instructions as each assignment is made. In devising learning strategies, follow the procedure that was described earlier in this chapter: analyze, plan, implement, monitor, modify. When you analyze, take into account not only the material to be learned and the nature of the tests you will give but also the cognitive characteristics of the learners.

EXAMPLE

In a middle school or high school class, analyze each text chapter, and decide what kind of exam you intend to use to evaluate your students' understanding. Perhaps draw up a list of key points, print these on the board, and announce that they will be emphasized on exam questions. Explain what kinds of test questions you intend to ask, and give some suggestions on the best ways to study in order to be able to answer such questions. Announce the date of the exam well in advance. Schedule supervised study sessions during class periods. Give your students specific suggestions about learning strategies that they might use during each study session. At least a week or so before the exam, give a practice quiz featuring questions similar to those that will be on the exam, and have students note points they know and don't know. Tell them to concentrate on material that is incompletely learned and recommend troubleshooting learning strategies. Give a follow-up quiz, and repeat the monitor-modify procedure.

The next section describes several ways that you can use computer-based technology to improve your students' learning skills.

@ APPLYING TECHNOLOGY TO TEACHING

Using Technology to Aid Information Processing

Computer-based instructional technology can help students develop learning strategies, including metacognitive skills, in addition to helping them learn content. Accordingly, we now want to suggest a few ways in which computers can be used to help students improve their information-processing skills.

Computer-based learning shifts the dynamic of teacher-student relationships because computers can take on many preliminary or ancillary tasks, such as keeping records, monitoring the pace of instruction, and delivering raw content for the student to work with. This shift allows teachers to concentrate more fully on facilitating the students' use of the content and development of learning strategies (Collins, 1991). Teachers may have more time and flexibility to make decisions about what students should learn and to model metacognitive skills for students. Even tutorial and drill programs are more successful when used by students in conjunction with feedback and problem-solving advice from the teacher, which extends their effectiveness beyond simply rote presentation of material.

APPLYING TECHNOLOGY TO TEACHING, *continued*

Some educational programs focus primarily on teaching learning tactics. For example, a program called *Mind-Step 1* teaches students from sixth grade to college how to create and use mnemonic devices. *Mind-Step 2* extends the lessons in *Mind-Step 1* with analysis and memorization of poetry and text, development of good listening habits, and remembering of visual information. *Fundamentals of Outlining* is a tutorial program that teaches students how to outline correctly and how to recognize and write titles, main topics, subtopics, details, and subpoints. *Mystery Master Murder by Dozen* is a deductive reasoning game that encourages the development of notetaking skills. And *Plan Ahead* is a tutorial that teaches students how to schedule their own time (EPIE Institute, 1993).

An additional way in which computers can help students is through programs that prompt them to think about how various ideas and pieces of information are interrelated or that allow them to create their own "databases" of related ideas. You may recall that we discussed this thought process earlier in the chapter in the sections on elaborative encoding and schema formation. Another phrase commonly used to refer to schema formation is *mental model building.* Computer programs that seem to foster this process are *HyperCard* for the Apple Macintosh computer and *ToolBook* for IBM-type computers. Both programs have similar features. The basic unit of information (called a "card" in HyperCard and a "page" in ToolBook) is essentially one computer screen, which can contain information just as an index card or book page might be. The information can consist of text, pictures, audio, or video. Collections of cards or pages can be linked together by means of simple point-and-click buttons to create a "stack" or "book."

Ready-made programs can be purchased on a wide variety of subjects, but the true strength of these programs is that students can create such programs for themselves and in the process apply and develop cognitive skills. To create a meaningful stack or book, students need to come up with a plan for organizing the information according to criteria or characteristics they choose. To use a simple example: if you had several dozen names in a stack called "business associates," you could sort them by state, area code, gender, occupation, interests, position within their company, and so on. (See Kozma, 1991, for a general discussion of this type of program.) The fact that the information is put into a context promotes the development of multiple memory codes and supportive connections between codes for better retrieval (Grabe and Grabe, 1995). And the database can be expanded with new branches when students determine that new information doesn't quite fit the existing structure—corresponding to their own development of new schemata.

Statistics programs, lab programs, and three-dimensional rendering programs can be used to help students get a better understanding of abstract concepts through graphic illustrations. Many seventh- and eighth-grade students, for example, do not understand certain graphic representations. When asked to draw a graph depicting how fast a bicyclist travels uphill, downhill, and on flat stretches, their products represented the hills and valleys rather than the bicyclist's speed. That is, they drew an ascending line to represent the bicyclist's speed going uphill without realizing that such a line represented the downhill portion of the journey since it indicated increasing speed. In effect, they were drawing pictures that represented the exact opposite of what they were asked to represent. This graph interpretation skill was significantly improved when students worked with computers that were connected to a variety of sensors (temperature probes, microphones, and motion sensors, for example). As students applied a source of energy to one of the sensors—heating up and allowing to cool down a beaker of water, for example, a corresponding graphic representation was instantly created on the computer screen (Kozma, 1991).

Finally, the growing number of large computer databases, both on the Internet and on commercially published CD-ROM discs such as *Compton's Encyclopedia* and *SoftwareToolworks U.S. Atlas,* offer students the opportunity to hone cognitive skills by searching and retrieving information. Choosing the subject of the search, selecting key words, and assessing the results of the search all can provide students with practice in self-questioning and note-taking techniques.

Resources for Further Investigation

The Nature of Information-Processing Theory

For more on how information-processing theory relates to teaching and learning, read Chapter 1 of *Cognitive Classroom Learning* (1986). Written by Thomas André and Gary Phye, and titled "Cognition, Learning, and Education," the chapter compares information processing with behavioral learning theory, describes the nature of memory stores and control processes, and discusses the value of an information-processing perspective for educational practice.

Another source of information is *The Cognitive Psychology of School Learning* (2d ed., 1993), by Ellen Gagné, Carol Walker Yekovich, and Frank Yekovich. The goal of these authors is to help educators use information-processing theory and research to answer the questions "What shall we teach?" and "How shall we teach?" Chapters 12–15 describe how to use this knowledge base to teach reading, writing, mathematics, and science, respectively.

A collection of ERIC (Education Resources Information Center) digests on information processing can be found at gopher://inet.ed.gov:12002/7waisrc%3A/EricDigests?information processing.

Memory Structures and Processes

Norman Spear and David Riccio describe various aspects of memory structures and processes in *Memory: Phenomena and Principles* (1994). As the title suggests, Alan Searleman and Douglas Herrmann cover the same ground, plus such additional topics as the role of social factors in memory, individual differences in memory, and changes in memory ability, in *Memory from a Broader Perspective* (1994). Alan Baddeley provides a detailed account of memory phenomena in *Human Memory: Theory and Practice* (1990). If you have ever wondered if your memory for everyday events is better or worse than most other people's, you might want to take the Everyday Memory Questionnaire on pages 234 and 235 of Baddeley's book.

Metacognition

If you would like to know more about the nature of metacognition and its role in memory, eyewitness testimony, and problem solving; its development in adulthood and old age; and the neuropsychology of metacognition, take a look at *Metacognition: Knowing About Knowing* (1994), edited by Janet Metcalfe and Arthur Shimamura. If teaching reading is going to be one of your future responsibilities, you may glean some useful ideas from Ruth Garner, *Metacognition and Reading Comprehension* (1987).

A collection of ERIC digests on metacognition can be found on-line at gopher://inet.ed.gov:12002/7waisrc%3A/EricDigests?metacognitive strategies.

Learning Tactics and Strategies

One of the most popular (and useful) memory improvement books available is *The Memory Book* (1974), by Harry Lorayne and Jerry Lucas. They explain why and how you should think up ridiculous associations, offer suggestions for using substitute words, provide techniques for learning foreign and English vocabulary, and describe ways to remember names and faces.

Bernice Bragstad and Sharyn Stumpf (offer practical advice and instructional materials for teachers of study skills in *A Guidebook for Teaching Study Skills and Motivation* (2d ed., 1987).

Meredith Gall, Joyce Gall, Dennis Jacobsen, and Terry Bullock outline why it is important to teach students study skills, summarize underlying theories of information processing and motivation, and describe how a school or district can implement a study skills program in *Tools for Learning: A Guide to Teaching Study Skills* (1990).

In Part C of *Teaching Reading, Writing, and Study Strategies* (3d ed., 1983), H. Alan Robinson describes patterns of writing (text structures) and associated comprehension tactics for four major content areas: science, social studies, English, and mathematics.

A complete list of projects on cognitive skills development approved by the Department of Education for national dissemination for elementary through high school educators is found on-line at the Department of Education's gopher server, gopher://gopher.ed.gov:70/00/programs/NDN/edprog94/eptw10. The site is maintained by the National Diffusion Network and is equivalent to its "Educational Programs That Work," twentieth edition print catalogue.

Individual Differences in Memory

One of the most striking accounts of supernormal memory is provided by Alexander Luria, *The Mind of a Mnemonist: A Little Book About a Vast Memory* (1968). Luria describes his experiments and experiences over a period of almost thirty years with the man he refers to as S, who could recall nonsense material he had not seen for fifteen years. Charles Thompson, Thaddeus Cowan, and Jerome Frieman describe a series of studies done with Rajan Mahadevan, who earned a place in the *Guinness Book of World Records* by memorizing the first 31,811 digits of pi, in *Memory Search by a Memorist* (1993). Additional articles about people with unusually proficient memory capability can be found in *Memory Observed* (1982), edited by Ulric Neisser.

Robert Kail describes memory differences among normal children, as well as differences between normal and retarded children in *The Development of Memory in Children* (3d ed., 1990). Also briefly discussed is the phenomenon of the idiot savants—individuals who are below average on all measures of ability except one, in which they far surpass almost all other individuals—and the reliability of children's eyewitness testimony. Leon Miller describes musical savants, mentally retarded individuals who can perfectly reproduce musical passages on an instrument after one hearing, in *Musical Savants: Exceptional Skill in the Mentally Retarded* (1989).

Summary

1. Information-processing theory attempts to explain how individuals acquire, store, recall, and use information.
2. A popular model of information processing is composed of three memory stores and a set of control processes that determine the flow of information from one memory store to another. The memory stores are the sensory register, short-term memory, and long-term memory. The control processes are recognition, attention, maintenance rehearsal, elaborative rehearsal, and retrieval.
3. The sensory register holds information in its original form for two or three seconds, during which time we may recognize and attend to it further.
4. Recognition involves noticing key features of a stimulus and integrating those features with relevant information from long-term memory.
5. Attention is a selective focusing on a portion of the information in the sensory register. Information from long-term memory influences what we focus on.
6. Short-term memory holds about seven bits of information for about twenty seconds (in the absence of rehearsal). It is often called working memory because it contains information we are conscious of.
7. Information can be held in short-term memory indefinitely through the use of maintenance rehearsal, which is rote repetition of information.
8. Information is transferred from short-term memory to long-term memory by the linking of the new information to related information in long-term memory. This process is called elaborative rehearsal.
9. Elaborative rehearsal is based partly on organization. This involves grouping together, or chunking, items of information that share some important characteristic.
10. Elaborative rehearsal is also based on meaningfulness. Meaningful learning occurs when new information that is clearly written and logically organized is consciously related to information the learner currently has stored in long-term memory.
11. Long-term memory is thought to be an unlimited storehouse of information from which nothing is ever lost.
12. Many psychologists believe the information in long-term memory is organized in the form of schemata. A schema is a generalized abstract structure of information. When schemata are absent or crudely formed, learning and recall problems occur.
13. Contrary to popular belief, students remember much of the information they learn in school, especially if it was well learned to start with and if it was learned in a meaningful fashion.
14. Metacognition refers to any knowledge an individual has about how humans think and the circumstances that affect thinking.
15. Metacognitive knowledge increases gradually with experience. This helps explain why junior high and high school students are more flexible and effective learners than primary grade students.
16. A learning strategy is a general plan that specifies the resources one will use, when they will be used, and how one will use them to achieve a learning goal.
17. A learning tactic is a specific technique one uses to help accomplish an immediate task-related objective.

18. Most teachers provide little or no direct instruction to students in the formulation and use of strategies and tactics.

19. Learning tactics can be classified as memory directed or comprehension directed. The former are used when accurate storage and retrieval of information are important. The latter are used when comprehension of ideas is important.

20. Two types of memory-directed tactics are rehearsal and mnemonic devices. Since most forms of rehearsal involve little or no encoding of information, they are not very effective memory tactics. Because mnemonic devices organize information and provide built-in retrieval cues, they are effective memory tactics.

21. Popular mnemonic devices include rhymes, acronyms, acrostics, the loci method, and the keyword method.

22. Two effective comprehension tactics are self-questioning and notetaking.

23. The components of a learning strategy are metacognition, analysis, planning, implementation, monitoring, and modification.

24. Learning strategy training raises the reading comprehension scores of both average and below-average readers.

Key Terms

information-processing theory *(317)*
sensory register (SR) *(320)*
recognition *(320)*
attention *(322)*
short-term memory (STM) *(322)*
maintenance rehearsal *(323)*
elaborative rehearsal *(323)*
long-term memory (LTM) *(325)*
schemata *(326)*
metacognition *(332)*
learning strategy *(334)*
learning tactic *(334)*
mnemonic device *(335)*
distributed practice *(346)*
serial position effect *(346)*
massed practice *(347)*

Discussion Questions

1. Can you think of any personal, everyday experiences that illustrate the nature of one or more of the three memory stores? Have you recently, for instance, retrieved a long-dormant memory because of a chance encounter with an associated word, sound, or smell?

2. Information-processing psychologists have expressed disappointment that the results of their research on memory stores and processes, learning tactics, and learning strategies have not been widely implemented by teachers. Is this complaint consistent with your experience? Can you recall any instances when you were taught how to use a variety of learning tactics to formulate different strategies? How about out of school? Did you acquire any such skills without the help of a classroom teacher?

3. Many teachers have said that they would like to teach their students more about the nature and use of learning processes but that they don't have time because of the amount of subject material they must cover. What can you do as a teacher to avoid this pitfall?

4. A major problem in training students to use learning strategies and tactics is getting the youngsters to spend the time and effort required to master these skills. Suppose some students expressed their lack of interest, saying their own methods would be just as effective (although you know full well they would not be). How would you convince these students otherwise?

CHAPTER 10

Cognitive Learning Theories and Problem Solving

Key Points

These key points will help you learn the important information in this chapter. To help you study, they also appear in the margins of the pages, next to the text where they are discussed.

THE NATURE OF MEANINGFUL LEARNING

- Bruner: students should learn the structure of a field of study
- Discover how ideas relate to each other and to existing knowledge
- Meaningful reception learning: integrate new ideas into existing knowledge schemes
- When relationships are ignored, reception learning can be nonmeaningful
- Meaningful learning depends on nature of the task, learner's set
- Advance organizer helps relate new ideas to existing schemes
- Constructivist view: meaningful learning due to personal interpretation of ideas, experiences
- Construction of ideas comes largely from discussion and debate
- Constructivism aided by cognitive apprenticeship, realistic tasks, multiple perspectives

THE NATURE OF PROBLEM SOLVING

- Well-structured problems: clearly stated, known solution procedures, known evaluation standards
- Ill-structured problems: vaguely stated, unclear solution procedures, vague evaluation standards
- Issues: ill-structured problems that arouse strong feelings
- Problem finding depends on curiosity, dissatisfaction with status quo
- Problem framing depends on knowledge of subject matter, familiarity with problem types
- Inert knowledge due to learning isolated facts under limited conditions
- Studying worked examples is an effective solution strategy

- Solve simpler version of problem first; then transfer process to harder problem
- Break complex problems into manageable parts
- Work backward when goal is clear but beginning state is not
- Analogous problems must be very similar to target problem
- Evaluate solutions to well-structured problems by estimating or checking

SUGGESTIONS FOR TEACHING IN YOUR CLASSROOM

- Comprehension of subject matter critical to problem solving

TRANSFER OF LEARNING

- Early view of transfer based on degree of similarity between two tasks
- Positive transfer: previous learning makes later learning easier
- Negative transfer: previous learning interferes with later learning
- Specific transfer due to specific similarities between two tasks
- General transfer due to use of same cognitive strategies
- Low-road transfer: previously learned skill automatically applied to similar current task
- High-road transfer: formulate rule from one task and apply to related task
- Low-road and high-road transfer produced by varied practice at applying skills, rules, memory retrieval cues

When you begin to teach, you may devote a substantial amount of class time to having students learn information discovered by others. But the acquisition of a storehouse of facts, concepts, and principles is only part of what constitutes an appropriate education. Students must also learn how to *find, evaluate,* and *use* what they need to know to accomplish whatever goals they set for themselves. In other words, students need to learn how to be effective problem solvers. One justification for teaching problem-solving skills in *addition* to ensuring mastery of factual information is that life in technologically oriented countries is marked by speedy change. New products, services, and social conventions are rapidly introduced and integrated into our lifestyles. Microcomputers, videocassette recorders, microwave ovens, anticancer drugs, and in vitro fertilization, to name just a few examples, are relatively recent innovations that significantly affect the lives of many people.

But change, particularly rapid change, can be a mixed blessing. On the one hand, new products and services such as those just mentioned can make life more convenient, efficient, and enjoyable. On the other hand, they can make life more complicated and problematic. Factory automation, for example, promises increased efficiency and productivity (which contribute to our standard of living), but it also threatens the job security of thousands of workers. Advances in medical care promise healthier and longer lives, but they introduce a host of moral, ethical, legal, and economic problems.

The educational implication that flows from these observations is clear: if we are to benefit from our ability to produce rapid and sometimes dramatic change, our schools need to invest more time, money, and effort in teaching students how to be effective problem solvers. As Lauren Resnick, a past president of the American Educational Research Association, argues:

> We need to identify and closely examine the aspects of education that are most likely to produce ability to adapt in the face of transitions and breakdowns. Rather than training people for particular jobs—a task better left to revised forms of on-the-job training—school should focus its efforts on preparing people to be good *adaptive learners*, so that they can perform effectively when situations are unpredictable and task demands change. (1987, p. 18)

Resnick's argument, which echoes many others, is not without some justification. According to estimates made by the Carnegie Foundation, big business spends up to $100 billion a year on corporate classrooms that try to develop the thinking skills corporate management believes the schools have failed to teach (Ruggiero, 1988).

Good problem solvers share two general characteristics: a well-organized, meaningful fund of knowledge and a systematic set of problem-solving skills. Historically, cognitive learning theories have been particularly useful sources of ideas for imparting both. In this chapter, then, we will examine the issue of meaningful learning from three cognitive perspectives: that of Jerome Bruner, that of David Ausubel, and that of constructivism, a contemporary view that is consistent with many of the ideas of Bruner and Ausubel. We will then go on to describe the nature of the problem-solving process and what you can do to help your students become better problem solvers. We will conclude by describing the circumstances under which learned capabilities are applied to new tasks, a process known as transfer of learning.

The Nature of Meaningful Learning

For as long as there have been schools, educators have wrestled with the questions "What should students learn?" and "How should they learn it?" The debates that have occurred both in the past and at present over these two questions are usually not framed in either/or terms. Most people agree that learning should in some degree encompass problem-solving skills, creativity, basic intellectual skills (such as reading, writing, and computation), and knowledge of basic subject matter (such as history, geography, and science). Many people also agree that students should pursue their own natural interests and self-discovery of facts and problem-solving procedures as well as memorize a predetermined body of knowledge. Whatever differences exist among theorists are a matter of emphasis. The emphasis favored by psychologist Jerome Bruner is twofold: students should understand the structure of a body of knowledge rather than memorize names, dates, places, rules, formulas, and so on as isolated fragments; and they should learn how to discover what they need to know.

BRUNER: THE IMPORTANCE OF STRUCTURE AND DISCOVERY

Bruner's interest in meaningful learning and the discovery approach began with his studies on perception (1951) and thinking (Bruner, Goodnow, & Austin, 1956). A subsequent book, *The Process of Education* (1960), became

The essence of the approach to teaching and learning advocated by Bruner is that meaningful learning occurs when students are permitted to make their own discoveries.

a classic statement on education; when it was published, it triggered an interest in school learning in general, which Bruner discussed further in *Toward a Theory of Instruction* (1966) and *The Relevance of Education* (1971).

Bruner: students should learn the structure of a field of study

Structure One of the major points emphasized in *The Process of Education* is that teachers should assist students in grasping the structure of a field of study. Understanding the **structure** of a subject means understanding its basic or fundamental ideas and how they relate to one another. Ideas that are truly fundamental share a number of characteristics: they can be simply represented as a diagram, picture, verbal statement, or formula (as in Albert Einstein's formula for relativity, $E = mc^2$); they can be represented in more than one sensory modality; and they are applicable to a wide range of new problems.

The operant conditioning principle of reinforcement is an example of a fundamental idea. It is simple to understand and to state, it can be expressed as a simple verbal proposition or illustrated on film, and it helps explain the learning of habits, verbal skills, attitudes, motor skills, and behavior in home, work, play, and school settings. Good versus evil is another fundamental idea that appears repeatedly in varied forms in religion, literature, art, and philosophy. Bruner suggests that when students are helped to grasp the structure of a field of study, they are more likely to remember what they learn, comprehend principles that can be applied in a variety of situations, and be prepared for mastering more complex knowledge. As we will see a bit later in this chapter, an understanding of structure is critical to effective problem solving and transfer of learning.

Discovery Learning Another point stressed by Bruner is that too much school learning takes the form of step-by-step study of verbal or numerical statements or formulas that students can reproduce on cue but are unable to use outside the classroom. When students are presented with such highly structured materials as linear computer-assisted instruction programs, Bruner argues, they become too dependent on other people for guidance and approval. Furthermore, they are likely to think of learning as something done only to earn a reward.

Instead of using techniques that feature preselected and prearranged materials, teachers should, according to Bruner, confront children with problems and help them seek solutions either on their own or in group discussion. True learning, says Bruner, involves "figuring out how to use what you already know in order to go beyond what you already think" (1983, p. 183). Like Jean Piaget, Bruner argues that the conceptions that children arrive at on their own are usually more meaningful than those proposed by others and that students do not need to be rewarded when they seek to make sense of things that puzzle them. Bruner maintains, in addition, that when children are given a substantial amount of practice in finding their own solutions to problems, they not only develop problem-solving skills but also acquire confidence in their own learning abilities as well as a propensity to function later in life as problem solvers. They learn *how* to learn *as* they learn.

This approach to education is sometimes called **discovery learning** (or *discovery teaching* if you prefer to look at it from the instructor's point of view). Like the idea mentioned earlier that any subject can be taught to any child, Bruner's position on discovery learning is often misunderstood. He does not suggest that students should discover every fact or principle or formula they may need to know. Discovery is simply too inefficient a process to be used that widely, and learning from others can be as meaningful as personal discovery. Rather, Bruner argues that certain types of outcomes—understanding the ways in which ideas connect with one another, the possibility of solving problems on our own, and how what we already know is relevant to what we are trying to learn—are the essence of education and can best be achieved through personal discovery.

Discover how ideas relate to each other and to existing knowledge

As an example of this discovery approach, Bruner describes an incident in which a student is asked to explain the purpose of a compass (the instrument used to draw perfect circles). When the student refers to it as a steadying tool, the other children in the class quickly think of other devices that serve the same purpose, such as a camera tripod or a cane. Another example is Bruner's approach to teaching geography in the elementary grades. Instead of having a group of fifth graders memorize a set of geography facts, he gave them blank outline maps that showed the location of rivers, lakes, mountains, valleys, plains, and so on. Their task was to figure out where the major cities, railways, and highways might be located. The students were not permitted to consult books or other maps; they had to figure out locations on their own by drawing on their prior knowledge and reasoning ability.

Evaluations of the Discovery Approach Discovery methods have been evaluated most often in the area of science education. Programs like *Elementary Science Study, Science—A Process Approach,* and *Science Curriculum*

The essence of Ausubel's approach to teaching and learning is that meaningful learning occurs when information is organized and presented in such a way that it relates easily to the student's existing knowledge base, and when a student adopts a meaningful learning set.

Improvement Study stress hands-on activities in which students must use reasoning strategies to solve various problems. Since students work in small groups, these activities provide numerous opportunities for discussion and argument. Research at the elementary, middle, and high school levels has produced mostly positive findings (see, for example, Bredderman, 1982; Glasson, 1989). On average, students in activity-based science programs scored at the 70th percentile on tests of science processes, whereas students in traditional science classes scored at the 50th percentile. Low-achieving students gained the most from activity-based programs. They outscored the typical student in the comparison class on process tests by 34 percentile ranks (Bredderman, 1982).

AUSUBEL: THE IMPORTANCE OF MEANINGFUL RECEPTION LEARNING

Like Jerome Bruner, David Ausubel stresses the importance of linking new information to existing knowledge schemes as a requirement for meaningful learning. In fact, on the flyleaf of *Educational Psychology: A Cognitive View* (Ausubel, Novak, & Hanesian, 1978), Ausubel states, "If I had to reduce all of educational psychology to just one principle, I would say this: the most important single factor influencing learning is what the learner already knows. Ascertain this and teach him accordingly."

But while Bruner emphasizes the importance of discovery in meaningful learning, Ausubel emphasizes the importance of good-quality expository teaching. According to Ausubel, good-quality expository teaching involves presenting to the learner what is to be learned in more or less final form. In other words, the information (in a lecture or reading passage, for example) should be organized and stated in such a way that it can be easily related to students' existing knowledge schemes. Most of the behavioral learning techniques described in Chapter 8 are examples of good expository teaching. In programmed instruction or computer-assisted instruction, for instance, the material to be learned is organized and presented to the learner in a predetermined step-by-step fashion that allows for easy assimilation into existing knowledge schemes.

This ease of assimilation is the goal of Ausubel's expository teaching, and he calls this goal **meaningful reception learning** (that is, the integration of new ideas into existing knowledge schemes). Not all reception learning is meaningful, however. Rote, or nonmeaningful, learning occurs when students are presented with a mass of information for which few relationships are provided. In the study of history, for example, students often memorize the dates of certain events (such as the American Civil War), what happened during those events (such as battles between opposing armies, for example), and the roles of major figures (such as Ulysses S. Grant and Robert E. Lee). Ausubel maintains that while such material has meaningful components, it will not be learned as a meaningful whole so long as it remains unconnected to related knowledge schemes that the student already possesses. Hence, the components are memorized in more or less verbatim fashion and tend to be quickly forgotten. In contrast, a reading passage or lecture that is designed to produce meaningful reception learning would explain how these events were related to political, social, and economic factors as well as to something students may already know (such as the circumstances surrounding a different civil war or a disagreement among family members).

Meaningful reception learning: integrate new ideas into existing knowledge schemes

When relationships are ignored, reception learning can be nonmeaningful

Ausubel notes that, contrary to arguments offered by some theorists, reception learning is not invariably rote learning and discovery learning is not necessarily meaningful. It is possible—and definitely desirable—for students working through a program or studying a chapter in a text to search for meaning. In some forms of discovery learning, however, particularly where students are given a series of similar problems to solve in quick succession, they may unthinkingly apply a formula as they search for solutions.

Factors in Meaningful Reception Learning Whether a student engages in meaningful rather than rote learning, Ausubel suggests, is a function of two factors: the nature of the learning task and the learner's intention, or learning set. A poorly written program *or* repetitive discovery projects may virtually force a student to resort to rote memorization or unthinking application of a formula. And many students may use a rote memorization approach to learn logically organized programs or to solve excellent discovery problems simply because they believe that memorization is the only way to learn.

Meaningful learning depends on nature of the task, learner's set

To understand why students adopt a rote or meaningful learning set, you will need to be aware of what they already know about a topic. This argument of Ausubel is similar to the information-processing principle that any individual's perception of a stimulus will be a function of background experiences. It is also similar to Piaget's observation that every child's cognitive structure is unique. All of these views emphasize that teachers should take into account a particular learner's thinking processes at a particular time and in a particular situation.

Advance organizer helps relate new ideas to existing schemes

Advance Organizers To help students adopt a meaningful, rather than a rote, learning set, Ausubel recommends that teachers use **advance organizers.** As the name suggests, advance organizers are introductory materials that provide an organizing structure to help students relate new information to existing knowledge schemes. Because no two students are likely to have identical cognitive structures, advance organizers need to be more abstract, more general, and more inclusive than the material to be learned. Advance organizers usually are relatively brief passages written in familiar terms, although schematic diagrams and illustrations can also be used. Studies of advance organizers show that they have their strongest positive effects on measures of comprehension and problem solving rather than on measures of retention (Mayer, 1979).

Potential Limitations Every theory has its potential limitations, and Ausubel's is no exception. The main weakness of meaningful reception learning is that the learner is largely responsible for establishing a meaningful learning set. Thus, it is possible for students to approach a task in a manner that they believe will produce genuine understanding when in fact all they will attain is a vague and superficial level of understanding. Students need to recognize those occasions when they do not understand the structure of a subject and be willing to do something about it. Students who have been trained to think strategically, as described in Chapter 8, are least likely to mistake superficial or rote learning for meaningful learning.

Summary Comparison with Bruner Both Bruner and Ausubel agree that schools should promote meaningful learning. Bruner believes there is a legitimate place for good-quality texts and lectures, just as Ausubel sees value in learning through discovery. The major difference between them and their advocates centers on how much in-school time students should devote to acquiring information created by others versus how much time they should devote to gaining experience solving problems. Bruner argues that children who gain considerable experience solving problems in school will be better equipped to solve problems outside of the classroom. And Ausubel argues (along with B. F. Skinner) that teachers are better off spending class time presenting subject matter as efficiently as possible. If problem-solving skills are deemed important, they should be taught systematically.

A CONSTRUCTIVIST VIEW OF MEANINGFUL LEARNING

Many of Bruner's and Ausubel's ideas about the discovery approach and meaningful learning, as well as Piaget's ideas about cognitive development, can be found in a contemporary view of learning that we first mentioned in Chapter 1—**constructivism.** To understand the nature of constructivism, consider first the opposite perspective, a view of learning that might be called *objectivism.* The objectivist view basically holds that all knowledge exists outside and independently of people, that some people (experts and teachers, for example) possess knowledge that others (novices and students, for example) do not, and that knowledge can be transferred from one person to another with such fidelity that the student comes to know what the teacher knows (Bednar, Cunningham, Duffy, & Terry, 1991).

The constructivist view of learning holds that meaningful learning occurs when students have to use previously learned knowledge and skill to solve realistic problems in a realistic context.

Facets of Constructivism The constructivist view has several facets. The first, and perhaps most basic, is that meaningful learning is the active creation of knowledge structures (for example, concepts, rules, hypotheses, associations) from personal experience. In other words, each learner builds a personal view of the world by using existing knowledge, interests, attitudes, goals, and the like to select and interpret currently available information. As Rochel Gelman (1994) points out, this assumption highlights the importance of what educational psychologists call entering behavior—the previously learned knowledge and skill that students bring to the classroom.

Depending on the particular characteristics that are active in students when teachers present a lesson, students may ignore the information, attend to one or more parts of it, or add other information from their own experiences. Gelman vividly demonstrated this by asking fourth, fifth, and seventh graders to explain why there are two numbers in a fraction. Despite the fact that these students had been taught in the primary grades what the teachers deemed to be necessary prerequisite knowledge, many of them provided unsatisfactory answers, such as "Because if there weren't two numbers then you wouldn't have a fraction" and "The top one explains how many of the bottom ones there are." As Ausubel, Novak, & Hanesian (1978) point out, if we do not try to get some sense of what students are bringing to a learning task, we may not be pleased with the understanding of it that they construct.

A second facet is that the essence of one person's knowledge can never be *totally* transferred to another person because knowledge is the result of a personal interpretation of experience that is influenced by such factors as the learner's age, gender, race, ethnic background, and knowledge base. When knowledge is transferred from one person to another, some aspects of it are invariably "lost in translation." The area of musical performance provides an apt illustration of this aspect of constructivism. Although a piano teacher

Constructivist view: meaningful learning due to personal interpretation of ideas, experiences can tell a student volumes about how and why a piece should be performed in a particular way, the teacher cannot tell the student *everything*. The interpretation of a composition is constructed from such factors as the performer's knowledge of the composer's personality and motives, the nature of the instrument or instruments for which the composition was written, and the nature of the music itself. Since performers assign different meanings to such knowledge, different (yet equally valid) interpretations of the same composition result. Think, for example, of the many different ways in which you have heard "The Star-Spangled Banner" sung. Although listeners may prefer one version over another, there is no one correct way to sing this song.

The third facet follows directly from the second. Does constructivism necessarily mean that everyone walks around with a personal, idiosyncratic view of the world and that consensus is impossible? A few minutes of reflection should tell you that the answer is no. And if you recall what you read in Chapter 4, you will recognize that the cultures and societies to which people belong channel and place limits on the views people have of the world around them. Consequently, individuals make observations, test hypotheses, and draw conclusions about a variety of events that are largely consistent with one another (Cognition and Technology Group at Vanderbilt, 1991). Of course, there are many instances when people cannot reconcile their views and so "agree to disagree." For example, the world recently observed the fiftieth anniversary of the atomic bombing of Hiroshima. Although everyone agreed on the basic facts of the event, there was sharp disagreement about why the bomb was dropped, whether it was necessary, and what exactly the anniversary should be observing. In matters such as these truth is where it always is for the constructivist—in the mind of the beholder.

Construction of ideas comes largely from discussion and debate

The fourth and final facet of constructivism that we will discuss has to do with the formation and changing of knowledge structures. Additions to, deletions from, or modifications of these interpretations come mainly from the sharing of multiple perspectives. Systematic, open-minded discussions and debates are instrumental in helping individuals create personal views (Bednar et al., 1991; Cunningham, 1991). As we have seen in previous chapters, scholars form and reform their positions on aspects of theory or research as a result of years of discussion and debate with colleagues. The debate between the Piagetians and the Vygotskians in Chapter 2 is a good example of this facet. Accordingly, and as Bruner argued some thirty years ago, students need to be provided with the conditions that will allow them to construct their own interpretation of key information and experiences.

Conditions That Foster Constructivism The conditions that constructivists typically mention include a cognitive apprenticeship between student and teacher, a use of realistic problems and conditions, and an emphasis on multiple perspectives (Bednar et al., 1991). The first condition, that of a cognitive apprenticeship, was illustrated in Chapter 9 when we described the reciprocal teaching program of Annemarie Palincsar and Ann Brown (1984). Its main feature is that the teacher models a cognitive process that students are to learn and then gradually turns responsibility for executing the process over to students as they become more skilled.

The second condition is that students be given learning tasks set in realistic contexts. A realistic context is one in which students must solve a meaningful problem by using a variety of skills and information. The example we provided earlier of Bruner requiring fifth graders to specify the location of cities, railways, and highways by thinking as a geographer would is an example of this condition. Bruner's constructivist approach to teaching is nicely summarized in the following statement:

> To instruct someone in [a] discipline is not a matter of getting him to commit results to mind. Rather, it is to teach him to participate in the process that makes possible the establishment of knowledge. We teach a subject not to produce little living libraries on the subject, but rather to get a student to think mathematically for himself, to consider matters as an historian does, to take part in the process of knowledge-getting. Knowing is a process, not a product. (1966, p. 72)

The third condition fostering constructivism is that students should view ideas and problems from multiple perspectives. The rationale for this condition is twofold: most of life's problems are multifaceted, and the knowledge base of experts is a network of interrelated ideas. The problem of becoming an effective teacher is a good example of the need for multiple perspectives. As we mentioned in Chapter 1, being an effective teacher requires the mastery of many skills and disciplines so that classroom problems (such as why a particular student does not perform up to expectations) can be analyzed and attacked from several perspectives. We have tried to help you develop an integrated knowledge base by constantly making cross-references throughout the text. For example, the topic of learning strategies is discussed primarily in Chapter 9 but is also mentioned in Chapters 7 and 12 because of its relationship to instructional objectives and the demands of classroom tests, respectively.

Constructivism aided by cognitive apprenticeship, realistic tasks, multiple perspectives

An Example of Constructivist Teaching A group of researchers from Vanderbilt University, called the Cognition and Technology Group at Vanderbilt (CTGV), devised an interesting set of instructional materials that incorporate the constructivist principles just mentioned. Called *The Adventures of Jasper Woodbury,* it is an experimental video disk–based series designed to promote problem solving, reasoning, and effective communication among middle school students. Each story in the series is a fifteen- to twenty-minute adventure that involves Jasper Woodbury and other characters. At the end of each story the characters are faced with a problem that students must solve before they are allowed to see how the characters in the video solved the problem.

The adventures are arranged in pairs so that the experimenters can assess how well students use the problem-solving skills they learned in the first video. The first pair concerns planning a trip, the second pair involves using statistics to create a business plan, and the third pair involves meaningful uses of geometry. In the course of solving the problem posed in the video, students become involved in activities such as generating subgoals, identifying relevant information, cooperating with others, discussing the advantages and disadvantages of possible solutions, and comparing perspectives (CTGV, 1992a, 1992b).

Despite the complexity of these problems and the fact that Jasper students received less direct basic math instruction than control students, they performed quite well. On tests of such basic math concepts as units of time, units of distance, area, decimals, and fractions, both groups improved at the same rate. But Jasper students scored significantly higher than the control students on word problems, tests of planning, and attitudes towards math (CTGV, 1992a, 1992b).

While you may not have access to a program as technologically advanced as the Jasper series, there are other techniques you can use to foster meaningful learning within a constructivist framework. One that is particularly well suited to developing, comparing, and understanding different points of view is the classroom discussion (Rabow, Charness, Kipperman, & Radcliffe-Vasile, 1994; Schiever, 1991). Because this format also allows students to deal with realistic problems and to exercise cognitive skills taught by the teacher, it is an excellent general-purpose method for helping students construct (or discover, depending on your preference) a meaningful knowledge base. Now let's turn our attention to specific Suggestions for Teaching that describe ways to emphasize meaningful learning in your classroom.

Suggestions for Teaching in Your Classroom

Using a Discovery/Constructivist Approach to Meaningful Learning

1. Arrange the learning situation so that students are exposed to different perspectives on a problem or an issue.

a. Ask students to discuss familiar topics or those that are matters of opinion.

b. Provide necessary background information by asking all students to read all or part of a book, take notes on a lecture, or view a film.

2. Structure discussions by posing a specific question; by presenting a provocative, topic-related issue; or by asking students to choose topics or subtopics.

a. In some cases encourage students to arrive at conclusions already reached by others.

b. In other cases present a controversial topic for which there is no single answer.

3. If time is limited and if only one topic is to be covered, ask students to form a circle and have an all-class discussion.

a. Ask questions that stimulate students to apply, analyze, synthesize, and evaluate.

b. Allow sufficient time for initial responses, and then probe for further information (if appropriate).

c. When selecting students to recite, use techniques likely to sustain steady but nonthreatening attention. At the same time, guard against the temptation to call primarily on bright, articulate, assertive students.

4. If abundant time is available and if a controversial subdivided topic is to be discussed, divide the class into groups of five or so, and arrange for all members in each group to have eye contact with every other group member.

1. **Arrange the learning situation so that students are exposed to different perspectives on a problem or an issue.**

This is the crux of the discovery approach and the constructivist view of learning. The basic idea is to *arrange* the elements of a learning task and *guide* student actions so that students discover, or construct, a personally meaningful conception of a problem or issue. In some cases you may present a topic that is a matter of opinion or that all students are sure to know something about. In other cases you might structure the discussion by exposing all participants to the same background information.

Journal Entry
Ways to Arrange for Discovery to Take Place

a. **Ask students to discuss familiar topics or those that are matters of opinion.**

EXAMPLES

"What are some of the techniques that advertising agencies use in television commercials to persuade us to buy certain products?"

"What do you think is the best book you ever read, and why do you think so?"

b. **Provide necessary background information by asking all students to read all or part of a book, take notes on a lecture, or view a film.**

EXAMPLES

After the class has read *Great Expectations,* ask, "What do you think Dickens was trying to convey when he wrote this novel? Was he just trying to tell a good story, or was he also trying to get us to think about certain kinds of relationships between people?"

"After I explain some of the principles of electrical currents, I'm going to ask you to suggest rules for connecting batteries in series and in parallel. Then, we'll see how well your rules work."

2. **Structure discussions by posing a specific question; by presenting a provocative, topic-related issue; or by asking students to choose topics or subtopics.**

It is important to structure a discovery session by giving students something reasonably specific to discuss; otherwise, they may simply engage in a disorganized and desultory bull session. You might supply direction in the following ways.

a. **In some cases encourage students to arrive at conclusions already reached by others.**

Thousands of books provide detailed answers to such questions as "What is human about human beings? How did they get that way? How can they be made more so?" But constructivists believe that answers mean more when they are constructed by the individual, not supplied ready-made by others. As you look over lesson plans, therefore, you might try to select some questions for students to answer by engaging in discussion rather than by reading or listening to what others have already discovered. In searching for such topics, you might take into account the techniques described by Bruner. Here is a list of those techniques, together with an example of each one. In your Reflective Journal you might describe similar applications that you could use when you begin to teach. Keep in mind that students often acquire a deeper understanding of ideas and issues when they have had appropriate previous experience.

- *Emphasize contrast.* In an elementary school social studies unit on cultural diversity, say, "When you watch this film on Mexico, look for customs and ways of living that differ from ours. Then we'll talk about what these differences are and why they may have developed."
- *Stimulate informed guessing.* In a middle school unit on natural science, you might say, "Suppose we wanted to figure out some kind of system to classify trees so that we could later find information about particular types. What would be the best way to do it?" After students have developed a classification scheme, show them schemes developed by specialists.
- *Encourage participation.* In a high school political science class, illustrate the jury system by staging a mock trial. (Note that the use of a simulation satisfies the constructivist criterion of realistic tasks and contexts.)
- *Stimulate awareness.* In a high school English class, ask the students to discuss how the author developed the plot.

b. **In other cases present a controversial topic for which there is no single answer.**

Discussions might center on provocative issues about which there are differences of opinion. One caution here is to avoid topics (such as premarital sex or legalized abortion) that parents may not want discussed in school, either because they are convinced it is their prerogative to discuss them with their children or because they feel that students may be pressured to endorse your opinion because you assign grades. You should not avoid controversy, but neither should you go out of your way to agitate students and their parents.

Another caution is to avoid selecting issues that provoke more than they instruct. You may be tempted to present a highly controversial topic and then congratulate yourself at the end of the period if most students engaged in heated discussion. But if they simply argued enthusiastically about something that had nothing to do with the subject you are assigned to teach, you cannot honestly claim to have arranged an instructive exchange of ideas. A final caution relates to a characteristic of formal thought described in Chapter 2: there may be a tendency for secondary school students to engage in unrestrained theorizing when they first experience the thrill of being able to deal with hypotheses and possibilities. Thus, you may have to remind some students to take into account realities when they discuss controversial issues involving tangled background circumstances or conflicts of interest.

EXAMPLES

In a middle school science class, ask students to list arguments for and against attempting to alter the genetic code of human beings.

In a high school political science class, ask students to list arguments for and against democratic forms of government.

3. If time is limited and if only one topic is to be covered, ask students to form a circle and have an all-class discussion.

You may sometimes wish to have the entire class discuss a topic. Such discussions are most likely to be successful if all students have eye contact with each other. The simplest way to achieve this is to ask all students to form a circle. Next, invite responses to the question you have posed. As students make remarks, serve more as a moderator than as a leader. Try to keep the discussion on the topic, but avoid directing it toward a specific predetermined end result. If one or more students tend to dominate the discussion, say something like "Kim and Carlos have given us their ideas. Now I'd like to hear from the rest of you." If an aggressive student attacks or belittles something said by a classmate, say something like "It's good to *believe* in a point of view, but let's be friendly as we listen to other opinions. This is supposed to be a discussion, not an argument or a debate."

Journal Entry
Ways to Supervise Discussion Sessions

Factors that lead to successful or unsuccessful discussions are often idiosyncratic, but there are certain procedures you might follow to increase the likelihood of success.

a. Ask questions that stimulate students to apply, analyze, synthesize, and evaluate.

When you first structure a discussion session, but also when it is under way, take care to ask questions likely to elicit different points of view. If you ask students to supply information (for example, "When did Charles Dickens write *Great Expectations*?"), the first correct response will lead to closure. You may end up asking a series of questions leading to brief answers—the equivalent of a program or a fill-in exam. Meredith Gall (1970) reviewed dozens of studies of classroom recitation sessions and found consistent evidence that up to 80 percent of all questions asked by teachers stressed facts and knowledge. When one intends to encourage students to construct personally meaningful interpretations of the issues or to develop skills as deductive thinkers, it is preferable to ask questions likely to tap higher levels of thinking.

EXAMPLES

"You just learned how to calculate the area of a circle. Think of as many different ways as you can of how you might be able to use that bit of knowledge if you were a do-it-yourself home owner." (Application)

"Last month we read a novel by Dickens; this month we read a play by Shakespeare. What are some similarities in the way each author developed the plot of his story?" (Synthesis)

b. Allow sufficient time for initial responses, and then probe for further information (if appropriate).

Current research finds that many teachers fail to allow enough time for students to respond to questions. Quite often instructors wait only one second before repeating the question, calling on another student, or answering the question themselves. When teachers wait at least three seconds after asking a question, students are more likely to participate; their responses increase in frequency, length, and complexity; and their achievement improves. There are changes in teacher behavior as well. As a function of waiting longer, teachers ask more complex questions and have higher expectations for the quality of students' responses (Ormrod, 1995).

One possible explanation for improved student recitation when teachers wait longer for a response is that reflective thinkers have an opportunity to figure out what they want to say. But even impulsive thinkers probably welcome a few more seconds of thinking time. It seems logical to expect that snap answers will be more superficial than answers supplied after even a few seconds of reflection.

In addition to giving students ample time to make an initial response, you should encourage them to pursue an idea. If it seems appropriate, probe for further information or clarification of a point by asking students who give brief or incomplete answers to explain how or why they arrived at a conclusion or to supply additional comments.

EXAMPLE

"Well, Keesha, I'm sure a gardener might sometimes need to figure the area of a circle, but can you give a more specific example? If you can't think of one right away, put up your hand as soon as you can describe a specific situation where it would help to know the area of a circular patch of lawn or soil."

c. **When selecting students to recite, use techniques likely to sustain steady but nonthreatening attention. At the same time, guard against the temptation to call primarily on bright, articulate, assertive students.**

The way you moderate student contributions may not only determine how successful the discussion will be; it may also influence how students feel about themselves and each other. Jacob Kounin (1970) points out that when a teacher first names a student and then asks a question, the rest of the class may tend to turn its attention to other things. The same tendency to "tune out" may occur if a teacher follows a set pattern of calling on students (for example, by going around a circle). To keep all the students on their toes, therefore, you might ask questions first and then, in an unpredictable sequence, call on those who volunteer to recite, frequently switching from one part of the room to another. As you look around the room before selecting a volunteer, remember Skinner's criticism that a few students may make all the discoveries. Guard against the temptation to call primarily on students you expect to give good or provocative answers. Repeatedly ignoring students who may be a bit inarticulate or unimaginative may cause them and their classmates to conclude that you think they are incompetent. These students may then lose interest in and totally ignore what is taking place.

4. **If abundant time is available and if a controversial or subdivided topic is to be discussed, divide the class into groups of five or so, and arrange for all members in each group to have eye contact with every other group member.**

When students are invited to engage in small-group discussions, it may be necessary for the teacher to occasionally remind some groups to explore the assigned topic rather than engage in social chitchat.

A major limitation of any kind of discussion is that only one person can talk at a time. You can reduce this difficulty by dividing the class into smaller groups before asking them to exchange ideas. A group of about five seems to work best. If only two or three students are interacting with each other, the exchange of ideas may be limited. If there are more than five, not all members will be able to contribute at frequent intervals.

One way to form groups, particularly if students have suggested subtopics, is to ask them to list in order their first three subject preferences. (Mention at the start that it is unlikely that all the students in the class will get their first choice.) Then, you can divide by referring to the lists. One advantage of this technique is that students embark on a discovery session with the feeling that they have chosen to do so. Another advantage is that you can arrange group membership to a certain extent since students won't know how many of their classmates listed a particular topic as first choice. You might break up potentially disruptive pairings and also spread around talkative, creative, and thoughtful students.

> ***Journal Entry***
> Techniques for Arranging Small-Group Discussions

Another way to divide the class, particularly if all groups are to discuss the same topic, is to ask all students in a row to form a group. Or have the class count off from one to five. After all students have counted off, ask all "ones" to move to one part of the room, "twos" to another part, and so on. You can manage to achieve different assortments of students by having the class count off in different ways each time.

The Nature of Problem Solving

As with most of the topics covered in this book, an extensive amount of theorizing and research on problem solving has been conducted over the years. We will focus our discussion on the types of problems that students are typically required to deal with, the cognitive processes that play a central role in problem solving, and various approaches to teaching problem solving in the classroom.

Let's begin by asking what we mean by the terms *problem* and *problem solving*. Most, if not all, psychologists would agree that "a problem is said to exist when one has a goal and has not yet identified a means for reaching that goal"(Gagné, Yekovich, & Yekovich, 1993, p. 211). **Problem solving,** then, is the identification and application of knowledge and skills that result in goal attainment. Although this definition encompasses a wide range of problem types, we will focus on three types that students frequently encounter both in school and out.

THREE COMMON TYPES OF PROBLEMS

In the first category are the well-structured problems of mathematics and science—the type of problems that students from kindergarten through middle school are typically required to solve. **Well-structured problems** are clearly formulated, can be solved by recall and application of a specific procedure (called an *algorithm*), and result in a solution that can be evaluated against a well-known, agreed-on standard (Hamilton & Ghatala, 1994). Examples of well-structured problems are

Well-structured problems: clearly stated, known solution procedures, known evaluation standards

$5 + 8 =$ ______

$732 - 485 =$______

$8 + 3x = 40 - 5x$

In the second category are the ill-structured problems often encountered in everyday life and in disciplines such as economics or psychology. **Ill-structured problems** are more complex, provide few cues pointing to solution procedures, and have less definite criteria for determining when the problem has been solved (Hamilton & Ghatala, 1994). Examples of ill-structured problems are how to identify and reward good teachers, how to improve access to public buildings and facilities for persons with physical handicaps, and how to increase voter turnout for primary and general elections.

Ill-structured problems: vaguely stated, unclear solution procedures, vague evaluation standards

The third category includes problems that are also ill-structured but differ from the examples just mentioned in two respects. First, these problems tend to divide people into opposing camps because of the emotions they arouse. Second, the primary goal, at least initially, is not to determine a course of action but to identify the most reasonable position. These problems are often referred to as **issues** (Ruggiero, 1988). Examples of issues are capital punishment, gun control, and nondenominational prayer in classrooms. Beginning with the freshman year in high school, students usually receive more opportunities to deal with ill-structured problems and issues.

Issues: ill-structured problems that arouse strong feelings

HELPING STUDENTS BECOME GOOD PROBLEM SOLVERS

Despite the differences that exist among well-structured problems, ill-structured problems, and issues, recent theory and research suggest that good problem solvers employ the same general approach when solving one or another of these problem types (see, for example, Bransford & Stein, 1993; Gagné et al., 1993; Gick, 1986; Krulik & Rudnick, 1993; Nickerson, 1994;

Ruggiero, 1988). When used to solve ill-structured problems or to analyze issues, this approach consists of five steps or processes (although the solution of well-structured problems may call only for the implementation of steps 2, 4, and 5):

1. Realize that a problem exists.
2. Understand the nature of the problem.
3. Compile relevant information.
4. Formulate and carry out a solution.
5. Evaluate the solution.

We will discuss each of these steps in the next few pages, along with some specific techniques that you can use to help your students become good problem solvers.

Step 1: Realize That a Problem Exists Most people assume that if a problem is worth solving, they won't have to seek it out; it will make itself known. Like most assumptions, this one is only partly true. Well-structured problems are often thrust on us by teachers, in the form of in-class exercises or homework, or by supervisors at work. Ill-structured problems and issues, however, often remain hidden from most people. It is a characteristic of good problem solvers that they are more sensitive to the existence of problems than most of their peers (Okagaki & Sternberg, 1990).

The keys to problem recognition, or *problem finding* as it is sometimes called, are curiosity and dissatisfaction. You need to question why a rule, procedure, or product is the way it is or to feel frustrated or irritated because something does not work as well as it might. The organization known as Mothers Against Drunk Driving, for example, was begun by a woman who, because her daughter had been killed in a traffic accident by a drunk driver, was dissatisfied with current, ineffective laws. This organization has been instrumental in getting state legislatures to pass laws against drunk driving that mandate more severe penalties. As another example, John Bransford and Barry Stein (1993) mention a business that, by taking a critical look at its record-keeping procedure, was able to eliminate the generation of 120 tons of paper per year.

Problem finding depends on curiosity, dissatisfaction with status quo

Problem finding does not come readily to most people, possibly because schools emphasize solving well-structured problems and possibly because most people have a natural tendency to assume that things work as well as they can. Like any cognitive process, however, problem recognition can improve with instruction and practice. Students can be sensitized in a number of ways to the absence or flaws and shortcomings of products, procedures, rules, or whatever. We will make some specific suggestions about improving problem recognition and the other problem-solving processes a bit later in Suggestions for Teaching in Your Classroom.

Step 2: Understand the Nature of the Problem The second step in the problem-solving process is perhaps the most critical. The problem solver has to construct an *optimal* representation or understanding of the nature of a problem or issue. The preceding sentence stresses the word *optimal* for two reasons. First, most problems can be expressed in a number of ways. Written problems, for example, can be recast as pictures, equations, graphs, charts, or diagrams. Second, because the way we represent the problem determines the amount and type of solution-relevant information we recall from long-term memory, some representations are better than others. For obvious reasons, problem-solving researchers often refer to this process as **problem representation** or **problem framing.**

Problem framing depends on knowledge of subject matter, familiarity with problem types

To achieve an optimal understanding of a problem, an individual needs two things: a high degree of knowledge of the subject matter (facts, concepts, and principles) on which the problem is based and familiarity with that particular type of problem. This background will allow the person to recognize important elements (words, phrases, and numbers) in the problem statement and patterns of relationships among the problem elements. This recognition, in turn, will activate one or more solution-relevant schemes from long-term memory. It is just this level of knowledge of subject matter and problem types that distinguishes the high-quality problem representations of the expert problem solver from the low-quality representations of the novice. Experts typically represent problems in terms of one or more basic patterns or underlying principles, whereas novices focus on limited or superficial surface features of problems.

To give you a clearer idea of the nature and power of an optimal problem representation, consider the following situation. When novices are given a set of physics problems to solve, they sort them into categories on the basis of some noticeable feature. For example, they group together all problems that involve the use of an inclined plane or all the ones that involve the use of pulleys or all those that involve friction. Then, novices search their memory for previously learned information. The drawback to this approach is that, while two or three problems may involve the use of an inclined plane, their solutions may depend on the application of different laws of physics. Experts, in contrast, draw on their extensive and well-organized knowledge base to represent groups of problems according to a common underlying principle, such as conservation of energy or Newton's third law (Gagné et al., 1993; Gick, 1986).

Inert knowledge due to learning isolated facts under limited conditions

An important aspect of the problem-solving process is the ability to activate relevant schemes (organized collections of facts, concepts, principles, and procedures) from long-term memory when they are needed. The more relevant and powerful the activated scheme is, the more likely it is that an effective problem solution will be achieved. But as many observers of education have pointed out, acquiring this ability is often easier said than done. John Bransford argues that standard educational practices produce knowledge that is *inert.* That is, it can be accessed only under conditions that closely mimic the original learning context (Bransford, Sherwood, Vye, & Rieser, 1986). Richard Feynman, a Nobel Prize–winning physicist, made the same observation in describing how his classmates at the Massachusetts Institute of Technology failed to recognize the application of a previously learned mathematical formula: "They didn't put two and two together. They didn't even know what they 'knew.' I don't know what's the matter with people: they don't learn by understanding; they learn by some other way—by rote, or something. Their knowledge is so fragile!" (1985, p. 36). To overcome this limitation of inert and fragile knowledge, teachers need to present subject matter in a highly organized fashion, and students need to learn more about the various conditions under which their knowledge applies.

Step 3: Compile Relevant Information For well-structured problems that are relatively simple and familiar (such as arithmetic drill problems), this step in the problem-solving process occurs simultaneously with problem representation. In the process of defining a problem, we very quickly and easily recall from long-term memory all the information that is needed to achieve a solution. As problems and issues become more complex, however, we run into two difficulties: the amount of information relevant to the solution becomes too great to keep track of mentally, and there is an increasing chance that we may not possess all the relevant information. As a result, we are forced to compile what we know in the form of lists, tables, pictures, graphs, and diagrams, and so on and to seek additional information from other sources.

The key to using yourself as an information source is the ability to accurately retrieve from long-term memory information that will aid in the solution of the problem. We need to think back over what we have learned in other somewhat similar situations, make a list of some other form of representation of those ideas, and make a judgment as to how helpful that knowledge might be. Techniques for ensuring accurate and reliable recall were discussed in Chapter 9.

In addition to relying on our own knowledge and experience to solve problems, we can draw on the knowledge and experience of friends, colleagues, and experts. According to Vincent Ruggiero, "Investigating other people's views calls for little talking and a lot of careful listening. We do well, in such cases, to ask questions rather than make statements" (1988, p. 39). The main purpose of soliciting the views of others about solutions to problems and positions on issues is to identify the reasons and evidence those people offer in support of their positions. This skill of asking questions and analyzing responses is quite useful in debates and classroom discussions of controversial issues.

Step 4: Formulate and Carry Out a Solution When you feel you understand the nature of a problem or issue and possess sufficient relevant information, you are ready to attempt a solution. The first step is to consider which of several alternative approaches is likely to be most effective. The literature on problem solving mentions quite a few solution strategies. We will discuss five that we think are particularly useful.

Study worked examples. This approach may strike you as so obvious that it hardly merits attention. But it is worth mentioning for two reasons. First, obvious solution strategies are the ones that are most often overlooked. Second, it is a very effective solution strategy. Mary Gick (1986) cites almost a dozen studies in which learners improved their ability to solve a variety of problems by studying similar problems whose solutions had already been worked out. The beneficial effect is thought to be due to the learners' acquisition of a general problem schema.

Studying worked examples is an effective solution strategy

In order to become proficient at carrying out a proposed solution to a problem or evaluating the adequacy of a solution, students need many opportunities to practice these skills.

Solve simpler version of problem first; then transfer process to harder problem

Work on a simpler version of the problem. This is another common and very effective approach. Geometry offers a particularly clear example of working on a simpler problem. If you are having difficulty solving a problem of solid geometry (which involves three dimensions), work out a similar problem in plane geometry (two dimensions), and then apply the solution to the three-dimensional example (Nickerson, 1994; Polya, 1957). Architects and engineers employ this approach when they construct scaled-down models of bridges, buildings, experimental aircraft, and the like. Scientists do the same thing by creating laboratory simulations of real-world phenomena.

Break complex problems into manageable parts

Break the problem into parts. The key to this approach is to make sure you break the problem into manageable parts. Whether you can do this will depend largely on how much subject-matter knowledge you have. The more you know about the domain from which the problem comes, the easier it is to know how to break a problem into logical, easy-to-handle parts.

At least two benefits result from breaking a problem into parts: doing so reduces the amount of information you have to keep in short-term memory to a manageable level, and the method used to solve one part of the problem can often be used to solve another part. Bransford and Stein (1993) use the following example to illustrate how this approach works.

Problem: what day follows the day before yesterday if two days from now will be Sunday?

1. What is today if two days from now will be Sunday? (Friday)
2. If today is Friday, what is the day before yesterday? (Wednesday)
3. What day follows Wednesday? (Thursday)

Work backward when goal is clear but beginning state is not

Work backward. This is a particularly good solution strategy to use whenever the goal is clear but the beginning state is not. Bransford and Stein (1993) offer the following example. Suppose you arranged to meet someone at a restaurant across town at noon. When should you leave your office to be sure of arriving on time? By working backward from your destination and arrival time (it takes about ten minutes to find a parking spot and walk to the restaurant; it takes about thirty minutes to drive to the area where you would park; it takes about five minutes to walk from your office to your car), you would more quickly and easily determine when to leave your office (about 11:15) than if you had worked the problem forward.

Solve an analogous problem. If you are having difficulty solving a current problem, possibly because your knowledge of the subject matter is incomplete, it may be useful to think of a similar problem about a subject in which you are more knowledgeable. Solve the analogous problem, and then use the same method to solve the current problem. In essence, this is a way of making the unfamiliar familiar.

Although solving analogous problems is a very powerful solution strategy, it can be difficult to employ, especially for novices. In our earlier discussion of understanding the problem, we made the point that novices represent problems on the basis of superficial features, whereas experts operate from knowledge of underlying concepts and principles. The same is true of analogies. Novices are more likely than experts to use superficial analogies (Gick, 1986).

A potential way around this problem is to provide students with good analogies. This approach does work, but in a limited way. For students to recognize the usefulness of the analogy, it must mimic the target problem in both structure and surface details. The evidence for this conclusion comes largely from a series of studies by Mary Gick and Keith Holyoak (for example, Gick & Holyoak, 1980, 1983; Holyoak & Koh, 1987).

Analogous problems must be very similar to target problem

In the initial experiments, college students read a story about a general who wanted to capture a fortress. If the general used his entire army, the attack would succeed. However, many of the surrounding villages would be destroyed during the attack because of mines planted along the roads leading to the fortress. This outcome was unacceptable. The general's solution was to divide his army into smaller groups that could slip through the minefields, send each group along a different road, and have them converge on the fortress at the same time.

The students were then given a second story to read that concluded with a problem for them to solve. The second story was about a patient with an inoperable stomach tumor. The patient's doctor could destroy the tumor with a beam of high intensity x-rays, but healthy surrounding tissue would be destroyed in the process. Although a beam of lower intensity would not damage healthy tissue, neither would it destroy the tumor. The problem posed to the students was how to use radiation to destroy the tumor without destroying the healthy tissue at the same time. Only 30 percent of the students realized that just as the general solved his problem by dividing his forces and having them converge on the fortress simultaneously, the doctor could destroy the tumor by using several beams of low-intensity radiation aimed from different directions.

In the later study (Holyoak & Koh, 1987) students first read a story about a physics lab that used an expensive light bulb. The filament, enclosed in a permanently sealed bulb, was broken. It could be repaired with a high-intensity laser beam. This solution was unacceptable, however, because a high-intensity beam would also shatter the glass. The problem was solved by using several lower-intensity beams aimed at the filament. As before, students then read the inoperable-tumor story. Because the details of the light bulb and tumor stories were very similar, the outcome in this case was dramatically different. Almost 70 percent of these students were able to solve the tumor problem. This figure was increased to 75 percent when the subjects were told that the first story could help them solve the problem in the second story.

Step 5: Evaluate the Solution The last step in the problem-solving process is to evaluate the adequacy of the solution. For relatively simple, well-structured problems where the emphasis is on producing a correct response, two levels of evaluation are available to the problem solver. The first is to ask whether, given the problem statement, the answer makes sense. For example, if the problem reads $75 \times 5 = ?$ and the response is 80, a little voice inside the problem solver's head should say that the answer cannot possibly be right. This signal should prompt a reevaluation of the way the problem was represented and the solution procedure that was used (for example, "I misread the times sign as a plus sign and added when I should have multiplied"). The second level of evaluation is to use an alternative algorithm (a fixed procedure used to solve a problem) to check the accuracy of the solution. This is necessary because an error in the carrying out of an algorithm can produce an incorrect response that is "in the ballpark." For example, a common error in multiple-column subtraction problems is to subtract a smaller digit from a larger one regardless of whether the small number is in the minuend (top row) or the subtrahend (bottom row) (Mayer, 1987), as in

Evaluate solutions to well-structured problems by estimating or checking

$$\begin{array}{r} 522 \\ -\underline{418} \\ 116 \end{array}$$

Since this answer is off by only 12 units, it "looks right." The flaw can be discovered, however, by adding the answer to the subtrahend to produce the minuend.

The evaluation of solutions to ill-structured problems is likely to be more complicated and time consuming for at least two reasons. First, the evaluation should occur both before and after the solution is implemented. Although many flaws and omissions can be identified and corrected beforehand, some will slip through. There is much to be learned by observing the effects of our solutions. Second, because these problems are complex, often involving a dozen or more variables, some sort of systematic framework should guide the evaluation. Vincent Ruggiero suggests a four-step procedure (1988, pp. 44–46). The first step is to ask and answer a set of basic questions. Imagine, for example, that you have proposed a classroom incentive system (a token economy, perhaps) to enhance student motivation. You might ask such questions as, How will this program be implemented? By whom? When? Where? With what materials? How will the materials be obtained?

The second step is to identify imperfections and complications. Is this idea, for example, safe, convenient, efficient, economical, and compatible with existing policies and practices? The third step is to anticipate possible negative reactions from other people (such as parents and your school principal). The fourth step is to devise improvements.

The Suggestions for Teaching in Your Classroom section contains guidelines and examples that will help you improve the problem-solving skills of your students.

Suggestions for Teaching in Your Classroom

Teaching Problem-Solving Techniques

1. Teach students how to identify problems.
2. Teach students how to represent problems.
3. Teach students how to compile relevant information.
4. Teach several methods for formulating problem solutions.
5. Teach students the skills of evaluation.

1. Teach students how to identify problems.

Since the notion of finding problems is likely to strike students as an unusual activity, you may want to introduce this skill in gradual steps. One way to start is to have students list different ways in which problems can be identified. Typical responses are to scan newspaper and magazine articles, observe customer and employee behavior in a store, watch traffic patterns in a local area, and interview local residents, including, for instance, teachers, business owners, police, clergy, or government officials. A next step is to have students carry out their suggested activities in order to gain an understanding of the status quo and to find out how people identify problems. They may learn, for example, that a principal periodically has lunch with a teacher in order to learn of conditions that decrease the teacher's effectiveness.

2. Teach students how to represent problems.

The ability to construct a good representation of a problem is based on a command of the subject matter surrounding the problem and familiarity with the particular type of problem. As the work of Jerome Bruner and David Ausubel indicates, students need to acquire a genuine understanding of many of the associations, discriminations, concepts, and rules of a discipline before they can effectively solve problems in that subject-matter area. Too often, students are taught to state principles on cue, but they reveal by further responses that they do not understand what they are saying. The classic illustration of this all too common trap was given by William James in his *Talks to Teachers:*

> A friend of mine, visiting a school, was asked to examine a young class in geography. Glancing at the book, she said: "Suppose you should dig a hole

> in the ground, hundreds of feet deep, how should you find it at the bottom—warmer or colder than on top?" None of the class replying, the teacher said: "I'm sure they know, but I think you don't ask the question quite rightly. Let me try." So, taking the book, she asked: "In what condition is the interior of the globe?" and received the immediate answer from half the class at once: "The interior of the globe is in a condition of igneous fusion." (1899, p. 150)

If these students had genuinely understood concepts and principles regarding the composition of the earth, instead of having simply memorized meaningless phrases, they would have been able to answer the original question.

Comprehension of subject matter critical to problem solving

Different problem types lend themselves to particular forms of representation. Verbal reasoning problems that are based on relationships among categories, for example, can usually be represented by a set of intersecting circles known as a Venn diagram.

EXAMPLE PROBLEM

The government wants to contact all druggists, all gun store owners, and all parents in a town without contacting anyone twice. Based on the following statistics, how many people must be contacted?

Druggists	10
Gun store owners	5
Parents	3,000
Druggists who own gun stores	0
Druggists who are parents	7
Gun store owners who are parents	3

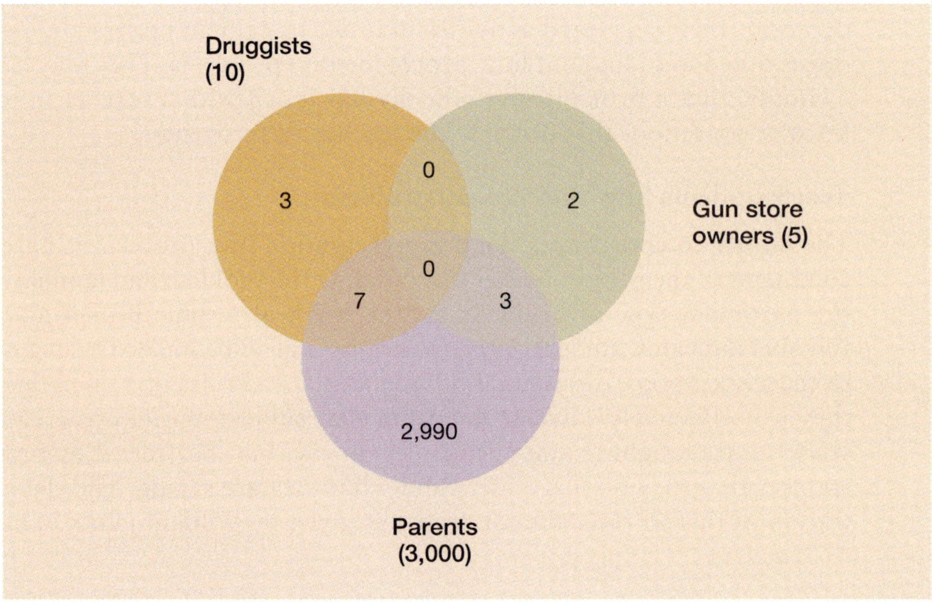

Solution Using Venn Diagram

The total number of people who must be contacted is 2990 + 7 + 3 + 3 + 2 = 3,005 (adapted from Whimbey & Lochhead, 1991, p. 102).[1]

Verbal reasoning problems that describe transactions can take the form of a flow diagram.

EXAMPLE PROBLEM

Sally loaned $7.00 to Betty. But Sally borrowed $15.00 from Estella and $32.00 from Joan. Moreover, Joan owes $3.00 to Estella and $7.00 to Betty. One day the women got together at Betty's house to straighten out their accounts. Which woman left with $18.00 more than she came with?

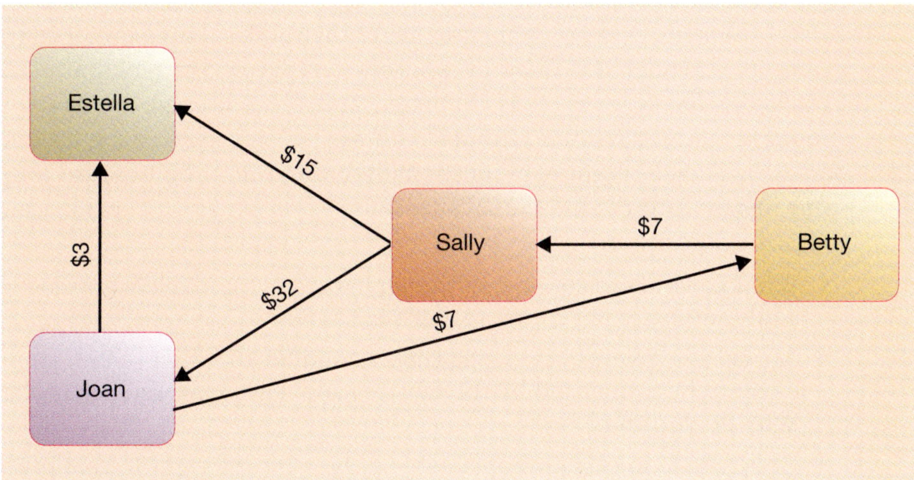

Solution Using Flow Diagram

From the diagram, it is clear that Estella left with $18.00 more than she came with (adapted from Whimbey & Lochhead, 1991, p. 126).

3. **Teach students how to compile relevant information.**

Good problem solvers start with themselves when compiling information to solve a problem or evidence to support a position on an issue. They recognize the importance of recalling earlier-learned information (metacognitive knowledge) and are adept at doing so (cognitive skill). Poor problem solvers, by contrast, lack metacognitive knowledge, cognitive skills, or both. If their

1. Excerpts and diagrams in this section are adapted from *Problem Solving and Comprehension*, Fifth Edition, by A. Whimbey and J. Lochhead, 1991.

deficiency is metacognitive, they make little or no effort to recall solution-relevant memories, even when the information was recently learned, because they do not understand the importance of searching long-term memory for potentially useful knowledge. Even if a student poor in problem solving recognizes the value of searching long-term memory for relevant information, he may still be handicapped because of inadequate encoding and retrieval skills.

To minimize any metacognitive deficiency, make sure your instruction in problem-solving methods emphasizes the importance of retrieving and using previously learned knowledge. To minimize retrieval problems, make sure *you* recall and implement the Suggestions for Teaching in Your Classroom that we offered in the preceding chapter.

If a student does not possess all the relevant information needed to work out a solution or to analyze an issue, you will have to guide her toward individuals and sources that can help. In referring students to individuals, select people who are judged to be reasonably knowledgeable about the subject, are careful thinkers, and are willing to share their ideas (Ruggiero, 1988). As an example, consider the issue of whether certain books (such as the novels *Catcher in the Rye,* by J. D. Salinger, and *Tom Sawyer,* by Mark Twain) should be banned from a school's reading list. In interviewing an interested person, students might ask questions like the following because they allow some insight into the individual's reasoning process and the evidence used to support his position:

- What general effects do you think characters in novels who rebel against adult authority have on a reader's behavior?
- Are certain groups of people, such as middle and high school students, likely to be influenced by the motives and actions of such characters? Why do you think so?
- Does a ban on certain books violate the authors' right to free speech?
- Does a book ban violate the principle of academic freedom? Why?
- Is it the proper role of a school board to prevent or discourage students from exposure to certain ideas during school hours?

If a reasonably informed person is not available, recognized authorities can often be interviewed by phone. If a student chooses this tactic, Ruggiero suggests calling or writing in advance for an appointment, preparing questions in advance, and asking permission to tape-record the interview.

Obviously, in addition to or in lieu of personal interviews, students can find substantial information in a good library. For example, you can steer them toward books by recognized authorities, research findings, court cases, and interviews with prominent individuals in periodicals. While the Internet potentially contains a vast amount of information on any particular topic, warn students about using material gathered there indiscriminately. As with any medium, there are more and less reliable sources, and only material from reputable sources should be gathered. One additional benefit is that an extra layer of problem-solving activity is introduced when students must decide how to gather and evaluate on-line information.

4. **Teach several methods for formulating problem solutions.**

Earlier we mentioned five methods for formulating a problem solution: study worked examples, work on a simpler version of the problem, break the problem into parts, work backward, and solve an analogous problem. At the end of the chapter, under Resources for Further Investigation, we recommend several recently published books on problem solving that, taken together, provide numerous examples of each method. We encourage you to check out one or more of those references and other sources as demonstrations of worked problems and as opportunities for you to practice your own problem-solving skills so that you will be well prepared to teach each of these five methods.

5. **Teach students the skills of evaluation.**

Solutions to well-structured problems are usually evaluated through the application of an estimating or checking routine. Such procedures can be found in any good mathematics text. The evaluation of solutions to ill-structured problems and analyses of issues, however, is more complex and is less frequently taught. Ruggiero (1988) lists the following twelve habits and skills as contributing to the ability to evaluate complex solutions and positions:

- Being open-minded about opposing points of view.
- Selecting proper criteria of evaluation. Violations of this skill abound. A current example is the use of standardized achievement test scores to evaluate the quality of classroom instruction.
- Understanding the essence of an argument. To foster this skill, Ruggiero recommends that students be taught how to write a *précis,* which is a concise summary of an oral argument or a reading passage.
- Evaluating the reliability of sources.
- Properly interpreting factual data (for example, recognizing that an increase in a state's income tax rate from 4 to 6 percent is an increase not of 2 percent but of 50 percent).
- Testing the credibility of hypotheses. On the basis of existing data, hypotheses can range from highly improbable to highly probable.
- Making important distinctions (for instance, between preference and judgment, emotion and content, appearance and reality).
- Recognizing unstated assumptions (for example, that because two events occur close together in time, one causes the other; that what is clear to us will be clear to others; that if the majority believes something, it must be true).
- Detecting fallacies (for instance, stereotyping, faulty analogies, strawman arguments [those that are easily refuted because they are deliberately weak], or overgeneralizing).
- Evaluating arguments.
- Making sound judgments.
- Recognizing when evidence is insufficient.

Transfer of Learning

Throughout Chapters 8, 9, and 10, we indicated that classroom instruction should be arranged in such a way that students independently apply the knowledge and problem-solving skills they learn in school to similar but new situations. This capability is typically valued very highly by educators. Referred to as **transfer of learning,** it is the essence of being an autonomous learner and problem solver. In this section, we will examine the nature of transfer and discuss ways in which you can help bring it about.

THE NATURE AND SIGNIFICANCE OF TRANSFER OF LEARNING

The Theory of Identical Elements During the early 1900s, it was common practice for high school students and colleges to require that students take such subjects as Latin, Greek, and geometry. Because they were considered difficult topics to learn, mastery of them was expected to improve a student's ability to memorize, think, and reason. These enhanced abilities were then expected to facilitate the learning of less difficult subjects. The rationale behind this practice was that the human mind, much like any muscle in the body, could be exercised and made stronger. A strong mind, then, would learn things that a weak mind would not. This practice, known as the *doctrine of formal discipline,* constituted an early (and incorrect) explanation of transfer.

In 1901 Edward Thorndike and Robert Woodworth proposed an alternative explanation of how transfer occurs. They argued that the degree to which knowledge and skills acquired in learning one task can help someone learn another task depends on how similar the two tasks are (if we assume that the learner recognizes the similarities). The greater the degree of similar-

If teachers want students to apply what they learn in the classroom in other settings in the future, they should create tasks and conditions that are similar to those that students will encounter later.

ity is between the tasks' stimulus and response elements (as in riding a bicycle and riding a motorcycle), the greater the amount of transfer will be. This idea became known as the **theory of identical elements.**

Early view of transfer based on degree of similarity between two tasks

Positive, Negative, and Zero Transfer In time, however, other psychologists (among them Osgood, 1949; Ellis, 1965) identified different types of transfer and the conditions under which each type prevailed. A useful distinction was made among positive transfer, negative transfer, and zero transfer (Ormrod, 1995).

The discussion up to this point has been alluding to **positive transfer,** defined as a situation in which prior learning aids subsequent learning. According to Thorndike's analysis, positive transfer occurs when a new learning task calls for essentially the same response that was made to a similar, earlier-learned task. The accomplished accordion player, for instance, probably will become a proficient pianist faster than someone who knows how to play the drums or someone who plays no musical instrument at all, all other things being equal. Similarly, the native English speaker who is also fluent in French is likely to have an easier time learning Spanish than is someone who speaks no foreign language.

Positive transfer: previous learning makes later learning easier

Negative transfer is defined as a situation in which prior learning interferes with subsequent learning. It occurs when two tasks are highly similar but require different responses. A tennis player learning how to play racquetball, for example, may encounter problems at first because of a tendency to swing the racquetball racket as if it were a tennis racket. Primary grade children often experience negative transfer when they encounter words that are spelled alike but pronounced differently (as in "I will *read* this story now since I *read* that story last week").

Negative transfer: previous learning interferes with later learning

Zero transfer is defined as a situation in which prior learning has no effect on new learning. It can be expected when two tasks have different stimuli and different responses. Learning to conjugate Latin verbs, for example, is not likely to have any effect on learning how to find the area of a rectangle.

Specific and General Transfer The preceding description of positive transfer, while useful, is somewhat limiting because it is unclear whether transfer from one task to another is due to specific similarities or to general or nonspecific similarities. Psychologists (as described by Ellis, 1978, pp. 249–250) decide whether transfer is due to specific or general factors by setting up learning tasks such as the following for three different but equivalent groups of learners.

	Initial Task	*Transfer Task*
Group 1	Learn French	Learn Spanish
Group 2	Learn Chinese	Learn Spanish
Group 3		Learn Spanish

If on a Spanish test, group 1 scores higher than group 2, the difference is attributed to **specific transfer** of similarities between French and Spanish (such

Specific transfer due to specific similarities between two tasks

General transfer due to use of same cognitive strategies

as vocabulary, verb conjugations, and sentence structure). If groups 1 and 2 score the same but both outscore group 3, the difference is attributed to nonspecific or **general transfer** of similarities between the two tasks since Chinese shares no apparent specific characteristics with French or Spanish. In this case it is possible that learners use cognitive strategies—such as imagery, verbal elaboration, and mnemonic devices—when learning a foreign language and that these transfer to the learning of other foreign languages. Such nonspecific transfer effects have also been demonstrated for other classroom tasks, such as problem solving and learning from text (Ellis, 1978; Royer, 1979).

CONTEMPORARY VIEWS OF SPECIFIC AND GENERAL TRANSFER

Gavriel Salomon and David Perkins (1989) offer a current treatment of specific and general transfer under the labels *low-road transfer* and *high-road transfer*, respectively.

Low-road transfer: previously learned skill automatically applied to similar current task

Low-Road Transfer **Low-road transfer** refers to a situation in which a previously learned skill or idea is almost automatically retrieved from memory and applied to a highly similar current task. For example, a student who has mastered the skill of two-column addition and correctly completes three-column and four-column addition problems with no prompting or instruction is exhibiting low-road transfer. Another example is a student who learns how to tune up car engines in an auto shop class and then almost effortlessly and automatically carries out the same task as an employee of an auto repair business.

Two conditions need to be present for low-road transfer to occur. First, students have to be given ample opportunities to practice using the target skill. Second, practice has to occur with different materials and in different settings. The more varied the practice is, the greater is the range of tasks to which the skill can be applied. If, for example, you want students to be good notetakers, give them instruction and ample practice at taking notes from their biology, health, and English textbooks. Once they become accomplished notetakers in these subjects, they will likely apply this skill to other subjects in an almost automatic fashion. The auto mechanic who has learned to change the spark plugs in a Chrysler, a Toyota, and a Mercedes-Benz should be able to do the same job as efficiently in a Ford, a Buick, or a Nissan. In essence, what we are describing is the behavioral principle of generalization. Since the transfer task is similar in one or more respects to the practice task, this type of transfer is also called *near transfer.* To understand how people transfer prior knowledge and skills to new situations that look rather different from the original task, we will need to explore the nature of high-road transfer.

High-Road Transfer **High-road transfer** involves the conscious, controlled, somewhat effortful formulation of an "abstraction" (that is, a rule, a schema, a strategy, or an analogy) that allows a connection to be made between two tasks. For example, an individual who learns to set aside a certain number of hours every day to complete homework assignments and study for upcoming exams formulates the principle that the most efficient way to accomplish a task is to break it down into small pieces and work at each piece according to a set schedule. As an adult, the individual uses this principle to successfully deal with complex tasks at work and at home. As another example, imagine a student who, after much observation and thought, has finally developed a good sense of what school is and how one is supposed to behave there. In other words, this student has developed a school schema. Such a schema would probably be made up of actors (teachers and students), objects (desks, chalkboards, books, pencils), and events (reading, listening, writing, talking, drawing). Since this is an idealized abstraction, actual classrooms may contain fewer or greater numbers of these characteristics in varying proportions. Even so, with this schema a student could walk into most any instructional setting (another school classroom, a training seminar, or a press briefing, for example) and readily understand what was going on, why it was going on, and how one should behave. Of course, with repeated applications of schemata, rules, strategies, and the like, the behaviors become less conscious and more automatic. What was once a reflection of high-road transfer becomes low-road transfer.

High-road transfer: formulate rule from one task and apply to related task

Salomon and Perkins (1989) refer to this deliberate, conscious, effortful formulating of a general principle or schema that can be applied to a variety of different-looking but fundamentally similar tasks as *mindful abstraction.* The *mindful* part of the phrase indicates that the abstraction must be thought about and fully understood for high-road transfer to occur. That is, people must be aware of what they are doing and why they are doing it. Recall our earlier discussion in this chapter (p. 376) of inert knowledge and Richard Feynman's observations of how his classmates at the Massachusetts Institute of Technology failed to recognize the application of a previously learned mathematical formula because it was initially learned for use only in that course.

Teaching for Low-Road and High-Road Transfer To enhance both low-road and high-road transfer, Salomon and Perkins (1989) offer four suggestions:

Low-road and high-road transfer produced by varied practice at applying skills, rules, memory retrieval cues

1. Provide students with multiple opportunities for varied practice.
2. Give students opportunities to solve problems that are similar to those they will eventually have to solve.
3. Teach students how to formulate a general rule, strategy, or schema that can be used in the future with a variety of similar problems.
4. Give students cues that will allow them to retrieve from memory earlier-learned information that can be used to make current learning easier.

If there is one thing we hope you have learned from this discussion of transfer of learning, it is this: *if you want transfer, teach for transfer.* As you can see, students have to be carefully prepared and coached to use the information and skills they learn in school. If you expect transfer, be it low road or high road, to occur on its own, you will be disappointed most of the time.

The next section illustrates how you can use computer programs and the Internet to help students improve their problem-solving skills.

C A S E   I N   P R I N T

Solving Problems with the Help of Technology

The computer, with its capacity for almost unlimited networking and information gathering, is a natural tool for students to use in the kinds of higher-order thinking processes we've described in this chapter. (p. 392)

"Teachers Bet Computers Will Spark Love of Learning"

COCO MCCABE

Boston Sunday Globe 8/13/95

Last May, for a school assignment on the Holocaust, Hamilton eighth-grader Justin Budrow decided to prove to his classmates that as horrifying as that episode was, there is a chance it could happen again.

But he didn't take the old-fashioned route of a written report dug out of texts and illustrated by pictures held in front of class. He went to a computer in the lab at Wenham's Bessie Buker Middle School, plugged in a program called Hypercard Studio and set to work pulling together some of the latest news events from around the country. . . .

How was it?

"Spectacular," he says with obvious delight. "I learned a lot about the subject and how to pull it together. Once you get going, you can't stop and want to learn how to do new things."

Around the North Weekly region teachers are betting that that kind of enthusiasm will be contagious this coming school year as they introduce more students to new computer programs and networks that allow them to learn in ways never imagined by their parents.

When former President Richard Nixon died last year, students at one of the elementary schools in Haverhill turned to their computers to learn something about him. They searched the CD encyclopedia files for his name and heard a recording of him insisting "I am not a crook."

. . . At Beverly High School, seniors in an advanced German class logged regularly onto the Internet and pored over pages of correspondence—all in German—from their peers in schools scattered around Germany. They chatted about Oklahoma, the 50th anniversary of World War II, and how minorities are treated.

"Kids enjoy anything you put on a computer. In a book, it's boring," says German teacher Clifford Kent, who spent a good deal of timing poking around on the Internet looking for just this kind of connection for his students.

While school districts around the region offer varying degrees of computer capability to their students, the question of how to enter the 21st century fully prepared with new technology is on the minds of many administrators. Networked computers and multi-media presentations are part of the latest wave.

"I don't think it's a choice any longer," says Cheryl Forster, director of program development for Ipswich schools and instrumental in developing a five-year technology plan that includes providing each grade at the elementary level with a cluster of computers, printers, and access to the Internet. In the past, some school districts saw the introduction of advanced technologies as a sign of prestige while others viewed it as superfluous, says Forster. No longer. Conscientious school districts understand the role of technology, she says.

But the task of gearing up to bring this new world of information into the classrooms may seem daunting. According to the Center for Educational Leadership and Technology (CELT), the average amount spent statewide on technology is $30 per student a year—or half of 1 percent of the $5,500 per pupil foundation budget established by the state's new Education Reform Act.

CELT, a nonprofit research organization hired by the state Department of Education to help each school district put together a technology plan, says spending in this area should be three or four times that amount.

"You need a certain critical mass of technology to get an improvement," says CELT's executive director, John Phillipo. He uses the analogy of telephones not becoming truly useful until everyone had one. The same is true for the latest technology: It doesn't become effective until there is enough in place to impact student learning, he says.

School districts are trying to head in that direction, maybe not at the pace—yet—that CELT proposes, but with increasing momentum and often in the hands of teachers inspired to bring as much of this new world to their students as possible. . . .

It's a tool that has inspired Kevin O'Reilly, a history teacher at Hamilton-Wenham Regional High School, to take highlights from his recent sabbatical and create a computer program designed to engage his students in a thoughtful exploration of the Industrial Revolution.

"My most driving force in being a teacher is to get students to think. I prefer to have students be confronted with problems and think them through," says O'Reilly. "I think computers have possibilities we don't really understand yet. It's like being in 1520 when printing presses were starting."

The program O'Reilly is developing—including photographs gathered during his sabbatical and scanned in—will guide students to make hypotheses about what caused industrialization in different countries. It tosses in historical events and asks students to figure out what impact they might have had on a country's progress. And students are asked to make economic decisions: in France in 1815 taxes have been wiped out. What will you do? Impose new ones? Print money?

"A lot of people, once you give them a taste of what technology can do, they go off. Once you empower the teachers, they empower the students," says Jill Bonina, technology coordinator for Hamilton-Wenham High.

Questions and Activities

1. In Chapter 2 you learned that cognitive development is based partly on open-ended interactions among students. Consequently, people who envision students spending a large part of the school day working by themselves on computers fear that computer technology will have an adverse effect on cognitive growth. How can you use the information in the accompanying article to fashion a response?

2. In the article, a high school history teacher planned to use computer technology to help students formulate hypotheses about what caused industrialization in different countries. Based on what you learned in Chapter 2 about stages of cognitive development, what types of students are most likely and least likely to have difficulty with such an assignment?

3. The article points out that in 1995 in Massachusetts the average amount spent statewide on technology was .5 percent of the per-student yearly allotment. Such real-life considerations may well place limitations on the use of technology in your own teaching situation. Imagine that in such a situation you volunteered to appear before the local school board to plead for an increased percentage of the budget to be given to technology in the classroom. Compose the most persuasive arguments possible. Now also imagine that—even if your arguments are successful—they will take several years to be implemented. In the meantime, you must make efficient use of extremely limited computer resources. Draw up some ideas and plans to demonstrate how you might work most creatively and resourcefully with other teachers and the school library to make the best use of the few computers that are available.

4. To become familiar with the rewards and pitfalls of identifying and collecting information from the Internet, select a topic and see how much information you can collect in one hour.

@ APPLYING TECHNOLOGY TO TEACHING

Using Technology to Improve Problem-Solving Skills

In our initial discussion about the nature of problem solving, and again in the Suggestions for Teaching section, we pointed out that solving ill-structured problems and issues often requires identifying and synthesizing a great deal of widely scattered information. When this task is approached traditionally, students are usually limited to a nearby library or two and spend many hours searching through volumes of reference material. The sheer magnitude of the task and the difficulty in finding a wide array of relevant material may well rob students of the motivation to enthusiastically engage future problem solving tasks.

But the computer, with its capacity for almost unlimited networking and information gathering, is a natural tool for students to use in the kinds of higher-order thinking processes we've described in this chapter. Several testimonials to the power of computer technology appear in the Case in Print article on the previous page. For example, one eighth-grade student said about a presentation he prepared on the Holocaust using computer technology, "I learned a lot about the subject and how to pull it together. Once you get going, you can't stop and want to learn how to do new things."

A variety of well-designed computer programs exist that can help students acquire and refine one or more problem-solving skills. The 1991 edition of *Only the Best: Preschool–Grade 12* (Neill & Neill, 1990) and the 1991–1992 edition of *The Latest and Best of TESS: The Educational Software Selector* (EPIE Institute, 1991) describe several programs that you may want to consider using. We will briefly describe a few of them here to give you an idea of their goals and characteristics.

In *Blockers and Finders,* students attempt to move small animals called finders along a path on a 4-by-4 grid toward a particular destination. This seemingly straightforward task is complicated by hidden blockers, such as arrows and detours, that force students to take a different path. The skill this program attempts to develop is inference. By using available information, students can determine the best path to take. This program has different levels of difficulty that allow it to be used from the first grade on.

The Secret Island of Dr. Quandary, an action-adventure game, challenges thinking skills and reflexes and features a variety of brain teasers for hours of perplexing fun. Explore a chemistry lab that shoots flames and acid balls that burn—if you are not quick! Discover a frog idol that guards its treasure until you can find the secret to satisfying its appetite. Puzzle solutions change each time you play. This game includes three levels of difficulty, five island layouts, and fourteen almost infinitely variable puzzles.

Snooper Troops 1—G.P. Ghost is similar in nature to *The Secret Island of Dr. Quandary.* The Kim family has moved into an old mansion in which strange things happen. Students play the role of detective and try to figure out who is scaring the Kim family and why. Players question suspects, search houses for clues, and use something called the Snoopnet computer to gather information. This program can be used in grades 3 through 12. An almost identical program for students in grades 5 through 12, *Snooper Troops 2—Disappearing Dolphin,* is also available.

About *TesselMania!:* Artist M. C. Escher produced intricate interlocking figures of fish, birds, lizards, and other creatures in patterns called *tessellations.* Creating a tessellation involves designing a motif (tile) that will cover a plane without leaving any gaps or overlaps (kind of like tiling a bathroom floor!). In this problem-solving program, which builds planning, geometry, communication, and creative skills, students provide the creativity and *TesselMania!* provides the tools for making the geometry and the art.

Microsoc *Thinking Games,* a six-disk series, helps players understand and apply language concepts and develop vital problem-solving skills. Each program taps a different thinking process using three innovative games, such as constructing analogies or finding commonalities in various situations, and three to four levels of difficulty, which makes the series appropriate for all students.

Resources for Further Investigation

Bruner on Education

Toward a Theory of Instruction (1966) is Jerome Bruner's most concise and application-oriented book on teaching; it provides general descriptions of his view on teaching and learning and specific descriptions of materials he used in structuring the discovery approach. To learn more about Bruner, his ideas, and the circumstances that led him to study such topics as perception, concept formation, problem solving, cognitive development, and discovery learning, read *In Search of Mind: Essays in Autobiography* (1983).

Ausubel's Meaningful Reception Learning

David Ausubel provides detailed explanations of meaningful reception learning in *The Psychology of Meaningful Verbal Learning* (1963), *School Learning: An Introduction to Educational Psychology* (Ausubel and Robinson, 1969, Chapter 3), and *Educational Psychology: A Cognitive View* (Ausubel et al., 2d ed., 1978, Chapters 2 and 4).

Constructivism

In *The Young Child as Scientist: A Constructivist Approach to Early Childhood Science Education* (1991), Christine Chaillé and Lory Britain start from the premise that young children learn and solve problems in much the same way as scientists do—they actively construct conceptions of the world on the basis of a constant process of theorizing and experimenting. From this perspective the authors describe how to create a constructivist learning environment for the purpose of teaching science to preschool and primary grade children.

Constructivism in Education (1995), edited by Leslie Steffe and Jerry Gale, is a massive (550 pages) collection of chapters on various aspects of constructivism.

Several chapters describe the relationship between constructivism and technology, and several others describe constructivist approaches to teaching science and mathematics.

Given the importance of interpersonal interaction to the constructivist position and the flexibility of classroom discussions as an instructional tool, you might want to read *William Fawcett Hill's Learning Through Discussion* (3d ed., 1994), by Jerome Rabow, Michelle Charness, Johanna Kipperman, and Susan Radcliffe-Vasile. A compact book at only 67 pages, it nevertheless provides a wealth of practical information on how to structure and run discussion groups in the classroom.

An excellent source of on-line information about programs for developing creativity and problem-solving skills is the Educational Software Institute Online, which can be found at http://www.bonsai.com/q/@009412dqkyxt/edsoftcat/htdocs/esihome.html. This organization can be contacted directly at 4213 South 94th Street, Omaha, NE 68127, 1-800-955-5570.

Problem-Solving Processes

In *Teaching Thinking Across the Curriculum* (1988), Vincent Ryan Ruggiero describes a model for solving problems and analyzing issues, discusses teaching objectives and methods, identifies obstacles to students' cognitive development, details assignments that can be used in a variety of courses, demonstrates how instructors can design additional course-specific thinking assignments, and offers guidelines for developing a thinking skills program.

Encouraging students to become involved in extracurricular activities that require logical and/or creative thinking is often a successful way to motivate practice of problem solving skills. For example, the Junior States of America involves students in simulating and exploring the workings of democratic institutions; while the Model United Nations leads to discussions of current world events.

Gary Woditsch designed *The Thoughtful Teacher's Guide to Thinking Skills* (1991) to help kindergarten through college teachers improve their students' thinking skills. According to the author, "Every page of this guide aims at classroom impact, regardless of whether that classroom happens to serve a college, a kindergarten, or somewhere in between. That impact is meant to flow from the reader's strengthened grasp of what constitutes and what advances skillful thought" (p.vii).

In *Reasoning and Problem Solving: A Handbook for Elementary School Teachers* (1993), Stephen Krulik and Jesse Rudnick discuss the nature of higher-order thinking skills, present general approach to problem solving, provide steps teachers should follow when teaching problem solving, and offer hands-on materials and resources for problem-solving instruction.

In two handbooks—*Teaching Thinking Skills: A Handbook for Elementary School Teachers* (1991a) and *Teaching Thinking Skills: A Handbook for Secondary School Teachers* (1991b)—Barry Beyer provides a comprehensive account of the nature of a variety of thinking skills, including problem solving, and how they can be taught.

Summary

1. Bruner believes that meaningful learning occurs when students grasp the structure of a field of study (the nature of fundamental ideas and how they relate to one another) and when they discover these relationships themselves.
2. Ausubel believes that meaningful learning occurs when students receive information organized so that it can be easily related to their current knowledge schemes. Students also need to adopt a meaningful learning set.
3. To help students adopt a meaningful learning set, teachers could, according to Ausubel, construct and provide advance organizers. An advance organizer is introductory material that is more abstract, more general, and more inclusive than the material that is to be learned. It is intended to provide an organizing structure that helps students relate new ideas to existing knowledge schemes.

4. The constructivist view holds that meaningful learning occurs when people actively construct personal knowledge structures, that only part of a teacher's understanding of some concept or issue can be transferred to students through direct instruction, that the knowledge structures of different people have much in common, and that the formation and changing of knowledge structures come mainly from peer interaction.

5. Three conditions that support constructivism are a cognitive apprenticeship between teacher and student, the use of realistic learning tasks, and exposure to multiple perspectives.

6. The classroom discussion is an instructional technique that teachers can use to support a constructivist view of meaningful learning as it allows students to share different perspectives of realistic problems.

7. The types of problems that students most often come into contact with are well-structured problems, ill-structured problems, and issues. Well-structured problems are clearly stated and can be solved by applying previously learned procedures, and their solutions can be accurately evaluated. Ill-structured problems are often vaguely stated, they cannot always be solved by applying previously learned procedures, and their solutions cannot always be evaluated against clear and widely accepted criteria. Issues are like ill-structured problems, but with two differences: they arouse strong emotions that tend to divide people into opposing camps, and they require that one determine the most reasonable position to take before working out a solution.

8. A general problem-solving model is composed of five steps: realize that a problem exists, understand the nature of the problem, compile relevant information, formulate and carry out a solution, and evaluate the solution.

9. The keys to realizing that a problem exists are to be curious about why things are the way they are and to be dissatisfied with the status quo.

10. Understanding the nature of a problem, also known as problem representation or problem framing, requires a high level of knowledge about the subject matter surrounding the problem and familiarity with the particular type of problem.

11. A problem solver can compile relevant information by searching long-term memory, retrieving solution relevant information, and representing that information as lists, tables, pictures, graphs, diagrams, and so on. In addition, friends, colleagues, and experts can be tapped for information.

12. A problem solver can formulate solutions by studying worked examples, working on a simpler version of the problem, breaking the problem into parts, working backward, or solving an analogous problem.

13. A problem solver can evaluate solutions for well-structured problems by estimating or checking and solutions for ill-structured problems by answering a set of basic questions that deal with who, what, where, when, why, and how; by identifying imperfections and complications; by anticipating possible negative reactions; and by devising improvements.

14. Transfer of learning occurs when the learning of new information or skills is influenced by previously learned information or skills.

15. An early view of transfer was based on Thorndike and Woodworth's theory of identical elements. This theory holds that transfer of learning is a function of how many elements two tasks have in common. The greater the similarity is, the greater is the degree of transfer.

16. Positive transfer occurs when a new learning task is similar to a previously learned task and calls for a similar response. Negative transfer occurs when a new learning task is similar to a previously learned task but calls for a different response. Zero transfer occurs when previously learned information or skills are so dissimilar to new information or skills that they have no effect on how quickly the latter will be learned.

17. Positive transfer that is due to identifiable similarities between an earlier-learned task and a current one is referred to as specific transfer. Positive transfer that is due to the formulation, use, and carryover of cognitive strategies from one task to another is referred to as general transfer.
18. A current view of specific transfer is called low-road transfer. It is produced by giving students many opportunities to practice a skill in different settings and with different materials.
19. A current view of general transfer is called high-road transfer. It is produced by teaching students how to formulate a general rule, strategy, or schema that can be used in the future with a variety of problems that are fundamentally similar to the original.

Key Terms

structure *(360)*
discovery learning *(361)*
meaningful reception learning *(363)*
advance organizers *(364)*
constructivism *(364)*
problem solving *(374)*
well-structured problems *(374)*
ill-structured problems *(374)*
issues *(374)*
problem representation *(376)*
problem framing *(376)*
transfer of learning *(386)*
theory of identical elements *(387)*
positive transfer *(387)*
negative transfer *(387)*
zero transfer *(387)*
specific transfer *(387)*
general transfer *(388)*
low-road transfer *(388)*
high-road transfer *(388)*

Discussion Questions

1. According to Jerome Bruner, to foster meaningful learning (and guide students away from rote learning), teachers should help students discover how the basic ideas of a subject relate to one another and to what students already know. Can you recall a class in which the instructor made use of discovery techniques? What did the instructor do? How did you react? Was the learning outcome as meaningful as Bruner suggests? How could you tell? How might you use similar techniques?
2. David Ausubel argues that to steer students toward meaningful learning, teachers should provide information that has been organized so that it can be easily related to students' existing knowledge schemes. Can you recall one or more instances when a lecture or text was organized this way? How did you react? Was the learning outcome as meaningful as Ausubel suggests? How could you tell? How might you use similar techniques?
3. Critics of American education argue that contemporary students are poor problem solvers because they receive little systematic instruction in problem-solving processes. How would you rate the quantity and quality of the instruction you received in problem solving? In terms of the five steps discussed in this chapter, which ones were you taught? What can you do to ensure that your students become good problem solvers?
4. Educational psychologists who have studied transfer have said to teachers that if they want transfer, they should teach for transfer. What do you think this statement means?

CHAPTER 11

Motivation

Key Points

These key points will help you learn the important information in this chapter. To help you study, they also appear in the margins of pages, next to the text where they are discussed.

Behavioral Views of Motivation

- Behavioral view of motivation: reinforce desired behavior
- Social learning view of motivation: identification, imitation, vicarious reinforcement
- Extrinsic motivation occurs when learner does something to earn external reward
- Intrinsic motivation occurs when learner does something to experience inherently satisfying results
- Excessive use of external rewards may lead to temporary behavior change, materialistic attitudes, decreased intrinsic motivation
- Intrinsic motivation undermined by rewarding performance when interest is high, rewards held out in advance, quality of performance ignored
- Intrinsic motivation enhanced when reward is given according to predetermined standard or is consistent with individual's level of skill
- Give rewards sparingly, especially on tasks of natural interest

Cognitive Views of Motivation

- Cognitive-developmental view of motivation: strive for equilibration, master the environment
- Need for achievement revealed by desire to attain goals that require skilled performance
- High-need achievers prefer moderately challenging tasks
- Low-need achievers prefer very easy or very hard tasks
- Unsuccessful students attribute success to luck, easy tasks; failure, to lack of ability
- Successful students attribute success to effort, ability; failure, to lack of effort
- Students with entity beliefs motivated to get high grades, avoid failure

- Students with incremental beliefs motivated to meaningfully learn, improve skills
- Often difficult to arouse cognitive disequilibrium
- Need for achievement difficult to assess on basis of short-term observations
- Faulty attributions difficult to change due to beliefs about ability

THE HUMANISTIC VIEW OF MOTIVATION

- People are motivated to satisfy deficiency needs only when those needs are unmet
- Self-actualization depends on satisfaction of lower needs, belief in certain values
- When deficiency needs are not satisfied, person likely to make bad choices
- Encourage growth choices by enhancing attractions, minimizing dangers
- Teachers may be able to satisfy some deficiency needs but not others

THE ROLE OF SELF-PERCEPTIONS IN MOTIVATION

- Self-concept is description of self; self-esteem is value we place on that description
- High self-esteem due to being competent at valued tasks, reinforcement from others
- Self-esteem declines when students move from elementary grades to middle school and from middle school to high school
- Self-efficacy affects choice of goals, expectations of success, attributions for success and failure
- Raise self-esteem by helping students become better learners

THE IMPACT OF COOPERATIVE LEARNING ON MOTIVATION

- Competitive reward structures may decrease motivation to learn
- Cooperative learning characterized by heterogeneous groups, positive interdependence, promotive interaction, individual accountability
- Cooperative-learning effects likely due to stimulation of motivation, cognitive development, meaningful learning

The last three chapters provided you with several explanations of *how* people learn and suggested techniques for helping students achieve objectives. In this chapter we will try to answer the question of *why* students strive (or don't strive) for academic achievement—that is, What motivates students? The importance of motivation was vividly pointed out by Larry Cuban, a Stanford University professor of education who returned to teach a high school class for one semester after a sixteen-year absence. Of this experience, he says, "If I wanted those students to be engaged intellectually, then every day—and I *do* mean *every* day—I had to figure out an angle, a way of making connections between whatever we were studying and their daily lives in school, in the community, or in the nation" (1990, pp. 480–481). Cuban's comment about the importance of motivating students is as applicable to the elementary and middle school teacher as it is to the high school teacher. Researchers have consistently found that interest in school in general decreases the most between fourth and fifth grades, while interest in specific subjects decreases the most between sixth and seventh grades. Declines in motivation have also been found among girls when they move from a kindergarten through eighth-grade school to a traditional high school setting (Anderman & Maehr, 1994).

Motivation is typically defined as the forces that account for the arousal, selection, direction, and continuation of behavior. Nevertheless, many teachers have at least two major misconceptions about motivation that prevent them from using this concept with maximum effectiveness. One misconception is that some students are unmotivated. Strictly speaking, that is not an accurate statement. As long as a student chooses goals and expends a certain amount of effort to achieve them, he is, by definition, motivated. What teachers really mean is that students are not motivated to behave in the way teachers would like them to behave. The second misconception is that one person can directly motivate another. This view is inaccurate because motivation comes from within a person. What you *can* do, with the help of the various motivation theories discussed in this chapter, is create the circumstances that *influence* students to do what you want them to do.

Many factors determine whether the students in your classes will be motivated or not motivated to learn. You should not be surprised to discover that no single theoretical interpretation of motivation explains all aspects of student interest or lack of it. Different theoretical interpretations do, however, shed light on why some students in a given learning situation are more likely to want to learn than others. Furthermore, each theoretical interpretation can serve as the basis for the development of techniques for motivating students in the classroom. Several theoretical interpretations of motivation —some of which are derived from discussions of learning presented earlier— will now be summarized.

Behavioral Views of Motivation

OPERANT CONDITIONING AND SOCIAL LEARNING THEORY

The Effect of Reinforcement In Chapter 8 we discussed Skinner's emphasis of the role of reinforcement in learning. After demonstrating that organisms tend to repeat actions that are reinforced and that behavior can be shaped by reinforcement, Skinner developed the technique of programmed instruction to make it possible for students to be reinforced for every correct response. Supplying the correct answer—and being informed by the program that it *is* the correct answer—motivates the student to go on to the next frame; and as the student works through the program, the desired terminal behavior is progressively shaped.

Following Skinner's lead, many behavioral learning theorists devised techniques of behavior modification. Students are motivated to complete a task by being promised a reward of some kind. Many times the reward takes the form of praise or a grade. Sometimes it is a token that can be traded in for some desired object; and at other times the reward may be the privilege of engaging in a self-selected activity.

Behavioral view of motivation: reinforce desired behavior

Operant conditioning interpretations of learning help reveal why some students react favorably to particular subjects and dislike others. For instance, some students may enter a required math class with a feeling of delight, while others may feel that they have been sentenced to prison. Skinner

Providing students with positive reinforcers after they exhibit a desired response may serve to motivate them to make the same response in the future, because the reinforcer tells students that their responses are acceptable.

suggests that such differences can be traced to past experiences. He would argue that the student who loves math has been shaped to respond that way by a series of positive experiences with math. The math hater, in contrast, may have suffered a series of negative experiences.

Social learning view of motivation: identification, imitation, vicarious reinforcement

The Power of Persuasive Models Social learning theorists, such as Albert Bandura, call attention to the importance of observation, imitation, and vicarious reinforcement (expecting to receive the same reinforcer that we see someone else get for exhibiting a particular behavior). A student who identifies with and admires a teacher of a particular subject may work hard partly to please the admired individual and partly to try becoming like that individual. A student who observes an older brother or sister reaping benefits from earning high grades may strive to do the same with the expectation of experiencing the same or similar benefits. A student who notices that a classmate receives praise from the teacher after acting in a certain way may decide to imitate such behavior to win similar rewards. As we pointed out in Chapter 8, both vicarious reinforcement and direct reinforcement can raise an individual's sense of self-efficacy for a particular task, which, in turn, leads to higher levels of motivation.

LIMITATIONS OF THE BEHAVIORAL VIEW

While approaches to motivation based on positive reinforcement are often useful, you should be aware of the disadvantages that can come from overuse or misuse of such techniques. Most of the criticisms of the use of reinforcement as a motivational incentive stem from the fact that it represents **extrinsic motivation.** That is, the learner decides to engage in an activity (such as participate in class, do homework, study for exams) to earn a reward that is not inherently related to the activity (such as receive praise from the teacher, earn a high grade, or enjoy the privilege of doing something different). By contrast, students under the influence of **intrinsic motivation** study a subject or acquire a skill because it produces such inherently positive consequences as becoming more knowledgeable, competent, and independent.

Extrinsic motivation occurs when learner does something to earn external reward

Intrinsic motivation occurs when learner does something to experience inherently satisfying results

Although extrinsic motivation is widespread in society (individuals are motivated to engage in many activities because they hope to win certificates, badges, medals, public recognition, prizes, or admiration from others), this approach has at least three potential dangers. First, changes in behavior may be temporary. As soon as the extrinsic reward has been obtained, the student may revert to such earlier behaviors as studying inconsistently, turning in poor-quality homework, and disrupting class with irrelevant comments and behaviors. Second, students may develop a materialistic attitude toward learning. They may think (or say), "What tangible reward will I get if I agree to learn this information?" If the answer is "none," they may decide to make little or no effort to learn it. Third, giving students extrinsic rewards for completing a task may lessen whatever intrinsic motivation they may have for that activity (Kohn, 1993).

Excessive use of external rewards may lead to temporary behavior change, materialistic attitudes, decreased intrinsic motivation

This last disadvantage, which is referred to as the *undermining effect,* has been extensively investigated by researchers. It appears that giving students rewards may indeed decrease their intrinsic motivation for a task, but only when (1) initial interest in the activity is very high, (2) the rewards used are not reinforcers (meaning they do not increase the desired behavior), (3) the rewards are held out in advance as incentives, and, most important, (4) the rewards are given simply for engaging in an activity (Cameron & Pierce, 1994; Chance, 1992).

However, there are two instances in which external rewards can enhance intrinsic motivation. First, when rewards are given according to some predetermined standard of excellence, when the task is moderately challenging, and when the reward is relatively large, intrinsic interest in the task is likely to increase. Second, intrinsic motivation can be enhanced when the task is moderately challenging and the size of the reward is consistent with the individual's perceived level of skill. If a student wins first prize in a science fair, for example, and believes that her project was truly superior to those of the other participants, a large reward may cause the student to maintain a strong interest in science (Morgan, 1984).

Intrinsic motivation undermined by rewarding performance when interest is high, rewards held out in advance, quality of performance ignored

Intrinsic motivation enhanced when reward is given according to predetermined standard or is consistent with individual's level of skill

Why do external rewards undermine intrinsic motivation when they are given just for performing a task? One possible reason is that human beings have an innate drive to be competent (an idea we will discuss in the next section), and rewards that are given irrespective of quality of performance say nothing about an individual's level of competence on moderately difficult tasks. The second possibility is that beginning in early childhood we learn to equate the promise of a reward with the performance of an unpleasant activity. Students may therefore come to believe that "if somebody promises me a reward to do something, it will probably be unpleasant." Furthermore, the type of reward seems to make no difference. Tangible rewards (such as toys and candy) and social rewards (such as praise and honors) can be equally effective in undermining or enhancing intrinsic motivation. These results strongly suggest that teachers should avoid the indiscriminate use of rewards for influencing classroom behavior, particularly when an activity seems to be naturally interesting to students. Instead, rewards should be used to provide students with information about their level of competence on tasks they have not yet mastered (Morgan, 1984).

Give rewards sparingly, especially on tasks of natural interest

Cognitive Views of Motivation

Cognitive views stress that human behavior is influenced by the way people think about themselves and their environment. The direction that behavior takes can be explained by four influences: the inherent need to construct an organized and logically consistent knowledge base, one's expectations for successfully completing a task, the factors that one believes account for success and failure, and one's beliefs about the nature of cognitive ability.

THE IMPACT OF COGNITIVE DEVELOPMENT

This view is based on Jean Piaget's principles of equilibration, assimilation, accommodation, and schema formation. Piaget proposes that children possess an inherent desire to maintain a sense of organization and balance in their conception of the world (equilibration). A sense of equilibration may be experienced if a child assimilates a new experience by relating it to an existing scheme, or the child may accommodate by modifying an existing scheme if the new experience is too different.

In addition, individuals will repeatedly use new schemes because of an inherent desire to master their environment. This explains why young children can, with no loss of enthusiasm, sing the same song, tell the same story, and play the same game over and over and why they repeatedly open and shut doors to rooms and cupboards with no seeming purpose. It also explains why older children take great delight in collecting and organizing almost everything they can get their hands on and why adolescents who have begun to attain formal operational thinking will argue incessantly about all the unfairness in the world and how it can be eliminated (Stipek, 1993).

Cognitive-developmental view of motivation: strive for equilibration; master the environment

THE NEED FOR ACHIEVEMENT

Have you ever decided to take on a moderately difficult task (like take a course on astronomy even though you are a history major and have only a limited background in science) and then found that you had somewhat conflicting feelings about it? On the one hand, you felt eager to start the course, confident that you would be pleased with your performance. But on the other hand, you also felt a bit of anxiety because of the small possibility of failure. Now try to imagine the opposite situation. In reaction to a suggestion to take a course outside your major, you flat out refuse because the probability of failure seems great, while the probability of success seems quite small.

In the early 1960s John Atkinson (1964) proposed that such differences in achievement behavior are due to differences in something called the *need for achievement.* Atkinson described this need as a global, generalized desire to attain goals that require some degree of competence. He saw this need as being partly innate and partly the result of experience. Individuals with a high need for achievement have a stronger expectation of success than they do a fear of failure for most tasks and therefore anticipate a feeling of pride in accomplishment. When given a choice, high-need achievers seek out moderately challenging tasks because they offer an optimal balance between challenge and expected success. By contrast, individuals with a low need for achievement avoid such tasks because their fear of failure greatly outweighs their expectation of success, and they therefore anticipate feelings of shame. When faced with a choice, they typically opt either for relatively easy tasks because the probability of success is high or rather difficult tasks because there is no shame in failing to achieve a lofty goal.

Need for achievement revealed by desire to attain goals that require skilled performance

High-need achievers prefer moderately challenging tasks

Low-need achievers prefer very easy or very hard tasks

Atkinson's point about taking fear of failure into account in arranging learning experiences has been made more recently by William Glasser in *Control Theory in the Classroom* (1986) and *The Quality School* (1990). Glasser argues that for people to succeed at life in general, they must first experience success in one important aspect of their lives. For most children, that one important part should be school. But the traditional approach to evaluating learning, which emphasizes comparative grading (commonly called "grading on the curve"), allows only a minority of students to achieve A's and B's and feel successful. The self-worth of the remaining students (who may be quite capable) suffers, which depresses their motivation to achieve on subsequent classroom tasks (Covington, 1985).

EXPLANATIONS OF SUCCESS AND FAILURE: ATTRIBUTION THEORY

Some interesting aspects of success and failure are revealed when students are asked to explain why they did or did not do well on some task. The four reasons most commonly given stress ability, effort, task difficulty, and luck. To explain a low score on a math test, for example, different students might make the following statements:

"I just have a poor head for numbers." (Lack of ability)

"I didn't really study for the exam." (Lack of effort)

"That test was the toughest I've ever taken." (Task difficulty)

"I guessed wrong about which sections of the book to study." (Luck)

Because students *attribute* success or failure to the factors just listed, research of this type contributes to what is referred to as **attribution theory.**

Students with long histories of academic failure and a weak need for achievement typically attribute their success to easy questions or luck and their failures to lack of ability. Ability is a stable attribution (that is, people expect its effect on achievement to be pretty much the same from one task to another), while task difficulty and luck are both external attributions (in other words, people feel they have little control over their occurrence). Research has shown that stable attributions, particularly ability, lead to expectations of future success or failure, whereas internal attributions (those under personal control) lead to pride in achievement and reward attractiveness following success or lead to shame following failure. Because low-achieving

Unsuccessful students attribute success to luck, easy tasks; failure, to lack of ability students attribute failure to low ability, future failure is seen as more likely than future success. In addition, ascribing success to factors beyond one's control diminishes the possibility of taking pride in achievement and placing a high value on rewards. Consequently, satisfactory achievement and reward may have little effect on the failure-avoiding strategies that poor students have developed over the years.

Successful students attribute success to effort, ability; failure, to lack of effort

Success-oriented students (high-need achievers), in contrast, typically attribute success to ability and effort and failure to insufficient effort. Consequently, failure does not diminish expectancy of success, feelings of competence, or reward-attractiveness for these students. They simply resolve to work harder in the future (Graham & Weiner, 1993).

BELIEFS ABOUT THE NATURE OF COGNITIVE ABILITY

Throughout the primary and elementary grades, most children believe that academic ability is closely related to effort; if one works hard, one succeeds and becomes "smarter." But as these same children reach the middle school and high school grades, many of them adopt a different view. Cognitive ability now comes to be seen as a trait—a fixed, stable part of a person that basically cannot be changed. It is not uncommon, for example, to hear older children and adolescents talk about peers who do or do not have "it" (Anderman & Maehr, 1994). Why this change occurs, and why it occurs in some individuals but not others, is not entirely known, but the increased emphasis on norm-referenced grading procedures (which we will discuss in the next chapter) is suspected of playing a major role. One casualty of this belief is motivation for learning.

Carol Dweck, who has done extensive research on this topic (see, for example, Cain & Dweck, 1995; Henderson & Dweck, 1990), has found that students can be placed into one of two categories based on their beliefs about

Students who believe that success in the classroom is based on intellectual skills that can be improved with practice are likely to be more motivated to participate in class and persist in the face of difficulties than are students who believe that intelligence is a fixed capacity.

the nature of cognitive ability. On the one hand are students who subscribe to what Dweck calls an *entity theory* because they talk about intelligence (another term for cognitive ability) as if it were a thing or an entity that has fixed characteristics. On the other hand are students who believe that intelligence can be improved through the use of new thinking skills. Dweck describes these students as subscribing to an *incremental theory* to reflect their belief that intelligence can be gradually improved by degrees or increments.

Students who believe that intelligence is an unchangeable thing are primarily motivated to prove their ability by getting high grades and praise and by avoiding low grades and criticism. They report feeling bright or capable when they do not make major mistakes on a test or assignment or when they are among the first students to turn in a paper. If their confidence in their ability is low, they are likely to avoid challenging tasks. If avoidance is not possible, they become discouraged at the first sign of difficulty. This, in turn, produces anxiety, ineffective problem solving, and withdrawal from the task (as a way to avoid concluding that one lacks ability and thereby maintain some self-esteem). According to attribution theory, entity theorists should continue this pattern since success is not attributed to effort, but failure is attributed to low ability.

Students with entity beliefs motivated to get high grades, avoid failure

Those who believe that intelligence is a fixed trait and who are highly confident of their ability are likely to demonstrate such mastery-oriented behaviors as seeking challenges and persisting in the face of difficulty. Both high-confidence and low-confidence entity theorists strive to achieve high grades in order to be praised for their brightness. When confronted with a new task, their initial thought is likely to be "Am I smart enough to do this?" They may forgo opportunities to learn new ideas and skills if they think they will become confused and make mistakes.

Students with incremental beliefs tend to be motivated to acquire new and more effective cognitive skills. They seek challenging tasks and do not give up easily because they see obstacles as a natural part of the learning process. They often tell themselves what adults have told them for years— "Think carefully," "Pay attention," and "Try to recall useful information that was learned earlier." They seem to focus on the questions "How do you do this?" and "What can I learn from this?" Errors are seen as opportunities for useful feedback.

Students with incremental beliefs motivated to meaningfully learn, improve skills

LIMITATIONS OF COGNITIVE VIEWS

Cognitive Development While cognitive development theory can be useful as a means for motivating students, it has a major limitation: it is not always easy or even possible to induce students to experience a cognitive disequilibrium sufficient to stimulate them to seek answers. This is particularly true if an answer can be found only after comparatively dull and unrewarding information and skills are mastered. (How many elementary school students, for example, might be expected to experience a self-impelled urge to learn English grammar or to acquire skill in mathematics?) You are likely to gain some firsthand experience with the difficulty of arousing cognitive disequilibrium the first time you ask students to respond to what you hope will be a

Often difficult to arouse cognitive disequilibrium

provocative question for class discussion. Some students may experience a feeling of intellectual curiosity and be eager to clarify their thinking, but others may stare out the window or do homework for another class.

Need for Achievement Perhaps the major problem that teachers have in using Atkinson's theory of need for achievement is the lack of efficient and objective instruments for measuring its strength. Although you could probably draw reasonably accurate conclusions about whether a student has a high or low need for achievement by watching that student's behavior over time and in a variety of situations, you may not be in a position to make extensive observations. And the problem with short-term observations is that a student's achievement orientation may be affected by more or less chance circumstances. A student might do well on a first exam in a course, for example, because the teacher gave in-class time for study and happened to offer advice at a crucial point during the study period. The high score on that test might inspire the student to work for an A in that class. But if that exam happened to be scheduled the day after a two week bout with the flu, the student might not be well prepared and could end up with a C or D grade. Such a poor performance might cause the student to forget about the A and concentrate instead on obtaining a C.

Need for achievement difficult to assess on basis of short-term observations

Attribution Theory and Beliefs About Ability The major implication of the idea that faulty attributions are at least partly responsible for sabotaging students' motivation for learning is to teach students to make more appropriate attributions. But this is likely to be a substantial undertaking requiring a concerted, coordinated effort. One part of the problem in working with students who attribute failure to lack of ability is that ability tends to be seen as a stable factor that is relatively impervious to change. The other part of the problem is that the same students often attribute their success to task difficulty and luck, two factors that cannot be predicted or controlled because they are external and random. Ideas about how to teach students to make more appropriate attributions for success and failure can be found in *Enhancing Motivation: Change in the Classroom* (1976), by Richard deCharms. An additional limitation is that attribution training is not likely to be fully effective with elementary school children. For them, two individuals who learn the same amount of material are equally smart despite the fact that one person has to work twice as long to achieve that goal. Older children and adolescents, however, have a better grasp of the concept of efficiency; they see ability as something that influences the amount and effectiveness of effort (Stipek, 1993).

Faulty attributions difficult to change due to beliefs about ability

The Humanistic View of Motivation

Abraham Maslow earned his Ph.D. in a psychology department that supported the behaviorist position. After he graduated, however, he came into contact with Gestalt psychologists (a group of German psychologists whose work during the 1920s and 1930s laid the foundation for the cognitive theories of the 1960s and 1970s), prepared for a career as a psychoanalyst, and became interested in anthropology. As a result of these various influences, he came to the conclusion that American psychologists who endorsed the behaviorist position had become so preoccupied with overt behavior and objectivity that they were ignoring other important aspects of human existence (hence the term *humanistic* to describe his views). When Maslow observed the behavior of especially well-adjusted persons—or *self-actualizers,* as he called them—he concluded that healthy individuals are motivated to *seek* fulfilling experiences.

MASLOW'S THEORY OF GROWTH MOTIVATION

Maslow describes seventeen propositions, discussed in Chapter 1 of *Motivation and Personality* (3d ed., 1987), that he believes would have to be incorporated into any sound theory of *growth motivation* (or *need gratification*) to meet them. Referring to need gratification as the most important single principle underlying all development, he adds that "the single, holistic principle that binds together the multiplicity of human motives is the tendency for a new and higher need to emerge as the lower need fulfills itself by being sufficiently gratified" (1968, p. 55). He elaborates on this basic principle by proposing a five-level hierarchy of needs. *Physiological* needs are at the bottom of the hierarchy, followed in ascending order by *safety, belongingness and love, esteem,* and *self-actualization* needs (see Figure 11.1). This order reflects differences in the relative strength of each need. The lower a need is in the hierarchy, the greater is its strength because when a lower-level need is activated (as in the case of extreme hunger or fear for one's physical safety), people will stop trying to satisfy a higher-level need (such as esteem or

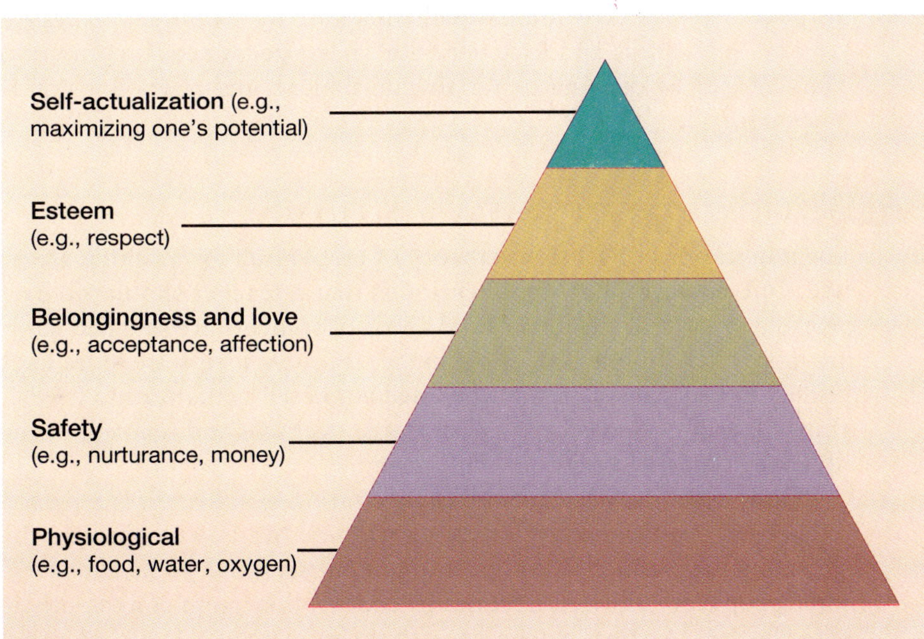

FIGURE 11.1 *Maslow's Hierarchy of Needs*

SOURCE: Maslow (1943).

self-actualization) and focus on satisfying the currently active lower-level need (Maslow, 1987).

The first four needs (physiological, safety, belongingness and love, and esteem) are often referred to as **deficiency needs** because they motivate people to act only when they are unmet to some degree. Self-actualization, by contrast, is often called a **growth need** because people constantly strive to satisfy it. Basically, **self-actualization** refers to the need for self-fulfillment—the need to develop all of one's potential talents and capabilities. For example, an individual who felt she had the capability to write novels, teach, practice medicine, and raise children would not feel self-actualized until all of these goals had been accomplished to some minimal degree. Because it is at the top of the hierarchy and addresses the potential of the whole person, self-actualization is discussed more frequently than the other needs.

People are motivated to satisfy deficiency needs only when those needs are unmet

Maslow originally felt that self-actualization needs would automatically be activated as soon as esteem needs were met, but he changed his mind when he encountered individuals whose behavior did not fit this pattern. He concluded that individuals whose self-actualization needs became activated held in high regard such values as truth, goodness, beauty, justice, autonomy, and humor (Feist, 1990).

Self-actualization depends on satisfaction of lower needs, belief in certain values

In addition to the five basic needs that compose the hierarchy, Maslow describes cognitive needs (such as the needs to know and to understand) and aesthetic needs (such as the needs for order, symmetry, or harmony). While not part of the basic hierarchy, these two classes of needs play a critical role in the satisfaction of basic needs. Maslow maintains that such conditions as the freedom to investigate and learn, fairness, honesty, and orderliness in interpersonal relationships are critical because their absence makes satisfaction of the five basic needs impossible. (Imagine, for example, trying to satisfy your belongingness and love needs or your esteem needs in an atmosphere characterized by dishonesty, unfair punishment, and restrictions on freedom of speech.)

IMPLICATIONS OF MASLOW'S THEORY

The implications of Maslow's theory of motivation for teaching are provocative. One down-to-earth implication is that a teacher should do everything possible to see that the lower-level needs of students are satisfied so that they are more likely to function at the higher levels. Students are more likely to be primed to seek satisfaction of the esteem and self-actualization needs, for example, if they are physically comfortable, feel safe and relaxed, have a sense of belonging, and experience self-esteem.

Only when the need for self-actualization is activated is a person likely to choose wisely when given the opportunity. Maslow emphasizes this point by making a distinction between *bad choosers* and *good choosers*. When some people are allowed freedom to choose, they seem consistently to make wise choices. Most people, however, frequently make self-destructive choices. An insecure student, for example, may choose to attend a particular college more on the basis of how close it is to home than on the quality of its academic programs.

When deficiency needs are not satisfied, person likely to make bad choices

Growth, as Maslow sees it, is the result of a never-ending series of situations offering a free choice between the attractions and dangers of safety and those of growth. If a person is functioning at the level of growth needs, the choice will ordinarily be a progressive one. Maslow adds, however, that "the environment (parents, therapists, teachers) . . . . can help by making the growth choice positively attractive and less dangerous, and by making the regressive choice less attractive and more costly" (1968, pp. 58–59). This point can be clarified by a simple diagram Maslow uses to illustrate a situation involving choice (1968, p. 47).

Enhance the dangers		Enhance the attraction
Safety	←—person—→	Growth
Minimize the attractions		Minimize the dangers

This diagram emphasizes that if you set up learning situations that impress students as dangerous, threatening, or of little value, they are likely to play it safe, make little effort to respond, or even try to avoid learning. If, however, you make learning appear appealing, minimize pressure, and reduce possibilities for failure or embarrassment, your students are likely to be willing, if not eager, to do an assigned task.

Encourage growth choices by enhancing attractions, minimizing dangers

LIMITATIONS OF MASLOW'S THEORY

While Maslow's speculations are thought-provoking, they are also sometimes frustrating. You may conclude, for instance, that awareness of his hierarchy of needs will make it possible for you to do an excellent job of motivating your students, only to discover that you don't know exactly how to apply what you have learned. Quite often, for example, you may not be able to determine precisely which of a student's needs are unsatisfied. Even if you *are* quite sure that a student lacks interest in learning because he feels unloved or insecure, you may not be able to do much about it. A girl who feels that her parents do not love her or that her peers do not accept her may not respond to your efforts. And if her needs for love, belonging, and esteem are not satisfied, she is less likely to be in the mood to learn.

Teachers may be able to satisfy some deficiency needs but not others

Then again, there will be times when you can be quite instrumental in helping satisfy certain deficiency needs. The development of self-esteem, for example, is closely tied to successful classroom achievement for almost all students. Although you may not be able to feed students when they are hungry or protect them from physical danger, you can always take steps to help them learn more effectively.

The Role of Self-Perceptions in Motivation

Current interest in the effects of self-perceptions on school motivation and achievement runs high and seems to have been prompted by such developments as a better understanding of the nature of self-concept and self-esteem, the introduction by Bandura of the self-efficacy concept, advances in the measurement of self-perceptions, and the consistent finding of a positive relationship among self-perceptions, motivation, and school achievement. Much of this interest can be traced to ideas published during the 1960s and 1970s by psychologists such as Abraham Maslow, Carl Rogers, and Arthur Combs. These individuals stressed that how students saw and judged themselves and others played an important part in determining how motivated they were and how much they learned.

In Chapter 3 we introduced and briefly discussed the notions of self-concept, self-esteem, and self-efficacy as important aspects of children's emotional and cognitive development. In Chapter 8 we described in even more detail the nature of self-efficacy and its role in learning. We will now revisit each of these concepts because of their relationship to motivation.

SELF-CONCEPT, SELF-ESTEEM, AND SELF-EFFICACY

To briefly review, self-concept is the nonevaluative picture people have of themselves. It begins to be revealed when people make such statements as "I am a sixth grader," "I am five feet one inches tall," or "My favorite subject is history." Current theory and research support a notion of self-concept as being made up of separate parts that are hierarchically arranged. That is, individuals have a nonacademic self-concept and an academic self-concept. One's academic self-concept can be broken down into a mathematical/academic self-concept and a verbal/academic self-concept. Each of these can be further subdivided into subject-specific self-concepts (Marsh, Byrne, & Shavelson, 1992).

Self-concept is description of self; self-esteem is value we place on that description

Self-esteem refers to the evaluative judgments we make of the various parts that make up our self-concept. A person's level of self-esteem can be inferred from such comments as "I think I'm pretty smart at math," "I'm too short for my age," "I'm not much good at making new friends," and "My ability to speak and understand a foreign language is about average" (Beane, 1994; Harter, 1988). Another way of thinking about the relationship between self-concept and self-esteem is that the former describes who you are, whereas the latter indicates how you feel about that identity.

Self-efficacy is like self-esteem in that it involves an evaluative judgment. But self-efficacy judgments are different because they refer only to how capable a person thinks he is at organizing and carrying out a specific course of action (Bandura, 1986; Schunk, 1995). Thinking of yourself as ugly because your nose seems to be too big for your face or as being smarter than most other people is a self-esteem judgment. Believing yourself highly capable of learning how to use a computer program or incapable of figuring out how to solve quadratic equations is a self-efficacy judgment.

THE ROLE OF SELF-CONCEPT/SELF-ESTEEM IN MOTIVATION AND LEARNING

Over the years researchers have consistently found a moderately positive relationship (called a correlation) between measures of self-esteem and school achievement. Students who score relatively high on measures of self-esteem tend to have higher-than-average grades. But, as the saying goes, correlation

Students who have a positive self-concept tend to be intrinsically motivated. They have a high level of curiosity, are interested in schoolwork, and prefer moderately challenging tasks.

does not imply causation. The fact that students with high self-esteem scores tend to have high grades is not sufficient grounds for concluding that high self-esteem causes high achievement. It is just as plausible that high achievement causes increased self-esteem or that increases in both variables are due to the influence of a third variable. Recent work on the antecedents and consequences of self-esteem has begun to shed some light on what causes what.

Susan Harter (1988), on the basis of her own research and that of others, proposes the causal explanation depicted in Figure 11.2. Harter believes that achieving an acceptable level of competence in school, valuing academic success (which most students do), and being given support and positive

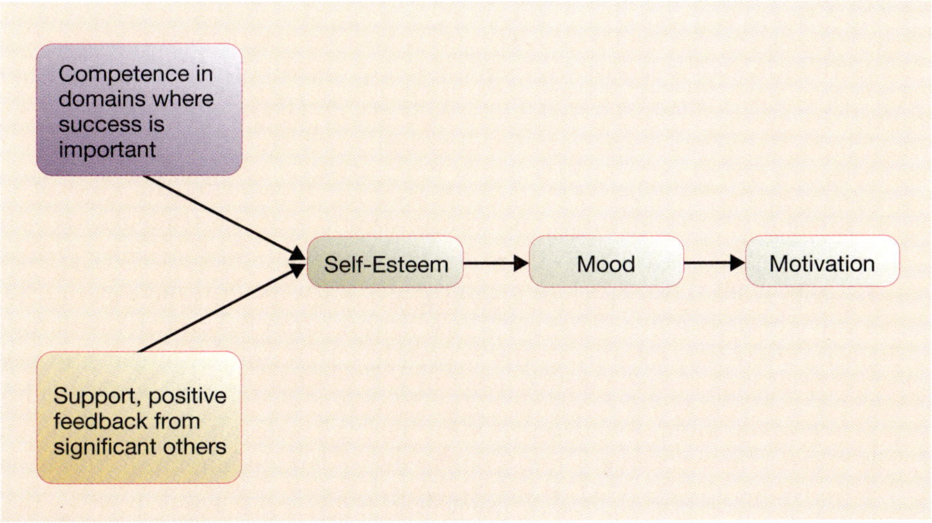

FIGURE 11.2 *Causes and Consequences of Academic Self-Esteem*

SOURCE: Adapted from Harter (1988).

High self-esteem due to being competent at valued tasks, reinforcement from others

feedback for one's academic accomplishments by parents, teachers, and friends are the primary determinants of a positive self-concept (high self-esteem). A positive self-concept contributes, in turn, to feeling satisfied and pleased about one's accomplishments, which contributes to the development of intrinsic motivation. Such students are likely to be curious about many things, to find schoolwork interesting, and to prefer moderately challenging tasks. This motivational orientation leads to high levels of achievement, which maintain high levels of self-esteem, and so on.

In contrast, children with relatively low levels of achievement see themselves as less competent than their peers and tend to feel badly about their performance. This attitude leads to a more extrinsic motivation orientation in which students show little interest or pleasure in classroom learning, avoid challenging tasks when they have the opportunity to do so, and reduce their efforts in subjects where they are having difficulty keeping up with others. This, of course, leads to low grades and a perpetual pattern of low self-esteem, low motivation, and low grades.

In one study Harter found that seventh graders who placed a high value on academic success but who felt their learning skills weren't developing rapidly enough for them to keep up with teachers' demands had lower levels of self-esteem than did peers who were able to tell themselves that school success wasn't that important. The fact that Harter found this phenomenon among seventh graders is noteworthy given the often-cited declines in motivation that occur when students move from the elementary to the middle school or junior high grades and from the middle school or junior high to the high school grades. These transitions require students to deal with a larger and less familiar peer group, several teachers who are seen only for a short time each day, greater academic demands, and a more competitive reward system (Anderman & Maehr, 1994; Lipka, Hurford, & Litten, 1992).

Self-esteem declines when students move from elementary grades to middle school and from middle school to high school

THE ROLE OF SELF-EFFICACY IN MOTIVATION AND LEARNING

An individual's sense of self-efficacy can affect motivation to learn in at least three ways, each of which we will discuss briefly.

Choice of Learning Goals One way is by influencing the kind of learning goals a student chooses. According to one scheme, students may choose a task mastery, ego/social, or work-avoidant goal. Task mastery goals involve doing what is necessary to meaningfully learn the information and skills that have been assigned. They are chosen more often by students with high levels of self-efficacy than by students with low levels of self-efficacy. In pursuit of task mastery goals, high efficacy students will use a variety of encoding techniques, do more organizing of information to make it meaningful, review and practice more frequently, monitor their understanding more closely, and formulate more effective learning strategies. Ego/social goals involve doing what is necessary to please the teacher and one's parents. This may mean memorizing large amounts of information to get a high test grade without necessarily understanding the ideas or how they relate to each other or doing assignments neatly and exactly according to directions. Students who choose ego/social goals tend to have lower levels of self-efficacy. Work-avoidant goals involve, as the term suggests, trying to get by with as little work as possible. This goal is also selected more often by students with low levels of self-efficacy (Schunk, 1995).

Outcome Expectations A second way in which self-efficacy can affect motivation is in terms of the outcomes that students expect. Those with high levels of self-efficacy more often expect a positive outcome. As a result, they tend to be more willing to use the more complex and time-consuming learning skills mentioned previously and to persist longer in the face of difficulties. Those with lower levels of self-efficacy are more likely to expect a disappointing outcome, tend to use simpler learning skills, and are likely to give up more quickly when tasks demand greater cognitive efforts (Bandura, 1993; Schunk, 1995).

Attributions A third way in which self-efficacy influences motivation is through the reasons students cite to explain why they succeeded or failed at a task. Those with a high level of self-efficacy for a subject are likely to attribute failure to insufficient effort (and so vow to work harder the next time) but credit their success to a combination of ability and effort. Their low self-efficacy peers are likely to explain their failures by saying that they just don't have the ability to do well in this subject, but they will chalk their successes up to an easy task or luck. As we pointed out earlier in this chapter, this attribution pattern undercuts motivation since it ascribes success to unstable factors that cannot be controlled but ascribes failure to a stable factor that is internal and often viewed as unchangeable (Bandura, 1993; Schunk, 1995).

Self-efficacy affects choice of goals, expectations of success, attributions for success and failure

IMPLICATIONS OF RESEARCH ON SELF-PERCEPTIONS

According to current research, enhanced self-esteem does not lead to higher levels of motivation and achievement, but higher levels of achievement can increase future motivation and self-esteem. Furthermore, there is essentially no support for the claims made by the designers of special curriculum programs that they can raise students' levels of self-esteem. A major implication that follows from these two statements is that educators should focus instead on altering the entire school environment so as to maximize the amount of meaningful learning that takes place (Beane, 1994; Kohn, 1994). We have already offered several suggestions for doing just that in Chapters 8, 9, and 10. We will offer some additional suggestions in the next section when we take up cooperative learning and in the next chapter when we discuss mastery learning. And, as you will see from Case in Print, which describes one solution to altering a whole-school environment, sometimes the most effective way to enhance students' self-perceptions is to start with teachers' ideas about students' competence.

Raise self-esteem by helping students become better learners

LIMITATIONS OF THE SELF-PERCEPTIONS APPROACH

One problem with using students' views of themselves as a way of influencing their motivation and learning is the lack of useful, commercially prepared measures of self-efficacy and self-esteem. Most of the available instruments

Helping Teachers Develop Students' Self-Efficacy, Self-Esteem, and Motivation

Achieving an acceptable level of competence in school, valuing academic success..., and being given support and positive feedback for one's academic accomplishments by parents, teachers, and friends are the primary determinants of a positive [academic] self-concept (high [academic] self-esteem). A positive self-concept contributes, in turn, to feeling satisfied and pleased about one's accomplishments, which contributes to the development of intrinsic motivation. (pp. 211–212)

"Instituting Efficacy: Self-Esteem Principles May Be Tested at Burke High"

ESTHER SHEIN

Boston Sunday Globe 6/18/95

One of the first calls Steven Leonard made when he was named headmaster of Boston's Jeremiah E. Burke High School was to the Lexington-based Efficacy Institute. Leonard, who earlier this month was given the formidable task of helping the Burke regain its accreditation, has trained at the institute himself, and he was confident it could help his teachers.

His confidence is based not just on his own experience. Since it was founded 10 years ago, the Efficacy Institute has trained some 20,000 teachers in 64 school districts across the state. Its teaching is based on the principle that intelligence is a developmental process, not something a person is born with. It tries to instill the notion in teachers that all students have the ability to learn when teachers believe in the students' capabilities and the students are given confidence.

If he can come up with the $300 per-person training fee for the institute's four-day training sessions, Leonard said, Efficacy training will be a requirement for all teachers who remain at the Burke next fall.

"Efficacy is part of the solution," he said in a recent interview. "After you eliminate...the staff people that can't perform or don't want to perform in ways that are essential to educating children, you get to the realization that, in many, if not most, cases, teachers have been left in the lurch as far as professional development in teaching the contemporary child."

Efficacy founder Jeff Howard said he will work closely with Leonard to train the Burke's teachers. But he said the city, in turn, needs to make an investment in the school building to show the students it cares about their welfare.

"The City of Boston ought to be ashamed of how it's treated that building," said Howard, a Harvard-educated social psychologist, "and the deplorable conditions the faculty has had to work under."

Another hurdle, Howard said, is helping teachers overcome a high level of frustration. They have become demoralized, he said, because society no longer views the teaching profession as prestigious.

"It's a terrible state for teachers to be in," he said. "They desperately want to be great teachers again—everybody wants to be effective in their work—and our secret weapon is that we help them feel effective again."

Another burden placed on teachers, Howard said, is the notion that there's an "unequal distribution of intelligence, and that the kinds of kids that go to inner-city schools...don't have a lot of intelligence."

That, he said, puts teachers "in a tough situation. They're given these kids that nobody thinks can learn much, and then they're given the mandate that they have to teach them."

Efficacy's role, according to Howard, is to "explode that bind. The underlying premise is all wrong." All students can learn, he said, if they are perceived to have the right attitude. But before that can happen, he said, the teachers' own attitude has to change.

"They have the capacity to be some of the best professionals in American society," Howard said of the teachers. "They have potential to be creative, disciplined, highly skilled, lifelong learners, but they have to believe in themselves and the kids. American society makes that hard; we make it easy."

Mia Roberts, director of community services for the institute, said much of the frustration lies in the fact that "kids come into school now with lots of other needs," including emotional and health issues.

Consequently, she said, the teachers become "educators, counselors, psychologists and moms and dads all rolled into one...and that can be very overwhelming."

Efficacy stresses, she said, that "all people are capable of brilliance and no one has limits. Human capabilities...can be developed throughout life."

That idea has become almost a religious belief for Jesse Solomon, a math teacher at Brighton High School who first learned about the institute while doing a college internship there.

"Having someone unconditionally believe in your intelligence can only be a positive thing," he said. "It turns kids around at best, and allows them small successes at worst."

Solomon believes he has always had a positive attitude toward his students, but he said Efficacy helped him translate that into action.

"Everything you see in your classroom sends a million messages a day," Solomon said, including messages about high expectations. But if those messages come from someone who believes in them, he said, the students are more likely to perform effectively.

Solomon recalled a middle-school student he taught for two years. For no particular reason, Solomon said, the student did poorly his first year.

"Showing him that I had a belief in him that wasn't going to go away...caused him to put in hard work," Solomon said. "He came to school every day, and he graduated as a competent and confident student, more so than when I first met him."

Solomon attributes the turnaround to the student's increased motivation level and the desire to "make himself get smarter. The work has to be well-designed and supported, but I think that's the only way to get smarter."

Solomon said Efficacy also taught him the importance of creating networks with other teachers.

"No change or reform is going to come without those networks," he said. Calling teaching "a very isolated profession," Solomon said it would be cathartic for teachers to meet once a week after school to discuss issues such as dealing with students, developing curricula together or even reading articles about education.

"Often," he said, "there's no built-in time to share what you do professionally or no time to discuss their craft."

...The new headmaster said his challenge is to change the misperception that "some kids make it and some kids don't, and those who flunk are dumb...and the kids who make it are smart."

Leonard said Efficacy helps teachers understand that, many times, what's perceived as their failure is really "the failure of school systems and the university community to prepare teachers to do the job of urban education in 1995."

Even the best teachers will be deemed ineffective if they're asked to perform at levels that "exhaust their physical or mental resources, and right now that's what's being asked of many teachers—especially in urban environments—where issues of poverty are becoming more demanding and resources are decreasing."

Questions and Activities

1. The philosophy of the Efficacy Institute is that students' intellectual capabilities can be improved through systematic efforts that combine high-quality instruction and positive feedback from teachers about students' competence. This is the same idea as Dweck's incremental theory of intelligence. Do you share that belief? If so, what evidence can you cite in support of it? If you don't share that belief, can you explain why not?

2. Mia Roberts, the director of community services for the Efficacy Institute, noted that one of the challenges for teachers is that "kids come into school now with lots of other needs," and that these needs include emotional and health issues. As we pointed out earlier in the chapter, Maslow's theory suggests that as long as a person's deficiency needs are unmet, growth needs will not be activated. One implication of this analysis is that teachers need to be aware of students' unmet deficiency needs. What steps can you take to increase the likelihood that you will notice and attend to a student's physiological, safety, belongingness, and esteem needs?

3. If you have the opportunity to work with a low-achieving student, systematically provide the type of positive feedback described in the article and note any subsequent changes in the student's behavior. Ask the student whether his or her self-efficacy and beliefs about intelligence changed as a function of your comments.

assess global self-concept/global self-esteem. But as we mentioned earlier, the more narrow the measure of self-perception is (such as math self-esteem, self-efficacy for understanding medieval literature), the better it predicts motivation and achievement. One solution to this limitation is to prepare the same kinds of instruments that researchers use. This is not as difficult as it might seem. Some researchers use a relatively small set of questions ("How good are you at math?" "If you were to rank all the students in your math class from the worst to the best, where would you put yourself?" "Compared to your other school subjects, how good are you at math?") and ask students to rate themselves on a 7-point scale that may range from "not at all good" to "very good" (Stipek, 1993).

Another problem is that whatever success you may have in changing the sense of self-esteem and self-efficacy of students is likely to be slow in coming. This conclusion follows from two others. One is that changes in self-perception are best made by helping students become more effective learners than by constantly telling them they should feel good about themselves. The second conclusion is that learning how to use the cognitive skills that result in meaningful learning takes time because of their complexity and the doubts that some students will have about their ability to master these skills.

The Impact of Cooperative Learning on Motivation

Classroom tasks can be structured so that students are forced to compete with one another, work individually, or cooperate with one another to obtain the rewards that teachers make available for successfully completing these tasks. Traditionally, competitive arrangements have been assumed to be superior to the other two in increasing motivation and learning. But reviews of the research literature by David Johnson and Roger Johnson (Johnson & Johnson, 1995; Johnson, Johnson, & Smith, 1995) found cooperative arrangements to be far superior in producing these benefits. In this section we will describe cooperative-, competitive, and individual learning arrangements (sometimes called goal structures or reward structures), identify the elements that make up the major approaches to cooperative learning, and examine the effect of cooperative learning on motivation, achievement, and interpersonal relationships.

TYPES OF CLASSROOM REWARD STRUCTURES

Competitive Competitive goal structures are typically norm referenced. (If you can't recall our discussion of the normal curve in Chapter 5, now might be a good time for a quick review.) This traditional practice of grading on the curve predetermines the percentage of A, B, C, D, and F grades regardless of the actual distribution of test scores. Because only a small percentage of students in any group can achieve the highest rewards and because this accomplishment must come at some other students' expense, competitive goal structures are characterized by negative interdependence. Students try to outdo one another, view classmates' failures as an advantage, and come to believe that the winners deserve their rewards because they are inherently better (Johnson, Johnson, & Holubec, 1994; Johnson et al., 1995).

Some researchers have argued that competitive reward structures lead students to focus on ability as the primary basis for motivation. This orientation is reflected in the question "Am I smart enough to accomplish this task?" When ability is the basis for motivation, competing successfully in the classroom may be seen as relevant to self-esteem (since nobody loves a loser), difficult to accomplish (since only a few can succeed), and uncertain (success depends on how everyone else does). These perceptions may cause some students to avoid challenging subjects or tasks, to give up in the face of difficulty, to reward themselves only if they win a competition, and to believe that their own successes are due to ability, whereas the successes of others are due to luck (Ames & Ames, 1984; Dweck, 1986).

Competitive reward structures may decrease motivation to learn

Individualistic Individualistic goal structures are characterized by students working alone and earning rewards solely on the quality of their own efforts. The success or failure of other students is irrelevant. All that matters is whether the student meets the standards for a particular task (Johnson et al., 1994; Johnson et al., 1995). Thirty students working by themselves at computer terminals are functioning in an individual reward structure. According to Carole Ames and Russell Ames (1984), individual structures lead students to focus on task effort as the primary basis for motivation (as in "I can do this if I try"). Whether a student perceives a task as difficult depends on how successful she has been with that type of task in the past.

Cooperative Cooperative goal structures are characterized by students working together to accomplish shared goals. What is beneficial for the other students in the group is beneficial for the individual and vice versa. Because students in cooperative groups can obtain a desired reward (such as a high grade or a feeling of satisfaction for a job well done) only if the other students in the group also obtain the same reward, cooperative goal structures are characterized by positive interdependence. Also, all groups may receive the same rewards, provided they meet the teacher's criteria for mastery. For example, a teacher might present a lesson on map reading, then give each group its own map and a question-answering exercise. Students then work with each other to ensure that all know how to interpret maps. Each student then takes a quiz on map reading. All teams whose average quiz scores meet a preset standard receive special recognition (Johnson et al., 1994; Johnson et al., 1995; Slavin, 1995).

Cooperative structures lead students to focus on effort and cooperation as the primary basis of motivation. This orientation is reflected in the statement "We can do this if we try hard and work together." In a cooperative atmosphere, students are motivated out of a sense of obligation: one ought to try, contribute, and help satisfy group norms (Ames & Ames, 1984). William Glasser, whose ideas we mentioned earlier, is a fan of cooperative learning. He points out that student motivation and performance tend to be highest for such activities as band, drama club, athletics, the school newspaper, and the yearbook, all of which require a team effort (Gough, 1987). We would also like to point out that cooperative-learning and reward structures are consistent with the constructivist approach discussed in Chapters 1, 2, and 10 since they encourage inquiry, perspective sharing, and conflict resolution.

Cooperative reward structures are more likely to motivate almost all students in a class to study and develop positive attitudes toward learning than are competitive or individualistic arrangements.

ELEMENTS OF COOPERATIVE LEARNING

Over the past twenty years different approaches to cooperative learning have been proposed by different individuals. The three most popular are those of David Johnson and Roger Johnson (Johnson et al., 1994), Robert Slavin (1994, 1995), and Shlomo Sharan and Yael Sharan (Sharan, 1995; Sharan & Sharan, 1994). To give you a general sense of what cooperative learning is like and to avoid limiting you to any one individual's approach, the following discussion is a synthesis of the main features of each approach.

Group Heterogeneity The size of cooperative-learning groups is relatively small and as heterogeneous as circumstances allow. The recommended size is usually four to five students. At the very least, groups should contain both males and females and students of different ability levels. If possible, different ethnic backgrounds and social classes should be represented as well.

Group Goals/Positive Interdependence A specific goal, such as a grade or a certificate of recognition, is identified for the group to attain. Students are told that they will have to support one another because the group goal can be achieved only if each member learns the material being taught (in the case of a task that culminates in an exam) or makes a specific contribution to the group's effort (in the case of a task that culminates in a presentation or a project).

Promotive Interaction This element is made necessary by the existence of positive interdependence. Students are shown how to help each other overcome problems and complete whatever task has been assigned. This may involve episodes of peer tutoring, temporary assistance, exchanges of information and material, challenging of each other's reasoning, feedback, and encouragement to keep one another highly motivated.

Individual Accountability This feature stipulates that each member of a group has to make a significant contribution to achieving the group's goal. This may be satisfied by achieving a minimal score on a test, having the group's test score be the sum or average of each student's quiz scores, or having each member be responsible for a particular part of a project (such as doing the research and writing for a particular part of a history report).

Cooperative learning characterized by heterogeneous groups, positive interdependence, promotive interaction, individual accountability

Interpersonal Skills Positive interdependence and promotive interaction are not likely to occur if students do not know how to make the most of their face-to-face interactions. And you can safely assume that the interpersonal skills most students possess are probably not highly developed. As a result, they have to be taught such basic skills as leadership, decision making, trust building, clear communication, and conflict management. The conflict that arises over differences of opinion, for example, can be constructive if it is used as a stimulus to search for more information or to rethink one's conclusions. But it can destroy group cohesion and productivity if it results in students stubbornly clinging to a position or referring to each other as "stubborn," "dumb," or "nerdy."

Equal Opportunities for Success Because cooperative groups are heterogeneous with respect to ability and their success depends on positive interdependence, promotive interaction, and individual accountability, it is important that steps be taken to ensure that all students have an opportunity to contribute to their team. You can do this by awarding points for degree of improvement over previous test scores, having students compete against comparable members of other teams in a game- or tournament-like atmosphere, or giving students learning assignments (such as math problems) that are geared to their current level of skill.

Team Competition This may seem to be an odd entry in a list of cooperative-learning components, especially in light of the comments we made earlier about the ineffectiveness of competition as a spur to motivation. But we're not being contradictory. The main problem with competition is that it is rarely used appropriately. When competition occurs between well-matched competitors, is done in the absence of a norm-referenced grading system, and is not used too frequently, it can be an effective way to motivate students to cooperate with each other.

DOES COOPERATIVE LEARNING WORK?

The short answer to this question is yes. In the vast majority of studies, forms of cooperative learning have been shown to be more effective than non-cooperative reward structures in raising the levels of variables that contribute to motivation, in raising achievement, and in producing positive social outcomes.

Effect on Motivation Because a student's sense of self-esteem can have a strong effect on motivation (a point we made in the last section of this chapter), this variable has been examined in several cooperative-learning studies.

The results are encouraging, yet confusing. Slavin (1995) found that in eleven of fifteen studies, cooperative learning produced bigger increases in some aspect of self-esteem (general self-esteem, academic self-esteem, social self-esteem) than the noncooperative method with which it was compared. But these effects were not consistent across studies. Some researchers would report increases in academic self-esteem or social self-esteem, but others would find no effect. Adding to the confusion is the conclusion drawn by Johnson and Johnson (1995) that cooperative learning consistently produced higher self-efficacy scores than did competitive or individualistic conditions. Such inconsistencies may reflect weaknesses in the self-esteem instruments that were used (self-ratings are not always accurate), weaknesses in the designs of the studies (many cooperative-learning studies last anywhere from a few days to a few weeks, yet changes in self-esteem happen slowly), or differences in specific cooperative-learning programs. Perhaps future research will clarify this issue.

Another way in which cooperative learning contributes to high levels of motivation is in the proacademic attitudes that it fosters among group members. Slavin (1995) cites several studies in which students in cooperative-learning groups felt more strongly than did other students that their groupmates wanted them to come to school every day and work hard in class.

Probably because of such features as promotive interaction and equal opportunities for success, cooperative learning has been shown to have a positive effect on motivation inducing attributions. Students in cooperative-learning groups were more likely to attribute success to hard work and ability than to luck (Slavin, 1995).

A strong indicator of motivation is the actual amount of time students spend working on a task. Most studies have found that cooperative-learning students spend significantly more time on-task than do control students (Johnson et al., 1995; Slavin, 1995).

Effect on Achievement Slavin (1995) examined several dozen studies that lasted four or more weeks and that used a variety of cooperative-learning methods. Overall, students in cooperative-learning groups scored about one-fourth of a standard deviation higher on achievement tests than did students taught conventionally. This translates to an advantage of 10 percentile ranks (60th percentile for the average cooperative-learning student versus 50th percentile for the average conventionally taught student). But the beneficial effect of cooperative learning varied widely as a function of the particular method used. The best performances occurred with two techniques called Student Teams-Achievement Divisions and Teams-Games-Tournaments. The cooperative-learning features that seem to be most responsible for learning gains are group goals and individual accountability.

David Johnson, Roger Johnson, and Karl Smith (1995) also reviewed much of the cooperative-learning literature but drew a somewhat different conclusion. They found that the test scores of students in the cooperative-learning groups were about two-thirds of a standard deviation higher than the test scores of students in competitive or individualistic situations. This translates to an advantage of 25 percentile ranks (75th versus 50th). It's not clear why Slavin's analysis produced a somewhat lower estimate of the size of the advantage produced by cooperative learning. It may be due in part to differences in the studies cited by each; Slavin focused on studies lasting at least four weeks. It may also be due to differences in the cooperative techniques used by various researchers.

In addition to achievement outcomes, researchers have also assessed the impact of cooperative learning on problem solving. Given the complex nature of problem solving and the multiple resources that a cooperative group has at its disposal, one would logically expect cooperative learning to have a positive effect on this outcome as well. This hypothesis was confirmed by Zhining Qin, David Johnson, and Roger Johnson (1995). After reviewing forty-six studies, they concluded that students of all age levels (elementary, secondary, college, adult) who worked cooperatively outscored students who worked competitively. The average student in a cooperative group solved more problems correctly than 71 percent of the students who worked competitively.

Effect on Social Relationships In most studies students exposed to cooperative learning were more likely than students who learned under competitive or individualistic conditions to name a classmate from a different race, ethnic group, or social class as a friend or to label such individuals as "nice" or "smart." In some studies the friendships that were formed were deemed to be quite strong. A similar positive effect was found for students with mental disabilities who were mainstreamed. Finally, the cooperations skills that students learn apparently transfer. Cooperative-learning students were more likely than other students to use the cooperative behaviors they were taught when they worked with new classmates (Johnson & Johnson, 1995; Slavin, 1995).

Students who learn cooperatively tend to be more highly motivated to learn because of increased self-esteem, the proacademic attitudes of groupmates, appropriate attributions for success and failure, and greater on-task behavior. They also score higher on tests of achievement and problem solving and tend to get along better with classmates of different racial, ethnic, and social class backgrounds. This last outcome should be of particular interest to those of you who expect to teach in areas marked by cultural diversity.

WHY DOES COOPERATIVE LEARNING WORK?

When researchers attempt to explain the widespread positive effects that are typically found among studies of cooperative learning, they usually cite one or more of the following explanations (Slavin, 1995).

Motivational Effect The various features of cooperative learning, particularly positive interdependence, are highly motivating because they encourage such achievement-oriented behaviors as trying hard, attending class regularly, praising the efforts of others, and receiving help from one's groupmates. Learning is seen as an obligation and a valued activity because the group's success is based on it and one's groupmates will reward it.

Cognitive-Developmental Effect According to Lev Vygotsky, collaboration promotes cognitive growth because students model for each other more advanced ways of thinking than any would demonstrate individually. According to Jean Piaget, collaboration among peers hastens the decline of egocentrism and allows the development of more advanced ways of understanding and dealing with the world.

Cooperative-learning effects likely due to stimulation of motivation, cognitive development, meaningful learning

Cognitive Elaboration Effect As we saw in Chapter 9, new information that is elaborated (restructured and related to existing knowledge) is more easily retrieved from memory than is information that is not elaborated. A particularly effective means of elaboration is explaining something to someone else.

Now that you are familiar with interpretations of motivation, it is time to consider in the Suggestions for Teaching that follow how the information and speculations you've learned can be converted into classroom practice.

Suggestions for Teaching in Your Classroom

Motivating Students to Learn

1. Use behavioral techniques to help students exert themselves and work toward remote goals.

2. Make sure that students know what they are to do, how to proceed, and how to determine when they have achieved goals.

3. Do everything possible to satisfy deficiency needs—physiological, safety, belongingness, and esteem.
   a. Accommodate the instructional program to the physiological needs of your students.
   b. Make your room physically and psychologically safe.
   c. Show your students that you take an interest in them and that they belong in your classroom.
   d. Arrange learning experiences so that all students can gain at least a degree of esteem.

4. Enhance the attractions and minimize the dangers of growth choices.

5. Direct learning experiences toward feelings of success in an effort to encourage an orientation toward achievement, a positive self-concept, and a strong sense of self-efficacy.
   a. Make use of objectives that are challenging but attainable and, when appropriate, that involve student input.
   b. Provide knowledge of results by emphasizing the positive.

6. Try to encourage the development of need achievement, self-confidence, and self-direction in students who need these qualities.
   a. Use achievement-motivation training techniques.
   b. Use cooperative-learning methods.

7. Try to make learning interesting by emphasizing activity, investigation, adventure, social interaction, and usefulness.

1. Use behavioral techniques to help students exert themselves and work toward remote goals.

Maslow's hierarchy of needs calls attention to the reasons that few students come to school bursting with eagerness to learn. Only students with all their deficiency needs satisfied are likely to experience a desire to know and understand. But even growth-motivated students may not fully appreciate the need to master certain basic skills before they can engage in more exciting and rewarding kinds of learning. And as we noted earlier, the information that appropriately administered reinforcement provides about one's level of competence contributes to high levels of self-esteem. Accordingly, you may often need to give your students incentives to learn. Techniques you might use for this purpose were described in Chapter 8. They include shaping, modeling, token economies, and contingency contracting.

EXAMPLES

Arrange for students to observe that classmates who persevere and complete a task receive a reinforcer of some kind. (But let this occur more or less naturally. Also, don't permit students who have finished an assignment to engage in attention-getting or obviously enjoyable self-chosen activities; those who are still working on the assignment may become a bit resentful and therefore less inclined to work on the task at hand.)

Draw happy faces on primary grade students' papers, give check marks as students complete assignments, write personal comments acknowledging good work, and assign bonus points.

Develop an individual reward menu, or contract with each student based on the Premack principle (Grandma's rule). After passing a spelling test at a particular level, for example, each student might be given class time to work on a self-selected project.

Journal Entry
Using Behavior Modification Techniques to Motivate

When making use of such motivational techniques, you might do your best to play down overtones of manipulation and materialism. Point out that rewards are used in almost all forms of endeavor to induce people to work toward a goal. Just because someone does something to earn a reward does not mean that the activity should never be indulged in for intrinsic reasons. For example, athletes often compete to earn the reward of being members of the best team, but they still enjoy the game.

2. **Make sure that students know what they are to do, how to proceed, and how to determine when they have achieved goals.**

Many times students do not exert themselves in the classroom because they say they don't know what they are supposed to do. Occasionally such a statement is merely an excuse for goofing off, but it may also be a legitimate explanation for lack of effort. Recall from Chapter 9 that knowing what one is expected to do is important information in the construction of a learning strategy. You should use the techniques described in Chapter 7 to take full advantage of the values of instructional objectives. In terms of motivation, objectives should be clear, understood by all members of the class, and attainable in a short period of time. For reasons illustrated by behavioral theorists' experiments with different reinforcement schedules, students are more likely to work steadily if they are reinforced at frequent intervals. If you set goals that are too demanding or remote, lack of reinforcement during the early stages of a unit may derail students, even if they started out with good intentions. Whenever you ask students to work toward a demanding or remote goal, try to set up a series of short-term goals.

Journal Entry
Ways to Arrange Short-Term Goals

EXAMPLE

One way to structure students' learning efforts is to follow the suggestions offered by Raymond Wlodkowski for drawing up a personal contract. He recommends that such a contract should contain four elements. A sample contract from Wlodkowski (1978, p. 57) is presented here, with a description of each element in brackets.

Date ________________

1. Within the next two weeks I will learn to multiply correctly single-digit numbers ranging between 5 and 9, e.g., 5 × 6, 6 × 7, 7 × 8, 8 × 9, 9 × 5. [What the student will learn]
2. When I feel prepared, I will ask to take a mastery test containing 50 problems from this range of multiplication facts. [How the student can demonstrate learning]
3. I will complete this contract when I can finish the mastery test with no more than three errors. [The degree of proficiency to be demonstrated]
4. My preparation and study will involve choosing work from the workbook activities, number games, and filmstrip materials. [How the student will proceed]

Signed ________________________

3. Do everything possible to satisfy deficiency needs—physiological, safety, belongingness, and esteem.

a. Accommodate the instructional program to the physiologiacl needs of your students.

Journal Entry
Ways to Satisfy Physiological Needs

EXAMPLES

Be aware that your students may occasionally be hungry or thirsty. (This point sounds obvious, but it is frequently forgotten.) If conditions allow, permit snacks on an individual basis, or have a routine or occasional nonroutine snack break.

Have a change of pace or a break when appropriate. With young children, make allowance for a flexible nap-time.

Schedule demanding activities when students are fresh; schedule relaxing activities toward the end of a period or day.

Be prepared for greater restlessness before lunch and just before dismissal time at the end of the day.

Make a habit of checking the room temperature. Ask students if the room is too warm or too cool.

b. **Make your room physically and psychologically safe.**

The need for safety is likely to be satisfied by the general classroom climate you establish, although physical factors of safety may be involved, particularly with young students. In one kindergarten, for example, several children were worried about the possibility of fire after seeing television news coverage of a fire in a school. In most cases, however, you can best ensure safety by establishing a relaxed, secure classroom environment.

EXAMPLES

If you see that a student fears something (for example, bullies on the playground, fire, enclosed places), explain that you will offer protection or that adequate precautionary measures have been taken.

Establish a classroom atmosphere in which students know what to expect and can relax about routines. Do everything you can to make your room a place that is psychologically safe. Be alert to things you do that are unnecessarily threatening. Try to see classroom assignments and activities from your students' point of view in an effort to detect anxiety-producing situations.

As much as possible, establish classroom routines in which students can take the initiative. Don't require recitation; wait for students to volunteer. Don't force students to participate in new activities; let them try such activities when they feel ready.

Journal Entry
Ways to Satisfy Safety Needs

c. **Show your students that you take an interest in them and that they belong in your classroom.**

EXAMPLES

Learn and use names as fast as you can.

Keep detailed records for individual students, and refer to specific accomplishments.

Whenever possible, schedule individual tutorial or interview sessions so that you can interact with all students on a one-to-one basis. If a student

Journal Entry
Ways to Satisfy Belongingness Needs

Theorists like Abraham Maslow, who argue that deficiency needs such as belongingness and self-esteem must be satisfied before students will be motivated to learn, call attention to the importance of positive teacher-student relationships in the classroom.

is absent because of an extended illness, send a get-well card signed by the entire class.

To encourage class spirit, schedule group planning sessions or sharing.

d. **Arrange learning experiences so that all students can gain at least a degree of esteem.**

Journal Entry
Ways to Satisfy Esteem Needs

EXAMPLES

Play down comparisons; encourage cooperation and self-competition. (Evaluation techniques that encourage self-competition will be provided in the next chapter in an analysis of mastery learning.)

Permit students to work toward individual goals.

Provide opportunities to students who possess culture-specific talents (such as storytelling, singing, dancing, or weaving) to demonstrate and teach them to others.

Give unobtrusive individual assistance to students who are experiencing problems.

4. Enhance the attractions and minimize the dangers of growth choices.

When you first begin to teach, you might keep a copy of Maslow's diagram of a choice situation in your top desk drawer. Refer to it when the need arises, and ask yourself, "Am I setting tasks up to encourage effort, or am I encouraging students *not* to try?" If you establish situations that generate pressure, tension, or anxiety, your students will choose safety and do their best to remain uninvolved. But if you minimize risks and make learning seem exciting and worthwhile, even the less secure students may join in.

EXAMPLES

Don't penalize guessing on exams.

Don't impose restrictions or conditions on assignments if they will act as dampers. For example, avoid insisting that "you must hand in all papers typed, with no erasures or strikeovers." Some students may not even start a report under such conditions.

Avoid "do or die" situations, such as single exams or projects.

To encourage free participation, make it clear that you will not grade students on recitation.

Point out and demonstrate the values of learning and the limitations and disadvantages (dangers) of not learning. For example, explain to students that knowing how to multiply and divide is necessary for personal bookkeeping and that errors in doing so could lead to difficulties.

Remain aware of the disadvantages of inappropriate or excessive competition. If competition becomes excessive in a school situation, students may think of learning only as a means to an end (being better than others or finishing first). As a result, students may become more interested in their relative position in a class than in their actual performance. Only a few students will be able to experience success, and the tendency to make safety, rather than growth, choices will be increased. To avoid these disadvantages, encourage students to compete against themselves. Try to give each student some experience with success by arranging situations in which all students have a fairly equal chance in a variety of activities, and make use of group competitive situations that stress fun rather than winning.

EXAMPLES

Have students set their own goals, and keep private progress charts.

Use portfolio assessment (see Chapter 12), which involves keeping a separate folder for each student rather than a grade book that indicates only relative performance.

Give recognition for such virtues as punctuality and dependability.

Give recognition for skill in arts and crafts and in music.

Journal Entry
Ways to Encourage Self-Competition

5. **Direct learning experiences toward feelings of success in an effort to encourage an orientation toward achievement, a positive self-concept, and a strong sense of self-efficacy.**

To feel successful, an individual must first establish goals that are neither so low as to be unfulfilling nor so high as to be impossible and then know that the goals have been achieved. This is a two-step process: establishing goals and receiving knowledge of results.

a. **Make use of objectives that are challenging but attainable and, when appropriate, that involve student input.**

Although in many instructional situations, you may find it necessary to set goals yourself, when it is possible and instructionally appropriate, you can use goals to heighten motivation as well. In these instances you are likely to get a better reaction if you invite your students to participate in selecting objectives or at least in thinking along with you as you explain why the objectives are worthwhile. This will tend to shift the emphasis from extrinsic to intrinsic motivation.

To help students suggest appropriate objectives, you may want to use the techniques recommended by Robert Mager. You might assist your students in stating objectives in terms of a time limit, a minimum number of correct responses, a proportion of correct responses, or a sample of actions.

EXAMPLES

"How many minutes do you think you will need to outline this chapter? When you finish, we'll see that film I told you about."

"George, you got six out of ten on this spelling quiz. How many do you want to try for on the retest?"

Journal Entry
Ways to Encourage Students to Set Their Own Objectives

b. **Provide knowledge of results by emphasizing the positive.**

To experience success (as a basis for establishing a realistic level of aspiration), your students must receive detailed information about their performance. Comments on the quality of a presentation, participation in a debate, papers and projects of various kinds, or answers on an exam may make the difference between feelings of success and feelings of failure. Accordingly, you should do your best to comment favorably on successful performance and avoid calling attention to failure, particularly the kind that is already apparent.

Behavioral theorists have proposed that for praise to shape behavior, it should be provided only after performance of designated activities, and it should be specific. Humanistic theorists (Purkey & Stanley, 1991, 1994) add that it should be sincere and credible. Jere Brophy (1981), however, suggests that classroom teachers rarely use praise as an effective or desirable form of reinforcement. Brophy recommends that teachers use praise in the following ways:

Journal Entry
Ways to Supply Positive Feedback

- As a spontaneous expression of surprise or admiration. ("Why, Juan! This report is really excellent!")
- As compensation for criticism or as vindication of a prediction. ("After your last report, Lily, I said I knew you could do better. Well, you *have* done better. This is really excellent.")
- As an attempt to impress all members of a class. ("I like the way Nguyen just put his books away so promptly.")
- As a transition ritual to verify that an assignment has been completed. ("Yes, Maya, that's very good. You can work on your project now.")
- As a consolation prize or as encouragement to students who are less capable than others. ("Well, Josh, you kept at it, and you got it finished. Good for you!")

Many of these uses of praise do not serve to reinforce student behavior in specific ways. Quite often, however, various forms of praise may influence a student's self-concept and attitude toward learning. High achievers tend to attribute failure to lack of effort and resolve to try harder. Low achievers often attribute failure to lack of ability and assume nothing can be done about it. Brophy suggests that teachers may shape such reactions by the ways they supply praise (and criticism). In an effort to help teachers become aware of some of the unexpected aspects of praise, Brophy drew up the guidelines for effective praise listed in Table 11.1.

6. Try to encourage the development of need achievement, self-confidence, and self-direction in students who need these qualities.

Despite your efforts to provide appropriate incentives, gratify deficiency needs, enhance the attractions of growth choices, and arrange learning experiences to produce a realistic level of aspiration and a feeling of success, some of your students will still lack confidence in their ability to learn. In such cases you may try to help students acquire a general motive to achieve.

a. Use achievement-motivation training techniques.

A technique described by John Nicholls (1979) allows students opportunities to schedule their own classroom learning. For example, students can be given

TABLE 11.1 *Guidelines for Effective Praise*

Effective Praise	Ineffective Praise
1. Is delivered contingently	1. Is delivered randomly or unsystematically
2. Specifies the particulars of the accomplishment	2. Is restricted to global positive reactions
3. Shows spontaneity, variety, and other signs of credibility; suggests clear attention to the student's accomplishment	3. Shows a bland uniformity, which suggests a conditional response made with minimal attention
4. Rewards attainment of specified performance criteria (which can include effort criteria, however)	4. Rewards mere participation, without consideration of performance process or outcomes
5. Provides information to students about their competence or the value of their accomplishments	5. Provides no information at all or gives students information about their status
6. Orients students toward better appreciation of their own task-related behavior and thinking about problem solving	6. Orients students towards comparing themselves with others and thinking about competing
7. Uses students' own prior accomplishments as the context for describing present accomplishments	7. Uses the accomplishments of peers as the context for describing students' present accomplishments
8. Is given in recognition of noteworthy effort or success at tasks that are difficult (for *this* student)	8. Is given without regard to the effort expended or the meaning of the accomplishment (for *this* student)
9. Attributes success to effort and ability, implying that similar successes can be expected in the future	9. Attributes success to ability alone or to external factors such as luck or easy task
10. Leads students to expend effort on the task because they enjoy the task and/or want to develop task-relevant skills	10. Leads students to expend effort on the task for external reasons—to please the teacher, win a competition or reward, etc.
11. Focuses students' attention on their own task-relevant behavior	11. Focuses students' attention on the teacher as an external authority figure who is manipulating them
12. Fosters appreciation of and desirable attributions about task-relevant behavior after the process is completed	12. Intrudes into the ongoing process, distracting attention from task-relevant behavior

SOURCE: Brophy (1981).

responsibility for deciding when to work on a particular assignment and for how long. This gives them the feeling they are working on a task because they want to, not because someone told them to. According to Nicholls, researchers have found greater continuing interest in learning tasks under self-evaluation and greater frequencies of assignment completion when opportunities for self-scheduling were increased.

b. **Use cooperative-learning methods.**

As we pointed out earlier in this chapter and previous ones, cooperative-learning methods have proven effective in increasing motivation for learning and self-esteem, redirecting attributions for success and failure, fostering positive feelings toward classmates, and increasing performance on tests of comprehension, reasoning, and problem solving (Johnson & Johnson, 1995; Johnson et al., 1995; Slavin, 1995). Accordingly, you may want to try one or more of the cooperative-learning techniques described by Johnson and Johnson (Johnson et al., 1994) and Slavin (1995). To familiarize you with these methods, we will briefly describe the Student Teams-Achievement Divisions (STAD) method devised by Slavin and his associates at Johns Hopkins University.

STAD is one of the simplest and most flexible of the cooperative-learning methods, having been used in grades 2 through 12 and in such diverse subject areas as math, language arts, social studies, and science. As with other cooperative-learning methods, students are assigned to four- or five-member groups, with each group mirroring the make-up of the class in terms of ability, background, and gender. Once these assignments are made, a four-step cycle is initiated: teach, team study, test, and recognition. The teaching phase begins with the presentation of material, usually in a lecture-discussion format. Students should be told what it is they are going to learn and why it is important. During team study, group members work cooperatively with teacher-provided worksheets and answer sheets. Next, each student *individually* takes a quiz. Using a scoring system that ranges from 0 to 30 points and reflects degree of individual improvement over previous quiz scores, the teacher scores the papers. Each team receives one of three recognition awards, depending on the average number of points earned by the team. For example, teams that average 15 to 19 improvement points receive a GOODTEAM certificate, teams that average 20 to 24 improvement points receive a GREATTEAM certificate, and teams that average 25 to 30 improvement points receive a SUPERTEAM certificate.

May Seagoe found that students respond with interest to school situations that are active, investigative, adventurous, social, and useful. Having members of a fifth-grade class play the roles of state government officials is an activity that includes almost all these features.

The cooperative methods developed by the Johnsons are similar to those developed by Slavin, but with two exceptions: these methods place a greater emphasis on teaching students how to productively work together, and they recommend using team grades, rather than certificates or other forms of recognition, as positive reinforcers.

7. **Try to make learning interesting by emphasizing activity, investigation, adventure, social interaction, and usefulness.**

More than twenty-five years ago, May Seagoe suggested an approach to motivation that is based on students' interests and that is consistent with many of the motivation theories mentioned in this chapter. Among the "points of appeal that emerge from studies of specific interests," she lists the following:

> (a) the opportunity for overt bodily *activity,* for manipulation, for construction, even for observing the movement of animals and vehicles of various sorts; (b) the opportunity for *investigation,* for using mental ingenuity in solving puzzles, for working problems through, for creating designs, and the like; (c) the opportunity for *adventure,* for vicarious experiences in make believe, in books, and in the mass media; (d) the opportunity for *social assimilation,* for contacts with others suitable to the maturity level of the child (ranging from parallel play to discussion and argument), for social events and working together, for human interest and humanitarianism, and for conformity and display; and (e) the opportunity for use of the new in real life, making the new continuous with past experience and projecting it in terms of future action. (1970, p. 25)

One approach that incorporates most or all of these features, and that can be used with preschool and primary grade children, is the project approach. Lillian Katz and Sylvia Chard (1989) define a project as an in-depth study of a particular topic that one or more children undertake and that extends over a period of days or weeks. Projects may involve an initial discussion that captures the students' interest (for example, discussing how a house is built); dramatic play; drawing, painting, and writing; group discussions; field trips; construction activities; and investigation activities. Because projects are based on children's natural interests and involve a wide range of activities, they are more likely to be intrinsically motivating.

As you think about how you are going to organize your lesson plans for each day and each period, you might ask yourself: "Are there ways that I can incorporate activity, investigation, adventure, social interaction, and usefulness into this presentation?" "Are there projects that I can assign to students, particularly as cooperative groups, that incorporate most of these features?" Here are some examples of techniques you might use.

ACTIVITY

Have several students go to the board. Give a rapid-fire series of problems to be solved by those at the board as well as those at their desks. After five problems, have another group of students go to the board, and so on.

Journal Entry
Ways to Make Learning Active

Think of ways to move out of the classroom legitimately every now and then. Teach geometry, for instance, by asking the class to take several balls of string and lay out a baseball diamond on the side lawn of the school.

INVESTIGATION

Journal Entry
Ways to Promote Investigation

In elementary grade classrooms (and in some middle school and high school classrooms), set up a variety of learning centers with themes such as library, games, social science, cultural appreciation, computer use, and organize these with provocative displays and materials. For example, your social science center could be stocked with maps, charts, and documents (Charles, 1972). Your computer center might include educational software or game programs; student-created publications made with desktop publishing or word processing programs; a computer equipped with modem, communications software, Internet or commercial on-line service access; and lists of appropriate and interesting on-line sites.

In middle school and high school classrooms, you might arrange centers that pertain to different aspects of a single subject. In a science class, for example, you might have an appreciation center stressing aesthetic aspects of science, a display center calling attention to new developments in the field, a library center consisting of attractive and provocative books, and so on.

ADVENTURE

Journal Entry
Ways to Make Learning Seem Adventurous

Occasionally, use techniques that make learning entertaining and adventurous. Such techniques might be particularly useful when you introduce a new topic. You might employ devices used by advertisers and the creators of *Sesame Street,* for instance. Use intensity, size, contrast, and movement to attract attention. Make use of color, humor, exaggeration, and drama to introduce a new unit. Use audiovisual devices of all kinds—multimedia exhibits, tapes, charts, models. Take students by surprise by doing something totally unexpected.

The night before you introduce a new unit, redecorate part of the room. Then ask the class to help you finish it.

Arrange a "Parade of Presidents" in which each student selects a president of the United States and presents a State of the Union message to the rest of the class, with the rest of the class taking the part of members of Congress.

Hand out a dittoed sheet of twenty questions based on articles in each section of a morning newspaper. Students compete against themselves to discover how many of the questions they can answer in the shortest period of time. (Typical questions: "Why is the senator from Mississippi upset?" "Who scored the most points in the UCLA–Notre Dame basketball game?" "What did Lucy say to Charlie Brown?")

SOCIAL INTERACTION

Have students pair off and ask each other questions before an exam. Do the same with difficult-to-learn material by suggesting that pairs cooperate in developing mnemonic devices, preparing flashcards, and engaging in the like to help each other master information.

Organize an end-of-unit extravaganza in which individuals and groups first present or display projects and then celebrate by having refreshments.

Journal Entry
Ways to Make Learning Social

USEFULNESS

Continually point out that what is being learned can be used outside of class. Ask students to keep a record of how they use what they learn outside of class.

Develop exercises that make students aware that what they are learning has transfer value. Have students in an English class write a job application letter, for instance; have math students balance a checkbook, fill out an income tax form, or work out a yearly budget; have biology students think about ways they can apply what they have learned to avoid getting sick.

Journal Entry
Ways to Make Learning Useful

Resources for Further Investigation

Surveys of Motivational Theories

In a basic survey text, *Motivation to Learn: From Theory to Practice* (2d ed., 1993), Deborah Stipek discusses reinforcement theory, social cognitive theory, intrinsic motivation, need for achievement theory, attribution theory, and perceptions of ability. In Appendix 2-A, she presents a rating form and scoring procedure with which teachers can identify students who may have motivation problems. Appendix 3-A is a self-rating form that teachers can use to keep track of how often they provide rewards and punishments.

A useful summary of motivation theories and techniques can be found in the Worcester Polytechnic University's WWW site for teacher development, at http://www.wpi.edu/~isg_501/motivation.html.

Self-Perceptions

In *When the Kids Come First* (1987), James Beane and Richard Lipka describe the kinds of organizational, curricular, and instructional features that contribute to positive self-perceptions among middle school students. The same two authors cover the same issue, but in more detail and over a wider age range (childhood through adulthood), in *Self-Concept, Self-Esteem, and the Curriculum* (1986).

Four studies on the relationship between self-esteem and achievement done recently at the University of Queensland in Australia can be found on-line at http://www.cltr.uq.oz.au:8000/nllia/rd531. These studies focus on language learning in particular and are of interest because of their currency and detail.

The on-line psychology library at the University of California, Berkeley, is an excellent resource for researching further aspects of motivation and self-perception. It is located at gopher://library.berkeley.edu:70/00/resdbs/educ/psycinfo.

Cooperative Learning

The New Circles of Learning: Cooperation in the Classroom and School (1994), by David Johnson, Roger Johnson, and Edythe Johnson Holubec is a brief (105 pages) and readable description of the basic elements of the authors' version of cooperative learning. In *Cooperative Learning: Theory, Research, and Practice* (2d ed., 1995), Robert Slavin describes the cooperative-learning techniques that he favors, analyzes the research evidence that supports their use, and provides detailed directions on how to use them.

Cooperative learning is sufficiently flexible that it can be used at all level of education. Four books that describe how to use cooperative methods for specific grade levels are *Cooperative Learning in the Early Childhood Classroom* (1991), by Harvey Foyle, Lawrence Lyman, and Sandra Thies; *Cooperative Learning in the Elementary Classroom* (1993), by Lawrence Lyman, Harvey Foyle, and Tara Azwell; *Cooperative Learning in Middle-Level Schools* (1991), by Jerry Rottier and Beverly Ogan; and *Secondary Schools and Cooperative Learning* (1995), edited by Jon Pederson and Annette Digby.

Finally, a collection of forty-eight articles that originally appeared in the journal *Educational Leadership* between 1985 and 1991 can be found in *Cooperative Learning and the Collaborative School* (1991), edited by Ronald Brandt.

Motivational Techniques for the Classroom

Motivation and Teaching: A Practical Guide (1978), by Raymond Wlodkowski, and *Eager to Learn* (1990), by Raymond Wlodkowski and Judith Jaynes, are a good source of classroom application ideas. *Motivating Students to Learn: Overcoming Barriers to High Achievement* (1993), edited by Tommy Tomlinson, devotes four chapters to elementary school and four chapters to high school motivation issues.

Two sources of information on motivation techniques and suggestions for teaching are found at Columbia University's Institute for Learning Technologies, which contains documents, papers, and unusual projects and activities that could be used to increase student motivation; and at Northwestern University's Institute for Learning Sciences Engines for Education on-line program, which allows educators to pursue a number of questions about students, learning environments, and successful teaching through a hyperlinked database. The Institute for Learning Technologies is found at http://www.ilt.columbia.edu/ilt/. The Institute for Learning Sciences is found at http://www.ils.nwu.edu/.

Summary

1. Motivation is the willingness to expend a certain amount of effort to achieve a particular goal.
2. Behavioral views of motivation are based on the desire of students to obtain a positive reinforcer (in the case of operant conditioning theory) or to imitate an admired individual because of vicarious reinforcement (in the case of social learning theory).
3. A potential limitation of operant conditioning theory is its emphasis on extrinsic sources of motivation. The learner is motivated to attain a goal in order to receive a reward that is not inherently related to the activity. This may produce only temporary changes in behavior, a materialistic attitude toward learning, and an undermining of whatever intrinsic motivation a student may have for a particular task.
4. The condition that is most likely to undermine a student's intrinsic interest in a task is rewarding the student for simply engaging in an activity regardless of the quality of the student's response. Thus, teachers should reward students only for significant behaviors that require the skilled use of recently learned information and skills.

5. Cognitive views of motivation emphasize the effect of various kinds of thinking on students' academic behavior.

6. The cognitive development view holds that people are inherently driven to overcome gaps, inconsistencies, or contradictions between what they know and what they experience.

7. Atkinson proposes that people are motivated by a need for achievement, which is a general desire to attain goals that require some degree of competence. An individual's level of need is determined by the extent to which he emphasizes an expectation of success or a fear of failure. Individuals with a high need to achieve have a greater expectation of success than they do a fear of failure. They prefer moderately difficult tasks because such tasks provide an optimal balance between the possibility of failure and the expectation of success. Individuals with a low need to achieve are dominated by a fear of failure. Consequently, they prefer either very easy tasks (because success is assured) or very difficult tasks (because there is no shame in failing to do well at them).

8. Research on attribution theory found marked differences between high achievers and low achievers. High achievers attribute success to ability and effort and failure to insufficient effort. Low achievers attribute success to luck or task difficulty and failure to lack of ability.

9. Some students are less motivated than others because they subscribe to what Dweck calls an entity theory of cognitive ability. Because they believe that intelligence is a fixed capacity, they tend to avoid challenging tasks if uncertain of success. Students who subscribe to an incremental theory tend to pursue more meaningful learning opportunities because they think of intelligence as something that can be improved through experience and corrective feedback.

10. One limitation of the cognitive view is that teachers may not always find it possible to induce a sense of disequilibrium in students.

11. A problem with need for achievement theory is the lack of instruments with which to measure it and the unreliability of short-term observations.

12. A limitation of attribution theory and beliefs about ability is the difficulty of changing students' faulty attribution patterns and beliefs about the nature of cognitive ability.

13. Maslow's humanistic view of motivation is based on a person satisfying a hierarchical sequence of deficiency needs (physiological, safety, belongingness and love, and esteem) so that the individual can satisfy her self-actualization needs.

14. A limitation of the humanistic view is that the teacher may not always find it possible to identify a student's unmet deficiency needs or to satisfy them once they are identified.

15. Factors that appear to determine one's level of self-esteem are being competent at a valued task and being given support and positive feedback for one's accomplishments from significant others. High self-esteem contributes to feeling satisfied about one's accomplishments, which leads to the development of intrinsic motivation.

16. Declines in self-esteem have been found in some students when they move from the elementary to the middle school or junior high grades and from the middle school or junior high to the high school grades.

17. A student's level of self-efficacy—how capable one believes one is to perform a particular task—affects motivation by affecting the learning goals that are chosen, the outcome the student expects, and the attributions the student makes for success and failure.

18. Since self-esteem and self-efficacy are most directly affected by performance accomplishments, teachers should arrange instruction to maximize learning for all students.

19. Cooperative reward structures are characterized by group heterogeneity, group goals and positive interdependence, promotive interaction, individual accountability, interpersonal skills, equal opportunities for success, and team competition.

20. Cooperative-learning arrangements appear to be superior to individualistic and competitive arrangements for improving students' motivation for learning, achievement, problem solving, and interpersonal relationships.

Key Terms

extrinsic motivation *(401)*
intrinsic motivation *(401)*
attribution theory *(403)*
deficiency needs *(408)*
growth need *(408*
self-actualization *(408)*

Discussion Questions

1. At the beginning of this chapter, we drew a distinction between extrinsic motivation (doing something solely to obtain a reward offered by someone else) and intrinsic motivation (doing something solely because it brings pleasure or satisfaction). What percentage of your behavior do you think stems from intrinsic motivation? From extrinsic motivation? Do you think it is possible to change this ratio? How? Are any of your ideas applicable to the classroom?
2. Maslow states that for individuals to be motivated to satisfy self-actualization needs, deficiency needs have to be satisfied first. Has this been the case in your own experience? If not, how was it different?
3. Students with a high need to achieve usually attribute success to effort and ability and failure to lack of effort. If you think of yourself as fitting this pattern, how did you get this way? Is there anything from your own experiences that you can use to help students develop this attributional pattern?
4. Have you ever experienced a competitive reward structure in school? Were your reactions to it positive or negative? Why? Would you use it in your own classroom? For what purpose and under what circumstances?
5. Have you ever experienced a cooperative reward structure in school? Were your reactions to it positive or negative? Why? Would you use it in your own classroom? For what purpose and under what circumstances?

Part 4

Evaluating Performance

CHAPTER 12 *Assessment of Classroom Learning*

CHAPTER 12

Assessment of Classroom Learning

Key Points

These key points will help you learn the important information in this chapter. To help you study, they also appear in the margins of pages, next to the text where they are discussed.

The Role of Assessment in Teaching

- Measurement: assigning numbers to things according to rules to create a ranking
- Evaluation: making judgments about the value of a measure
- Summative evaluation: measure achievement; assign grades
- Formative evaluation: monitor progress; plan remedial instruction
- Tests can positively affect many aspects of students' learning
- Moderate testing produces more learning than no testing or infrequent testing

Ways to Measure Student Learning

- Written tests measure degree of knowledge about ideas
- Selected-response tests objectively scored and efficient but usually measure lower levels of learning
- Short-answer tests easy to write but measure lower levels of learning
- Essay tests measure higher levels of learning but are hard to grade consistently
- Performance tests measure ability to use knowledge and skills to solve realistic problems, produce products
- Performance tests may vary in degree of realism
- Reliability and validity of performance tests not yet firmly established

Ways to Evaluate Student Learning

- Norm-referenced grading: compare one student to others
- Norm-referenced grading based on absence of external criteria
- Norm-referenced grading can be used to evaluate advanced levels of learning
- Criterion-referenced grading: compare individual performance to stated criteria
- Criterion-referenced grades provide information about strengths and weaknesses
- Expectations of a normal distribution lead to low aspirations
- Mastery approach: give students multiple opportunities to master goals at own pace
- Mastery learning has several potential limitations
- Mastery learning does not eliminate competition and comparisons

Improving Your Grading Methods: Assessment Practices to Avoid

- Be aware of and avoid faulty measurement and grading practices

Suggestions for Teaching in Your Classroom

- Necessary to obtain a representative sample of behavior when testing
- Table of specifications helps ensure an adequate sample of content, behavior
- Elementary grade students tested as much for diagnostic, formative evaluation purposes as for summative purposes
- Rating scales and checklists make evaluations of performance more systematic
- Item analysis tells about difficulty, discriminability of multiple-choice items

Chapters 2 through 6 of this book acquainted you with information relating to phase one of the learning and instruction model on which this book is based: taking into account what students are like and allowing for individual differences in characteristics and abilities. Chapter 7 was devoted to phase two: specifying what is to be learned in the form of appropriate types of instructional objectives. Chapters 8 through 11 summarized information intended to assist you to achieve phase three: applying what psychologists have discovered about learning and motivation to help students master instructional objectives. In this chapter the fourth and final phase in the model will be analyzed: assessing learning to determine whether students have achieved instructional objectives.

The Role of Assessment in Teaching

Assessing student learning is something that every teacher has to do, usually quite frequently. Written tests, book reports, research papers, homework exercises, oral presentations, question-and-answer sessions, science projects, and artwork of various sorts are just some of the ways in which teachers measure student learning, with written tests accounting for about 45 percent of a typical student's course grade (Green & Stager, 1986/1987). It is no surprise, then, that the typical teacher can spend between one-third and one-half of her class time engaged in one or another type of measurement activity (Stiggins, 1994). Yet despite the amount of time teachers spend assessing student learning, it is a task that most of them dislike and that few do well. One reason is that many teachers have little or no in-depth knowledge of assessment principles (Crooks, 1988; Hills, 1991; Stiggins, Griswold, & Wikelund, 1989). Another reason is that the role of assessor is seen as being inconsistent with the role of teacher (or helper). Since teachers with more training in assessment use more appropriate assessment practices than do teachers with less training (Green & Stager, 1986/1987), a basic goal of this chapter is to help you understand how such knowledge can be used to reinforce, rather than work against, your role as teacher. Toward that end, we will begin by defining what we mean by the term *assessment* and by two key elements of this process, *measurement* and *evaluation*.

WHAT IS ASSESSMENT?

Broadly conceived, classroom assessment involves two major types of activities: collecting information about how much knowledge and skill students have learned (measurement) and making judgments about the adequacy or acceptability of each student's level of learning (evaluation). Both the measurement and evaluation aspects of classroom assessment can be accomplished in a number of ways. To determine how much learning has occurred, teachers can, for example, have students take exams, respond to oral questions, do homework exercises, write papers, solve problems, and make oral presentations. Teachers can then evaluate the scores from those activities by comparing them either to one another or to an absolute standard (such as an A equals 90 percent correct). Throughout much of this chapter we will explain and illustrate the various ways in which you can measure and evaluate student learning.

Measurement: assigning numbers to things according to rules to create a ranking

Measurement **Measurement** is the assignment of numbers to certain attributes of objects, events, or people according to a rule-governed system. For our purposes, we will limit the discussion to attributes of people. For example, we can measure someone's level of typing proficiency by counting the number of words the person accurately types per minute or someone's level of mathematical reasoning by counting the number of problems correctly solved. In a classroom or other group situation, the rules that are used to assign the numbers will ordinarily create a ranking that reflects how much of the attribute different people possess (Linn & Gronlund, 1995).

Evaluation: making judgments about the value of a measure

Evaluation **Evaluation** involves using a rule-governed system to make judgments about the value or worth of a set of measures (Linn & Gronlund, 1995). What does it mean, for example, to say that a student answered eighty out of one hundred earth science questions correctly? Depending on the rules that are used, it could mean that the student has learned that body of knowledge exceedingly well and is ready to progress to the next unit of instruction or, conversely, that the student has significant knowledge gaps and requires additional instruction.

WHY SHOULD WE ASSESS STUDENTS' LEARNING?

This question has several answers. We will use this section to address four of the most common reasons for assessment: to provide summaries of learning,

Classroom assessments serve several purposes. They provide information about the extent to which students have acquired the knowledge and skills that have recently been taught, they indicate whether students are understanding and keeping up with the pace of instruction, they may identify the particular cause of a student's learning difficulties, and they help students effectively regulate their study efforts.

to provide information on learning progress, to diagnose specific strengths and weaknesses in an individual's learning, and to motivate further learning.

Summative Evaluation The first, and probably most obvious, reason for assessment is to provide to all interested parties a clear, meaningful, and useful summary or accounting of how well a student has met the teacher's objectives. When testing is done for the purpose of assigning a letter or numerical grade, it is often called **summative evaluation** since its primary purpose is to sum up how well a student has performed over time and at a variety of tasks.

Summative evaluation: measure achievement; assign grades

Formative Evaluation A second reason for assessing students is to monitor their progress. The main things that teachers want to know from time to time is whether students are keeping up with the pace of instruction and are understanding all of the material that has been covered so far. For students whose pace of learning is either slower or faster than average or whose understanding of certain ideas is faulty, you can introduce supplementary instruction (a workbook or a computer-based tutorial program), remedial instruction (which may also be computer based), or in-class ability grouping (recall that we discussed the benefits of this arrangement in Chapter 6). Because the purpose of such assessment is to facilitate or form learning and not to assign a grade, it is usually called **formative evaluation.**

Formative evaluation: monitor progress; plan remedial instruction

Diagnosis A third reason follows from the second. If you discover a student who is having difficulty keeping up with the rest of the class, you will probably want to know why in order to determine the most appropriate course of action. This purpose may lead you to construct an assessment (or to look for one that has already been made up) that will provide you with specific diagnostic information.

Effects on Learning A fourth reason for assessment of student performance is that it has potentially positive effects on various aspects of learning and instruction. As Terence Crooks points out, classroom assessment guides students' "judgment of what is important to learn, affects their motivation and self-perceptions of competence, structures their approaches to and timing of personal study (e.g., spaced practice), consolidates learning, and affects the development of enduring learning strategies and skills. It appears to be one of the most potent forces influencing education" (1988, p. 467).

Tests can positively affect many aspects of students' learning

Proof of Crooks's contention that classroom testing helps students consolidate their learning (despite students' arguments to the contrary) was offered by Robert Bangert-Drowns, James Kulik, and Chen-Lin Kulik (1991). They analyzed the results of forty studies conducted in actual classrooms and drew the following conclusions:

1. Students who were tested more frequently (six or seven tests over the course of a semester) scored about one-fourth of a standard deviation higher on a final exam than did students who were tested less frequently. This translated to an advantage of 9 percentile ranks for the more frequently tested students.
2. The advantage was even larger (20 percentile ranks) when students who were tested several times were compared to students who were never tested.
3. As students took more tests over the course of a semester, they generally scored higher on a final exam, but the increases became successively smaller for each additional test. The benefit of taking multiple tests seemed to peak by the sixth or seventh test.

Moderate testing produces more learning than no testing or infrequent testing

Ways to Measure Student Learning

Just as measurement can play several roles in the classroom, teachers have several ways to measure what students have learned. Which type of measure you choose will depend, of course, on the objectives you have stated. For the purposes of this discussion, objectives can be classified in terms of two broad categories: knowing about something (for example, that knots are used to secure objects, that dance is a form of social expression, that microscopes are used to study things too small to be seen by the naked eye) and knowing how to do something (for example, tie a square knot, dance the waltz, operate a microscope). Measures that attempt to assess the range and accuracy of someone's knowledge are usually called written tests. And measures that attempt to assess how well somebody can do something are often referred to as performance tests. Again, keep in mind that both types have a legitimate place in a teacher's assessment arsenal. Which type is used, and to what extent, will depend on the purpose or purposes you have for assessing students. In the next two sections, we will briefly examine the nature of both types.

WRITTEN TESTS

As we indicated at the beginning of this chapter, teachers spend a substantial part of each day assessing student learning, and much of this assessment activity involves giving and scoring some type of written test. Most written

Most of the tests that students take are written tests composed of multiple-choice and short-answer items. Written tests are efficient in that many items can be asked in a short space of time and they can be quickly and reliably scored. But they tend to be used to measure the lowest level of Bloom's taxonomy.

tests are composed of one or more of the following item types: selected response (multiple choice, true-false, and matching, for example), short answer, and essay. They are designed to measure how much people know about a particular subject. In all likelihood, you have taken hundreds of these types of tests in your school career thus far. In the next couple of pages, we will briefly describe the main features, advantages, and disadvantages of each test.

Written tests measure degree of knowledge about ideas

Selected-Response Tests

CHARACTERISTICS. Selected-response tests are so named because the student reads a relatively brief opening statement (called a stem) and selects one of the provided alternatives as the correct answer. Selected-response tests are typically made up of multiple-choice, true-false, or matching items. Quite often all three item types are used in a single test. Selected-response tests are sometimes called "objective" tests because they have a simple and set scoring system. If alternative (b) of a multiple-choice item is keyed as the correct response and the student chose alternative (d), the student is marked wrong, regardless of how much the teacher wanted the student to be right. But that doesn't mean selected-response items are totally free of subjective influences. After all, whoever created the test had to make subjective judgments about which areas to emphasize, how to word items, and which items to include in the final version. Finally, selected-response tests are typically used when the primary goal is to assess what might be called foundational knowledge. This is the basic factual information and cognitive skills that students need in order to do such high-level tasks as solve problems and create products (Stiggins, 1994).

ADVANTAGES. A major advantage of selected-response tests is efficiency—a teacher can ask many questions in a short period of time. Another advantage is ease and reliability of scoring. With the aid of a scoring template (such as a multiple-choice answer sheet that has holes punched out where the correct answer is located), many tests can be quickly and uniformly scored.

Selected-response tests objectively scored and efficient but usually measure lower levels of learning

DISADVANTAGES. Because items that reflect the lowest level of Bloom's Taxonomy (verbatim knowledge) are the easiest to write, most teacher-made tests are composed almost entirely of knowledge-level items (a point we made initially in Chapter 7). As a result, students focus on verbatim memorization rather than on meaningful learning. Another disadvantage is that, while we get some indication of what students know, such tests tell us nothing about what students can do with that knowledge.

Short-Answer Tests

CHARACTERISTICS. Instead of selecting from one or more alternatives, the student is asked to supply a brief answer consisting of a name, word, phrase, or symbol. Like selected-response tests, short-answer tests can be scored quickly, accurately, and consistently, thereby giving them an aura of objectivity. They are primarily used for measuring foundational knowledge.

ADVANTAGES. Short-answer items are relatively easy to write, so a test, or part of one, can be constructed fairly quickly. They allow for either broad or in-depth assessment of foundational knowledge since students can respond to many items within a short space of time. Since students have to supply an answer, they have to recall, rather than recognize, information.

Short-answer tests easy to write but measure lower levels of learning

DISADVANTAGES. This item type has the same basic disadvantages as the selected-response items. Because these items ask only for short verbatim answers, students are likely to limit their processing to that level, and these items provide no information about how well students can use what they have learned. In addition, unexpected but plausible answers may be difficult to score.

Essay Tests

CHARACTERISTICS. The student is given a somewhat general directive to discuss one or more related ideas according to certain criteria. One example of an essay question is "Compare operant conditioning theory and information-processing theory in terms of basic assumptions, typical research findings, and classroom applications."

ADVANTAGES. Essay tests reveal how well students can recall, organize, and clearly communicate previously learned information. When well written, essays tests call on such higher-level abilities as analysis, synthesis, and evaluation. Because of these demands, students are more likely to try to meaningfully learn the material over which they are tested.

DISADVANTAGES. Consistency of grading is likely to be a problem. Two students may have essentially similar responses, yet receive different letter or numerical grades. These test items are also very time consuming to grade. And because it takes time for students to formulate and write responses, only a few questions at most can be given.

Essay tests measure higher levels of learning but are hard to grade consistently

PERFORMANCE TESTS

In recent years many teachers and measurement experts have argued that the typical written test should be used far less often because it reveals little or nothing of the depth of students' knowledge and how students use their knowledge to work through questions, problems, and tasks. The solution that these experts have proposed is to use one or more of what are called performance tests.

Performance tests attempt to assess how well students use foundational knowledge to perform complex tasks under more or less realistic conditions. At the low end of the realism spectrum, students may be asked to construct a map, interpret a graph, or write an essay under highly standardized conditions. That is, everyone completes the same task in the same amount of time and under the same conditions. At the high end of the spectrum, students may be asked to conduct a science experiment, produce a painting, or write an essay under conditions that are similar to those of real life. For example, students may be told to produce a compare-and-contrast essay on a particular topic by a certain date, but the resources students choose to use, the number of revisions they make, and when they work on the essay are left unspecified. As we noted in Chapter 5, when performance testing is conducted under such realistic conditions, it is also called *authentic assessment* (Meyer, 1992). Another term that is often used to encompass both performance testing and authentic assessment, and to distinguish them from traditional written tests, is *alternative assessment.* In this section we will first define the four different types of performance tests and then look at their most important characteristics.

Performance tests measure ability to use knowledge and skills to solve realistic problems, produce products

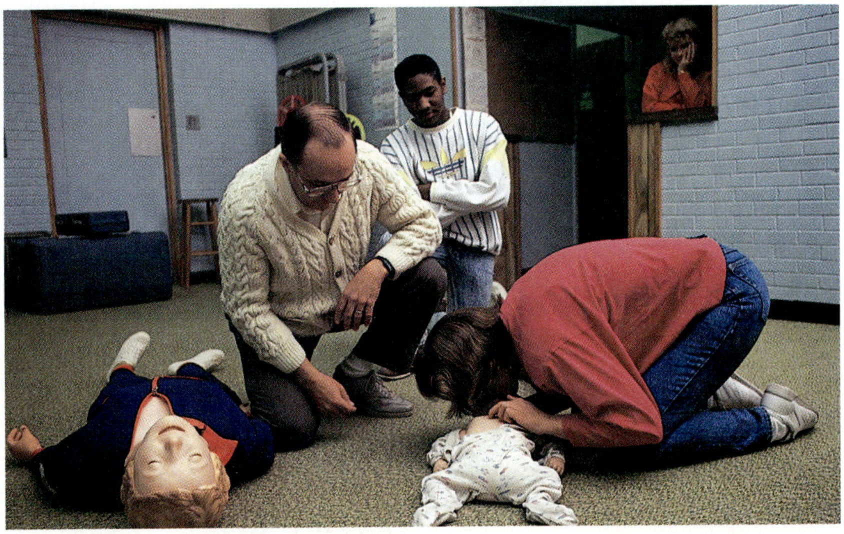

Performance tests assess how well students complete a task under realistic conditions.

Types of Performance Tests Currently, there are four ways in which the performance capabilities of students are typically assessed: direct writing assessments, portfolios, exhibitions, and demonstrations.

DIRECT WRITING ASSESSMENTS. These tests ask students to write about a specific topic ("Describe the person whom you admire the most, and explain why you admire that person.") under a standard set of conditions. Each essay is then scored by two or more people according to a set of defined criteria.

PORTFOLIOS. A portfolio may contain one or more pieces of a student's work, some of which demonstrate different stages of completion. For example, a student's writing portfolio may contain business letters; pieces of fiction; poetry; and an outline, rough draft, and final draft of a research paper. Through the inclusion of various stages of a research paper, both the process and the end product can be assessed. Portfolios can also be constructed for math and science as well as for projects that combine two or more subject areas. Often the student is involved in the selection of what is included in his portfolio. The portfolio is sometimes used as a showcase to illustrate exemplary pieces, but it also works well as a collection of pieces that represent a student's typical performances. In its best and truest sense, the portfolio functions not just as a housing for these performances but also as a means of self-expression, self-reflection, and self-analysis for an individual student (Templeton, 1995).

EXHIBITIONS. Exhibitions involve just what the label suggests—a showing of such products as paintings, drawings, photographs, sculptures, videotapes, and models. As with direct writing assessments and portfolios, the products a student chooses to exhibit are evaluated according to a predetermined set of criteria.

DEMONSTRATIONS. In this type of performance testing, students are required to show how well they can use previously learned knowledge or skills to solve a somewhat unique problem (such as conducting a scientific inquiry to answer a question or diagnosing the cause of a malfunctioning engine and describing the best procedure for fixing it) or perform a task (such as reciting a poem, performing a dance, or playing a piece of music).

Characteristics of Performance Tests Performance tests are different from traditional written tests in that they require the student to make an active response, are more like everyday tasks, contain problems that involve many variables, clearly state the criteria for acceptable performance, are closely related to earlier instructional activities, and emphasize formative evaluation.

EMPHASIS ON ACTIVE RESPONDING. As we pointed out previously, the goal of performance testing is to gain some insight into how competently students can carry out various tasks. Consequently, such tests focus on processes (that is, the underlying skills that go into a performance), products (an observable outcome such as a speech or a painting), or both. For example, a speech teacher may be interested in assessing how well students use gestures, pauses, and changes in voice pitch and volume; the accuracy and comprehensiveness of the content of their speeches; or both (Linn & Gronlund, 1995). A science teacher may want to know if students can use their knowledge of electric circuitry to determine the types of electrical elements that are inside a set of boxes (Shavelson & Baxter, 1992).

Degree of Realism. Although performance tests strive to approximate everyday tasks, not every test needs to be or can be done under the most realistic circumstances. How realistic the conditions should be depends on such factors as time, cost, availability of equipment, and the nature of the skill being measured. Imagine, for example, that you are a third-grade teacher and one of your objectives is that students will be able to determine how much change they should receive after making a purchase in a store. If this is a relatively minor objective, or if you do not have a lot of props available, you might simply demonstrate the situation with actual money and ask the students to judge whether the amount of change received was correct. If, however, you consider this to be a major objective and you have the props available, you might set up a mock store and have each student make a purchase using real money (Gronlund, 1993).

Performance tests may vary in degree of realism

For middle school and high school teachers who would like to use a problem-solving type of performance assessment but who have neither the necessary time nor the resources, computer-based simulations are becoming increasingly available. One recent development, for example, is IMMEX (Interactive Multi-Media Exercises), a Windows-based software system that allows the rapid construction of computer-based problem-solving experiences in many disciplines without the need for formal software programming. These "simulations" are the basis for an on-line analysis of student performance. The program uses a database to record students' use of the simulations and provide a measure of student performance. A separate component, IMMEX ANALYSIS, electronically reconstructs individual student's or groups of students' performances from this database, thereby offering a unique cognitive perspective on their problem-solving strategies. This type of program could make realistic performance assessment more practical and economical (in terms of time) for teachers.

Emphasis on Complex Problems. To properly assess how well students can use foundational knowledge and skills in a productive way, the questions and problems they are given should be sufficiently open-ended and ill-structured (Wiggins, 1993). The "Rescue at Boone's Meadow" problem that we described in Chapter 10 is a good example of a complex and somewhat ill-structured task. It has several interrelated parts, provides few cues as to how the problem might be solved, and contains some uncertainty about what constitutes an appropriate solution.

Clearly Stated Criteria. To plan a course of action and monitor their academic progress, students need to have a clear idea of the types of behavior that represent the range from unacceptable to exceptional performance (Wiggins, 1993). This can be done with a combination of verbal descriptions and actual examples of the desired behavior. As we noted in Chapter 9, planning and monitoring are two components of strategic learning. Thus, if you want to help students be strategic learners, provide them with the measurement conditions that make that behavior possible. While this type of preparation is unfortunately not a common part of everyday classroom testing, it is typically used in the performing arts, the studio arts, athletics, and vocational education. As Gene Maeroff observes, "A young pianist who is asked to master Beethoven's 'Für Elise' becomes proficient by practicing the piece, knowing all the while that his examination will consist of playing it" (1991, p. 274).

CLOSE RELATIONSHIP BETWEEN TEACHING AND TESTING. All too often students walk out of an exam in a state of high frustration (if not anger) because the content and format of the test seemed to have little in common with what was covered in class and the way in which it was taught. It's the old story of teaching for one thing and testing for something else. Performance testing strives for a closer match between teaching and testing. For example, if in giving an oral book report, a student is expected to speak loudly and clearly enough for everyone to hear, to speak in complete sentences, to stay on the topic, and to use pictures or other materials to make the presentation interesting, the student needs to be informed of these criteria, and classroom instruction should be organized around them. By the same token, the assessment of students' performances should be limited to just the criteria emphasized during instruction (Maeroff, 1991). One reason that proponents of performance testing push for this feature is because it has always been a standard part of successful programs in sports and the arts. Football coaches, for example, have long recognized that if they want their quarterback to know when during a game to attempt a pass and when not to (the equivalent of a final exam), they must provide him with realistic opportunities to practice making this particular type of decision. Perhaps you recall our mentioning in Chapter 10 that realistic and varied practice are essential if students are to transfer what they learn in an instructional setting to an applied setting.

GREATER USE OF FORMATIVE EVALUATION. Earlier we pointed out that tests can be used as a source of feedback to help students improve the quality of their learning efforts. Because many real-life performances and products are the result of several feedback and revision cycles, performance testing often includes this feature as well. As anyone who has ever done any substantial amount of writing can tell you (and your author is no exception), a satisfactory essay, story, or even personal letter is not produced in one attempt. Usually, there are critical comments from oneself and others and subsequent attempts at another draft. If we believe that the ability to write well, even among people who do it for a living, is partly defined by the ability to profitably use feedback, why should this be any different for students (Wiggins, 1993)?

Some Concerns About Performance Assessment As we noted in Chapter 5, many states are either using performance tests or are planning to do so as part of their mandated statewide assessment programs. Connecticut, for example, uses a range of performance-based assessments in science, foreign language, drafting, and small-engine repair. In 1992 Vermont implemented a portfolio-based assessment of students' writing and mathematical skills. In Kentucky fourth-, eighth-, and twelfth-grade students compile writing portfolios and take performance tests in science, social studies, and math (O'Neil, 1992). In addition, many teachers and schools have begun integrating performance assessments into their normal classroom testing activities.

There is no question that alternative assessment methods have excited educators and will be used with increasing frequency in future years. But some of the same features that make these new assessment methods attractive also create problems that may or may not be solvable. For example, evaluating portfolios, exhibits, and demonstrations is time consuming, labor intensive, and expensive. In addition, there are questions about the reliability (consistency of performance) and validity (how accurately the test measures its target) of such measures. It is difficult to obtain reliable and valid measures of some characteristic by judging the quality of portfolios, performances, and exhibitions because there is as yet no consensus as to what a portfolio should include, how large a portfolio should be, what standards should be used to judge products and performances, and whether all students should be assessed under precisely the same conditions (Linn, 1994; Maeroff, 1991; Wiggins, 1993; Worthen, 1993).

The few research finding currently available suggest that the proponents of performance assessment have their work cut out for them. Richard Shavelson and Gail Baxter (1992) investigated the reliability and validity of different kinds of science assessments for fifth and sixth graders. The good news was that several raters had little problem agreeing on the quality of students' performances as they worked through three science investigations (a form of reliability known as *interrater reliability*). The troubling news was that students' scores were very inconsistent from task to task (thereby producing a relatively low level of a form of reliability known as *internal consistency*). Thus, to get a clear picture of whether a student understands the use of basic scientific principles, understands how to do scientific projects of a particular type, or can only complete the particular science project that is contained in the assessment, a number of tasks may be needed. This calls the feasibility of performance assessment into question since it becomes even more expensive and time consuming.

Reliability and validity of performance tests not yet firmly established

John Herman, Maryl Gearhart, and Eva Baker (1993) found that the writing portfolios of first-, third-, and fourth-grade children could be consistently scored by trained raters and that the same rating scale could be used to score different types of writing products. But they also reported two troubling findings. One was that the pieces students wrote in class for inclusion in their portfolios were scored higher than a narrative they wrote in thirty minutes under standardized conditions (an example of a direct writing assessment). The researchers could not determine which writing sample was a better estimate of students' writing ability. The second problem was that overall portfolio scores were substantially higher than the aggregate scores of the individual items that made up the portfolio—truly a case of the whole being greater than the sum of its parts. Whatever the cause of this effect, it suggests that those who are selected to rate portfolios need to be given rational, clear, and comprehensive directions.

Ways to Evaluate Student Learning

Once you have collected all the measures you intend to collect—for example, test scores, quiz scores, homework assignments, special projects, and laboratory experiments—you will have to give the numbers some sort of value (the essence of evaluation). As you probably know, this is most often done by using an A to F grading scale. Typically, a grade of A indicates superior performance; a B, above-average performance; a C, average performance; a D, below-average performance; and an F, failure. There are two general ways to approach this task. One approach involves comparisons among students. Such forms of evaluation are called norm-referenced since students are identified as average (or normal), above average, or below average. An alternative approach is called criterion-referenced because performance is interpreted in terms of defined criteria. (As you may recall, these concepts were initially discussed in Chapter 5.) Although both approaches can be used, we favor criterion-referenced grading for reasons we will mention shortly.

NORM-REFERENCED GRADING

A **norm-referenced grading** system assumes that classroom achievement will naturally vary among a group of heterogeneous students because of differences in such characteristics as prior knowledge, learning skills, motivation, and aptitude. Under ideal circumstances (hundreds of scores from a diverse group of students), this variation produces a bell-shaped, or "normal," distribution of scores that ranges from low to high, has few tied scores, and has only a very few low scores and only a very few high scores. For this reason, norm-referenced grading procedures are also referred to as "grading on the curve."

Norm-referenced grading: compare one student to others

The Nature of Norm-Referenced Grading As with the interpretation of standardized test scores, course grades are determined through a comparison of each student's level of performance to the normal, or average, level of other, similar students in order to reflect the assumed differences in amount of learned material. The comparison may be to all other members of the student's class that year, or it may be to the average performance of several classes stretching back over several years. It is probably better for teachers to use a broad base of typical student performance made up of several classes as grounds for comparison than to rely on the current class of students. Doing so avoids two severe distorting effects: when a single class contains many weak students, those with more well-developed abilities will more easily obtain the highest grades; and when the class has many capable students, the relatively weaker students are virtually predestined to receive low or failing grades (Hopkins & Antes, 1990; Kubiszyn & Borich, 1993).

The basic procedure for assigning grades on a norm-referenced basis involves just a few steps. First, determine what percentage of students will receive which grades. If, for example, you intend to award the full range of grades, you may decide to give A's to the top 15 percent, B's to the next 25 percent, C's to the middle 35 percent, D's to the next 15 percent, and F's to the bottom 10 percent. Second, arrange the scores from highest to lowest. Third, calculate which scores fall in which category, and assign the grades accordingly.

Of course, many other arrangements are also possible. How large or small you decide to make the percentages for each category will depend on such factors as the nature of the students in your class, the difficulty of your exams and assignments, and your own sense of what constitutes appropriate standards. Furthermore, a norm-referenced approach does not necessarily mean that each class will have a normal distribution of grades or that anyone will automatically fail. For example, it is possible for equal numbers of students to receive A's, B's, and C's if you decide to limit your grading system to just those three categories and award equal numbers of each grade. A norm-referenced approach simply means that the grading symbols being used indicate one student's level of achievement relative to other students.

Proponents of norm-referenced grading typically point to the absence of acceptable external criteria for use as a standard for evaluating and grading student performance. In other words, there is no good way to externally determine how much learning is too little, just enough, or more than enough for some subject. And if there is no amount of knowledge or set of behaviors that must be mastered by all students, then grades may be awarded on the basis of relative performance among a group of students (Hopkins & Antes, 1990).

Norm-referenced grading based on absence of external criteria

Advantages and Disadvantages of Norm-Referenced Grading There are at least two circumstances under which it may be appropriate to use norm-referenced measurement and evaluation procedures. You might, for example, wish to formulate a two-stage instructional plan in which the first stage involves helping all students master a basic level of knowledge and skill in a particular subject. Performance at this stage would be measured and evaluated against a predetermined standard (such as 80 percent correct on an exam). Once this has been accomplished, you could supply advanced instruction and encourage students to learn as much of the additional material as possible. Since the amount of learning during the second stage is not tied to a predetermined standard, and since it will likely vary because of differences in motivation and learning skills, a norm-referenced approach to grading can be used. This situation also fits certain guidelines for the use of competitive reward structures (discussed in Chapter 11) since everyone starts from the same level of basic knowledge.

Norm-referenced grading can be used to evaluate advanced levels of learning

Norm-referenced measurement and evaluation are also applicable in cases where students with the best chances for success are selected for a limited-enrollment program from among a large pool of candidates. One example is the selection of students for honors programs who have the highest test scores and grade-point averages (Hopkins & Antes, 1990).

The main disadvantage of the norm-referenced approach to grading is that there are few situations in which the typical public school teacher can appropriately use it. Either the goal is not appropriate (as in mastery of certain material and skills by all students or diagnosis of an individual student's specific strengths and weaknesses), or the basic conditions cannot be met (classes are too small and/or homogeneous). When a norm-referenced approach is used in spite of these limitations, communication and motivation problems are often created. Consider the example of a group of high school sophomores having a great deal of difficulty mastering German vocabulary and grammar. The students may have been underprepared, the teacher may be doing a poor job of organizing and explaining the material, or both factors may be at work. At any rate the top student averages 48 percent correct on all of the exams, quizzes, and oral recitations administered during the term. That student and a few others with averages in the high 40s will receive the A's. While these fortunate few may realize their knowledge and skills are incomplete, others are likely to falsely conclude that these students learned quite a bit about the German language since a grade of A is generally taken to mean superior performance.

At the other extreme we have the example of a social studies class in which most of the students are doing well. Because the students were well prepared by previous teachers, used effective study skills, were exposed to high-quality instruction, and were strongly motivated by the enthusiasm of their teacher, the final test averages ranged from 94 to 98 percent correct. And yet the teacher who uses a norm-referenced scheme would assign at least A's, B's, and C's to this group. Not only does this practice seriously damage the motivation of students who worked hard and performed well, but it also miscommunicates to others the performance of students who received B's and C's (Airasian, 1994).

Although higher standards generally lead to greater effort and more learning, students who perceive standards as unattainable are likely to become less motivated to learn. For the perennial low-achieving student or the student whose work is above average but not among the best, the A in a norm-referenced system is likely to be seen as unattainable. In addition, forcing students to compete for a limited number of top grades is antithetical to the goals of the cooperative-learning programs we described in the previous chapter and may have a negative impact on students' character development (Wynne & Walberg, 1985/1986). As one person who has studied this issue put it: "It is hard to see any justification before the final year or so of high school for placing much emphasis on using classroom evaluation for normative grading of student achievement" (Crooks, 1988, p. 468).

CRITERION-REFERENCED GRADING

A **criterion-referenced grading** system permits students to benefit from mistakes and to improve their level of understanding and performance. Furthermore, it establishes an individual (and sometimes cooperative) reward structure, which fosters motivation to learn to a greater extent than other systems.

Under a criterion-referenced system, grades are determined through comparison of the extent to which each student has attained a defined standard (or criterion) of achievement or performance. Whether the rest of the students in the class are successful or unsuccessful in meeting that criterion is irrelevant. Thus, any distribution of grades is possible. Every student may get an A or an F, or no student may receive these grades. For reasons we will discuss shortly, very low or failing grades tend to occur less frequently under a criterion-referenced system.

Criterion-referenced grading: compare individual performance to stated criteria

A common version of criterion-referenced grading assigns letter grades on the basis of the percentage of test items answered correctly. For example, you may decide to award an A to anyone who correctly answers at least 85 percent of a set of test questions, a B to anyone who correctly answers 75 to 84 percent, and so on down to the lowest grade. To use this type of grading system fairly, which means specifying realistic criterion levels, you would need to have some prior knowledge of the levels at which students typically perform. You would thus be using normative information to establish absolute or fixed standards of performance. However, although norm-referenced and criterion-referenced grading systems both spring from a normative database (that is, from comparisons among students), only the former system uses those comparisons to directly determine grades.

Criterion-referenced grading systems (and criterion-referenced tests) have become increasingly popular in recent years primarily because of three factors. First, educators and parents complained that norm-referenced tests and grading systems provided too little specific information about student strengths and weaknesses. Second, educators have come to believe that clearly stated, specific objectives constitute performance standards, or criteria, that are best assessed with criterion-referenced measures. Third, and perhaps most important, contemporary theories of school learning claim that most, if not all, students can master most school objectives under the right circumstances. If this assertion is even close to being true, then norm-referenced testing and grading procedures, which depend on variability in performance, will lose much of their appeal. This third notion underlies a particular criterion-referenced approach to measurement and evaluation that is often referred to as *mastery learning* and stems in large part from the work of John Carroll (1963) and Benjamin Bloom (1968, 1976).

Criterion-referenced grades provide information about strengths and weaknesses

A MASTERY APPROACH TO LEARNING AND INSTRUCTION

John Carroll (1963) supplied the impetus for the emergence of mastery learning. He proposed that the focus of instruction should be the time required for different students to learn a given amount of material. He suggested that teachers should allow more time and provide more and better instruction for students who learn less easily and less rapidly than their peers.

Benjamin Bloom (1968) used the Carroll model as the basis for a statement in favor of mastery learning. The traditional approach, he argues, promotes the concept that if a normal distribution of students (with respect to aptitude for a subject) is exposed to a standard curriculum, achievement after instruction will be normally distributed. This approach, Bloom maintains, causes both teachers and students to expect that only one-third of all students will adequately learn what is being taught, and this expectation in turn

Expectations of a normal distribution lead to low aspirations leads to a disastrous self-fulfilling prophecy. Here is the alternative Bloom suggests:

> Most students (perhaps over 90 percent) can master what we have to teach them, and it is the task of instruction to find the means which will enable our students to master the subject under consideration. Our basic task is to determine what we mean by mastery of the subject and to search for the methods and materials which will enable the largest proportion of our students to attain such mastery. (1968, p. 1)

Ingredients of a Successful Mastery Approach Carroll observes that "teaching ought to be a simple matter if it is viewed as a process concerned with the management of learning" (1971, p. 29). He suggests that the teacher's function is to follow this procedure:

Mastery approach: give students multiple opportunities to master goals at own pace

> Specify what is to be learned.
>
> Motivate students to learn it.
>
> Provide instructional materials [to foster learning].
>
> [Present] materials at a rate appropriate for different students.
>
> Monitor students' progress.
>
> Diagnose difficulties and provide remediation.
>
> Give praise and encouragement for good performance.
>
> Give review and practice.
>
> Maintain a high rate of learning over a period of time. (1971, pp. 29–30)

The following suggestions, which can be adapted for use at any grade level and in any subject area, are based on Carroll's outline.

1. Go through a unit of study, a chapter of a text, or an outline of a lecture, and pick out what you consider to be the most important points—

The classroom assessments that are associated with mastery learning focus as much on monitoring students' progress and diagnosing their learning difficulties as they do on measuring how much of some subject has been learned.

that is, those points you wish to stress because they are most likely to have later value or are basic to later learning.

Journal Entry
Trying Mastery Learning

2. List these points in the form of a goal card, instructional objectives (as described by Robert Mager [1984] or Robert Linn and Norman Gronlund [1995]), key points, or the equivalent. If appropriate, arrange the objectives in some sort of organized framework, perhaps with reference to the relevant taxonomy of educational objectives.

3. Distribute the list of objectives at the beginning of a unit. Tell your students that they should concentrate on learning those points and that they will be tested on them.

4. Consider making up a study guide in which you provide specific questions relating to the objectives and a format that students can use to organize their notes.

5. Use a variety of instructional methods and materials to explain and illustrate objectives-related ideas.

6. Make up exam questions based on the objectives and the study guide questions. Try to write several questions for each objective.

7. Arrange these questions into at least two (preferably three) alternate exams for each unit of study.

8. Make up tentative criteria for grade levels for each exam and for the entire unit or report period (for example, A—not more than one question missed on any exam; B—not more than two questions missed on any exam; C—not more than four questions missed on any exam).

9. Test students either when they come to you and indicate they are ready or when you feel they have all had ample opportunity to learn the material. Announce all exam dates in advance, and remind students that the questions will be based only on the objectives you have mentioned. Indicate the criteria for different grade levels, and emphasize that any student who fails to meet a desired criterion on the first try will have a chance to take an alternate form of the exam.

10. Grade and return the exams as promptly as possible, go over questions briefly in class (particularly those that caused problems for more than a few students), and offer to go over exams individually with students. Allow for individual interpretations, and give credit for answers you judge to be logical and plausible, even if they differ from the answers you expected.

11. Schedule alternate exams, and make yourself available for consultation and tutoring the day before. (While you are giving alternate exams, you can administer the original exam to students who were absent.)

12. If students improve their score on the second exam but still fall below the desired criterion, consider a safety valve option: invite them to provide you with a completed study guide (or the equivalent) when they take an exam the second time, or give them an open-book exam on the objectives they missed to see whether they can explain them in terms other than those of a written examination. If a student fulfills either of these options satisfactorily, give credit for one extra answer on the second exam.

13. To supplement exams, assign book reports, oral reports, papers, or some other kind of individual work that will provide maximum opportunity for student choice. Establish and explain the criteria you will use to evaluate these assignments, but stress that you want to encourage freedom of choice and expression. (Some students will thrive on free choice, but others are likely to feel threatened by open-ended assignments. To allow for such differences, provide specific directions for those who need them and general hints or a simple request that "original" projects be cleared in advance for the more independent thinkers.) Grade all reports Pass or Do Over, and supply constructive criticism on those you consider unsatisfactory. Announce that all Do Over papers can be reworked and resubmitted within a certain period of time. Have the reports count toward the final grade—for example, three reports for an A, two for a B, one for a C. (In addition, students should pass each exam at the designated level.) You might also invite students to prepare extra papers to earn bonus points to be added to exam totals.

This basic technique will permit you to work within a traditional A to F framework, but in such a way that you should be able, without lowering standards, to increase the proportion of students who do acceptable work. It will also permit you to make the most of the procedures suggested by Carroll and to use an individual reward structure.

Focus on Stating Objectives One of the advantages of a criterion-referenced approach to grading is that it focuses attention on instructional objectives. Even if you try to be conscientious about drawing up a table of specifications when preparing exams in a norm-referenced approach, you may still fail to measure objectives in a systematic or comprehensive way. With a mastery approach, however, you are following the recommendations made by those who urge use of instructional objectives. Mager (1984) offers these guidelines: (1) identify and describe the terminal behavior, (2) define the important conditions under which the behavior is to occur, and (3) define the criterion of acceptable performance. This is exactly the procedure you will follow if you use a mastery approach.

Stating objectives in precise terms and focusing on a specific terminal behavior at a specified level of performance also permit you to treat instruction as if it were a branching program. That is, some students may achieve unit objectives on their first try and go on to the next unit; but students who have problems reaching the desired criterion level on their first effort are given additional instruction and another opportunity to show that they can perform at an acceptable level. This approach is more likely to lead to understanding and to encourage transfer than any approach that permits only one try and reports results only in terms of relative position.

Criteria for Assigning Letter Grades One of the most crucial decisions in a mastery approach centers on the criteria you establish for different grade levels. If you hope to defend grades to parents, other teachers, and administrators, you should do everything possible to make sure that an A in your class is equivalent to an A in your colleagues' classes. James Block (1971) reports that the proportion of A grades in mastery classes is typically higher than in traditional classes not because of low standards but because more students are motivated to do A and B work. Therefore, you should be well prepared to defend your grades by retaining copies of exams and the keys used to evaluate them and by explaining the criteria for different grade levels. As Tom Kubiszyn and Gary Borich point out, "It is a curious fact of life that everyone presses for excellence in education, but many balk at marking systems that make attainment of excellence within everyone's reach" (1993, p. 156).

In establishing criteria, refer to the discussion on instructional objectives in Chapter 7, particularly the observations of Mager (pp. 247–249) and Gronlund (pp. 249–250). You might set up standards for an exam in terms of the percentage of correct answers, the number of correct answers provided within a given time limit, or a sample of applications. An approach that has worked well in practice is to make up ten-question exams, grade each answer plus or minus, and use these standards: zero or one wrong—A, two wrong—B, three wrong—C, four wrong—D.

As noted earlier, plus or minus grading has definite advantages. It not only provides a definite number of correct and incorrect answers but also simplifies and speeds up grading. If you make up exams with an equivalent number of questions but evaluate each on a 5-point scale, you will be forced to read each answer with great care and then make a studied judgment of its relative value. But if you use a plus or minus approach, you simplify both the judging and the totaling of the final score. In many cases you will find that the answer is obviously right or wrong and that you can evaluate it in a matter of seconds. You can also read more carefully those answers that are marginal; and if you eventually do mark them minus, you can do so knowing that the student will have another chance. Finally, it is obviously much simpler to count the number of wrong answers than to add up ten scores ranging in value from 1 to 5. With practice, you may find grading exams so quick that you will be able to provide feedback the next day.

Advantages and Disadvantages of Mastery Learning After briefly summing up the advantages of mastery learning, we'll take a look at some of its limitations. On the plus side, the research findings demonstrate that students taught under mastery conditions often learn more than students taught under nonmastery conditions. On a final exam in which all of the items directly reflected the objectives the students were required to learn, the typical student taught under mastery conditions outscored the typical nonmastery-taught student by 11–19 percentile ranks (depending on whose analysis of the research one chooses to cite). Although both low- and high-aptitude students benefit from a mastery approach, the improvement is greatest for low-aptitude students. Consequently, there is less variation in final exam scores in mastery classes than in nonmastery classes. The effect of mastery learning on standardized test scores was essentially zero, probably owing to the fact that many of the test items asked about things not covered by the mastery program's objectives (Kulik, Kulik & Bangert-Drowns, 1990; Slavin, 1987, 1990).

However, mastery learning is not without its problems, any one of which may limit its effectiveness. The following criticisms of mastery learning are derived from points made by Daniel Mueller (1973) and William Cox Jr. and Thomas Dunn (1979). (All of these limitations can be overcome, however, with effort and ingenuity.)

Mastery learning has several potential limitations

1. Mastery learning requires careful planning, preparation of several sets of evaluation materials, and extensive monitoring of student progress. Accordingly, it requires more teacher time and effort than conventional instruction.
2. The standard for mastery may be difficult to establish or defend.
3. Students may practice the "principle of least effort" by not studying for first exams on the assumption that they will pick up test-taking hints over time as they examine the questions. Accordingly, the teacher will have to administer and score several exams.
4. Since some students inevitably achieve mastery faster than others, it is necessary to devise alternative assignments for those who have passed tests at an acceptable level on the first try.

Being Realistic About Mastery Learning Although this discussion of mastery learning has been intended to make you enthusiastic about the approach, you should be aware that it is not a panacea. For one thing, some students will disappoint, if not infuriate, you by the lengths they will go to in trying to beat the system—even after you have done everything in your power to make the system fair, just, and sensible. And students who find it difficult to learn may feel even more inadequate under a mastery approach than under a traditional one. When every opportunity to learn is provided and slow students are still unable to respond and do as well as their classmates, it is more difficult for them to blame the system.

Mastery learning does not eliminate competition and comparisons

Mastery learning reduces competition and comparisons, but it does not eliminate them. Students who learn easily will meet the criterion for an A with little effort; they are likely to go through the required sequence so rapidly that they have considerable time for independent study. But those who learn slowly will engage in a constant battle to keep up with the required work. Because fortunate students learn faster and can engage in more self-selected study, they will probably get further and further ahead of their less capable classmates. Despite suggestions that prestige colleges ought to practice open admissions, it is most unlikely that they will do so. Furthermore, the number of jobs at the top of a scale based on interest, pay, and influence will always be limited. A mastery approach cannot by itself alter the fact that students who learn easily and rapidly are still likely to be rewarded with admission to the best colleges and to get the best jobs. Even so, you may discover that a mastery approach is well worth the extra time, effort, and trouble it requires. A greater proportion of your students will probably learn more, enjoy school more, develop better attitudes toward learning, and feel more confident and proud of themselves than they would under comparative grading techniques.

PUTTING CRITERION-REFERENCED GRADING INTO PRACTICE

Converting Scores into Letter Grades To practice criterion-referenced grading, look at Figure 12.1 (p. 460), which has two elements. On the left side of the figure, you see a representative page from a teacher's grade book depicting one way a teacher at any grade level might record grades when using mastery learning. Notice that there are two columns under each exam heading in this figure. The page has room for two scores because a mastery approach urges students to find out what errors they made on the first try on an exam, ask for clarification, study further (with or without teacher assistance), and take an alternate form of the exam in an effort to improve their score. The obvious advantage of this policy is that students who do less well than they had hoped on a first exam will feel motivated to try harder instead of giving up, which is a common response when an exam is given only once. On the right side of the figure, you'll see the information that was distributed to these students on the first day of the report period. You can figure their grades using the data presented on the left side.

Next, follow a similar procedure for Figure 12.2 (p. 461), using the set of instructions on the right side of that figure to calculate the grade for each student in the accompanying grade book. For both figures, compare your mastery grades with those assigned by classmates to identify any arithmetic errors that might have been made. Finally, speculate about how students would respond to a mastery approach as compared to norm-referenced grading techniques.

Guidelines for Implementation As you implement a criterion-referenced grading approach, the following guidelines and practical suggestions should help you organize your time and work.

1. Try to set aside a specified period one day each week for exams. When deciding how many exams to give, be sure to allow at least two days for each exam. If possible, also schedule at least one make-up exam day.

2. Grade and return papers and exams as soon as possible so that students will know whether to study for a second try. If you use a point-per-exam approach, it is preferable to make up multiple-choice exams that can be graded as quickly as students finish them. If you prefer short-essay questions, try using plus or minus grading. It is considerably simpler and faster than point grading.

3. On second-exam days, allow students who were satisfied with grades earned on the first try to work on projects or to engage in individualized study.

4. Start using grade standards that reflect the traditional pattern of 90 percent and above for an A, 80 to 89 percent for a B, and so forth. If it turns out that fewer than 10 percent of your students are earning A's after the first exam, it is possible that these standards are too high and should be lowered. Before you draw that conclusion, however, realize

	1st Exam		2nd Exam		3rd Exam		Exam	Projects			Extra Project	Grade
	1st Try	2nd Try	1st Try	2nd Try	1st Try	2nd Try	Total Points	1	2	3		
Adams, Ann	16	18	17	18	18			P	P	P		
Baker, Charles	13	14	14		10	14		P				
Cohen, Matthew	14	16	15	16	17			P	P			
Davis, Rebecca	19		19		20			P	P	P		
Evans, Deborah	16	18	17	18	16	18		P	P	P		
Ford, Harold	15	16	17		15			P	P			
Grayson, Lee	10	13	12	14	12	15		P				
Hood, Barbara	16		17		15			P	P			
Ingalls, Robert	16	18	16		15			P	P			
Jones, Thomas	11	14	12	16	15			P				
Kim, David	18		19		19			P	P	P		
Lapine, Craig	14	16	18		16			P	P			
Moore, James	17		17		17			P	P			
Nguyen, Tuan	17	18	19		16	17		P	P	P		
Orton, John	10	10	11		9							
Peck, Nancy	14		15		14			P				
Quist, Ann	16	18	17	18	18			P	P	P		
Richards, Mary	16		17		15			P	P			
Santos, Maria	13		15		14			P				
Thomas, Eric	15	16	15	17	15			P	P			
Wong, Yuen	14		15		16			P				
Vernon, Joan	11	14	13	14	12	14		P				
Zacharias, Saul	16	18	17		16	19		P	P	P		

Instructions for Determining Your Grade in Social Studies

Your grade in social studies this report period will be based on three exams (worth 20 points each) and satisfactory completion of up to three projects.

Here are the standards for different grades:

A—Average of 18 or more on three exams, plus three projects at Pass level

B—Average of 16 or 17 on three exams, plus two projects at Pass level

C—Average of 14 or 15 on three exams, plus one project at Pass level

D—Average of 10 to 13 on three exams

F—Average of 9 or less on three exams

Another way to figure your grade is to add together points as you take exams. This may be the best procedure to follow as we get close to the end of the report period. Use this description of standards as a guide:

A—At least 54 points, plus three projects at Pass level

B—48 to 53 points, plus two projects at Pass level

C—42 to 47 points, plus one project at Pass level

D—30 to 41 points

F—29 points or less

If you are not satisfied with the score you earn on any exam, you may take a different exam on the same material in an effort to improve your score. (Some of the questions on the alternate exam will be the same as those on the original exam; some will be different.) Projects will be graded P (Pass) or DO (Do Over). If you receive a DO on a project, you may work to improve it and hand it in again. You may also submit an *extra* project, which may earn up to 3 points of bonus credit (and can help if your exam scores fall just below a cutoff point). As you take each exam and receive a Pass for each project, record your progress on this chart.

First Exam		Second Exam		Third Exam		Project 1	Project 2	Project 3	Extra Project	Grade
1st Try	2nd Try	1st Try	2nd Try	1st Try	2nd Try					

FIGURE 12.1 *Page from a Teacher's Grade Book and Instructions to Students: Mastery Approach Featuring + or – Grading*

	1st Exam		2nd Exam		3rd Exam		Projects			Grade
	1st Try	2nd Try	1st Try	2nd Try	1st Try	2nd Try	1	2	3	
Adams, Ann	~~2~~	1	1		1		P	P	P	
Baker, Charles	~~4~~	3	~~4~~	3	~~5~~	3	P			
Cohen, Matthew	3		3		~~4~~	3	P			
Davis, Rebecca	2		2		2		P	P		
Evans, Deborah	3		~~4~~	3	3		P			
Ford, Harold	~~6~~	3	~~4~~	3	~~4~~	3	P			
Grayson, Lee	~~2~~	1	~~2~~	1	1		P	P	P	
Hood, Barbara	1		0		1		P	P	P	
Ingalls, Robert	~~3~~	2	2		~~3~~	2	P	P		
Jones, Thomas	~~5~~	4	4		4					
Kim, David	0		1		0		P	P	P	
Lapine, Craig	~~4~~	3	3		3		P			
Moore, James	~~3~~	2	2		2		P	P		
Nguyen, Tuan	~~3~~	2	~~3~~	2	~~3~~	2	P	P		
Orton, John	~~3~~	2	2		2		P	P		
Peck, Nancy	~~2~~	1	~~2~~	1	1		P	P		
Quist, Ann	~~3~~	2	~~4~~	2	2		P	P		
Richards, Mary	~~2~~	1	~~2~~	1	1		P	P	P	
Santos, Maria	~~4~~	2	~~3~~	2	~~3~~	2	P	P		
Thomas, Eric	~~2~~	1	1		1		P	P	P	
Wong, Yuen	~~4~~	3	3		3		P			
Vernon, Joan	~~5~~	3	~~4~~	3	~~4~~	3	P			
Zacharias, Saul	~~3~~	1	~~2~~	1	~~3~~	1	P	P	P	

Instructions for Determining Your Grade in Social Studies

Your grade in social studies this report period will be based on scores on three exams and successful completion of up to three projects. The exams will consist of ten questions each, and your answers will be graded plus or minus. The projects will be graded P (Pass) or DO (Do Over). Here are the standards for different grades:

A—Miss not more than one question on any exam, plus three projects at Pass level

B—Miss not more than two questions on any exam, plus two projects at Pass level

C—Miss not more than three questions on any exam, plus one project at Pass level

D—Miss four questions on any exam

F—Miss five or more questions on all three exams

If you are not satisfied with the grade you earn on any exam, you may take a different form of the exam to try and improve your score. (Some of the questions on the alternate form of the exam will be the same as those on the original exam; some will be different.) You may hand in an extra project, which may earn up to two bonus points (and can help if you fall just below the cutoff point on one or two exams).

FIGURE 12.2 *Page from a Teacher's Grade Book and Instructions to Students: Mastery Approach Featuring Point Grading*

that there are several possible causes of poor test performance and low test grades and that the other possibilities should be examined before you alter grading practices. You may find, for example, that several test items were vaguely worded, that some items did not adequately reflect course objectives, that the students did not prepare properly for the test, that they did not understand the material, or that you did not allow sufficient time for them to master the material. If you find that one or more of these factors could be responsible for lower than expected grades, apply corrective action, and observe the effect on another exam before lowering your standards.

Improving Your Grading Methods: Assessment Practices to Avoid

Earlier in this chapter we noted that the typical teacher has little systematic knowledge of assessment principles and as a result may engage in a variety of inappropriate testing and grading practices. We hope that the information in this chapter will help you become more proficient than most of your colleagues at these tasks. (In addition, we strongly encourage you to take a course in classroom assessment if you have not already done so.) To reinforce what you have learned here, we will now describe some of the more common inappropriate testing and grading practices committed by teachers. The following list is based largely on the observations of Robert Lynn Canady and Phyllis Riley Hotchkiss (1989) and John Hills (1991).

Be aware of and avoid faulty measurement and grading practices

1. *Worshiping averages.* Some teachers mechanically average all scores and automatically assign the corresponding grade, even when they know an unusually low score was due to an extenuating circumstance. Allowances can be made for physical illness, emotional upset, and the like; students' lowest grade can be dropped, or they can repeat the test on which they performed most poorly. While objectivity in grading is a laudatory goal, it should not be practiced to the extent that it prevents you from altering your normal procedures when your professional judgment indicates an exception is warranted.

Another shortcoming of this practice is that it ignores measurement error. No one can construct the perfect test, and no person's score is a true indicator of knowledge and skill. Test scores represent estimates of these characteristics. Accordingly, giving a student with an average of 74.67 a grade of D when 75 is the minimum needed for a C pretends the test is more accurate than it really is. This is why it is so important to conduct an item analysis of your tests. If you discover several items that are unusually difficult, you may want to make allowances for students who are a point or two from the next highest grade (and modify the items if you intend to use them again). We describe a simple procedure for analyzing your test items in the next Suggestions for Teaching section.

2. *Using zeros indiscriminately.* The sole purpose of grades is to communicate to others how much of the curriculum a student has mastered. When teachers also use grades to reflect their appraisal of a student's work habits or character, the validity of the grades is lessened. This oc-

curs most dramatically when students receive zeros for assignments that are late (but are otherwise of good quality), incomplete, or not completed according to directions and for exams on which students are suspected of cheating. This is a flawed practice for two reasons. First, and to repeat what we said in point 1, there may be good reasons that projects and homework assignments are late, incomplete, or different from what was expected. You should try to uncover such circumstances and take them into account. The second reason for not automatically giving zeros is that they cause communication problems. If a student who earns grades in the low 90s for most of the grading period is given two zeros for one or more of the reasons just mentioned, that student could easily receive a D or an F. Such a grade is not an accurate reflection of what was learned. If penalties are to be given for work that is late, incomplete, or not done according to directions and for which there are no extenuating circumstances, they should be clearly spelled out far in advance of the due date, and they should not seriously distort the meaning of the grade. For students suspected of cheating, for example, a different form of the exam can be given.

3. *Providing insufficient instruction before testing.* For a variety of reasons, teachers occasionally spend more time than they had planned on certain topics. In an effort to "cover the curriculum" prior to a scheduled exam, they may significantly increase the pace of instruction or simply tell students to read the remaining material on their own. The low grades that typically result from this practice will unfortunately be read by outsiders (and this includes parents) as a deficiency in students' learning ability when in fact they more accurately indicate a deficiency in instructional quality.

4. *Teaching for one thing but testing for another.* This practice takes several forms. For instance, teachers may provide considerable supplementary material in class through lecture, thereby encouraging students to take notes and study them extensively, but base test questions almost entirely on text material. Or if teachers emphasize the text material during class discussion, they may take a significant number of questions from footnotes and less important parts of the text. A third form of this flawed practice is to provide students with simple problems or practice questions in class that reflect the knowledge level of Bloom's Taxonomy but to give complex problems and higher-level questions on a test. Remember what we said at the end of Chapter 10: if you want transfer, then teach for transfer.

5. *Using pop quizzes to motivate students.* If you recall our discussion of reinforcement schedules from Chapter 8, you will recognize that surprise tests represent a variable interval schedule and that such schedules produce a consistent pattern of behavior in humans under certain circumstances. Being a student in a classroom is not one of those circumstances. Surprise tests produce an undesirable level of anxiety in many students and cause others to simply give up. If you sense that students are not sufficiently motivated to read and study more consistently, consult the previous chapter for better ideas on how to accomplish this goal.

6. *Keeping the nature and content of the test a secret.* Many teachers scrupulously avoid giving students any meaningful information about the type of questions that will be on a test or what the test items will cover.

The assumption that underlies this practice is that if students have been paying attention in class, have been diligently doing their homework, and have been studying at regular intervals, they will do just fine on a test. But they usually don't—and the main reason can be seen in our description of a learning strategy (Chapter 9). A good learning strategist first analyzes all of the available information that bears on attaining a goal. But if certain critical information about the goal is not available, the rest of the strategy (planning, implementing, monitoring, and modifying) will suffer.

7. *Keeping the criteria for assignments a secret.* This practice is closely related to the previous one. Students may be told, for example, to write an essay on what the world would be like if all diseases were eliminated and to give their imagination free rein in order to come up with many original ideas. But when the papers are graded, equal weight is given to spelling, punctuation, and grammatical usage. If these aspects of writing are also important to you and you intend to hold students accountable for them, make sure that fact is clearly communicated to them.

8. *Shifting criteria.* Teachers are sometimes disappointed in the quality of students' tests and assignments and decide to change the grading criteria as a way to "shock" students into more appropriate learning behaviors. For example, a teacher may have told students that mechanics will count for one-third of the grade on a writing assignment. But when the teacher discovers that most of the papers contain numerous spelling, punctuation, and grammatical errors, she may decide to let mechanics determine one-half of the grade. As we indicated before, grades should not be used as a motivational devicc or as a way to make up for instructional oversights. There are far better ways to accomplish these goals.

The following Suggestions for Teaching should help you properly implement the assessment concepts and research findings that were presented in this chapter.

Suggestions for Teaching in Your Classroom

Effective Assessment Techniques

1. As early as possible in a report period, decide when and how often to give tests and other assignments that will count toward a grade, and announce tests and assignments well in advance.

2. Prepare a content outline and/or a table of specifications of the objectives to be covered on each exam, or otherwise take care to obtain a systematic sample of the knowledge and skill acquired by your students.

3. Consider the purpose of each test or measurement exercise in light of the developmental characteristics of the students in your classes and the nature of the curriculum for your grade level.

4. Decide whether a written test or a performance test is most appropriate.

5. Make up and use a detailed answer key.

   a. Evaluate each answer by comparing it to the key.

   b. Be willing and prepared to defend the evaluations you make.

6. During and after the grading process, analyze questions and answers in order to improve future exams.

In order for students to effectively plan how they will master your objectives, they need to know as early as possible how many tests they will have to take, when the tests will occur, what types of items each test will contain, and what content they will be tested on.

1. **As early as possible in a report period, decide when and how often to give tests and other assignments that will count toward a grade, and announce tests and assignments well in advance.**

If you follow the suggestions for formulating objectives presented in Chapter 7, you should be able to develop a reasonably complete master plan that will permit you to devise a course outline even though you have only limited experience with teaching and/or a text or unit of study. In doing so, you will have not only a good sense of the objectives you want your students to achieve but also the means by which achievement will be assessed.

Before the term actually starts is a good time to block out the number of tests you will give in that term. Recall that research cited earlier has shown that students who take six or seven tests per term (two or three per grading period) learn more than students who are tested less frequently or not at all. Don't assume, however, that if giving three tests per grading period is good, then giving five or six tests is better. A point of diminishing returns is quickly reached after the fourth test.

Journal Entry
Announcing Exams and Assignments

If you announce at the beginning of a report period when you intend to give exams or set due dates for assignments, you not only give students a clear idea of what they will be expected to do, but you also give yourself guidelines for arranging lesson plans and devising, administering, and scoring tests. (If you will be teaching elementary students, it will be better to announce exams and assignments for a week at a time rather than providing a long-range schedule.)

For the most part it is preferable to announce tests well in advance. Pop quizzes tend to increase anxiety and tension and to force students to cram on isolated sections of a book on a day-by-day and catch-as-catch-can basis. Simple homework assignments or the equivalent are more likely to encourage more careful and consistent study than pop quizzes. When tests are announced, it is useful to students to know exactly what material they will be held responsible for, what kinds of questions will be asked, and how much tests will count toward the final grade. Research indicates that students who are told to expect (and who receive) an essay test or a multiple-choice test score slightly higher on an exam than students who do not know what to expect or who are led to expect one type of test but are given another type (Lundeberg & Fox, 1991).

For term papers or other written work, list your criteria for grading the papers (for example, how much emphasis will be placed on style, spelling and punctuation, research, individuality of expression). In laboratory courses most students prefer a list of experiments or projects and some description of how they will be evaluated (for example, ten experiments in chemistry, fifteen drawings in drafting, five paintings in art, judged according to posted criteria).

2. Prepare a content outline and/or a table of specifications of the objectives to be covered on each exam, or otherwise take care to obtain a systematic sample of the knowledge and skill acquired by your students.

The more precisely and completely goals are described at the beginning of a unit, the easier and more efficient assessment (and teaching) will be. The use of a clear outline will help ensure an adequate sample of the most significant kinds of behavior.

When the time comes to assess the abilities of your students, you can't possibly observe and evaluate all relevant behavior. You can't listen to more than a few pages of reading by each first grader, for example, or ask high school seniors to answer questions on everything discussed in several chapters of a text. Because of the limitations imposed by large numbers of students and small amounts of time, your evaluation will have to be based on a sample of behavior—a three- or four-minute reading performance and questions covering points made in only a few sections of text material assigned for an exam. It is therefore important to try to obtain a representative, accurate sample.

Necessary to obtain a representative sample of behavior when testing

Psychologists who have studied measurement and evaluation often recommend that as teachers prepare exams they use a **table of specifications** to note the types and numbers of test items to be included so as to ensure thorough and systematic coverage. You can draw up a table of specifications by first listing along the left-hand margin of a piece of lined paper the important topics that have been covered. Then insert appropriate headings from the taxonomy of objectives for the cognitive domain (or for the affective or psychomotor domain, if appropriate) across the top of the page. An example of such a table of specifications for the information discussed so far in this chapter is provided in Figure 12.3. A computer spreadsheet program such as Microsoft Excel is an ideal tool for creating a table of specifications. Doing your work on the computer gives you the ability to save and modify it for future use.

Journal Entry
Using a Table of Specifications

Test specialists often recommend that you insert in the boxes of a table of specifications the percentage of test items that you intend to write for each topic and each type of objective. This practice forces you to think about both the number and the relative importance of your objectives before you start teaching or writing test items. Thus, if some objectives are more important to you than others, you will have a way of ensuring that these are tested more thoroughly. If, however, a test is going to be brief and emphasize all objec-

Table of specifications helps ensure an adequate sample of content, behavior

Topic	Objectives					
	Knows	Comprehends	Applies	Analyzes	Synthesizes	Evaluates
Nature of measurement and evaluation						
Purposes of measurement and evaluation						
Types of written tests						
Nature of performance tests						

FIGURE 12.3 *Example of a Table of Specifications for Material Covered So Far in This Chapter*

tives more or less equally, you may wish to put a check mark in each box as you write questions. If you discover that you are overloading some boxes and that others are empty, you can take steps to remedy the situation. The important point to realize is that by taking steps to ensure that your tests cover what you want your students to know, you will be increasing the tests' validity.

For reasons to be discussed shortly, you may choose not to list all of the categories in the taxonomy for all subjects or at all grade levels. Tables of specifications that you draw up for your own use, therefore, may contain fewer headings across the top of the page than those in the table illustrated in Figure 12.3. Because the levels of the cognitive domain taxonomy are represented by words that have very specific meaning (knows, applies, analyzes), you may find it helpful to refer to the tables of objectives and outcomes for the three taxonomies included in Chapter 7 (Tables 7.1, 7.2, and 7.3, pp. 251–253).

The primary reason for using various types of instructional objectives to plan evaluation, for drawing up a table of specifications, or for referring to the lists just provided is to make your evaluations of student understanding and abilities comprehensive and systematic. Without some sort of rationale, you might simply make up questions on material that strikes you as testable.

You also might fall into the extremely common trap of writing questions that test a limited range of outcomes. Recall the statement by Benjamin Bloom quoted in Chapter 7: "It is estimated that over 90 percent of test questions that U.S. public school students are now expected to answer deal with little more than information" (1984, p. 13). Bloom stresses the word *now* to emphasize that, even though over one million copies of the taxonomy for the cognitive domain have been sold, very few teachers seem to be using them. Subsequent research (e.g., Stiggins, Griswold, & Wikelund, 1989) supports Bloom's contention that most of the test items used by teachers reflect verbatim recall. This pattern occurs most often among teachers of science, social studies, and language arts and least often among mathematics teachers.

3. **Consider the purpose of each test or measurement exercise in light of the developmental characteristics of the students in your classes and the nature of the curriculum for your grade level.**

In addition to considering different uses of tests and other forms of measurement when you plan assessment strategies, you should think about the developmental characteristics of the students you plan to teach and the nature of the curriculum at your grade level. As noted in the discussion of Jean Piaget's theory in Chapter 2, there are significant differences among preoperational, concrete operational, and formal thinkers. Furthermore, because primary grade children are asked to master a curriculum that is substantially different from the curriculum upper elementary and secondary school students are expected to learn, different forms of measurement should be used at each level.

Primary grade children are asked to concentrate on learning basic skills, and their progress—or lack of it—will often be apparent even if they are not asked to take tests. A second grader who can read only a few words, for instance, will reveal that inability each time she is asked to read. Upper elementary grade and middle school students are asked to improve and perfect their mastery of skills in reading, writing, and arithmetic and also to study topics in the sciences, social studies, and other subjects. Success in dealing with many subjects, learning materials, and tests often depends on skill in reading. A fifth grader who is a slow reader, for instance, might not be able to get through an assigned chapter or answer all the questions on a multiple-choice test in the allotted time. Because performance in several subjects must be reported, many separate assessments have to be made. In all of the elementary grades, there is usually an emphasis on helping as many students as possible master the curriculum. Thus, tests may be used as much to diagnose weaknesses and chart improvement (a formative evaluation function) as to establish grades.

Elementary grade students tested as much for diagnostic, formative evaluation purposes as for summative purposes

At the secondary level, many subjects are arranged in sequence; in addition, the process of identifying students most likely to go on to college begins at this time. Thus, comparisons of students become more systematic and direct. It is often desirable (or necessary) to discover if a student who takes Math I, for instance, is ready to go on to Math II. Colleges and universities may request that high schools establish particular grading standards to facilitate the selection of candidates who apply for admission. If a school does not maintain sufficiently high standards, graduates may encounter problems when they apply for admission to certain institutions of higher learning.

4. **Decide whether a written test or a performance test is most appropriate.**

As you think about which types of questions to use in a particular situation, consider the student characteristics and curriculum differences noted earlier.

In the primary grades, you may not use any written tests in the strict sense. Instead you might ask your students to demonstrate skills, complete exercises (some of which may be similar to completion tests), and solve simple problems (often on worksheets). In the upper elementary and middle school grades you may need to use or make up dozens of measurement instruments since many subjects must be graded. Accordingly, it may be necessary to make extensive use of completion, short-answer, and short-essay items that can be printed on the board or on a ditto master. If you find it impossible or impractical to make up a table of specifications for each exam, at least refer to instructional objectives or a list of key points as you write questions. At the secondary level, you might do your best to develop some sort of table of specifications for exams not only to ensure measurement of objectives at various levels of the taxonomy but also to remind yourself to use different types of items.

Journal Entry
Using Different Types of Test Items

In certain elementary and middle school subjects and in skill or laboratory subjects at the secondary level, performance tests may be more appropriate than written tests. At the primary grade level, for instance, you may be required to assign a grade in oral reading. In a high school home economics class, you may grade students on how well they produce a garment or a soufflé. In a woodshop class, you may base a grade on how well students construct a piece of furniture. In such cases you can make evaluations more systematic and accurate by using rating scales and checklists and by attempting to equate (or at least take into account) the difficulty level of the performance to be rated.

Rating scales and checklists make evaluations of performance more systematic

To evaluate a product such as a garment or piece of furniture, you might use a checklist that you devised and handed out at the beginning of a course. Such a checklist should state the number of possible points that will be awarded for various aspects of the project—for example, accuracy of measurements and preparation of component parts, neatness of assembly, quality of finishing touches, and final appearance. To evaluate a performance, you might use the same approach, announcing beforehand how heavily you intend to weigh various aspects of execution. In music, for instance, you might note possible points to be awarded for tone, execution, accuracy, and interpretation. For both project and performance tasks, you might multiply the final score by a difficulty factor. (You have probably seen television coverage of Olympics events in which divers and gymnasts have their performance ratings multiplied by such a difficulty factor.)

5. Make up and use a detailed answer key.

a. Evaluate each answer by comparing it to the key.

One of the most valuable characteristics of a test is that it permits comparison of the permanently recorded answers of all students to a fixed set of criteria. A complete key not only reduces subjectivity; it can also save you much time and trouble when you are grading papers and/or defending your evaluation of questions.

For short-answer, true-false, matching, or multiple-choice questions, you should devise your key as you write and assemble the items. With planning

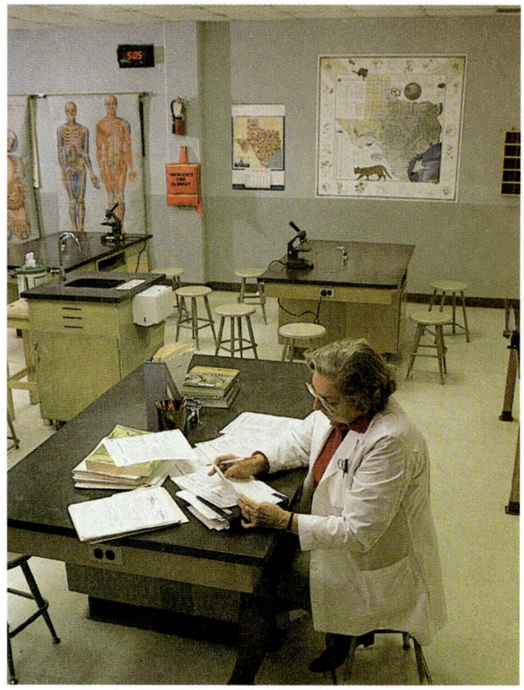

The onerous chore of grading papers can be speeded up and simplified if plus-minus grading is used.

Journal Entry
Preparing a Detailed Key

and ingenuity, you can prepare a key that will greatly simplify grading. For essay questions, you should also prepare answers as you write the questions. If you ask students to write answers to a small number of comprehensive essay questions, you are likely to maximize the consistency of your grading process by grading all answers to the first question at one sitting, then grading all answers to the second question, and so on. If a test consists of eight or ten short-essay items (which can usually be answered in a half-hour or so), you would have to do too much paper shuffling to follow such a procedure. One way to speed up the grading of short-essay exams (so that you can evaluate up to thirty tests in a single session of forty minutes or so) is to use plus or minus grading. If you use a point scale to grade short-essay answers, you will spend an agonizing amount of time deciding just how much a given answer is worth. But with practice, you should be able to write short-essay questions and answers (on your key) that can be graded plus or minus.

To develop skill in writing such questions, make up a few formative quizzes that will not count toward a grade. Experiment with phrasing questions that require students to reveal that they either know or don't know the answer. Prepare your key as you write the questions. When the time comes to grade papers, simply make a yes or no decision about the correctness of each answer. With a felt-tip pen, make a bold check over each satisfactory answer on an exam, and simply tally the number of checks when you have read all the answers. (Counting up to eight or ten is obviously a lot quicker and easier than adding together various numbers of points for eight or ten answers.) Once you have developed skill in writing and evaluating short-essay questions that can be graded plus or minus, prepare and use summative exams. If you decide to use this type of exam, guard against the temptation to write items that measure only knowledge. Use a table of specifications, or otherwise take steps to write at least some questions that measure skills at the higher levels of the taxonomy for the cognitive domain.

b. **Be willing and prepared to defend the evaluations you make.**

You will probably get few complaints if you have a detailed key, and when exams are returned, you can explain to the class how each answer was graded. To a direct challenge about a specific answer to an essay or short-essay question, you might respond by showing complainers an answer that received full credit and inviting them to compare it with their own.

A major disadvantage of multiple-choice items is that it is very difficult to go over a multiple-choice test in class. Going over a fifty-item test could take hours even if just one or two students are divergent thinkers or particularly argumentative. Because of such factors, instructors often simply report or post scores on multiple-choice exams. The unfortunate result of such a policy is that it encourages students to think only about a score, not about what they have learned (or failed to learn). Students also reason that as soon as a test is completed, the purpose for learning what was covered on the exam has been served, and information might as well be forgotten.

Perhaps the best way to encourage students to think about what has been covered in multiple-choice questions, instead of concentrating only on the score, is to prepare a feedback booklet (see the Study Guide that accompanies this text, for an example). As you write each multiple-choice question, also write a brief explanation as to why you feel the answer is correct and why the distracters are incorrect. If you follow this policy (which takes less time than you might expect), you can often improve the questions as you write your defense of the answer. If you go a step farther (to be described in the next point), you can obtain information to use in improving questions after they have been answered. This is a good policy to follow with any exam, multiple choice or otherwise.

6. During and after the grading process, analyze questions and answers in order to improve future exams.

If you prepare sufficient copies of feedback booklets for multiple-choice exams, you can supply them to all students when you hand back scored answer sheets (and copies of the question booklets). After students have checked their papers and identified and examined questions that were marked wrong, invite them to select up to three questions that they wish to challenge. Even after they read your explanation in the feedback booklet, many students are likely to feel that they selected a different answer than you did for logical and defensible reasons. Permit them to write out a description of the reasoning behind their choices. If an explanation seems plausible, give credit for the answer. If several students chose the same questions for comment, you have evidence that the item needs to be revised. (It's also possible that the information reflected in the item was not directly related to your objectives or was poorly taught.)

If you follow the procedure of supplying feedback booklets, it is almost essential to prepare at least two forms of every exam. After writing the questions, arrange them into two tests. Make perhaps half of the questions the same, half unique to each exam. (If you have enough questions, you might prepare three forms.) If you teach multiple sections, give the first form to period 1, the next form to period 2, and thereafter use the forms in random order. This procedure will reduce the possibility that some students in later classes will have advance information about most of the questions on the test. (Having two or more forms also equips you to use a mastery approach.)

Journal Entry
Analyzing Test Items

If you find that you do not have time to prepare feedback booklets, you might invite students to select three answers to defend as they record their choices when taking multiple-choice exams. This will supply you with information about ambiguous questions, even though it will not provide feedback to students. It may also provide you with useful information about how well the items were written.

Item analysis tells about difficulty, discriminability of multiple-choice items

Turning back to multiple-choice questions, you may also want to use simple versions of item-analysis techniques that measurement specialists use to analyze and improve this type of item. These techniques will allow you to estimate the difficulty level and discriminating power of each item. To do so, try the following steps suggested by Gronlund (1993):

- Rank the test papers from highest score to lowest score.
- Select approximately the top one-third, and call this the upper group. Select approximately the bottom one-third, and call this the lower group. Set the middle group of papers aside.
- For each item, record the number of students in the upper group and in the lower group who selected the correct answer and each distracter as follows:

Item 1. Alternatives	A	B*	C	D	E
Upper Group	0	6	3	1	0
Lower Group	3	2	2	3	0

* = correct answer

- Estimate the item difficulty by calculating the percentage of students who answered the item correctly. The difficulty index for the preceding item is 40 percent (8/20 x 100). Note that the smaller the percentage is, the more difficult the item is.
- Estimate the item discriminating power by subtracting the number in the lower group who answered the item correctly from the number in the upper group, and divide by one-half of the total number of students included in the item analysis. For the preceding example, the discrimination index is 0.40 (6 - 2 ÷ 10). When the index is positive, as it is here, it indicates that more students in the upper group than in the lower group answered the item correctly. A negative value indicates just the opposite.

As you can see, this type of item analysis is not difficult to do, nor is it likely to be very time consuming. It is important to remember, however, that the benefits of item analysis can quickly be lost if you ignore certain limitations. One is that you will be working with relatively small numbers of students. Therefore, the results of item analysis are likely to vary as you go from class to class or from test to test with the same class. Because of this variation, you should retain items that a measurement specialist would discard or revise. In general, you should retain multiple-choice items whose difficulty index lies between 50 and 90 percent and whose discrimination index is positive (Gronlund, 1988). Another limitation is that you may have objectives that everyone must master. If you do an effective job of teaching these objectives, the corresponding test items are likely to be answered correctly by nearly every student. These items should be retained rather than revised to meet arbitrary criteria of difficulty and discrimination.

Resources for Further Investigation

Suggestions for Constructing Written and Performance Tests

For specific suggestions on ways to write different types of items for paper-and-pencil tests of knowledge and on methods for constructing and using rating scales and checklists to measure products, performances, and procedures, consult one or more of the following books: *Measurement and Evaluation in Teaching* (7th ed., 1995), by Robert Linn and Norman Gronlund; *How to Make Achievement Tests and Assessments* (5th ed., 1993), by Norman Gronlund; *Classroom Assessment: What Teachers Need to Know* (1995), by W. James Popham; *Student-Centered Classroom Assessment* (1994), by Richard Stiggins; *Classroom Assessment* (2d ed., 1994), by Peter Airasian; and *Practical Aspects of Authentic Assessment* (1994), by Bonnie Campbell Hill and Cynthia Ruptic.

The Learning Resources Development Center (LRDC) at the University of Pittsburgh publishes a large number of briefs, articles, and reviews related to assessment and learning, particularly emphasizing cognitive-based approaches. An on-line resource of the LRDC can be found at http://www.lrdc.pitt.edu/publications.html. The most extensive on-line database of assessment information is the ERIC/AE Test Locater, which is found at www.cua.edu/www/eric_ae/testcol.html. It includes numerous topics, reviews of tests, suggestions and digests relating to alternative assessment, and broader standards and policy-making information as it relates to evaluation and assessment of students.

Writing Higher-Level Questions

As Benjamin Bloom and others point out, teachers have a disappointing tendency to write test items that reflect the lowest level of the taxonomy—knowledge. To avoid this failing, carefully read Part 2 of *Taxonomy of Educational Objectives: The Classification of Educational Goals, Handbook I: Cognitive Domain* (1956), edited by Benjamin Bloom, Max Englehart, Edward Furst, Walker Hill, and David Krathwohl. Each level of the taxonomy is clearly explained and followed by several pages of illustrative test items.

Analyzing Test Items

Norman Gronlund briefly discusses item-analysis procedures for norm-referenced and criterion-referenced tests in Chapter 6 of *How to Make Achievement Tests and Assessments* (5th ed., 1993). For norm-referenced multiple-choice tests, these include procedures for assessing the difficulty of each item, the discriminating power of each item, and the effectiveness of each alternative answer. For criterion-referenced tests, they include a measure for assessing the effects of instruction. More detailed discussions of item-analysis procedures can be found in Chapter 8 of *Educational Testing and Measurement: Classroom Application and Practice* (4th ed., 1993), by Tom Kubiszyn and Gary Borich.

Question Mark Software, based in Britain, produces a software program that can help teachers generate quality test items. Information on the software can be found at http://www.qmark.com or by calling the U.S. distributor at 800-863-3950.

Mastery Learning

If you would like to read comprehensive analyses of mastery learning, look for one of these books: *Human Characteristics and School Learning* (1976), by Benjamin Bloom; *All Our Children Learning* (1981), by Benjamin Bloom; *Improving Student Achievement Through Mastery Learning Programs* (1985), edited by Daniel Levine; and *Building Effective Mastery Learning Schools* (1989), by James Block, Helen Efthim, and Robert Burns.

Summary

1. Classroom assessment, which involves the measurement and evaluation of student learning, accounts for anywhere between one-third and one-half of a teacher's class time.

2. Measurement involves ranking individuals according to how much of a particular characteristic they possess. Evaluation involves making judgments about the value or worth of a set of measures.

3. Teachers give tests and assign grades to communicate to others how well students have mastered the teacher's objectives, to find out if students are keeping up with and understanding the learning material, to diagnose students' strengths and weaknesses, and to positively affect students' approaches to studying.

4. Research indicates that students who take four to six exams a term learn more than students who take fewer or no exams.

5. Written tests are used to measure how much knowledge people have about some topic. Test items can be classified as selected response (multiple choice, true-false, matching), short answer, and essay.

6. Selected-response tests are efficient to administer and score but tend to reflect the lowest level of the cognitive domain taxonomy and provide no information about what students can do with the knowledge they have learned.

7. Short-answer tests measure recall, rather than recognition, of information and allow for comprehensive coverage of a topic, but they have the same disadvantages of selected-response tests.

8. Essay tests measure such high-level skills as analysis, synthesis, and evaluation but are difficult to grade consistently, are time consuming to grade, and allow only limited coverage of material.

9. Performance tests are used to measure how well students use basic knowledge to perform a particular skill or produce a particular product under somewhat realistic conditions.

10. Performance tests emphasize active responding, realistic conditions, complex problems, clearly stated criteria, a close relationship between teaching and testing, and use of test results for formative evaluation purposes.

11. Performance tests have not yet demonstrated that student performances and products can be measured reliably (consistently) and validly (accurately).

12. When grades are determined according to a norm-referenced system, each student's level of performance is compared to the performance of a group of similar students. A norm-referenced scheme is used by those who feel that external criteria for determining the adequacy of performance are unavailable.

13. In a criterion-referenced grading system, each student's level of perform-

ance is compared to a predetermined standard.

14. Related to criterion-referenced measurement and evaluation is the concept of mastery learning. As proposed by John Carroll and Benjamin Bloom, mastery learning holds that student achievement is largely a function of the amount of time a student is allotted for learning.
15. The potential benefits of measurement and evaluation activities can be undermined by any one of several inappropriate testing and grading practices.
16. To be sure that the number of various types of items on a test is consistent with your instructional objectives, prepare a table of specifications.
17. For primary and elementary grade students, the formative evaluation purpose of tests should be emphasized at least as much as the summative purpose.
18. Item-analysis procedures exist to determine the difficulty and discriminability of multiple-choice items.

Key Terms

measurement *(440)*
evaluation *(440)*
summative evaluation *(441)*
formative evaluation *(441)*
performance tests *(445)*
norm-referenced grading *(450)*
criterion-referenced grading *(452)*
table of specifications *(466)*

Discussion Questions

1. Because students in American schools feel considerable pressure to obtain high grades, a significant number of them feel driven to cheat. Knowing that you will almost certainly have to give tests and assign grades on one basis or another, what might you do to reduce your students' tendency to cheat?
2. Over the last ten to twelve years you have probably taken hundreds of classroom tests. What types of tests best reflected what you learned? Why?
3. A norm-referenced approach to grading is often called grading on the curve. Have you ever taken a class in which grades were determined in this fashion? Did you feel that your grade accurately reflected how much you had learned? If not, explain why the grade was too low or too high.
4. Proponents of mastery learning argue that most students can master most subjects if they receive good-quality instruction and are allowed sufficient time to learn the material. On the basis of your own experience, would you agree with this assumption? Why or why not?

Part 5

Maintaining an Effective Learning Environment

CHAPTER 13
Classroom Management

CHAPTER 13

Classroom Management

Key Points

These key points will help you learn the important information in this chapter. To help you study, they also appear in the margins of pages, next to the text where they are discussed.

AUTHORITARIAN, LAISSEZ-FAIRE, AND AUTHORITATIVE APPROACHES TO CLASSROOM MANAGEMENT

- Authoritative approach to classroom management superior to permissive and authoritarian approaches

PREVENTING PROBLEMS: TECHNIQUES OF CLASSROOM MANAGEMENT

- Ripple effect: group response to a reprimand directed at an individual
- Teachers who show they are "with it" head off discipline problems
- Being able to handle overlapping activities helps maintain classroom control
- Teachers who continually interrupt activities have discipline problems
- Keeping entire class involved and alert minimizes misbehavior
- Identify misbehavers; firmly specify constructive behavior
- Well-managed classroom: students complete clear assignments in busy but pleasant atmosphere
- Effective teachers plan how to handle classroom routines
- During first weeks, have students complete clear assignments under your direction
- Assertive discipline: teach desired behaviors, give positive reinforcement, invoke discipline plan if necessary

MANAGING THE MIDDLE, JUNIOR HIGH, AND HIGH SCHOOL CLASSROOM

- Manage behavior of adolescents by making and communicating clear rules and procedures

Suggestions for Teaching in Your Classroom

- Establish, call attention to, and explain class rules the first day
- Establish a businesslike but supportive classroom atmosphere

Techniques for Dealing with Behavior Problems

- Use supportive reactions to help students develop self-control
- Give criticism privately; then offer encouragement
- I-message: tell how you feel about an unacceptable situation
- Determine who owns a problem before deciding on course of action
- No-lose method: come to mutual agreement about a solution to a problem

Suggestions for Teaching in Your Classroom

- Be prompt, consistent, reasonable when dealing with misbehavior
- First ignore misbehavior, and then stress rewards; use punishment as a last resort

Violence in American Schools

- Male aggressiveness due to hormonal and cultural factors
- Middle school and junior high boys with low grades may feel trapped
- Misbehavior of high school students may reveal lack of positive identity
- School violence can be reduced by improving student achievement levels
- Violence less likely when students invited to participate in making decisions

By now you have no doubt begun to realize what we pointed out in Chapter 1—teaching is a complex enterprise. It is complex for the following reasons:

- Students vary in their physical, social, emotional, cognitive, and cultural characteristics
- Systematic preparations have to be made to ensure that students master the objectives that teachers lay out
- Learning occurs gradually and only with extensive and varied practice
- Different students learn at different rates
- Students are motivated to learn (or not learn) by different factors
- Learning can be measured and evaluated in a variety of ways.

If not managed properly, an endeavor as complex as teaching can easily become chaotic.

Recall, for example, our account in Chapter 1 of those individuals who taught in private schools without the benefit of a good teacher education program. They felt unprepared to handle the many problems that typically arise when one teaches groups of students and were very dissatisfied with the experience. To avoid the same fate, you will have to become familiar with different ways of managing the various behaviors that your students will exhibit. To appreciate the role you will play as the manager of a diverse group of students, think of yourself as the equivalent of an orchestra conductor. An orchestra is, of course, a collection of musicians who vary in terms of the instrument they play, the years of experience they have, the way they prefer to play, and how they think a particular piece should sound. It is the conductor's job to understand all these factors and manage them in such a way that the outcome is a performance that pleases both performer and audience.

Before describing the various management techniques that you may have reason to use at one time or another, we would like to make you aware of several general factors that influence how students behave in classrooms: the types of tasks you assign, the structure you provide for these tasks, and the learning goals you choose to emphasize.

First, you should realize that the types of learning tasks your students are assigned can affect their behavior in class. Behavior problems are often related to learning tasks that are characterized by a high degree of ambiguity (that is, are like the ill-defined problems we described in Chapter 10) and that carry with them a high risk, such as of receiving a poor grade. But don't avoid engaging your students in such tasks because many of the learning tasks you most want your students to undertake inevitably involve these two characteristics. For instance, most application and problem-solving tasks are high in both ambiguity and risk (Doyle, 1983). Instead, present such tasks to your students in a way that lessens their discomfort. Students who understand what is expected of them, see the task as a meaningful one, and feel as confident as possible that they have the skills to meet challenging demands are less likely to be behavior problems. Most of the Suggestions for Teaching mentioned in Chapters 4–12 meet these criteria and should help you structure learning situations that are both thought-provoking and nonthreatening.

Second, recognize that a traditional view of a well-managed classroom, which includes the notions of students working silently at their desks (or in front of their computers), speaking only when spoken to, and providing verbatim recitations of what the teacher and textbook said, is incompatible with the contemporary views of learning and motivation described in Chapters 9, 10, and 11. If some of your goals are for students to acquire a meaningful knowledge base, to become proficient problem solvers, and to learn how to work productively with others, then you have to accept the idea that these goals are best met in classrooms that are characterized by a fair amount of autonomy, physical movement, and social interaction (McCaslin & Good, 1992).

Authoritarian, Laissez-Faire, and Authoritative Approaches to Classroom Management

You may recall from Chapter 3 that Diana Baumrind (1971, 1991) found that parents tended to exhibit one of three styles in managing the behavior of their children: authoritarian, laissez-faire (or permissive), or authoritative. These three styles can be applied as well to a teacher's actions in the classroom. We will quickly review Baumrind's categories and then take a brief look at how teachers' approaches to management, too, can be characterized by these styles.

Authoritarian parents establish rules for their children's behavior and expect them to be blindly obeyed. Explanations of why a particular rule is necessary are almost never given. Instead, rewards and punishments are given for following or not following rules. Laissez-faire parents represent the other extreme. They impose few controls. They allow their children to make many basic decisions (such as what to eat, what to dress, when to go to bed) and provide advice or assistance only when asked. Authoritative parents provide rules but discuss the reasons for them, teach their children how to meet them, and reward children for exhibiting self-control. Authoritative parents also cede more responsibility for self-governance to their children as the children demonstrate increased self-regulation skills. This style, more so than the other two, leads to internalization of the parents' norms and to maintenance of intrinsic motivation for following them in the future.

You can probably see the parallel between Baumrind's work and classroom management. Teachers who adopt an authoritarian style tend to have student compliance as their main goal ("Do what I say because I say so") and make heavy use of rewards and punishments to produce that compliance. Teachers who adopt a permissive style rely heavily on students identifying with and respecting them as their main approach to classroom management ("Do what I say because you like me and respect my judgment"). Teachers who adopt an authoritative style have as their main goal students who can eventually regulate their own behavior. By explaining the rationale for classroom rules and by adjusting those rules as students demonstrate the ability to appropriately govern themselves, authoritative teachers hope to convince students that adopting the teacher's norms for classroom behavior as their own will lead to the achievement of valued academic goals ("Do what I say because doing so will help you learn more"). The students of authoritative teachers better understand the need for classroom rules and tend to operate within them most of the time (McCaslin & Good, 1992).

Authoritative approach to classroom management superior to permissive and authoritarian approaches

The first part of this chapter will describe guidelines you might follow to establish and maintain an effective learning environment in which you make coordinated use of the techniques described in earlier chapters. Even if you do an excellent job of "getting it all together," however, certain factors and conditions will be beyond your control. Inevitably, some students will fail to respond to your efforts as positively as others. Accordingly, you will occasionally need to deal with disruptive behavior. The second part of this chapter will describe a variety of techniques you might use to handle such types of behavior and will conclude with an analysis on the reasons for school violence. The emphasis in both parts will be on helping you become an authoritative manager of classroom behavior.

Preventing Problems: Techniques of Classroom Management

KOUNIN'S OBSERVATIONS ON GROUP MANAGEMENT

Interest in the significance of classroom management was kindled when Jacob Kounin wrote a book titled *Discipline and Group Management in Classrooms* (1970). Kounin noted that he first became interested in group management when he reprimanded a college student for blatantly reading a newspaper in class. Kounin was struck by the extent to which the entire class responded to a reprimand directed at only one person, and he subsequently dubbed this the **ripple effect.** Chances are you can recall a situation when you were diligently working away in a classroom and the teacher suddenly

Ripple effect: group response to a reprimand directed at an individual

Jacob Kounin found that teachers who were "with it" could deal with overlapping situations, maintained smoothness and momentum in class activities, used a variety of activities, kept the whole class involved, and had few discipline problems.

became quite angry at a disruptive classmate. If you felt a bit tense after the incident (even though your behavior was blameless) and tried to give the impression that you were a paragon of student virtue, you have had personal experience with the ripple effect.

Once his interest in classroom behavior was aroused, Kounin supervised a series of observational and experimental studies of student reactions to techniques of teacher control. In analyzing the results of these various studies, he came to the conclusion that the following classroom management techniques appear to be most effective.

Teachers who show they are "with it" head off discipline problems

1. *Show your students that you are "with it."* Kounin coined the term **withitness** to emphasize that teachers who prove to their students that they know what is going on in a classroom usually have fewer behavior problems than teachers who appear to be unaware of incipient disruptions. An expert at classroom management will nip trouble in the bud by commenting on potentially disruptive behavior before it gains momentum. An ineffective teacher may not notice such behavior until it begins to spread and then perhaps hopes that it will simply go away. At first glance Kounin's suggestion that you show that you are with it might seem to be in conflict with operant conditioning's prediction that nonreinforced behavior will disappear. If the teacher's reaction is the only source of reinforcement in a classroom, ignoring behavior may cause it to disappear. In many cases, however, a misbehaving student gets reinforced by the reactions of classmates. Therefore, ignoring behavior is much less likely to lead to extinction of a response in a classroom than in controlled experimental situations.

Journal Entry
Learning to Deal with Overlapping Situations

2. *Learn to cope with overlapping situations.* When he analyzed videotapes of actual classroom interactions, Kounin found that some teachers seemed to have one-track minds. They were inclined to deal with only one thing at a time, and this way of proceeding caused frequent interruptions in classroom routine. One primary grade teacher observed by

Kounin, for example, was working with a reading group when she noticed two boys on the other side of the room poking each other. She abruptly got up, walked over to the boys, berated them at length, and then returned to the reading group. By the time she returned, however, the children in the reading group had become bored and listless and were tempted to engage in mischief of their own.

Kounin concluded that withitness and skill in handling overlapping activities seemed to be related. An expert classroom manager who is talking to children in a reading group, for example, might notice two boys at the far side of the room who are beginning to scuffle with each other. Such a teacher might in midsentence tell the boys to stop and make the point so adroitly that the attention of the children in the reading group does not waver. You might carry out a self-analysis of how you handle overlapping situations when you first begin to teach. If you find that you tend to focus on only one thing at a time, you might make an effort to develop skills in coping with two or more situations simultaneously.

Being able to handle overlapping activities helps maintain classroom control

3. *Strive to maintain smoothness and momentum in class activities.* This point is related to the previous one. Kounin found that some teachers caused problems for themselves by constantly interrupting activities without thinking about what they were doing. Some teachers whose activities were recorded on videotape failed to maintain the thrust of a lesson because they seemed unaware of the rhythm of student behavior (that is, they did not take into account the degree of student inattention and restlessness but instead moved ahead in an almost mechanical way). Others flip-flopped from one activity to another. Still others would interrupt one activity (for example, a reading lesson) to comment on an unrelated aspect of classroom functioning ("Someone left a lunch bag on the floor"). There were also some who wasted time dwelling on a trivial incident (making a big fuss because a boy lost his pencil). And a few teachers delivered individual, instead of group, instructions ("All right, Charlie, you go to the board. Fine. Now, Rebecca, you go to the board"). All these types of teacher behavior tended to interfere with the flow of learning activities.

Journal Entry
Learning How to Maintain Momentum

Teachers who continually interrupt activities have discipline problems

You might carry out a movement analysis of your own teaching from time to time. Think about how you handle a class for a period or a day, and see if you can recall incidents of the sort just described. To counteract such tendencies, you might endeavor to maintain a smooth flow of activities in the following class periods and days. If you succeed in doing so, this smooth flow may become habitual.

4. *Try to keep the whole class involved, even when you are dealing with individual students.* Kounin found that some well-meaning teachers had fallen into a pattern of calling on students in a predictable order and in such a way that the rest of the class served as a passive audience. Unless you stop to think about what you are doing during group recitation periods, you might easily fall into the same trap. If you do, the "audience" is almost certain to become bored and may be tempted to engage in troublemaking activities just to keep occupied. Some teachers, for example, call on students to recite by going around a circle, or going up and down rows, or by following alphabetical order. Others call on a child first and then ask a question. Still others ask one child to recite at length (read an entire page, for example). All these techniques tend to

spotlight one child in predictable order and cause the rest of the class members to tune out until their turn comes. You are more likely to maintain interest and limit mischief caused by boredom if you use techniques such as the following:

Keeping entire class involved and alert minimizes misbehavior

- Ask a question, and after pausing a few seconds to let everyone think about it, pick out someone to answer it. With subsequent questions, call on students in an unpredictable order so that no one knows when she will be asked to recite. (If you feel that some students in a class are very apprehensive about being called on, even under relaxing circumstances, you can either ask them extremely easy questions or avoid calling on them at all.)
- If you single out one child to go to the board to do a problem, ask all other students to do the same problem at their desks, and then choose one or two at random to compare their work with the answers on the board.

Journal Entry
Ways to Keep the Whole Class Involved

- When dealing with lengthy or complex material, call on several students in quick succession (and in unpredictable order), and ask each to handle one section. In a primary grade reading group, for example, have one child read a sentence; then pick someone at the other side of the group to read the next sentence and so on.
- Use props in the form of flashcards, mimeographed sheets, or workbook pages to induce all students to respond to questions simultaneously. Then, ask students to compare answers. (One ingenious elementary school teacher observed by Kounin had each student print the ten digits on cards that could be inserted in a slotted piece of cardboard. She would ask a question such as "How much is 8 and 4?"; she would pause a moment while the students arranged their answers in the slots and then say, "All show!")

5. *Introduce variety, and be enthusiastic, particularly with younger students.* After viewing videotapes of different teachers, Kounin and his associates concluded that some teachers seemed to fall into a deadly routine much more readily than others. They followed the same procedure day after day and responded with the same, almost reflexive comments. At the other end of the scale were teachers who introduced variety, responded with enthusiasm and interest, and moved quickly to new activities when they sensed that students either had mastered or were satiated by a particular lesson. It seems logical to assume that students will be less inclined to sleep, daydream, or engage in disruptive activities if they are exposed to an enthusiastic teacher who varies the pace and type of classroom activities. Kounin pointed out, however, that variety may be most appropriate in elementary school classrooms because older students may be interested in thoroughly analyzing complex ideas and may be bothered if they are interrupted too frequently.

6. *Be aware of the ripple effect. When criticizing student behavior, be clear and firm, focus on behavior rather than on personalities, and try to avoid angry outbursts.* If you take into account the suggestions just made, you may be able to reduce the amount of student misbehavior in your classes. Even so, some behavior problems are certain to occur. When you deal with these, you can benefit from Kounin's research on the ripple effect. On the basis of observations, questionnaires, and experi-

mental evidence, he concluded that "innocent" students in a class are more likely to be positively impressed by the way the teacher handles a misbehavior if the following conditions exist:

- The teacher identifies the misbehaver and states what the unacceptable behavior is. ("Jorge! Don't flip that computer disk at Jamal.")
- The teacher specifies a more constructive behavior. ("Please put the computer disk back in the storage box.")
- The teacher explains why the deviant behavior should cease. ("If the computer disk gets broken or dirty, no one else will be able to use it, and we'll have to try to get a new one.")
- The teacher is firm and authoritative and conveys a no-nonsense attitude. ("All infractions of classroom rules will result in an appropriate punishment—no ifs, ands, or buts.")
- The teacher does not resort to anger, humiliation, or extreme punishment. Kounin concluded that extreme reactions did not seem to make children behave better. Instead, anger and severe reprimands upset them and made them feel tense and nervous. ("Roger, I am deeply disappointed that you used obscene language in your argument with Michael. Such behavior is simply unacceptable in my classroom.")
- The teacher focuses on behavior, not on personality. (Say, "Ramona, staring out the window instead of reading your textbook is unacceptable behavior in my classroom" rather than "Ramona, you're the laziest student I have ever had in class.")

Identify misbehavers; firmly specify constructive behavior

UNIVERSITY OF TEXAS STUDIES OF GROUP MANAGEMENT

Stimulated by Kounin's observations, members of the Research and Development Center for Teacher Education at the University of Texas at Austin instituted a series of studies on classroom management. The basic procedure followed in most studies was to first identify very effective and less effective teachers by using a variety of criteria (often stressing student achievement), ratings, and observations. Then classroom management techniques used by very effective teachers were analyzed in detail. In some studies (for example, Brophy, 1979; Good, 1982), basic characteristics of well-managed classrooms were described. They can be summarized as follows:

1. Students know what they are expected to do and generally experience the feeling that they are successful doing it.
2. Students are kept busy engaging in teacher-led instructional activities.
3. There is little wasted time, confusion, or disruption.
4. A no-nonsense, work-oriented tone prevails, but at the same time there is a relaxed and pleasant atmosphere.

Well-managed classroom: students complete clear assignments in busy but pleasant atmosphere

These conclusions can be related to information presented in earlier chapters. The first point can be interpreted as supporting the use of instructional objectives that are stated in such a way that students know when they have achieved them. It might also be interpreted as supporting the use of mastery learning evaluation procedures. The next three points stress student productivity under teacher guidance and a no-nonsense, work-oriented atmosphere. These outcomes are more likely when teachers use procedures recommended by behavioral and cognitive psychologists.

Another set of studies carried out by the Texas researchers led to two recent books on group management, one for elementary school teachers (Evertson, Emmer, Clements, & Worsham, 1994) and the other for secondary school teachers (Emmer, Evertson, Clements, & Worsham, 1994). You may wish to examine the appropriate book for your grade level (complete titles and names of authors are given in Resources for Further Investigation), but for now we will provide the following summary of basic keys to management success stressed in both volumes.

Effective teachers plan how to handle classroom routines

1. On the first day with a new class, very effective teachers clearly demonstrate that they have thought about classroom procedures ahead of time. They have planned first-day activities that make it possible for classroom routine to be handled with a minimum of confusion. They also make sure students understand why the procedures are necessary and how they are to be followed.
2. A short list of basic classroom rules is posted and/or announced, and students are told about the penalties they will incur in the event of misbehavior.
3. During the first weeks with a new group of students, effective teachers have students engage in whole-group activities under teacher direction. Such activities are selected to make students feel comfortable and successful in their new classroom.

During first weeks, have students complete clear assignments under your direction

4. After the initial shakedown period is over, effective teachers maintain control by using the sorts of techniques described by Kounin: they show they are with it, cope with overlapping situations, maintain smoothness and momentum, and avoid ignoring the rest of the class when dealing with individual students.
5. Effective teachers give clear directions, hold students accountable for completing assignments, and give frequent feedback.

ASSERTIVE DISCIPLINE

This list of factors calls attention to the importance of being thoroughly prepared the first days you meet with a new class. You should not only have thought about how you are going to handle classroom routine; you should also have planned learning activities likely to make students feel comfortable and successful. You should give students clear assignments, convey the message that they will be responsible for completing them, and provide supportive feedback so that they are aware they have completed work successfully. A specific version of this general approach is the Assertive Discipline program of Lee Canter (1989).

Canter's program has three parts and is modeled after the classroom management practices of master teachers. The first part, *teaching students how to behave,* has two general steps. First, establish specific directions for each activity. For an all-class discussion, for example, you may want students to raise their hands and be recognized before speaking. For a cooperative-learning session, you may want students to stay in their seats and work quietly. Second, make sure students know how to behave. You can accomplish this by writing the desired behaviors on the board, demonstrating them, asking students to restate them, questioning students to verify that they understand the rules, and immediately engaging them in the activity.

The second part of Assertive Discipline is *providing positive reinforcement* for good behavior. Canter suggests that whenever you notice a student who is following the rules, point it out and compliment her. For example, if Maria has followed the rules laid down for a class discussion, you might say, "Maria raised her hand and patiently waited to be called on. Very good, Maria." Although this part of the program is either omitted or deemphasized by some teachers, Canter feels it is as important as the other two parts.

Assertive discipline: teach desired behaviors, give positive reinforcement, invoke discipline plan if necessary

The third and final part of the program is *invoking the discipline plan.* This involves the use of aversive consequences, but only after students have been taught the desired behaviors and positive reinforcement has been given. Canter suggests that teachers refrain from using aversive consequences until at least two students have been positively reinforced for behaving appropriately. A discipline plan should include no more than five aversive consequences for misbehavior, each of which is slightly more severe than the last one. For example, the first time a rule is broken, the student is warned. The second and third infractions result in ten-minute and fifteen-minute time-outs, respectively. The fourth infraction results in a call to the parents. And if the rule is broken a fifth time, the student must visit the principal. Although there are a variety of aversive consequences that you can use, avoid those that might cause psychological or physical harm (ridicule and paddling, for example) for the reasons we gave in Chapter 8.

Managing the Middle, Junior High, and High School Classroom

Most of the classroom management techniques and suggestions we have discussed so far are sufficiently general that they can be used in a variety of classroom settings and with primary through secondary grade students. Nevertheless, teaching preadolescents and adolescents is sufficiently different from teaching younger students that the management of the middle school, junior high, and high school classroom requires a slightly different emphasis and a few unique practices.

Classroom management has to be approached somewhat differently in the secondary grades (and in those middle schools that change classes several times a day) because of the segmented nature of education for these grades. Instead of being in charge of the same twenty-five to thirty students all day, most junior high or high school teachers (and some middle school teachers) are responsible for as many as five different groups of twenty-five to thirty students for about fifty minutes each. This arrangement results in a wider range of individual differences, a greater likelihood that these teachers will see a wide range of behavior problems, and a greater concern with efficient use of class time.

Because middle school, junior high, and high school students move from one teacher to another every fifty minutes or so, it is important to establish a common set of rules that govern various activities and procedures and to clearly communicate the reasons for those rules.

Because of the special nature of adolescence, relatively short class times, and consecutive classes with different students, middle school, junior high, and high school teachers must concentrate their efforts on preventing misbehavior. Edmund Emmer, Carolyn Evertson, Barbara Clements, and Murray Worsham (1994), in *Classroom Management for Secondary Teachers* (3d ed.), discuss how teachers can prevent misbehavior by carefully organizing the classroom environment, establishing clear rules and procedures, and delivering effective instruction.

According to Emmer and his associates, the physical features of the classroom should be arranged to optimize teaching and learning. They suggest an environment in which (1) the arrangement of the seating, materials, and equipment is consistent with the kinds of instructional activities the teacher favors; (2) high traffic areas, such as the teacher's desk and the pencil sharpener, are kept free of congestion; (3) the teacher can easily see all students; (4) frequently used teaching materials and student supplies are readily available; and (5) students can easily see instructional presentations and displays.

In too many instances teachers spend a significant amount of class time dealing with misbehavior, rather than with teaching and learning, either because students are never told what is expected of them or because rules and procedures are not communicated clearly. Accordingly, Emmer et al. suggest that classroom rules be specifically stated, discussed with students on the first day of class, and, for seventh, eighth, and ninth grades, posted in a prominent place. Sophomores, juniors, and seniors should be given a handout on which the rules are listed. Some examples of these basic rules follow:

Bring all needed materials to class.

Be in your seat and ready to work when the bell rings.

Respect and be polite to all people.

Do not talk or leave your desk when someone else is talking.

Respect other people's property.

Obey all school rules.

You may also want to allow some degree of student participation in rule setting. You can ask students to suggest rules, arrange for students to discuss why certain classroom rules are necessary, and perhaps allow students to select a few rules. This last suggestion should be taken up cautiously, however. Because middle school and secondary teachers teach different sets of students, having a different set of rules for each class is bound to cause confusion for you and hard feelings among some students. You may find yourself admonishing a student for breaking a rule that applies to a different class, and some students will naturally want to know why they cannot do something that is allowed in another class.

In addition to rules, various procedures need to be formulated and communicated. Procedures differ from rules in that they apply to a specific activity and are usually directed at completing a task rather than completing a behavior. To produce a well-run classroom, you will need to formulate efficient procedures for beginning-of-the-period tasks (such as taking attendance and allowing students to leave the classroom), use of materials and equipment (such as the encyclopedia, dictionary, and pencil sharpener), learning activities (such as discussions, seatwork, and group work), and end-of-the-period tasks (such as handing in seatwork assignments, returning materials and equipment, and making announcements).

Manage behavior of adolescents by making and communicating clear rules and procedures

Much of what Emmer and his associates mention in relation to the characteristics of effective instruction has been described in earlier chapters. For example, they recommend that short-term (daily, weekly) and long-term (semester, annual) lesson plans be formulated and coordinated, that instructions and standards for assignments be clear and given in a timely manner, that feedback be given at regular intervals, and that the grading system be clear and fairly applied.

The following Suggestions for Teaching will help you become an effective manager of student behavior in the classroom.

Suggestions for Teaching in Your Classroom

Techniques of Classroom Management

1. Show you are confident and prepared the first day of class.

2. Think ahead about how you plan to handle classroom routine, and explain basic procedures the first few minutes of the first day.

3. Establish class rules, call attention to them, and explain why they are necessary.

4. Begin class work the first day with an instructional activity that is clearly stated and can be completed quickly and successfully.

5. During the first weeks with a new group of students, have them spend most of their time engaging in whole-class activities under your direction.

6. Give clear instructions, hold students accountable for carrying them out, and provide frequent feedback.

7. Continually demonstrate that you are competent, well prepared, and in charge.

8. Be professional but pleasant, and try to establish a businesslike but supportive classroom atmosphere.

1. **Show you are confident and prepared the first day of class.**

The first few minutes with any class are often crucial. Your students will be sizing you up, especially if they know you are a new teacher. If you act scared and unsure of yourself, you will probably be in for trouble. Even after years of experience, you may find that confronting a roomful of strange students for the first time is a bit intimidating. You will be the center of attention and may feel the equivalent of stage fright. To switch the focus of attention and to begin identifying your students as individuals rather than as a threatening audience, you might consider using this strategy. Hand out 4-by-6-inch cards as soon as everyone is seated, and ask your students to write down their full names, the names they prefer to be called, what their hobbies and favorite activities are, and a description of the most interesting experience they have ever had. (For primary grade students who are unable to write, substitute brief oral introductions.)

As they write, you will be in a position to make a leisurely scrutiny of your students as individuals. Recognizing that you are dealing with individuals should reduce the tendency to feel threatened by a group. Perhaps you have read about singers who pick out a single, sympathetic member of the audience and sing directly to her. The sea of faces as a whole is frightening. The face of the individual is not. Even if you are not bothered by being the center of attention, you might still consider using this card technique to obtain information that you can use to learn names rapidly and to individualize instruction. Whatever you do during the first few minutes, it is important to give the impression that you know exactly what you are doing. The best way to pull that off is to be thoroughly prepared.

2. **Think ahead about how you plan to handle classroom routine, and explain basic procedures the first few minutes of the first day.**

Journal Entry
Planning How to Handle Routines

The Texas researchers found that very effective teachers demonstrated from the first moment with a new group of students that they knew how to handle the details of their job. They also conveyed the impression that they expected cooperation. To demonstrate that you are a confident, competent instructor, you should plan exactly how you will handle classroom routines. You will pick up at least some ideas about the details of classroom management during student-teaching experiences, but it might be worth asking a friendly experienced teacher in your school for advice about tried-and-true procedures that have worked in that particular school. (You might also read one of the books on classroom management recommended at the end of this chapter.)

Try to anticipate how you will handle such details as taking attendance, assigning desks, handing out books and materials, permitting students to go to the restroom during class, and so forth. If you don't plan ahead, you will

Research has shown that effective teachers call attention to and explain class rules on the first day of class.

have to come up with an improvised policy on the spur of the moment, and that policy might turn out to be highly inefficient or in conflict with school regulations.

3. **Establish class rules, call attention to them, and explain why they are necessary.**

Very effective teachers observed by the Texas researchers demonstrated an authoritative approach to classroom management by explaining class rules the first day of school. Some teachers list standard procedures on a chart or bulletin board; others simply state them the first day of class. Either technique saves time and trouble later because all you have to do is refer to the rule when a transgression occurs. The alternative to this approach is to interrupt the lesson and disturb the whole class while you make a hurried, unplanned effort to deal with a surprise attack. Your spur-of-the-moment reaction may turn out to be clumsy and ineffective.

Establish, call attention to, and explain class rules the first day

When you introduce rules the first day, take a positive, nonthreatening approach. If you spit rules out as if they were a series of ultimatums, students may feel you have a chip on your shoulder, which the unwritten code of the classroom obligates them to try knocking off. One way to demonstrate your good faith is to invite the class to suggest necessary regulations and explain why they should be established. Whatever your approach, encourage understanding of the reasons for the rules. You can make regulations seem desirable, rather than restrictive, if you discuss why they are needed. Reasonable rules are much more likely to be remembered and honored than pronouncements that seem to be the whims of a tyrant.

EXAMPLES

"During class discussion, please don't speak out unless you raise your hand and are recognized. I want to be able to hear what each person has to say, and I won't be able to do that if more than one person is talking."

"During work periods, I don't mind if you talk a bit to your neighbors. But if you do it too much and disturb others, I'll have to ask you to stop."

"If you come in late, go to your desk by walking along the side and back of the room. It's disturbing—and not very polite—to walk between people who are interacting with each other."

4. **Begin class work the first day with an instructional activity that is clearly stated and can be completed quickly and successfully.**

When selecting the very first assignment to give to a new class, refer to the suggestions for preparing instructional objectives proposed by Robert Mager and Norman Gronlund (Chapter 7), and arrange a short assignment that can be successfully completed before the end of the period. Clearly specify what is to be done, and perhaps state the conditions and criteria for determining successful completion. In addition, mention an activity (such as examining the assigned text) that students should engage in after they have completed the assignment. In the elementary grades, you might give a short assignment that helps students review material covered in the preceding grade. At the secondary level, pick out an initial assignment that is short, interesting, and does not depend on technical knowledge.

EXAMPLES

"Your teacher from last year told me that most of you were able to spell all of the words on the list I am going to read. Let's see if you can still spell those words. If you have trouble with certain ones, we can work together to come up with reminders that will help you remember the correct spelling."

"The first chapter in our natural science text for this fall is about birds. I want you to read the first ten pages, make a list of five types of birds that are described, and prepare your own set of notes about how to recognize them. At 10:30 I am going to hold up pictures of ten birds, and I want you to see if you can correctly identify at least five of them."

In a high school history class, ask students to write a brief description of a movie they have seen that depicted historical events. Then ask them to indicate whether they felt the film interpretation was accurate.

5. **During the first weeks with a new group of students, have them spend most of their time engaging in whole-class activities under your direction.**

The very effective teachers observed by the Texas researchers followed the strategy just described, which makes sense when you stop to think about it. You can't expect students to adjust to the routine of a new teacher and classroom in just a few days. Accordingly, it would be wise to make sure students have settled down before asking them to engage in relatively unstructured activities like discovery learning. Furthermore, group discussions or cooperative-learning arrangements usually work out more successfully when the participants have a degree of familiarity with one another and a particular set of background factors (such as a chapter in a text). Thus, as you plan activities during the first weeks with a new class, prepare instructional objectives that ask students to complete assignments under your direction. Postpone using the techniques just mentioned until later in the report period.

6. **Give clear instructions, hold students accountable for carrying them out, and provide frequent feedback.**

All three of these goals can be achieved by making systematic use of instructional objectives as described in Chapter 7 and by putting into practice the model of instruction described throughout this book.

7. **Continually demonstrate that you are competent, well prepared, and in charge.**

As students work at achieving instructional objectives, participate in group discussions, or engage in any other kind of learning activity, show them that you are a competent classroom manager. Arrange periods so that there will be a well-organized transition from one activity to the next, maintain smoothness and momentum, and don't waste time. Use a variety of teaching approaches so that you please some of your students some of the time, and use techniques recommended by behavioral, cognitive, and humanistic psychologists. Show you are with it by being alert for signs of mischief or disruptive behavior, and handle such incidents quickly and confidently by using the techniques described later in this chapter and in the "Becoming a Reflective Teacher" section of the next chapter.

8. **Be professional but pleasant, and try to establish a businesslike but supportive classroom atmosphere.**

If you establish classroom routines in a competent fashion and keep your students busy working to achieve clearly stated instructional objectives, you should be able to establish a no-nonsense, productive atmosphere. At the same time, you should strive to make your room an inviting and pleasant place to be. Keep in mind the points made in Chapters 3 and 11 regarding the importance of self-esteem, self-efficacy, and interpersonal relationships. Put yourself in the place of students thrust into a strange classroom with an unfamiliar instructor. Try to identify with your students so that you can appreciate how they feel if they do or say something embarrassing or have difficulty with class work.

Establish a businesslike but supportive classroom atmosphere

One of the best ways to get students to respond positively to you and make them feel welcome in your classroom is to learn their names as quickly as possible (even if you have five sections of secondary school students to teach). To accomplish this feat, refer to the cards mentioned in point 1. Use the information that students have provided, perhaps supplemented by your own notes or sketches about distinctive physical and facial features, to establish associations between names and faces. Before and after every class period the first few days, flip through your pile of cards, try to picture the appearance of the students, and practice using their names. Refer to the description of mnemonic devices in Chapter 9. Once you have learned a student's name, use it as often as possible to maintain the memory trace. Greet students by name as they come in the door, use their names when asking them to recite or carry out some task, and speak to them personally when you hand back assignments.

Another way to make students feel at home in your classroom is to try establishing a feeling of class spirit. One way to do this is to have a brief *sharing* period—similar to the sharing time you may remember from your kindergarten days—at the beginning of each period. Invite students to describe recent interesting experiences they have had or to give announcements about extracurricular activities. If a member of the class is injured in an accident or suffers a lengthy illness, buy a get-well card, and have every member of the class sign it before sending it off.

Techniques for Dealing with Behavior Problems

If you follow the procedures just discussed, you should be able to establish a well-managed classroom. As noted at the beginning of this chapter, however, you are likely to encounter occasional incidents of misbehavior. Even if you do everything possible to prevent problems from developing, you are still likely to have to deal with disruptive behavior. Therefore, techniques for handling disruptive behavior, the extent of disciplinary problems, and some of the factors that lead to misbehavior are topics that merit attention.

Signals such as staring at a misbehaving student or putting a finger to one's lips are examples of the influence techniques suggested by Redl and Wattenberg.

INFLUENCE TECHNIQUES

In *Mental Hygiene in Teaching* (1959), Fritz Redl and William Wattenberg describe a list of behavior management interventions called *influence techniques*. This list was modified by James Walker and Thomas Shea in *Behavior Management: A Practical Approach for Educators* (1991). In the following sections and subsections, based on the ideas of both sets of individuals, we will offer specific examples roughly reflecting a least-direct to most-direct ordering. Some of these examples are based on ideas noted by Redl and Wattenberg; some are based on the ideas of Walker and Shea; some are the results of reports by students and teachers; some are based on personal experience. You might use the Journal Entries to pick out or devise techniques that seem most appropriate for your grade level or that you feel comfortable about.

The value of these techniques is that they appeal to self-control and imply trust and confidence on the part of the teacher. However, they may become ineffective if used too often, and that is why so many different techniques will be described. The larger your repertoire is, the less frequently you will have to repeat your various gambits and ploys.

Planned Ignoring As we pointed out in Chapter 8, you might be able to extinguish inappropriate attention-seeking behaviors by merely ignoring them. Such behaviors include finger snapping, body movements, book dropping, hand waving, and whistling. If you plan to use this technique, make sure the student is aware that he is engaging in the behavior and that the behavior does not interfere with the efforts of other students.

EXAMPLE

Carl has recently gotten into the habit of tapping his pencil on his desk as he works on an assignment as a way to engage you in a conversation that is unrelated to the work. The next several times Carl does this, do not look at him or comment on his behavior.

Signals In some cases a subtle signal can put an end to budding misbehavior. The signal, if successful, will stimulate the student to control herself. (Note, however, that this technique should not be used too often and that it is effective only in the early stages of misbehavior.)

Journal Entry
Signals to Use to Nip Trouble in the Bud

EXAMPLES

Clear your throat.

Stare at the offender.

Stop what you are saying in midsentence and stare.

Shake your head (to indicate no).

Say, "Someone is making it hard for the rest of us to concentrate" (or the equivalent).

Proximity and Touch Control Place yourself close to the misbehaving student. This makes a signal a bit more apparent.

Use supportive reactions to help students develop self-control

EXAMPLES

Walk over and stand near the student.

With an elementary grade student, it sometimes helps if you place a gentle hand on a shoulder or arm.

Interest Boosting Convey interest in the misbehaver. This relates the signal to schoolwork.

EXAMPLE

Ask the student a question, preferably related to what is being discussed. (Questions such as "Ariel, are you paying attention?" or "Don't you agree, Ariel?" invite wisecracks. *Genuine* questions are to be preferred.) Go over and examine some work the student is doing. It often helps if you point out something good about it and urge continued effort.

Humor Humor is an excellent, all-around influence technique, especially in tense situations. However, remember that it should be *good*-humored humor—gentle and benign rather than derisive. Avoid irony and sarcasm.

EXAMPLES

"Shawn, for goodness' sake, let that poor pencil sharpener alone. I heard it groan when you used it just now."

Perhaps you have heard someone say, "We're not laughing *at* you; we're laughing *with* you." Before you say this to one of your students, you might take note that one second grader who was treated to that comment unhinged the teacher by replying, "I'm not laughing."

Helping over Hurdles Some misbehavior undoubtedly occurs because students do not understand what they are to do or lack the ability to carry out an assignment.

EXAMPLES

Try to make sure your students know what they are supposed to do.

Arrange for students to have something to do at appropriate levels of difficulty.

Have a variety of activities available.

Program Restructuring In Chapter 1 we noted that teaching is an art because lessons do not always proceed as planned and must occasionally be changed in midstream. The essence of this technique is to recognize when a lesson or activity is going poorly and to try something else.

EXAMPLES

Journal Entry
Ways to Help Students Exhibit Acceptable Behavior

"Well, class, I can see that many of you are bored with this discussion of the pros and cons of congressional term limits. Let's turn it into a class debate instead, with the winning team getting 50 points toward its final grade."

"I had hoped to complete this math unit before the Christmas break, but I can see that most of you are too excited to give it your best effort. Since today is the last day before the break, I'll postpone the lesson until school resumes in January. Let's do an art project instead."

Antiseptic Bouncing Sometimes a student will get carried away by restlessness, uncontrollable giggling, or the like. If you feel that this is nonmalicious behavior and due simply to lack of self-control, ask the student to leave the room. (You may have recognized that antiseptic bouncing is virtually identical to the *time-out* procedure described by behavior modification enthusiasts.)

EXAMPLES

"Nancy, please go down to the principal's office and sit on that bench outside the door until you feel you have yourself under control."

Some high schools have "quiet rooms"—supervised study halls that take extra students any time during a period, no questions asked.

Physical Restraint Students who lose control of themselves to the point of endangering other members of the class may have to be physically restrained. However, such restraint should be protective, not punitive; that is, don't shake or hit. This technique is most effective with younger children; such control is usually not appropriate at the secondary level.

EXAMPLE

If a boy completely loses his temper and starts to hit another child, lead him gently but firmly away from the other students, or sit him in a chair, and keep a restraining hand on his shoulder.

Direct Appeals When appropriate, point out the connection between conduct and its consequences. This technique is most effective if done concisely and infrequently.

EXAMPLES

"We have a rule that there is to be no running in the halls. Scott forgot the rule, and now he's down in the nurse's office having his bloody nose taken care of. It's too bad Mr. Harris opened his door just as Scott went by. If Scott had been walking, he would have been able to stop in time."

"If everyone would stop shouting, we'd be able to get this finished and go out to recess."

Criticism and Encouragement On those occasions when it is necessary to criticize a particular student, do so in private if possible. When public criticism is the only possibility, do your best to avoid ridiculing or humiliating the student. Public humiliation may cause the child to resent you or hate school, to counterattack, or to withdraw. Because of the ripple effect, it may also have a negative impact on innocent students (although nonhumiliating public criticism has the advantage of setting an example for other students). One way to minimize the negative aftereffects of criticism is to tack on some encouragement in the form of a suggestion as to how the backsliding can be replaced by more positive behavior.

Give criticism privately; then offer encouragement

EXAMPLES

If a student doesn't take subtle hints (such as stares), you might say, "Levar, you're disturbing the class. We all need to concentrate on this." It sometimes adds punch if you make this remark while you are writing on the board or helping some other student.

Act completely flabbergasted, as though the misbehavior seems so inappropriate that you can't comprehend it. A kindergarten teacher used this technique to perfection. She would say, "Adam! Is that you?" (Adam has been belting Lucy with a shovel.) "I can't believe my eyes. I wonder if you would help me over here." Obviously, this gambit can't be used too often, and the language and degree of exaggeration have to be altered a bit for older students. But indicating that you *expect* good behavior and providing an immediate opportunity for the backslider to substitute good deeds can be very effective.

Defining Limits In learning about rules and regulations, children go through a process of testing the limits. Two-year-olds particularly, when they have learned how to walk and talk and manipulate things, feel the urge to assert their independence. In addition, they need to find out exactly what the house rules are. (Does Mommy *really* mean it when she says, "Don't take the pots out of the cupboard"? Does Daddy *really* mean it when he says, "Don't play with that hammer"?) Older children do the same thing, especially with new teachers and in new situations. The technique of defining limits includes not only establishing rules (as noted earlier) but also enforcing them.

EXAMPLES

Establish class rules, with or without the assistance of students, and make sure they are understood.

When someone tests the rules, show that they are genuine and that there *are* limits.

Postsituational Follow-Up Classroom discipline occasionally has to be applied in a tense, emotion-packed atmosphere. When this happens, it often helps to have a postsituational discussion—in private if an individual is involved, with the whole class if it was a groupwide situation.

When confronted by a student, it is usually better to arrange for a private conference or appeal to an outside authority than to engage in a showdown in front of the class.

EXAMPLES

In a private conference: "Leila, I'm sorry I had to ask you to leave the room, but you were getting kind of carried away."

"Well, everybody, things got a bit wild during those group work sessions. I want you to enjoy yourselves, but we practically had a riot going, didn't we? And that's why I had to ask you to stop. Let's try to hold it down to a dull roar tomorrow."

Marginal Use of Interpretation Analysis of behavior can sometimes be made *while* it is occurring rather than afterward. The purpose here is to help students become aware of potential trouble and make efforts to control it.

EXAMPLE

To a restless and cranky prelunch class, you might say, "I know that you're getting hungry and that you're restless and tired, but let's give it all we've got for ten minutes more. I'll give you the last five minutes for some free visiting time."

I-MESSAGES

In *Teacher and Child,* Haim Ginott offers a cardinal principle of communication: "Talk to the situation, not to the personality and character" (1972, p. 84). Instead of making derogatory remarks about the personalities of two boys who have just thrown bread at each other, Ginott suggests that as a teacher you deliver an **I-message** explaining how you feel. Don't say, "You are a couple of pigs"; say, "I get angry when I see bread thrown around. This room needs cleaning." According to Ginott, guilty students who are told why a teacher is angry will realize the teacher is a real person, and this realization will cause them to strive to mend their ways. Ginott offers several examples of the cardinal principle of communication in Chapter 4 of *Teacher and Child.* And in Chapter 6 he offers some observations on discipline. Seek alternatives to punishment. Try not to diminish a misbehaving student's self-esteem. Try to provide face-saving exits.

Journal Entry
Using I-Messages

I-message: tell how you feel about an unacceptable situation

PROBLEM OWNERSHIP

In *TET: Teacher Effectiveness Training* (1974), Thomas Gordon suggests that teachers try to determine who *owns* a problem before they decide how to handle that problem. If a student's misbehavior (such as disrupting the smooth flow of instruction with inappropriate comments or joking remarks) results in the teacher feeling annoyed, frustrated, or angry at not being able to complete a planned lesson, the teacher owns the problem and must respond by doing something to stop the disruptive behavior. But if a student expresses anger or disappointment about some classroom incident (getting a low grade on an exam), that student owns the problem.

Journal Entry
Speculating About Problem Ownership

Determine who owns a problem before deciding on course of action

Gordon suggests that failure to identify problem ownership may cause teachers to intensify difficulties unwittingly, even as they make well-intended efforts to diminish them. If a student is finding it difficult to concentrate on schoolwork because her needs are not satisfied, the situation will not be ameliorated if the teacher orders, moralizes, or criticizes. According to Gordon, such responses act as roadblocks to finding solutions to student-owned problems because they tend to make the student feel resentful and misunderstood.

The preferred way to deal with a student who owns a problem is to use what Gordon calls **active listening.** The listener is *active* in the sense that interest is shown and the talker is encouraged to continue expressing feelings; the listener does *not* actively participate by interpreting, explaining, or directing. The listener *does* respond, however, by recognizing and acknowledging what the student says.

For teacher-owned problems—those that involve misbehavior that is destructive or in violation of school regulations—Gordon agrees with Ginott that I-messages are appropriate. Instead of ordering, threatening, moralizing, using logic, offering solutions, or commenting on personal characteristics, teachers should explain why they are upset. Proof of the effectiveness of I-messages takes the form of anecdotes reported in *TET* and provided by teachers who used the technique successfully. A principal of a continuation school for dropouts, for example, reported that a group of tough boys responded very favorably when he told them how upset he became when he saw them break some bottles against the school wall.

Almost invariably the anecdotes reported in *TET* refer to the success of a teacher's first try at delivering an I-message. It seems likely that at least part of the technique's success the first time it is used could be attributed to surprise or novelty. But it is also possible that extensive use of the technique might stir up, rather than calm down, troublemakers. Instead of saying, "Gee! We never realized you felt that way!" they might say, "We're getting awfully tired of hearing about your troubles!"

NO-LOSE METHOD

Journal Entry
Trying the No-Lose Method

Thomas Gordon (1974) also urges teachers to try resolving conflicts in the classroom by using the **no-lose method.** If either person in a conflict loses, there is bound to be resentment. If you tell a girl who is fooling around during a work period that she must settle down or stay after school, *she* loses. If you make a halfhearted and unsuccessful effort to control her and then try to cover up your failure by ignoring her and working with others, *you* lose. In Gordon's method, the preferred procedure is to talk over the problem and come up with a mutually agreeable compromise solution. He offers this six-step procedure for coming up with no-lose solutions, a procedure that is similar to the one we described in Chapter 10:

No-lose method: come to mutual agreement about a solution to a problem

1. Define the problem.
2. Generate possible solutions.
3. Evaluate the solutions.
4. Decide which solution is best.
5. Determine how to implement the solution.
6. Assess how well the solution solved the problem. (1974, p. 228)

To put this procedure into practice with an individual, you might approach a boy who is disruptive during a work period and engage in a dialogue something like this:

You: You're making such a ruckus over here by talking loudly and shoving others that I can't hear the group I'm working with.

Student: I think this workbook junk is stupid. I already know how to do these problems. I'd rather work on my science project.

You: Well, suppose we try this. You do one page of problems. If you get them all correct, we'll both know you can do them, and you should be free to work on your science project. If you make some mistakes, that means you need more practice. Suppose you do a page and then ask me to check it. Then we can take it from there. How does that sound?

Some general guidelines you might consider when you find it necessary to resort to disciplinary techniques appear in Suggestions for Teaching in Your Classroom.

Suggestions for Teaching in Your Classroom

Handling Problem Behavior

1. Have a variety of influence techniques planned in advance.
2. Be prompt, consistent, and reasonable.
3. Avoid threats.
4. Whenever you have to deal harshly with a student, make an effort to reestablish rapport.
5. Consider making occasional use of behavior modification techniques.
6. When you have control, ease up some.

1. Have a variety of influence techniques planned in advance.

You may save yourself a great deal of trouble, embarrassment, and strain if you plan ahead. When first-year teachers are asked which aspects of teaching bother them most, classroom control is almost invariably near the top of the list. Perhaps a major reason is that problems of control frequently erupt unexpectedly, and they often demand equally sudden solutions. If you lack experience, your shoot-from-the-hip reactions may be ineffective. Initial attempts at control that are ineffective tend to reinforce misbehavior, and you will find yourself trapped in a vicious circle. Yet this sort of trap can be avoided if specific techniques are devised ahead of time. Being familiar with several of the techniques mentioned in the preceding section will prepare you for the inevitable difficulties that arise.

However, if you find yourself forced to use prepared techniques too often, some self-analysis is called for. How can you prevent so many problems from developing? Frequent trouble is an indication that you need to work harder at motivating your class. Also, check on your feelings when you mete out punishment. Teachers who really like students and want them to learn consider control techniques a necessary evil and use them only when they will provide a better atmosphere for learning. If you find yourself looking for trouble or perhaps deliberately luring students into misbehaving, or if you discover yourself gloating privately or publicly about an act of punishment, stop and think. Are you using your power to build up your ego or giving vent to personal frustration rather than paying attention to your students needs?

Journal Entry
Analyzing Feelings After Dealing with Troublemakers

2. **Be prompt, consistent, and reasonable.**

No attempt to control behavior will be effective if it is remote from the act that provokes it. If a troublemaker is to comprehend the relationship between behavior and counterreaction, one must quickly follow the other. Don't postpone dealing with misbehaving students or make vague threats to be put into effect sometime in the future (such as not permitting the students to attend an end-of-the-year event). By that time, most students will have forgotten what they did wrong. They then feel resentful and persecuted and may conclude that you are acting out of sheer malice. A frequent reaction is more misbehavior in an urge to get even. (In such situations guilty students are not likely to remember that you are the one doing the evening up.) However, retribution that is too immediate, that is applied when a student is still extremely upset, may also be ineffective. At such times it is often better to wait a bit.

Journal Entry
Being Prompt, Consistent, and Reasonable in Controlling the Class

Being consistent about classroom control can save a lot of time, energy, and misery. Strictness one day and leniency the next, or roughness on one student and gentleness with another, invite all students to test you every day just to see whether this is a good day or a bad day or whether they can get away with something more frequently than others do. Establishing and enforcing class rules are an excellent way to encourage yourself to be consistent.

Be prompt, consistent, reasonable when dealing with misbehavior

Harshness in meting out retribution encourages, rather than discourages, more extreme forms of misbehavior. If students are going to get into a lot of trouble for even a minor offense, they will probably figure they should get their money's worth. Several hundred years ago in England all offenses—from picking pockets to murder—were punishable by death. The petty thief quickly became a murderer; it was a lot easier (and less risky) to pick the pocket of a dead man and, since the punishment was the same, eminently more sensible. The laws were eventually changed to make punishment appropriate to the degree of the offense. Keep this in mind when you dispense justice.

3. **Avoid threats.**

If at all possible, avoid a showdown in front of the class. In a confrontation before the whole group, you are likely to get desperate. You may start out with a "Yes, you will," "No, I won't" sort of duel and end up making a threat on the spur of the moment. Frequently, you will not be able to make good on the threat, and you will lose face. It's far safer and better for everyone to settle extreme differences in private. When two people are upset and angry with each other, they look silly at best and completely ridiculous at worst. You lose a great deal more than a student does when this performance takes place in front of the class. In fact, a student may actually gain prestige by provoking you successfully.

Perhaps the worst temptation of all is to try getting back at the entire class by making a blanket threat of a loss of privilege or detention. It hardly ever works and tends to lead to a united counterattack by the class. One elementary school teacher had the reputation of telling her students at least once a year that they would not be allowed to participate in the Spring Play-Day if they didn't behave. By the time students reached this grade, they had been tipped off by previous students that she always made the threat but never carried it out. They behaved accordingly.

4. Whenever you have to deal harshly with a student, make an effort to reestablish rapport.

If you must use a drastic form of retribution, make a point of having a confidential conference with your antagonist as soon as possible. Otherwise, she is likely to remain an antagonist for the rest of the year. It's too much to expect chastised students to come to you of their own volition and apologize. You should set up the conference and then explain that the punishment has cleared the air as far as you are concerned. You shouldn't be surprised if a recalcitrant student doesn't respond with signs or words of gratitude. Perhaps some of the causes of misbehavior lie outside of school, and something you did or said may have been merely the last straw. Even if you get a sullen reaction, at least indicate your willingness to meet punished students more than halfway.

Journal Entry
Ways to Reestablish Rapport

At the elementary level, you can frequently make amends simply by giving the child some privilege—for example, passing out paper or being hall monitor at recess. One teacher made it a point to praise a child for some positive action shortly after a severe reprimand.

5. Consider making occasional use of behavior modification techniques.

Many of the procedures that have been noted here—in particular, stating rules, using techniques planned in advance, and being prompt and consistent—are employed in a highly systematic fashion in the behavior modification approach to classroom control. In Chapter 8 you were acquainted with the techniques of behavior modification, including the suggestion that you follow this procedure when confronted by inappropriate behavior, as when two boys engage in a mild argument that stops and starts several times:

Journal Entry
Experimenting with Behavior Modification

> First, ignore the behavior. (It may extinguish because of lack of reinforcement.)
>
> Second, remind the class that those who finish the assignment early will earn 5 bonus points and be allowed to see a film.
>
> Third, approach the boys and tell them (privately and nicely) that they are disturbing others and making life difficult for themselves. If they do not complete the assignment in the allotted time, they will have to make it up some other time.

Fourth, resort to punishment by informing the boys (in a firm but not nasty way) that they must leave the classroom immediately and report to the vice principal to be assigned to a study hall for the rest of the class period. Tell them they will have to complete the assignment when the rest of the class has free time.

First ignore misbehavior, and then stress rewards; use punishment as a last resort

Fifth, point out that once the work is made up, they will be all caught up and in a good position to do satisfactory work for the rest of the report period.

The techniques just described are appropriate for secondary school students. The following behavior modification procedure for maintaining classroom control in the primary grades is recommended by Wesley Becker, Siegfried Engelmann, and Don Thomas:

> Specify in a positive way the rules that are the basis for your reinforcement. Emphasize the behavior you desire by praising children who are following the rules. Rules are made important by providing reinforcement for following them.
>
> Rules may be different for different kinds of work, study, or play periods.
>
> Limit the rules to five or less.
>
> As the children learn to follow the rules, repeat them less frequently, but continue to praise good classroom behavior.
>
> Relate the children's performance to the rules. Praise behavior, not the child.
>
> Be specific about behavior that exemplifies paying attention or working hard. . . .
>
> Relax the rules between work periods. . . .
>
> Catch the children being good. Reinforce behavior incompatible with that which you wish to eliminate. Reinforce behavior that will be most beneficial to the child's development. In the process of eliminating disruptive behavior, focus on reinforcing tasks important for social and cognitive skills.
>
> Ignore disruptive behavior unless someone is getting hurt. Focus your attention on the children who are working well in order to prompt the correct behavior from the children who are misbehaving.
>
> When you see a persistent problem behavior, look for the reinforcer. It may be your own behavior. (1971, p. 171)

6. **When you have control, ease up some.**

It is extremely difficult, if not impossible, to establish a controlled atmosphere after allowing anarchy. Don't make the mistake of thinking you will be able to start out without any control and suddenly take charge. It may work, but in most cases you will have an armed truce or a cold war on your hands. It is far better to adopt the authoritative approach of starting out on the structured side and then easing up a bit after you have established control.

Violence in American Schools

HOW SAFE ARE OUR SCHOOLS?

You have probably read or heard reports about the frequency of crime in the United States, particularly among juveniles. One recent report noted that of all persons arrested for serious crimes, 43 percent were between the ages of seven and eighteen, despite the fact that this age group accounts for only 20 percent of the population. The peak age for committing crime among this group is fourteen (Wiles & Bondi, 1993). Since the kinds of behaviors one observes in schools tends to reflect trends in society at large, it is natural that a certain amount of violent behavior occurs on school grounds and during school hours. The Department of Justice, for example, estimates that approximately one hundred thousand children carry guns to school each day, that more than two thousand students are physically attacked on school grounds in any given hour of the school day, and that approximately nine hundred teachers are threatened and almost forty are physically attacked in any given hour of the school day (Lantieri, 1995). Other studies of school violence report that among thirteen- to nineteen-year-olds 20 percent reported seeing confrontations between students that involved a knife; 7 percent said they had seen an incident involving a gun; 83 percent had witnessed fistfights; and 55 percent said they had seen other students destroy school property (Quarles, 1993).

Although these figures are alarming, they need to be put in perspective. Bear in mind that violent behavior is more likely to occur in some schools than in others. The highest levels of violence are found in schools that are located in high-crime areas, that have large student populations and large class sizes, that have a high proportion of male students, that are run by administrators who lack firmness, that contain a high number of low-achieving students, and that have students who feel they have little control over what happens to them (Baker, 1985; Quarles, 1993).

These figures are consistent with student perceptions. In 1990 high school sophomores from low-socioeconomic-status (SES) families were twice as likely as sophomores from high-SES families to feel unsafe at school (11 percent versus 5 percent). A similar difference was noted for public school students (11 percent felt unsafe) versus Catholic school students (4 percent felt unsafe) (Office of Educational Research and Improvement, 1993). In addition, the overall frequency of violent behavior may be decreasing. Between 1980 and 1990 the proportion of high school sophomores who felt unsafe in their schools decreased from 12 percent to 8 percent (Office of Educational Research and Improvement, 1993).

Although these studies reveal a disquieting level of school violence, particularly in certain schools, they also suggest that most teachers are likely to be physically safe in their own classroom. Nevertheless, school violence is a problem that directly or indirectly touches every student and teacher. Accordingly, you should be aware of the various explanations of school violence and the steps that can be taken to reduce its frequency.

ANALYZING REASONS FOR VIOLENCE

Physiological Factors The research just cited noted that the level of violence was highest in secondary schools with a high proportion of male students. One of the clear-cut gender differences that has been repeatedly supported by consistent evidence (reviewed by Parke & Slaby, 1983) is that males are more aggressive than females. While the causes of this difference cannot be traced precisely, it is likely due to hormonal as well as cultural factors. *Hormone* in the Greek means "to arouse" or "to urge on," which reflects the fact that these substances are released in the bloodstream and arouse reactions in various parts of the body. The male sex hormone androgen arouses high energy and activity levels. Moreover, because of long-established cultural expectancies, males in our society are encouraged to assert themselves in physical ways. As a result, tendencies toward high energy and activity levels aroused by male sex hormones may be expressed in the form of aggressiveness against others.

Male aggressiveness due to hormonal and cultural factors

Gender-Related Cultural Factors As noted in the discussion of age-level characteristics in Chapter 3, there is also evidence that young girls in our society are encouraged to be dependent and to be eager to please adults, while young boys are encouraged to assert their independence (Block, 1973; Fagot, 1978). Furthermore, it appears that boys are more likely than girls to be reinforced for assertive and illegal forms of behavior. Martin Gold and Richard Petronio (1980, p. 524) speculate that delinquency in our society seems to have a masculine character. They suggest that the range of delinquent behavior that will be admired by peers is narrower for females than for males and that boys are more likely to achieve recognition by engaging in illegal acts. The same reasoning may well apply to disruptive behavior in the classroom. A boy who talks back to the teacher or shoves another boy in a skirmish in the cafeteria is probably more likely to draw a favorable response from peers than is a girl who exhibits the same behavior. Thus, there are a variety of factors that predispose boys to express frustration and hostility in physical and assertive ways.

Research findings indicate that impersonal and punitively oriented schools have higher than average levels of school violence. Consequently, one preventive technique suggested by some experts is to involve students in some aspects of school and classroom decision-making and to treat students with respect.

Academic Factors Boys also seem more likely than girls to experience feelings of frustration and hostility in school. For a variety of reasons (more rapid maturity, desire to please adults, superiority in verbal skills) girls earn higher grades, on the average, than boys do. A low grade almost inevitably arouses feelings of resentment and anger. In fact, any kind of negative evaluation is a very direct threat to a student's self-esteem. Thus, a middle school, junior high, or high school boy who has received an unbroken succession of low grades and is unlikely to graduate may experience extreme frustration and anger. Even poor students are likely to be aware that their chances of getting a decent job are severely limited by the absence of a high school diploma.

At the same time, high school students who have never developed successful study habits and who are saddled with a low grade-point average may feel that they can do nothing about the situation unless there is a continuation school or the equivalent to attend. Older high school boys who do not have opportunities to attend special schools can escape further humiliation by dropping out of school; but middle school and junior high boys cannot legally resort to the same solution, which may partially explain why violent acts are twice as frequent in seventh, eighth, and ninth grades as in the upper grades.

Middle school and junior high boys with low grades may feel trapped

Psychosocial Factors Other explanations of disruptive classroom behavior are supplied by Erik Erikson's observations on identity. A teenager who has failed to make a clear occupational choice, who is confused about gender roles, or who does not experience acceptance "by those who count" may decide to establish a negative identity. Instead of striving to behave in ways that parents and teachers respond to in positive ways, negative identity teenagers may deliberately engage in opposite forms of behavior.

Misbehavior of high school students may reveal lack of positive identity

James Marcia's identity status concept (1980, 1991) may also help you understand why certain students cause problems in class. Individuals in foreclosure who have accepted parental values may well be model students. Those in a moratorium state who are experiencing identity crises of different kinds may feel impelled to release frustration and anger. But even students who are not experiencing identity problems, either because they are too young to be concerned or because they have resolved their identity conflicts, may misbehave because they need to release frustration and tension.

School Environment Factors So far we have mentioned the role of hormonal, gender-related cultural, academic, and personality factors in school violence. Each of these explanations places the responsibility for violent behavior largely or entirely on the individual. Other explanations focus instead on schools that are poorly designed and do not meet the needs of their students. Violent behavior, in this view, is seen as a natural (though unacceptable) response to schools that are too large, impersonal, and competitive; that do not enforce rules fairly or consistently; that use punitive ways of resolving conflict; and that impose an unimaginative, nonmeaningful curriculum on students (Zwier & Vaughan, 1984). Dona Kagan (1990) reports that students who are at risk of dropping out of school believe that their teachers neither care about them nor consider them capable of academic success. Ironically, the self-esteem and motivation of a large proportion of these students improve after they leave school to the extent that they enroll in General Equivalency Diploma or job training programs. Similar observations on the characteristics of schools that have low levels of violence are stressed by Eugene Howard, an authority on school climate and discipline, who writes:

> Schools with positive climates are places where people care, respect, and trust one another; and where the school as an institution cares, respects, and trusts people. In such a school people feel a high sense of pride and ownership which comes from each individual having a role in making the school a better place . . . . Schools with positive climates are characterized by people-centered belief and value systems, procedures, rules, regulations, and policies. (1981, p.8)

REDUCING SCHOOL VIOLENCE

School violence can be reduced by improving student achievement levels

Classroom Tactics Several analyses of school violence (for example, Howard, 1981; Kagan, 1990; Zwier & Vaughan, 1984) suggest that academic achievement and school atmosphere can play a significant role in reducing school violence. To foster respectable levels of achievement by as many students as possible, teachers can make effective use of carefully selected objectives, help students establish at least short-term goals, use efficient instructional techniques (such as those advocated by behavioral theorists), teach students how to use learning strategies, and implement a mastery approach. If you show that students who do not do well on the first try at an assignment will receive your help and encouragement to improve their performance, you may be able to convert at least some resentment into a desire to achieve.

At the same time, it appears that students should be invited to participate in making at least some decisions about what is to be studied and about school and classroom rules. Constructivist techniques and contingency contracts, for example, permit some self-direction by students. Such tactics may ease students' fears that schooling is impersonal and that they have no control over what happens to them. As humanistic psychologists have argued, students seem to respond more positively to schooling when they are treated as individuals, when their feelings and opinions are taken into account, and when they are invited to participate in making decisions about how the school and the classroom function.

Programs to Reduce Violence and Improve Discipline Several states and many school districts have initiated programs to make schools safer places for students and teachers. One such program is the just community at the Birch Meadow Elementary School in Reading, Massachusetts (Murphy, 1988). You may recall reading (at the end of Chapter 2) about the just community concept as an extension of Lawrence Kohlberg's work on moral reasoning. The goal of the just community at Birch Meadow was to help students take responsibility for reducing undesirable behaviors (such as petty bickering among students, the development of cliques, and graffiti on restroom walls) and promoting more desirable actions (such as cooperative learning, cleanup activities, and the organization of fund-raising events).

Implementation of the just community concept involves two types of activities: circle meetings and student councils. Circle meetings are held in each classroom. The first meeting occurs on the first day of the school year and is devoted to establishing classroom rules and punishments. Subsequent meetings can be called at any time to deal with such issues as unfair treatment of some students by others (or by the teacher), classroom safety, and revisions of classroom rules. There were two student councils at Birch Meadow: one (the primary council) for kindergarten through grade 3 and the other (the intermediate council) for grades 4 and 5. Each class selects a representative to serve on the council. The councils meet separately with the principal in alternating weeks to decide on ways to make the atmosphere of the school more enjoyable. For example, the primary council conducted a playground cleanup campaign, and the intermediate council raised money to purchase an American flag for the school auditorium.

Violence less likely when students invited to participate in making decisions

A somewhat different approach to decreasing physical violence, particularly between students, is the Resolving Conflict Creatively Program (RCCP). Created by Linda Lantieri in 1985, the goal of the program is to teach students how to use nonviolent conflict resolution techniques in place of their more normal and more violent methods. Students are trained by teachers to monitor the school environment (such as the playground, the cafeteria, and hallways) for imminent or actual physical confrontations between students. For example, picture two students who are arguing about a comment that struck one as an insult. As the accusations and counter accusations escalate, one student threatens to hit the other. At that moment one or two other students who are wearing T-shirts with the word *mediator* printed across the front and back intervene and ask if the two students would like help in resolving their problem. The mediating students may suggest that they all move to a quieter area where they can talk. The mediators then establish certain ground rules, such as each student gets a turn to talk without being interrupted and that name calling is not allowed.

The goal of the RCCP is to teach students that they should listen to one another when disputes arise and actively work toward peaceful solutions. The program is currently being used in school districts in New York City, Anchorage, New Orleans, southern California, and New Jersey and is described by Lantieri as the largest school-based program of its kind in the country. In schools where the program has been implemented, teachers have noted less physical violence in their classrooms, fewer insults and verbal put-downs, and greater spontaneous use of conflict resolution skills (Lantieri, 1995). Given the unfamiliarity of these behaviors, several months may pass before changes are seen in students' behaviors. But given the alternative, this seems a small price to pay. A description of how conflict resolution and other violence reduction programs are being implemented in the schools is presented in Case in Print.

CASE IN PRINT

Fighting Violence with Nonviolence

Violent behavior, in this view, is seen as a natural (though unacceptable) response to schools that are too large, impersonal, and competitive; that do not enforce rules fairly or consistently; that use punitive ways of resolving conflict; and that impose an unimaginative, non-meaningful curriculum on students. . . . Several states and many school districts have initiated programs to make schools safer places for students and teachers. (pp. 507–508)

"Pathways to Peace"

MICKEY BACA

Merrimack Valley Sunday 3/5/95

At the Kelley Elementary School in Newburyport [MA], a fourth grader who flares up in anger is moved to a separate area of the room surrounded by restful scenes and posters. He is given drawing materials and earphones to listen to relaxation tapes until he cools off enough to discuss what sent him up the anger "escalator."

At Triton Regional School in Salisbury, two eighth graders involved in a shoving match in the hall sit down with a pair of student mediators to analyze what led to the scuffle. After nearly two hours, they emerge with a written agreement on how to avoid future strife.

At Newburyport's Nock Middle School, a couple of fifth graders who sometimes clash because one's mother buys her clothes at K-Mart rather than the more trendy Gap find themselves working together to solve a burglary case in a group lesson designed to build cooperation and understanding.

Like their counterparts around the country, local schools are turning to a variety of techniques to try to combat intolerance and violence in their students. . . .

. . ."There's a real culture in our society that reinforces violence," says Susan Fallon, health coordinator at Triton. "We're trying to create a culture that reinforces nonviolence."

For the past three years, the Triton School District—which includes Salisbury, Rowley and Newbury—has been training its staff and passing on to its students the latest techniques in violence prevention. Teachers have attended seminars on something called "conflict resolution skills"—methods to resolve disputes through nonviolent means such as better communication, collaboration and compromise. The idea, according to former state Rep. Barbara Hildt of Amesbury, who works in violence prevention and is participating in the Partnership effort, is to give students strategies to better manage anger, listen more, "talk about problems, not people," offer choices and work with others on problem solving.

Triton also has a peer mediation program in which students are trained to act as impartial middlemen in student conflicts to root out and hopefully defuse their causes. . . .

"They provide a neutral way to clarify what the problem is," says Fallon. "And to help each side understand the other's point of view.". . .

Under peer mediation at Triton, school staff advising the mediators take referrals about fights between students or even about conflicts that could lead to fights eventually. The referrals can come from a teacher, parent, bus driver, hallway monitor or a student who is either being picked on or perhaps has a friend facing conflict, according to Fallon. Mediation augments, but doesn't replace, regular school disciplinary consequences to violence. . . .

Staff advisors decide what's appropriate for mediation. Some things—like harassment cases or any kind of dating violence—are not, Fallon says. . . .

Fallon says one indication she sees that Triton's commitment to anti-violence training is paying off is the kids' willingness to use the relatively new peer mediation option. She and other educators say kids like the idea of sitting down with their peers rather than with adults to resolve their differences.

What's more, Fallon says, the results of mediation sessions are encouraging. "It can be truly moving. You can see some tough kids becoming choked up."

Over in Newburyport, where anti-violence training is less developed in the schools, officials have mixed reactions to the training trend.

Doug Lay, principal at the Nock Middle School, says some schools seem to have a positive track record with such training, but it's hard to say how effective things like conflict resolution training will be in the long run in changing middle school kids' views towards violence.

"I don't see that it's ever going to resolve all of the conflicts," he says.

What it will do, Lay says, is build a common vocabulary for nonviolent problem-solving and spell out ways to break down conflicts more objectively.

Given that framework, kids are willing to work at solving conflicts, Lay finds, and have also shown more of a willingness to seek the help of an adult when facing problems.

. . . [Newburyport High School] Principal Mary Lanard. . . sees a clear need for it at the high school, she says, particularly in the area of teaching kids to tolerate diversity.

"We're looking at ways we can make it easier for kids who are coming from other schools or who are different," Lanard says. "I think we're trying to make the school more humane."

At the elementary school level, Chris Morton, a fourth grade teacher at the Kelley School, a strong proponent of violence prevention training, says her students have been quick to pick up the conflict resolution lessons they've been getting since last year.

"I think we know it works when we begin seeing kids solve problems without violence," she says, noting that she does hear her students using the terminology of conflict resolution.

Morton says Newburyport elementary schools have also begun a unique "time out" process that really seems to help students better manage their anger. An area of the classroom is set up away from the rest of the class where angry students go to cool off and get in control by listening to relaxation tapes. The area also features posters that remind kids to do things like count backwards from 10 when they feel themselves getting angry.

For the most part, she says, kids are able to calm down in 15 or 20 minutes and are then ready to talk about the problem. . . .

One program that Lay says has been effective in promoting understanding and stemming conflicts at his school is an effort started last year, called Prime Time. Under that program, the school's student population is divided up into groups of roughly 16 that meet three mornings a week for 45 minutes.

Group advisors, including teachers and Lay himself, lead the groups in exercises that emphasize group cohesiveness, encourage students to share their thoughts and feelings and look at issues like peer pressure and conflict.

Like other area school officials, Lay doesn't see racial or cultural differences as a source of conflict among his students. His school population, and the population through Essex County, is pretty homogeneous in that respect.

What he does see is economic prejudices and stereotypes fueling conflict, Lay notes.

"Kids making fun of each other's clothing. Do you buy at the Gap or do you buy at K-Mart? You end up with a potentially polarized population."

The most important thing Lay believes school programs should teach kids is tolerance and respect of diversity. . . .

After only a year, Prime Time seems to be working. Lay says there's a lot more cohesiveness and a lot less tension and conflict among students this year.

Questions and Activities

1. According to two educators interviewed in this article, student-based conflict resolution strategies are not appropriate for dealing with certain types of problems and may not effectively resolve other types of conflicts. Do you agree with this view? If you do agree, what types of problems should student mediators not try to resolve? Why? Where peer mediation is appropriate, with which types of conflicts is it likely to be unsuccessful? Why? If you do not agree that peer mediation has its limits, explain why.

2. Although peer mediation is an attractive method for helping students peacefully resolve conflicts, it may not work effectively below a certain grade level. Review the discussion in Chapter 2 of Piaget's theory of cognitive development, note the lowest grade level below which you would not institute this type of program, and explain why.

3. Relate what you learned in Chapter 4 and elsewhere in this book about teaching in a culturally diverse classroom to the comments about diversity in this article. Do you agree with the educator who says that the most important things school programs can teach are tolerance and respect for diversity? Why or why not? As a classroom teacher with an awareness of issues related to cultural or economic diversity, how could you augment some of the strategies and policies described in this article?

4. To test the feasibility of peer mediation, try acting as a go-between the next time two friends or family members have a disagreement (with their permission of course). Ask each party to describe the source of the conflict, why the two parties have different views, what their feelings are, and what ideas they might have for resolving it.

Resources for Further Investigation

Classroom Management

Even though the second edition of *Mental Hygiene in Teaching,* by Fritz Redl and William Wattenberg, was published in 1959, it includes a particularly clear, concise, and well-organized analysis of influence techniques. Many of the techniques described have been used by teachers for years and will continue to be used as long as an instructor is asked to supervise a group of students.

More recent analyses of classroom control techniques can be found in *Classroom Management and Discipline* (1995), by Paul Burden; *Classroom Management for Elementary Teachers* (3d ed., 1994), by Carolyn Evertson, Edmund Emmer, Barbara Clements, and Murray Worsham; *Classroom Management for Secondary Teachers* (3d ed., 1994), by Edmund Emmer, Carolyn Evertson, Barbara Clements, and Murray Worsham; *Behavior Management: A Practical Approach for Educators* (5th ed., 1991), by James Walker and Thomas Shea; and *Elementary Classroom Management: Lessons from Research and Practice* (1993), by Carol Weinstein and Andrew Mignano Jr.

Discussions of classroom management that emphasize particular approaches or techniques can also be found. For instance, James Cangelosi emphasizes the use of methods that foster student cooperation in *Classroom Management Strategies: Gaining and Maintaining Students' Cooperation* (1988); and William Purkey and David Strahan emphasize the use of invitational learning in *Positive Discipline: A Pocketful of Ideas* (1986).

On-line resources for classroom management include Teacher Talk, a World Wide Web site at education.indiana.edu/cas/tt/tthmpg.html. It is maintained by the Indiana University Center for Adolescent Studies and is a journal with articles on many topics, including coverage of classroom management. In particular, it includes a self-survey to help you determine your classroom management style. The survey can be found at http://education.indiana.edu/cas/tt/v1i2/v1i2.html#what.

Teachers Edition Online is another resource with tips for classroom management (including a "Tip of the Day"), answers to teacher questions, and sample lesson plans. It's found at www.southwind.net/~lshiney/index.html.

Teachers Helping Teachers provides a "bulletin board" of postings by teachers about particular topics, including classroom management. Many of these first-person comments are insightful and relevant to most beginning teachers. The site can be found at http://north.pacificnet.net/~mandel/ClassroomManagement.html.

The AskERIC on-line database contains a large number of resources for classroom management. The search-able database is found at http://ericir.sunsite.syr.edu/. It can be searched for articles, ERIC digests, postings from newsgroups and classroom-related listservs, and so forth.

School Violence

For information on how to reduce school violence through the use of behavior modification techniques, psychodynamic and humanistic interventions, and the teaching of prosocial values and behaviors, read *School Violence* (1984), by Arnold Goldstein, Steven Apter, and Berj Harootunian. *Victimization in Schools* (1985), by Gary Gottfredson and Denise Gottfredson, describes research conducted at the Center for Social Organization of Schools at Johns Hopkins University on the nature and frequency of school violence; it also discusses possible solutions. And, finally, Chester Quarles describes how teachers can try to prevent school violence and deal with it when it does happen in *Staying Safe at School* (1993).

There are a number of on-line resources dedicated to educating educators, parents, and students about violence and its effects. One unusual site is Danger High, a simulation in which students are confronted with somewhat realistic situations and must solve problems. Developed by the Metro Nashville Police Department on a National Institute of Justice grant, it can be found at http://www.nashville.net/~police/dangerhi/.

Summary

1. Just as parents adopt either an authoritarian, a laissez-faire, (permissive), or an authoritative approach to raising children, teachers adopt one of these approaches to managing the behavior of students. The authoritative approach, which revolves around explaining the rationale for classroom rules and adjusting those rules as students demonstrate the ability for self-governance, produces the highest level of desirable student behavior.

2. Kounin, one of the early writers on classroom management, identified several effective classroom management techniques. Kounin emphasized being aware of the ripple effect, cultivating withitness, coping with overlapping activities, maintaining the momentum of a lesson, keeping the whole class involved in a lesson, using a variety of instructional techniques enthusiastically, focusing on the misbehavior of students rather than on their personalities, and suggesting alternative constructive behaviors.

3. Researchers at the University of Texas found that in well-managed classrooms students know what they are expected to do and do it successfully, are kept busy with teacher-designated activities, and exhibit little confusion or disruptive behavior. Such classrooms are marked by a work-oriented, yet relaxed and pleasant atmosphere.

4. Canter's Assertive Discipline program recommends that teachers teach students the behaviors they want them to exhibit, give them positive reinforcement, and, if the first two steps do not produce desirable results, invoke a discipline plan.

5. Redl and Wattenberg proposed a set of behavior management methods in 1959 called influence techniques that were designed to help teachers deal with classroom misbehavior.

6. Ginott suggests that teachers use I-messages when responding to misbehavior. These are statements that indicate to students how the teacher feels when misbehavior occurs. The aim is to comment on the situation rather than on the personality and character of the student.

7. Gordon recommends that teachers determine who owns a problem, use active listening when the student owns the problem, and resolve conflicts by using the no-lose method. The no-lose method involves discussing problem behaviors with the misbehaving student and formulating a mutually agreeable compromise solution.

8. School violence is most likely to occur in schools that are located in high-crime areas, that have large numbers of students and large class sizes, that have a high proportion of males, that are administered by permissive administrators, and that contain students with low levels of achievement and a history of substance abuse.

9. Possible explanations for misbehavior and violence, particularly among boys at the junior high and high school levels, include high levels of the male sex hormone androgen, a culture that encourages male aggression and independence, feelings of resentment and frustration over low levels of achievement, and difficulty in establishing a positive identity.

10. Other explanations for school violence focus on the characteristics and atmosphere of schools that are so large that they seem impersonal, that emphasize competition, that do not enforce rules fairly or consistently, that use punishment as a primary means of resolving conflict, and that offer a curriculum perceived as unimaginative and nonmeaningful.

11. Steps that classroom teachers can take to reduce school violence include providing students with well-conceived

objectives, helping students set short-term goals, using instructional techniques derived from behavioral learning theories, teaching students how to use learning strategies, using a mastery approach, and allowing students to make some decisions about classroom rules and what is to be studied.

12. Two schoolwide programs that may reduce violence and improve behavior are the just community, in which students are given responsibility for reducing undesirable behavior and increasing the frequency of desirable behavior, and the Resolving Conflict Creatively Program, in which students mediate disputes between other students to prevent physical violence.

Key Terms

ripple effect *(481)*
withitness *(482)*
I-message *(499)*
active listening *(500)*
no-lose method *(500)*

Discussion Questions

1. Can you recall any classes in which you experienced Kounin's ripple effect? Since this phenomenon simultaneously affects the behavior of several students, would you consider using it deliberately? Why?
2. Haim Ginott and Thomas Gordon recommend that when responding to misbehavior, teachers speak to the behavior and not the character of the student. How often have you seen this done? If it strikes you as a good approach that is not practiced often enough, what steps will you take to use it as often as possible with your own students?
3. Do you agree with the argument raised earlier that school violence can be caused by a nonmeaningful, unimaginative curriculum? If so, what can you do to make the subjects you teach lively, interesting, and useful?

CHAPTER 14

Becoming a Better Teacher by Becoming a Reflective Teacher

As you know from personal experience, some teachers are much more effective than others. Take a moment and think back to as many teachers as you can remember. How many of them were really outstanding in the sense that they established a favorable classroom atmosphere, were sensitive to the needs of students, and used a variety of techniques to help you learn? How many of them did an adequate job but left you bored or indifferent most of the time? How many of them made you dread entering their classrooms because they were either ineffective teachers or insensitive or even cruel in dealing with you and your classmates? Chances are you remember few outstanding teachers and had at least one who was incompetent or tyrannical (and perhaps several of them). You probably know from your experiences as a student that ineffective or vindictive teachers are often dissatisfied with themselves and with their jobs. It seems logical to assume a circular relationship in such cases: unhappy teachers often do a poor job of instruction; teachers who do a poor job of instruction are likely to be unhappy.

If you hope to be an effective teacher who enjoys life in the classroom (most of the time), you must be well prepared and willing to work. You will need a wide variety of skills, sensitivity to the needs of your students, and awareness of many instructional techniques. Each chapter in this book was written to help you acquire these various skills, sensitivities, and techniques.

In addition, and to return to a theme we introduced in Chapter 1, you will need to develop the reflective attitudes and abilities that help you formulate thoughtful instructional goals and plans, implement those plans, observe their effects, and judge whether your goals were met. This last chapter offers some suggestions you might use to enhance such attitudes and abilities.

Improving Your Reflection and Teaching Skills

In the introduction to Chapter 13, we suggested that you think of the classroom teacher as playing the same role as that of an orchestra conductor. This analogy is used frequently by scholars who study instructional processes. Jere Brophy and Carolyn Evertson, for example, note that "effective teaching involves *orchestration* of a large number of factors, continually shifting teaching behavior to respond to continually shifting needs" (1976, p. 139). They also note that "the most successful teachers looked upon themselves as diagnosticians and problem solvers" (1976, p. 45). Taken together, these two comments emphasize the point that to be consistently effective, you will need to observe and analyze what you do in the classroom and use different approaches with different groups of students.

There are a number of ways you can strive to become a more reflective and effective teacher. You might ask for students' evaluations or suggestions, employ peer or self-assessment techniques, or use your Reflective Journal and the questions and suggestions at the end of this chapter to both troubleshoot your teaching and systematically analyze your goals and techniques. Each of these will be discussed separately.

STUDENT EVALUATIONS AND SUGGESTIONS

In many respects students are in a better position to evaluate teachers than anyone else. They may not always be able to analyze *why* what a teacher does is effective or ineffective (even an experienced expert observer might have difficulty doing so), but they know, better than anyone else, whether they are responding and learning. Furthermore, students form their impressions after interacting with a teacher for hundreds or thousands of hours. Most principals or other adult observers may watch a teacher in action for only a few minutes at a time. It makes sense, therefore, to pay attention to and actively solicit opinions from students.

As a matter of fact, it will be virtually impossible for you to ignore student reactions. Every minute that school is in session, you will receive student feedback in the form of attentiveness (or lack of it), facial expressions, restlessness, yawns, sleeping, disruptive behavior, and the like. If a particular lesson arouses either a neutral or a negative reaction, this should signify to you that you need to seek a better way to present the same material in the future. If you find that you seem to be spending much of your time disciplining students, it will be worth your while to evaluate why and to find other methods.

In addition to analyzing the minute-by-minute reactions of your students, you may find it helpful to request more formal feedback. After completing a unit, you might ask, "I'd like you to tell me what you liked and disliked about the way this unit was arranged and give me suggestions for improving it if I teach it again next year."

A more comprehensive and systematic approach is to distribute a questionnaire or evaluation form and ask students to record their reactions anonymously. You might use a published form or devise your own. In either case a common format involves listing a series of statements and asking students to rate them on a 5-point scale. Some of the published forms use special answer sheets that make it possible to tally the results electronically. One disadvantage of many rating-scale evaluation forms is that responses may not be very informative unless you can compare your ratings to those of colleagues. If you get an overall rating of 3.5 on "makes the subject matter interesting," for example, you won't know whether you need to work on that aspect of your teaching until you discover that the average rating of other teachers of the same grade or subject was 4.2. Another disadvantage is that published evaluation forms may not be very helpful unless all other teachers use the same rating scale. Fortunately, this may be possible in school districts that use a standard scale to obtain evidence for use in making decisions about retention, tenure, and promotion.

Another disadvantage of many rating scales is indicated by the phrase *leniency problem*. Students tend to give most teachers somewhat above-average ratings on most traits. Although leniency may soothe a teacher's ego, wishy-washy responses do not provide the information needed to improve pedagogical effectiveness. To get around the leniency problem and to induce students to give more informative reactions, forced-choice ratings are often used. Figure 14.1 shows a forced-choice rating form, the Descriptive Ranking Form for Teachers, developed by Don Cosgrove (1959). This form is designed to let teachers know how students perceive their skill in four areas of performance: (1) knowledge and organization of subject matter, (2) adequacy of relations with students in class, (3) adequacy of plans and procedures in class, and (4) enthusiasm in working with students. If you decide to use this form, omit the numbers in brackets that follow each statement when you prepare copies for distribution to students. On your own copy of the form, write in those numbers, and use them to prepare your score in each of the four categories.

To calculate your index of effectiveness in each category of the Descriptive Ranking Form for Teachers, assign a score of 4 to the phrase in each group that is ranked 1, a score of 3 to the phrase marked 2, and so on. Then add together the scores for all phrases identified by the parenthetical number 1, and do the same for the other sets of phrases. The cluster of phrases that yields the highest score is perceived by your students to be your strongest area of teaching; the cluster that yields the lowest score is considered to be your weakest. A total of 30 points for all phrases indicated by the parenthetical number 1, for example, means that you ranked high in category 1 (knowledge and organization of subject matter). If, however, you get only 12 points for phrases identified by the parenthetical number 4, you will need to work harder at being enthusiastic when working with students.

Set a ______ Always on time for class [3]
______ Pleasant in class [2]
______ Very sincere when talking with students [4]
______ Well-read [1]

Set b ______ Contagious enthusiasm for subject [4]
______ Did not fill up time with trivial material [3]
______ Gave everyone an equal chance [2]
______ Made clear what was expected of students [1]

Set c ______ Classes always orderly [3]
______ Enjoyed teaching class [4]
______ Friendliness did not seem forced [2]
______ Logical in thinking [1]

Set d ______ Encouraged creativity [4]
______ Kept course material up to date [1]
______ Never deliberately forced own decisions on class [2]
______ Procedures well thought out [3]

Set e ______ Authority on own subject [1]
______ Friendly attitude toward students [4]
______ Marked tests very fairly [3]
______ Never criticized in a destructive way [2]

Set f ______ Good sense of humor [4]
______ Spaced assignments evenly [3]
______ Students never afraid to ask questions in class [2]
______ Well-organized course [1]

Set g ______ Accepted students' viewpoints with open mind [2]
______ Increased students' vocabulary by own excellent usage [1]
______ Students always knew what was coming up next day [3]
______ Students willingly worked for teacher [4]

Set h ______ Always knew what he was doing [3]
______ Appreciated accomplishment [4]
______ Did not ridicule wrong answers [2]
______ Well informed in all related fields [1]

Set i ______ Always had class material ready [3]
______ Covered subject well [1]
______ Encouraged students to think out answers [4]
______ Rules and regulations fair [2]

Set j ______ Always managed to get things done on time [3]
______ Course had continuity [1]
______ Made material significant [4]
______ Understood problems of students [2]

FIGURE 14.1 *The Descriptive Ranking Form for Teachers*

SOURCE: Cosgrove (1959).

Quite often a homemade form that covers specific points regarding your personal approach to teaching will provide useful information. You might ask a series of questions about specific points (Were there enough exams? Did you think too much homework was assigned?). Or you can ask students to list the three things they liked best, the three things they liked least, and what they would suggest you do to improve the way a particular unit is taught. When you ask students to respond to questions like these, not only do you usually get feedback about teaching techniques, but you also get ideas you might use to improve your teaching skill. (On a rating scale, if rated below average on an item such as "Examinations are too difficult," you may not know *why* you were rated low or what you might do to change things for the better.)

PEER AND SELF-ASSESSMENT TECHNIQUES

Observation Schedules While your students can supply quite a bit of information that can help you improve your teaching, they cannot always tell you about technical flaws in your instructional technique. This is especially true with younger students. Accordingly, you may wish to submit to a detailed analysis of your approach to teaching. Several observation schedules have been developed for this purpose. *The Flanders Interaction Analysis Categories* (Flanders, 1970) is perhaps the most widely used teacher behavior schedule, but ninety-eight others are described in *Mirrors for Behavior III: An Anthology of Observation Instruments* (1974), edited by Anita Simon and E. Gil Boyer.

As the title of the Flanders schedule indicates, it stresses verbal interactions between teacher and students. The following ten categories are listed on a record blank:

- accepts feelings
- praises or encourages
- uses student ideas
- asks questions
- lectures
- gives directions
- criticizes
- pupil talk—response
- pupil talk—initiation
- silence or confusion

A trained observer puts a check mark opposite one of these categories every three seconds during a period when teacher and students are interacting verbally. Once the observation is completed, it is a simple matter to tally checks

Soliciting comments about the effectiveness of one's teaching methods from students and colleagues and reflecting on these comments is an excellent way to become a better teacher.

Successful teachers constantly record and analyze how students respond to classroom activities and assignments. They are always striving to improve their effectiveness as instructors.

and determine the percentage of time devoted to each activity. Then, if a teacher discovers that a substantial amount of time was spent in silence or confusion and that only a tiny fraction of interactions involved praise or encouragement, she can make a deliberate effort to change for the better.

Perhaps the biggest problem with such observational approaches is the need for a trained observer. But it would be possible to team up with another teacher and act as reciprocal observers if you feel that a detailed analysis of your teaching style would be helpful.

Audiotaped Lessons If it is not possible for you to team up with a colleague, you might consider trying to accomplish the same goal through the use of audiotape. Your first step should be to decide which classes or parts of classes you want to record, for how long, and on what day of the week. The goal should be to create a representative sample of the circumstances under which you teach. Then, you should inform your students that you intend to tape-record a sample of your lessons over a period of several weeks to study and improve your instructional methods and that you will protect their confidentiality by not allowing anyone but you to listen to the tapes. Then you can analyze the tapes according to the same categories that make up the Flanders instrument as well as any others that might be of interest.

When this method was used with ten secondary student teachers, significant improvements in such behaviors as amount of time used for bringing a lesson to closure, waiting for students to formulate answers to questions (commonly referred to as wait-time), and making positive statements. The impact of listening to yourself as an outsider would can be appreciated from the following comment by one student teacher: "Now I'm just so much more aware of waiting. Before, I would address all questions to the class and whoever wanted could blurt out the answer. Whereas, now, I'm much more conscious of calling a name and waiting for a response for that person" (Anderson & Freiberg, 1995, p. 83).

Reflective Lesson Plans Finally, you may want to try something called reflective lesson plans (Ho, 1995). To do so, follow these four steps:

1. Divide a sheet of paper in half. Label the left-hand side "Lesson Plan." Label the right-hand side "Reflective Notes."
2. On the lesson plan side, note relevant identifying information (fourth period English, January 23, 9:00 A.M.; honors algebra; fourth-grade social studies), the objectives of the lesson, the tasks that are to be carried out in chronological order, the materials and equipment that are to be used, and how much time has been allotted for this lesson.
3. On the reflective notes side, write your thoughts about the worthwhileness of the objective that underlies the lesson, the adequacy of the materials, and how well you performed the basic mechanics of teaching as soon as possible after the lesson.
4. Make changes to the lesson plan based on your analysis of the reflective notes.

USING YOUR REFLECTIVE JOURNAL TO IMPROVE YOUR TEACHING

Research has shown that keeping a personal journal about one's teaching activities and outcomes helps teachers improve their effectiveness because it forces them to focus on what they do, why they do it, and what kinds of results are typically obtained.

In Chapter 1 we pointed out that we had written this book to be used in three ways: (1) as a text for a course in educational psychology, (2) as a source of practical ideas on how to apply psychology to teaching, and (3) as a means for improving your teaching effectiveness through thoughtful reflection. To help you use the text for this third purpose, we have placed in each chapter a number of marginal notes called Journal Entry. The Journal Entries offer a framework for you to use in developing your own set of guidelines for instruction.

To sum up what we originally described in Chapter 1: before or during student teaching, develop your own ideas about how to apply the information and techniques described in this book. One recommendation is that you use the Journal Entries as just what their name implies—page headings in your Reflective Journal. Under each, you can develop a two-part page or multipage entry. As was illustrated in the first half of Figure 1.2, the first part should contain your own teaching ideas, custom-tailored from the Suggestions for Teaching and from personal experience and other sources, to fit the grade level and subjects you expect to teach. With this part of the journal under way, you should feel reasonably well prepared when you first take charge of a class.

At this point it might be helpful to recall the teaching cycle we introduced in Chapter 1 and illustrated in Figure 1.3. In Chapter 1 we highlighted the process of assembling your Suggestions for Teaching and other ideas. A cycle

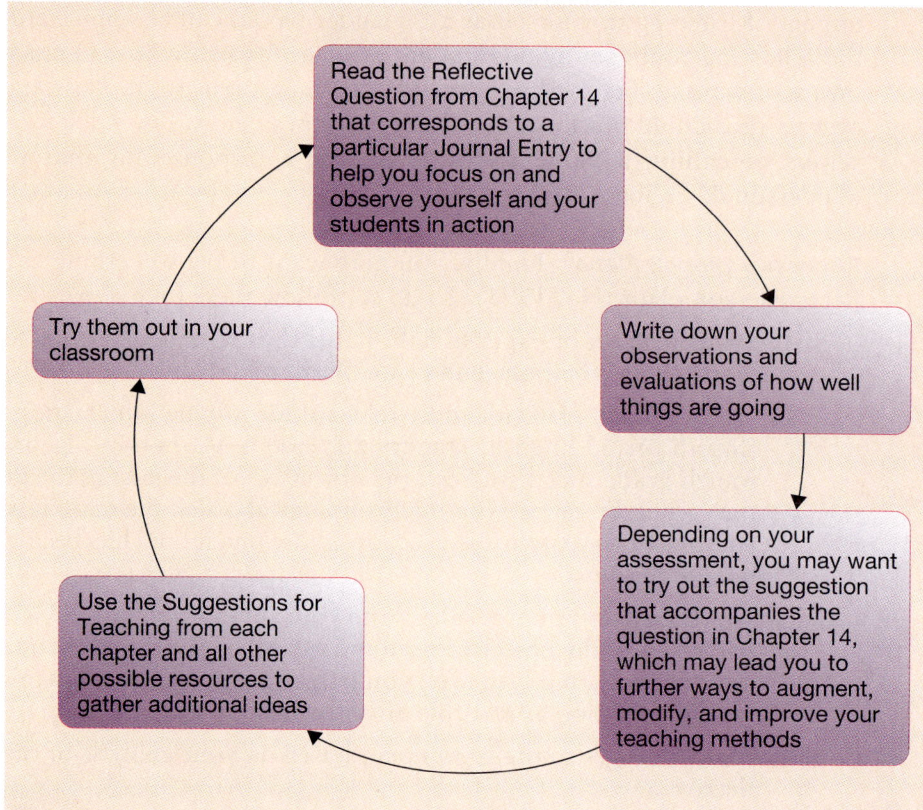

FIGURE 14.2 *How to Use Your Journal as Part of a Reflective Teaching Cycle: Focus on Reflectivity*

is, of course, a circle, and a circle has many different possible "jumping-in" points. Here, we reprint the cycle (see Figure 14.2) with a different jumping-in point emphasized, as we are now focused on the ongoing process of self-observation, reflection, and improvement of your teaching skills.

After a few weeks or months of experience, this deliberate effort to analyze and improve your teaching technique might begin. The information provided in the last section of this chapter, "Becoming a Reflective Teacher: Questions and Suggestions," is offered as a means for achieving this goal. Each question is designed to call your attention to a specific aspect of your teaching technique, to help you formulate relevant questions about your teaching, and to stimulate ideas you might use to improve your instructional skills. To help you coordinate the suggested reflective questions with the relevant text section, each question or set of questions appears next to a marginal Journal Entry, which is reprinted from the margins of text Chapters 2 through 13.

For example, let's say that you had some doubts about whether you were providing your students with appropriate reinforcement. Turning to page 534 of this chapter, you find under Chapter 8 the Journal Entry "Ways to Supply Reinforcement," which is a verbatim Journal Entry from Chapter 8. You might do two things at this point—you might flip back to that marginal note in Chapter 8 and reread the relevant text discussion; and you might focus on the questions that accompany that Journal Entry in this chapter. In this case the questions ask you to think about both the amount and type of reinforcement you supply to students.

Directly following the questions is at least one answer, written as if it were a specific suggestion you might make to yourself. You can use this suggestion to get restarted or headed in a new direction, if need be, with your teaching.

Both the questions and suggestions can be recorded in the reflections portion of your journal (the second part of the journal page) and used (1) as troubleshooting aids when you are confronted with a specific, identifiable problem and (2) as a basis for systematic evaluations. (Again, see Figure 1.2, paying attention to the second half of the figure.)

Recent research found that student teachers who were given questions as reflective prompts (for example, Why was this event significant? How did you react to this event? Why did you react that way? What did you learn from this event?) were more likely to note the reasons for their actions and to make judgments about the adequacy of their efforts than were students who were not given such prompts. According to one student:

> After your lesson, you may say, "it's over," and you may not think about it again. But with the reflective logs, you are forced to sit down and really think about what was something significant about the class and what did you do about it? So, I think it is important. Because if this assignment wasn't there, I probably would just go on and forget about the lesson, and this is not a good thing to do. (Tsangaridou & O'Sullivan, 1994, p. 23)

To become familiar with the questions and suggestions section as a tool for self-observation, make it a habit during the first year of your teaching career to set aside at least a few moments at the end of each school day for examining the questions for one chapter. If you feel that you might improve your teaching by concentrating on techniques highlighted by a particular question, plan a step-by-step campaign. The next day peruse the questions for the next chapter and so on. If you follow this procedure for a few weeks, you should systematically evaluate all aspects of teaching discussed in this book and also become thoroughly familiar with every section of your journal. Then, when you become aware of the need for improving some phase of instruction, you will know where to look for help, and you will have a good start toward devising your own step-by-step plan for solving a particular problem.

Becoming a Reflective Teacher: Questions and Suggestions

CHAPTER 2: STAGE THEORIES OF DEVELOPMENT

Questions Am I providing plenty of opportunities for younger students to develop a sense of autonomy? What else can I do to foster independence? Am I doing my best to minimize the emergence of feelings of doubt or shame?

Suggestions Check on how often I give children ample time to complete something on their own, how often I finish a task *for* a child.

> *Journal Entry*
> Ways to Apply Erikson's Theory (Preschool and Kindergarten)

Journal Entry
Ways to Apply Erikson's Theory (Elementary Grades)

Questions With older students, am I making it possible for feelings of initiative and accomplishment to emerge? Do I make students feel guilty by imposing unnecessary restrictions or regulations?

Suggestions Keep a record of how much time I spend directing activities and how much time I permit students to engage in self-selected activities.

Questions Am I arranging learning experiences so that students can complete assignments successfully and in such a way that they acquire feelings of genuine accomplishment? What can I do to minimize feelings of inferiority on the part of those who don't do as well as others?

Suggestions Arrange learning situations so that students compete against themselves and frequently experience a sense of successful achievement. Use the mastery learning techniques described in Chapter 12.

Journal Entry
Ways to Apply Erikson's Theory (Secondary Grades)

Questions What can I do to foster the development of a sense of identity? Do I take enough personal interest in individual students so that they feel they are being recognized as individuals?

Suggestions Keep a record of the number of times I recognize—say hello to, call on, smile at, talk with—each student in my classes. If I discover I have ignored some students, make it a point to address them by name and comment favorably on their work.

Questions Is there anything I can do in the courses I teach to help students begin to think about occupational choice? Can I provide specific job skills, or should I concentrate on helping students get ready for college not only by learning subject matter but also by becoming skilled students?

Suggestions Make a list of job skills, academic *and* nonacademic, that I can teach in my classes.

Questions Is it appropriate in the courses I teach to encourage analysis of gender roles so that each individual can develop a personal philosophy of how to deal with gender differences?

Suggestions Check to see if it would be appropriate to set up a discussion of male and female attitudes and achievement in the field of study I teach.

Questions Should I explain the concept of *psychosocial moratorium* to students and point out that there is no reason to panic if they are not positive about occupational choice by the time they graduate?

Suggestions Point out that some of the famous people in almost any field of endeavor floundered around before they settled on that particular career.

Questions How can I be tolerant of students who have chosen a negative identity? What can I do to avoid confirming a student's negative identity by reacting too harshly to impertinent or disruptive behavior? If I really have to put down a troublemaker, do I try to give him a chance to do something praiseworthy immediately afterward?

Suggestions Keep a record of what I say and to whom I say it when I really criticize students. Then, write out some guidelines for doing a more effective, positive job of handling the next incident involving a disruptive student. (Check Chapter 13 for ideas.)

Journal Entry
Ways to Apply Piaget's Theory (Preschool, Elementary, and Middle School Grades)

Questions Am I remaining aware of the fact that many of my students may be thinking in preoperational terms—that is, they tend to think of only one quality at a time and are incapable of mentally reversing actions? What can I do to arrange learning experiences that stress only one thing at a time and also feature physical manipulation of objects rather than mental manipulation of symbols?

Suggestions Ask veteran teachers about teaching materials and techniques that stress manipulation.

Questions What can I do to set up learning experiences so that students can learn through their own activities and also explain things to each other?

Suggestions Next week, set up some learning centers (tables with books, objects, and instructional materials in various areas of study and interest), and invite students to make and share discoveries.

Questions How can I avoid having students acquire merely verbal learning (that is, memorizing statements that they do not really understand)? What can I do to encourage students to concentrate on concepts and ideas they thoroughly comprehend?

Suggestions Give students frequent opportunities to explain ideas in their own way.

Questions Should I ask individual students to carry out some conservation tasks so that I can estimate if they are thinking at the preoperational level and also develop insight into how young children think?

Suggestions Working from the discussion of the preoperational stage of cognitive development, obtain and prepare the necessary materials so that you will be equipped to evaluate how students think.

Questions When confronted by a tattletale or when discussing classroom rules, do I keep in mind that students of this age are moral realists and that they will need separate rules for different situations and tend to concentrate on consequences rather than intentions?

Suggestions If students get needlessly upset over minor rule infractions, point out that sometimes it is better to change the rules slightly; then go on to another topic.

Journal Entry
Ways to Apply Piaget's Theory (Middle School and Secondary Grades)

Questions What can I do to allow for the fact that most students shift from concrete to formal thinking around the sixth grade or so and that they will sometimes think one way, sometimes the other? Should I use some of Piaget's experiments or class exercises to estimate how many students are capable of formal thinking?

Suggestions Review the Piagetian experiments described in Chapter 2, and obtain and prepare the necessary materials so that I will be equipped to evaluate how my students think.

Questions When students show that they are capable of formal thought, how can I teach problem-solving skills?

Suggestions Make a list of promising ways to teach problem solving after examining the section on that topic in Chapter 10, pages 374–380.

Questions Should I avoid presenting far-out hypothetical situations in order to hold down the tendency for inexperienced formal thinkers to concentrate more on possibilities than on realities? How can I encourage novice theorists to take realities into account?

Suggestions When selecting discussion topics, choose those that require students to deal with actual conditions and realistic problems, and avoid those that more or less *force* far-out theorizing.

Journal Entry
Ways to Encourage Moral Development

Questions Am I taking into account differences between the moral thinking of younger and older students?

Suggestions After referring to Tables 2.2 and 2.3, I might think about the kind of moral reasoning likely to be used by the students I teach.

Questions Am I taking into account differences between the moral thinking of male and female adolescents?

Suggestions Review Gilligan's analysis of adolescent moral development, and incorporate issues of interpersonal understanding and caring into classroom exercises and discussions of morality.

Questions Is it possible and appropriate for me in the next few days to introduce a classroom discussion of some aspect of morality?

Suggestions Refer to the techniques for arranging such discussions on page 76 of the text.

CHAPTER 3: AGE-LEVEL CHARACTERISTICS

PRESCHOOL AND KINDERGARTEN

Journal Entry
Active Games

Questions What games and exercises can I use to permit students to be active in reasonably controlled ways?

Suggestions Ask veteran teachers for energetic but safe game ideas.

Journal Entry
Riot-Stopping Signals and Activities

Questions What signals can I use to gain immediate attention, even when the noise and activity level are excessively high? What activities and games can I use to calm down students when they begin to get carried away?

Suggestions Pick out some piano chords to use as an "Attention!" signal, and select two or three calming activities to use.

Journal Entry
Allowing for Large-Muscle Control

Questions Are the pencils, crayons, brushes, and tools we have in the classroom large enough, or do students seem to have difficulty manipulating them?

Suggestions Make an inventory of objects that are held in the hand, and check to see if some of them seem hard for children to manipulate.

Journal Entry
How Much Control Is Necessary?

Questions Am I exerting too much control over my students? If I keep insisting on quiet play, am I doing it primarily for my own convenience? Should I stipulate that once a child gets out some blocks, finger paints, or the equivalent, she must play with these materials for at least a specified period of time? How can I help children become conscientious about cleaning up after they have engaged in activities that involve equipment?

Suggestions Keep a record of the amount of time students spend engaging in particular self-selected activities, and note what they do when they switch from one activity to another. (The chart opposite is an example.)

Suggested Form for Activities Record Sheet

Activity	Pupil	Date and Time	Termination Behavior
Easel Painting	*Mary*	*4/9/96 9:35–9:45*	*Put messy brushes on easel tray and went over to join Nancy in doll corner.*

Journal Entry Encouraging Girls to Achieve, Boys to Be Sensitive

Questions Are there books in our classroom library that depict girls or older females as weak, submissive, and lacking career choices? If so, should I dispose of them? Are there plenty of books that depict females engaging in a wide variety of careers? If girls in the class persist in playing with dolls, should I try to encourage them to engage in other activities?

Suggestions Carry out a time-sampling study (making brief observations of students at specific, predetermined times) to determine the proportion of girls and boys who engage in gender-stereotyped activities, such as girls playing with dolls. (Use the Activities Record Sheet form just outlined.)

Journal Entry Helping Students Understand Anger

Questions The last time a student became angry about something and hit someone, or the like, did I simply intervene and punish, or did I try to help the child understand the behavior? Should I use Ginott's technique of taking the child aside and asking questions intended to help him realize why the angry outburst occurred and, if possible, suggesting less destructive ways of letting off steam?

Suggestions Resolve to try Ginott's technique the next time I deal with an angry child.

Journal Entry Ways to Avoid Playing Favorites

Questions Am I reacting more positively to some students than to others and inadvertently causing jealousy and resentment? Do I respond more favorably to attractive, obedient students who show that they like me and less favorably to unattractive, troublemaking, or indifferent students? What can I do to be more positive toward students I find difficult to like? Should I make a systematic effort to spread my smiles and praise around more equitably so that all students get approximately the same number of positive reactions?

Suggestions Keep a record of the number of times I respond positively to each child in the class. If some children don't have a check mark opposite their names after one week, make sure they do by the end of the next week.

Journal Entry Handling Sharing

Questions Do all students get to participate in sharing? If not, how can I encourage shy children to gain some experience talking in front of others? Am I prepared in case someone starts to share the wrong things?

Suggestions Keep a record of sharing participation—who speaks up, what they say, how long they talk, how confident they are. A form for keeping track of which students participate and for how long appears on the next page.

Journal Entry Encouraging Competence

Questions Am I using techniques likely to lead my students to develop feelings of competence and self-confidence? How often and how successfully do I

Interact with individual students

Show interest in what children say and do

Suggested Form for Sharing Record Sheet

Name	Date	Topic	Duration	Attitude and Manner	Notes
Jane	*10/14*	*Kittens*	*30 seconds*	*Spoke so softly it was difficult to hear what she had to say. Looked at floor whole time.*	*Encourage her to talk more in small-group situations.*

Permit and encourage independence

Urge students to strive for more mature and skilled ways of doing things

Establish firm and consistent limits

Explain why restrictions are necessary

Show students that their achievements are admired and appreciated

Communicate sincere affection

Serve as a model of competence

Suggestions List these points on a sheet of paper, and try to keep a tally of the number of times I behave in the way described. Then, concentrate on one or two points, and make a deliberate effort to do a better job using that type of behavior. A form you might use for this project appears below.

Suggested Form for Analyzing Effectiveness in Encouraging Competence

Individual Interaction			
Name	Date	Time	Nature of Interaction
Jimmy	*11/16*	*2 min.*	*Noticed Jimmy was standing in middle of room sucking his thumb. Asked him if he had looked at any new books. Took him over to book corner and helped him pick out a book. Asked him to tell me about it later.*

PRIMARY GRADES

Journal Entry
Building Activity into Classwork

Questions Am I forcing students to sit still for too long? What can I do to give students legitimate reasons for moving around as they learn?

Suggestions Keep a record of the amount of "seat time" students have to put in before they are given the chance to move around.

Journal Entry
Safe but Strenuous Games

Questions Am I encouraging students to engage in safe but strenuous games during recess? When I am on playground duty, do I remain alert for reckless play? Have I found out the procedure to follow if a child is injured?

Suggestions Keep a time-sampling record of recess activities. Make sure I know my school's policy for dealing with injuries to students.

Questions Should I use sociometric techniques to become more aware of isolates? Should I try to help isolates develop skill and confidence in social situations by pairing them with popular children?

Journal Entry
Using Sociometric Techniques

Suggestions Make lists of children I think are popular and those I think are isolates. Then, ask children individually to tell me whom they like best, record their choices on a target diagram, and compare the sociometric responses to my predictions.

Questions At recess time do students engage in frequent arguments about rules? If so, what team games might be used to arouse interest but minimize quarrels? Should I ask students for their favorite games or consult books describing team games of various kinds? Should I find out what teachers of other grades do during recess to avoid duplication of recess activities?

Journal Entry
Enjoyable Team Games

Suggestions Ask the class to suggest games it would like to play.

Questions Am I alert for the possibility of feuds in the classroom? If I discover that some students seem to delight in antagonizing each other, what can I do to effect a truce? Have I thought about how to handle an honest-to-goodness fight?

Journal Entry
Handling Feuds and Fights

Suggestions Keep a record of arguments and fights. If some students get into an excessive number of altercations, try to persuade them to find other ways to let off steam. Try the conflict resolution techniques described in Chapter 13.

Questions Do I tend to use sarcasm with students who may take what I say too literally? Have I recently been excessively critical of individual students or the entire class? Have I ever ridiculed or publicly humiliated a student? If so, what can I do to prevent myself from engaging in such activities in the future?

Journal Entry
Avoiding Sarcasm and Extreme Criticism

Suggestions At the end of each day, analyze any extreme or critical statements I have made. (If I can't remember all critical remarks, make it a policy to write them down.) Ask myself if my anger was justified, and try to remember how the victim (or victims) reacted.

Questions Do I use a fair rotation scheme so that all students—not just favorites—get a chance to handle enjoyable responsibilities? Do I give students enough chances to help out? What other classroom responsibilities can I add to those already assigned?

Journal Entry
Spreading Around Responsibilities

Suggestions Ask the class to suggest ways to spread around enjoyable responsibilities, and keep a Responsibility Record to make sure every student gets a fair share of the most popular responsibilities.

Questions Have I used an effective technique recently for handling hopelessly wrong answers? If not, what should I say the next time this occurs?

Journal Entry
Ways to Handle Wrong Answers

Suggestions Ask veteran teachers how they handle wrong answers.

ELEMENTARY GRADES

Questions Do I inadvertently reinforce existing gender differences in motor skill performance by letting students always choose their own games and activities?

Journal Entry
Minimizing Gender Differences in Motor Skill Performance

Suggestions During recess, arrange games and competitions that involve both genders and different types of motor skills. Look for opportunities in class to engage both boys and girls in art and craft, singing, dancing, and instrumental playing activities.

> *Journal Entry*
> Moderating the Power of Peer Group Norms

Questions Am I ignoring the fact that peer group norms influence children to engage in behaviors that are contrary to adult norms and that may get them into trouble?

Suggestions As part of social studies lessons, discuss the pros and cons of students formulating their own rules of conduct. Look for both positive and negative examples in the daily newspaper (such as college fraternity hazing rituals that result in serious injury or death).

> *Journal Entry*
> Ways to Improve Students' Self-Concept

Questions What can I do to help students develop and maintain a strong self-concept?

Suggestions Keep in mind Erikson's observation that the primary developmental task for school-age children is to feel competent and industrious. Then, review from Chapters 9 and 10 the observation that many students lack good learning and problem-solving skills. Finally, go back to Chapter 12 and look again at the procedures for establishing mastery of objectives. Use this knowledge to help students master a variety of learning skills and subject matter.

> *Journal Entry*
> Allowing for Differences in Cognitive Style

Questions What can I do to allow for differences in cognitive style?

Suggestions Follow the suggestions made on pages 98–99.

MIDDLE SCHOOL GRADES

> *Journal Entry*
> Helping Students Adjust to the Growth Spurt

Questions Do any students seem to be upset about the timing of the growth spurt—fast-maturing girls or slow-maturing boys in particular? Is there anything I can do to help them adjust (for example, explain about the spurt, point out that things will eventually even out, urge them to engage in activities that do not depend on size or strength)?

Suggestions Pick out the three most mature and least mature girls and boys, and check to see if they seem bothered by their atypicality.

> *Journal Entry*
> Helping Early and Late Maturers Cope

Questions Have I paid any attention to the behavior of late-maturing boys and early-maturing girls?

Suggestions Make it a point to pick out the least mature boys and most mature girls in the class. Observe them to determine if they seem to exhibit the sorts of behavior reported in Table 3.5. If late-maturing boys or early-maturing girls seem bothered, try to give them opportunities to gain status and self-confidence by succeeding in schoolwork or by taking on classroom responsibilities.

> *Journal Entry*
> Ways to Promote Social Sensitivity

Questions Are there certain students who seem to lack social skills to the point that they offend others?

Suggestions Privately, and as subtly as possible, talk to such students about how what they do influences the reactions of others. Urge them to make an effort to take into account the feelings of others.

Questions Am I treating girls as if they are not capable of mastering math and science? Is there anything I can do to encourage girls to consider a career that is based on math or science?

Journal Entry
Encouraging Girls to Excel in Math and Science

Suggestions Complete a list of women who have become prominent in math or science-based careers, and emphasize the employment opportunities that exist for women who are interested in these areas.

HIGH SCHOOL

Questions Do some of the students in my classes seem extremely depressed most of the time?

Journal Entry
Helping Students Overcome Depression

Suggestions Make it a point to show such students that I care about them. Use teaching techniques to encourage them to work toward—and achieve—a series of personal, short-term goals.

CHAPTER 4: UNDERSTANDING CULTURAL DIVERSITY

Questions Am I using teaching techniques with educationally disadvantaged students that improve both basic and higher-level skills?

Journal Entry
Using Productive Teaching Techniques

Suggestions Compare my instructional practices with those on pages 146–148. Incorporate points from both of these lists into my teaching practices.

Questions Have I thought about ways to reduce the impact of factors that lead to the creation of a self-fulfilling prophecy?

Journal Entry
Ways to Minimize Subjectivity

Suggestions Consult the guidelines for reducing subjectivity mentioned under Suggestions for Teaching in Your Classroom 3a, 3b, and 3c. Try out techniques that seem promising.

Questions Do my students seem to be poorly informed about the contributions made to society by different ethnic groups?

Journal Entry
Ways to Promote Awareness of Contributions of Ethnic Minorities

Suggestions Implement the suggestions on page 149 for increasing awareness of the contributions of ethnic minorities.

Questions Are my students puzzled and dismayed by conflicts among such ethnic groups as African Americans, Korean Americans, Jewish Americans, Native Americans, and Hispanic Americans?

Journal Entry
Ways to Help Students Explore Conflicts Between Cultures

Suggestions Have students prepare and present reports on the history, values, customs, and behavior patterns of each group. Then, use this information in an all-class discussion to explain why such conflicts occur, whether they are productive, and how destructive conflicts can be avoided in the future.

CHAPTER 5: ASSESSING STUDENT VARIABILITY

Journal Entry
Using Standardized Tests

Questions Will I have to administer any standardized tests to my students during this report period?

Suggestions Find out if any tests are scheduled. A few days before any test is to be given, review Suggestions for Teaching in Your Classroom on pages 187–190. Review those suggestions once again before looking over test profiles and discussing scores with students.

Journal Entry
Explaining Test-Taking Skills

Questions Is a standardized test scheduled to be given in the near future?

Suggestions The day before the test is scheduled, explain test-taking skills to the class by covering the points noted on pages 187–188.

Journal Entry
Interpreting Test Scores

Questions Do I understand my students' test scores well enough to avoid misinterpreting and misusing them?

Suggestions Review the user's manual of the test your students took as well as a basic text on standardized testing, and compare each student's score with the work done by that student in class over a period of several weeks.

CHAPTER 6: DEALING WITH STUDENT VARIABILITY

Journal Entry
Helping Mildly Retarded Students Deal with Frustration

Questions Do I pay enough attention to the kinds of frustrations faced by students with mild retardation?

Suggestions Make it a point to observe how children with mild retardation react when instructional activities tend to call attention to differences in learning ability. If the poorest learners in the group seem disappointed or upset, try to figure out ways to help them cope with their inability to do schoolwork as easily as others.

Journal Entry
Combating the Tendency to Communicate Low Expectations

Questions Do I tend to communicate the impression that students with mild retardation are not really capable of learning?

Suggestions Examine the list of tendencies and antidotes included under point 2 on page 216. If I recognize that I tend to react in some of the ways listed as tendencies, use the antidote suggested to combat that tendency.

Journal Entry
Giving Students with Mild Retardation Simple Assignments

Questions When I assign class work, do I take into account that students with mild retardation cannot cope with complex tasks?

Suggestions Prepare some cards that outline simple tasks that can be completed quickly, and ask children with retardation to work on such assignments when more capable students are involved with more complex tasks.

Journal Entry
Giving Students with Mild Retardation Proof of Progress

Questions Have I set up lessons in such a way that students with mild retardation will know that they have made at least some progress?

Suggestions Develop a chart or personal learning diary so that students can record tangible indications of progress as they complete assignments.

Journal Entry
Helping Students with Learning Disabilities Improve Basic Learning Processes

Questions Do some of my students with learning disabilities seem to have a particularly difficult time getting to work or making adequate progress once they get started?

Suggestions Refer to the suggestions on pages 220–221 for structuring both the classroom environment and the learning tasks that I assign as a way of helping students compensate for their disability.

Questions Do any of my students with a behavior disorder keep to themselves even though classmates try to interact with them?

Suggestions Instead of lecturing or guiding a discussion, use simulations and games that require cooperation among participants.

> **Journal Entry**
> Activities and Materials that Encourage Cooperation

Questions Am I too busy to help withdrawn students become more outgoing?

Suggestions Have a high-achieving, outgoing student tutor a withdrawn student in a subject that gives the withdrawn student difficulty.

> **Journal Entry**
> Getting Students to Initiate Interaction with a Withdrawn Child

Questions Am I doing a conscientious job of planning individualized study projects for gifted and talented learners?

Suggestions The next time I ask students to work on a project, explain the contract approach, and invite gifted and talented learners (in particular) to discuss independent learning with me individually.

> **Journal Entry**
> Individual Study for the Gifted and Talented

CHAPTER 7: DEVISING AND USING OBJECTIVES

Questions Have I consulted the "Taxonomy of Educational Objectives: Cognitive Domain" when drawing up lesson plans?

Suggestions The next time I plan a unit, refer to the headings and questions listed in the abridged version of the taxonomy for the cognitive domain presented on pages 242–244. List the kinds of things I would like students to learn, and use the headings of the taxonomy to organize them. Also, check the list of categories and specific-outcome verbs in Table 7.1.

> **Journal Entry**
> Using the Taxonomy of Cognitive Objectives

Questions Am I making a systematic approach to identifying affective objectives?

Suggestions Look over the "Taxonomy of Educational Objectives: Affective Domain" (pp. 245–246), and list some of the habits and attitudes I should try to foster. Then describe specific ways I might encourage students to achieve those affective objectives. Also, check the list of categories and specific outcome verbs in Table 7.2.

> **Journal Entry**
> Using the Taxonomy of Affective Objectives

Questions Am I being systematic about teaching psychomotor skills?

Suggestions Look over the "Taxonomy of Educational Objectives: Psychomotor Domain" (pp. 246–247), and list some of the psychomotor skills I should try to foster. Also, check the list of categories and specific outcome verbs in Table 7.3.

> **Journal Entry**
> Using the Taxonomy of Psychomotor Objectives

CHAPTER 8: BEHAVIORAL AND SOCIAL LEARNING THEORIES

Questions Did I do anything today that shaped undesirable forms of student behavior?

Suggestions The next time the class is listless or uncooperative or the next time a student is rebellious, analyze what I said and did before and after I noticed the behavior to determine if I inadvertently shaped it. If it appears that I *did* cause problems for myself, resolve to avoid making the same mistake again.

> **Journal Entry**
> Checking on Causes of Behavior

> *Journal Entry*
> Ways to Supply Reinforcement

Questions Am I not using reinforcement often enough, or am I overusing certain types of reinforcement, thereby causing them to become ineffective?

Suggestions Make a list of dozens of different ways I can supply reinforcement. Then try to recall at the end of the day how often I supplied reinforcement and what type.

> *Journal Entry*
> Ways to Supply Immediate Feedback

Questions The last time I asked the class to learn factual material, did I supply specific and immediate feedback?

Suggestions The next time I plan a lesson that requires students to supply many right answers, make it a point to arrange things so that feedback is frequent, specific, and immediate.

> *Journal Entry*
> Ways to Encourage Perseverance

Questions Am I taking advantage of the Premack principle (Grandma's rule)?

Suggestions Invite students to draw up their own reward menus, and then let them reinforce themselves after they have completed tedious tasks or tough assignments.

> *Journal Entry*
> Ways to Use Behavior Modification to Maintain Control

Questions Can I do a more effective job of controlling the class if I use behavior modification techniques?

Suggestions Pick out a common type of discipline problem (for example, two students scuffling), and plan how to handle it using behavior modification techniques. Then, the next time that kind of trouble occurs, try out the planned techniques, and make any adjustments that seem necessary.

CHAPTER 9: INFORMATION-PROCESSING THEORY

> *Journal Entry*
> Techniques for Capturing Attention

Questions Do I make sure I have everyone's attention before I present a lesson? Do I use innovative ways to present something new?

Suggestions Experiment with attention-getting techniques such as those described on page 345. Spend a few moments trying to come up with a distinctive grabber when I am getting ready to present something new.

> *Journal Entry*
> Techniques for Maintaining Attention

Questions Am I able to maintain everyone's attention once I get it?

Suggestions Use a variety of teaching methods and materials—flashcards, board work, student teams, class projects, problems that require unusual forms of thinking—to keep interest and attention at high levels.

> *Journal Entry*
> Techniques for Increasing Attention Span

Questions Can my students learn to increase their attention spans?

Suggestions Experiment with games such as those described on page 345. Play two taped messages simultaneously, and ask students to listen to one while ignoring the other. Then see how well they can answer factual questions about the message they were supposed to be listening to.

> *Journal Entry*
> Ways to Use Chunking to Facilitate Learning

Questions Am I presenting hard-to-learn material in small enough chunks and in study periods of appropriate duration?

Suggestions Examine hard-to-learn material to see if it can be divided into chunks. Set up distributed study periods so that students can learn material in bite-sized chunks.

Questions Are there sets of information my students need to learn that can be grouped into related categories?

Suggestions Examine text chapters and lesson plans, and look for ways to organize material that needs to be memorized into groups so that one item leads to an association with other items.

Journal Entry
Organizing Information into Related Categories

Questions Are my students searching for meaning as they learn, or do they seem to resort to rote memorization?

Suggestions Give a brief explanation of elaborative rehearsal, and present students with a planned exercise so that they get practice elaborating on new information by relating it to what they already know. Then have students tell each other how they searched for meaningful associations, and urge them to use the same technique on their own.

Journal Entry
Ways to Stress Meaningfulness

Questions Do my students have difficulty recalling important information for discussions, oral presentations, and tests?

Suggestions Schedule a series of sessions on how to memorize. Explain how experts use memory aids, and give an example of each of the mnemonic devices listed in my journal. Whenever possible, supply mnemonics to help students learn. Ask students to develop mnemonics on their own and to share these with the rest of the class.

Journal Entry
Ways to Teach Memory Tactics

Questions Do my students have difficulty understanding the meaning of what they read or of what I present in class?

Suggestions Schedule a series of sessions on how to study. Explain the purpose and mechanics of self-questioning and notetaking (see pages 338–339). Provide opportunities for students to practice these skills on material they have been assigned to read. Give corrective feedback as needed. Also consider preparing graphic displays of ideas like the concept maps in the *Study Guide* that accompanies this text.

Journal Entry
Ways to Teach Comprehension Tactics

Questions Are my students likely to benefit from the use of learning strategies?

Suggestions Read the description of learning strategies on pages 340–342. If it seems likely that my students will be able to formulate a strategy as described or a variation of it, explain the basic procedures, and have them give it a try. After they have experimented with the strategy, ask them to discuss how it worked and how it might be improved.

Journal Entry
Ways to Teach Learning Strategies

CHAPTER 10: COGNITIVE LEARNING THEORIES AND PROBLEM SOLVING

Questions When I set up a discovery session, do I arrange the situation so that it helps students gain insight?

Suggestions The next time I plan a discovery session, think about how to present background information, or otherwise arrange things so that students are likely to grasp new relationships.

Journal Entry
Ways to Arrange for Discovery to Take Place

Journal Entry
Ways to Supervise Discussion Sessions

Questions Am I doing an effective job supervising all-class discussions?

Suggestions Make up a checklist of steps to follow in supervising discovery sessions that involve the entire class. Include such things as arrangements of desks and chairs, kinds of questions to ask, a reminder to wait at least three seconds for students to respond, phrases to use when probing for more complete or revealing answers, and a strategy for calling on students so that everyone remains alert but no one feels threatened or ignored.

Journal Entry
Techniques for Arranging Small-Group Discussions

Questions Am I doing an effective job arranging small-group discussions?

Suggestions Make up a checklist of steps to follow in setting up and supervising small-group discussions. Include ideas on how to organize the groups, how to select a moderator and recorder, what to do while the groups interact, and when to intervene.

CHAPTER 11: MOTIVATION

Journal Entry
Using Behavior Modification Techniques to Motivate

Questions Am I making use of behavior modification techniques to help students stick with material that is not intrinsically interesting?

Suggestions Consider setting up a series of tasks so that students are aware of their progress. Supply positive reinforcement in the form of verbal and written comments.

Journal Entry
Ways to Arrange Short-Term Goals

Questions Am I expecting my students to work toward remote goals?

Suggestions Try developing the equivalent of a goal card, or use some variation of contingency contracting.

Journal Entry
Ways to Satisfy Physiological Needs

Questions Am I taking into account the physiological needs of my students?

Suggestions List specific ways to make sure students' physiological needs are satisfied. For example, let students go to the bathroom as often as they (legitimately) need to. At frequent intervals ask students if the room seems too cold or warm. And consider scheduling a snack-time, or urge students to have a snack between classes.

Journal Entry
Ways to Satisfy Safety Needs

Questions Am I doing something that causes students to worry about their physical or psychological safety?

Suggestions Make up a list of safety-need do's and don'ts. For example, don't make students attempt any activity if they act apprehensive. But do make it a point to be sympathetic and supportive after students have had a bad experience.

Journal Entry
Ways to Satisfy Belonging Needs

Questions Do my students give the impression that they feel welcome, relaxed, and accepted when they enter my classroom?

Suggestions Next month, schedule some sort of activity, such as a brief personal planning session, that gives me a chance to interact individually with every student in class.

Journal Entry
Ways to Satisfy Esteem Needs

Questions Am I inadvertently putting down some of my students?

Suggestions Look for ways to play down public comparisons. Consider using cooperative learning and mastery learning arrangements. Try to individualize assignments so that all students can improve.

Questions Am I remembering the disadvantages of competitive reward structures?

Suggestions Have students keep private progress charts. Give recognition for good performance in a variety of activities. Follow the next two suggestions for encouraging students to set their own goals and finding a variety of ways to supply positive feedback.

> *Journal Entry*
> Ways to Encourage Self-Competition

Questions Am I permitting my students to participate in setting individual objectives?

Suggestions Urge students to set goals for themselves by stating objectives in terms of a time limit, a number or proportion of correct responses, or a sample of actions. (Refer to the examples on page 427.)

> *Journal Entry*
> Ways to Encourage Students to Set Their Own Objectives

Questions Am I supplying plenty of positive feedback and in the most effective ways? When I use praise, do I use techniques that Brophy suggests are likely to be effective?

Suggestions Over a period of days, keep a record of how I use praise. Then, analyze those praise responses with reference to the points raised by Brophy and the information summarized in Table 11.1.

> *Journal Entry*
> Ways to Supply Positive Feedback

Questions Am I giving my students enough chances to be active as they learn?

Suggestions Examine the examples of active learning on pages 431–432, and plan ways to use one or more of such techniques during the next few days.

> *Journal Entry*
> Ways to Make Learning Active

Questions Are there ways that I can give my students greater opportunities to investigate?

Suggestions Consider the possibility of setting up investigation centers in the room. Take the entire class to the library, and have students select books in an area of interest. Ask the class to suggest possible field trips or guest lecturers.

> *Journal Entry*
> Ways to Promote Investigation

Questions Are there ways that I can legitimately and effectively use some "show biz" techniques in my classroom?

Suggestions As I plan each new unit, think about dramatic or unexpected ways to introduce it.

> *Journal Entry*
> Ways to Make Learning Seem Adventurous

Questions Am I giving my students opportunities to engage in social interaction as they learn?

Suggestions Have students team up and study for exams or prepare reports. Consider the use of role-playing or simulation games.

> *Journal Entry*
> Ways to Make Learning Social

Questions Am I making sure that my students are aware that what they are learning is useful or potentially useful?

Suggestions Frequently point out how what is being learned can be used. Devise class exercises that demonstrate the potential value of what is being learned.

> *Journal Entry*
> Ways to Make Learning Useful

CHAPTER 12: ASSESSMENT OF CLASSROOM LEARNING

Journal Entry
Trying Mastery Learning

Questions Do some students seem to be losing motivation because of low test scores?

Suggestions Read the section on mastery learning on pages 453–458. Think about the possibility of using a mastery approach. If it will not be in conflict with school regulations, try out a mastery grading system some time during this report period.

Journal Entry
Announcing Exams and Assignments

Questions The last time I introduced a unit, did I explain what would be covered and tell students when and how they would be evaluated?

Suggestions The next time I plan a unit, make out a syllabus to be distributed the first day. Outline what will be covered, note in capital letters the days on which exams are scheduled, describe the types of items each test will contain, and explain how grades will be determined.

Journal Entry
Using a Table of Specifications

Questions Have I thought about using a table of specifications when I prepare exams?

Suggestions Look over the description of how to use a table of specifications on pages 466–467. If it appears that using such techniques will help improve exams in the subject(s) I teach, experiment with these techniques when preparing the next exam.

Journal Entry
Using Different Types of Test Items

Questions Am I using a variety of test items on my exams?

Suggestions Analyze all recent tests I have given, and prepare a record of which types of items I have used. If I have overemphasized some types and ignored others, prepare a table of specifications for the next exam to make sure that I use a variety of items.

Journal Entry
Preparing a Detailed Key

Questions The last time I corrected an exam, did I use a complete key?

Suggestions The next time I write exam questions, include a key that I can use in evaluating those questions. Then put myself in the position of a student, and check to see if the question clearly asks for the information listed in the key.

Journal Entry
Analyzing Test Items

Questions Have I analyzed the items on exams to weed out confusing or ineffective items and identify particularly good ones?

Suggestions The next time I give an exam, ask students to help me identify good and bad questions. Do the same as I grade papers. Identify or record on index cards questions that seem to be particularly effective.

CHAPTER 13: CLASSROOM MANAGEMENT

Journal Entry
Learning to Deal with Overlapping Situations

Questions Am I "with it" in terms of knowing what is going on in my classroom, or do I have a one-track mind?

Suggestions Carry out a self-analysis of how I deal with simultaneous activities. Make it a point to look around the room continually as I carry out one activity, and keep an eye out for signs of incipient problems. Practice ways to handle more than one thing at a time. List some techniques to use to prove I'm "with it: if I see two boys starting to shove each other just before I turn to write something on the board, tell them to stop as I write with my back turned. Start a sentence, insert a comment directed at the troublemaker, and go right on with the rest of the sentence.

Questions Do I flip-flop from one activity to another or unnecessarily interrupt the flow of an activity?

> ***Journal Entry***
> Learning How to Maintain Momentum

Suggestions The next time I am tempted to interrupt what we are doing to comment on some unrelated incident or activity, fight down the impulse, and keep things flowing. Also, make an effort to build momentum into class activities as I draw up plans for the day or period.

Questions Am I using techniques that tend to cause some members of the class to tune out?

> ***Journal Entry***
> Ways to Keep the Whole Class Involved

Suggestions Make up a list of ways to keep everybody involved. Call on students in unpredictable order. Ask questions first, and then call on students. Ask several students to respond in quick succession. Have all students in the class respond to questions one way or another.

Questions Have I made a conscious effort to anticipate and plan for how to handle class routines?

> ***Journal Entry***
> Planning How to Handle Routines

Suggestions Ask an experienced teacher to describe typical classroom routines in our school and explain how he handles them. Then draw up my own detailed description of how I intend to manage my classroom.

Questions What signals might I use to communicate to potential troublemakers that I am with it?

> ***Journal Entry***
> Signals to Use to Nip Trouble in the Bud

Suggestions Clear my throat. Pause a few seconds in midsentence, and stare at the misbehaving students. Move and stand near troublemakers. Direct a question at a student who is beginning to engage in disruptive behavior. Make a lighthearted remark about what is going on.

Questions What techniques can I use to help potential troublemakers control themselves?

> ***Journal Entry***
> Ways to Help Students

Suggestions Remind them of what they are supposed to be doing. Set up routines designed to minimize temptation. Send a student who seems on the verge of getting into trouble on an errand. Prepare the class by stressing the need for control when a potentially explosive activity is imminent.

Questions Am I applying Ginott's fundamental principle of communication, and am I using I-messages?

> ***Journal Entry***
> Using I-Messages

Suggestions Just after I reprimand students, jot down what I said. Then check to see if I criticized personality or character rather than the situation. If I *did* tell students they were lazy or sloppy or something similar, make a resolution to deliver an I-message the next time I face a similar situation; in short, tell the student or the class how I feel about it.

Questions Have I ever tried to figure out who "owns" a problem before dealing with it?

> ***Journal Entry***
> Speculating About Problem Ownership

Suggestions Starting tomorrow, try to classify the ownership of problems as soon as I become aware of them. If students are doing something disruptive or destructive, use an appropriate influence technique to handle it in an authoritative way. If the problem seems to be due to feelings of confusion, inadequacy, or incompetence, try active listening.

Journal Entry
Trying the No-Lose Method

Questions Am I trying to seek compromises when conflicts develop, or am I being too authoritarian?

Suggestions The next time I run into a conflict with an individual student or the entire class, try the no-lose method. That is, define the problem, ask for and propose solutions, and come to mutual agreement about a solution.

Journal Entry
Analyzing Feelings After Dealing with Troublemakers

Questions How do I feel after I really have to put down a student?

Suggestions The next time I deal harshly with a student, make it a point to examine the emotional aftereffects I experience. If I am pleased and smug, should I be? If I am upset, what might I do to avoid experiencing similar emotional tension in the future?

Journal Entry
Being Prompt, Consistent, and Reasonable in Controlling the Class

Questions Am I being prompt, consistent, and reasonable in my efforts to maintain control of the class?

Suggestions Carry out a personal survey of how prompt and consistent I am as a disciplinarian. Perhaps ask the class to tell me in anonymous statements if they think punishments are reasonable.

Journal Entry
Ways to Reestablish Rapport

Questions The last time I sharply criticized a student, did I later make a move to effect a reconciliation?

Suggestions The next time I have to deal harshly with a student, make it a point to tell or show the individual that as far as I am concerned, bygones are bygones and I am not holding a grudge. Then, try to give that student a chance to do something constructive.

Journal Entry
Experimenting with Behavior Modification

Questions Have I tried using a behavior modification approach to handle discipline problems?

Suggestions Write down and put into practice a series of steps to follow when dealing with classroom misbehavior. State rules or a description of what needs to be done to gain reinforcement. Perhaps invite students to prepare individual reward menus. Praise those who are doing what they should be doing. If negative behavior does not extinguish when it is ignored, point out unfortunate consequences that might occur if that behavior continues. At the same time, stress the desirability of completing the task and gaining reinforcement.

Resources for Further Investigation

Reflective Teaching

Among the many recently published books on reflection in teaching, you might take a look at *Interwoven Conversations: Learning and Teaching Through Critical Reflection* (1991), by Judith Newman. Written in an interesting narrative form, this book describes the author's inquiry into her own pedagogical assumptions, teaching practices, and contradictions between beliefs and practices. Another book is *Teachers and Teaching: From Classroom to Reflection* (1992), edited by Tom Russell and Hugh Munby. The four topics covered by this book are "Reflection in Teaching," "Reflection in Cases in Teaching," "Narrative in Reflection," and "Reflection in the Context of Teacher Education." Chapter 1 of *Reflective Teaching for Student Empowerment* (1993), by Dorene Ross, Elizabeth Bondy, and Diane Kyle, describes the essence of reflective teaching, explains why reflection is essential in teaching, and describes the knowledge and skills one must learn in order to teach reflectively. Judy Eby notes that her book *Reflective Planning, Teaching, and Evaluation: K–12* (1994) is intended to help beginning and practicing teachers improve their performance through a process of self-discovery. The first five chapters of *Becoming a Reflective Teacher* (1994), by Leonard Kochendorfer, are designed to help readers reflect on and challenge their concepts of schooling and teaching. The last three chapters describe a model of teacher-based action research that teachers can use to investigate the validity of their conclusions. Finally, *Reports from the Classroom: Cases for Reflection* (1995), by Sarah Huyvaert, presents thirty-two case reports, each written by a practicing classroom teacher. Each report describes a classroom incident between either the teacher and a student, the teacher and an administrator, or the teacher and another teacher. Following the incident the teacher reflects on how the incident was handled (sometimes well, but sometimes not).

Glossary

accommodation The process of creating or revising a scheme to fit a new experience. (*See* **schemes**)

achievement batteries Sets of tests designed to assess performance in a broad range of subjects.

active listening A way of dealing with a problem-owning student by showing interest and encouraging the talker to continue expressing feelings.

adaptation The process, described by Piaget, of creating a good fit or match between one's conception of reality and one's real-life experiences. (*See* **assimilation** *and* **accommodation**)

adolescent egocentrism The introspective, inward turning of a high school student's newly developed powers of thought, with a tendency to project one's self-analysis onto others. (*See* **egocentrism**)

advance organizers Introductory materials that provide an organizing structure to help students relate new information to existing knowledge schemes. (*See* **meaningful reception learning**)

affective domain taxonomy A classification of instructional outcomes that concentrates on attitudes and values.

aptitude tests Tests intended to give educators some idea of the level of knowledge and skill a student could acquire with effective instruction.

assimilation The process of fitting new experience into an existing scheme. (*See* **schemes**)

attention The selective focusing on a portion of the information currently stored in the sensory register. (*See* **sensory register**)

attribution theory A body of research into the ways that students explain their success or failure, usually in terms of ability, effort, task difficulty, and luck.

authentic assessment (*See* **performance-based assessment**)

authoritarian parents Parents who make demands and wield power without considering their children's point of view.

authoritative parents Parents who provide models of competence to be imitated, based on confidence in their own abilities.

behavior disorder (*See* **emotional disturbance**)

behavior modification The use of operant conditioning techniques to modify behavior, generally by making rewards contingent on certain actions. (Also called *contingency management. See* **operant conditioning**)

between-class ability grouping Assigning students of similar learning ability to separate classes based on scores from standardized intelligence or achievement tests.

branching program A teaching program with supplementary sets of questions that enables students to master troublesome points.

cognitive domain taxonomy A classification scheme of instructional outcomes that stresses knowledge and intellectual skills, including comprehension, application, analysis, synthesis, and evaluation. (Also called *Bloom's taxonomy*)

cognitive style A tendency or preference to respond to a variety of intellectual tasks and problems in a particular fashion.

competency test A test to determine a student's ability to handle basic subjects.

computer-assisted instruction (CAI) Teaching methods that use interactive software as an aid to learning.

conservation The recognition that certain properties stay the same despite a change in appearance or position.

constructivism The view that meaningful learning is the active creation of knowledge structures, rather than a mere transferring of objective knowledge from one person to another.

contingency contracting A behavior-strengthening technique that specifies desirable behaviors and consequent reinforcement.

cooperative learning An approach that uses small heterogeneous groups for purposes of mutual help in the mastery of specific tasks.

criterion-referenced grading A system in which grades are determined on the basis of whether each student has attained a defined standard of achievement or performance.

criterion-referenced tests Tests in which students are evaluated according to how well they have mastered specific objectives in various well-defined skill areas.

cultural pluralism A set of tenets based on three principles: 1) every culture has its own internal coherence, integrity, and logic; 2) no culture is inherently better or worse than another; and 3) all persons are to some extent culture-bound.

culture A description of the ways a group of people perceives the world; formulates beliefs; evaluates objects, ideas, and experiences; and behaves.

decentration The ability to think of more than one quality of an object or problem at a time. (*See* **perceptual centration**)

deficiency needs The first four levels (physiological, safety, belongingness or love, and self-esteem) in Maslow's hierarchy of needs, so called because these needs cause people to act only when they are unmet to some degree.

depression An emotional disorder characterized by self-deprecation, crying spells, and suicidal thoughts, afflicting between 7 to 28 percent of all adolescents.

diagnostic test A single-subject achievement test intended to identify the source of a problem in basic subjects and perhaps in study skills. (*See* **single-subject achievement test**)

direct reinforcement A situation in which an individual watches a model perform, imitates the behavior, and is reinforced by the model or some other individual.

discovery learning A teaching strategy that encourages children to seek solutions to problems either on their own or in group discussion.

discrimination A process in which individuals learn to notice the unique aspects of seemingly similar situations, and thus learn different ways of responding.

distributed practice The practice of breaking up learning tasks into small, easy-to-manage pieces that are learned over several relatively brief sessions.

early language development The phase of language learning in which children tend to stick to their own rules, despite efforts to correct them.

early-maturing boy A boy whose early physical maturation typically draws favorable adult responses and promotes confidence and poise, thus contributing to leadership and popularity with peers. (*See* **late-maturing boy**)

early-maturing girl A girl whose early physical maturation typically makes her socially out of step with her peers. (*See* **late-maturing girl**)

educational psychology The branch of psychology that specializes in understanding how different factors affect the classroom behavior of both teachers and students.

egocentrism The difficulty a young child may find in taking another person's point of view.

elaborative rehearsal A process that consciously relates new information to knowledge already stored in long-term memory. (Also called *elaborative encoding*. *See* **long-term memory**)

emotional disturbance An emotional condition in which inappropriate aggressive or withdrawal behaviors are exhibited over a long period of time and to a marked degree, adversely affecting a child's educational performance.

epigenetic principle The notion that a child's personality develops as the ego progresses through a series of interrelated stages, much as the human body takes shape during its fetal development.

equilibration The tendency to organize schemes to allow better understanding of experiences. (*See* **schemes**)

ethnic group A collection of people who identify with one another on the basis of such characteristics as ancestral origin, race, religion, language, values, political or economic interests, and behavior patterns.

evaluation The use of a rule-governed system to make judgments about the value or worth of a set of measures.

extinction The weakening of a target behavior by ignoring it.

extrinsic motivation A form of incentive based on a system of rewards not inherent in a particular activity. (*See* **intrinsic motivation**)

foreclosure status An adolescent identity status marked by the unquestioning endorsement of parents' goals and values.

formative evaluation A type of assessment that monitors a student's progress in order to faciliate learning rather than assign a grade.

frames The individual steps in a teaching program. (*See* **programmed instruction**)

full inclusion The practice of eliminating pull-out programs (those outside the classroom) and providing regular teachers with special training, so as to keep special needs students in regular classrooms. (Also called *inclusion* and *full mainstreaming*)

gender roles An awareness among young children that shows up clearly in the toys and activities that boys and girls prefer.

generalization The learned ability to respond in similar ways to similar stimuli.

general objectives Objectives that use the three taxonomies (cognitive, affective, and psychomotor) to describe types of behavior that would demonstrate a student's learning. (*See* **taxonomy**)

general transfer A situation in which prior learning aids subsequent learning due to the use of similar cognitive strategies.

gifted and talented student A student who shows unusual ability in a variety of ways and who may require services not ordinarily provided by his or her school.

grade equivalent score A measurement that interprets test performance in terms of grade levels.

group test of scholastic aptitude A test administered by a school district as part of its annual or semi-annual testing program that attempts to measure ability to cope with the intellectual demands of classroom tasks.

growth need A yearning for personal fulfillment that people constantly strive to satisfy. (*See* **self-actualization**)

growth spurt The rapid and uneven physical growth that besets adolescents during the middle school years.

high-road transfer A situation involving the conscious, controlled, somewhat effortful formulation of an "abstraction" (that is, a rule, a schema, a strategy, or an analogy) that allows a connection to be made between two tasks.

identity achievement status An adolescent identity status marked by self-chosen commitments with respect to at least some aspects of identity.

identity diffusion status An adolescent identity status marked by the avoidance of choices pertaining to jobs, roles, or values, and the readiness to change one's position in response to negative or positive feedback.

ill-structured problems Vaguely stated problems with unclear solution procedures and vague evaluation standards. (*See* **well-structured problems**)

I-message A first-person statement by a teacher that emphasizes the teacher's feelings about a situation rather than his or her feelings about the students.

individual intelligence test A test such as the Stanford-Binet or the Wechsler Intelligence Scale for Children, used to predict how students will cope with academic demands in classroom settings.

individualized education program (IEP) A written statement describing an educational program designed to meet the unique needs of a child with a particular disability.

information-processing theory An area of study that seeks to understand how people acquire, store, and recall information, and how their current knowledge guides and determines what and how they will learn.

interindividual variation The ways that individuals differ from each other at any given point in time.

interpersonal reasoning The ability to understand the relationship between motives and behavior among a group of people.

intraindividual variation The ways a given individual changes over time or acts differently in different situations.

intrinsic motivation A form of incentive inherent in a particular activity, such as the positive consequence of becoming more competent or knowledgeable. (*See* **extrinsic motivation**)

irreversibility The inability of a young child to mentally reverse physical or mental processes, such as pouring water from a tall, thin glass back into a short, squat one.

issues Ill-structured problems that arouse strong feelings. (*See* **ill-structured problems**)

Joplin Plan An ability grouping technique that combines students of different grade levels according to their standardized test scores. (*See* **regrouping**)

late-maturing boy A boy whose delayed physical maturation typically causes inferiority feelings and leads to bossy and attention-getting behavior. (*See* **early-maturing boy**)

late-maturing girl A girl whose delayed physical maturation typically makes her more poised than others her age and elicits praise from elders, thus conferring leadership tendencies. (*See* **early-maturing girl**)

learning disability Problems in otherwise mentally fit students who are unable to respond to certain aspects of the curriculum presented in regular classrooms because of disorders in one or more basic psychological processes.

learning strategy A general plan that a learner formulates for achieving a somewhat distant academic goal.

learning tactic A specific technique that a learner uses to accomplish an immediate learning objective.

least restrictive environment A requirement under the 1994 Code of Federal Regulations that disabled children be provided with education in the least restrictive setting possible, usually by including them in regular classrooms. (*See* **mainstreaming**)

linear program A teaching program whose sequence of steps is formulated to ensure that every response will be correct, as there is only one path to the terminal behavior.

long-term memory (LTM) Storehouse of permanently recorded information in an individual's memory.

low-road transfer A situation in which a previously learned skill or idea is almost automatically retrieved from memory and applied to a highly similar current task. (*See* **high-road transfer**)

mainstreaming The policy of placing students with disabilities in regular classes.

maintenance rehearsal A rather mechanical process that uses mental and verbal repetition to hold information in short-term memory for some immediate purpose. Also called *rote rehearsal* or *repetition*. (*See* **short-term memory**)

massed practice An approach to learning that emphasizes a few long, infrequently spaced study periods.

mastery learning An approach that assumes most students can master the curriculum if certain conditions are established: (a) sufficient aptitude, (b) sufficient ability to understand instruction, (c) a willingness to persevere, (d) sufficient time, and (e) good-quality instruction.

meaningful reception learning The integration of new ideas into existing knowledge schemes by way of drawing relationships between otherwise disconnected facts and existing knowledge schemes.

measurement The assignment of numbers to certain attributes of objects, events, or people according to a rule-governed system.

melting pot A term referring to the assimilation of diverse ethnic groups into one national mainstream.

mental retardation A condition in which learning proceeds at a significantly slow rate, is limited to concrete experiences, and is accompanied by difficulty functioning in social environments.

metacognition Knowledge about the operations of cognition and how to use them to achieve a learning goal.

mnemonic device A memory-directed tactic that helps a learner transform or organize information to enhance its retrievability.

morality of constraint Piaget's term for the moral thinking of children up to age ten or so, in which they hold sacred rules that permit no exceptions and make no allowance for intentions. (Also called *moral realism*)

morality of cooperation Piaget's term for the moral thinking of children eleven or older, based on flexible rules and considerations of intent. (Also called *moral relativism*)

moratorium status An adolescent identity status marked by various kinds of identity crises, often involving experimentation and restless searching.

multicultural education An approach to learning and teaching that seeks to foster an understanding of and mutual respect for the values, beliefs, and practices of different cultural groups.

multidisciplinary assessment team A group of people involved in determining the nature of a child's disability, typically consisting of a school psychologist, guidance counselor, classroom teacher, school social worker, school nurse, learning disability specialist, physician, and psychiatrist.

negative identity Defiant or destructive behavior engaged in by a young person who is unable to overcome role confusion, often expressed as hostility towards roles offered as desirable by one's family or community.

negative reinforcement A way of strengthening a target behavior by removing an aversive stimulus after a particular behavior is exhibited. (*See* **positive reinforcement**)

negative transfer A situation in which one's prior learning interferes with subsequent learning. (*See* **positive transfer**)

no-lose method A conflict-resolving procedure that involves discussing problems and coming up with a mutually agreeable compromise.

normal curve The bell-shaped distribution of scores that tends to occur when a particular characteristic is measured in thousands of people.

norm group A sample of individuals carefully chosen to reflect the larger population of students for whom a test is intended.

norm-referenced grading A system of grading that assumes classroom achievement will vary among a group of heterogeneous students because of such differences as prior knowledge, learning skills, motivation, and aptitude, and so compares the score of each student to the scores of other students in order to determine grades.

norm-referenced test A test in which individual performance is evaluated with reference to the performance of a norm group.

observational learning A form of learning that de-emphasizes the role of reinforcement by attributing initial changes in behavior to the observation and imitation of a model. (*See* **social learning theory**)

operant conditioning The theory of behavior developed by B. F. Skinner, based on the fact that organisms respond to their environments in particular ways to obtain or avoid particular consequences.

organization The tendency to systematize and combine processes into coherent general systems.

outcome-based education (OBE) An approach to generating instructional objectives that are not based on a set curriculum, and in which the desired outcome drives the curriculum rather than the other way around.

peer tutoring An approach to learning that involves the teaching of one student by another, based on evidence that a child's cognitive growth benefits from exposure to alternative cognitive schemes.

percentile rank A score that indicates the percentage of students who are at or below a given student's achievement level, providing specific information about relative position.

perceptual centration The tendency to focus attention on only one characteristic of an object or aspect of a problem or event at a time.

performance tests An assessment system that attempts to gauge how well students can use basic knowledge and skill to perform complex tasks or solve problems under more or less realistic conditions. (Also called *performance-based assessment* and *authentic assessment*)

permissive parents Parents who make few demands on their children and fail to discourage immature behavior, thus reflecting their own tendency to be disorganized, inconsistent, and lacking in confidence.

play behavior Kinds of free play observed in preschool children and described by Parten as consisting of six types: unoccupied, solitary, onlooker, parallel, associative, and cooperative.

positive reinforcement A way of strengthening a target behavior (increasing and maintaining the probability that a particular behavior will be repeated) by supplying a positive stimulus immediately after a desired response. (*See* **negative reinforcement**)

positive transfer A situation in which prior learning aids subsequent learning, when for example a new learning task calls for essentially the same response that was made to a similar, earlier-learned task. (*See* **negative transfer**)

Premack principle A shaping technique that allows students to indulge in a favorite activity after completing a set of instructional objectives. (Also called *Grandma's rule*. *See* **shaping**)

problem representation/framing The process of finding ways to express a problem so as to recall the optimal amount of solution-relevant information from long-term memory. (*See* **long-term memory**)

problem solving The identification and application of knowledge and skills that result in goal attainment.

programmed instruction A method of instruction developed by B. F. Skinner that presents specially designed written material to students in a predetermined sequence.

psychological androgyny An acquired sense of gender that combines traditional masculine and feminine traits.

psychomotor domain taxonomy A classification of instructional outcomes that focuses on physical abilities and skills.

psychosocial moratorium A period of identity development marked by a delay of commitment, ideally a time of adventure and exploration having a positive, or at least neutral, impact on the individual and society.

punishment A method of weakening a target behavior by presenting an aversive stimulus after the behavior occurs.

recognition A cognitive process that involves noting key features of a stimulus and relating them to previously stored information in an interactive manner.

reflective teaching A way of teaching that blends artistic and scientific elements through thoughtful analysis of classroom activity.

regrouping A form of ability grouping that brings together students of the same age, ability, and grade but from different classrooms, for instruction in a specific subject, usually reading or mathematics.

reliability Consistency in test results, related to the assumption that human characteristics are relatively stable over short periods of time.

response cost The withdrawal of previously earned positive reinforcers as a consequence of undesirable behavior, often used with a token economy. (*See* **token economy**)

ripple effect The extent to which an entire class responds to a reprimand directed at only one student.

role confusion Uncertainty as to what behaviors will elicit a favorable reaction from others.

schema An abstract information structure by which our store of knowledge is organized in long-term memory. (*See* **long-term memory**)

scheme An organized pattern of behavior or thought that children formulate as they interact with their environment, parents, teachers, and agemates.

self-actualization The movement towards full development of a person's potential talents and capabilites.

self-concept A self-description of one's physical, social, emotional, and cognitive attributes. (*See* **self-image** and **self-esteem**)

self-efficacy The degree to which people believe they are capable or prepared to handle particular tasks.

self-esteem The evaluative judgments made about self-attributed qualities. (*See* **self-image** and **self-concept**)

self-fulfilling prophecy The tendency of students to achieve the levels expected of them by their teachers. (Also called the *Pygmalion effect*)

self-image A mental self-portrait composed of self-concept and self-esteem elements. (*See* **self-concept** and **self-esteem**)

self-reinforcement A situation in which the individual strives to meet personal standards and does not depend on or care about the reactions of others.

sensory register (**SR**) The primary memory store that records temporarily (for one to three seconds) an incoming flow of data from the sense receptors.

serial position effect The tendency to learn and remember words at the beginning and end of a list more easily than those in the middle.

sexually transmitted diseases (**STDs**) Contagious diseases, such as HIV/AIDS, gonorrea, and herpes, that are spread by sexual contact.

shaping Learning complex behaviors by reinforcing successive approximations to the terminal behavior.

short-term memory (**STM**) The second temporary memory store, which holds about seven bits of information for about twenty seconds. (Also called *working memory*)

single-subject achievement test A test designed to assess learning or achievement in a particular basic school subject, such as reading or math.

social class An individual's or a family's relative standing in society, determined by such factors as income, occupation, education, place of residence, types of associations, manner of dress, and material possessions.

social learning theory A theory, exemplified in the work of Albert Bandura, that deemphasizes the role of reinforcement in learning by attributing initial changes in behavior to the observation and imitation of a model. (Also called *observational learning*)

socioeconomic status (**SES**) A quantifiable level of social standing, determined by the federal government on the basis of a person's income, occupation, and education. (*See* **social class**)

special-purpose achievement test A test to determine specific qualifications, such as the College-Level Examination Program or the National Teacher Examination.

specific objectives Objectives that specify the behavior to be learned, the conditions under which it will be exhibited, and the criterion for acceptable performance.

specific transfer A situation in which prior learning aids subsequent learning because of specific similarities between two tasks.

spontaneous recovery The reappearance of a seemingly extinguished behavior. (*See* **extinction**)

standard deviation A statistic that indicates the degree to which scores in a group of tests differ from the average or mean.

standardized tests Assessment tools designed by people with specialized knowledge and applied to all students under the same conditions.

stanine score A statistic reflecting a division of a score distribution into nine groups, with each stanine being one-half of a standard deviation unit.

structure The fundamental ideas of a particular subject or field of study, and how they relate to one another.

summative evaluation Testing done for the purpose of assigning a letter or numerical grade to sum up a student's performance at a variety of tasks over time.

table of specifications A table used in exam preparation that notes types and numbers of included test items, ensuring systematic coverage of the subject matter.

taxonomy A classification scheme with categories arranged in hierarchical order.

teaching as an art A way of teaching that involves intangibles such as emotions, values, and flexibility.

teaching as a science A way of teaching based on scientific methods such as sampling, control, objectivity, publication, and replication.

test score pollution Test-related practices that cause scores to fluctuate but which are unrelated to what the test measures.

theory of identical elements The theory that a similarity between the stimulus and response elements in two different tasks accounts for transfer of learning from one task to the other. (*See* **transfer of learning**)

time-out A procedure that weakens a target behavior by temporarily removing the opportunity for the behavior to be rewarded.

token economy A behavior strengthening technique that uses items of no inherent value to "purchase" other items perceived to be valuable.

transfer of learning A student's ability to apply knowledge and problem-solving skills learned in school to similar but new situations.

T score A standardized test score that ranges from 0 to 100 and uses a preselected mean of 50 to avoid negative values. (*See* **z score**)

validity The extent to which a test measures what it claims to measure.

vicarious reinforcement A situation in which the observer anticipates receiving a reward for behaving in a given way because someone else has been so rewarded.

well-structured problems Clearly formulated problems with known solution procedures and known evaluation standards. (*See* **ill-structured problems**)

within-class ability grouping A form of ability grouping that involves the division of a single class of students into two or three groups for reading and math instruction.

withitness An attribute of teachers who prove to their students that they know what is going on in a classroom and as a result have fewer discipline problems than teachers who lack this characteristic.

zero transfer A situation in which prior learning has no effect on new learning.

zone of proximal development (ZPD) Vygotsky's term for the difference between what a child can do on his or her own versus what can be accomplished with some assistance.

z score A standardized test score that tells how far a given raw score differs from the mean in standard deviation units. (*See* **T score**)

References

Achenbach, T. M., & Edelbrock, C. S. (1983). *Manual for the child behavior checklist and revised child behavior profile*. Burlington, VT: University of Vermont.

Adelson, J. (1972). The political imagination of the young adolescent. In J. Kagan & R. Coles (Eds.), *Twelve to sixteen: Early adolescence*. New York: Norton.

Adelson, J. (Ed.). (1980). *Handbook of adolescent psychology*. New York: Wiley.

Adelson, J. (1986). *Inventing adolescence: The political psychology of everyday schooling*. New Brunswick, NJ: Transaction Books.

Ainsworth, M. D. S., & Wittig, B. A. (1972). Attachment and exploratory behavior of one-year-olds in a strange situation. In B. M. Foss (Ed.), *Determinants of infant behavior* (Vol. 4). New York: Wiley.

Airasian, P. W. (1994). *Classroom assessment* (2d ed.). New York: McGraw-Hill.

Allen, H. A., Splittgerber, F. L., & Manning, M. L. (1993). *Teaching and learning in the middle school*. New York: Merrill.

Almy, M.C., Chittenden, E., & Miller, P. (1996). *Young children's thinking*. New York: Teachers College Press.

Ambert, A. N. (Ed.). (1991). *Bilingual education and English as a second language: A research handbook, 1988–1990*. New York: Garland.

Ames, C., & Ames, R. (1984). Systems of student and teacher motivation: Toward a qualitative definition. *Journal of Educational Psychology, 76*(4), 535–556.

Ames, N. L., & Miller, E. (1994). *Changing middle schools: How to make schools work for young adolescents*. San Francisco: Jossey-Bass.

Amiram, R., Bar-Tal, D., Alona, R., & Peleg, D. (1990). Perception of epistemic authorities by children and adolescents. *Journal of Youth and Adolescence, 19*(5), 495–510.

Anastasi, A. (1988). *Psychological testing* (6th ed.). New York: Macmillan.

Anderman, E. M., & Maehr, M. L. (1994). Motivations and schooling in the middle grades. *Review of Educational Research, 64*(2), 287–309.

Anderson, J. B., & Freiberg, H. J. (1995). Using self-assessment as a reflective tool to enhance the student teaching experience. *Teacher Education Quarterly, 22*(1), 77–91.

Anderson, R. C. (1984). Some reflections on the acquisition of knowledge. *Educational Researcher, 13*(9), 5–10.

André, M. E. D. A., & Anderson, T. H. (1978/1979). The development and evaluation of a self-questioning study technique. *Reading Research Quarterly, 14*(4), 605–623.

Andre, T., & Phye, G.D. (1986). Cognition, Learning, and Education. In G.D. Phye & T. Andre (Eds.), *Cognitive classroom learning*. Orlando, FL: Academic Press.

Appleton, N. (1983). *Cultural pluralism in education*. New York: Longman.

Archer, S. L. (1982). The lower age boundaries of identity development. *Child Development, 53*(6) 1551–1556.

Archer, S. L. (1991). Identity development, gender differences in. In R. M. Lerner, A. C. Peterson, & J. Brooks-Gunn (Eds.), *Encyclopedia of adolescence.* New York: Garland.

Arias, M. B., & Casanova, U. (Eds.). (1993). *Bilingual education: Politics, practice, and research.* Chicago: National Society for the Study of Education.

Armstrong, T. (1994). *Multiple intelligences in the Classroom.* Alexandria, VA: Association for Supervision and Curriculum Development.

Atkinson, J. W. (1964). *An introduction to motivation.* Princeton, NJ: Van Nostrand.

Atkinson, R. C. (1975). Mnemotechnics in second language learning. *American Psychologist, 30*(2), 821–828.

Atkinson, R. C., & Raugh, M. R. (1975). An application of the mnemonic keyword method to the acquisition of a Russian vocabulary. *Journal of Experimental Psychology: Human Learning and Memory, 104*(2), 126–133.

Atkinson, R. C., & Shiffrin, R. M. (1968). Human memory: A proposed system and its control processes. In K. W. Spence & J. T. Spence (Eds.), *The psychology of learning and motivation* (Vol. 2). New York: Academic Press.

Ausubel, D. P. (1963). *The psychology of meaningful verbal learning.* New York: Grune & Stratton.

Ausubel, D. P., Novak, J. D., & Hanesian, H. (1978). *Educational psychology: A cognitive view* (2d ed.). New York: Holt, Rinehart & Winston.

Ausubel, D. P., & Robinson, F. G. (1969). *School learning: An introduction to educational psychology.* New York: Holt, Rinehart & Winston.

Baddeley, A. (1990). *Human memory: Theory and practice.* Boston: Allyn & Bacon.

Baines, L., Baines, C., & Masterson, C. (1994). Mainstreaming: One school's reality. *Phi Delta Kappan, 76*(1), 39–40, 57–64.

Baker, E. T., Wang, M. C., & Walberg, H. J. (1994/1995). The effects of inclusion on learning. *Educational Leadership, 52*(4), 33–35.

Baker, K. (1985). Research evidence of a school discipline problem. *Phi Delta Kappan, 66*(7), 482–487.

Baldwin, A. Y. (1991). Ethnic and cultural issues. In N. Colangelo & G. A. Davis (Eds.), *Handbook of gifted education.* Boston: Allyn & Bacon.

Balk, D. E. (1995). *Adolescent Development.* Pacific Grove, CA: Brooks/Cole.

Bandura, A. (1982). Self-efficacy mechanism in human agency. *American Psychologist, 37*(2), 122–147.

Bandura, A. (1986). *Social foundations of thought and action: A social cognitive theory.* Englewood Cliffs, NJ: Prentice-Hall.

Bandura, A. (1989). Human agency in social cognitive theory. *American Psychologist, 44*(9), 1175–1184.

Bandura, A. (1993). Perceived self-efficacy in cognitive development and functioning. *Educational Psychologist, 28*(2), 117–148.

Bandura, A., Ross, D., & Ross, S. (1961). Transmission of aggression through imitation of aggressive models. *Journal of Abnormal and Social Psychology, 63*(3), 375–382.

Bandura, A., Ross, D., & Ross, S. (1963a). Imitation of film mediated aggressive models. *Journal of Abnormal and Social Psychology, 66*(1), 3–11.

Bandura, A., Ross, D., & Ross, S. (1963b). A comparative test of the status envy, social power, and secondary reinforcement theories of identificatory learning. *Journal of Abnormal and Social Psychology, 67*(6), 527–534.

Bangert-Drowns, R. L., Kulik, J. A., & Kulik, C.-L. (1985). Effectiveness of computer-based education in secondary schools. *Journal of Computer-Based Instruction, 12*(3), 59–68.

Bangert-Drowns, R. L., Kulik, J. A., & Kulik, C.-L. (1991). Effects of frequent classroom testing. *Journal of Educational Research, 85*(2), 89–99.

Banks, J. A. (1991). *Teaching strategies for ethnic studies* (5th ed.). Boston: Allyn & Bacon.

Banks, J. A. (1993). The canon debate, knowledge construction, and multicultural education. *Educational Researcher, 22*(5), 4–14.

Banks, J. A. (1994a). *An introduction to multicultural education.* Boston: Allyn & Bacon.

Banks, J. A. (1994b). *Multiethnic education: Theory and practice* (3d ed.). Boston: Allyn & Bacon.

Banks, J. A. (1994c). Transforming the mainstream curriculum. *Educational Leadership, 51*(8), 4–8.

Bartlett, F. C. (1932). *Remembering.* London: Cambridge University Press.

Baumrind, D. (1971). Current patterns of parental authority. *Developmental Psychology Monographs, 4*(1, Pt. 2), 1–103.

Baumrind, D. (1991). Parenting styles and adolescent development. In R. M. Lerner, A. C. Peterson, & J. Brooks-Gunn (Eds.), *Encyclopedia of adolescence.* New York: Garland.

Beane, J. A. (1994). Cluttered terrain: The schools' interest in the self. In T. M. Brinthaupt & R. P. Lipka (Eds.), *Changing the self: Philosophies, techniques, and experiences.* Albany: State University of New York Press.

Beane, J. A., & Lipka, R. P. (1986). *Self-concept, self-esteem, and the curriculum.* New York: Teachers College Press.

Beane, J. A., & Lipka, R. P. (1987). *When the kids come first.* Columbus, OH: National Middle Schools Association.

Beck, A. T. (1972). *Depression: Causes and treatment.* Philadelphia: University of Pennsylvania Press.

Becker, W. C., Englemann, S., & Thomas, D. R. (1971). *Teaching: A course in applied psychology.* Chicago: Science Research Associates.

Bednar, A. K., Cunningham, D., Duffy, T. M., & Perry, J. D. (1991). Theory into practice: How do we link? In G. J. Anglin (Ed.), *Instructional technology: Past, present, and future.* Englewood, CO: Libraries Unlimited.

Bee, H. (Ed.). (1978). *Social issues in developmental psychology* (2d ed.). New York: Harper & Row.

Beilin, H., & Pufall, P. B. (Eds.). (1992). *Piaget's theory: Prospects and possibilities.* Hillsdale, NJ: Lawrence Erlbaum.

Beirne-Smith, M. (1991). Peer tuturing in arithmetic for children with learning disabilities. *Exceptional children, 57*(4), 330–337.

Beirne-Smith, M., Patton, J. R., & Ittenbach, R. (1994). *Mental retardation* (4th ed.). New York: Merrill.

Bellezza, F. S. (1981). Mnemonic devices: Classification, characteristics, and criteria. *Review of Educational Research, 51*(2), 247–275.

Bem, S. L. (1975). Sex-role adaptability: One consequence of psychological androgyny. *Journal of Personality and Social Psychology, 31*(4), 634–643.

Bem, S. L. (1976). Sex-typing and androgyny: Further explorations of the expressive domain. *Journal of Personality and Social Psychology, 34*(5), 1016–1023.

Benbow, C. P. (1991). Mathematically talented children: Can acceleration meet their educational needs? In N. Colangelo & G. A. Davis (Eds.), *Handbook of gifted education.* Boston: Allyn & Bacon.

Bender, W. N. (1995). *Learning disabilities: Characteristics, identification, and teaching strategies* (2d ed.). Boston: Allyn & Bacon.

Bennett, C. I. (1995). *Comprehensive multicultural education: Theory and practice* (3d ed.). Boston: Allyn & Bacon.

Bergen, D. J., & Williams, J. E. (1991). Sex stereotypes in the United States revisited: 1972–1988. *Sex Roles, 24*(7/8) 413–423.

Berger, S. L. (Ed.). (1992). *Programs and practices in gifted education.* Reston, VA: Council for Exceptional Children.

Berko, J. (1958). The child's learning of English morphology. *Word, 14*(1–2), 150–177.

Berliner, D. C. (1986). In pursuit of the expert pedagogue. *Educational Researcher, 15*(7), 5–13.

Berliner, D. C. (1992). Telling the stories of educational psychology. *Educational Psychologist,* 27 (2), 143–161.

Best, R. (1983). *We've all got scars.* Bloomington, IN: Indiana University Press.

Beyer, B. K. (1991a). *Teaching thinking skills: A handbook for elementary school teachers.* Boston: Allyn & Bacon.

Beyer, B. K. (1991b). *Teaching thinking skills: A handbook for secondary school teachers.* Boston: Allyn & Bacon.

Bilsker, D., & Marcia, J. E. (1991). Adaptive regression and ego identity. *Journal of Adolescence, 14*(1), 75–84.

Bjork, R. A. (1979). Information processing analysis of college teaching. *Educational Psychologist, 14,* 15–23.

Blais, D. M. (1988). Constructivism: A theoretical revolution in teaching. *Journal of Developmental Education, 11*(3), 2–7.

Blatt, M., & Kohlberg, L. (1978). The effects of classroom moral discussion upon children's level of moral development. In L. Kohlberg & E. Turcel (Eds.), *Recent research in moral development.* New York: Holt, Rinehart & Winston.

Block, Ja. H. (1971). Operating procedures for mastery learning. In J. H. Block (Ed.), *Mastery learning: Theory and practice.* New York: Holt, Rinehart & Winston.

Block, Ja. H., Efthim, H. E., & Burns, R. B. (1989). *Building effective mastery learning schools.* New York: Longman.

Block, Je. H. (1973). Conceptions of sex role: Some cross-cultural and longitudinal perspectives. *American Psychologist, 28*(6), 512–529.

Block, Je. H. (1976). Issues, problems and pitfalls in assessing sex differences. *Merrill-Palmer Quarterly, 22*(4), 283–308.

Bloom, B. S. (1968). Learning for mastery. *Evaluation Comment, 1*(2), 1–12.

Bloom, B. S. (1976). *Human characteristics and school learning.* New York: McGraw-Hill.

Bloom, B. S. (1981). *All our children learning.* New York: McGraw-Hill.

Bloom, B. S. (1984). The two sigma problem: The search for methods of group instruction as effective as one-to-one tutoring. *Educational Researcher, 13*(6), 4–16.

Bloom, B. S., Englehart, M. B., Furst, E. J., Hill, W. H., & Krathwohl, D. R. (Eds.). (1956). *Taxonomy of educational objectives: The classification of educational goals. Handbook I: Cognitive domain.* New York: McKay.

Blumenthal, S. J., & Kupfer, D. J. (1988). Overview of early detection and treatment strategies for suicidal behavior in young people. *Journal of Youth and Adolescence, 17*(1), 1–22.

Blustein, D. L., & Palladino, D. E. (1991). Self and identity in late adolescence: A theoretical and empirical investigation. *Journal of Adolescent Research, 6*(4), 437–453.

Blythe, T., & Gardner, H. (1990). A school for all intelligences. *Educational Leadership, 47*(7), 33–37.

Bolin, F. S. (1990). Helping student teachers think about teaching: Another look at Lou. *Journal of Teacher Education, 41*(1), 10–19.

Bond, C. L., Miller, M. J., & Kennon, R. W. (1987). Study skills: Who is taking the responsibility for teaching? *Performance & Instruction, 26*(7), 27–29.

Borker, S. R. (1987). Sex roles and labor force participation. In D. B. Carter (Ed.), *Current conceptions of sex roles and sex typing.* New York: Praeger.

Bower, G. H., Clark, M. C., Lesgold, A. M., & Winzenz, D. (1969). Hierarchical retrieval schemes in recall of categorized word lists. *Journal of Verbal Learning and Verbal Behavior, 8*(3), 323–343.

Bowman, B. T. (1989). Educating language-minority children: Challenges and opportunities. *Phi Delta Kappan, 71*(2), 118–120.

Boyer, C. B., & Hein, K. (1991). Sexually transmitted diseases in adolescence. In R. M. Lerner, A. C. Peterson, & J. Brooks-Gunn (Eds.), *Encyclopedia of adolescence.* New York: Garland.

Boyer, E. L. (1983). *High school.* New York: Harper & Row.

Bracey, G. W. (1983). On the compelling need to go beyond minimum competency. *Phi Delta Kappan, 64*(10), 717–721.

Bragstad, B. J., & Stumpf, S. M. (1987). *A guidebook for teaching study skills and motivation* (2d ed.). Boston: Allyn & Bacon.

Brandt, R. S. (Ed.). (1991). *Cooperative learning and the collaborative school.* Alexandria, VA: Association for Supervision and Curriculum Development.

Brandt, R. S. (1944). On educating for diversity: A conversation with James A. Banks. *Educational Leadership, 51* (8), 28–31.

Bransford, J. D., & Stein, B. S. (1993). *The ideal problem solver* (2d ed.). New York: W. H. Freeman.

Bransford, J. D., Sherwood, R., Vye, N., & Rieser, J. (1986). Teaching thinking and problem solving: Research foundations. *American Psychologist, 41*(10), 1078–1089.

Brantlinger, E. A., & Guskin, S. L. (1985). Implications of social and cultural differences for special education with specific recommendations. *Focus on Exceptional Children, 18*(1), 1–12.

Braun, C. (1976). Teacher expectations: Sociopsychological dynamics. *Review of Educational Research, 46*(2), 185–213.

Bredderman, T. (1982). Activity science—the evidence shows it matters. *Science and Children, 20*(1), 39–41.

Brittain, C. V. (1967). An exploration of the bases of peer compliance and parent-compliance in adolescence. *Adolescence, 2*(8), 445–458.

Brody, N. (1992). *Intelligence* (2d ed.). San Diego, CA: Academic Press.

Brooks, J. G. (1990). Teachers and students: Constructivists forging new connections. *Educational Leadership, 47*(5), 68–71.

Brooks-Gunn, J., & Furstenberg, F. F., Jr. (1989). Adolescent sexual behavior. *American Psychologist, 44*(2), 249–257.

Brophy, J. E. (1979). Teacher behavior and its effects. *Journal of Educational Psychology, 71*(6), 733–750.

Brophy, J. E. (1981). Teacher praise: A functional analysis. *Review of Educational Research, 51*(1), 5–32.

Brophy, J. E. (1983). Research on the self-fulfilling prophecy and teacher expectations. *Journal of Educational Psychology, 75*(5), 631–661.

Brophy, J. E., & Alleman, J. (1991). Activities as instructional tools: A framework for analysis and evaluation. *Educational Researcher, 20*(4), 9–23.

Brophy, J. E., & Evertson, C. M. (1976). *Learning from teaching.* Boston: Allyn & Bacon.

Broverman, I. K., Vogel, S. R., Broverman, D. M., Clarkson, F. E., & Rosenkrantz, P. S. (1972). Sex–role stereotypes: A current appraisal. *Journal of Social Issues, 29*(2), 59–78.

Brown, A. L., Campione, J. C., & Day, J. D. (1981). Learning to learn: On training students to learn from text. *Educational Researcher, 10*(2), 1424.

Brown, C. A. (1982). Sex typing in occupational preferences of high school boys and girls. In I. Gross, J. Downing, & A. d'Heurle (Eds.), *Sex role attitudes and cultural change.* Dordrecht, Holland: D. Reidel Publishing Company.

Brown, R. (1973). *A first language: The early stages.* Cambridge, MA: Harvard University Press.

Bruner, J. S. (1951). Personality dynamics and the process of perceiving. In R. R. Blake & G. V. Ramsey (Eds.), *Perception: An approach to personality.* New York: Ronald Press.

Bruner, J. S. (1960). *The process of education.* New York: Vintage Books.

Bruner, J. S. (1966). *Toward a theory of instruction.* New York: Norton.

Bruner, J. S. (1971). *The relevance of education.* New York: Norton.

Bruner, J. S. (1983). *In search of mind: Essays in autobiography.* New York: Harper & Row.

Bruner, J. S., Goodnow, J. J., & Austin, G. A. (1956). *A study of thinking.* New York: Wiley.

Bryant, P. E. (1984). Piaget, teachers, and psychologists. *Oxford Review of Education, 10*(3), 251–259.

Burch, C. B. (1993). Teachers vs. professors: The university's side. *Educational Leadership, 51*(2), 68–76.

Burden, P. R. (1995). *Classroom management and discipline.* New York: Longman.

Bureau of the Census. (1975). *Historical statistics of the United States, colonial times to 1970.* Washington, DC: Department of Commerce.

Bureau of the Census. (1993a). *Statistical abstract of the United States, 1993:*

The national data book. Washington, DC: Department of Commerce.

Bureau of the Census. (1993b). *1990 census of population: Social and economic characteristics*. Washington, DC: Department of Commerce.

Bybee, R.W. & Sund, R.B. (1982). *Piaget for educators* (2d ed.). Columbus, OH: Merrill.

Byrd, D. E. (1990). Peer tutoring with the learning disabled: A critical review. *Journal of Educational Research, 84(*2), 115–118.

Cain, K. M., & Dweck, C. S. (1995). The relation between motivational patterns and achievement cognitions through the elementary school years. *Merrill-Palmer Quarterly, 41*(1), 25–52.

Cameron, J., & Pierce, W. D. (1994). Reinforcement, reward, and intrinsic motivation: A meta-analysis. *Review of Educational Research, 64*(3), 363–423.

Canady, R. L., & Hotchkiss, P. R. (1989). It's a good score! Just a bad grade. *Phi Delta Kappan, 71*(1), 68–71.

Cangeolsi, J. S. (1988). *Classroom management strategies: Gaining and maintaining students' cooperation*. New York: Longman.

Canter, L. (1989). Assertive discipline—more than names on the board and marbles in a jar. *Phi Delta Kappan, 71*(1), 57–61.

Carney, R. N., Levin, J. R., & Levin, M. E. (1994). Enhancing the psychology of memory by enhancing memory of psychology. *Teaching of Psychology, 21*(3), 171–174.

Carrasquillo, A. L. (1991). *Hispanic children and youth in the United States: A resource guide*. New York: Garland.

Carrasquillo, A. L. (1994). *Teaching English as a second language: A resource guide*. New York: Garland.

Carroll, J. B. (1963). A model of school learning. *Teachers College Record, 64*, 723–733.

Carroll, J. B. (1971). Problems of measurement related to the concept of learning for mastery. In J. H. Block (Ed.), *Mastery learning: Theory and practice*. New York: Holt, Rinehart & Winston.

Carter, D. B. (1987). The role of peers in sex role socialization. In D. B. Carter (Ed.), *Current conceptions of sex roles and sex typing*. New York: Praeger.

Case, R. (1975). Gearing the demands of instruction to the developmental capacities of the learner. *Review of Educational Research, 45*(1), 59–88.

Cassidy, J., & Johnson, N. (1986). Federal and state definitions of giftedness: Then and now. *Gifted Child Today, 9*(6), 15–21.

Chaillé, C., & Britain, L. (1991). *The young child as scientist: A constructivist approach to early childhood science education*. New York: HarperCollins.

Chance, P. (1992). The rewards of learning. *Phi Delta Kappan, 74*(3), 200–207.

Chance, P. (1993). Sticking up for rewards. *Phi Delta Kappan, 74*(10), 787–790.

Charles, C. M. (1972). *Educational psychology: The instructional endeavor*. St. Louis, MO: Mosby.

Chinn, P.C., & Plata, M. (1987/1988). Multicultural education: Beyond ethnic studies. *Teacher Education and Practice, 4*(2), 7–10.

Clausen, J. (1975). The social meaning of differential physical and sexual maturation. In S. Dragastin & G. H. Elder, Jr. (Eds.), *Adolescence in the life cycle*. New York: Wiley.

Coates, D. L., & van Widenfeldt, B. (1991). Pregnancy in adolescence. In R. M. Lerner, A. C. Peterson, & J. Brooks-Gunn (Eds.), *Encyclopedia of adolescence*. New York: Garland.

Cognition and Technology Group at Vanderbilt. (1991). Some thoughts about constructivism and instructional design. *Educational Technology, 31*(9), 16–18.

Cognition and Technology Group at Vanderbilt. (1992a). The Jasper series: A generative approach to improving mathematical thinking. In K. Sheingold, L. G. Roberts, & S. M. Malcolm (Eds.), *This year in school science 1991: Technology for teaching and learning*. Washington, DC: American Association for the Advancement of Science.

Cognition and Technology Group at Vanderbilt. (1992b). The Jasper series as an example of anchored instruction: Theory, program description, and assessment data. *Educational Psychologist, 27*(3), 291–315.

Cohen, P. A., Kulik, J. A., & Kulik, C.-L. (1982). Education outcomes of tutoring: A meta-analysis of findings. *American Educational Research Journal, 19*(2), 237–248.

Colangelo, N., & Davis, G. A. (Eds.). (1991). *Handbook of gifted education.* Boston: Allyn & Bacon.

Coleman, J. C. (1980). Friendship and the peer group in adolescence. In J. Adelson (Ed.), *Handbook of adolescent psychology.* New York: Wiley.

Collins, A. (1991). The role of computer technology in restructuring schools. *Phi Delta Kappan, 73*(1), 28–36.

Colton M. E., & Gore, S. (Eds.). (1991). Adolescent stress. New York: Aldine de Gruyter.

Conger, J.J. (1991). *Adolescence and youth* (4th ed.). New York: HarperCollins.

Connell, J. P., Halpern-Felsher, B. L., Clifford, E. L., Crichlow, W., & Usinger, P. (1995). Hanging in there: Behavioral, psychological, and contextual factors affecting whether African American adolescents stay in school. *Journal of Adolescent Research, 10*(1), 41–63.

Conoley, J. C., & Kramer, J. J. (Eds.). (1989). *Tenth mental measurements yearbook.* Lincoln, NE: Buros Institute of Mental Measurements.

Consortium for Research on Black Adolescence (1990). *Black adolescence: Current issues and annotated bibliography.* Boston: Hall.

Cooper, H. M. (1979). Pygmalion grows up: A model for teacher expectation, communication, and performance influence. *Review of Educational Research, 49*(3), 389–410.

Cosgrove, D. J. (1959). Diagnostic ratings of teacher performance. *Journal of Educational Psychology, 50*(5), 200–204.

Covington, M. V. (1985). Strategic thinking and the fear of failure. In J. W. Segal, S. F. Chipman, & R. Glaser (Eds.), *Thinking and learning skills* (Vol. 1). Hillsdale, NJ: Lawrence Erlbaum.

Cox, W. F., Jr., & Dunn, T. G. (1979). Mastery learning: A psychological trap? *Educational Psychologist, 14*, 2429.

Crain, W. (1992). *Theories of development: Concepts and applications* (3rd ed.). Englewood Cliffs, NJ: Prentice-Hall.

Crockett, L. J. (1991). Sex roles and sex–typing in adolescence. In R. M. Lerner, A. C. Peterson, & J. Brooks–Gunn (Eds.), *Encyclopedia of adolescence.* New York: Garland.

Cronbach, L. J. (1990). *Essentials of psychological testing* (5th ed.). New York: Harper & Row.

Crooks, T. J. (1988). The impact of classroom evaluation practices on students. *Review of Educational Research, 58*(4), 438–481.

Cruickshank, D. R. (1990). *Research that informs teachers and teacher educators.* Bloomington, IN: Phi Delta Kappa Educational Foundation.

Csikszentmihalyi, M., & Larson, R. (1984). *Being adolescent.* New York: Basic Books.

Cuban, L. (1986). *Teachers and machines: The classroom use of technology since 1920.* New York: Teachers College Press.

Cuban, L. (1990). What I learned from what I had forgotten about teaching: Notes from a professor. *Phi Delta Kappan, 71*(6), 479–482.

Cunningham, D. J. (1991). In defense of extremism. *Educational Technology, 31*(9), 26–27.

Damon, W. (1988). *The moral child.* New York: Free Press.

Damon, W., & Hart, D. (1988). *Self-understanding in childhood and adolescence.* New York: Cambridge University Press.

Damon, W., & Phelps, E. (1991). Peer collaboration as a context for cognitive growth. In L. T. Landsmann (Ed.), *Culture, schooling, and psychological development.* Norwood, NJ: Ablex.

Dasen, P., & Heron, A. (1981). Cross–cultural tests of Piaget's theory. In H. C. Triandis & A. Heron (Eds.), *Handbook of cross–cultural psychology, developmental psychology* (Vol. 4). Boston: Allyn & Bacon.

Davies, L. J. (1984). Teaching university students how to learn. *Improving University and College Teaching, 31*(4), 160–165.

Dawe, H. A. (1984). Teaching: A performing art. *Phi Delta Kappan, 65*(8), 548–552.

Dawson, M. M. (1987). Beyond ability grouping: A review of the effectiveness of ability grouping and its alternatives. *School Psychology Review, 16*(3), 348–369.

deCharms, R. (1976). *Enhancing motivation: Change in the classroom.* New York: Irvington.

Dempster, F. N. (1988). The spacing effect: A case study in the failure to apply the results of psychological research. *American Psychologist, 43*(8), 627–634.

Department of Education (1995). *To assure the free appropriate public education of all children with disabilities: seventeenth annual report to Congress on the implementation of the Individuals with Disabilities Education Act.* Washington, DC: Author.

DeVillars, R. A., Faltis, C. J., & Cummins, J. P. (Eds.). (1994). *Cultural diversity in schools: From practice to rhetoric.* Albany: State University of New York Press.

diSibio, M. (1982). Memory for connected discourse: A constructivist view. *Review of Educational Research, 52*(2), 149–174.

Doll, C. A. (1987). *Evaluating educational software.* Chicago: American Library Association.

Douvan, E., & Adelson, J. (1966). *The adolescent experience.* New York: Wiley.

Doyle, W. (1983). Academic work. *Review of Educational Research, 53*(2), 159–200.

Driscoll, M. P. (1994). *Psychology of learning and instruction.* Boston: Allyn & Bacon.

Duchastel, P. C., & Merrill, P. F. (1973). The effects of behavioral objectives on learning: A review of empirical studies. *Review of Educational Research, 43*(1), 53–69.

Duell, O. K. (1986). Metacognitive skills. In G. D. Phye & T. Andre (Eds.), *Cognitive classroom learning.* Orlando, FL: Academic Press.

Durkin, K. (1985). *Television, sex roles and children.* Milton Keynes, England: Open University Press.

Dusek, J. B. (1987). Sex roles and adjustment. In D. B. Carter (Ed.), *Current conceptions of sex roles and sex typing.* New York: Praeger.

Dusek, J. B. (1991). *Adolescent development and behavior* (2d ed.). Englewood Cliffs, NJ: Prentice-Hall.

Dweck, C. S. (1986). Motivational processes affecting learning. *American Psychologist, 41*(10), 1040–1048.

Dwyer, C. A. (1982). The role of schools in developing sex role attitudes. In I. Gross, J. Downing, & A. d'Heurle (Eds.), *Sex role attitudes and cultural change.* Dordrecht, Holland: D. Reidel Publishing.

Ebel, R. L., & Frisbie, D. A. (1991). *Essentials of educational measurement* (5th ed.). Englewood Cliffs, NJ: Prentice-Hall.

Eby, J. W. (1994). *Reflective planning, teaching, and evaluation: K–12.* New York: Merrill.

Edmunds, R. D. (Ed.). (1980). *American Indian leaders: Studies in diversity.* Lincoln: University of Nebraska Press.

Elkind, D. (1968). Cognitive development in adolescence. In J. F. Adams (Ed.), *Understanding adolescence.* Boston: Allyn & Bacon.

Elkind, D. (1989). Developmentally appropriate practice: Philosophical and practical implications. *Phi Delta Kappan, 71*(2), 113–117.

Ellis, A., & Fouts, J. (1993). *Research on educational innovations.* Princeton Junction, NJ: Eye on Education.

Ellis, H. C. (1965). *The transfer of learning.* New York: Macmillan.

Ellis, H. C. (1978). *Fundamentals of human learning, memory, and cognition* (2d ed.). Dubuque, IA: William C. Brown.

Elrich, M. (1994). The stereotype within. *Educational Leadership, 51*(8), 12–15.

Emmer, E. T., Evertson, C. M., Clements, B. S., & Worsham, M. E. (1994). *Classroom management for secondary teachers* (3d ed.). Boston: Allyn & Bacon.

EPIE Institute. (1993). *The latest and best of TESS: The educational software selector.* Hampton Bays, NY: The EPIE Institute.

Epstein, H. T. (1980). Brain growth and cognitive functioning. In D. R. Steer (Ed.), *The emerging adolescent: Characteristics and educational implications.* Columbus, OH: National Middle School Association.

Erdelyi, M. H., & Goldberg, B. (1979). Let's now sweep repression under the rug: Towards a cognitive psychology of repression. In J. Kihlstrom & F. Evans (Eds.), *Functional disorders of memory.* Hillsdale, NJ: Lawrence Erlbaum.

Ericsson, K. A., Chase, W. G., & Faloon, S. (1980). Acquisition of a memory skill. *Science, 208*, 1181–1182.

Erikson, E. H. (1963). *Childhood and society* (2d ed.). New York: Norton.

Erikson, E. H. (1968). *Identity: Youth and crisis.* New York: Norton.

Evans, E. D., & Richardson, R. C. (1995). Corporal punishment: What teachers should know. *Teaching Exceptional Children, 27*(2), 33–36.

Evans, R. I. (1967). *Dialogue with Erik Erikson.* New York: Harper & Row.

Evertson, C. M., Emmer, E. T., Clements, B. S., & Worsham, M. E. (1994). *Classroom management for elementary teachers* (3d ed.). Boston: Allyn & Bacon.

Fagot, B. I. (1978). The influence of sex of child on parental reactions to toddler children. *Child Development, 49*(2), 459–465.

Fagot, B. I., & Leinbach, M. D. (1987). Socialization of sex roles within the family. In D. B. Carter (Ed.), *Current conceptions of sex roles and sex typing.* New York: Praeger.

FairTest. (1990). *Standardized tests and our children: A guide to testing reform.* Cambridge, MA: National Center for Fair and Open Testing.

Fantuzzo, J. W., Polite, K., & Grayson, N. (1990). An evaluation of reciprocal peer tutoring across elementary school settings. *Journal of School Psychology, 28*(4), 309–323.

Fantuzzo, J. W., Riggio, R. E., Connelly, S., & Dimeff, L. A. (1989). Effects of reciprocal peer tutoring on academic achievement and psychological adjustment: A component analysis. *Journal of Educational Psychology, 81*(2), 173–177.

Faw, H. W., & Waller, T. G. (1976). Mathemagenic behaviors and efficiency in learning from prose materials. *Review of Educational Research, 46*(4), 691–720.

Feather, N. T. (1980). Values in adolescence. In J. Adelson (Ed.), *Handbook of adolescent psychology.* New York: Wiley.

Feingold, A. (1988). Cognitive gender differences are disappearing. *American Psychologist, 43*(2), 95–103.

Feist, J. (1990). *Theories of personality* (2d. ed). Fort Worth, TX: Holt, Rinehart & Winston.

Ferguson, P., & Womack, S. T. (1993). The impact of subject matter and education coursework on teaching performance. *Journal of Teacher Education, 44*(1), 55–63.

Feuer, M. J., Fulton, K., & Morison, P. (1993). Better tests and testing practices: Options for policy makers. *Phi Delta Kappan, 74*(7), 530–533.

Feynman, R. P. (1985). *"Surely you're joking, Mr Feynman."* New York: Norton.

First, J. M. (1988). Immigrant students in U.S. public schools: Challenges with solutions. *Phi Delta Kappan, 70*(3), 205–210.

Fitzgerald, J. (1995). English-as-a-second-language learners' cognitive reading processes: A review of the research in the United States. *Review of Educational Research, 65*(2), 145–190.

Flanders, N. A. (1970). *Analyzing teacher behavior.* Reading, MA: Addison-Wesley.

Flavell, J. H. (1976). Metacognitive aspects of problem solving. In L. B. Resnick (Ed.), *The nature of intelligence.* Hillsdale, NJ: Lawrence Erlbaum.

Flavell, J. H. (1987). Speculations about the nature and development of metacognition. In F. E. Weinert & R. H. Kluwe (Eds.), *Metacognition, moti-*

vation, and understanding. Hillsdale, NJ: Lawrence Erlbaum.

Flinders, D. J. (1989). Does the "art of teaching" have a future? *Educational Leadership, 46*(8), 16–20.

Foot, H. C., Shute, R. H., & Morgan, M. J. (1990). Theoretical issues in peer tutoring. In H. C. Foot, M. J. Morgan, & R. H. Shute (Eds.), *Children helping children.* Chichester, England: John Wiley & Sons.

Foster, D. W. (1982). *Sourcebook of Hispanic culture in the United States.* Chicago: American Library Association.

Foyle, H. C., Lyman, L., & Thies, S. A. (1991). *Cooperative learning in the early childhood classroom.* Washington, DC: National Education Association.

Franca, V. M., Keer, M. M., Reitz, A. L., & Lambert, D. (1990). Peer tutoring among behaviorally disordered students: Academic and social benefits to tutor and tutee. *Education and Treatment of Children, 13*(2), 109–128.

Frank, S. J., Pirsch, L. A., & Wright, V. C. (1990). Late adolescents' perceptions of their relationships with their parents: Relationships among deidealization, autonomy, relatedness, and insecurity and implications for adolescent adjustment and ego identity status. *Journal of Youth and Adolescence, 19*(6), 571–588.

Frasier, M. M. (1991). Disadvantaged and culturally diverse gifted students. *Journal for the Education of the Gifted, 14*(3), 234–245.

Friedenberg, E. Z. (1963). *Coming of age in America: Growth and acquiescence.* New York: Vintage Books.

Furst, E. J. (1981). Bloom's taxonomy of educational objectives for the cognitive domain. *Review of Educational Research, 51*(4), 441–453.

Furth, H. G. (1970). *Piaget for teachers.* Englewood Cliffs, NJ: Prentice–Hall.

Gable, R. A., & Warren, S. F. (Ed.). (1993). *Strategies for teaching students with mild to severe mental retardation.* Baltimore, MD: Paul H. Brookes.

Gage, N. L. (1984). What do we know about teaching effectiveness? *Phi Delta Kappan, 66*(2), 87–93.

Gagné, E. D., Yekovich, C. W., & Yekovich, F. R. (1993). *The cognitive psychology of school learning* (2d ed.). New York: HarperCollins.

Gall, M. D. (1970). The use of questions in teaching. *Review of Educational Research, 40*(5), 707–721.

Gall, M. D., Gall, J. P., Jacobsen, D. R., & Bullock, T. L. (1990). *Tools for learning: A guide to teaching study skills.* Alexandria, VA: Association for Supervision and Curriculum Development.

Gallagher, J. J. (1985). *Teaching the gifted child.* (3d ed.). Boston: Allyn and Bacon.

Gallagher, P. A. (1995). *Teaching students with behavior disorders: Techniques and activities for classroom instruction* (2d ed.). Denver: Love.

Gallatin, J. (1980). Political thinking in adolescence. In J. Adelson (Ed.), *Handbook of adolescent psychology.* New York: Wiley.

Gallimore, R., & Tharp, R. (1990). Teaching mind in society: Teaching, schooling, and literate discourse. In L. C. Moll (Ed.), *Vygotsky and education: Instructional implications and applications of sociohistorical psychology.* Cambridge, England: Cambridge University Press.

García, E. (1994). *Understanding and meeting the challenge of student cultural diversity.* Boston: Houghton Mifflin.

Gardner, H. (1983). *Frames of mind: The theory of multiple intelligences.* New York: Basic Books.

Gardner, H., & Hatch, T. (1989). Multiple intelligences go to school. *Educational Researcher, 18*(8), 410.

Garfinkel, B. D., Crosby, E., Herbert, M. R., Matus, A. L., Pfeifer, J. K., & Sheras, P. L. (1988). *Responding to adolescent suicide.* Bloomington, IN: Phi Delta Kappa Educational Foundation.

Garner, R. (1987). *Metacognition and reading comprehension.* Norwood, NJ: Ablex.

Garrod, A. (Ed.). (1993). *Approaches to moral development: New Research and emerging themes.* New York: Teachers College Press.

Geisenger, K. F. (Ed.). (1992). *Psychological testing of Hispanics*. Washington, DC: American Psychological Association.

Gelman, R. (1994). Constructivism and supporting environments. In D. Tirosh (Ed.), *Implict and explicit knowledge: An educational approach*. Norwood, NJ: Ablex.

Gelman, R., & Baillargeon, E. E. (1983). A review of some Piagetian concepts. In J. H. Flavell & E. M. Markman (Eds.) *Handbook of child development: Vol. III Cognitive development* (4th ed.). New York: Wiley.

Getzels, J. W., & Jackson, P. W. (1962). *Creativity and intelligence*. New York: Wiley.

Gick, M. L. (1986). Problem-solving strategies. *Educational Psychologist, 21*(1, 2), 99–120.

Gick, M. L., & Holyoak, K. J. (1980). Analogical problem solving. *Cognitive Psychology, 12*(3), 306–355.

Gick, M. L., & Holyoak, K. J. (1983). Schema induction and analogical transfer. *Cognitive Psychology, 15*(1), 1–38.

Gilligan, C. (1979). Women's place in man's life cycle. *Harvard Educational Review*, *49*(4), 431–446.

Gilligan, C. (1982). *In a different voice: Psychological theory and women's development*. Cambridge, MA: Harvard University Press.

Gilligan, C. (1987). Adolescent development reconsidered. In C.E. Irwin, Jr. (Ed.), *Adolescent social behavior and health*. San Francisco: Jossey-Bass.

Gilligan, C. (1988). Exit–voice dilemmas in adolescent development. In C. Gilligan, J. Ward, J. Taylor, & B. Bardige (Eds.), *Mapping the moral domain: A contribution of women's thinking to psychological theory and education*. Cambridge, MA: Harvard University Press.

Ginott, H. (1965). *Between parent and child*. New York: Macmillan.

Ginott, H. (1972). *Teacher and child*. New York: Macmillan.

Ginsburg, H. P., & Opper, S. (1988). *Piaget's theory of intellectual development* (3d ed.). Englewood Cliffs, NJ: Prentice–Hall.

Glaser, R. (1976). Components of a psychology of instruction: Toward a science of design. *Review of Educational Research, 46*(1), 1-24.

Glasser, W. (1986). *Control theory in the classroom*. New York: Harper & Row.

Glasser, W. (1990). *The quality school*. New York: Harper & Row.

Glasson, G. E. (1989). The effects of hands-on and teacher demonstration laboratory methods on science achievement in relation to reasoning ability and prior knowledge. *Journal of Research in Science Teaching, 26*(2), 121–131.

Gold, M., & Petronio, R. J. (1980). Delinquent behavior in adolescence. In J. Adelson (Ed.), *Handbook of adolescent psychology*. New York: Wiley.

Goldstein, A. P., Apter, S. J., & Harootunian, B. (1984). *School violence*. Englewood Cliffs, NJ: Prentice-Hall.

Goldstein, A. P., Sprafkin, R. P., Gershaw, N. J., & Nein, P. (1980). *Skill-streaming the adolescent: A structured learning approach to teaching prosocial skills*. Champaign, IL: Research Press.

Gollnick, D. A., & Chinn, P. C. (1994). *Multicultural education in a pluralistic society* (4th ed.). New York: Merrill.

Good, T. (1982). *Classroom research: What we know and what we need to know* (R&D Report No. 9018). Austin: University of Texas, Research and Development Center for Teacher Education.

Good, T. L., & Brophy, J. (1995). *Contemporary educational psychology* (5th ed.). New York: Longman.

Goodlad, J. I. (1984). *A place called school*. New York: McGraw-Hill.

Gordon, S., & Gilgun, J. F. (1987). Adolescent sexuality. In V. B. van Hasselt & M. Hersen (Eds.), *Handbook of adolescent psychology*. New York: Pergamon Press.

Gordon, T. (1974). *TET: Teacher effectiveness training*. New York: McKay.

Gottfredson, G. D., & Gottfredson, D. C. (1985). *Victimization in schools*. New York: Plenum Press.

Gough, P. B. (1987). The key to improving schools: An interview with William

Glasser. *Phi Delta Kappan, 69*(9), 656–662.

Gould, S. J. (1981). *The mismeasure of man.* New York: Norton.

Grabe, M., & Grabe, C. (1995). *Integrating technology for meaningful learning.* Boston: Houghton Mifflin.

Graham, S., & Weiner, B. (1993). Attributional applications in the classroom. In T. M. Tomlinson (Ed.), *Motivating students to learn: Overcoming barriers to high achievement.* Berkeley, CA: McCutchan.

Green, K. E., & Stager, S. F (1986/1987). Testing: Coursework, attitudes, and practices. *Educational Research Quarterly, 11*(2), 48–55.

Gronlund, N. E. (1959). *Sociometry in the classroom.* New York: Harper & Row.

Gronlund, N. E. (1993). *How to make achievement tests and assessments* (5th ed.). Boston:Allyn & Bacon.

Gronlund, N. E. (1995). *How to write and use instructional objectives* (5th ed.).Englewood Cliffs, NJ: Merrill.

Gruber, E., & Vonèche, J. J. (Eds.). (1977). *The essential Piaget: An interpretive reference and guide.* New York: Basic Books.

Guild P. (1994). The culture/learning style connection. *Educational Leadership, 51*(8), 16–21.

Guilford, J. P. (1967). *The nature of human intelligence.* New York: McGraw-Hill.

Guralnick, M. J. (1986). The peer relations of young handicapped and nonhandicapped children. In P. S. Strain, M. J. Guralnick, & H. M. Walker (Eds.), *Children's social behavior: Development, assessment, and modification.* Orlando, FL: Academic Press.

Gutek, G. L. (1992). *Education and schooling in America* (3d ed.). Boston: Allyn & Bacon.

Haberman, M., & Dill, V. (1993). The knowledge base on retention vs. teacher ideology: Implications for teacher preparation. *Journal of Teacher Education, 44*(5), 352–360.

Hakuta, K., & Garcia, E. E. (1989). Bilingualism and education. *American Psychologist, 44*(2), 374–379.

Hakuta, K., & Gould, L. J. (1987). Synthesis of research on bilingual education. *Educational Leadership, 44*(6), 38–45.

Haladyna, T. M., Nolan, S. B., & Haas, N. S. (1991). Raising standardized achievement test scores and the origins of test score pollution. *Educational Researcher, 20*(5), 2–7.

Hall, G. S. (1904). *Adolescence: Its psychology and its relations to physiology, anthropology, sociology, sex, crime, religion, and education* (2 vols.). New York: Appleton.

Hall, R. V., Axlerod, S., Foundopoulos, M., Shellman, J., Campbell, R. A., & Cranston, S. S. (1971). The effective use of punishment to modify behavior in the classroom. *Educational Technology, 11*(4), 24–26.

Halmi, K. A. (1987). Anorexia nervosa and bulimia. In V. B. van Hasselt & M. Hersen (Eds.), *Handbook of adolescent psychology.* New York: Pergamon Press.

Halpern, D. F. (1992). *Sex differences in cognitive abilities* (2d ed.). Hillsdale, NJ: Lawrence Erlbaum.

Hamilton, R., & Ghatala, E. (1994). *Learning and instruction.* New York: McGraw-Hill.

Han, E. P. (1995). Reflection is essential in teacher education. *Childhood Education, 71*(4), 228–230.

Haney, W. M., Madaus, G. F., & Lyons, R. (1993). *The fractured marketplace for standardized testing.* Boston: Kluwer Academic Publishers.

Hansgen, R. D. (1991). Can education become a science? *Phi Delta Kappan, 72(9)*, 689–694.

Harding, C. G., & Snyder, K. (1991). Tom, Huck, and Oliver Stone as advocates in Kohlberg's just community: Theory–based strategies for moral–based education. *Adolescence, 26*(102), 319–330.

Harrow, A. J. (1972). *A taxonomy of the psychomotor domain: A guide for developing behavioral objectives.* New York: McKay.

Harter, S. (1988). Developmental processes in the construction of the self. In T. D. Yawkey & J. E. Johnson (Eds.), *Integrative processes and socialization: Early to middle childhood* (pp. 45–78). Hillsdale, NJ: Lawrence Erlbaum. (155.418 / I616)

Harter, S. (1990). Self and identity development. In S. S. Feldman & G. R. Elliot (Eds.), *At the threshold: The developing adolescent* (pp. 352–387). Cambridge, MA: Harvard University Press.

Hartshorne, H., & May, M. A. (1929). *Studies in service and self-control.* New York: Macmillan.

Hartshorne, H., & May, M. A. (1930a). *Studies in deceit.* New York: Macmillan.

Hartshorne, H., & May, M. A. (1930b). *Studies in the organization of character.* New York: Macmillan.

Hartup, W. W. (1989). Social relationships and their developmental significance. *American Psychologist, 44*(2), 120–126.

Hassett, J. (1984). Computers in the classroom. *Psychology Today, 18*(9), 22–28.

Hatton, N., & Smith, D. (1995). Reflection in teacher education: Towards definition and implementation. *Teaching and Teacher Education, 11*(1), 33–49.

Heidemann, S., & Hewitt, D. (1992). *Pathways to play.* St. Paul, MN: Redleaf Press.

Henderson, V. L., & Dweck, C. S. (1990). Motivation and achievement. In S. S. Feldman & G. R. Elliott (Eds.), *At the threshold: The developing adolescent.* Cambridge, MA: Harvard University Press.

Henry, M. A. (1986). Strengths and needs of first-year teachers. *The Teacher Educator, 22* (2), 10–18.

Herman, J. L., Gearhart, M., & Baker, E. L. (1993). Assessing writing portfolios: Issues in the validity and meaning of scores. *Educational Assessment, 1*(3), 201–224.

Hersh, R. H., Paolitto, D. P., & Reimer, J. (1979). *Promoting moral growth: From Piaget to Kohlberg.* New York: Longman.

Hetherington, E. M., & Parke, R. D. (1993). *Child psychology: A contemporary viewpoint* (4th ed.). New York: McGraw-Hill.

Higbee, K. L. (1979). Recent research on visual mnemonics: Historical roots and educational fruits. *Review of Educational Research, 49*(4), 611–630.

Highet, G. (1957). *The art of teaching.* New York: Vintage Books.

Hill, B. C., & Ruptic, C. A. (1994). *Practical aspects of authentic assessment.* Norwood, MA: Christopher-Gordon.

Hill, J. P. (1987). Research on adolescents and their families: Past and prospect. In C. E. Irwin, Jr. (Ed.), *Adolescent social behavior and health.* San Francisco: Jossey-Bass.

Hills, J. R. (1991). Apathy concerning grading and testing. *Phi Delta Kappan, 72*(7), 540–545.

Ho, B. (1995). Using lesson plans as a means of reflection. *ELT Journal, 49*(1), 66–70.

Hodgson, J. W., & Fischer, J. L. (1979). Sex differences in identity and intimacy development in college youth. *Journal of Youth and Adolescence, 8*(1) 37–50.

Hoffer, T. B. (1992). Middle school ability grouping and student achievement in science and mathematics. *Educational Evaluation and Policy Analysis, 14*(3), 205–227.

Hoffman, M. L. (1980). Moral development in adolescence. In J. Adelson (Ed.), *Handbook of adolescent psychology.* New York: Wiley.

Hoge, R. D., & Renzulli, J. S. (1993). Exploring the link between giftedness and self-concept. *Review of Educational Research, 63*(4), 449–465.

Holmes, C. T. (1989). Grade level retention effects: A meta-analysis of research studies. In L. A. Shepard & M. L. Smith (Eds.), *Flunking grades: Research and policies on retention.* London: Falmer Press.

Holyoak, K. J., & Koh, K. (1987). Surface and structural similarity in analogical transfer. *Memory & Cognition, 15*(4), 332–340.

Hopkins, C. D., & Antes, R. L. (1990). *Classroom measurement and evaluation* (3d ed.). Itasca, IL: F. E. Peacock.

Horan, J. J., & Strauss, L. K. (1987). Substance abuse in adolescence. In V. B. van Hasselt & M. Hersen (Eds.), *Handbook of adolescent psychology*. New York: Pergamon Press.

Horowitz, F., & O'Brien, M. (1986). Gifted and talented children: State of knowledge and directions for research. *American Psychologist, 41(*10), 1147–1152.

Houston, W. R., & Williamson, J. L. (1992–1993). Perceptions of their preparation by 42 Texas elementary school teachers compared with their responses as student teachers. *Teacher Education and Practice, 8*(2), 27–42.

Howard, E. R. (1981). School climate improvement—rationale and process. *Illinois School Research and Development, (18)*1, 8–12.

Howe, C. K. (1994). Improving the achievement of Hispanic students. *Educational Leadership, 51*(8), 42–44.

Hoyenga, K. B., & Hoyenga, K. T. (1993). *Gender-related differences: Origins and outcomes*. Boston: Allyn & Bacon.

Hughes, F. P. (1991). *Children, play, and development*. Boston: Allyn & Bacon.

Hughes, F. P., & Noppe, L. D. (1991). *Human development across the life span*. New York: Macmillan.

Hunt, N., & Marshall, K. (1994). *Exceptional children and youth*. Boston: Houghton Mifflin.

Huyvaert, S. (1995). *Reports from the classroom: Cases for reflection*. Boston: Allyn & Bacon.

Hyde, J. S. (1986). Gender differences in aggression. In J. S. Hyde & M. C. Linn (Eds.), *The psychology of gender*. Baltimore: Johns Hopkins University Press.

Idstein, P. (1993). Swimming against the mainstream. *Phi Delta Kappan, 75*(4), 336–340.

Irvin, J. L. (Ed.). (1992). *Transforming middle level education*. Boston: Allyn & Bacon.

Irwin, C. E., Jr., & Millstein, S. G. (1991). Risk-taking behaviors during adolescence. In R. M. Lerner, A. C. Peterson, & J. Brooks-Gunn (Eds.), *Encyclopedia of adolescence*. New York: Garland.

Jackson, S., & Bosma, H. (1990). Coping and self in adolescence. In H. Bosma & S. Jackson (Eds.), *Coping and self-concept in adolescence*. New York: Springer-Verlag.

James, W. (1899). *Talks to teachers on psychology: And to students on some of life's ideals*. New York: Holt.

Janzen, R. (1994). Melting pot or mosaic? *Educational Leadership, 51*(8), 9–11.

Johnson, D. W., & Johnson, R. T. (1995). Cooperative learning and nonacademic outcomes of schooling: The other side of the report card. In J. E. Pederson & A. D. Digby (Eds.), *Secondary schools and cooperative learning*. New York: Garland.

Johnson, D. W., Johnson, R. T., & Holubec, E. J. (1994). *The new circles of learning: Cooperation in the classroom and school*. Alexandria, VA: Association for Supervision and Curriculum Development.

Johnson, D. W., Johnson, R. T., & Smith, K. A. (1995). Cooperative learning and individual student achievement in secondary schools. In J. E. Pedersen & A. D. Digby (Eds.), *Secondary schools and cooperative learning*. New York: Garland.

Johnson, R. E. (1975). Meaning in complex learning. *Review of Educational Research, 45*(3), 425–460.

Jones, M. C. (1957). The later careers of boys who were early- or late- maturing. *Child Development, 28*(1), 113–128.

Jones, M. C. (1965). Psychological correlates of somatic development. *Child Development, 36*(4), 899–911.

Kagan, D. M. (1990). How schools alienate students at risk: A model for examining proximal classroom variables. *Educational Psychologist, 25*(2), 102–125.

Kagan, J. (1964a). *Developmental studies of reflection and analysis.* Cambridge, MA: Harvard University Press.

Kagan, J. (1964b). Impulsive and reflective children. In J. D. Krumbolz (Ed.), *Learning and the educational process.* Chicago: Rand McNally.

Kail, R. (1990). *The development of memory in children* (3d ed.). San Francisco: Freeman.

Kalbaugh, P., & Haviland, J. M. (1991). Formal operational thinking and identity. In R. M. Lerner, A. C. Peterson, & J. Brooks–Gunn (Eds.), *Encyclopedia of adolescence.* New York: Garland Publishing.

Kamii, C. (1984). Autonomy: The aim of education envisioned by Piaget. *Phi Delta Kappan, 65*(6), 410–415.

Kaplan, J. S. (1991). *Beyond behavior modification: A cognitive-behavioral approach to behavior management in the school* (2d ed.). Austin, TX: Pro-Ed.

Katz, L. G., & Chard, S. C. (1989). *Engaging children's minds: The project approach.* Norwood, NJ: Ablex Publishing.

Kaufmann, J. M. (1993). *Characteristics of emotional and behavioral disorders of children and youth* (5th ed.). New York: Merrill.

Kellogg, J. B. (1988). Forces of change. *Phi Delta Kappan, 70*(3), 199–204.

Kelly, M. L., & Carper, L. B. (1988). Home-based reinforcement procedures. In J. C. Witt, S. N. Elliott, & F. M. Gresham (Eds.), *Handbook of behavior therapy in education.* New York: Plenum Press.

Ketterlinus, R. D., & Lamb, M. E. (1994). *Adolescent problem behaviors: Issues and research.* Hillsdale, NJ: Lawrence Erlbaum.

Keyser, D. J., & Sweetland, R. C. (Eds.). (1984–1991). *Test critiques* (Vols. 1–8). Austin, TX: Pro-Ed.

Khalili, A., & Shashaani, L. (1994). The effectiveness of computer applications: A meta-analysis. *Journal of Research on Computing in Education, 27*(1), 48–61.

King, A. (1992a). Comparison of self-questioning, summarizing, and note-taking-review as strategies for learning from lectures. *American Educational Research Journal, 29*(2), 303–323.

King, A. (1992b). Facilitating elaborative learning through guided student-generated questioning. *Educational Psychologist, 27*(1), 111–126.

Kirk, S. A., Gallagher, J. J., & Anastasiow, N. J. (1993). *Educating exceptional children* (7th ed.). Boston: Houghton Mifflin.

Klauer, K. (1984). Intentional and incidental learning with instructional texts: A meta-analysis for 1970–1980. *American Educational Research Journal, 21*(2), 323–339.

Knapp, M. S., & Shields, P. M. (1990). Reconceiving academic instruction for the children of poverty. *Phi Delta Kappan, 71*(10), 753–758.

Knapp, M. S., Shields, P. M., & Turnbull, B. J. (1995). Academic challenge in high-poverty classrooms. *Phi Delta Kappan, 76*(10), 770–776.

Kochendorfer, L. (1994). *Becoming a reflective teacher.* Washington, DC: National Education Association.

Kohlberg, L. (1963). The development of children's orientations toward a moral order: 1. Sequence in the development of moral thought. *Vita Humana, 6,* 11–33.

Kohlberg, L. (1969). Stage and sequence: The cognitive–developmental approach to socialization. In D. A. Goslin (Ed.), *Handbook of socialization theory and research.* Chicago: Rand McNally.

Kohlberg, L. (1976). Moral stages and moralization: The cognitive–developmental approach. In T. Lickona (Ed.), *Moral development and behavior: Theory, research, and social issues.* New York: Holt, Rinehart & Winston.

Kohlberg, L. (1978). Revisions in the theory and practice of moral development. In W. Damon (Ed.), *New directions for child development: Moral development* (No.2). San Francisco: Jossey–Bass.

Kohlberg, L. (1985). The just community approach to moral education in theory and practice. In M. W. Berkowitz & F. Oser (Eds.), *Moral education: Theory and application.* Hillsdale, NJ: Lawrence Erlbaum.

Kohn, A. (1993). Rewards versus learning: A response to Paul Chance. *Phi Delta Kappan, 74*(10), 783–787.

Kohn, A. (1994). The truth about self-esteem. *Phi Delta Kappan, 76*(4), 272–283.

Kounin, J. S. (1970). *Discipline and group management in classrooms.* New York: Holt, Rinehart & Winston.

Kozma, R. B. (1991). Learning with media. *Review of Educational Research, 61*(2), 179–212.

Kramer, L.R. (1992). Young adolescents' perceptions of school. In J.L. Irvin (Ed.), *Transforming middle level education.* Boston: Allyn & Bacon.

Krathwohl, D. R., Bloom, B. S., & Masia, B. B. (1964). *Taxonomy of educational objectives. Handbook II: Affective domain.* New York: McKay.

Krulik, S., & Rudnick, J. A. (1993). *Reasoning and problem solving: A handbook for elementary school teachers.* Boston: Allyn & Bacon.

Kubiszyn, T., & Borich, G. (1993). *Educational measurement and testing: Classroom application and practice* (4th ed.). New York: HarperCollins.

Kulik, J. A., & Kulik, C.-L. (1984). Effects of accelerated instruction on students. *Review of Educational Research, 54*(3), 409–426.

Kulik, J. A., & Kulik, C.-L. (1991). Ability grouping and gifted students. In N. Colangelo & G. A. Davis (Eds.), *Handbook of gifted education.* Boston: Allyn & Bacon.

Kulik, J. A., Kulik, C.-L., & Bangert-Drowns, R. L. (1985). Effectiveness of computer-based education in elementary schools. *Computers in Human Behavior, 1*(1), 59–74.

Kulik, C.-L., Kulik, J. A., & Bangert-Drowns, R. L. (1990). Effectiveness of mastery learning programs. *Review of Educational Research, 60*(2), 265–299.

Ladson-Billings, G. (1994). What we can learn from multicultural education research. *Educational Leadership, 51*(8), 22–26.

Lambert, B. G., & Mounce, N. B. (1987). Career planning. In V. B. van Hasselt & M. Hersen (Eds.), *Handbook of adolescent psychology.* New York: Pergamon Press.

Langone, J. (1990). *Teaching students with mild and moderate learning problems.* Boston: Allyn & Bacon.

Lantieri, L. (1995). Waging peace in our schools: Beginning with the children. *Phi Delta Kappan, 76*(5), 386–388.

Lazear, D. G. (1992). *Teaching for multiple intelligences.* Bloomington, IN: Phi Delta Kappa Educational Foundation.

Leadbeater, B. (1991). Relativistic thinking in adolescence. In R. M. Lerner, A. C. Peterson, & J. Brooks-Gunn (Eds.), *Encyclopedia of adolescence.* New York: Garland Publishing.

LeFrancois, G. (1995). *Of children: An introduction to child development* (8th ed.). Belmont, CA: Wadsworth.

Lepper, M. R., & Chabay, R. W. (1985). Intrinsic motivation and instruction: Conflicting views on the role of motivational processes in computer-based education. *Educational Psychologist, 20*(4), 217–230.

Lepper, M. R., & Gurtner, J.-L. (1989). Children and computers: Approaching the twenty-first century. *American Psychologist, 44*(2), 170–178.

Lerner, J. (1993). *Learning disabilities: Theories, diagnosis, and teaching strategies* (6th ed.). Boston: Houghton Mifflin.

Lerner, J. W., Lowenthal, B., & Lerner, S. R. (1995). *Attention deficit disorders: Assessment and teaching.* Pacific Groves, CA: Brooks/Cole.

Lessow-Hurley, J. (1991). *A commonsense guide to bilingual education.* Alexandria, VA: Association for Supervision and Curriculum Development.

Levin, J. R. (1982). Pictures as prose-learning devices. In A. Flammer & W. Kintsch (Eds.), *Advances in psychology. Vol. 8: Discourse processing.* Amsterdam: North-Holland.

Levine, D. U. (Ed.). (1985). *Improving student achievement through mastery learning programs.* San Francisco: Jossey-Bass.

Levine, D. U., & Havighurst, R. J. (1992). *Society and education* (8th ed.). Boston: Allyn & Bacon.

Leyser, Y., Frankiewicz, L. E., & Vaughn, R. (1992). Problems faced by first–year teachers: A survey of regular and special educators. *Teacher Educator, 28*(1), 36–45.

Liao, Y.-K. (1992). Effects of computer-assisted instruction on cognitive outcomes: A meta-analysis. *Journal of Research on Computing in Education, 24*(3), 367–380.

Lickona, T. (1976). Research on Piaget's theory of moral development. In T. Lickona (Ed.), *Moral development and behavior: Theory, research, and social issues*. New York: Holt, Rinehart & Winston.

Linn, R. L. (1994). Performance assessment: Policy promises and technical measurement standards. *Educational Researcher, 23*(9), 4–14.

Linn, R. L., & Gronlund, N. E. (1995). *Measurement and assessment in teaching* (7th ed.). Englewood Cliffs, NJ: Merrill.

Lipka, R. R., Hurford, D. P., & Litten, M. J. (1992). Self in school: Age and school experience effects. In R. P. Lipka & T. M Brinthaupt (Eds.), *Self-perspectives across the life span*. (Albany: State University of New York Press.

Little, J. K. (1967). The occupations of non-college youth. *American Educational Research Journal, 4*(2), 147–153.

Livingston, C., & Borko, H. (1989). Expert–novice differences in teaching: A cognitive analysis and implications for teacher education. *Journal of Teacher Education, 40*(4), 36–42.

Livson, N., & Peskin, H. (1980). Perspectives on adolescence from longitudinal research. In J. Adelson (Ed.), *Handbook of adolescent psychology*. New York: Wiley.

Lockwood, A. (1978). The effects of values clarification and moral development curricula on school age subjects: A critical review of recent research. *Review of Educational Research, 48*(3), 325–364.

Loftus, E. F., & Loftus, G. R. (1980). On the permanence of stored information in the brain. *American Psychologist, 35*(5), 409–420.

Long, J. D., Frye, V. H., & Long, E. W. (1989). *Making it till Friday: A Guide to Successful Classroom Management* (4th ed.). Pennington, NJ: Princeton Book.

Lorayne, H., & Lucas, J. (1974). *The memory book*. New York: Ballantine Books.

Lundeberg, M. A., & Fox, P. W. (1991). Do laboratory findings on test expectancy generalize to classroom outcomes? *Review of Educational Research, 61*(1), 94–106.

Luria, A. R. (1968). *The mind of a mnemonist: A little book about a vast memory*. New York: Ballantine Books.

Lyman, L., Foyle, H. C., & Azwell, T. S. (1993). *Cooperative learning in the elementary classroom*. Washington, DC: National Education Association.

Maccoby, E. E., & Jacklin, C. N. (1974). *Psychology of sex differences*. Stanford, CA: Stanford University Press.

Maeroff, G. I. (1991). Assessing alternative assessment. *Phi Delta Kappan, 73*(4), 272–281.

Mager, R. F. (1962). *Preparing instructional objectives*. Palo Alto, CA: Fearon.

Mager, R. F. (1984). *Preparing instructional objectives* (rev. 2d ed.). Belmont, CA: Pitman Learning.

Maker, C. J. (1982). *Curriculum development for the gifted*. Rockville, MD: Aspen Systems.

Mantzicopoulos, P., & Morrison, D. (1992). Kindergarten retention: Academic and behavioral outcomes through the end of second grade. *American Educational Research Journal, 29*(1), 182–198.

Marcia, J. E. (1966). Development and validation of ego identity status. *Journal of Personality and Social Psychology, 3*(5), 551–558.

Marcia, J. E. (1967). Ego identity status: Relationship to change in self–esteem, "general adjustment," and authoritarianism. *Journal of Personality, 35*(1), 119–133.

Marcia, J. E. (1980). Identity in adolescence. In J. Adelson (Ed.), *Handbook of adolescent psychology*. New York: Wiley.

Marcia, J. E. (1991). Identity and self–development. In R. M. Lerner, A. C. Peterson, & J. Brooks–Gunn (Eds.), *Encyclopedia of adolescence.* New York: Garland Publishing.

Marsh, H. W., Byrne, B. M., & Shavelson, R. J. (1992). A multidemensional, hierarchical self-concept. In T. M Brinthaupt & R. P. Lipka (Eds.), *The self: Definitional and methodological issues.* Albany: State University of New York Press.

Marsh, H. W., Chessor, D., Craven, R., & Roche, L. (1995). The effects of gifted and talented programs on academic self-concept: The big fish strikes again. *American Educational Research Journal, 32*(2), 285–319.

Marsh, R. S., & Raywid, M. A. (1994). How to make detracking work. *Phi Delta Kappan, 76*(4), 314–317.

Maslow, A. H. (1943). A theory of human motivation. *Psychological Review, 50* (4), 370–396.

Maslow, A. H. (1968). *Toward a psychology of being* (2d ed.). Princeton, NJ: Van Nostrand.

Maslow, A. H. (1987). *Motivation and personality* (3d ed.). New York: Harper & Row.

Mayer, R. E. (1979). Can advance organizers influence meaningful learning? *Review of Educational Research, 49*(2), 371–383.

Mayer, R. E. (1987). Learnable aspects of problem solving: Some examples. In D. E. Berger, K. Pezdek, & W. P. Banks (Eds.), *Applications of cognitive psychology: Problem solving, education, and computing.* Hillsdale, NJ: Lawrence Erlbaum.

McCaslin, M., & Good, T. L. (1992). Compliant cognition: The misalliance of management and instructional goals in current school reform. *Educational Researcher, 21*(3), 4–17.

McConnell, S. R., & Odom, S. L. (1986). Sociometrics: Peer-referenced measures and the assessment of social competence. In P. S. Strain, M. J. Guralnick, & H. M. Walker (Eds.), *Children's social behavior: Development, assessment, and modification.* Orlando, FL: Academic Press.

McLaughlin, T. F., & Williams, R. L. (1988). The token economy. In J. C. Witt, S. N. Elliott, & F. M. Gresham (Eds.), *Handbook of behavior therapy in education.* New York: Plenum Press.

Means, B., & Knapp, M. S. (1991). Introduction: Rethinking teaching for disadvantaged students. In B. Means, C. Chelemer, & M. S. Knapp (Eds.), *Teaching advanced skills to at-risk students.* San Francisco: Jossey-Bass.

Meisels, S. J., & Liaw, F–R. (1993). Failure in grade: Do retained students catch up? *Journal of Educational Research, 87*(2), 69–77.

Melton, R. F. (1978). Resolution of conflicting claims concerning the effect of behavioral objectives on student learning. *Review of Educational Research, 48*(2), 291–302.

Mercer, C. D. (1991). *Students with learning disabilities* (4th ed.). New York: Merrill.

Messick, S. (1989). Meaning and values in test validation: The science and ethics of assessment. *Educational Researcher, 18*(2), 5–11.

Metcalfe, J., & Shimamura, A. P. (1994). *Metacognition: Knowing about knowing.* Cambridge, MA: MIT Press.

Mevarech, Z., & Susak, Z. (1993). Effects of learning with cooperative-mastery method on elementary students. *Journal of Educational Research, 86*(4), 197–205.

Meyer, C. A. (1992). What's the difference between authentic and performance assessment? *Educational Leadership, 49*(8), 39–40.

Milgram, J. (1992). A portrait of diversity: The middle level student. In J.L. Irvin (Ed.), *Transforming middle level education.* Boston: Allyn & Bacon.

Miller, D. (1993). Making the connection with language. *Arithmetic Teacher, 40*(6), 311–316.

Miller, L. K. (1989). *Musical savants: Exceptional skill in the mentally retarded.* Hillsdale, NJ: Lawrence Erlbaum.

Miller, P. H. (1993). *Theories of developmental psychology* (3d ed.). New York: W. H. Freeman.

Miller, P. Y., & Simon, W. (1980). The development of sexuality in adolescence.

In J. Adelson (Ed.), *Handbook of adolescent psychology*. New York: Wiley.

Mitchell, J. J. (1990). *Human growth and development: The childhood years*. Calgary, Alberta: Detselig Enterprises.

Mitchell, J. V., Jr. (Ed.). (1985). *Ninth mental measurements yearbook*. Highland Park, NJ: Gryphon Press.

Moely, B. E., Hart, S. S., Leal, L., Santulli, K. A., Rao, N., Johnson, T., & Hamilton, L. B. (1992). The teacher's role in facilitating memory and study strategy development in the elementary school classroom. *Child Development, 63*(3), 653–672.

Moll, L. C. (Ed.). (1990). *Vygotsky and education: instructional implications and applications of sociohistorical psychology*. New York: Cambridge University Press.

Morgan, M. (1984). Reward-induced decrements and increments in intrinsic motivation. *Review of Educational Research, 54*(1), 5–30.

Morris, P. (1977). Practical strategies for human learning and remembering. In M. J. A. Howe (Ed.), *Adult Learning*. New York: Wiley.

Morris, R. B. (Ed.). (1961). *Encyclopedia of American history*. New York: Harper & Row.

Mortimer, J. T. (1991). Employment. In R. M. Lerner, A. C. Peterson, & J. Brooks-Gunn (Eds.), *Encyclopedia of Adolescence*. New York: Garland.

Mueller, D. J. (1973). The mastery model and some alternative models of classroom instruction and evaluation: An analysis. *Educational Technology, 13*(5), 5–10.

Murphy, D. F. (1988). The just community at Birch Meadow Elementary School. *Phi Delta Kappan, 69*(6), 427–428.

Murphy, J. (1987). Educational influences. In V. B. van Hasselt & M. Hersen (Eds.), *Handbook of adolescent psychology*. New York: Pergamon Press.

Mussen, P. H., & Jones, M. C. (1957). Self-conceptions, motivations, and interpersonal attitudes of late and early maturing boys. *Child Development, 28*(2), 243–256.

Nagy, P., & Griffiths, A. K. (1982). Limitations of recent research relating Piaget's theory to adolescent thought. *Review of Educational Research, 52*(4), 513–556.

Natriello, G., McDill, E. L., & Pallas, A. M. (1990). *Schooling disadvantaged children: Racing against catastrophe*. New York: Teachers College Press.

Neill, S. B., & Neill, G. W. (1990). *Only the best: Preschool–grade 12*. New York: R. R. Bowker.

Neisser, U. (1976). *Cognition and reality*. San Francisco: Freeman.

Neisser, U. (1982). *Memory observed*. San Francisco: Freeman.

Newman, B. M., & Newman, P. R. (1991). *Development through life: A psychosocial approach* (5th ed.). Pacific Grove, CA: Brooks/Cole.

Newman, F., & Holzman, L. (1993). *Lev Vygotsky: Revolutionary scientist*. London: Routledge.

Newman, J. M. (1991). *Interwoven conversations: Learning and teaching through critical reflection*. Toronto: Ontario Institute for Studies in Education.

Nicholls, J. G. (1979). Quality and inequality in intellectual development: The role of motivation in education. *American Psychologist, 34*(11), 1071–1084.

Nickerson, R. S. (1994). The teaching of thinking and problem solving. In R. J. Sternberg (Ed.), *Thinking and problem solving*. San Diego, CA: Academic Press.

Nieto, S. (1992). *Affirming diversity*. New York: Longman.

Norman, D. A., & Rumelhart, D. E. (1970). A system for perception and memory. In D. A. Norman (Ed.), *Models of human memory*. New York: Academic Press.

Novak, M. (1971). Rise of unmeltable ethnics. In M. Friedman (Ed.), *Overcoming middle class rage*. Philadelphia: Westminster Press.

Nuttall, E. V. (1987). Survey of current practices in the psychological assessment of limited-English-proficiency handicapped children. *Journal of School Psychology, 25*(l), 53–61.

Nye, R. D. (1979). *What is B. F. Skinner really saying?* Englewood Cliffs, NJ: Prentice-Hall.

Oakes, J. (1985). *Keeping track: How schools structure inequality.* New Haven: Yale University Press.

Oakes, J. (1992). Can tracking research inform practice? Technical, normative, and political considerations. *Educational Researcher, 21*(4), 12–21.

Oakes, J., & Lipton, M. (1992). Detracking schools: Early lessons from the field. *Phi Delta Kappan, 73*(6), 448–454.

Oakes, J., Quartz, K. H., Gong, J., Guiton, G., & Lipton, M. (1993). Creating middle schools: Technical, normative, and political considerations. *Elementary School Journal, 93*(5), 461–480.

Ochse, R., & Plug, C. (1986). Cross-cultural investigation of the validity of Erikson's theory of personality development. *Journal of Personality and Social Psychology, 50*(6), 1240–1252.

Offer, D., & Offer, J. B. (1975). *From teenage to young manhood: A psychological study.* New York: Basic Books.

Office of Educational Research and Improvement. (1993, Spring/Summer). *OERI Bulletin.* Washington, DC: Department of Education.

Office of the Federal Register. (1994). *Code of Federal Regualtions 34. Parts 300 to 399.* Washington, DC: Author.

Ogbu, J. U. (1992). Understanding cultural diversity and learning. *Educational Researcher, 21*(8), 5–14.

Ohanian, S. (1990). PL 94142: Mainstream or quicksand? *Phi Delta Kappan, 72*(3), 217–222.

Okagaki, L., & Sternberg, R. J. (1990). Teaching thinking skills: We're getting the context wrong. In D. Kuhn (Ed.), *Developmental perspectives on teaching and learning thinking skills.* Basel, Switzerland: S. Karger.

Okagaki, L., & Sternberg, R. J. (Eds.). (1991). *Directors of development: Influences on the development of children's thinking.* Hillsdale, NJ: Lawrence Erlbaum.

O'Neil, J. (1992). Putting performance assessment to the test. *Educational Leadership, 49*(8), 14–19.

Ormrod, J. E. (1995). *Human learning* (2d ed.). Englewood Cliffs, NJ: Merrill.

Ornstein, A. C., & Levine, D. U. (1993). *Foundations of education* (5th ed.). Boston: Houghton Mifflin.

Osgood, C. E. (1949). The similarity paradox in human learning: A resolution. *Psychological Review, 56*(3), 132–143.

Overton, W. F, & Byrnes, J. P. (1991). Cognitive development. In R. M. Lerner, A. C. Peterson, & J. Brooks–Gunn (Eds.), *Encyclopedia of Adolescence.* New York: Garland Publishing.

Palincsar, A., & Brown, A. L. (1984). Reciprocal teaching of comprehension-fostering and comprehension-monitoring activities. *Cognition and Instruction, 1*(2), 117–175.

Pallas, A. M., Natriello, G., & McDill, E. L. (1989). The changing nature of the disadvantaged population: Current dimensions and future trends. *Educational Researcher, 18*(5), 16–22.

Paris, S. G., Cross, D. R., & Lipson, M. Y. (1984). Informed strategies for learning: A program to improve children's reading awareness and comprehension. *Journal of Educational Psychology, 76*(6), 1239–1252.

Paris, S. G., Lawton, T. A., Turner, J. C., & Roth, J. L. (1991). A developmental perspective on standardized achievement testing. *Educational Researcher, 20*(5), 12–20.

Paris, S. G., & Oka, E. R. (1986). Children's reading strategies, metacognition, and motivation. *Developmental Review, 6*(1), 25–56.

Parke, R. D., & Slaby, R. G. (1983). The development of aggression. In E. M. Hetherington (Ed.), *Handbook of child psychology: Socialization, personality, and social development* (Vol. 4). New York: Wiley.

Parten, M. B. (1932). Social participation among preschool children. *Journal of Abnormal and Social Psychology, 27*(3), 243–269.

Patterson, G. R., DeBaryshe, B. D., & Ramsey, E. (1989). A developmental perspective on antisocial behavior. *American Psychologist, 44*(2), 329–335.

Pederson, J. E., & Digby, A. D. (Eds.).(1995). *Secondary schools and cooperative learning.* New York: Garland.

Peltier, G. L. (1991). Why do secondary schools continue to track students? *Clearing House, 64*(4), 246–247.

Penfield, W. (1969). Consciousness, memory, and man's conditioned reflexes. In K. Pribram (Ed.), *On the biology of learning.* New York: Harcourt Brace Jovanovich.

Peskin, H. (1967). Pubertal onset and ego functioning. A psychoanalytic approach. *Journal of Abnormal Psychology, 72*(1), 1–15.

Peskin, H. (1973). Influence of the developmental schedule of puberty on learning and ego functioning. *Journal of Youth and Adolescence, 2*(4), 273–290.

Peterson, A. C. (1988). Adolescent development. In M. R. Rosenzweig & L. W. Porter (Eds.), *Annual review of psychology* (Vol. 39, pp. 583–607). Palo Alto, CA: Annual Reviews.

Peterson, A. C., & Taylor, B. (1980). The biological approach to adolescence. In J. Adelson (Ed.), *Handbook of adolescent psychology.* New York: Wiley.

Petti, T. A., & Larson, C. N. (1987). Depression and suicide. In V. B. van Hasselt & M. Hersen (Eds.), *Handbook of adolescent psychology.* New York: Pergamon Press.

Phye, G. D. & Andre, T. (Eds.). (1986). *Cognitive classroom learning: Understanding, thinking, and problem solving.* New York: Academic Press.

Piaget, J. (1952a). *The language and thought of the child.* London: Routledge & Kegan Paul.

Piaget, J. (1952b). *The origins of intelligence in children.* New York: International Universities Press.

Piaget, J. (1965). *The moral judgment of the child* (M. Gabain, Trans.). Glencoe, IL: Free Press. (Original work published 1932.)

Piaget, J., & Inhelder, B. (1956). *The child's conception of space.* London: Routledge & Kegan Paul.

Piaget, J., & Inhelder, B. (1969). *The psychology of the child.* New York: Basic Books.

Piechowski, M. M. (1991). Emotional development and emotional giftedness. In N. Colangelo & G. A. Davis (Eds.), *Handbook of gifted education.* Boston: Allyn & Bacon.

Polya, G. (1957). *How to solve it* (2d ed.). Princeton, NJ: Princeton University Press.

Popham, W. J. (1995). *Classroom assessment: What teachers need to know.* Boston: Allyn & Bacon.

Porter, A. C., & Brophy, J. (1988). Synthesis of research on good teaching: Insights from the work of the Institute for Reserarch on Teaching. *Educational Leadership, 45*(8), 74–85.

Power, C. (1981). Moral education through the development of the moral atmosphere of the school. *Journal of Educational Thought, 15(*1), 419.

Power, C. (1985). Democratic moral education in the large public high school. In M. W. Berkowitz & F. Oser (Eds.), *Moral education: Theory and application.* Hillsdale, NJ: Lawrence Erlbaum.

Premack, D. (1959). Toward empirical behavior laws: 1. Positive reinforcement. *Psychological Review, 66*(4), 219–233.

Pressley, M., Levin, J. R., & Delaney, H. D. (1982). The mnemonic keyword method. *Review of Educational Research, 52*(1), 61–91.

Price, R. V. (1991). *Computer-aided instruction: A guide for authors.* Pacific Grove, CA: Brooks/Cole.

Purkey, W. W., & Stanley, P. H. (1991). *Invitational teaching, learning, and living.* Washington, DC: National Education Association.

Purkey, W. W., & Stanley, P. H. (1994). *The inviting school treasury: 1001 ways to invite student success.* New York: Scholastic.

Purkey, W. W., & Strahan, D. B. (1986). *Positive discipline: A pocketful of ideas.* Columbus, OH: National Middle Schools Association.

Putnam, J. W. (Ed.).(1993). *Cooperative learning and strategies for inclusion.* Baltimore, MD: Paul H. Brookes.

Qin, Z., Johnson, D. W., & Johnson, R. T. (1995). Cooperative versus competitive efforts and problem solving. *Re-*

view of Educational Research, 65(2), 129–143.

Quarles, C. L. (1993). *Staying safe at school.* Thousand Oaks, CA: Corwin Press.

Quay, H. C. (1986). Classification. In H. C. Quay & J. S. Werry (Eds.), *Psychopathological disorders of childhood* (3d ed.). New York: Wiley.

Queen, J. A., & Gretes, J. A. (1982). First year teachers' perceptions of their preservice training. *Phi Delta Kappan, 64* (3), 215–216.

Rabow, J., Charness, M. A., Kipperman, J., & Radcliffe-Vasile, S. (1994). *William Fawcett Hill's learning through discussion* (3d ed.). Thousand Oaks, CA: Sage.

Raison, J., Hanson, L. A., Hall, C., & Reynolds, M. C. (1995). Another school's reality. *Phi Delta Kappan, 76*(6), 480–482.

Ratner, C. (1991). *Vygotsky's sociohistorical psychology and its contemporary applications.* New York: Plenum Press.

Raudenbush, S. W. (1984). Magnitude of teacher expectancy effects on pupil IQ as a function of the credibility of expectancy induction: A synthesis of findings from 18 experimenters. *Journal of Educational Psychology, 76*(1), 85–97.

Raudenbush, S. W., Rowan, B., & Cheong, Y. F. (1993). Higher order instructional goals in secondary schools: Class, teacher, and school influences. *American Educational Research Journal, 30*(3), 523–553.

Raugh, M. R., & Atkinson, R. C. (1975). A mnemonic method for learning a second-language vocabulary. *Journal of Educational Psychology, 67*(1), 1–16.

Redl, F., & Wattenberg, W. W. (1959). *Mental hygiene in teaching* (2d ed.). New York: Harcourt Brace Jovanovich.

Reis, S. M., & Renzulli, J. S. (1985). *The secondary triad model.* Mansfield Center, CT: Creative Learning Press.

Renzulli, J. S., & Reis, S. M. (1985). *The schoolwide enrichment model.* Mansfield Center, CT: Creative Learning Press.

Resnick, L. B. (1987). Learning in school and out. *Educational Researcher, 16*(9), 13–20.

Retish, P., Hitchings, W., Horvath, M., & Schmalle, B. (1991). *Students with mild disabilities in the secondary school.* New York: Longman.

Reynolds, A. J. (1992). Grade retention and school adjustment: An exploratory analysis. *Educational Evaluation and Policy Analysis, 14*(2), 101–122.

Robinson, H. A. (1983). *Teaching reading, writing, and study strategies* (3d ed.). Boston: Allyn and Bacon.

Rogers, D. (1972). *The psychology of adolescence* (2d ed.). New York: Appleton-Century-Crofts.

Rogers, J. (1993, May). The inclusion revolution. *Phi Delta Kappa Research Bulletin, 11,* 1–6.

Rogoff, B. (1990). *Apprenticeship in thinking: Cognitive development in social context.* New York: Oxford University Press.

Rosenshine, B., & Meister, C. (1994). Reciprocal teaching: A review of the research. *Review of Educational Research, 64*(4), 479–530.

Rosenthal, R. (1985). From unconscious experimenter bias to teacher expectancy effects. In J. B. Dusek (Ed.), *Teacher expectations.* Hillsdale, NJ: Lawrence Erlbaum.

Rosenthal, R., and Jacobson, L. (1968). *Pygmalion in the classroom.* New York: Holt, Rinehart & Winston.

Ross, D. D., Bondy, E., & Kyle, D. W. (1993). *Reflective teaching for student empowerment.* New York: Macmillan.

Rotheram-Borus, M. J., & Koopman, C. (1991). AIDS and adolescents. In R. M. Lerner, A. C. Peterson, & J. Brooks-Gunn (Eds.), *Encyclopedia of adolescence.* New York: Garland.

Rottier, J., & Ogan, B. J. (1991). *Cooperative learning in middle-level schools.* Washington, DC: National Education Association.

Rowan, B. (1994). Comparing teachers' work with work in other occupations: Notes on the professional status of teaching. *Educational Researcher, 23*(6), 4–17.

Royer, J. M. (1979). Theories of the transfer of learning. *Educational Psychologist, 14*, 53–72.

Royer, J. M., & Cable, G. W. (1975). Facilitated learning in connected discourse. *Journal of Educational Psychology, 67*(1), 116–123.

Royer, J. M., & Cable, G. W. (1976). Illustrations, analogies, and facilitative transfer in prose learning. *Journal of Educational Psychology, 68*(2), 205–209.

Rubin, K. H., Maioni, T. L., & Hornung, M. (1976). Free play behavior in middle- and lower-class preschoolers: Parten and Piaget revisited. *Child Development, 47*(2), 414–419.

Rubin, L. J. (1985). *Artistry in teaching.* New York: Random House.

Ruggiero, V. R. (1988). *Teaching thinking across the curriculum.* New York: Harper & Row.

Russell, T., & Munby, H. (Eds.). (1992). *Teachers and teaching: From classroom to reflection.* London: Falmer Press.

Rutter, M. (1990). Changing patterns of psychiatric disorders during adolescence. In J. Bancroft & J. M. Reinisch (Eds.), *Adolescence and puberty.* New York: Oxford University Press.

Sadker, M. P., & Sadker, D. M. (1982). *Sex equity handbook for schools.* New York: Longman.

Sadker, M. P., & Sadker, D. M. (1991). *Teachers, schools, and society* (2d ed.). New York: Random House.

Salomon, G., & Perkins, D. N. (1989). Rocky roads to transfer: Rethinking mechanisms of a neglected phenomenon. *Educational Psychologist, 24*(2), 113–142.

Sameroff, A., & McDonough, S. C. (1994). Educational implications of developmental transitions: Revisiting the 5- to 7-year shift. *Phi Delta Kappan, 76*(3), 189–193.

Samuda, R. J., Kong, S. L., Cummins, J., Lewis, J., & Pascual-Leone, J. (1991). *Assessment and placement of minority students.* Toronto: C. J. Hogrefe.

Sanders-Phillips, K. (1989). Prenatal and postnatal influences on cognitive development. In G. L. Berry & J. K. Asamen (Eds.), *Black students: Psychosocial issues and academic achievement.* Newbury Park, CA: Sage.

Sauvé, D. (1985). Guide to microcomputer courseware for bilingual education (rev. & exp.). Rosslyn, Va: National Clearinghouse for Bilingual Education.

Scales, P. (1993). How teachers and education deans rate the quality of teacher preparation for the middle grades. *Journal of Teacher Education, 44*(5), 378–383.

Scarcella, R. (1990). *Teaching language minority students in the multicultural classroom.* Englewood Cliffs, NJ: Prentice-Hall.

Scarr, S., Weinburg, R. A., & Levine, A. (1986). *Understanding development.* San Diego, CA: Harcourt Brace Jovanovich.

Schab, F. (1991). Schooling without learning: Thirty years of cheating in high school. *Adolescence, 26*(104), 839–848.

Schiever, S. W. (1991). *A comprehensive approach to teaching thinking.* Boston: Allyn & Bacon.

Schlaefli, A., Rest, J. R., & Thoma, S. J. (1985). Does moral education improve moral judgment? A meta-analysis of intervention studies using the Defining Issues Test. *Review of Educational Research, 55*(3), 319–352.

Schon, A. D. (1987). *Educating the reflective practitioner.* San Francisco: Jossey-Bass.

Schultz, T. (1989). Testing and retention of young children: Moving from controversy to reform. *Phi Delta Kappan, 71*(2), 125–129.

Schunk, D. H. (1981). Modeling and attributional effects on children's achievement: A self-efficacy analysis. *Journal of Educational Psychology, 73*(1), 93–105.

Schunk, D. H. (1987). Peer models and children's behavioral change. *Review of Educational Research, 57*(2), 149–174.

Schunk, D. H. (1991). *Learning theories: An educational perspective.* New York: Macmillan.

Schunk, D. H. (1995). Self-efficacy and education and instruction. In J. E.

Maddux (Ed.), *Self-efficacy, adaptation, and adjustment.* New York: Plenum Press.

Schunk, D. H., & Hanson, A. R. (1989). Peer models: Influences on children's self-efficacy and achievement. *Journal of Educational Psychology, 77*(3), 313–322.

Seagoe, M. V. (1970). *The learning process and school practice.* Scranton, PA: Chandler.

Seagoe, M. V. (1975). *Terman and the gifted.* Los Altos, CA: Kaufmann.

Searleman, A., & Herrmann, D. (1994). *Memory from a broader perspective.* New York: McGraw-Hill.

Seligman, M. E. P. (1975). *Helplessness: On depression, development, and death.* San Francisco: Freeman.

Selman, R. L. (1980). *The growth of interpersonal understanding: Developmental and clinical analyses.* New York: Academic Press.

Selmes, I. (1987). *Improving study skills.* London: Hodder and Stoughton.

Semb, G. B., & Ellis, J. A. (1994). Knowledge taught in school: What is remembered? *Review of Eductional Research, 64*(2), 253–286.

Serafica, F. C., & Rose, S. (1982). Parents' sex role attitudes and children's concepts of femininity and masculinity. In I. Gross, J. Downing, & A. d'Heurle (Eds.), *Sex role attitudes and cultural change.* Dordrecht, Holland: D. Reidel Publishing Co.

Sharan, S. (1995). Group investigation: Theoretical foundations. In J. E. Peterson & A. D. Digby (Eds.), *Secondary schools and cooperative learning.* New York: Garland.

Sharan, Y., & Sharan, S. (1994). Group investigation in the cooperative classroom. In S. Sharan (Ed.), *Handbook of cooperative learning methods.* Westport, CT: Greenwood Press.

Shavelson, R. J., & Baxter, G. P. (1992). What we've learned about assessing hands-on science. *Educational Leadership, 49*(8), 20–25.

Shook, S. C., LaBrie, M., Vallies, J., McLaughlin, T. F., & Williams, R. L. (1990). The effects of a token economy on first grade students' inappropriate social behavior. *Reading Improvement, 27*(2), 96–101.

Shulman, L. S. (1986). Those who understand: Knowledge growth in teaching. *Educational Research, 15*(2), 4–21.

Siegler, R. S. (1994). Cognitive variability: A key to understanding cognitive development. *Current Directions in Psychological Science, 3*(1), 1–5.

Sigelman, C. K., & Shaffer, D. R. (1991). *Life–span human development.* Pacific Grove, CA: Brooks Cole.

Simon, A., & Boyer, E. G. (Eds.). (1974). *Mirrors for behavior III: An anthology of observation instruments.* Wyncote, PA: Communication Materials Center.

Simpson, E. J. (1966). The classification of educational objectives: Psychomotor domain. *Illinois Teacher of Home Economics,* 10(4), 111–144.

Simpson, M. L. (1984). The status of study strategy instruction: Implications for classroom teachers. *Journal of Reading, 29*(2), 136–143.

Skinner, B. F. (1948). *Walden two.* New York: Macmillan.

Skinner, B. F. (1968). *The technology of teaching.* New York: Appleton-Century-Crofts.

Skinner, B. F. (1976). *Particulars of my life.* New York: Knopf.

Skinner, B. F (1979). *The shaping of a behaviorist.* New York: Knopf.

Skinner, B. F. (1983). *A matter of consequences.* New York: Knopf.

Skinner, B. F. (1984). The shame of American education. *American Psychologist, 39*(9), 947–954.

Skinner, B. F. (1986). Programmed instruction revisited. *Phi Delta Kappan, 68*(2), 103–110.

Slavin, R. E. (1987). Mastery learning reconsidered. *Review of Educational Research, 57*(2), 175–213.

Slavin, R. E. (1989). PET and the pendulum: Faddism in education and how to stop it. *Phi Delta Kappan, 79*(10), 752–758.

Slavin, R. E. (1990b). Achievement effects of ability grouping in secondary schools: A best-evidence synthesis. *Review of Educational Research, 60*(3), 471–500.

Slavin, R. E. (1990a). Mastery learning re-reconsidered. *Review of Educational Research, 60*(2), 300–302.

Slavin, R. E. (1994). Student teams-achievement divisions. In S. Sharan (Ed.), *Handbook of cooperative learning methods.* Westport, CT: Greenwood Press.

Slavin, R. E. (1995). *Cooperative learning: Theory, research, and practice* (2d ed.). Boston: Allyn & Bacon.

Sleeter, C. E., & Grant, C. A. (1994). *Making choices for multicultural education* (2d ed.). New York: Merrill.

Smelter, R. W., Rasch, B. W., & Yudewitz, G. J. (1994). *Phi Delta Kappan, 76*(1), 35–38.

Smilansky, S. (1968). *The effects of sociodramatic play on disadvantaged preschool children.* New York: Wiley.

Smith, D. D. (1989). *Teaching students with learning and behavior problems* (2d ed.). Englewood Cliffs, NJ: Prentice-Hall.

Smith, K., Johnson, D. W., & Johnson, R. T. (1981). Can conflict be constructive? Controversy versus concurrence seeking in learning groups. *Journal of Educational Psychology, 73*(5), 651–663.

Smith, M. L. (1991). Put to the test: The effects of external testing on teachers. *Educational Researcher, 20*(5), 8–11.

Smith, M. L., & Shepard, L. A. (1987). What doesn't work: Explaining policies of retention in the early grades. *Phi Delta Kappan, 69*(2), 129–134.

Snow, R. E. (1986). Individual differences and the design of educational programs. *American Psychologist, 41*(10), 1029–1039.

Snow, R. E. (1992). Aptitude testing: Yesterday, today, and tomorrow. *Educational Psychologist, 27*(1), 5–32.

Snowman, J. (1986). Learning tactics and strategies. In G. D. Phye & T. Andre (Eds.), *Cognitive classroom learning: Understanding, thinking, and problem solving.* New York: Academic Press.

Snowman, J. (1987, October). *The keys to strategic learning.* Paper presented at the annual meeting of the Mid-Western Educational Research Association, Chicago, IL.

Soldier, L. L. (1989). Cooperative learning and the Native American student. *Phi Delta Kappan, 71*(2), 161–163.

Spady, W. G. (1988). Organizing for results: The basis of authentic restructuring and reform. *Educational Leadership, 46*(2), 4–8.

Spady, W. G., & Marshall, K. J. (1991). Beyond traditional outcome-based education. *Educational Leadership, 49*(2), 67–72.

Spear, N. E., & Riccio, D. C. (1994). *Memory: Phenomena and principles.* Boston: Allyn & Bacon.

Spear, R. C. (1992). Appropriate grouping practices for middle level students. In J. L. Irvin (Ed.), *Transforming middle level education.* Boston: Allyn & Bacon.

Sprinthall, N. A., Sprinthall, R. C. (1987). *Educational psychology; A developmental approach* (4th ed.). New York: Random House.

Sprinthall, N. A., Sprinthall, R. C., & Oja, S. N. (1994). *Educational psychology: A developmental approach* (6th ed.). New York: McGraw–Hill.

Stainback, S., & Stainback, W. (Ed.). (1992). *Curriculum considerations in inclusive classrooms.* Baltimore, MD: Paul H. Brookes.

Standing, L. (1973). Learning 10,000 pictures. *Quarterly Journal of Experimental Psychology, 25*(2), 207–222.

Standing, L., Conezio, J., & Haber, R. (1970). Perception and memory for pictures: Single trial learning of 2500 visual stimuli. *Psychonomic Science, 19*(2), 73–74.

Staub, D., & Peck, C. A. (1994/1995). What are the outcomes for nondisabled students? *Educational Leadership, 52*(4), 36–40.

Steffe, L. P., & Gale, J. (Eds.). (1995). *Constructivism in education.* Hillsdale, NJ: Lawrence Erlbaum.

Stephen, J., Fraser, E., & Marcia, J. E. (1992). Moratorium–achievement (mama) cycles in lifespan identity development: Value orientations and reasoning system correlates. *Journal of Adolescence, 15*(3), 283–300.

Sternberg, R. J. (1988). *The triarchic mind: A new theory of human intelligence.* New York: Viking.

Stiffman, A. R., Earls, F., Robins, L. N., Jung, K. G., & Kulbok, P. (1987). Adolescent sexual activity and pregnancy: Socioenvironmental problems, physical health, and mental health. *Journal of Youth and Adolescence, 16*(5), 497–509.

Stiggins, R. J. (1994). *Student-centered classroom assessment.* New York: Merrill.

Stiggins, R. J., Griswold, M. M., & Wikelund, K. R. (1989). Measuring thinking skills through classroom assessment. *Journal of Educational Measurement, 26*(3), 233–246.

Stipek, D. J. (1993). *Motivation to learn: From theory to practice* (2d ed.). Boston: Allyn & Bacon.

Stitt, B. A. (1988). *Building gender fairness in schools.* Carbondale: Southern Illinois University Press.

Stronge, J. H., Lynch, C. D., & Smith, C. R. (1987). Educating the culturally disadvantaged gifted student. *School Counselor, 34*(5), 336–344.

Strother, D. B. (1986). Suicide among the young. *Phi Delta Kappan, 67*(10), 756–759.

Sulzer-Azaroff, B., & Mayer, G. R. (1986). *Achieving educational excellence: Using behavioral strategies.* New York: Holt, Rinehart & Winston.

Susman, E. J. (1991). Stress and the adolescent. In R. M. Lerner, A. C. Peterson, & J. Brooks-Gunn (Eds.), *Encyclopedia of adolescence.* New York: Garland.

Tanner, J. M. (1972). Sequence, tempo, and individual variation in growth and development of boys and girls aged twelve to sixteen. In J. Kagan & R. Coles (Eds.), *Twelve to sixteen: Early adolescence.* New York: Norton.

Taylor, C. A. (1989). *Guidebook to multicultural resources.* Madison, WI: Praxis.

Templeton, S. (1995). *Children's literacy: Contexts for meaningful learning.* Boston: Houghton Mifflin.

Thoma, S. J. (1986). Estimating gender differences in the comprehension and preference of moral issues. *Developmental Review*, 6(2), 165–180.

Thompson, C. P., Cowan, T. M., & Frieman, J. (1993). *Memory search by a memorist.* Hillsdale, NJ: Lawrence Erlbaum.

Thorndike, E. L., & Woodworth, R. S. (1901). The influence of improvement in one mental function upon the efficiency of other functions. *Psychological Review, 8*, 247–261.

Tidwell, R. (1989). Academic success and the school dropout: A minority perspective. In G. L. Berry & J. K. Asamen (Eds.), *Black students: Psychosocial issues and academic achievement.* Newbury Park, CA: Sage.

Tomchin, E. M., & Impara, J. C. (1992). Unraveling teachers' beliefs about grade retention. American *Educational Research Journal, 29*(1), 199–223.

Tomlinson, T. M. (Ed.). (1993). *Motivating students to learn: Overcoming barriers to high achievement.* Berkeley, CA: McCutchan.

Tonemah, S. (1987). Assessing American Indian gifted and talented students' abilities. *Journal for the Education of the Gifted, 10*(3), 181–194.

Triandis, H. C. (1986). Toward pluralism in education. In S. Modgil, G. K. Verma, K. Mallick, & C. Modgil (Eds.), *Multicultural education: The interminable debate.* London: Falmer.

Tsangaridou, N., & O'Sullivan, M. (1994). Using pedagogical reflective strategies to enhance reflection among preservice physical education teachers. *Journal of Teaching in Physical Education, 14*(1), 13–33.

Tudge, J. R. H., & Rogoff, B. (1989). Peer influences on cognitive development: Piagetian and Vygotskian perspectives. In M.H. Bornstein & J.S. Bruner (Eds.), *Interaction in human development.* Hillsdale, NJ: Lawrence Erlbaum.

Tudge, J. R. H., & Winterhoff, P. A. (1993). Vygotsky, Piaget, and Bandura: Perspectives on the relations between the social world and cognitive development. *Human Development, 36*(2), 61–81.

Tulving, E., & Pearlstone, Z. (1966). Availability vs. accessibility of information in memory for words. *Journal of Verbal Learning and Verbal Behavior, 5*(4), 381-391.

Udrey, J. R. (1990). Hormonal and social determinants of adolescent sexual initiation. In J. Bancroft & J. M. Reinisch (Eds.), *Adolescence and puberty*. New York: Oxford University Press.

Valli, L. (1993). Teaching before and after professional preparation: The story of a high school mathematics teacher. *Journal of Teacher Education, 44*(2), 107–118.

van der Voort, T. H. A. (1986). *Television violence: A child's-eye view.* Amsterdam: North-Holland.

van Hasselt, V. B., & Hersen, M. (Eds.). (1987). *Handbook of adolescent psychology*. New York: Pergamon Press.

Vargas, J. (1986). Instructional design flaws in computer-assisted instruction. *Phi Delta Kappan, 67*(10), 738–744.

Vasquez, J. A. (1990). Teaching to the distinctive traits of minority students. *Clearing House, 63*(7), 299–304.

Vitz, P C. (1990). The use of stories in moral development: New psychological reasons for an old educational method. *American Psychologist, 45*(6), 709–720.

Vondracek, F. W., Schulenberg, J., Skorikov, V., Gillespie, L. K., & Wahlheim, C. (1995). The relationship of identity status to career indecision during adolescence. *Journal of Adolescence, 18*(1), 17–30.

Voyat, G. (1983). *Cognitive development among Sioux children.* New York: Plenum Press.

Vygotsky, L. S. (1986). *Thought and language* (A. Kozulin, Trans.). Cambridge, MA: MIT Press. (Original work published 1934.)

Wadsworth, B. J. (1989). Piaget's theory of cognitive and affective development (4th ed.). New York: Longman.

Walberg, H. J. (1990). Productive teaching and instruction: Assessing the knowledge base. *Phi Delta Kappan, 71*(6), 470–478.

Walberg, H. J., Schiller, D., & Haertel, G. D. (1979). The quiet revolution in educational research. *Phi Delta Kappan, 61*(3), 179–182.

Walker, H. M., Colvin, G., & Ramsey, E. (1995). *Antisocial behavior in school: Strategies and best practices.* Pacific Groves, CA: Brooks/Cole.

Walker, J. E., & Shea, T. M. (1991). *Behavior management: A practical approach for educators* (5th ed.). New York: Macmillan.

Walsh, W. B., & Betz, N. E. (1995). *Tests and assessment* (3d ed.). Englewood Cliffs, NJ: Prentice-Hall.

Waterman, A. S. (1988). Identity status theory and Erikson's theory: Communalities and differences. *Developmental Review, 8*, 185–208.

Waterman, A. S., & Archer, S. L. (1990). A life–span perspective on identity formation: Developments in form, function, and process. In P. B. Baltes, D. L. Featherman, & R. M. Lerner (Eds.), *Life–span development and behavior* (Vol. 10, pp. 30–57). Hillsdale, NJ: Erlbaum.

Watson, J. B. (1913). Psychology as the behaviorist views it. *Psychological Review, 20*, 158–177.

Watson, M. F., & Protinsky, H. (1991). Identity status of black adolescents: An empirical investigation. *Adolescence, 26*(104), 963–966.

Wechsler, D. (1975). Intelligence defined and undefined: A relativistic appraisal. *American Psychologist, 30*(2), 135–139.

Wechsler, D. (1981).*Wechsler adult intelligence scale—revised.* New York: Psychological Corporation.

Wechsler, D. (1991). *Wechsler intelligence scale for children—III.* New York: Psychological Corporation.

Weiner, I. B. (1975). Depression in adolescence. In F. F Flach & S. C. Draghi (Eds.), *The nature and treatment of depression.* New York: Wiley.

Weinstein, C. S., & Mignano, A. J., Jr. (1993). *Elementary classroom management: Lessons from research and practice.* New York: McGraw-Hill.

Wellman, H. M., & Gelman, S. A. (1992). Cognitive development: Foundational theories of core domains. In M.R. Rosenzweig & L. W. Porter

(Eds.), *Annual Rreview of Psychology* (Vol. 43, pp. 337–375). Palo Alto, CA: Annual Reviews.

Westerman, D. A. (1991). Expert and novice teacher decision making. *Journal of Teacher Education, 42*(4), 292–305.

Wheatley, G. H. (1991). Constructivist perspectives on science and mathematics learning. *Science Education, 75*(1), 9–21.

Wheelock, A. (1992). *Crossing the tracks: How "untracking" can save America's schools.* New York: New Press.

Wheelock, A. (1994). *Alternatives to tracking and ability grouping.* Arlington, VA: American Association of School Administrators.

Whimbey, A., & Lochhead, J. (1991). *Problem solving and comprehension* (5th ed.). Hillsdale, NJ: Lawrence Erlbaum.

White, B. L., & Watts, J. C. (1973). *Experience and environment: Major influences on the development of the young child.* Englewood Cliffs, NJ: Prentice-Hall.

Whitmore, J. (1987). Conceptualizing the issue of underserved populations of gifted students. *Journal for the Education of the Gifted, 10*(3), 141–153.

Wicks-Nelson, R., & Israel, A. C. (1991). *Behavior disorders of childhood* (2d ed.). Englewood Cliffs, NJ: Prentice-Hall.

Wiggins, G. (1993). Assessment: Authenticity, context, and validity. *Phi Delta Kappan, 75*(3), 200–214.

Wilen, D. K., & Sweeting, C. (1986). Assessment of limited English proficiency Hispanic students. *School Psychology Review, 15*(1), 59–75.

Wiles, J., & Bondi, J. (1993). *The essential middle school* (2d ed.). New York: Macmillan.

Williams, J. E., & Best, D. L. (1990). *Measuring sex stereotypes: A multination study* (rev. ed.). Newbury Park, CA: Sage.

Willig, A. C. 91985). A meta-analysis of selected studies on the effectiveness of bilingual education. *Review of Educational Research, 55*(3), 269–318.

Willis, J., Hovey, L., & Hovey, K. G. (1987). *Computer simulations: A source book to learning in an electronic environment.* New York: Garland.

Witkin, H. A., Moore, C. A., Goodenough, D. R., & Cox, P. W. (1977). Field-dependent and field-independent cognitive styles and their educational implications. *Review of Educational Research, 47*(1), 1–64.

Wlodkowski, R. J. (1978). *Motivation and teaching: A practical guide.* Washington, DC: National Education Association.

Wlodkowski, R. J., & Jaynes, J. H. (1990). *Eager to learn.* San Francisco: Jossey-Bass.

Woditsch, G. A. (1991). *The thoughtful teacher's guide to thinking skills.* Hillsdale, NJ: Lawrence Erlbaum.

Wong, B. Y. L. (1985). Self-questioning instructional research: A review. *Review of Educational Research, 55*(2), 227–268.

Wood, F. W., & Zabel, R. H. (1978). Making sense of reports on the incidence of behavior disorders/emotional disturbance in school-aged populations. *Psychology in the Schools, 15*(1), 45–51.

Woodring, P (1957). *A fourth of a nation.* New York: McGraw–Hill.

Worthen, B. R. (1993). Critical issues that will determine the future of alternative assessment. *Phi Delta Kappan, 74*(6), 444–454.

Wuthrick, M. A. (1990). Blue jays win! Crows go down in defeat! *Phi Delta Kappan, 71*(7), 553–556.

Wynn, R. L., & Fletcher, C. (1987). Sex role development and early educational experiences. In D. B. Carter (Ed.), *Current conceptions of sex roles and sex typing.* New York: Praeger.

Wynne, E. A., & Walberg, H. J. (1985/1986). The complementary goals of character development and academic excellence. *Educational Leadership, 43*(4), 15–18.

Yates, F. A. (1966). *The art of memory.* London: Routledge & Kegan Paul.

Ysseldyke, J. E., & Algozzine, B. (1995).

Special education: A practical approach for teachers (3d ed.). Boston: Houghton Mifflin.

Zimmerman, B. J., & Blotner, R. (1979). Effects of model persistence and success on children's problem solving. *Journal of Educational Psychology, 71*(4), 508–513

Zimmerman, B. J., & Ringle, J. (1981). Effects of model persistence and statements of confidence on children's self-efficacy and problem solving. *Journal of Educational Psychology, 73*(4), 485–493.

Zwier, G., & Vaughan, G. M. (1984). Three ideological orientations in school vandalism research. *Review of Educational Research, 54*(2), 263–292.

Author/Source Index

Subject Index

Credits

p. 3, *photo*: D. Degnan/H. Armstrong Roberts; **p. 6,** *photo*: C. Bachmann/The Image Works; **p. 9,** *photo*: Gene Peach/The Picture Cube; **p. 12,** *photo*: Elizabeth Crews; **p. 14,** *photo*: Frank Siteman/The Picture Cube; **p. 19,** *photo*: James Wilson/Woodfin Camp & Associates; **p. 36,** *photo*: Bob Daemmrich; **p. 40,** *Case in Print*: Micky Baca, *Merrimack Valley Sunday,* Amesbury, MA, 8-7-94; **p. 43,** *photo*: Grant Le Duc/Monkmeyer Press; **p. 50,** *photo*: Martha Cooper; **p. 55,** *photo*: Robert Finken/The Picture Cube; **p. 65,** *photo*: D. Young Wolff/Photo Edit; **p. 74,** *photo*: Kindra Cineff/The Picture Cube; **p. 84,** *photo*: Elizabeth Crews; **p. 85,** *photo*: K. B. Kaplan/The Picture Cube; **p. 93,** *photo*: Geoffrey Biddle; **p. 98,** *photo*: Susie Fitzhugh; **p. 98,** *photo*: Erica Stone; **p. 104,** *photo*: D. Young Wolff/Photo Edit; **p. 106,** *photo*: Paul Conklin/Photo Edit; **p. 108,** *photo*: John Curtis/D. Donne Bryant Stock; **p. 111,** *photo*: Richard Hutchings/Photo Edit; **p. 122,** *photo*: Elizabeth Crews; **p. 125,** *photo*: Rhoda Sidney/Stock Boston; **p. 135,** *photo*: C. Bernsau/The Image Works; **p. 136,** *photo*: D. Young Wolff/Photo Edit; **p. 139,** *photo*: Diane Graham-Henry/Tony Stone Worldwide; **p. 142,** *Case in Print*: Reprinted with permission of the St. Louis Post-Dispatch, copyright © 1995; **p. 152,** *photo*: Bob Daemmrich/Stock Boston; **p. 161,** *photo*: Bob Daemmrich; **p. 162,** *photo*: Jim Harrison/Stock Boston; **p. 174,** *photo*: Ray Stott/The Image Works; **p. 176,** *photo*: Charles Gupton/Stock Boston; **p. 177,** *left photo*: D. Young Wolff/Photo Edit; **p. 177,** *right photo*: Laura Druskis/Stock Boston; **p. 178,** *Case in Print*: "Intelligence Goes Way Beyond Test Scores" by Charles M. Madigan, 4/24/94. © Copyrighted Chicago Tribune Company. All rights reserved. Used with permission; **p. 184,** *photo*: Bill Bachann/The Image Works; **p. 185,** *Figure 5.4*: Shavelson, R.J. and G.P. Baxter "What We've Learned About Assessing Hands-On Science." *Educational Leadership,* 49, 8: 21. Copyright © 1992 by ASCD. Reprinted by permission. All rights reserved; **p. 199,** *photo*: Don and Pat Valenti/Tony Stone Worldwide; **p. 204,** *photo*: Will McIntyre/Photo Researchers; **p. 208,** *photo*: Bodhan Hrynewych/Stock Boston; **p. 215,** *photo*: Paul Conklin; **p. 223,** *photo*: Michael Newman/Photo Edit; **p. 229,** *photo*: Bob Daemmrich/The Image Works; **p. 242–244,** *text*: From *Taxonomy of Educational Objectives: Handbook I: Cognitive Domain,* Benjamin S. Bloom, Ed. Copyright © 1956, renewed 1984 by Longman Publishers. Reprinted with permission; **p. 243,** *left photo*: Bob Daemmrich/Stock Boston; **p. 243,** *right photo*: Robert

Finken/The Picture Cube; **p. 244,** *photo*: Billy Barnes/Stock Boston; **p. 245–246,** *text*: From *Taxonomy of Educational Objectives: Handbook II: Affective Domain,* David R. Krathwohl, Ed. Copyright © 1964, renewed 1992. Reprinted with permission; **p. 246,** *photo*: Bob Daemmrich/Tony Stone Worldwide; **p. 246–247,** *text*: From Simpson, E.J. (1996). *The Classification of Educational Objectives: Psychomotor Domain. Illinois Teacher of Home Economics,* 10 (4). Reprinted with permission; **p. 247–249,** *text*: Reprinted with permission from *Preparing Instructional Objectives,* Revised 2nd ed. by Robert F. Mager, © 1984. Published by The Center for Effective Performance, 4250 Perimeter Park South, Suite 131, Atlanta, GA 30341. (770) 458-4080; **p. 248,** *photo*: Bob Daemmrich; **p. 255,** *photo*: Charles Gupton/Stock Boston; **p. 261,** *photo*: Bruce Forster; **p. 268,** *Case in Print*: Reprinted by permission of Associated Press; **p. 268,** *Case in Print*: Reprinted with permission of the St. Louis Post-Dispatch, copyright © 1994; **p. 269,** *photo*: Will and Deni McIntyre/Photo Researchers; **p. 279,** *photo*: Lawrence Migdale/Stock Boston; **p. 285,** *photo*: Elizabeth Crews; **p. 290,** *Case in Print*: Reprinted with permission of the author; **p. 292,** *photo*: Bob Daemmrich/The Image Works; **p. 302,** *photo*: Jeffrey Myers/Stock Boston; **p. 311,** *Table 8.2*: From "Instructional Design Flaws in Computer-Assisted Instruction" by J.S. Vargas, 1986 *Phi Delta Kappan,* 67, p. 744. Copyright © 1986 by Phi Delta Kappa. Adapted by permission; **p. 321,** *photo*: Dennis MacDonald/Photo Edit; **p. 324,** *Figure 9.2*: From G.H. Bower, M.C. Clark, A.M. Lesgold, and D. Winzenz, "Hierarchical Retrieval Schemes in Recall of Categorized Word Lists." *Journal of Verbal Learning and Verbal Behavior,* 1969, 8, 323–343. Copyright 1969 by Academic Press. Reproduced by permission of the publisher and the authors; **p. 325,** *photo*: Ralf Finn-Hestoff/SABA; **p. 327,** *photo*: Bob Daemmrich/The Image Works; **p. 329,** *photo*: Elizabeth Crews; **p. 330,** *Case in Print*: From *Newsweek*, September 26, 1994 and © 1994, Newsweek, Inc. All rights reserved. Reprinted by permission; **p. 339,** *Table 9.1*: From King, A. (1992), "Facilitating elaborative learning through guided student-generated questioning." *Educational Psychologist,* 27 (1). Used with permission; **p. 341,** *photo*: Rich Friedman/Black Star; **p. 349,** *photo*: Elizabeth Crews; **p. 360,** *photo*: Bachmann/The Image Works; **p. 362,** *photo*: Seth Resnick/Stock Boston; **p. 365,** *photo*: Tony Savino/The Image Works; **p. 373,** *photo*: Elizabeth Crews; **p. 378,** *photo*: Elizabeth Crews; **p. 383,** *Flow Diagram*: Adapted from A. Whimbey and J. Lochhead, *Problem Solving and Comprehension,* Fifth Edition, © 1991. Used with permission; **p. 386,** *photo*: Robert E. Daemmrich/Tony Stone Images; **p. 390,** *Case in Print*: Reprinted with permission of the author; **p. 400,** *photo*: Bob Daemmrich/The Image Works; **p. 404,** *photo*: John Harding/Time Magazine; **p. 411,** *photo*: M. Greenlar /The Image Works; **p. 414,** *Case in Print*: Reprinted with permission of the author; **p. 418,** *photo*: Bob Daemmrich/The Image Works; **p. 425,** *photo*: Susie Fitzhugh; **p. 429,** *Table 11.1*: Jere Brophy. "Teacher Praise: A Functional Analysis," *Review of Educational Research,* 51, No. 1 (1981), 5–32. Copyright © 1981. American Educational Research Association, Washington, D.C. Used with permission; **p. 430,** *photo*: Richard Hutchings; **p. 441,** *photo*: Jean Claude LeJeune; **p. 443,** *photo*: Bob Daemmrich/Stock

Boston; **p. 445,** *photo*: Dembinsky Photo Associates; **p. 454,** *photo*: D. Young Wolff/Photo Edit; **p. 465,** *photo*: Bob Daemmrich/The Image Works; **p. 470,** *photo*: Bob Daemmrich; **p. 482,** *photo*: B. Daemmrich/The Image Works; **p. 488,** *photo*: B. Daemmrich/The Image Works; **p. 491,** *photo*: David Young Wolff/Photo Edit; **p. 494,** *photo*: Junebug Clark/Photo Researchers; **p. 498,** *photo*: Bob Daemmrich; **p. 504,** *text*: From Becker, W.G., Englemann, S., and Thomas, D.R., *Teaching: A Course in Applied Psychology*. © 1991 by Science Research Associates; **p. 506,** *photo*: Frank Siteman/Monkmeyer Press; **p. 510,** *Case in Print*: Micky Baca, *Merrimack Valley Sunday,* Amesbury, MA, 3-5-95. **p. 519,** *photo*: Mary Kate Denny/Photo Edit; **p. 520,** *photo*: Frank Siteman/Stock Boston; **p. 521,** *photo*: Michael Newman.

STUDENT RESPONSE FORM

What do you think of this book? The authors and publisher would like to know what you think of this eighth edition of *Psychology Applied to Teaching*. Your comments will help us not only in improving the next edition of this book but also in developing other texts. We appreciate very much your taking a few minutes to respond to the following questions. When you have indicated your reactions, please send this form to: College Marketing, Houghton Mifflin Company, 222 Berkeley Street, Boston, MA 02116.

1. On a ten-point scale, with 10 as the highest rating and 1 as the lowest, how do you rate the following features of *Psychology Applied to Teaching*?
Overall rating compared to all other texts you have read ____
Interest level compared to all other texts you have read ____
Readability compared to other texts ____
Clarity of presentation of concepts and information ____
Value of the *Key Points* as a learning aid ____
Usefulness of *Suggestions for Teaching in Your Classroom* ____
Usefulness of *Resources for Further Investigation* ____
Usefulness of *Applying Technology to Teaching* ____
Usefulness of *Case in Print* ____
Usefulness of *Journal Entries* and Suggestions for Developing a Reflective Journal ____
Usefulness of *Becoming a Reflective Teacher: Questions and Suggestions* ____
Helpfulness of summary *tables* and *diagrams* ____
Interest level and pedagogical effectiveness of the *illustrations* ____

2. Do you intend to sell this book ____ or keep it for future reference ____ ?
(Please insert an X in the appropriate space.)

3. Have you used (or do you intend to refer to) *Becoming a Reflective Teacher: Questions and Suggestions* to improve your teaching effectiveness?
Yes ____ No ____

4. Please turn to the table of contents and list here the numbers of all chapters that were assigned by your instructor.

____

5. If not all chapters were assigned, did you read any others on your own? Please indicate chapter numbers you read on your own.

____

6. Were there any topics that were not covered that you thought should have been covered?

____

7. Please indicate the number of each of the following types of exams that your instructor asked you to take:
multiple choice ____ short-answer ____ essay ____ oral ____ other ____
(if other, please specify)____

8. Did your instructor give you the opportunity to compare your test answers to the answers provided by the person who wrote the questions?
Yes ____ No ____

9. Were you required to write a term paper ____ or complete some sort of term project?
(Please specify the nature of the term project) ______________________________

10. Did you use the Study Guide? Yes ____ No ____
On a ten-point scale, how do you rate the usefulness of the Study Guide? ____
Did your instructor ask you to use the Study Guide? ____ or did you obtain it on your own? ____

11. Are you attending a two-year college ____, four-year college ____, university ____ ?

12. What was your class standing at the time you took the course in educational psychology?
Freshman ____ Sophomore ____ Junior ____ Senior ____ Graduate ____

13. Is your college or university on the quarter system ____ or the semester system ____ ?

14. Do you have access to your own computer at your university? ____

15. How often do you use the Internet? ____
What sites do you visit? ____

16. To what extent is multimedia incorporated in your classes? ____________________
____

17. If you had a chance to talk to the authors of this book just before they started to prepare the next edition, what suggestions would you give them for improving *Psychology Applied to Teaching*?
____
____
____

INDEX TO CASE IN PRINT

Each **Case in Print** feature uses a recent news article to demonstrate how an idea or technique in the chapter was applied by educators. These selections demonstrate the real-world relevance of psychological theory and research.